The Writer's Craft

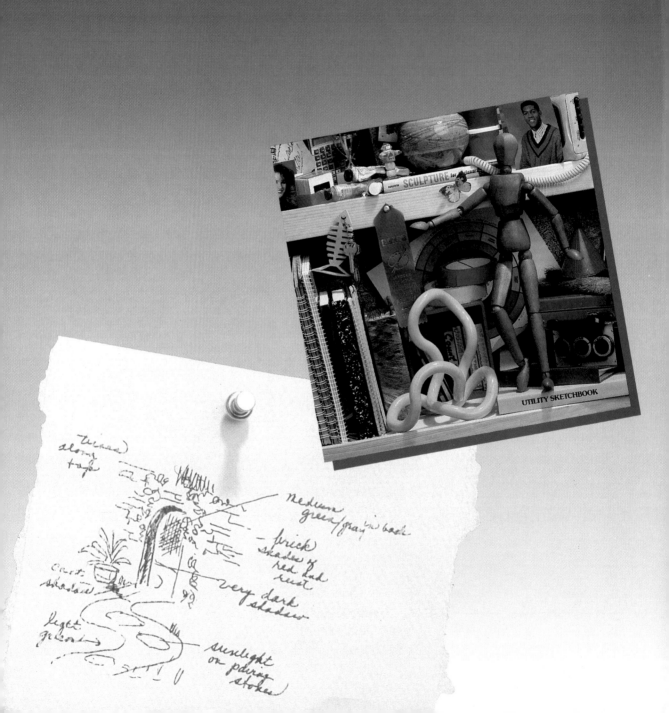

The Writer's Craft

SENIOR AUTHOR
SHERIDAN BLAU
University of California at Santa Barbara

CONSULTING AUTHOR
PETER ELBOW
University of Massachusetts at Amherst

SPECIAL CONTRIBUTING AUTHOR
DON KILLGALLON
Baltimore County Public Schools

SENIOR CONSULTANTS
Arthur Applebee
State University of New York at Albany

Judith Langer
State University of New York at Albany

ML McDougal, Littell & Company
Evanston, Illinois

Dallas • Phoenix • Columbia, SC

SENIOR AUTHOR

Sheridan Blau, Senior Lecturer in English and Education and former Director of Composition, University of California at Santa Barbara; Director, South Coast Writing Project; Director, Literature Institute for Teachers

The Senior Author, in collaboration with the Consulting Author, helped establish the theoretical framework of the program and the pedagogical design of the Workshop prototypes. In addition, he guided the development of the spiral of writing assignments, served as author of the Literary Workshops, and directed the Contributing Authors in the completion of Guided Assignments.

CONSULTING AUTHOR

Peter Elbow, Professor of English, University of Massachusetts at Amherst; Fellow, Bard Center for Writing and Thinking

The Consulting Author, in collaboration with the Senior Author, helped establish the theoretical framework for the series and the pedagogical design of the Writer's Workshops. He also provided material for use in the Writing Handbooks and reviewed selected units for consistency with current research and the philosophy of the series.

SENIOR CONSULTANTS

These consultants reviewed lesson prototypes to ensure consistency with current research. In addition, they reviewed and provided editorial advice on the completed Writer's Workshops.

Arthur N. Applebee, Professor of Education, State University of New York at Albany; Director, Center for the Learning and Teaching of Literature; Senior Fellow, Center for Writing and Literacy

Judith A. Langer, Professor of Education, State University of New York at Albany; Co-director, Center for the Learning and Teaching of Literature; Senior Fellow, Center for Writing and Literacy

SPECIAL CONTRIBUTING AUTHOR

Don Killgallon, English Chairman, Educational Consultant, Baltimore County Public Schools. Mr. Killgallon conceptualized, designed, and wrote all of the features on sentence composing.

ACADEMIC CONSULTANTS

In collaboration with the Consulting Author and Senior Author, the Academic Consultants helped shape the design of the Workshops. They also reviewed selected Workshops and mini-lessons to ensure appropriateness for the writing classroom.

Linda Lewis, Writing Specialist, Fort Worth Independent School District

John Parker, Professor of English, Vancouver Community College

CONTRIBUTING AUTHORS

C. Beth Burch, Visiting Assistant Professor in English Education, Purdue University, Indiana, formerly English Teacher with Lafayette High School

Sandra Robertson, English Teacher, Santa Barbara Junior High School in California; Fellow and teacher-consultant of the South Coast Writing Project and the Literature Institute for Teachers, both at the University of California, Santa Barbara

Linda Smoucha, formerly English Teacher, Mother Theodore Guerin High School, River Grove, IL

Carol Toomer Boysen, English Teacher, Williams School, Oxnard, California; Fellow and teacher-consultant of the South Coast Writing Project and the Literature Institute for Teachers

Richard Barth-Johnson, English Teacher, Scattergood Friends School, West Branch, Iowa; National Writing Project Fellow

John Phreaner, formerly Chairman of the English Department at San Marcos High School, Santa Barbara; Co-director of the South Coast Writing Project and the Literature Institute for Teachers

Wayne Swanson, Educational Materials Specialist, Chicago, IL

Joan Worley, Assistant Professor of English and Director of the Writing Center at the University of Alaska, Fairbanks; National Writing Project Fellow

Cherryl Armstrong, Assistant Professor of English at California State University, Sacramento; National Writing Project Fellow

Valerie Hobbs, Co-director of the Program in Intensive English, University of California, Santa Barbara; Fellow of the South Coast Writing Project and the Literature Institute for Teachers

STUDENT CONTRIBUTORS

Sarah Cazabon, Watertown, MA; Stephen Elsasser, Cedar Rapids, IA; Stacia Graham, Seattle, WA; Tamara Huffstutter, Birmingham, AL; Mike Hulfberg, Seattle, WA; Anne Lacy, Birmingham, AL; Maria Lopes, Jamaica Plain, NJ; Laurie McEachern, Jackson, MS; Brian Myers, Jackson, MS; Amy Rosanbalm, Hillsboro, OR; Tamiha Smith, Northfield, IL; Michele Sobarnia, Northfield, IL; Brendon Stahl, Watertown, MA; Stephanie Tubbs, Tuscaloosa, AL; Stephanie Yessayan, Watertown, MA.

TEACHER REVIEWERS

Dr. Joanne Bergman, English Teacher, Countryside High School, Clearwater, FL

Regina Dalicandro, English Department Chairperson, Mather High School, Chicago, IL

Becky Ebner, Trainer for the New Jersey Writing Project in Texas; English Teacher, Clark High School, San Antonio, TX

Sister Sheila Holly, S.S.J., M.A., English Department Chairperson, Saint Maria Goretti High School, Philadelphia, PA

Dr. William J. Hunter, Assistant Principal, English Department, John Jay High School, Brooklyn, NY

Margaret N. Miller, Language Arts Consultant (6-12); Library Coordinator (K-12), Birdville I.S.D., Fort Worth, TX

Janet Rodriguez, English Teacher, Clayton Valley High School, Concord, CA

Mark Rougeux, English and Journalism Teacher; Newspaper Advisor, Glenville High School, Cleveland, OH

Bennie Malroy Sheppard, English Teacher, High School for Law Enforcement and Criminal Justice, Houston, TX

Sue Wilson, English Department Chairperson, Wade Hampton High School, Greenville, SC

ISBN 0-8123-8670-1
Copyright © 1995 by McDougal, Littell & Company
Box 1667, Evanston, Illinois 60204
All rights reserved. Printed in the United States of America.

1 2 3 4 5 6 7 8 9 10 – DCI – 99 98 97 96 95 94

Contents Overview

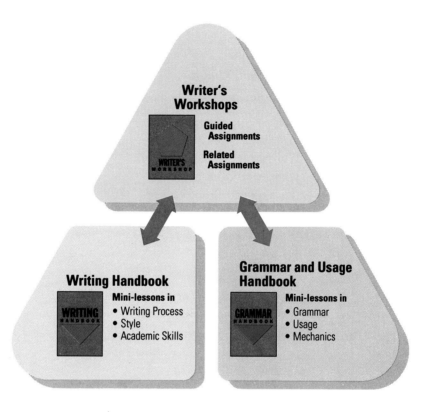

Writer's
Workshops

Guided
Assignments

Related
Assignments

WRITER'S
WORKSHOP

Writing Handbook

Mini-lessons in
• Writing Process
• Style
• Academic Skills

WRITING
HANDBOOK

Grammar and Usage
Handbook

Mini-lessons in
• Grammar
• Usage
• Mechanics

GRAMMAR
HANDBOOK

You are an individual. You think and act in ways that are uniquely your own. This book recognizes that individuality. On every page you will be encouraged to discover techniques best suited to your own personal writing style. Just as important, you will learn to think your way through every writing task.

In each of the Writer's Workshops, you will experiment with ideas and approaches as you are guided through a complete piece of writing. Cross-references to the Handbooks will allow you to find additional help when you need it. Then, as you write, you will discover what you think about yourself—and about the world around you.

Table of Contents

For more in-depth treatment of each stage of the writing process, see the Writing Handbook, pages 317–419.

Writer's Workshops

Observation and Description

Narrative and Literary Writing

Informative Exposition: Classification

Informative Exposition: Analysis

Informative Exposition: Synthesis

Persuasion

Writing About Literature

Reports

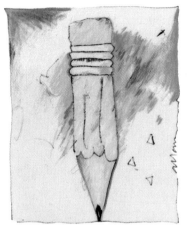

Writing for Assessment

Writing Handbook Mini-lessons

WRITING PROCESS

Prewriting

Drafting

Revising and Publishing

Grammar and Usage Handbook Mini-lessons

Getting Ready to Write

WRITING TO LEARN

I never would have expected to learn anything about myself while writing, but I did.

Brendon Stahl, student
Watertown, Massachusetts

Unexpectedly, Brendon discovered one of the most important and exciting reasons to write—learning something new. He found out that writing not only enables you to share what you already know, it also provides a chance to explore what you are not sure of and to make meaning out of confusion. You can write to revive a memory or record a new thought, to share your feelings with a friend or explore them by yourself, to describe your own experiences or to imagine you are someone else. If you ever made a list of pros and cons to help you make a decision or wrote down your feelings in order to sort them out, you were writing to make meaning, writing to learn. You were using writing as a process of discovery in which you try out and discard ideas, play with possible solutions to problems, and search for connections. Writing, as you will have learned, is thinking on paper.

Learning to Write

Writing is not a mysterious activity. It is a natural process that everyone can learn and adapt to fit his or her own needs. To write you will not need to develop a whole new set of mental muscles. You can use skills that you apply every day in thinking and speaking. You only need to recognize what those skills are, strengthen some, and learn when and how to apply others. In helping you learn to write, this book gives you the practice you need to hone those skills and to use them to keep learning and growing.

USING THIS BOOK

> For the things we have to learn before we can do them,
> we learn by doing them.
>
> **Aristotle**

That statement is just as true now as it was twenty-four centuries ago in Aristotle's Greece; and it is particularly true of writing. You are not born knowing how to write. It is a skill you must learn by doing it, not by reading about it. This book will allow you to do just that.

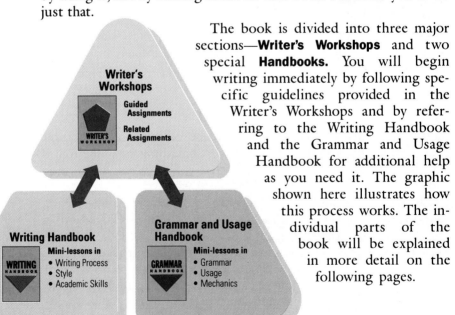

The book is divided into three major sections—**Writer's Workshops** and two special **Handbooks.** You will begin writing immediately by following specific guidelines provided in the Writer's Workshops and by referring to the Writing Handbook and the Grammar and Usage Handbook for additional help as you need it. The graphic shown here illustrates how this process works. The individual parts of the book will be explained in more detail on the following pages.

Writer's Workshops

Each writer's workshop focuses on a specific kind of writing or a specific writing strategy. You will have an opportunity to explore each writing type or strategy in three different settings—a guided assignment and two related assignments.

Guided Assignments The guided assignments offer detailed suggestions for doing a specific piece of writing. As you write, you will decide which, if any, of these suggestions will help you complete your writing. If you have questions that are not answered in the guided assignment itself, or if you need more help, explanation, or practice, you can turn to the handbooks at the back of the book. At each step in your writing process,
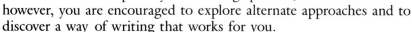
however, you are encouraged to explore alternate approaches and to discover a way of writing that works for you.

Related Assignments Each guided assignment is accompanied by two related writing applications that can be done instead of, or in addition to, the main assignment. The related assignments build on and extend the skills presented in the guided assignments. While the guided assignments offer many suggestions for completing your writing, the related assignments allow you to explore the process on your own, make your own decisions, and solve your own problems. Like the guided assignments, the related assignments refer you to specific handbook sections for additional help and encourage you to explore your personal writing process. You also may refer to the guided assignment in the workshop for help specifically related to that type of writing.

Additional Writing Opportunities At regular intervals throughout the book, you will find the **Sketchbook** and **Sentence Composing** features, which provide additional opportunities to write. The Sketchbooks give you a chance just to try out and have fun with your ideas without worrying about presenting them in finished form or even sharing them with anyone if you do not want to. The Sentence Composing feature provides sentences from professional writers that you can use as models to improve your own writing technique and style.

Handbooks

Writing must be learned, but everyone learns by different means and needs different help in the process. This text offers that help in the form of two handbooks—the **Writing Handbook,** a resource you can consult for information about the writing process, style, and academic skills, and the **Grammar and Usage Handbook,** which covers grammar, usage, and mechanics.

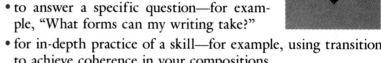

The guided assignments include cross-references to appropriate handbook sections, and you can consult these, or any other sections, at any point in your writing process. You can use the handbooks two ways as you complete a writing activity:

- to answer a specific question—for example, "What forms can my writing take?"
- for in-depth practice of a skill—for example, using transitions to achieve coherence in your compositions.

Making the Book Work for You

There is no single correct way to use this book—the right way is the way that helps you complete a specific piece of writing. Every writer and writing activity is different, so you will probably use this book differently at different times. Your way of using the book will not necessarily be the same as that of your classmates. Since no two writers and no two writing tasks are identical, that's entirely appropriate.

For example, a writer who already knows the characteristics of persuasive writing and the techniques used to write it probably would need very little of the help provided in the guided assignment. As the teacher directs, that writer might even do one of the related assignments in the persuasion workshop instead of the guided assignment.

However, this same writer may need a great deal of practice in creating believable characters and using dialogue, for example. He or she might need to follow the guided assignment for narrative writing closely and work through all the exercises in several handbook sections to master the relevant skills and create a satisfactory narrative.

In this book you'll find not only all the information you might need in learning to write, but also the opportunity to choose when and how you use it.

You are a member of a community that has been expanding as you have grown—from your family to your friends, neighborhood, school, city or town, country, and beyond. In all your activities you have learned to strike a balance between your needs as an individual and those of the community. In writing, too, you will learn to weigh your need for privacy and your need for an audience in the larger community of readers and writers.

Writing is a unique activity that offers you the benefits of both working alone and working with others. You can think things through by yourself and try out feelings and ideas you don't want to share. You can also ask others to help or respond to your writing at any stage. Every time you write, you can find the balance that works best for you.

Working Alone

A major advantage of working alone is the chance to explore your ideas and ways of expressing them without worrying about correctness, clarity, or criticism from readers. You can focus all your attention on your work and get it exactly the way you want it. You can work alone no matter what type of writing you are doing—a journal entry that will never be shared, or the early drafts of a piece that others eventually will read. Working alone is an important aspect of writing, because no matter how many references you consult or how many people you ask for advice, you alone are responsible for the words that finally appear on your paper.

Working Collaboratively

Because much of your writing will be school-related, you often will be writing not only for, but also with, other people. Collaborative writing can offer several advantages over working alone. It can provide a rich source of different ideas and points of view; a supportive, helpful atmosphere; and a safe testing ground for new reflections and approaches. You can work with both your teacher and your classmates in a variety of ways as you write.

Your Teacher as Co-writer   Your teacher is not only your most experienced reader, but also a writer as well, and can be an important source of help during your writing process. He or she can provide examples of good writing and offer general guidelines that work for many writers. Your teacher can also serve as a "test audience" for your work, helping you evaluate problems and find solutions that work for you.

Your Classmates as Co-planners and Peer Readers You can also work together with your classmates in many ways during the writing process. One way to get experience in writing with others is to do collaborative planning, in which you discuss your ideas for a writing activity with your peers. In addition, your teacher may suggest that you work collaboratively to brainstorm various approaches to your writing and solutions to problems. You can also collaborate later in the writing process as your teacher permits.

Your classmates also are a good source of specific feedback on your writing. Because you are all in the same situation and probably are somewhat apprehensive about sharing your writing, you can be understanding and helpful peer readers for one another.

Working Within the Larger Community

In writing outside the classroom, too, you will need to strike a comfortable balance between working alone and working collaboratively. Think about the bustling atmosphere of a newspaper office, with writers and editors working alone at their computer terminals in a large room, but stopping often to ask a question or share an idea. In the business and academic worlds as well, people often write alone, but usually discuss their ideas with colleagues at some point. Many times, however, their writing is actually done in committees or teams.

This textbook is a good example. It was written by many people working alone and together in a variety of ways—sharing ideas, writing separate parts of the book individually, working with others to make the parts fit together, or just responding to one another's work. The skills you will learn in this book will prepare you to become a fully contributing member of the community of writers, in the classroom and beyond.

USING LEARNING LOGS, JOURNALS, AND WRITING PORTFOLIOS

Learning a new fact, mastering a skill, or completing a project can be a source of excitement and pride that you will want to share with others. There are several ways that you can share your sense of accomplishment and savor and benefit from the learning process you went through.

Learning Logs

Keeping track of what you are learning is important no matter what the specific knowledge is—writing a play, playing a musical instrument, doing a chemistry experiment, or learning a foreign language. A **learning log** is a place for you to record and reflect on the knowledge you have gained—from living in the world, from studying in your classes, and from your own thinking. The log is more than just a record of information—it can also be a powerful learning tool. Writing what you have learned often provides a new perspective and reveals connections that you otherwise might not have noticed.

Journals

> I keep a journal of all my spontaneous thoughts, so that when I get a chance I can put these thoughts into writing.
> **Tamara Huffstutter, student**
> **Birmingham, Alabama**

A **journal** is your own private place for your writing. You can use a journal any way you wish. It can be a way both to collect ideas and to get extensive writing practice.

Examples of ways you can use your journal include the following:

- for enjoyment
- to free your imagination
- to help clear your mind
- for the freedom, privacy, and safety to experiment and develop as a writer
- to try out writing ideas and approaches that are not fully formed and that you would be afraid to share with a reader
- as a sourcebook for clippings, photos, conversations, observations, or other authors' works that you find interesting and that may provide writing ideas. (Some writers keep these materials in a separate **writer's file**.)

There are no rules for keeping a journal. Some writers just talk to themselves on paper. Their journals include entries of unformed ideas or impressions that will never be developed, or personal experiences or feelings that later turn into a story or poem. Others include completed pieces of imaginative writing, such as science-fiction stories, humorous essays, or poems not done for an audience, but purely for personal pleasure. No matter how you use your journal, however, it can provide ideas for writing and help you develop both those ideas and your skills as a writer.

Writing Portfolios

A good way to showcase and share what you have written as well as to track your writing progress is to keep a **writing portfolio,** a collection of finished pieces of writing and selected notes and drafts. You also can keep a separate **working folder** of your writing in progress and later transfer the finished piece to your portfolio. You may want to attach a note to your work, reflecting on your writing process and evaluating the results.

You can use a writing portfolio to analyze how your writing process has changed—or remained the same—and to discover how your personal writing style has developed. The portfolio can also be used by your teacher to evaluate individual pieces of writing, track your development as a writer, and identify where you still need work. Specific opportunities for using your portfolio are offered throughout this book. A writing portfolio is like a personal history book in which you record your progress as a writer and your development as a person. Understanding that process can help you to continue to learn and grow.

Thinking Through Your Writing Process

How do you learn about yourself and the world around you? Reading, asking questions, observing, and experiencing are all methods you may have used at various times. Writing is another important source of knowledge. It is a way not only of communicating your thoughts, but also of clarifying and understanding them. It is not just the making of sentences and paragraphs, it is the making of meaning. Writing, like any other learning activity, is a process, and it uses skills that you have already mastered and apply every day in thinking and speaking.

THE STAGES OF THE WRITING PROCESS

No two people look, dress, or act exactly alike. Similarly, no two people write alike, and individuals even write differently in different situations. Therefore, the writing process varies greatly. Most writers, however, go through four basic stages:

- prewriting
- drafting and discovery
- revising and proofreading
- publishing and presenting

Prewriting   Prewriting is the time to explore ideas and collect materials from a variety of sources. During prewriting, you examine what you already know about your writing activity and what you need to find out. You begin to think about the writing variables—the general purpose and specific or personal goals of your writing, your audience, and the form your writing will take.

Drafting and Discovery   Drafting is the time to get your ideas down on paper without worrying about making mistakes. You should feel free to change your mind and to try various approaches, even those that don't seem to be working. You may be able to clarify your writing variables at this stage and, eventually, you will discover not only what you want to say, but even ideas you had never thought of before. As you write your draft, you may find that you are also doing some revising, or that you must do more prewriting activities to rethink your writing plan or gather more information.

Revising and Proofreading   Revising involves reviewing the purpose and specific personal goals of your writing and determining whether you have met them. This is the time to look at your writing with fresh eyes, and perhaps to have others respond to it as well. During this stage you will evaluate the content, structure, and mechanics of your writing and make any necessary changes.

Publishing and Presenting   During this stage of the writing process, you may share your completed writing with others, if you wish. This sharing can take many forms, such as an oral presentation or publication in a newspaper or magazine. You are encouraged to share your writing at every stage of the process, however, not only after it is completed.

These stages of the writing process are not separate steps that must be completed one at a time. the entire process is flexible and can be modified depending on the individual writer and the writing activity. For example, some people like to plan and organize their thoughts carefully before they put pencil to paper; others prefer to develop their ideas as they write. Likewise, individual writing activities have specific requirements. A research report, for example, involves a very different approach from a personal essay. The flexibility of the writing process is illustrated in the following diagram.

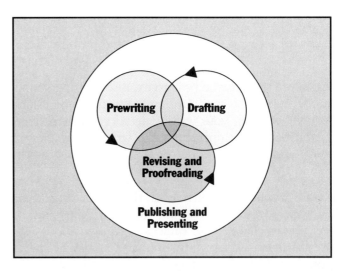

However, writing is more than just completing these steps, regardless of the order in which you complete them. It is a basic strategy for approaching new knowledge and solving problems. Writing is a way of learning and growing.

A good way to understand the flexibility of the writing process is to follow the approaches used by different writers. Two students, Kate and Jon, had just finished reading *The Snows of Kilimanjaro* by Ernest Hemingway, in which a mountain figures as a major character. Their English teacher asked them to extend their response to the literature by writing a paper on the general topic of mountains. As you follow the steps Kate and Jon go through, notice how each student adapts the writing process to suit his or her individual interests and learning styles.

Prewriting

As they began their writing activity, both Kate and Jon explored ideas they might like to pursue. In the process, they considered their writing variables—the topic, general purpose and personal goals, audience, and form of their writing—and how they could best gather and develop information.

Choosing a Topic   Kate had been very moved by *The Snows of Kilimanjaro* and wondered what drew the dying man's thoughts to the mountain's summit as he approached death. "The mountain must have represented something like freedom to him," she thought. "I'm not sure I understand that, though, because I would be terrified at the thought of climbing that mountain. I wonder what kind of people mountain climbers are and how I would handle the dangers they face." She decided that writing about the qualities that make a successful mountain climber would be a good way to answer those questions and would help her understand not only her own fears, but Hemingway's book as well.

On the other hand, a friend helped Jon choose his topic, although he was not aware that that's what he was doing at the time. While they were looking at photographs from a camping trip, his friend kept turning back to the picture of an unusual rock formation called Devil's Tower. "That looks like a fake mountain from a horror story." Jon immediately agreed, and realized that Devil's Tower would be the perfect setting for a story of his own. He then did some freewriting, recalling his observations and experiences at Devil's Tower, and reflecting on what they might mean. In the process, his writing idea began to take shape.

Devil's Tower—long, vertical stripes, as if a huge cat had sharpened its claws on it. No, not a cat—it was a bear! The ranger told us that story at the campfire program. Stone spirits raised the tower to save Sioux girls from an attacking bear. I could use that legend as the basis for my story.

Establishing a Purpose and Personal Goals   A piece of writing can have one or several purposes, the most common of which are **to express yourself, to inform, to tell a story,** and **to persuade.** For example, the purpose of an article explaining how weather conditions affect climbers would be to inform. A personal narrative by an adventurer who had spent several months in the mountains of Alaska might have three purposes: to tell an interesting story, to express the writer's feelings about the experience, and to persuade readers to support efforts to preserve the Alaskan wilderness.

Besides determining the general purpose of a piece of writing, writers at some point must also decide on their **specific** or **personal goals.** An example of a personal goal would be to understand and explain the experience of climbing a mountain for the first time, or to re-create the ominous atmosphere of Devil's Tower. Many writers determine their purpose and personal goals early in the writing process by asking themselves questions such as these:

• What do I really want to accomplish in this piece?
• How do I want my audience to respond to it?

Kate did not feel ready to answer those questions at this stage in her writing process and decided to postpone the decision about her personal goals until she had explored her idea more fully.

ONE STUDENT'S PROCESS   KATE

I don't understand what makes people even think about climbing mountains, so I want to learn more about their personalities and the situations that challenge them. However, I don't know yet exactly what I want to accomplish in my writing or how I want my audience to respond.

Jon, on the other hand, was already clear about his purpose and personal goals.

ONE STUDENT'S PROCESS   JON

Devil's Tower was an eerie and impressive place. I remember thinking that something remarkable could happen there at any moment. Since I want to convey that atmosphere to my readers, my story should be more than just an entertaining adventure. The events should be mysterious and magical, like the Sioux legend.

Identifying Your Audience Knowing who will read your writing can help you determine both what you write and how you write it. Sometimes your audience is chosen for you. For example, if you are planning to present an account of your first climbing expedition to a mountaineering club, your audience is the club members, and you should include information appropriate to people familiar with the sport. At other times, you can choose your audience, or even decide that you don't want to share your writing at all.

You don't have to identify your audience before beginning to write; sometimes you may decide to write just for yourself and tailor your work for a specific audience later. In general, however, thinking about your readers early in the writing process will help you communicate your ideas most effectively. You may find it helpful to ask yourself questions such as these:

- What aspects of my topic will my readers find most interesting?
- What do my readers already know about the topic and what do they need to know?
- What approach and language will best engage my readers and communicate to them?

Although Kate and Jon's writing would be submitted to their English teacher, part of their assignment was to find an additional place to submit their papers and to write for that audience. Notice how they dealt differently with their decisions about this writing variable.

ONE STUDENT'S PROCESS

KATE

Even though I am not sure about the overall purpose of my writing, I do know that it fits perfectly into the "adventure" theme of the next school magazine. The readers of that magazine are the high school students and faculty and maybe some parents, too. Those people will have a wide range of interests and backgrounds; so, as I explore my topic, I should probably think about the information that will be most useful to a general audience.

Our teacher said that the National Council of Teachers of English sponsors a writing contest for high-school students every year. That would be a good place to submit my story, but I don't know any of the details. Right now I'm really excited about my writing and keep thinking of new ideas. I don't want to stop now to make telephone calls or do research about the contest. I'll do that later and also continue to think about other possible audiences for my writing.

Choosing a Form   The **form** is the type of writing in which you express your ideas. Common forms of writing are stories, poems, plays, letters, essays, articles, reports, and speeches. Like the other writing variables, the form of your writing may not be clear before you begin to write. In many cases, however, you discover the appropriate form as you consider your topic, purpose, and audience.

In fact, considering and determining the form of her writing helped Kate clarify her purpose and the personal goals that she wanted to achieve.

ONE STUDENT'S PROCESS

KATE

I think I would like to try writing a profile of a typical mountain climber. This could be a composite portrait drawn from several individual climbers. It would cover both physical and emotional traits and would show how each is necessary on a climb.

It has suddenly become clear to me that what I want to accomplish in this paper is to understand from the inside out how a mountain climber thinks and feels. I want to express this understanding in a way that will help my readers understand and experience it as well.

Jon, on the other hand, decided not to make a decision about the form of his writing at this stage.

I could tell my story as a fantasy, since it includes many magical elements. I could also write a suspense story or even a narrative poem.

Right now, I think I'll just let my ideas flow. When I see where they take me, I'll know better which form will be most effective.

Gathering and Developing Information Although Kate and Jon have taken very different approaches to their writing activity so far, both felt that they needed to gather more information about their topics before proceeding.

Kate made a rough outline to guide her research.

The Making of a Mountain Climber

I. What do mountain climbers do?
  A. Physical requirements and training
  B. Emotional factors
II. What personal qualities do mountain climbers share?
  A. Family background and upbringing
  B. Education, activities, and other interests
  C. Personality

Jon developed his writing by **inquiring,** or asking questions, about his topic. He then answered his own questions by **inventing,** or freeing his imagination to come up with creative ideas. Notice how generating this information enabled him to decide on a form for his writing.

<u>Who are the characters?</u>
   Stan, eighteen, and his brother Mike, fifteen
<u>Where does the story take place?</u>
   on a backpacking trip near Devil's Tower, Wyoming
<u>What happens?</u>
   The boys meet an old man on the trail. He tells them the legend of the Great Bear, whose claws made the ridges in the tower. The boys stalk the bear. The bear stalks them. They eventually have to climb the tower to escape.
<u>How does the story end?</u>
   I haven't figured this out yet.
   I realize now that with all these suspenseful elements, this would make a good mystery story.

Drafting and Discovery

The next stage of the writing process, drafting, involves getting what is in your head on paper. It is the time to try different ways of expressing your ideas, to change direction, jump ahead, or backtrack and start over. It is not a time to worry about making mistakes or being unclear. It is the time when you make meaning from your ideas and the information you have gathered and start to write.

As you experiment with your ideas, you probably will make discoveries that will lead you to evaluate, rethink, and change your draft. You may find that you need to do more research, choose a different form or purpose for your writing, or even reassess your topic entirely. You should feel free to revise your writing as much or as little as you wish during this stage of the writing process.

Thinking as You Draft Whatever drafting method you use, you should keep the following questions in mind:

Ideas
   • In what direction is your writing taking you?
   • Are you developing the idea you originally had in mind, focusing on one aspect of it, or dealing with a new idea?

Organization
- How do your ideas relate to one another?
- What way of organizing them would best express that relationship?
- Have you provided all the necessary information?

Peer Response

Your peers can help you at any stage of your writing process, from finding a topic—as Jon's friend did—to choosing an audience or form, to evaluating how effectively you have communicated your ideas. However, it is often especially helpful to ask your peers to read and respond to your draft.

After Jon finished the draft of his story, he set it aside for a few days. When he reread it, he felt dissatisfied but could not decide what to change. Jon asked several of his peers to respond to the following questions.

- What parts did you like best? Least?
- What was going through your head as you read my story?
- What message do you think I am trying to get across? Summarize it for me.
- Why do you think I chose to write this story?
- What did you want to know more about? What parts are too long?
- Did you have any trouble following any part of my story?

We will continue to follow Jon through his writing process. Here is part of his story, with some of the responses his peer readers gave.

JON

Stan and Mike couldn't sleep that night. Devil's Tower loomed above them. The deep gashes on its flanks frightened the boys. The wind howling in the trees sounded like the growling of the great bear in the Sioux legend. I don't know if I want to go through with this Mike said under his breath.

Why had that old Indian told them the story of the two Sioux girls attacked by a bear and the formation of the tower? His voice still seemed to be casting a spell over them as he began the legend: "Once long, long ago. . . ." Only suddenly that time didn't seem so long ago, it felt like it was happening to them, there and then.

The girls had fled to the top of a small rock and begged the stone spirits to save them. Suddenly the rock had begun to grow, lifting them into the air. In its rage, the bear clawed the growing tower of rock.

I don't understand why the boys are at Devil's Tower.

I like this image. It reminds me of a ghost story I heard as a kid.

This paragraph is confusing to me. It seems out of place.

Revising and Proofreading

Having evaluated his draft himself and gotten responses to it from several peer readers, Jon was ready to begin revising his writing.

One of your most important tasks in revising your writing is to determine whether you have achieved your personal goals and communicated your ideas to your intended audience. Carefully consider the comments of your peer readers, but remember that you do not have to incorporate their suggestions. Before changing your draft to address a peer reader's comment, make sure the change would help you to achieve your purpose and improve your writing. Then decide if you must work on the content, the structure, or the mechanics of your writing—or on any combination of these elements—to accomplish the change.

Content To assess the basic message of your writing, you must loop back to the beginning of your writing process and review your general purpose and specific goals. As you wrote, you may have discovered new information or a new outlook on your topic, or you may have realized that you could not go any farther. Your peer readers also may have found problems with the content. Specific questions that should help you assess the substance of your writing are shown in the "Checklist for Rethinking Content" on page 392.

Structure If what you said does not seem to be a problem, but responses from your peer readers indicate that you have not communicated your message clearly, you will need to rework the structure or organization of your writing. See the questions in the "Checklist for Reworking Structure" on page 393.

Mechanics Errors in punctuation, capitalization, spelling, grammar, and usage also can hamper communication of your message. Checking for such errors, called **copy-editing** or **proofreading,** usually is the last step in revising your writing. Consult the "Checklist for Refining Mechanics" on page 394 for specific guidelines to follow.

You can use **proofreading** and **revising marks** such as those shown on page 394 to indicate major changes to your writing, such as reorganization of content, or minor revisions, such as spelling corrections. Jon used several of these marks in revising a paragraph in his story. Notice how he responded to his peer readers' comments and that he made additional changes in content and organization as well as in mechanics and usage.

Stan and Mike couldn't sleep that night. Devil's Tower loomed above them. The deep gashes on its ~~flanks frightened the boys.~~ *seemed to be bleeding in the shadows cast by the moon.* The wind howling in the trees sounded like the growling of the great bear in the Sioux legend. *¶ The thought of climbing the tower tomorrow, as they planned, gave Mike the chills.*

"I don't know if I want to go through with this," Mike said under his breath. *"I know what you mean," Stan answered. "The furrows in the tower remind me of that old Indian's wrinkled face in the firelight."*

Why had that ~~Old Indian~~ *he* told them the story of the two Sioux girls attacked by a bear and the formation of the tower? His voice still seemed to be casting a spell over them as he began the legend: "Once long, long ago . . ." Only suddenly that time didn't seem so long ago, it felt like it was happening to them, there and then.

The girls had fled to the top of a small rock and begged the stone spirits to save them. Suddenly the rock had begun to grow, lifting them into the air. In its rage, the bear clawed the growing tower of rock.

Margin notes:
- I need to show why they are afraid.
- I need a transition here and dialogue would help, too.
- This should appear earlier in the story when the boys meet the old Indian and he tells them the legend.

Publishing and Presenting

The last stage of the writing process is sharing your writing with others. Although you may do some writing only for yourself—for example, a journal entry or a sketch for your portfolio that you do not complete at the time—usually you will be writing to be read.

There are many ways to share your writing with readers or listeners other than your teachers or peers, such as those described in the following list.

- **Readers' Circles** Read your writing with several other writers in your class and discuss your responses to it.
- **Writing Exchange Groups** As a class, share your writing with students at your own or other schools.
- **Collected Writings** Publish a collection of student writing on a particular topic or of a particular type.
- **The Print Media** Submit your writing to your local or school newspaper or to a national magazine that accepts student writing.
- **Other Media** Use music, slides, videos, mime, or dance to accompany an oral presentation of your writing.
- **Performances** Dramatize a story or poem and present it to your class or school assembly.
- **Writing Portfolios** Keep your writing in a portfolio for your own reference and enjoyment or to share with others from time to time.

Learning From Your Writing Process

Thinking about the process you have gone through in completing a piece of writing can be a real learning experience and can help you continue to grow as a writer. In assessing your progress, ask yourself questions such as these:

- What did I learn from writing about my topic?
- Which aspects of the writing process were easiest for me? Which were most difficult?
- Which aspects are getting easier?
- What problems did I solve as I wrote? How can I improve my writing process the next time?
- What similarities or differences in style do I see in this piece compared with others in my writing portfolio?
- What features of my peers' writing or professional writers' work would I like to try myself?
- How can I apply the skills I have learned?

Record the answers to several of these questions and attach them to the finished piece of writing in your portfolio. Over a period of time, you will become increasingly aware of your progress as a writer. You will also realize firsthand how flexible the writing process is and how it may change as you do.

Sketchbook

For writers, just as for artists, sketchbooks are places to try out ideas. Use the words and images presented on the Sketchbook pages throughout this book as starting points for writing. See what thoughts they bring to mind. Then try something out and have fun with it. You may find that these sketches give you ideas you'd like to work on later. But for now, just see where your thoughts take you.

What if your refrigerator, or other household appliances, came to life? What would they say? What would they do? How would you react?

Additional Sketches

Tell the story of the time in your life when you were most happy—or perhaps most calmly content or serene.

Relive an adventure you experienced.

Personal and Expressive Writing

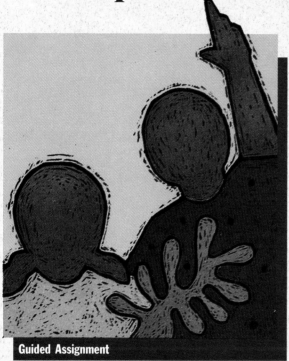

Guided Assignment
AUTOBIOGRAPHICAL INCIDENT

Related Assignment
FAMILY HISTORY

Related Assignment
TALL TALE

There is a particular individual whom you know better than anyone else—you. Therefore, only you can understand the ideas, memories, and feelings that are all tied up with who you are, where you've been, and where you hope you're going. Through personal and expressive writing, you can explore your thoughts and experiences in more depth. The guided assignment in this workshop will give you the chance to write an autobiographical incident. In the related assignments, you will explore your memories by putting together a family history and stretch one incident into a humorous tall tale.

Autobiographical Incident

FROM

AKÉ: THE YEARS OF CHILDHOOD

BY WOLE SOYINKA

Many memories make wonderful stories. When people tell these stories, they tell about themselves—who they were, who they became. When memories are written down to be shared with others, they become autobiographical essays.

In an autobiographical essay about his childhood, Nigerian author Wole Soyinka described events that in retrospect often seemed humorous and unusual. In this excerpt, he is three years old. As you read, look for the way he uses tone, dialogue, and point of view to bring an incident to life.

There was a birthday party for one of the Canon's[1] children. Only the children of the parsonage were expected but I passed the secret to Osiki and he turned up at the party in his best *buba*[2]. The entertainments had been set up out of doors in front of the house. I noticed that one of the benches was not properly placed, so that it acted like a see-saw when we sat on it close to the two ends. It was an obvious idea for a game, so, with the help of some of the other children, we carried it to an even more uneven ground, rested its middle leg on a low rock outcrop and turned it into a proper see-saw. We all took turns to ride on it.

For a long time it all went without mishap. Then Osiki got carried away. He was a bigger boy than I, so that I had to exert a lot of energy to raise him up, lifting myself on both hands and landing with all possible weight on my seat. Suddenly, while he was up in his turn, it entered his head to do the same. The result was that I was catapulted up very sharply while he landed with such force that the leg of the bench broke on his side. I was flung in the air, sailed over his head and saw, for one long moment, the Canon's square residence rushing out to meet me.

It was only after I had landed that I took much notice of what I had worn to the party. It was a yellow silk *dansiki*,[3] and now I saw with some surprise that it had turned a bright crimson, though not yet entirely. But the remaining yellow was rapidly taking on the new colour. My hair on the left side was matted with blood and dirt and, just before the afternoon was shut out and I fell asleep, I wondered if it was going to be possible to squeeze the blood out of the *dansiki* and pump it back through the gash which I had located beneath my hair.

The house was still and quiet when I woke up. One moment there had been the noise, the shouts and laughter and the bumpy ride of the see-saw, now silence and semi-darkness and the familiar walls of mother's bedroom. Despite mishaps, I reflected that there was something to be said for birthdays and began to look forward to mine. My only worry now was whether I would have recovered sufficiently to go to school and invite all my friends. . . . Then there was another worry. I had noticed that some of the pupils had been kept back in my earlier class and were still going through the same lessons as we had all learnt during my first year in school. I developed a fear that if I remained too long at home, I would also be sent back to join them. When I thought again of all the blood I had lost, it seemed to me that I might actually be bed-ridden for the rest of the year. Everything depended on whether or not the blood on my *dansiki* had been saved up and restored to my head. I raised it now and turned towards the mirror; it was difficult to tell because of the heavy bandage but I felt quite certain that my head had not shrunk to any alarming degree.

The bedroom door opened and mother peeped in. Seeing me awake she entered, and was followed in by Father. . . . I studied their faces intently as they asked me how I felt, if I had a headache or a fever and if I would like some tea. Neither would touch on the crucial question, so finally I decided to put an end to my suspense. I asked them what they had done with my *dansiki*.

"It's going to be washed," mother said, and began to crush a half-tablet in a spoon for me to take.

"What did you do with the blood?"

She stopped, they looked at each other. Father frowned a little and reached forward to place his hand on my forehead. I shook my head anxiously, ignoring the throb of pain this provoked.

"Have you washed it away?" I persisted.

Again they looked at each other. Mother seemed about to speak but fell silent as my father raised his hand and sat on the bed, close to my head. Keeping his eyes on me he drew out a long, "No-o-o-o-o."

I sank back in relief. "Because, you see, you mustn't. It wouldn't matter if I had merely cut my hand or stubbed my toe or something like that—not much blood comes out when that happens. But I saw this one, it was too much. And it comes from my head. So you must squeeze it out and pump it back into my head. That way I can go back to school at once."

My father nodded agreement, smiling. "How did you know that was the right thing to do?"

I looked at him in some surprise. "But everybody knows."

Then he wagged his finger at me. "Ah-ha, but what you don't know is that we have already done it. It's all back in there, while you were asleep. I used Dipo's feeding-bottle to pour it back."

I was satisfied. "I'll be ready for school tomorrow," I announced.

I was kept home another three days. I resumed classes with my head still swathed in a bandage. . . .

¹Canon: priest
²buba: a loose fitting outer garment
³dansiki: a loose-fitting tunic

Think AND Respond

In this excerpt, Wole Soyinka recalls not only a serious accident, but also the curious worries he had about the event. Why do you think he chose to write about this incident? What techniques does he use to help the reader see events from his point of view, both as a child and as an adult? What ideas for a subject does his autobiographical essay bring to your mind?

INVITATION
— TO —
Write

Wole Soyinka wrote an autobiographical essay about an accident he had as a boy and its aftermath. Now use the activities below to write an essay about an incident or series of events in your life.

In this assignment you will be writing about one subject you know better than any other: your own experience. Everyone has a rich store of memories. By tapping into that wealth of raw materials, you can find a precious memory well worth writing about.

Writing an essay about an autobiographical incident allows you to share with your readers an experience from your life and to explore why the experience had meaning for you. You may also discover just how much that incident from your past affects who you are today. You will probably write best about the memories you have strong feelings about, but since this will be a class assignment, you may want to choose less private memories.

PREWRITE AND EXPLORE

HANDBOOKS
FOR HELP & PRACTICE

Writing Variables, pp. 317–321
Personal Techniques, pp. 322–324
Exploring Ideas, pp. 330–332

1. Examine your memories. We replay some memories over and over again in our minds, like a favorite videotape. Yet our memories are better than tapes because our brain stores smells, tastes, and emotions in addition to sights and sounds. Try some of the following activities to help you explore your memories.

Exploratory Activities

• **Listing** Divide a sheet of paper into three vertical columns labeled *People, Places,* and *Things.* Quickly list all the memories in each category that come to mind. One word or phrase is adequate. When you've filled all three columns, you'll have a great catalog of memories to browse through.

- **Recalling**   Remember events in your past by writing a series of phrases, each beginning with "the time when. . . ." Your phrases might include such things as "the time when I found a $50 bill," "the time when I hit a home run with the bases loaded," or "the time when I lost my dad's car keys."

- **Life map**   Make a road map of your life. Start with your birth and draw figures or symbols for important events in your life up till now. For example, you might put in crossroads at points where you went one direction instead of another. You might put in mountains or rivers to stand for times when you faced obstacles. Share your map with a partner, explaining the different points along the way. Seeing your partner's map may help you remember other points you want to add to your own map.

- **Special days**   List special days, such as birthdays and Thanksgiving, Halloween, New Year's Eve, and other holidays. Try recalling memorable things that happened on or near each of the days, either recently or long ago, and make short notes about the events. Something memorable happened to Wole Soyinka at a birthday party, and years later he created a humorous auto-biographical essay based on the experience.

- **Reading literature**   Like Wole Soyinka, many writers have found inspiration in their personal experiences. Think of autobiographical works you have read recently, such as Maya Angelou's *I Know Why the Caged Bird*

PROBLEM
S O L V I N G

**How will I
find ideas?**

Sings, Ernesto Galarza's *Barrio Boy,* or Dylan Thomas's "A Child's Christmas in Wales." What ideas do these works give you for topics you could write about?

You should now have a variety of memories to choose from. Free-write on several of them to see where they take you. You also might look in "Apply Your Skills" on page 40 or at the ideas you experimented with in the Sketchbook on page 24 for additional topics.

2. Choose a topic. By now you probably have in mind a memory that you would like to write about. How can you tell whether this particular memory will be a good choice for your essay?

Here are questions you may want to consider:

- Do I remember this incident clearly enough to write about it?
- Will the telling of this memory reveal something significant about who I am?
- Am I comfortable sharing this memory with my classmates and teacher?

If the answer to any of these questions is no, consider choosing another memory to write about.

 Writer's Choice You may choose to focus on something that happened to you personally, or you may decide to write about an event you witnessed but did not participate in.

3. Examine your purpose and your audience. When you write an autobiographical incident essay, you don't have to say exactly what you learned from the experience. Nevertheless, if the memory is so important that you chose it out of all the many moments of your life, then you should show the reader how and why it affected you.

Autobiographical writing is different from narrating a made-up story in that the reader of an autobiographical piece learns something about who the author is as a person. The reader doesn't want just to find out what happened; the reader also wants to know what impact the event had—and maybe still has—on the writer.

One student, Renee, found a topic by drawing a life map. She decided that she had strong feelings about the time her best friend moved away. She explored her feelings by asking herself a series of questions. Throughout this assignment, you will follow Renee's progress as she writes an autobiographical essay.

PROBLEM SOLVING

How can I decide if my topic is a good choice?

Writing
—TIP—

For this essay, don't worry too much about finding a memory that will fascinate your readers. If you pick a memory that honestly tells about you, that's enough.

1. When did it take place?
   In 1988, when I was 13 years old.

2. Where did it happen?
   on a trail ride
      foggy
      twittering birds
      "clop" of horses hooves

3. What happened?
   I realized how much I missed my best friend Dena, but also how my friendship with Alexandria might grow.

4. How did I feel?
   sad
   confused
   hopeful

4. Explore your topic. Think about the details that will make your story come alive for your readers. Use the following suggestions to sketch out some ideas that you can use as guideposts when you begin to write.

- **Develop maps or clusters.** An effective way both to find out how clearly you remember the incident and to help you tell about it in an organized way is to jot down the events and details in related clusters or groupings. Such notes will not only make writing about the incident easier, they will also make following what happens easier for your readers. If you have ever listened to a long story told by someone who breaks off every minute to add some important detail he or she forgot, you know how frustrating a disorganized story can be. For information about clustering, see "Using Graphic Devices for Writing," pages 330–337.

- **List your characters.** Is there anyone other than you involved in this incident? Make a quick list of the other people. Soyinka's characters included Osiki, some unnamed children, and his mother and father. When you write the essay, you won't necessarily tell about each person, but you should show the reader what key characters are like. Soyinka, for example, showed Osiki's mischievousness by describing how he landed with all his weight on the end of the bench. Elements such as how people move, dress, and talk may add dimension to your essay. Also consider whether there are important conversations you should include as Soyinka did.

- **Think about your setting.** How important is the time and place of your incident? Could it have happened anywhere and at any time, or was the incident connected to a specific time and place? The answers to these questions will determine how much effort you should put into describing the setting. In his autobiographical essay, Wole Soyinka spent little time describing his setting, simply mentioning the birthday party, the bench, and his house and bed. He obviously did not think it was necessary to describe the exact time and place of the incident. In any case, the reader of your essay will probably want some idea of where and when your incident takes place.

1. Begin drafting. Get your story down on paper. Don't worry about how it comes out or looks; you can make improvements later. You may find that you lose interest in the first story you begin to write about. If this happens and you had other memories in mind, go ahead and begin writing a new story. Do more than just give a narration of what happened; also reflect on the meaning of what happened. The following strategies can help make your writing clear and vivid.

HANDBOOKS

FOR HELP & PRACTICE

Organization,
pp. 342–349
Adequate Detail,
pp. 405–406
Dialogue,
pp. 452–455

Strategies

- **Narration** Use some or all of the elements of the story—plot, character, and setting—to tell what happened and what impact the events had. Tell any background the reader needs to know as well as how events unfolded.
- **Description** Use language that appeals to the senses—sight, hearing, touch, taste, and smell—to reveal information about people, places, and things. Good descriptions can help you get below the surface of things and tell what people are thinking, what kind of mood a place creates, or how things came into existence. Wole Soyinka's description of how his yellow shirt became red with blood added a startling touch to his memoir and helped build the mood.
- **Dialogue** Use the words of characters to show rather than tell what people are like and what is going on. Dialogue brings variety to your writing as well. Soyinka used dialogue to move his story along as well as to show what characters were thinking and feeling.

PROBLEM

S O L V I N G

How can I make my autobiographical essay come alive?

2. Organize your draft. The usual way to retell an event is to use chronological order. Sometimes, though, you can grab the reader's interest better if you begin in the middle of the action. If you think you would like to start writing somewhere in the middle, choose a moment when you realized something important, or perhaps a moment when your outlook shifted. Then, in the course of your narrative, insert flashbacks, sentences or paragraphs that fill in the background information readers need to know about what led up to that incident.

Autobiographical
Incident

3. Take a break. Let your writing cool for a while. When you come back, reread your draft and consider how satisfied you are with it. Ask your peer readers for their reactions. Consider the following questions.

COMPUTER TIP

If you suddenly have an idea or recall an important detail while writing, hit the Page-Down key and write your idea. Then hit Page-Up to go back to your writing. When you finish the draft, you will have a collection of notes at the end of your document.

REVIEW YOUR WRITING

Questions for Yourself

- Does the story do justice to the experience as I remember it?
- Did I leave out any important details?
- Is there material that doesn't relate directly to the autobiographical incident that needs to be cut out?
- Does the writing sound like me?
- Will my readers understand why this memory is important to me?

Questions for Your Peer Readers

- Did my essay catch your interest right from the start?
- Is the order of events clear?
- Are there places where you got lost or confused?
- Is there more you would like to know about what happened?
- Can you point out examples of especially vivid descriptions of the events? of a scene? of a character?
- What does the essay tell you about the kind of person I am?
- Do the words used to tell the story sound like my own voice?
- Why do you think I chose to tell this story?

HANDBOOKS

FOR HELP & PRACTICE

Unity,
pp. 371–376
Self-Assessment,
p. 397
Peer Response,
pp. 398–401
Sharing Writing in
Progress,
pp. 417–418

REVISE YOUR WRITING

1. Evaluate your responses. If your peer readers point out weaknesses or confusing places in your essay, hear them out and learn as much about your writing from them as you can. Remember that you don't have to take all their advice. Also keep in mind that a well-written essay about an autobiographical incident generally displays these basic characteristics.

Standards for Evaluation

An effective autobiographical incident essay . . .

- focuses on a clear, well-defined incident or series of related events.
- uses such elements as plot, character, and setting as appropriate and develops these elements with specific details.
- makes clear the order in which events occurred even when the narrative begins in the middle and uses flashbacks.
- uses description or dialogue as appropriate.
- uses precise, vivid language.
- *shows* events rather than just *tells* about them.
- establishes and maintains a consistent tone and point of view.

Candle Walk: A holiday tradition preserved in rural southern communities

2. Problem-solve. After considering your peer readers' comments and your own evaluation, decide which responses you want to use and then rework your draft. Renee made these changes in part of her autobiographical incident essay in response to suggestions from one peer reader.

But now it was the day after, and there I sat in the cold window, bringing all the sorrow back. I needed comfort, but who would want to comfort me at 6:00 A.M.? Then, in a flash, I thought of Shariffa.

Quickly, I threw on my riding clothes and scribbled a note, letting my parents know I'd be back for breakfast. I slipped outside to the stable and saddled Shariffa. I rode down the street, noticing that all the houses were still dark. *and through a hayfield till I reached the canyon and from there climbed a steep hill,* I found myself at the entrance to a hayfield, a place I like to ride in often. I opened the gate and walked through, careful to stay on the trail and not step on any newly sprouted hay. I followed the trail into the canyon, where a streambed crisscrossed the trail. From there I turned up the hill to my right. After struggling to the top through the thick wet grass of the hill, *There* I got off Shariffa and let her graze on the weeds around me.

The point on which I stood usually gave a clear view of the valley for miles. Now, with the fog, I couldn't see anything but a little area around me. The trees *were dim, silhouettes,* looked fuzzy and I could hear birds *unseen were twittering sorrowfully, awaiting the sunrise.* waiting for the sun to come up.

I like this touch of mystery when we don't know who Shariffa is.

This helps me see what's going on, but it slows down the story.

I get a little feeling for the setting, but it would be nice to have an even clearer picture.

3. Proofread your work. Check your work for errors in grammar, punctuation, and spelling. Then make a clean copy of your autobiographical incident essay.

Grammar
——**TIP**——
Be sure any words your characters said are enclosed within opening and closing quotations marks. Do not use quotation marks to set off indirect quotations.

LINKING
GRAMMAR **AND** WRITING

Most of your autobiographical essay is probably written in the past tense, but some of it may describe feelings you have in the present. Be careful to avoid incorrect shifts in verb tense. Use the past tense to tell about past events. Use the present tense to tell about present events or feelings.

PROBLEM: After the game the autograph collector *was waiting* by the locker room. Suddenly he *sees* a player he *recognizes.*

REVISED: After the game the autograph collector *was waiting* by the locker room. Suddenly he *saw* a player he *recognized.*

PUBLISH AND PRESENT

- **Exchange essays with others.**   Share your essay with other writers in your class. This time, instead of helping each other edit and revise, just enjoy the finished pieces of writing and discuss your responses to them.
- **Create a class memory album.**   Put the autobiographical essays together in an album that can be checked out to one student at a time. You may want to add photographs to the album to accompany the essays.
- **Create your own memory album.**   Begin a collection of this and other autobiographical essays, including your family history, and some photographs. As the collection grows, it will be a great way to document and remember the moments that an ordinary photo album would not show. Save it for your own children to read someday!
- **Save your work in your writing portfolio.**   Compare this piece of writing with something you wrote a few months ago. How has your work changed?

HANDBOOKS
FOR HELP & PRACTICE

**Sharing Completed Writing,
pp. 418–419**

The Day After

Renee Richard

Opens in the middle of the story and then provides a flashback to key events

Gradually, sleep fell away and my eyes opened. I was lying on my bed and the red light of the clock across the room read a blurry 5:30 A.M. to my unfocused eyes. I stretched and tiptoed to the window. A dense fog cloaked the world. Realizing there would be no beautiful sunrise to hold my attention, I crept to the kitchen. Back in my window sipping cocoa, I stared out on the misty morning. Somehow, it suited me. . . .

Makes clear the order in which events occurred

Then I remembered. A hollow feeling took hold of me. I thought back to the day before. I was helping Dena and her family with the very last inspection of their house before they drove away, for good. Mrs. Hayes, my friend's mother, was standing in the hall, gazing around her.

"Is that all?" I asked.

Uses dialogue to convey what is happening and how people feel

"Yes, that's it. We're ready now," she answered mechanically. Her voice sounded weak, and she didn't look ready at all. Then we walked down the hill together. She gave me a hug, said good-bye, and climbed behind the wheel.

Dena was standing by the other door. We walked to each other and I chokingly said, "Bye, Dena."

"Bye, Renee," she echoed, "I love you." She hugged me and climbed into the passenger seat. The truck pulled away, and I could see Dena alternately waving and wiping away her tears.

Dena was my best friend. Only she seemed to love me simply as I was and for who I was. Knowing she would not be around anymore left me feeling empty and alone. As the truck disappeared, I thought, how could I ever replace a friendship like the one I had with Dena?

But now it was the day after, and there I sat in the cold window, bringing all the sorrow back. I needed comfort, but who would want to comfort me at 6:00 A.M.? Then, in a flash, I thought of Shariffa.

Quickly, I threw on my riding clothes and scribbled a note, letting my parents know I'd be back for breakfast. I slipped outside to the stable and saddled Shariffa.

I rode down the street and through a hayfield till I reached the canyon and from there climbed a steep hill, struggling to the top through thick, wet grass. There I got off Shariffa and let her graze on the weeds.

The point on which I stood usually gave a clear view of the valley for miles. Now, with the fog, I couldn't see anything but a little area around me. The trees were dim, fuzzy silhouettes, and unseen birds were twittering sorrowfully, awaiting the sunrise. My horse cropped the grass around my feet, every now and then glancing at me as if asking what was wrong.

Pretty soon, I got tired of just standing there. I got back on Shariffa, but somehow I still couldn't move. Instead of picking up the reins and riding away, I just sat there, and suddenly a picture of Alexandra flashed through my mind.

Alexandra had met Dena not long before me, and eventually the three of us had become inseparable. I always felt that Dena was the connecting link between us. Now I realized suddenly, Alex might turn out to be a real friend, maybe as good a friend as Dena—if I helped make our friendship happen. I would feel the sorrow of Dena's having left for a long time, but in the meantime I would find a new friendship growing.

The fog was lifting; in fact, it had been lifting the whole time I was sitting there. Not only was it lifting from the valley, it was lifting from my heart. In a few minutes, I could see the whole valley before me. I tugged Shariffa's head up from the grass and she cantered down the hill, heading for home. Shariffa pranced and snorted, then looked back at me, making sure I was all right. I told her thanks, even though she couldn't understand me.

Uses precise language, including vivid verbs

Uses description to establish setting and mood

Contains elements of plot, including a strong resolution

Autobiographical Incident   **39**

WRITER TO WRITER

I like writing because it is an intellectual activity that forces my mind to wander into my deepest innermost thoughts or feelings.

**Brian Myers, student
Jackson, Mississippi**

1. Reflect on your writing. Now that you have completed your autobiographical incident essay, think about the process you followed. Ask yourself the questions below and record your answers in your journal. Or you may prefer to attach the page with your answers to your essay.

- Did the writing change your perspective on the memory? If you were to write another autobiographical essay, what would you do the same? What would you do differently?
- Of all the essays you read (your own, the one by Wole Soyinka, ones written by your classmates), which did you like best? What qualities did you admire in it? What techniques did the writer use that you might apply to your own writing?

2. Apply your skills. Try one or more of the following activities to practice what you have learned in this Workshop.

- **Cross-curricular** Choose a person from history whom you particularly admire. Read about his or her childhood and write an autobiographical essay telling why you admire the person and how that person's life is similar to and different from your own.
- **Literature** Focus on a fictional character whom you particularly like who is described in the third person. Write an essay as if you were the character. Describe an incident from the novel or story from the character's point of view. You may want to pretend that the character is looking back at the incident after many years have passed.
- **Related assignments** Follow the suggestions on pages 44–52 to write a family history or a tall tale.

On the Lightside

SAILING EXPRESSIONS

Centuries ago, when the phrase "let the cat out of the bag" was first used, it had nothing to do with felines. Likewise, "mind your *p*'s and *q*'s" had nothing to do with the alphabet, and "the devil to pay" had nothing to do with Satan. These are just a few of the expressions that can be traced to life on early sailing ships.

"Letting the cat out of the bag" may seem like a harmless way to refer to giving away a secret, but its origin was far more ominous. On early sailing vessels, the "cat" in question was the cat-o'-nine tails, and when the ship's bosun let it out of the bag, it meant some sailor was in for a flogging.

"Minding one's *p*'s and *q*'s" was not part of a spelling lesson, either. When sailors went ashore, they were likely to congregate in the waterfront bars, where bartenders would tally the number of pints (*p*'s) and quarts (*q*'s) each man drank. The ship's quartermaster would warn the men before they left the ship about their *p*'s and *q*'s, hoping they would return to the ship somewhat sober.

The devil in "devil to pay" referred to a long seam running from stem to stern below the ship's main deck. "Paying" the devil was the term for the arduous task of caulking the seam and covering it with pitch.

Many other expressions, such as "first shot out of the locker," "son of a gun," and "pipe down," also sailed the high seas before finding a home on dry land.

Drawing by Donald Reilly. © 1982, The New Yorker Magazine, Inc.

"Hey, a whale! I mean thar she blows!"

Family History

OUR FAMILY'S BEGINNINGS

by Renée Dobkin Dushman

Have you ever wondered about your roots? Has a colorful or interesting story about a relative sparked your curiosity about the kind of world he or she lived in? Writing a family history can be a rewarding way to explore your personal past.

Here, Renée Dobkin Dushman traces her roots on her father's side of the family. As you read her account, look for details that make her ancestors and their world seem so vivid.

My family tree can be traced back to a little over one hundred years ago, when my grandfather, a Russian blacksmith named Jacob Dobkin, married Anna Padnos, one of thirteen brothers and sisters who lived near the town of Minsk. Since European Russia in the nineteenth century was not a comfortable place for Jews to live, Anna and Jacob, along with most of Anna's family, followed the dream of many Russian emigrants and came to America. The trip was so horrible that at one point Anna paid a stranger five dollars to care for her children in case she died. But after a long journey by train and boat, the family did arrive in America. Anna, Jacob, Eva, Lena, William, Louis, and Harry settled in Chicago.

The Padnos family came to America at an exciting time. They lived at 514 DeKoven St., made famous nineteen years earlier as the place where Mrs. O'Leary's cow knocked over the lantern that started the Chicago fire. Jane Addams had just founded Hull House nearby, one of the first settlement houses in the country. Benjamin Harrison was President,

and there were only thirty-eight states in the Union. John Peter Altgeld was running for governor, just four years after the Haymarket labor riots.

The family quickly adapted to the American way of life. Jacob Dobkin began making wagons for Studebaker. Brother Louis went out to the Wild West, worked as a blacksmith during the building of the railroads, and then came back east to become a tailor. Later he founded Padnos Metals in Holland, Michigan. The other brothers and sisters, and later their children, showed their own creativity by trying every profession from waiter to doctor to makers of bathtub gin (which they told everyone was cosmetics). They also entered whistling contests and dance marathons, invented the Skoot-Car and the Powell-lite, and built those long, long house trailers.

My ancestors were a colorful group: brave, adventurous, and full of laughter. As I have learned more about them, I have come to love them, and I feel a powerful tie to them even though some of them were born in another century.

Think *Respond*

Why do you think Renée Dushman wanted to learn about her ancestors? What details did she include in her history to make her family seem more real to a reader? What do you know about your own family, and how could you learn more? Would completing your family history reveal unexpected information about your ancestors? Which stories might be of interest to others?

INVITATION
—TO—
Write

Think again about the information given in the Dushman family history. Then write a history of your family, based on your own research and family interviews.

A family history, like a memoir, is a personal record of the past. Family histories include facts such as dates, places, and events; they also often provide descriptive details and entertaining anecdotes. The process of writing a family history can be full of challenges. For example, the history must be factual, but documentation is often hard to find. Surviving family members may recollect great stories and fascinating people, but memories (like mirrors) are often distorting. Or perhaps you cannot locate any family members to interview. Still, a family history provides both a record of family continuity and a sense of belonging.

RESEARCHING FAMILY HISTORY

HANDBOOKS
FOR HELP & PRACTICE

Other Techniques, pp. 327–329
Limiting a Topic, pp. 340–341

1. Begin your research. First make a list of relatives who may provide useful information, including those outside your area whom you must call or write. Leave room for names you discover as your research proceeds.

Next, list the different kinds of records you will want to examine: picture albums, scrapbooks, birth and marriage certificates, citizenship documents, death notices, correspondence, family trees, and so on. Also list places you could visit to attain information: cemeteries, former homes, places of worship, municipal buildings, and schools.

Finally, begin to list questions such as the following: Where did our ancestors live? When did they come here? What kinds of work did they do? What happened to them? What are the last names?

ROOTS: THE GIFT

Advertisement for the television adaptation of author Alex Haley's book *Roots: The Gift*

Writer's Choice   Could you use a questionnaire, perhaps with a cover letter explaining your project, to reach a greater number of relatives?

2. Talk to family members.   Involve your immediate family in the first discussion. Then reach out to grandparents, uncles and aunts, cousins, and more distant relatives or longtime family friends. Precise questions that refer to—or request—specific names, dates, places, and events may produce the most helpful responses. However, broader questions such as "What is your favorite memory of your grandfather?" may produce interesting, unexpected information. Encourage people to respond freely.

3. Study the records and sites.   In photo albums and scrapbooks, sort out people and events, noticing details such as settings, clothing, and activities. Scrutinize any available documents, and note names, places, and dates. If possible, visit key family sites. Cemeteries can reveal forgotten dates and, perhaps, names of additional family members. Former homes, schools, and places of work or worship may yield interesting information (even if you don't go inside). Record the details that might help you recreate the world in which your ancestors lived.

Writing
TIP

Tape your interviews, but keep a pencil handy for notes and questions as they occur to you.

Family History   **45**

Bedpost Doll, c.1850

©Schecter Lee/Esto

1. Narrow your focus. By this time you may have an overwhelming amount of information. Writing about everything you have learned would require work and many pages. With your teacher's permission, decide which approach is best for you: a history in a narrative form or some type of visual presentation.

In a narrative history, there are at least two ways to limit your focus. You could concentrate on just one or two generations—the generation of your grandparents and their children, for example, as Ms. Dushman did. Or you could focus on one family line—your mother, her mother, her grandmother, and so on.

Taking a different approach, you could create a visual record: a large family tree, going back as far as you wish or are able. You might show only dates of birth, marriage, and death for most people. However, you could highlight some especially interesting data— occupations, experiences, personalities—in brief annotations near the appropriate names. You could also provide illustrations— drawings, maps, photographs, documents.

2. If you choose the narrative form, write your first draft. Family histories are usually chronological, and the most interesting and enjoyable histories include anecdotes, personal recollections, and descriptive detail. Double-check dates, spellings, relationships, and other verifiable facts. Try to overcome the absence of information with plausible conjectures based on known information. With your narrative you may wish to include a simple family tree, as well as selected photographs, copies or sketches of documents, and a historical outline.

3. If you choose the chart form, draft your family tree. Use the trunk for lines of direct descent, large branches for aunts, uncles, and cousins, and smaller branches for more distant relatives. Even in this form, you may not want to include everyone. For example, if you come from a large family, you might include your immediate aunts and uncles and leave out more distant relatives. Look in history textbooks for lineage charts that can serve as models. Keep annotations brief and to the point. If you include illustrations, such as photographs, consider having reproductions or good photocopies made, so that the originals won't be lost or damaged.

Writing
TIP

You may want to attach a time line of historical events that affected your ancestors' lives.

1. Evaluate the scope of your history. If you include too many people or cover too long a time period in either a narrative or a family tree, you may wind up with just a list of facts in sentence form or with a chart that's impossible to read.

2. Evaluate the interest of your history. Check that you have included precise descriptions and interesting details that will enlighten the reader about particular people and events.

3. Review your history for clarity. Does your history follow chronological order? Is the sequence of generations and events easy to follow? Are the relationships between people always clear? Are your annotations brief and informative? Have you clearly indicated to which family members your notes and illustrations refer?

4. Get feedback from a friend. Ask a friend to read your history with these questions in mind: Which parts are particularly interesting? Which parts need changing? Why?

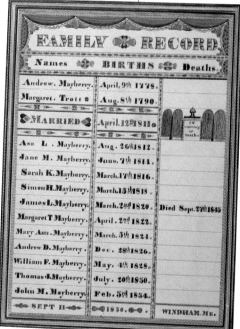

Collection of the Museum of American Folk Art, New York City. Gift of Mr. and Mrs. Philip M. Isaacson

Fraktur: Andrew Mayberry - Margaret Trott Family Record c.1850

• **Make copies of your family history.** Distribute copies to the people who assisted you in your research. Include visual materials such as photographs, records, and maps.

• **Make a classroom display.** Set aside a time when your narrative or family tree, accompanied by family photographs and records, can be displayed in the classroom. Be available at that time to answer questions.

• **Investigate genealogy groups.** Try to discover whether there are any genealogy groups who meet regularly to share information about family histories. Your local library will probably have information about such groups in your area. If so, plan to attend a meeting, and submit your history for their records.

TALL TALE AMERICA

By Walter Blair

A friend tells a preposterous story about a blind date and you laugh hysterically. Have you ever wondered what makes an obviously exaggerated story funny? Have you ever told this kind of story yourself? Wild characters and outrageous deeds make tall tales great fun to invent and to read.

Like many tall tales, this one is based on a real person, Davy Crockett, and a real event, a bright comet that appeared during his lifetime. As you read, notice how the storyteller begins with ordinary, believable details and ends with amazing exaggerations.

[One year a] Big Comet, which the scientific writers of that day say was all red and blue and yellow and green, took a running jump and started lickety split for the earth. Along the way, it kept giving off sparks, the way a big comet does, you know. It scooted past stars and through clouds, and kept right on coming.

Every night, after the cows were milked, the stock was watered, and the dinner things were washed and put away, people would go out in the yard—front or back, depending on which gave them the best view. They'd sit out there watching that comet getting bigger and bigger.

People began to get rather uneasy. In Washington, things were in even more of a dither than usual. Senators and [representatives] made speeches and passed laws against it, but the Big Comet kept sailing along, giving off sparks, and getting bigger and bigger. Even after the Committee for the Investigation of Falling Stars, Comets and Misplaced Planets had met five times and had taken testimony, it kept coming closer. And people kept getting more and more fidgety.

So the President of the United States, after a long Cabinet meeting, decided to do the only thing there was to do. [He asked Davy Crockett] to go up to the top of a mountain and do something drastic about that comet. . . .

Davy went up to the towering top of Cloud Mountain. That was a high mountain from which he could see almost to the Eastern seacoast. . . .

He waited until that Big Comet came in reaching distance, and then he grabbed it by the tail. It was a heavy comet, and it had been falling a long time, so it was hard to handle. Davy had to set his feet firmly and fairly wide apart, put his tongue in the corner of his mouth, and grunt a little. Then he swung it around his head seven times, getting up speed, you know.

Then he let go. The sparks hissed and flipped into the snow on the top of Cloud Mountain. But the Big Comet scooted, in a new direction, past the clouds and past the stars. And the people down below, sitting out in their yards, took pleasure in seeing that, for a change, it was getting smaller instead of bigger all the time.

And so far as is known, it never bothered people any more.

Think AND Respond

Why do you think the storyteller invented this tale? How did he subtly introduce humorous elements and exaggeration? Have you ever "stretched the truth" in order to make a point or to make someone laugh? What event or person do you know that could, with some clever exaggeration, make a good subject for a tall tale?

INVITATION
TO
Write

Davy Crockett's adventures provided the basis for hundreds of entertaining tall tales. Using some event or person you know as a starting point, write your own tall tale.

Tall tales are part of the oral tradition of many families and cultures. Like memoirs, tall tales may be based on real events, but exaggeration and creative invention twist reality into humorous, entertaining fiction. What tall tales have you heard others tell? Have you witnessed an event that might make a good tall tale?

I N V E N T I N G   A   T A L L   T A L E

HANDBOOKS
FOR HELP & PRACTICE

**Elaboration,
pp. 364–369**
**Literal/Figurative
Language,
pp. 425–426**

1. Get in the mood. Writing a tall tale is not a serious business, so relax! Before you begin your story, get yourself in the mood to exaggerate. Collaborate with others in a "comedy workshop," taking turns using the famous comic exchange:

> "I knew a guy who was *really* mean. . . . "
> "HOW MEAN WAS HE?"
> "He was *so* mean that he . . . "

For now, practice making up exaggerations like "Garfield was so hungry that he ate twenty-seven hamburgers, and five pans of lasagna for dessert" or "That horse was so fast that he looked like a tornado running down the track."

As you brainstorm, notice what kinds of exaggerations are funniest and most entertaining. After you've loosened up a little, apply your skill to characteristics and funny incidents related to people you know—including yourself.

2. Choose a character and a situation. Tall tales are usually written about one central character. Focus on family members or friends, and the funny or potentially funny stories you've heard about them. What might you make of the time your cousin saw a snake (that kept getting bigger and bigger each time he told about it)? What happened when your friend's computer seemed to develop a mind of its own?

3. Build up the character for your tall tale. Since exaggerations are funnier when they have some basis in reality, model your character on the real person you've chosen. List some of the qualities the real person has that you can exaggerate. For example, senators and congressmen are always making speeches and passing laws, but in the Crockett tall tale, they are pompously—and absurdly—passing laws against a comet.

 Writer's Choice Instead of a person, would you rather focus on a natural event, such as a terrible snowstorm, a heavy wind, or a heat wave?

4. Stretch the story. Take the situation you have chosen and push it to an extreme. For example, the story of your friend's computer could end up as a tale in which a computer refuses commands and talks back to the operator.

DRAFTING A TALL TALE

1. Jump right in. Tall tales are like carnival rides—they provide fun and laughter from the first moment. As the writer of the comet tale did, introduce your story with a sentence that sets a light mood and prepares the reader for the exaggeration to come.

2. Use vivid language. Describe the character and setting in lively, colorful language. You can use informal language, slang, or dialect.

3. Focus on action. Fill your story with vivid action verbs and humorous bits of detail. For instance, even as the comet sails along, it is *doing* things—scooting past stars and giving off sparks. Crockett, when he grabs the comet, has to "put his tongue in the corner of his mouth, and grunt a little." Move quickly from event to event, building to a climax.

4. Tie it all together. Wrap up your tall tale with an explanation of how the story was resolved. In the example, the Big Comet scoots off in a new direction, and everyone is pleased to see it "getting smaller instead of bigger."

Ichabod Crane, from Washington Irving's *Legend of Sleepy Hollow.* Illustration by Leonard Everett Fisher

Grammar
─ **TIP** ─

Like jokes, tall tales can be told in the present tense to help a reader picture the action more vividly.

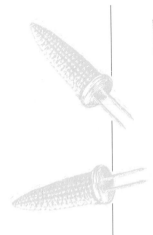

REVIEWING YOUR WRITING

1. Be sure your ideas are fresh and lively. Check that your exaggerations are imaginative enough to surprise and amuse your readers. Stay away from clichés. Don't say someone was "as tall as a tree" when you *could* say "tall enough to pick the pine cones from the top of a California redwood."

2. Avoid too much exaggeration. If your story is too absurd, your readers may lose interest. Check to see if your tale is real enough for readers to relate to.

3. Check that your tale makes sense. Make sure that events proceed in a logical order. Even a tall tale—with all its humor and exaggeration—must have a beginning, middle, and end.

PUBLISHING AND PRESENTING

- **Share your tale.** Tall tales can be especially effective when told aloud. Memorize yours and present it to one of your classes. Or tell it the next time you are around a table talking to your family or friends.
- **Start a "Tall Tale Club."** Meet with classmates and friends on a regular basis to share original tall tales. Explore volumes of folklore you may find in the library and read aloud tall tales from other cultures.

Sentence

Analyzing Sentences

The Sentence Composing lessons that follow each Writing Workshop show you how professional writers structure their sentences. By examining and imitating their work, you will learn ways to add variety, emphasis, and individuality to your own writing. The first two Sentence Composing lessons introduce you to the activities that will help you develop your sentence style: analyzing, imitating, unscrambling, combining, and expanding sentences. In the remaining lessons you will learn to use different types of phrases in new ways. Notice the variety and emphasis in the sentences that make up the description below.

MODELS

1. This is a snail shell, round, full, and glossy as a horse chestnut.

2. Comfortable and compact, it sits curled up like a cat in the hollow of my hand.

3. Milky and opaque, it has the pinkish bloom of the sky on a summer evening, ripening to rain.

Anne Morrow Lindbergh, *Gift From the Sea*

To analyze these sentences, break them into their parts. Then notice how each part relates to the others.

1. This is a snail shell, / round, full, / and glossy as a horse chestnut.
2. Comfortable and compact, / it sits curled up / like a cat / in the hollow of my hand.
3. Milky and opaque, / it has the pinkish bloom / of the sky on a summer evening, / ripening to rain.

A. Identifying Imitations   Break the sentences below each model into parts similar to those shown above. Then identify the sentence that has the same structure as the model.

Model: This is a snail shell, round, full, and glossy as a horse chestnut.

1. a. The novel, a story about overcoming obstacles, is a classic.
   b. Here is a good novel, fascinating, lively, and insightful as a wise man.

Model: Comfortable and compact, it sits curled up like a cat in the hollow of my hand.

2. a. Worn but precious, it leans like a tired traveler against the others in my bookcase.
   b. Alone, it waits to be picked up again, ready for another reader to unlock its treasures.

Model: Milky and opaque, it has the pinkish bloom of the sky on a summer evening, ripening to rain.

3. a. When the characters come to life once more, the pages will fill with action and insight for a new reader.
   b. Dog-eared and marked, it has the friendly feel of a familiar companion on a shared route, talking to pass the time.

B. Unscrambling Sentences   The sentence parts below are similar in structure to the parts of the models they follow. Unscramble each group of sentence parts. Then write them in an order that matches the order of their model. Punctuate them as the models are punctuated.

Model: This is a snail shell, round, full, and glossy as a horse chestnut.

1. a. and pale as a watercolor pastel
   b. this is a dried flower
   c. fragile, stiff

2. a. this is an antique bottle
   b. and old as a great-grandparent
   c. golden, smoky

Model: Comfortable and compact, it sits curled up like a cat in the hollow of my hand.

3. a. it beats rhythmically
   b. steady and strong
   c. in the hall of a comfortable home
   d. as a clock

4. a. at the hearth of a fireplace
   b. he lies stretched out
   c. ruffled and relaxed
   d. like a dog

Model: Milky and opaque, it has the pinkish bloom of the sky on a summer evening, ripening to rain.

5. a. it has the prancing gait
   b. muscular and lean
   c. high-stepping to win
   d. of a trotter in the ring

6. a. rusting to ruin
   b. broken and discarded
   c. it has the dejected look
   d. of a toy from childhood

C. Imitating Sentences Write a sentence that imitates the structure of each model sentence below. Major parts of each sentence are separated by slash marks (/). Examine each part, and see how it relates to the sentence parts before it and after it. Punctuate your sentences as the models are punctuated.

Example	This is a snail shell, / round, / full, / and glossy as a horse chestnut.
Student Sentence	That was a car crash, / sudden, / loud, / and chilling as a winter wind.

1. Standing straight and awkward / in her full-skirted red cotton dress, / Jade Snow was caught by surprise and without words.
   Jade Snow Wong, *Fifth Chinese Daughter*

2. We bounded into the house, / laden with snowballs, / and stopped at the open door of the smoke-filled room.
   Dylan Thomas, "A Child's Christmas in Wales"

3. With a sudden flick, / quick as lightning, / an apple left his hand / and hit Bill square on the nose.   **J.R.R. Tolkien, *The Fellowship of the Ring***

4. The Stones were always going out to dinner, / or entertaining at home, / or traveling about the country somewhere / in connection with Jim's work.
   Raymond Carver, "Neighbors"

5. As the boat bounced from the top of each wave, / the wind tore through the hair of the hatless men, / and as the craft plopped her stern down again, / the spray slashed past them.   **Stephen Crane, "The Open Boat"**

Application Write a paragraph to describe a small object like the seashell described by Lindbergh. In your paragraph, include sentences that imitate one or more of the model sentences in this lesson. Notice how these sentences add variety to your writing.

Grammar Refresher The model sentences at the beginning of this lesson are simple sentences; that is, each has only one independent clause. However, each sentence contains adjectives used in unusual positions. To learn more about adjectives, see Handbook 30, pages 541–545.

Sketchbook

The great American writer F. Scott Fitzgerald used his notebooks to record his thoughts and to try out descriptions, observations, and ideas, such as these descriptions of seasons.

Days of this February were white and magical, the nights were starry and crystalline. The town lay under a cold glory.

Spring came sliding up the mountain in wedges and spear points of green.

Abruptly it became full summer. After the last April storm someone came along the street one night, blew up the trees like balloons, scattered bulbs and shrubs like confetti, opened a cage full of robins and, after a quick look around, signaled up the curtain upon a new backdrop of summer sky.

Deep autumn had set in, with a crackling wind from the west.

THE NOTEBOOKS OF
F. SCOTT FITZGERALD

Choose a time of year and "try out" a description of how it looks and feels to you.

Additional Sketches

What will you look like 20 years from now?

Tell a dream you remember. Recreate what you saw, what you did, and what you felt.

Observation and Description

Guided Assignment
OBSERVING SITUATIONS AND SETTINGS

Related Assignment
INTERVIEW

Related Assignment
CHARACTER SKETCH

Have you ever written postcards to friends from a favorite vacation spot, telling them about some great new beach you discovered, a museum you visited, or a train ride you took? If you did, you undoubtedly used a common, powerful type of writing—description. Strong description can bring a subject to life, enabling readers to experience it just as the writer did.

In the following guided assignment, you will develop your powers of observation as you create a description of a situation or a setting. You will further sharpen your skills by conducting and describing an interview and then by writing a character sketch.

Observing Situations and Settings

from The Way to

RAINY MOUNTAIN

by N. Scott Momaday

Descriptive writing usually does not stand alone, but appears in the context of other types of writing. For example, N. Scott Momaday's *The Way to Rainy Mountain* is a personal narrative that contains many vivid descriptions of situations and events recalled from the author's Kiowa Indian background. In the excerpt you will read, Momaday describes his return to his grandmother's house after her death—and the vivid memories of childhood the visit stirred. As you read, notice how the author uses specific sensory details to give you vivid impressions of the situations and events he observed and remembered.

A single knoll rises out of the plain in Oklahoma, north and west of the Wichita Range. For my people, the Kiowas, it is an old landmark, and they gave it the name Rainy Mountain. The hardest weather in the world is there. Winter brings blizzards, hot tornadic winds arise in the spring, and in summer the prairie is an anvil's edge. The grass turns brittle and brown, and it cracks beneath your feet. There are green belts along the rivers and creeks, linear groves of hickory and pecan, willow and witch hazel. At a distance in July or August the steaming foliage seems almost to writhe in fire. Great green and yellow grasshoppers are everywhere in the tall grass, popping up like corn to sting the flesh, and tortoises crawl about on the red earth, going nowhere in the plenty of time. Loneliness is an aspect of the land. . . .

Once there was a lot of sound in my grandmother's house, a lot of coming and going, feasting and talk. The summers there were full of excitement and reunion. The Kiowas are a summer people; they abide the cold and keep to themselves, but when the season turns and the land becomes warm and vital they cannot hold still; an old love of going returns upon them. The aged visitors who came to my grandmother's house when I was a child were made of lean and leather, and they bore themselves upright. They wore great black hats and bright ample shirts that shook in the wind. They rubbed fat upon their hair and wound their braids with strips of colored cloth. . . . Their wives and daughters served them well. The women might indulge themselves; gossip was at once the mark and compensation of their servitude. They made loud and elaborate talk among themselves, full of jest and gesture, fright and false alarm. They went abroad in fringed and flowered shawls, bright beadwork and German silver. They were at home in the kitchen, and they prepared meals that were banquets.

There were frequent prayer meetings, and great nocturnal feasts. When I was a child I played with my cousins outside, where the lamplight fell upon the ground and the singing of the old people rose up around us and carried away into the darkness. There were a lot of good things to eat, a lot of laughter and surprise. And afterwards, when the quiet returned, I lay down with my grandmother and could hear the frogs away by the river and feel the motion of the air.

Now there is a funeral silence in the rooms, the endless wake of some final word. The walls have closed in upon my grandmother's house. When I returned to it in mourning, I saw for the first time in my life how small it was. It was late at night, and there was a white moon, nearly full. I sat for a long time on the stone steps by the kitchen door. From there I could see out across the land; I could see the long row of trees by the creek, the low light upon the rolling plains, and the stars of the Big Dipper. Once I looked at the moon and caught sight of a strange thing. A cricket had perched upon the handrail, only a few inches away from me. My line of vision was such that the creature filled the moon like a fossil. It had gone there, I thought, to live and die, for there, of all places, was its small definition made whole and eternal. A warm wind rose up and purled like the longing within me.

The next morning I awoke at dawn and went out on the dirt road to Rainy Mountain. It was already hot, and the grasshoppers began to fill the air. Still, it was early in the morning, and the birds sang out of the shadows. The long yellow grass on the mountain shone in the bright light, and a scissortail hied above the land. There, where it ought to be, at the end of a long and legendary way, was my grandmother's grave. Here and there on the dark stones were ancestral names. Looking back once, I saw the mountain and came away.

Think and Respond

N. Scott Momaday uses vivid sensory details to create a mood of affection, nostalgia, and pride as he describes situations and events that make up his family heritage. What details of sight, sound, and touch help you imagine events from his childhood? What descriptive details help reveal his feelings about the current situation at Rainy Mountain? What situations and events do you have memories of?

Art on page 58: *Pink and Green Mountains, No. 1,* 1917, by Georgia O'Keeffe (1887–1986)

INVITATION
— TO —
Write

N. Scott Momaday used sensory details to convey a vivid impression of situations and events in his family background. Now it is your turn to write a description of an interesting situation or setting.

Effective description uses sensory details to convey what a writer saw, heard, touched, tasted, or smelled so that the reader shares the same experience. A description sometimes occurs by itself, but more often it will be part of a larger piece of writing—a story, a letter, a newspaper article, or a police report, for example. A description of a political rally might make an exciting beginning to a history report on American elections. Describing the deadly effects of acid rain could persuade readers to take a stand on the issue of cleaner air.

PREWRITE AND EXPLORE

HANDBOOKS
FOR HELP & PRACTICE

Personal Techniques,
pp. 322–324

1. Look for ideas. Situations and settings to describe are all around you, and they are also in your memory and your imagination. One or more of the following activities can help you discover ideas.

Exploratory Activities

- **Listing people** Make a list of people you might like to describe and the types of situations in which they are at their best. Consider interesting people in the community, your acquaintances, your friends, your family, or even imaginary people.
- **Listing places** Imagine a map of the world, and then make a list of places you've been—including your hometown and other places you've lived. What situations and settings come to mind as you think about each place? You might also consider special places within your town where scenes from your childhood took place.

- **Recalling**   Food is often the center of social events and fond memories, so you might enjoy writing about a special meal, whether it took place at a traditional family event or a hot dog stand. Begin by brainstorming about a meal you remember vividly. In a timed freewriting, describe the food served, the guests who were present, the physical setting, the time of year—as much as you can remember.

- **Reading literature**   With other writers, recall descriptive passages from favorite works of fiction that made the author's words come to life. For example, did you feel cold and anxious as you read Jack London's "To Build a Fire"? Did you experience the terror of Sanger Rainsford in Richard Connell's "The Most Dangerous Game"? Copy particularly striking phrases into your journal. Give some thought to your own experiences. What situations have you been in where setting contributed to what happened?

2. Choose a topic.   Freewrite about one of the situations and settings you discovered through the Exploratory Activities to see if you want to proceed with it. You also might check your journal, the ideas you experimented with in the Sketchbook on page 56, or the suggestions in "Apply Your Skills" on page 71. Once you settle on a topic, focus it so you can manage your writing more easily. If you are writing about a person you know, for example, you might want to focus your description on a specific aspect of the person's life (your dad as a weekend fisherman) or on a specific time of the person's life (your best friend as a sixth-grader, your mother as a ten-year-old). Keep in mind that your goal is to create a **dominant impression** of what you describe. Narrowing your topic makes the dominant impression easier to create.

PROBLEM SOLVING

How can I find a manageable topic to describe?

3. Identify your specific goals.   What do you want to accomplish with this description? Are you using description to create a character, communicate a feeling about someone or something, or clarify a point for a report? Will your description help you remember or understand something or someone better?

4. Choose a context for writing.   Consider your purpose, and then decide how to present your description. The form it takes will influence the way you approach the task. Will your description be part of a story, an essay, or a report?

5. Gather descriptive details. A description without details is like a frame without a picture. You can't convey a vivid impression of a scene without providing sensory details. This means using details that engage any or all of the five senses—seeing, hearing, feeling, tasting, or smelling. To help you gather sensory details for your piece of descriptive writing, you might use the resources of observation, memory, imagination, or research.

Writer's Choice You can write an **objective** description in which you present facts about a person, place, or thing in a clear, logical way. Or, you can write a **subjective** description in which your goal is to create a mood or express an opinion about your subject. Your choice will depend on your purpose and the context you have chosen for your writing.

One student, James, decided to write a subjective description of a visit to his father's art studio. He wanted to describe the studio for readers in his class, but he also thought he would like his father to read it. His goal was to show his changing impressions of the place. To prepare himself for drafting, James brainstormed a list of details he remembered from his last visit to the studio. Throughout this lesson you will follow James's process in writing his description.

—driving down Main Street

—old run-down buildings

—near Motor Vehicle office, old brick building

—dusty—smell of dust in my nose

—dark, fumbling upstairs, lock hard to work

—didn't like it much—thinking why did Dad want to work in an old dumpy place like this?

—stairs steep, dirty; ragged carpet; stairs creaked

—stair railing wobbled, dangerously steep steps

—junky, decrepit

—padlock on door at top of stairs

—inside—huge room, no, the whole 3rd floor

—no walls dividing space, pillars in middle of room, windows at end of room

—neat patterns of light shining in through windows

—smell of paint

—bare room—heater, easel and table with paints

—white walls, bright

—Dad's paintings against the wall—field with barn, mountain in Italy, cliff and canyon

—leaving—lights off, one by one, room dark and dusty again

COMPUTER TIP

If your word processing program has a thesaurus, you may find it useful for identifying vivid synonyms.

DRAFT AND DISCOVER

1. Appeal to the senses. As you begin drafting, play with words and images that appeal to all the senses. For example, in the opening paragraph of Momaday's description, notice the vivid sensory words he uses to describe the "hot tornadic winds," the grass that "turns brittle and brown, and . . . cracks beneath your feet," and the "steaming foliage" that "seems almost to writhe in fire."

2. Show what you are describing. In descriptive writing, *showing* is vitally important. You may want to use some of these strategies to make your description come to life for your reader.

HANDBOOKS

FOR HELP & PRACTICE

Adequate Detail,
pp. 405–406

Concrete/Abstract
Language,
pp. 424–425

Literal/Figurative
Language,
pp. 425–426

Dialogue,
pp. 452–455

Strategies

- **Figurative language** You can create vivid, unforgettable images by looking for striking similarities in otherwise different things. Notice, for example, the pictures Momaday creates in your mind with his simile describing grasshoppers "popping like corn" and the metaphor in which he says that the hot, flat summer prairie "is an anvil's edge." Try creating your own vivid figures of speech to help readers experience your subject in fresh ways.

- **Action** Describe a person by revealing what he or she does. Doing so allows your readers to form an impression of your subject without direct input from you. Note how Momaday gives an impression of his grandmother's life by describing the actions of women in her world—serving others, feasting, gossiping, and adorning themselves with bright, warm colors.

- **Dialogue** People are known by what they say and how they say it. Include a person's words as a way of showing what that person is like. Don't forget to use words that describe **how** a person speaks. Words such as *giggles, whispers, roars, whines, sighs,* and *cajoles* can give vivid impressions of a person's personality.

3. Elaborate on Ideas. The following strategies can help you develop your description.

Strategies

- **Narration** A good way to build reader involvement in your description is to give it a narrative structure in which you describe events that occur over a period of time.

- **Contrast** To make your description more dramatic, you may want to contrast your subject with a person, place, or thing that is very different. Another way to use contrast is to show how a person, place, or thing is different at different times. Notice how Momaday contrasts the warmth, life, and joyous bustle of his grandmother's house with the silent, dark house he returns to after her death.

Giving the devil his do.

Writing
─TIP─

Use similes and metaphors carefully. Too many figures of speech crowded close together can have an unintentionally humorous effect.

4. Organize your description. Arrange your details in an order that will help readers imagine the subject and understand your impression of the subject. If you are describing a place, you might use spatial order, describing the scene from left to right, top to bottom, clockwise, or some other direction. A description of a person might be organized from the most important to the least important detail or from least important to most important. You can also structure your description so that your reader receives impressions in the order that you perceived them. This method of organization works particularly well in descriptions with a narrative structure.

James decided to give his description a narrative structure by describing his changing impressions during a visit he made to his father's art studio. He began his draft by describing his arrival at the studio and his first impressions of it.

PROBLEM

S O L V I N G

How can I
organize my
description?

ONE STUDENT'S PROCESS

My visit to my dad's art studio downtown was a good lesson for me in how wrong first impressions can be. I felt depressed as we drove down Main Street because not much is happening downtown these days. After passing several old, dilapidated buildings, Dad pulled over to the side of the street, and we lumbered out and onto the sidewalk. As we walked up to the dirty glass door between the Motor Vehicles Bureau and Republican headquarters, Dad fiddled with his keychain, trying to find the right key.

Eventually the door creaked open, and the smells of mold and dust filled my nose. There before us, climbing straight up, was a decrepit old stairway. The steps were warped, some bowing upward, some bowing down. Each step moaned a different sound as we made our way up.

5. Look over your work. When you finish your draft, put it aside for a while, and then review it. You can review the draft yourself, or ask some peer readers for help. The following questions can help you review your draft.

R E V I E W Y O U R W R I T I N G

Questions for Yourself

- Have I captured the picture I had in my mind?
- Does my description create the feeling I wanted?
- Do the details I chose help readers experience the subject in a way that won't confuse them?
- Do I show as well as tell? Do I use vivid details and original figures of speech?

Questions for Your Peer Readers

- Can you picture the subject I am describing?
- What feeling does my description give you about my subject?
- Which details help you imagine my subject most vividly?
- Which details do you think I could improve?

R E V I S E Y O U R W R I T I N G

HANDBOOKS

FOR HELP & PRACTICE

Peer Response,
pp. 398–401

1. Evaluate your responses. Read what your peer readers wrote about your description. Compare their remarks with your own honest evaluation of your draft. What advice will you accept? What changes do you want to make? Keep in mind that a well-written description generally displays certain basic characteristics.

OVERBOARD, © 1990. Reprinted
with permission. All rights reserved.

Standards for Evaluation

An effective description . . .

- has a specific focus and a clear sense of purpose.
- uses sensory details and precise verbs, nouns, and modifiers to create a vivid picture.
- uses figurative language when appropriate, but avoids clichés and trite expressions.
- maintains a consistent mood and point of view.

2. Problem-solve. Decide which responses you want to use and then rework your draft. James made the following changes in response to suggestions from one peer reader:

ONE STUDENT'S PROCESS

The sound of the door closing behind me sounded [echo] [slamming] [rang]

through the room and suddenly the smells of dust and

mold vanished as more livelier smells—the smell of oil [scents] [tangy aroma]

paints mingled with the smells of turpentine and brush [more pungent, penetrating odors]

cleaner—came through the empty space. [wafting]

The room before me was bear except for an old [bare] [ancient, rusted]

heater at the left end and an easle and small table with

paints on it way down at the far end. Walking toward

the easle Dad pulled on the string attatched to the bear [bare]

bulbs evenly spaced across the ceiling. As the lights

came on, the room took on a different look. The white [was transfomed .]

walls reflected the light, and the room became very

bright. a shimmering white palace. My feelings were transformed, too; I felt relaxed, dreamlike, as though I could be anywhere I wanted in the whole world .

> You noticed some good details, but could you use more vivid words to help me imagine the sound of the door and all the smells?

> Maybe you could punch up the part where the room changes.

> This really gave me a good feeling about your dad's studio.

3. Proofread your work. Make a clean copy that incorporates all your changes. Then look for errors in grammar, punctuation, and spelling. Correct these mistakes so that readers will not be distracted by them.

LINKING
GRAMMAR AND WRITING

Using Commas with Two or More Adjectives

Use commas between adjectives of equal rank that modify the same noun. To tell if the adjectives are of equal rank, try putting *and* between them or reversing their order. If the sentence still sounds natural and makes sense, then a comma is needed.

USE A COMMA:	We made our way down the dim, dusty stairway. (You could say "dim and dusty" or "dusty, dim.")
DO NOT USE A COMMA:	One painting showed a faded red barn. (You would not say "a faded and red barn" or a "red faded barn.")

PUBLISH AND PRESENT

HANDBOOKS
FOR HELP & PRACTICE

Sharing Completed Writing, pp. 418–419

- **Collaborate to prepare an oral reading.** Find some people in your class who wrote descriptions similar to yours, and then work together to prepare an oral reading for your class. Collaborate on an introduction that traces the themes that unite the descriptions.
- **Have an art student render your description in visual form.** Your English teacher and an art teacher might plan a joint exhibit of written descriptions and corresponding artwork. You also could create your own visual interpretation of your description.
- **Submit your description to your school's literary magazine.** You might also consider sending your description to a national publication that publishes student writing, such as *Writing* magazine. Ask your teacher's advice about submitting work.
- **Save your work in your writing portfolio.**

A Visit to the White Palace

James Scarcelli

My visit to my dad's art studio downtown was a good lesson for me in how wrong first impressions can be. I felt depressed as we drove down Main Street because not much is happening downtown these days. After passing some old, dilapidated buildings, Dad pulled over to the side of the street, and we lumbered out and onto the sidewalk. As we walked up to the dirty glass door between the Motor Vehicle Bureau and Republican headquarters, Dad fiddled with his keychain, trying to find the right key.

Eventually the door creaked open, and the smells of mold and dust filled my nose. There before us, climbing straight up, was a dusty old stairway. The steps were warped, some bowing upward, some bowing down. Each step moaned a different sound as we made our way up. Even though it was broad daylight outside, the stairway was dark as a cave, except for the thin stream of light filtering through the door on the street. I grasped the rail on the wall to steady myself on the uneven stairs, but over the years it had loosened from its mounting and now it rattled back and forth as I climbed.

I wondered to myself as we climbed to the third floor why Dad had picked this place for his studio. I knew artists don't need the cleanest place to work because they are going to mess it up with paint anyway, but this place seemed filthy. It looked as if any second it would fall apart from neglect.

Dad stuck the key into the padlock and opened the door. We stepped into the room. Well, it wasn't a room exactly, but an entire floor of the building. It was huge, as big as a basketball court. There were no dividing walls, just huge white pillars in a row, marching neatly

Focuses on a specific event and has a clear sense of purpose

Uses a narrative context to build reader involvement

Uses sensory details and precise words

Uses figurative language

Creates and maintains a consistent mood

Uses figurative language

down the middle of the room. At either end of the room, light shone through the huge old casement windows onto the soft, bare wooden floor.

The echo of the door slamming behind me rang through the room. Suddenly the smells of dust and mold vanished, as livelier scents—the tangy aroma of oil paints mingled with the more pungent, penetrating odors of turpentine and brush cleaner—came wafting across the empty space.

The room before me was bare except for an ancient, rusted heater at the left end and an easel and small table with paints on it way down at the far end. Walking toward the easel, Dad pulled on the strings attached to the bare bulbs evenly spaced across the ceiling. As the lights came on, the room was transformed. The white walls reflected the light, and the room became a shimmering white palace. My feelings were transformed, too; I felt relaxed, dreamlike, as though I could be anywhere I wanted in the whole world.

Dad showed me the paintings he had lined up against the wall, some finished, some just started. For the first time, I appreciated my dad's works. As I looked at the paintings, I felt I could walk inside one. I was out in a half-mown field looking at a faded red barn; in a little village on a rocky mountain in Italy; or looking off a cliff at a beautiful canyon far below.

After a couple of minutes, Dad's voice brought me back to the white palace. It was time to leave. Dad turned the lights off one by one, and the palace became once again a bare old room. We made our way down the dim, dusty stairway and out into the glaring light of day. As we stepped outside, a breath of fresh air welcomed me back to the "real" world. As the car pulled away from the curb, I looked up at those dusty windows on the third floor and thought, "What a surprising place!"

WRITER TO WRITER

Good writing is supposed to evoke sensation in the reader—not the fact that it's raining, but the feel of being rained upon.

E. L. Doctorow, novelist

Gene Kelly in the movie, *Singin' in the Rain*

1. Reflect on your writing. Write an informal letter to your teacher about your experience with writing a description. Tell your teacher how you felt about the writing assignment, about what went well for you and what was difficult. Talk about how you handled the specific requirements or problems generated by this assignment: how, for example, you chose a topic, how you revised to add sensory details, as the student writer did, or how you used contrast to add drama to your description, as both the student writer and N. Scott Momaday did in theirs. What did you learn from the models and from your own writing experience?

2. Apply your skills. Try one or more of the following activities.

FOR YOUR **PORTFOLIO**

- **Cross curricular** Imagine that you are a newspaper reporter on the scene at an important event in history. Write a news article in which you give an eyewitness description of the event.
- **Literature** Think of a story you have recently read, such as "The Ransom of Red Chief" by O. Henry or "The Possibility of Evil" by Shirley Jackson. Imagine what it would be like if that story took place in a different setting—a different place or time. Then rewrite a scene from the story as if it took place in the new setting you have imagined.
- **General** Work cooperatively with other students to create a travel guide to attractions in your community. Briefly describe attractions such as museums, sports arenas, historic sites, or parks that tourists should visit. Make sure your readers can "see" each attraction clearly.
- **Related Assignments** Follow the suggestions on pages 74–82 to write an interview and a character sketch.

Interview

Interview with
ANNE BANCROFT
by Lewis Funke and John E. Booth

Related ASSIGNMENT

Talk-show hosts, magazine editors, and reporters all share an important trade secret: everybody loves a good interview. Through interviews we can get a personal, even intimate view of a person we might otherwise never meet, much less get to know.

The actress Anne Bancroft, who is interviewed here, is famous for her roles as Helen Keller's teacher, Annie Sullivan, in the play and movie *The Miracle Worker,* and as Mrs. Robinson in the movie *The Graduate.* Notice, as you read this excerpt, how the interviewer asks questions that encourage Ms. Bancroft to talk freely, as she would to a close friend.

[Ms.] Bancroft was dressed entirely in black . . . [but she] is by no means a muted personality. . . . She obviously involves herself intensely in what she is doing.

Interviewer: You are one of the unusual young women, according to what I've read, whose parents actually favored their child's going into the theatre. . . . Why, I wonder, did they want you to [become an actress]?

Bancroft: Oh, well, I don't really know why, except that I think my mother always had kind of fantasies, you know, of herself going into the theatre, and then along came this daughter who would have done anything to please her mother, and therefore the mother saw a fulfillment of her own dreams in her child.

Interviewer: Did she act or sing?

Bancroft: She didn't, but I did, so that when I came along and started to express things that she had felt all her life—and I started to express them in songs and dancing, and through what I did as a child—it was then I could express the things she always wanted to express. . . .

Interviewer: What did you do in terms of singing and dancing and entertaining that gave [her] this feeling?

Bancroft: Ever since I was old enough to open my mouth, I was singing and dancing—and I'd rather do that than anything else in this world. I'd rather do that than eat or sleep, and I often did. You know, I'd be singing and my mother would be looking for me and I'd be on the street corner singing for somebody. Or else when she'd come in my room late at night, when I was supposed to be asleep, I'd be singing, or making up stories.

Interviewer: Where did you learn these songs?

Bancroft: Oh, I picked them up, like off the radio.

Interviewer: Why is it then that, as I gather also from what I've read, you began to think in terms of becoming a laboratory technician?

Bancroft: Because I just never in my wildest dreams ever thought that I ever would be an actress.

Interviewer: But you had been in the dramatic society at Christopher Columbus High School.

Bancroft: Yes, but not in my wildest dreams did I ever really think that—I mean, I thought it was like a fantasy, you know, like kids have fantasies, and I thought that's what it would remain all my life.

Think AND Respond

The interviewer focuses on the part Ms. Bancroft's mother played in her career. Why might the interviewer have chosen this detail from the actress's life to begin the interview? What effect do you think the strategy had on Ms. Bancroft? If you could interview anyone in the world, whom would you choose? What would you most want to know?

INVITATION TO Write

The interview with Anne Bancroft reveals aspects of the actress's life that her fans might not otherwise have known. Now plan and conduct an interview session of your own, one designed to bring out interesting details about a person you know.

An interview is a unique type of observation that has little to do with the sense of sight. Instead, a writer gathers details by asking questions and listening carefully to the answers. A good interviewer researches the subject's life beforehand, sets a focus for the interview, and prepares a list of questions that will encourage the subject to reveal himself or herself. If you plan and conduct an interview carefully, you may receive a fascinating glimpse into the life of the other person.

PLANNING THE INTERVIEW

HANDBOOKS
FOR HELP & PRACTICE

**Other Techniques,
pp. 327–329**
**Sharing Writing in
Progress,
pp. 417–418**
**Other Information
Sources,
pp. 495–496**

1. Choose a person to interview. Begin by thinking about friends, relatives, and other people you know. Consider someone who has an interesting job, hobby, or unusual life experience. Also think about interviewing people in the news, such as local celebrities or community leaders. Remember, however, that the person you interview does not have to be famous. If you need help in making a final selection, ask family members and friends for ideas, or check the local newspaper.

2. Make an appointment. Set up a time and place that will be convenient for the person you are interviewing. Try to make sure that you will have enough time and privacy to avoid being rushed or interrupted.

3. Prepare for the interview. Research both the person you are going to interview and, if you have a focus in mind, the topic on which you want to concentrate. The interviewers in the excerpt had clearly read about Ms. Bancroft's family background in preparation for their interview with her. They were also well-informed about the theater.

 Writer's Choice Do you want to take notes during the interview, or do you want to tape-record the session so that you have a complete and accurate record of everything that was said? As a courtesy, ask permission to use a tape recorder.

4. Make up a list of questions. Decide what you want to know, and compile a list of questions that will help you elicit the information. Avoid questions that can be answered with a simple yes or no. Instead, try questions that start with "Tell me about . . ." or "How do you . . ." or "What is . . ."

CONDUCTING AND WRITING THE INTERVIEW

1. Set the tone of the interview. Arrive on time, prepared and ready to get down to work. Introduce yourself and ask permission to take notes or set up your tape recorder. Begin with a friendly, open-ended question to help both of you relax and to get the conversation started. In the excerpt, for example, the interviewer asks about something remarkable in Ms. Bancroft's background—her mother wanted her to go into the theater. Because the question invites discussion, Ms. Bancroft and the interviewer are soon engaged in spontaneous conversation.

2. Relax and listen. Ask the questions you have prepared clearly and briefly, referring to your research notes, if necessary, to cite names, dates, and events. Listen carefully to the answers. Follow your sequence of questions as much as possible, but be flexible. You may want to ask for clarification and elaboration, or you may wish to pursue something new that comes up in the interview. Remember to thank your subject when the interview is over, and offer a draft of the interview for his or her review before publication.

3. Transcribe the tape. If the interview was fairly short, type it word-for-word from the tape, in question-and-answer form. If the interview was very long, just type up the major points at this stage. In either case, make a working copy you can write on, and save the original.

Barbara Walters interviewing Anwar Sadat

Writing
— **TIP** —

You may want to jot down important points, questions, or ideas on organization as you listen.

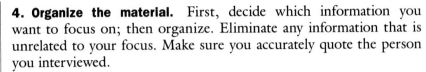

Writing TIP

Try writing each question and its answer on a separate index card. Then shuffle the cards to try out different organizations.

4. Organize the material. First, decide which information you want to focus on; then organize. Eliminate any information that is unrelated to your focus. Make sure you accurately quote the person you interviewed.

5. Select a format. Two basic formats are used to present interviews: a narrative article consisting of running text that quotes the subject liberally, or a series of questions and answers, like the Bancroft interview.

6. Write an introduction. After drafting the interview, write an introduction that provides necessary background information and sets the scene for the reader.

REVIEWING YOUR WRITING

1. Evaluate your audience's response. Ask two friends to read the interview aloud and try to listen objectively. Have you caught the "spirit" of the person you interviewed? Did you keep yourself in the background? Is the focus clear? Do you need to edit your questions more? Have you edited too much, so that answers are unclear or out of context?

2. Get feedback from the person you interviewed. Prepare a clean, typed draft, and ask the person you interviewed to review it. Make any changes that he or she requests.

PUBLISHING AND PRESENTING

- **Make arrangements for a guest speaker.** Invite the person you interviewed to come to school to talk to your class, and use information from your interview to make an impromptu introduction.
- **Share the interview with experts.** Share your interview with professionals who are in the same field or with people who are concerned with the same issue.
- **Seek out a wider audience.** Send the written interview to your school or local newspaper for publication. If the tape is of good quality, offer it to a local radio station for airing. For legal reasons, be sure you have the interviewee's permission to publish or broadcast your conversation.

76 Workshop 2

On the Lightside

DIAMONDS ARE A WORD'S BEST FRIEND

"The movie I saw last night was a smash hit."

"I had too much work, so I had to take a rain check."

"I liked that movie right off the bat, and the sequel is playing next Saturday, but I'm supposed to baby-sit. Could you pinch-hit for me and take my job?"

"I wish I could, but I'm writing a major-league term paper."

"Couldn't you take a seventh-inning stretch?"

"My report has to touch all the bases, so I'll be in all weekend."

"Well, I guess I struck out with you. I'll ask my brother."

Everyday expressions that come from the game of baseball are extremely common, and many date back to the turn of the century or even earlier. *Off (one's) base* meant "mistaken" or "wrong" from 1882 on and also suggested the meaning of "crazy" from about 1890 to 1910.

The *beanball,* a pitched baseball that comes near or hits the batter's head, has been written about since at least 1906. Today, people are more likely to complain that life has thrown them a *curveball.*

Around 1925, the underworld referred to a police informer as a *bat carrier.* During World War II, soldiers used the expressions "to bat the breeze" and "to bat one's gums" for idle gossip.

New baseball-related expressions come into use in each generation. Some quickly fade away, while others become permanent gems of the English language. As the ad says, (baseball) "diamonds are forever."

Character Sketch

FROM

The Hidden Songs of a Secret Soul

BY BOB GREENE

Have you ever heard or read a description of a stranger that was so vivid you felt you could recognize the person anywhere? A good character sketch can have that effect.

A character sketch is a portrait of a person, drawn in words. The writer focuses on one scene or incident that captures the essence of the subject. Here, Bob Greene sketches a co-worker at the pop-bottling plant where he worked part time during college. As you read, notice what characteristics Bob Greene saw in Lenny that his co-workers didn't see.

Lenny was the loneliest of dreamers. . . . [He] was a thin, slight man in his middle forties with a stammer and a sad face. . . .

He never said much, and for a while we didn't say much to him. We would come in after classes, nod hello to him, and start loading boxes. Lenny had spent most of his life being invisible; we sensed that without really thinking about it. He just seemed happy that we didn't rag him like the others did.

One afternoon, though, he started to talk. He didn't slow up what he was doing, but as he worked he began to ask us about the classes we took in school, the courses we were studying. He asked if any of us were studying English as a major; he wanted to know if any of us were studying the great poets. . . .

Lenny said, "Sometimes I write poems." . . .

We asked him that day if he would let us see his poems, and he said no. We kept it up, though; we wanted to see. Finally he said that he would like to let us see them, but that he was afraid that if he brought them in, the others would find out and make fun of him. . . .

One day he said that we could come home with him if we wished. . . . He lived in one room. There were not enough places for us to sit. He brought out a large scrapbook. The poems were inside.

They were written all in longhand, with a fountain pen. Even before we started to read them, they looked elegant. Lenny's hand moved with strokes full of flourish and style, confident and strong while Lenny was timid and quiet. And when we did begin to read, the poems were beautiful. The verses were long, and rich with imagery and detail. They told of love, and of spiritual triumphs, and of life in faraway places. They were music. We must have sat and read for an hour, saying nothing. When we finished and looked up, there was Lenny, in his rented room, staring away from us.

"Please never say anything to the others," he said.

We tried to tell him how good the poems were, how he should be proud of what he had done, and not ashamed to let anyone know, but he cut us off. . . .

The next day Lenny let us know, without a word, that we were not to talk about the poems again.

Think AND Respond

What does Bob Greene want the reader to understand about Lenny? What details does Greene include to help him accomplish his goal? Now think of people you know, even casually. Is there one who is particularly intriguing? Why? Could he or she be the subject of a character sketch?

INVITATION
— TO —
Write

Look again at Bob Greene's character sketch of Lenny.
Then create your own portrait of a person, highlighting
important aspects of the subject's personality.

Like any good description, a character sketch uses carefully chosen details to help bring the person to life. These details capture not only an individual's physical appearance, but also the personality—the distinctive traits and abilities that make up a person's character.

PLANNING THE CHARACTER SKETCH

HANDBOOKS
FOR HELP & PRACTICE

Limiting a Topic,
pp. 340–341
Point of View,
pp. 447–451

1. Decide on a subject. Because it's usually easier to write about what you know, you may wish to sketch someone who is or was special in your life—an uncle, a close friend, the teacher who actually made math fun. However, if you prefer, write about someone you don't know well but whose actions are particularly revealing in some way, as Lenny's were for Bob Greene. You can even choose a person you have only observed—on the street, in a store, at school, or even on television.

2. Describe your subject. List what you know about your subject. What does he or she look like? Describe physical details, such as facial features, style of dress, speech, or mannerisms. Then try to get beneath the surface appearance; identify the characteristics that make your subject unique. How does he or she behave toward other people? How does this person feel about himself or herself? What hidden talents or activities, like Lenny's secret love of poetry, might be part of the person?

3. Place your subject in a context. It often helps to place your subject in a particular setting—a time and place—to explain better how he or she behaves toward other people or reacts to a situation.

Think about what incident or setting best reveals the inner self of your subject. For example, in the excerpt, Greene gives two contrasting views of Lenny by showing him in two settings. At work he "never said much" and seemed to have "spent most of his life being invisible." On the other hand, at home, through his poetry, he was imaginative, confident, and romantic—someone who "should be proud of what he had done."

Writing
—**TIP**—

Try describing your subject to a small group of listeners. Their questions can help you discover more details.

DRAFTING THE CHARACTER SKETCH

1. Focus on a purpose. A writer's primary purpose in a character sketch is to share impressions of a particular person with the reader. In addition, however, a character sketch may be used to record a special experience that the writer shared with the person, to practice skills in observing and describing characters, or simply to entertain readers.

2. Show rather than tell. As you write, make the character come alive by using dialogue, descriptive detail, and anecdotes that reveal his or her personality and way of life. Greene describes Lenny's room by saying there weren't enough places to sit. He conveys Lenny's fear of being teased about his poems through just one remark: "Please never say anything to the others." He contrasts Lenny's poetry with Lenny's behavior and appearance.

 Writer's Choice What point of view will you use? As in Greene's sketch, first-person narration brings the reader in close touch with the writer, as if the two were conversing. On the other hand, third-person narration can be a compelling point of view for a character sketch, if you know the person well enough to imagine his or her thoughts and feelings.

3. Write a strong conclusion. For your conclusion try "saving the best for last." New details or a striking anecdote may provide a more effective ending than a simple summary of your subject's traits and accomplishments. If you are writing about a handicapped friend whose athletic skill and persistence you admire, you might wait until the end to reveal that he is confined to a wheelchair.

The Honeymooners

REVIEWING YOUR WRITING

1. Be sure your character sketch works. Ask your peer readers to respond to your sketch. Do they now know the person you have written about? Have you conveyed the important aspects of the person that you intended? Are the tone and point of view appropriate?

2. Check the details. Have you included a physical description? Perhaps one or two additional details would make the person's character more vivid. Is the setting clear? What could you add to complete your picture of the person?

3. Revise your draft. Consider your peer readers' suggestions and follow those that will strengthen your sketch. Then proofread for spelling, grammar, and mechanical errors.

COMPUTER TIP

Your magazine will look even more professional if you use a desktop publishing program to compose and lay out the character sketches.

PUBLISHING AND PRESENTING

- **Create a magazine.** Collect the character sketches written by members of your class into a kind of *People* magazine. If possible, illustrate it with photographs, drawings, or magazine pictures.
- **Present your character sketch to your class.** Perform it as a theater piece: a monologue or (with suitable revisions) a brief dialogue.

Sentence

Using Inverted Word Order

When you imitate sentences by accomplished writers, you learn structures and techniques that make your own writing more varied and effective. In this lesson, you will practice imitating sentences with an unusual word order.

Experienced writers sometimes emphasize certain sentences by changing the traditional order of words to one out of the ordinary. Compare the two sentences below.

              s   v

1. An iron <u>deer</u> <u>stood</u> outside, upon this lawn.

                     v   s

2. Outside, upon this lawn, <u>stood</u> an iron <u>deer</u>.
   Ray Bradbury, *The Martian Chronicles*

In the first sentence, the subject (underlined once) comes before the verb; this is traditional word order. In the second sentence, the verb (underlined twice) comes before the subject. This inverted word order is unusual enough to give the sentence extra emphasis.

Model: Outside, upon this lawn, stood an iron deer.
        Ray Bradbury, *The Martian Chronicles*

A. Identifying Imitations Some sentences below imitate the structure (not the content) of the model. Identify the imitations.

1. Together, in reserved seats, sat the nominee and his party.
2. They gathered, tired and hungry, for the celebration of harvest.
3. Downstairs, beside the toolbox, were the lost keys.
4. Dripping wet, the cat looked like a sewer rat with a collar.
5. Overhead, with its piercing whine, streaked the lone jet.

B. Unscrambling Sentences The sentence parts that follow are similar to those in the model. Unscramble the parts and then rewrite them to create sentences that imitate the model. Punctuate each sentence as the model is punctuated.

1. a. was the phantom's lair
   b. far below the opera house
   c. underneath

2. a. inside
   b. towered the cases of eggs
   c. in a refrigerated storage room

3. a. on the computer's screen
   b. were the rows of correct answers
   c. nearby

4. a. loomed a shaggy form
   b. far off
   c. by the edge of the clearing

5. a. on the rusty grate
   b. huddled the homeless man
   c. downstairs

6. a. below
   b. snaked the Rio Grande
   c. like a brown ribbon

C. Combining Sentences Combine each sentence pair to create one sentence that matches the model. To do this, find the modifying phrase (underlined) in the second sentence and insert it just before the verb (underlined) in the first sentence. Punctuate as the model is punctuated.

Example   Alone <u>stood</u> the victorious coach. The coach was <u>in the center of the court</u>.

Student Sentence   Alone, in the center of the court, stood the victorious coach.

1. There lies the tiny Swedish town of Abisko. Abisko is deep within the Arctic Circle.

2. In and out flew the Russian dancers. The dancers flew around their spinning partners.

3. High up soared the tiny biplane. The biplane soared straight toward the menacing clouds.

4. To the right raced a glacier-fed stream. The stream was sparkling in the sun.

5. Ahead lurked the mysterious stranger. The stranger was in the shadow of the doorway.

6. Far off bobbed a carved wooden chest. The chest bobbed on the inky surface of the water.

7. Upstairs stood the angry school principal. The principal was glowering down at me.

8. From the left rose his teammates' cheers. The cheers rose through the warm night air.

D. Expanding Sentences   Complete each sentence so that the verb comes before the subject, as it does in the model.

> ***Example***   Together, out of the wind. . . .
>
> ***Student Sentence***   Together, out of the wind, huddled the lost hikers.

1. Nearby, on the roof, . . .
2. Overhead, in the dark sky, . . .
3. Deep below, on the ocean floor, . . .
4. Outside, under the car, . . .
5. There, in the attic window, . . .

E. Imitating Sentences   Now that you are familiar with the sentence parts and their arrangement in the model, write three sentences of your own. Your sentences should imitate the model in structure, but not in content. Punctuate as the model is punctuated.

> ***Example***   Ahead, in the empty field, strolled a solitary deer.

Application   Write a short narrative paragraph that ends with one of the sentences you wrote for Exercise E. Notice how your inverted sentence adds emphasis to the end of your paragraph.

> ***Example***   Soon after sunrise, Lee parked his car in the hill country outside Austin and struck out to explore. He moved comfortably through the green terrain, as if he had been raised there instead of in the asphalt city. A faint rustling alerted him, and he stood still. Ahead, in the empty field, strolled a solitary deer.

Grammar Refresher   The sentences you have imitated in this exercise are simple sentences in which the order of subject and verb is inverted. Each sentence begins with two modifiers. For more on inversion of subject and verb, see Handbook 31, pages 573–575. For more on using phrases as modifiers, see Handbook 32, pages 586–589.

Sketchbook

We are usually given our names when we are infants, before much is known about us. But the Cree Indians also give people a name later in life based on something they did, something that happened to them, or some quality they had. This poem tells of one such name.

Indian Girl, by Robert Henri. ©1990 Indianapolis Museum of Art. Gift of Mrs. John N. Carey

QUIET UNTIL THE THAW
A CREE INDIAN NAMING POEM

Her name tells of how
    it was with her.
The truth is, she did not speak
    in winter.
Everyone learned not to
    ask her questions in winter,
    once this was known about her.
The first winter this happened
    we looked in her mouth to see
    if something was frozen. Her tongue
    maybe, or something else in there.
But after the thaw she spoke again
    and told it was fine for her that way.
So each spring we
    looked forward to that.

Write a poem or story that is a "naming poem" for you. Make up a name for yourself and use that as the title. Then tell the story of how you got this name.

Additional Sketches

Tell the story of your locker or some other familiar object.

Choose a song you like. Identify a few hints of structure or theme, and then write a song (or something song-like) that uses those features.

Narrative and Literary Writing

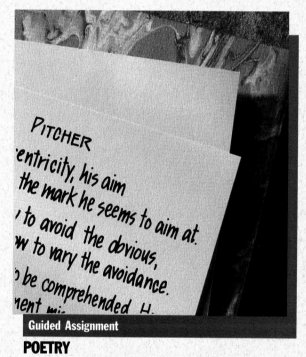

PITCHER

...entricity, his aim
...the mark he seems to aim at.
...to avoid the obvious,
...to vary the avoidance.
...be comprehended H...
...ent mi...

Guided Assignment

POETRY

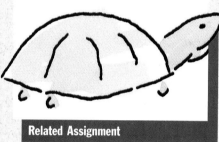

Related Assignment

STORY

Related Assignment

MONOLOGUE

hat can describe the sweetness of a peach? What can tell the tale of a soldier facing his first battle far from home? What can show you one person's experience of climbing Mt. Everest? Literature can do all these things as it calls forth the resources of the imagination to transform personal experience into works of narrative and imaginative power. Writers may focus on small events or large, on the blooming of a rose or the crossing of a continent, but their main resources—personal imagination and narrative skill—are always the same. In the three assignments that follow, you will call on your imagination and narrative skill and draw on your own experiences to create poems, stories, and monologues.

Guided ASSIGNMENT

Poetry

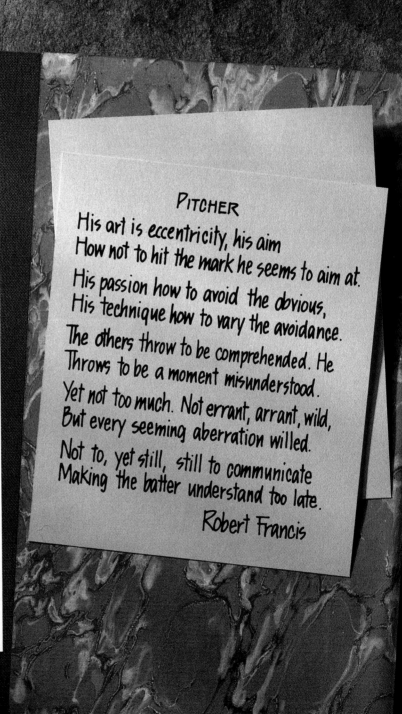

Poetry may be the most misunderstood form of writing. Many people think poems have to rhyme or be written in a particular form, or that only certain subjects are appropriate for poems. As the poems on this page show you, however, poets work with many options and few rules. Poems may be about any subject and may serve a variety of purposes. What most poems seem to share, however, is a desire to surprise and delight readers at the same time that they tell about an experience or insight. What purposes do the poems shown here seem to serve? Do some of them throw you curveballs, like the pitcher in the poem by Robert Francis?

PITCHER

His art is eccentricity, his aim
How not to hit the mark he seems to aim at.

His passion how to avoid the obvious,
His technique how to vary the avoidance.

The others throw to be comprehended. He
Throws to be a moment misunderstood.

Yet not too much. Not errant, arrant, wild,
But every seeming aberration willed.

Not to, yet still, still to communicate
Making the batter understand too late.

Robert Francis

For Valerie

Yesterday, stopped at the traffic light,
this lady comes over to the bike,
says "could you direct me to the Y?"
I tried, but couldn't remember street names,
so she puts on the extra helmet
and fifteen minutes later we were there.

Something in the way she held me,
tight about the waist; I knew it was you,
forty years from now — a red scarf
and blue jeans — catching a ride

Bobbie Copeland

ONE THOUSAND
NINE HUNDRED & SIXTY-EIGHT WINTERS

Got up this morning
Feeling good & black
Thinking black thoughts
Did black things
Played all my black records
And minded my own black business
Put on my best black clothes
Walked out my black door
And, Lord have mercy: white snow!

Jacqui Earley

Think AND Respond

Why does the pitcher in Robert
Francis's poem throw "to be
a moment misunderstood"?
Could the same thing be said
about poets? What do you think
inspired each poet to write what
he or she did? What ideas do
these poems give you for poems
you could write?

INVITATION
— TO —
Write

Poems like the ones you have just read tell a brief story, capture a moment of experience, or make a surprising observation. Use the activities that follow to help you write a poem of your own, drawing upon your own experiences, memory, imagination, feelings, or observations.

Contemporary poetry can take any form and may be written on any subject, yet poetry is a unique kind of writing. First, poetry is written in lines rather than in sentences. Like sentences, lines can be revised—shortened, lengthened, changed—in any way the poet chooses while working on a draft. Second, a poem is condensed, consolidated; there is space only for the most important details. Often a poem presents the center of a story or an experience. Third, a poem is the closest thing in words to music and to visual art. The sounds of words, their rhythms, the way lines look on the page, the mental images words evoke—these are all tools a poet may use in creating a poem. Finally, though sometimes poets begin writing when they have an idea, they most often begin with an image, or phrase, or feeling. Poets rarely plan what they will write before they begin composing. Many poets say they discover their poems as they draft.

In this assignment you will begin experimenting with poetry. You will write drafts of several poems and then choose one or two to revise. Like other poets, you will write from your own perspective and experience. This guided assignment will help you discover a poem that could be written only by you.

P R E W R I T E   A N D   E X P L O R E

1. Collect material for poems. Anything you pay close attention to can become a subject for poetry. In the following activities, you will begin looking and listening as a poet would. Use a section of your journal as a Poet's Notebook to record your ideas.

Exploratory Activities

- **Listening in** Jot down phrases that strike you as you talk to people or as you overhear other people talking. Bits of dialogue can provide the seeds of an idea.
- **Observing** Write phrases or lines describing things you notice at school, at home, or in your neighborhood.
- **Remembering images** In your mind, picture experiences from your recent past or childhood, moments and events that stand out in your memory as happy, sad, or amusing—not necessarily important moments, but interesting or surprising ones, like the one Bobbie Copeland drew upon for his poem "For Valerie." Make notes recording the details of your mental image. What do you see in your imagination? What do you hear, feel, taste, smell?

A perfect performance is a gymnast's most memorable moment.

Writing
—**TIP**—

Everyday language is filled with figures of speech, but most of these are so common ("big as a house" or "he's a snake in the grass") that they no longer stimulate the imagination. Avoid these "dead metaphors" or clichés in your writing.

- **Creating figures of speech** Pay attention to the special way you think or feel about certain people and events in your life and the nicknames you use for them. Nicknames and feelings can be a rich source for similes, metaphors, and other figures of speech. Do you think of lunchtime as a fashion parade? Do you sometimes feel like an alley cat at a pet show?
- **Reading literature** Reread the poems on pages 88–89, and read other contemporary poems such as "Miss Rosie" by Lucille Clifton, or "Foul Shot" by Edwin Hoey. Copy your favorite poems into your Poet's Notebook. Also, jot down lines or phrases of your own that occur to you as you read.

A student, Monica, collected the following notes in her Poet's Notebook. Throughout the remainder of this workshop you will follow Monica's process in writing a poem.

COMPUTER

COMPUTER TIP

Start a file for your own lines and phrases and for lines and phrases that strike you in the poems you read. The items in this file may spark ideas later when you start drafting your poems.

ONE STUDENT'S PROCESS

OBSERVING
Outside the elementary school the little kids are lined up dressed for the rain like miniature firefighters.

The poster's crooked on the wall above my head.

METAPHORS AND SIMILES
If I think about what might happen in five years, it's like looking into a long tunnel. I can't really see anything.

He's a hidden place in the mountains.

IMAGES OF WHAT I REMEMBER
The move into junior high: When I first walked into the cafeteria and didn't know anyone I felt like I was from outer space or the cafeteria was filled with people from outer space and the room looked bright white.

The fire: like a postcard picture of a sunset, only it was night.

2. Try collaborating. Meet with a group of classmates and read aloud passages from your Poet's Notebooks. First read aloud any of the published poems you have recorded in your notebook. Then share any of the prewriting you have done. Talk among yourselves about the different sources for poetry you have experimented with. Feel free to borrow lines or images from one another.

3. Choose a starting point. Look through your Poet's Notebook for a few ideas or phrases you want to explore. You may also find a topic in "Apply Your Skills" on page 101 or in the ideas you experiment with in the Sketchbook on page 86.

1. Begin by freewriting. Now that you've begun to think as a poet would, you're ready to begin writing quick drafts of poems. In these quick drafts, don't censor yourself. Write as much as you can. Most poets' early drafts are much longer than their final versions. To get started, try these techniques.

- **Write anything that comes to you.** Just begin writing. Listen to the rhythms of the words as you write them. Experiment with short lines, long lines, and lines that are the same length.
- **After a page or two, reread what you have written.** Read your freewriting and circle any lines or phrases you particularly like. Choose one or more of these lines or phrases to begin more freewriting. Pay attention to what seems to be emerging as the subject of your poem.
- **Write as much as you can.** Choose a subject from your freewriting and write as many lines as possible. Then set aside your quick draft without revising it.

Here is some of the freewriting Monica did in her notebook.

ONE STUDENT'S PROCESS

The cafeteria was filled with people from outer space
The room looked bright white
Maybe I was from outer space
I was from the outside
Outside that room
Where all the people knew each other
And there was nobody for me to talk to
I felt like I stood out and I bumped into the table
I set my tray down and I felt funny
The girl next to me was wearing a white shirt
  and the boy next to her
Was wearing a white shirt too
I was wearing dark blue

HANDBOOKS
FOR HELP & PRACTICE

Word Choice,
pp. 402–404
Sharing Writing in
Progress,
pp. 417–418
Literal/Figurative
Language,
pp. 425–426
Sound Devices,
pp. 427–428

PROBLEM
S O L V I N G

**How do I
decide which
details to include
in my poem?**

Writing
━TIP━

You can often use lines from one draft in another poem.

PROBLEM
S O L V I N G

How do I bring out what is important in my poem?

2. Ask for reactions. Share your quick-draft poems with your classmates. Read the poems aloud. Talk over with your classmates which poem you might focus on.

3. Choose one of your quick-draft poems. First reread all your quick-draft poems and circle lines and phrases you or your writing group particularly like. Decide which quick poem you want to work on.

4. Recopy your quick-draft. Recopying will give you a chance to pay close attention to what you have written so far and to determine what the poem seems to be saying.

5. Read the draft aloud. Listen to the words you have written so far and think about how you can begin to shape the poem.

6. Begin deleting, adding, and changing. Bring out what is important by getting rid of lines and phrases that seem unnecessary. Add new lines and phrases where you need them. You may wish to try some of the following strategies to help you shape your poem.

Strategies

- **Shape and form** The shape of your poem—the arrangement of short and long lines, and the use of stanzas to break up ideas—can enhance your message. You also may wish to experiment with the form of your poem. The poems on pages 88–89 are all written in free verse. If you want to explore a structured form, try out regular patterns of rhyme, rhythm, line length, and stanza construction, but don't let these elements limit your creativity.
- **Mood** Think about how you can use precise words and vivid images to create a mood. Do you want your poem to be humorous, sarcastic, ominous, angry, or solemn, or do you want to express some other emotion?
- **Sound devices** Poets take pleasure in playing with language, especially with the sounds of words. For example, Robert Francis describes a pitch as "not errant, arrant, wild,/But every seeming aberration willed," playfully repeating word sounds. Try using sound devices in your poem for your own delight and to give emphasis to your meaning. Use word repetition, alliteration (repeating initial sounds), onomatopoeia (words with imitative sounds), and other sound devices.

- **Figurative language**   Poems characteristically use figurative language—figures of speech that vividly re-create moments of life and help the poet to show rather than tell about experience. Metaphors, similes, and personification are all part of the language arsenal available for you to draw on as you write your poem.

Writer's Choice   Choose the sound devices and figurative language that suit your subject best and use them sparingly to most effectively express the structure and sense of your poem.

7. Focus on your poem.   Continue deleting, changing, and adding to your work, refining and clarifying the language and form. Give the poem your undivided attention. Many poets talk about the intense concentration of poetry writing. See if you can focus on the sounds of the words and your feelings about your subject for several minutes at a time as you work on the poem.

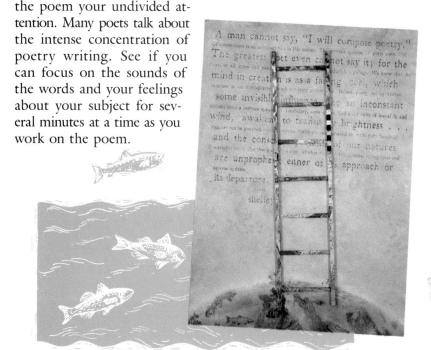

Illustrator John Stewart's background of working with poets is reflected in his art, which can be described as visual poetry.

8. Take a fresh look.   Put your draft away for a few days or at least a few hours. When you come back to your poem, sit back and read aloud what you have written. Read the poem a few times. Mark any lines you want to work on and put brackets around any words that seem extraneous to you. Make notes on what you want to ask your writing group to respond to. As you reread your poem, consider questions such as the following.

Questions for Yourself

- Does my poem make sense? Would it help to narrow the focus?

- What seems to be the "center" of my poem? Would it help to focus more on this material in my poem?

- Can I make my poem say some of what it wants to say indirectly? Could some parts of the poem be said metaphorically?

- Can I "see" parts of what is described in the poem? Do I need to add an image or images?

- What mood or feeling do I get from the poem? Would it be useful to enhance this mood or feeling by adding, deleting, or changing some of the words?

- Do my line breaks and/or stanza breaks make sense?

- Is every word necessary? If I eliminate some words, will the poem still hold together?

Questions for Your Peer Readers

- What words, phrases, or lines are most powerful for you?

- What do you think is the central idea or core meaning of my poem?

- What title would you give to my draft? Why?

- What mood or feeling characterizes my poem for you?

- What mental images does my poem create for you?

- Give a metaphoric response to my draft (e.g., "It's a trap-door.").

HANDBOOKS
FOR HELP & PRACTICE

**Unity,
pp. 371–375
Self-Assessment,
p. 397**

REVISE YOUR WRITING

1. Evaluate your responses. Keep in mind that readers may respond to and interpret your poem in different ways. This will be true when your poem is finished, too. However, as you prepare to revise your poem, keep in mind these characteristics generally found in poetry.

Standards for Evaluation

An effective poem . . .

- focuses on a single identifiable experience or event.
- uses precise and fresh language and no unnecessary words.
- uses sounds deliberately to support the meaning and effect of the poem.

2. Problem-solve. Rework your poem using the feedback from your classmates and your own response to your draft. Notice these changes Monica made as she revised a section of her poem.

ONE STUDENT'S PROCESS

The cafeteria is filled with people from outer space

Their faces are blurry

Blurry outer space junior high creatures

I can't really see in the bright white room
                                        a

It is like a junior high school landing zone

With junior high creatures floating off their chairs.
    # NEW STANZA
I bump into a table,

Like I don't fit.
                    ular   surrounded by
Like I'm a triangle and everything else is circles.
              ^   ^
                    ?   ?
No one like me, no room for me.
    #   NEW STANZA
    Where are all the familiar colors?
All the kids at my old high school had dark blue
    ^
T-shirts.

Here they wear white blouses,

and white pants,

Or blue jeans that are new.

The ideas really flow, but you might try separating them into stanzas so they would stand out more clearly.

These thoughts are really strong. Is there any way to make them stand out more?

Great images in the whole poem!

Poetry   **97**

3. Proofread your poem. Examine the punctuation of the poem to see if changing any of it would bring out the poem's rhythms or make the meaning of the poem clearer. Also check for misspellings that you did not intend. Then make a clean copy of your work that incorporates all your changes.

Grammar
—TIP—

Punctuation can help you clearly communicate with your reader, even in poetry.

GRAMMAR ᴀɴᴅ WRITING
Using Poetic License

Poets are granted "poetic license" when they write. This means they can take liberties with conventional forms in order to achieve a desired effect. This is particularly true of matters of capitalization. It is customary to begin each line of a poem with a capital letter, but some poets, such as Bobbie Copeland, use capitalization only to indicate new sentences. Other poets, such as e.e. cummings, choose not to use capitalization at all in some selections. Use your poetic license as you see fit, but use it consistently so you will not confuse or mislead your readers.

Le Dejeuner en fourrure (fur-covered cup, saucer, and spoon), by surrealist Meret Oppenheim. The Museum of Modern Art, New York City

See Grammar Handbook 38, pages 774–775 for additional help with capitalization in poetry.

PUBLISH AND PRESENT

- **Have a poetry reading.** Present the poems you and your classmates have just completed to another class. Beforehand, practice reading your poem aloud to make sure you use the phrasing and inflection you want when you present the poem.
- **Make a class poetry magazine.** Organize the poems by theme, mood, or in some other way that seems appropriate. Provide a table of contents listing poem titles and authors. Consider illustrating the magazine. Put the magazine in a special place in the classroom or in the library.
- **Make a poetry poster.** Write your poem on a large sheet of cardboard, illustrate it with a drawing or photograph, and display it on a bulletin board.
- **Make a poetry card.** Fold paper to form a note card and print your poem on the inside of the card. Illustrate the outside with a drawing or photograph. Display the card on a bulletin board or send it to someone with whom you would like to share your work.
- **Submit your poem to a literary magazine.** Send a copy of the poem to the school literary magazine or to a national magazine. A book like *Young Writer's Market* will help you find publications that welcome poetry submissions.
- **Save your work in your writing portfolio.** Read your poem in a month or two. See how you respond to it then.

HANDBOOKS
FOR HELP & PRACTICE

**Sharing Completed Writing,
pp. 418–419**

The Land of O's

Monica Moreno

Precise verbs, nouns, and modifiers create vivid pictures.

Cafeteria's filled with outer space people
Blurry faces in a bright white room
A junior high school landing zone
With creatures floating off their chairs.

I bump into a table,
Triangular, surrounded by circles.

Uses repetition to support meaning

No one like me?
No room for me?

Where are the familiar colors?
Dark blue T-shirts?
Here they wear white blouses,
And white pants, blue jeans that are new.

Form—lines broken into stanzas— emphasizes ideas.

I won't like anyone!
No one will like me!

Focuses on a single experience

They're sitting together on round, floating pillows
Laughing like it happens all the time.
I'm from the outside, or maybe I'm
Coming into outer space.

WRITER TO WRITER

When you write poetry you should remember that every poem is really a story. It should have a narrative that goes somewhere. The language should be public enough for people to understand, but private enough to be interesting. But when you are writing poetry, a little ambiguity is okay too. All good literature can be understood in more than one way.

Gary Soto, award-winning writer and poet

1. Reflect on your writing. Look back through all the writing you have done for this assignment and think about the process you went through to complete your poem. Ask yourself the questions below and record your answers in your journal.

- Did anything you experienced surprise you as you worked on your poem?
- What parts of the process did you enjoy most?
- How did your poem change as you were revising?
- What do you think of poetry writing?

2. Apply your skills. Try one or more of the following activities.

▶ FOR YOUR
PORTFOLIO

- **Cross-curricular** Many poems are "occasional poems" commemorating important public or personal events (Robert Frost's poem for the inauguration of President John F. Kennedy, for example). Select an occasion from any important moment in history—including the history of science or technology—and write a poem or speech commemorating the event.
- **Literature** Select a short story or fictional scene and turn it into a poem. One technique for doing this is the dramatic monologue in which one character speaks in his or her own voice. Add a note discussing how poems are like or unlike stories.
- **Related assignments** Follow the suggestions on pages 104–112 to write a short story or a monologue.

Story

Do you have a favorite short story, one that makes you laugh or cry, dream of the future, or become thoughtful every time you read it? Short stories, more than any other kind of narrative writing, are written for the pleasure people feel in reading about events and their meanings.

Ideas for stories are everywhere. The problem for a writer is deciding which story to tell and how best to tell it. As you read this story by James Thurber, notice how quickly you come to understand the relationship between the two main characters.

The Unicorn in the Garden
by James Thurber

Once upon a sunny morning a man who sat in a breakfast nook looked up from his scrambled eggs to see a white unicorn with a gold horn quietly cropping the roses in the garden. The man went up to the bedroom where his wife was still asleep and woke her. "There's a unicorn in the garden," he said. "Eating roses." She opened one unfriendly eye and looked at him. "The unicorn is a mythical beast," she said, and turned her back on him. The man walked slowly downstairs and out into the garden. The unicorn was still there; he was now browsing among the tulips. "Here, unicorn," said the man, and he pulled up a lily and gave it to him. The unicorn ate it gravely. With a high heart, because there was a unicorn in his garden, the man went upstairs and roused his wife again. "The unicorn," he said, "ate a lily." His wife sat up in bed and looked at him, coldly. "You are a booby," she said, "and I am going to have you put in the booby-hatch." The man, who had never liked the words "booby" and "booby-hatch," and who liked them even less on a shining morning when there was a unicorn in the garden, thought for a moment. "We'll see about that," he said. He walked over to the door. "He has a golden horn in the middle of his forehead," he told her. Then he went back to the garden to watch the unicorn; but the unicorn had gone away. The man sat down among the roses and went to sleep.

As soon as the husband had gone out of the house, the wife got up and dressed as fast as she could. She was very excited and there was a gloat in her eye. She telephoned the police and she telephoned a psychiatrist; she told them to hurry to her house and bring a strait-jacket. When the police and psychiatrist arrived they sat down in chairs and looked at her, with great interest. "My husband," she said, "saw a unicorn this morning." The police looked at the psychiatrist and the psychiatrist looked at the police. "He told me it ate a lily," she said. The psychiatrist looked at the police and the police looked at the psychiatrist. "He told

me it had a golden horn in the middle of its fore-head," she said. At a solemn signal from the psychiatrist, the police leaped from their chairs and seized the wife. They had a hard time subduing her, for she put up a terrific struggle, but they finally subdued her. Just as they got her into the strait-jacket, the husband came back into the house.

"Did you tell your wife you saw a unicorn?" asked the police. "Of course not," said the husband. "The unicorn is a mythical beast." "That's all I wanted to know," said the psychiatrist. "Take her away. I'm sorry, sir, but your wife is as crazy as a jay bird." So they took her away, cursing and screaming, and shut her up in an institution. The husband lived happily ever after.

Moral: Don't count your boobies until they are hatched.

Think AND Respond

What was Thurber trying to accomplish by writing his story in the style of a fable or fairy tale? How did he introduce humor? Did the story amuse you? Puzzle you? Make you think? What story could you tell about an unusual event or unusual relationship?

INVITATION
— TO —
Write

James Thurber wrote his brief and funny story about a husband, his wife, and a unicorn. Now write a short story of your own about anything you like, whether it be real or imaginary, serious or funny.

A short story allows you to invent characters or re-create people you've known, and then to decide what happens to them. As narrator, you can participate in the action or just observe and report it. You can set the story in a time and place you know, an entirely imaginary time and place, or one that combines the real and imaginary. Like all imaginative writing, stories touch our memories, feelings, desires, and dreams.

PLANNING YOUR SHORT STORY

HANDBOOKS
FOR HELP & PRACTICE

Writing Variables,
pp. 317–321
Starting Anywhere,
p. 352
Concluding a
Narrative,
pp. 388–389
Point of View,
pp. 447–451

1. Find an idea. You need to find a focus, something to narrow the many possibilities for stories. Any one of the elements common to all short stories—characters, plot, and setting—is a good place to start.

You might choose to start with a list of people who have interested or surprised you. When one person seems especially interesting, write the name of that person in the center of a sheet of paper to begin a cluster diagram. Circle the name and surround it with details—also circled—about the person's appearance, personality, character traits, hobbies, jobs—anything that brings him or her to life for you.

Similarly, you may first find a plot for your story: a series of events based on a conflict or problem that leads to a climax and a resolution. Look for problems that are familiar, such as curfews, grades, or family relationships. Ask yourself some "what if" questions. What if four friends were snowbound for a week in a small cabin? What if a mysterious stranger appeared in a small community?

If you decide to begin with the setting, it may help to list places you know well: your home, a store, a favorite spot to meet friends. Then imagine settings totally unlike places in your life. Draw maps or sketches to help "see" various settings. Now imagine characters in your setting and think of events that might happen there.

Wherever you begin, when you have established your plot, characters, and setting, you will have a general story idea.

2. Consider your purpose and audience. Will your short story be funny? Romantic? Mysterious? Who are your readers and how do you want them to react?

3. Develop your story idea. The characters, plot, and setting you identified probably need further development before you begin drafting. For example, suppose your purpose is to write a story of romantic misadventures. If your setting is a palace in India, your main character a student on vacation, and the plot a palace uprising, you still must decide what other characters might be needed to tell the story, and you may have to add more details to bring the time and place alive for your readers.

4. Create a chain of events. Think carefully about what happens—the chain of events that makes up the story's action. The problem your character faces gives you the beginning. The middle and the end come from possible solutions. Your story idea may not be complete as you start drafting, but if you can write down the first links in your chain of events, you will have the beginning of your plot.

Writing
—**TIP**—

If you want to combine the imaginary with a realistic setting, use an old story-telling trick that Thurber adopts from fairy tales and fables: begin with "Once upon a time."

1. Decide on the point of view. Who will tell your story? The Thurber story is told from a third-person point of view. The narrator, by observing all of the events but not participating in them, reports both the husband's activities in the garden and the wife's in the bedroom. With a third-person narrator, details of character (including thoughts), setting, and plot can be developed in as much depth as the writer wishes. A first-person narrator, on the other hand, is part of the story and creates a more personal and immediate tone.

2. Use chronological order. In most cases, you will want to relate the events in the order they occurred. Sometimes you will want to interrupt the action to describe a character or place. Just make sure that you keep the order of events clear when you return to the action of the story.

 Writer's Choice Do you want to use a flashback? You can create suspense by beginning the story in the middle of the action and then telling what happened earlier before revealing the conclusion.

3. Show, don't tell. Develop your characters through their actions and dialogue, not just by description. Thurber doesn't say, "The police and psychiatrist thought the wife was crazy." Instead, he shows how they seized her and put her in a strait-jacket. If it's vital to have an explosion in the palace kitchen, for example, present that event through the thoughts and actions of the characters.

4. Be selective. Stick to your goal. Tell the main story you had in mind and use only details that support your goal. Thurber doesn't sidetrack the reader into questions about mythical beasts, nor does he give long descriptions of the characters' qualities. He does, however, suggest a great deal about the relationship between the main characters through their actions.

REVIEWING YOUR WRITING

1. Evaluate the organization. Do you have a beginning, a middle, and an end? Have you established the setting early and clearly? Do you follow chronological order, or do you start right in the middle of events? If you use flashbacks, is the sequence of events clear to your audience?

2. Check the story elements.   Is the point of view consistent? Do the details you give about the characters and the setting further the story line? Have you told as much of the story as possible through the action and dialogue? Do your characters seem real and believable? Is the main character's problem resolved in an interesting and believable way?

3. Show your story to a friend.   Ask your friend if your story is interesting. Ask if you have succeeded in being funny, or mysterious, or romantic, or whatever you intended.

PUBLISHING AND PRESENTING

- **Gather classmates' stories into an anthology.**   Illustrate them with the authors' own drawings or photographs. Ask talented artists or photographers to illustrate the stories.
- **Organize a reading of selected stories.**   Invite audience comments.

Toni Morrison and John Cheever, both winners of the Pulitzer Prize and National Book Critics Circle Award

Monologue

Sammy's

M|O|N|O|L|O|G|U|E|

from *Dark at the Top of the Stairs*
by William Inge

Playwrights often show what characters are thinking by having them reveal their thoughts in a monologue—a one-sided conversation. A person giving a monologue is not expecting or inviting responses from others—he or she is simply thinking aloud.

In this monologue from *Dark at the Top of the Stairs*, Sammy, a very shy young man, uses a speech to his new friends to try to assure himself that things are not so bad in his life.

As you read, notice what Sammy actually says about himself, and consider what he might really feel but is not putting into words.

I always worry that maybe people aren't going to like me, when I go to a party. Isn't that crazy? Do you ever get kind of a sick feeling in the pit of your stomach when you dread things? Gee, I wouldn't want to miss a party for anything. But every time I go to one, I have to reason with myself to keep from feeling that the whole world's against me.

See, I've spent almost my whole life in military academies. My mother doesn't have a place for me, where she lives. She . . . she just doesn't know what else to do with me. But you mustn't misunderstand about my mother. She's really a very lovely person. I guess every boy thinks his mother is very beautiful, but my mother really is. She tells me in every letter she writes how sorry she is that we can't be together more, but she has to think of her work.

One time we were together, though. She met me in San Francisco once, and we were together for two whole days. She let me take her to dinner and to a show and to dance. Just like we were sweethearts. It was the most wonderful time I ever had. And then I had to go back to the old military academy.

Every time I walk into the barracks, I get kind of a depressed feeling. It's got hard stone walls. Pictures of generals hanging all over . . . oh, they're very fine gentlemen, but they all look so kind of hard-boiled and stern . . . you know what I mean. . . . Well, gee! I guess I've bored you enough, telling you about myself.

Think AND Respond

What do you learn about Sammy's character and fears through this monologue? How did the playwright create a realistic voice for Sammy? Think of a monologue that you could write that reveals the thoughts and concerns of a character you know well.

INVITATION
—TO—
Write

Sammy's monologue revealed a great deal about his character. Now write a monologue that reveals something about a familiar character from literature.

Like a poem, a monologue expresses personal thoughts, observations, or imaginings. Like many poems and all short stories, a monologue often tells a story. Because it presents the thoughts or words of a single speaker, a monologue is usually very personal and often deeply revealing.

P LANNING THE MONOLOGUE

HANDBOOKS

FOR HELP & PRACTICE

Varieties of Language, pp. 428–432

Oral Presentations, pp. 497–500

1. Choose a character. Make a list of your favorite literary characters—ones that made a vivid impression on you. The character you choose might be Shakespeare's Juliet or Romeo. Perhaps a character created by Mark Twain, Charles Dickens, or John Steinbeck appeals more to you. Whatever your choice, make sure you know the character well.

2. Focus on a goal. Think about what you want to communicate about the character you have chosen. What distinguishing traits or way of thinking does he or she possess? You will want to keep these characteristics in mind as you develop the monologue.

3. Choose a situation. Your character will have to talk about an incident or situation. Perhaps you can have Juliet continue to express her thoughts about Romeo, or you may want to have Huck Finn voice thoughts he might have had about his father.

4. Gather background information. In the excerpt, Sammy tells of his absent mother and his life at the military academy, background information that helps us understand his feelings. Think about what background information a reader or listener needs to know about the incident and the character you have chosen. Identify only essential information, such as the fact that the Capulets and the Montagues are feuding, or the kind of life Huck Finn's father leads. Make a list of these points to keep you on track while you are writing the monologue.

 Writer's Choice You may wish to choose a favorite character from the movies as the speaker of your monologue.

Jay Leno, comedian and TV personality

DRAFTING THE MONOLOGUE

1. Use language that reflects how your character would talk. You may not want to tackle the Shakespearean language of the original Juliet, but you would want to have her talk like an eager young person, not like the nurse or her mother. Be conversational. A monologue like Sammy's is meant to be spoken. Even monologues which contain characters who talk only to themselves are essentially conversational.

2. Avoid too much "telling." Let your character reveal the background information as he or she talks about personal feelings and concerns. Don't try to use all of the information you have. Tell what time it is or the character's age, for example, only if these details are necessary to the reader's understanding of the character's feelings and thoughts.

3. Look for ways to reveal character. A character's choice of words and the stories he or she chooses to tell can be especially revealing. In the excerpt, Sammy does not directly say that he is shy or that he dislikes the military academy, but the way he talks about himself and describes the academy make his feelings clear.

REVIEWING YOUR WRITING

1. Be sure you make a point about the character. Is your monologue more than just a first-person account of an event? Does it show an important aspect of the speaker's character?

2. Read your monologue to a friend. Ask what your friend thinks the monologue revealed about the character. Was the character believable? Compare your friend's response to the goal you set for yourself in writing the monologue. Use this feedback to revise your writing.

PUBLISHING AND PRESENTING

- **Give an oral reading.** Read your monologue to classmates. Invite the audience to discuss the character you chose.
- **Expand your monologue into a dramatic scene.** You may get ideas from *Dark at the Top of the Stairs,* which you can find at the library. Invite friends to read the various parts of your scene.

Sentence

Using Present Participial Phrases

Effective writers often use present participial phrases as modifiers. These phrases begin with a present participle, a verb form ending in *-ing*. They may also contain other words or even whole clauses (see model 3), related to the participle. These phrases often occur at the end of a sentence, describing in greater detail a noun mentioned earlier. Note that a comma precedes each phrase here.

MODELS

1. (Short)   She held the quilts securely in her arms, <u>stroking them</u>.
             Alice Walker, "Everyday Use"

2. (Medium) Just before supper Miguel came into the kitchen, <u>stamping the bits of dirty snow from his overshoes</u>.
             Durango Mendoza, "The Passing"

3. (Long)   First there was the local apple crop, <u>threatening to rot because the harvesters had all gone into the army or war factories</u>.
             John Knowles, *A Separate Peace*

A. Combining Sentences   Combine each sentence pair to form one sentence that ends with a present participial phrase. To do this, first find the present participial phrase in the second sentence. Then use a comma to join the phrase to the end of the first sentence.

Example   She had just returned from a week by the sea. She was recuperating from the strain of nursing so many nights.

Result   She had just returned from a week by the sea, recuperating from the strain of nursing so many nights.
Algernon Blackwood, "The Tradition"

1. Away she darted. She was stretching close to the ground.
Francis Parkman, *The Oregon Trail*

2. Bea bustled about. Bea was managing to keep up with both the conversation and the cooking.   **Eugenia Collier, "Sweet Potato Pie"**

3. Old Peg stopped short. Old Peg was hanging her head as if she, too, were at the limit of her strength.   **Dorothy Canfield, "The Heyday of the Blood"**

4. The water pelted windowpanes. The water was running down the charred west side where the house had been burned evenly free of its white paint
Ray Bradbury, "There Will Come Soft Rains"

5. Then the fish came alive, with his death in him, and rose high out of the water. The fish was showing all his great length and width and all his power and beauty.   **Ernest Hemingway, *The Old Man and the Sea***

B. Unscrambling Sentences   Find the present participial phrase in each group of words. (Hint: The present participial phrase will begin with an *-ing* word.) Then unscramble the sentence and write it out, with the present participial phrase at the end. Punctuate correctly.

1. a. in darkness
   b. listening
   c. he sat
   Algernon Blackwood,
   "The Tradition"

2. a. to make a pillow
   b. he rolled his trousers up
   c. putting the newspapers inside them
   Ernest Hemingway,
   The Old Man and the Sea

3. a. arguing about the fight
   b. a crowd of older men
   c. stood in front of the Garden
   Robert Lipsyte, *The Contender*

4. a. the women scattered toward their homes
   b. from the landing
   c. hurrying before the white-edged tide that would soon submerge the lower paths
   Kim Yong Ik, "The Sea Girl"

C. Imitating Sentences   Each model sentence contains a present participial phrase. Using your own words, write a sentence whose structure imitates that of the model.
   Important: Imitate as many of the sentence parts as possible, not just the underlined present participial phrase. Punctuate correctly.

1. We spent an odd day, <u>toiling in that railroad yard</u>.
   John Knowles, *A Separate Peace*

2. Two boys, in gym clothes and boxing shoes, were balancing themselves on their shoulders, <u>kicking their legs up in the air</u>.
   Robert Lipsyte, *The Contender*

3. Suddenly, he soared up out of the water in a fountain of spray, <u>turning as he fell</u>.   **Willard Price, *The Killer Shark***

4. The city was a great loom, <u>weaving its tangles and tufts of people into haphazard multicolored fabric</u>. **Patricia Grace, *Mutuwhenua***

5. The weather door of the smoking room had been left open to the North Atlantic fog, as the big liner rolled and lifted, <u>whistling to warn the fishing fleet</u>. **Rudyard Kipling, *Captains Courageous***

6. They would compose and sing as they went along, <u>consulting neither time nor tune</u>. **Frederick Douglass, *Narrative of the Life of Frederick Douglass***

D. Expanding Sentences Each sentence contains the beginning of a present participial phrase. Finish the sentences by completing the phrases. Make up content that fits in with the rest of the sentence. Then compare your sentences with the originals on page 311.

1. I spent as much time as I could alone in our room, trying. . . .
John Knowles, *A Separate Peace*

2. I dream I'm flying over a sandy beach in the early morning, touching. . . .
Toni Cade Bambara, "Raymond's Run"

3. For a long while we just stood there, looking. . . .
William Faulkner, "A Rose for Emily"

4. Jem threw open the gate and sped to the side of the house, slapped it with his palm and ran back past us, not waiting. . . .
Harper Lee, *To Kill a Mockingbird*

5. James had a library book on rocks, and they spent days just wandering around the park, filling. . . . **Robert Lipsyte, *The Contender***

6. Black clouds began to gather in the southwest, and he kept watching them, trying. . . . **James Hurst, "The Scarlet Ibis"**

Application Write a paragraph describing someone or something in action: a person running, a car gathering speed, a tree tossing in the wind. Use present participial phrases to add detail at the ends of several of your sentences. Punctuate your sentences correctly.

Grammar Refresher The model sentences in this lesson all contain present participial phrases. For more about present participles and participial phrases, see Handbook 32, pages 595–597.

Sketchbook

bobblegesture (bah' bul jes cher) n. The classroom behavior of not knowing the answer but raising one's hand anyway (after determining a sufficient number of other people have also raised their hands, thus reducing the likelihood of actually being called on).

chalktrauma (chawk' traw ma) n. The body's reaction to someone running his fingernails down a chalkboard.

cinemuck (si' ne muk) n. The combination of popcorn, soda, and melted chocolate which covers the floors of movie theaters.

hozone (ho' zohn) n. The place where one sock in every laundry load disappears to.

mittsquinter (mit' skwint ur) n. A ballplayer who looks into his glove after missing the ball, as if, somehow, the cause of the error lies there.

telecrastination (tel e kras tin ay' shun) n. The act of always letting the phone ring at least twice before you pick it up, even when you're only six inches away.

Rich Hall & Friends
SNIGLETS

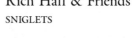

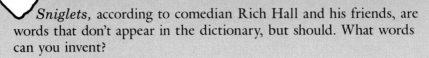

Sniglets, according to comedian Rich Hall and his friends, are words that don't appear in the dictionary, but should. What words can you invent?

Additional Sketches
Define yourself.
What famous person are you like? Why?

Informative Exposition: Classification

Guided Assignment
COMPARISON AND CONTRAST

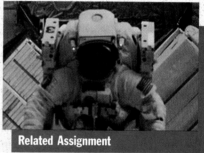

Related Assignment
DEFINITION

Related Assignment
ANALOGY

Suppose you have to pack up everything you own in order to move to another house. Most likely, you would sort your goods into categories and put each one into a labeled box. You know that this process of classification will save you time and effort in the end.

Classification, in fact, is a crucial skill for keeping every aspect of your life in order—including your thinking and writing. In this workshop's guided assignment, you will use this thinking skill to help you write an effective essay of comparison and contrast. You will then use the techniques learned through comparison to write definitions and to create analogies.

117

Comparison and Contrast

Guided ASSIGNMENT

When you compare and contrast, you identify similarities and differences. Without this ability, you could hardly understand the world. After all, only by making comparisons and detecting differences can you see the patterns that give the world meaning.

The poems "To an Athlete Dying Young" by A.E. Housman and "Ex-Basketball Player" by John Updike have obvious similarities, but they also have important differences. Look for these similarities and differences as you read.

To an Athlete Dying Young
by A.E. Housman

The time you won your town the race
We chaired you through the market-place;
Man and boy stood cheering by,
And home we brought you shoulder-high.

Today, the road all runners come,
Shoulder-high we bring you home,
And set you at your threshold down,
Townsman of a stiller town.

Smart lad, to slip betimes away
From fields where glory does not stay
And early though the laurel grows
It withers quicker than the rose.

Eyes the shady night has shut
Cannot see the record cut,
And silence sounds no worse than cheers
After earth has stopped the ears:

Now you will not swell the rout
Of lads that wore their honors out,
Runners whom renown outran
And the name died before the man.

So set before its echoes fade,
The fleet foot on the sill of shade,
And hold to the low lintel up
The still-defended challenge cup.

And round that early-laureled head
Will flock to gaze the strengthless dead,
And find unwithered on its curls
The garland briefer than a girl's.

Ex-Basketball Player
by John Updike

Pearl Avenue runs past the high-school lot,
Bends with the trolley tracks, and stops, cut off
Before it has a chance to go two blocks,
At Colonel McComsky Plaza. Berth's Garage
Is on the corner facing west, and there,
Most days, you'll find Flick Webb, who helps
    Berth out.

Flick stands tall among the idiot pumps—
Five on a side, the old bubble-head style,
Their rubber elbows hanging loose and low.
One's nostrils are two S's, and his eyes
An E and O. And one is squat, without
A head at all—more of a football type.

Once Flick played for the high-school team,
    the Wizards.
He was good: in fact, the best. In '46
He bucketed three hundred ninety points,
A county record still. The ball loved Flick.
I saw him rack up thirty-eight or forty
In one home game. His hands were like wild birds.

He never learned a trade, he just sells gas,
Checks oil, and changes flats. Once in a while,
As a gag he dribbles an inner tube,
But most of us remember anyway.
His hands are fine and nervous on the lug wrench.
It makes no difference to the lug wrench, though.

Off work, he hangs around Mae's Luncheonette.
Grease-grey and kind of coiled, he plays pinball,
Sips lemon cokes, and smokes those thin cigars;
Flick seldom speaks to Mae, just sits and nods
Beyond her face toward bright applauding tiers
Of Necco Wafers, Nibs, and Juju Beads.

Think AND Respond

In what ways are the two poems by John Updike and A.E. Housman alike and different? What feelings does each poem arouse in you and how do you think each poet created these effects? What relevance do you think the poems have for people who were never athletes or stars? If you were to write a comparison-contrast essay on some topic suggested by these poems, what would your essay be about?

INVITATION
TO
Write

While reading "Ex-Basketball Player" and "To an Athlete Dying Young," you may have gone through an automatic process of comparison-contrast—in your mind. Now share that process with an audience by writing a comparison and contrast of two or more subjects that interest you.

Comparison and contrast can turn up in many kinds of writing. A historian may compare two wars or two periods in a nation's history. Two characters in a piece of fiction may have similarities that lead them to friendship, or differences that create conflict. An advertising brochure may showcase the contrast between two products. The world abounds in people, places, and things with striking similarities and differences. Pick a pair that matter to you and bring their similarities or differences to the attention of others by writing a comparison and contrast essay.

PREWRITE AND EXPLORE

HANDBOOKS
FOR HELP & PRACTICE

Writing Variables,
pp. 317–321
Organizing Ideas,
pp. 333–337

1. Look for ideas. Think of items you might want to compare or contrast. They should be items with enough traits in common to make for a reasonable comparison. If you have trouble coming up with topics, you might find the following activities helpful.

Exploratory Activities

- **Listing** With a group of classmates, think about terms, objects, people, ideas, and other types of items that can be compared. Begin by listing as many items as you can in one column. Then, in a second column, list items to which they could be compared.
- **Freewriting** Think of a product, movie, or experience familiar to you but not to most of your classmates. What comparisons could you use to help them understand? Write down your ideas.

- **Similes and metaphors** In his poem "Ex-Basketball Player," John Updike compares Flick's hands to wild birds. Think of a friend or family member you know well. To what could you compare the person if you wanted to create a vivid descriptive image? Try to create a variety of similes and metaphors in five to ten minutes of freewriting.
- **Evaluating** Writers use comparison and contrast in reviews and evaluations. List areas in which you feel qualified to "be the judge," such as television programs, fashion, literature, animal behavior, or sports. Develop criteria or standards you would use to evaluate items in each category.
- **Reading literature** The poems "Ex-Basketball Player" and "To an Athlete Dying Young" can be compared and contrasted because they both deal with young athletes. Make a list of other pairs or groups of literary works that might be interesting to compare. Write down their essential similarities or differences that could become the basis for your writing.

PROBLEM

S O L V I N G

How can I find items to compare and contrast?

Writing
──TIP──

By discussing your plans with other writers, you can gain perspectives on your subject that you might not have discovered by yourself.

2. Choose a topic.   Before you decide on a topic, you may wish to freewrite on one or more of the ideas you uncovered in the exploratory activities to see if you want to proceed with any of them. Also, consult your journal, refer to the ideas in "Apply Your Skills" on page 132, or look back at the writing you did in the Sketchbook on page 116 for possible topics. Be sure that the topics you choose have enough features in common to make the comparison valid and interesting.

3. Try using collaborative planning.   Discuss your plans for writing your comparison-and-contrast essay with a partner. Consider the purpose, audience, and sources of information for your writing as a guide to your conversation.

- **Purpose**   What do you hope to achieve in your essay? Some possible purposes are:

  To evaluate a performance according to some standard
  To persuade readers to support a candidate or cause
  To define or explain concepts, issues, or processes
  To describe people, events, or objects

- **Audience**   Determining the needs of your audience can help you decide how much information to provide and how to focus your essay. For example, in comparing restaurants, you might emphasize different points to an audience of adult health food experts than to an audience of teenagers looking for a good place to go after a movie.

- **Sources of information**   How will you get the information you need for your essay? What resources will you use? How can you use interviews with experts, reading and library research, and direct observation?

PROBLEM
S O L V I N G

How can I organize my essay?

4. Explore your topic.   To organize your thoughts about the items you are comparing, consider making a chart or list. A Venn diagram, which enables you to use intersecting circles to find common and distinguishing characteristics, is one possibility (See Handbook 3, Using Graphic Devices). Another option is to make lists of similarities and differences, or problems and observations.

One student, Josh, made this list to compare "Ex-Basketball Player" and "To an Athlete Dying Young." Throughout this assignment you will track Josh's progress as he writes his essay.

Similarities:
  —Subjects of both poems are athletes who are past
    stars
  —Both poems sad, mournful
  —Anonymous athlete dies young as hero and Flick
    becomes pitiful has-been
Differences:
  —Lots of details about Flick vs. no details, not even
    name, for athlete
  —Updike poem informal, slangy, no rhyme vs. formal,
    rhyme etc.

Problems & Observations
  —Why does Housman say "smart boy"? Does he think
    the boy was lucky to die early?
  —6th stanza of Housman poem?
  —last line of Housman poem?
  —In Updike poem, why is Flick a failure? Is it only
    because he never learned a trade?
  —What are these two writers really saying about
    fame and glory?

Later in this workshop you will see how Josh used a number of these ideas and questions to develop his essay.

5. Share your findings. After you have made your charts or lists, meet with a partner or small group of writers to discuss what you have found. Use the feedback of others to help you round out your lists and solve any problems you found in exploring your topic.

Writer's Choice As you explore your writing topic, think about whether you want to focus on the similarities between the two items, the differences, or both. Your choice will depend on the purpose you want to achieve in writing your essay.

HANDBOOKS
FOR HELP & PRACTICE

Introductions,
pp. 352–355
Elaboration,
pp. 364–369

PROBLEM
S O L V I N G

What techniques
can I use to
explore the items
I am comparing?

1. Experiment with openers. Look over your prewriting notes and consider how you want to begin. For example, simply setting down a few plain sentences to identify your items may help you get started. You may find one or more of these strategies helpful.

Strategies

- **Definition** As a way to get your bearings, give a full definition of your items and the features that make them similar or set them apart.
- **Description** Describe each item in terms of one or more of the five senses.
- **Analogy** Think of a more familiar pair of items that are related to each other in the same way as the pair you are discussing. Compare your items to these more familiar ones.
- **Classification** Sort the features of your items into different categories and discuss each category.

Dresses, oil painting by
Lisa Milroy, 1985.
Saatchi Collection,
London

2. Think about the organization of your draft. There are two basic patterns for organizing comparisons. One is the **subject-by-subject** pattern, in which you discuss all the features of one subject and then discuss all the features of the other. The second pattern is the **feature-by-feature** pattern, in which you address each feature in turn, and show how the subjects are similar or different in terms of that feature. The following chart shows the two patterns.

Subject by Subject	**Feature by Feature**
Introduction	Introduction
Subject A	Feature 1
Feature 1	Subject A
Feature 2	Subject B
Subject B	Feature 2
Feature 1	Subject A
Feature 2	Subject B
Conclusion	Conclusion

COMPUTER TIP

Move paragraphs back and forth as a rough, quick way to decide which method of organization seems more effective for your topic.

After discussing his ideas with two other student writers, Josh began his draft by briefly describing the basis for his comparison. Then he went on to examine specific similarities and differences, quoting lines from the poems to illustrate his points. Here is the beginning of his unrevised draft.

ONE STUDENT'S PROCESS

"Ex-Basketball Player" by John Updike and "To an Athlete Dying Young" by A. E. Housman are two poems about athletes who have made their mark in particular sports: basketball and track. Both poems focus on what happens to the athletes after their moment of glory. They are both sad poems, and both express very similar themes—they both mourn the fleeting nature of success and fame.

Updike's basketball player and Housman's runner have both enjoyed applause. Housman's track star won a big race for his home town. Updike's Flick Webb was the best basketball player in the county.

3. Give your ideas some time to settle. Take a break for a few hours or a day. Then read your draft again, and share it with a peer reader. The following questions can help you evaluate the direction you want to take when you revise.

REVIEW YOUR WRITING

Questions for Yourself

- Does my introduction establish what items I will be comparing?

- Do I make my purpose clear in the introduction and keep to this purpose throughout the essay?

- Have I included all the details needed to complete my comparison? Do all my details support my purpose? Are any of them irrelevant or distracting?

- Have I presented my comparison in a way my readers will be able to follow?

Questions for Your Peer Readers

- Did you want to keep reading throughout my essay? If not, where did your interest flag?

- Did you understand what I was getting at throughout the essay? If not, which points did you find confusing?

- Can you think of any similarities or differences I left out, or do you disagree with any of the ones I included? Which ones? Why?

- Did you learn anything new from my essay, or did it change your mind in any way? How did it change your mind?

- Does my conclusion satisfy you? If not, why not?

REVISE YOUR WRITING

HANDBOOKS
FOR HELP & PRACTICE

Coherence,
pp. 376–385

1. Evaluate your responses. Review your own thoughts about your first draft as well as the responses of your peers. Then decide what kinds of revisions your essay needs. Keep in mind the following characteristics of a well-written comparison-and-contrast essay.

Standards for Evaluation

An effective essay of comparison and contrast . . .

- identifies clearly and precisely the items to be compared and contrasted.
- focuses on subjects with sufficient traits in common.
- discusses similarities and differences in the body of the essay, using specific and relevant details.
- follows a consistent and orderly plan of organization, dealing with the same features of both subjects under discussion.
- covers enough categories of information to give a complete view of the topic.
- uses transitional words and phrases to keep the relationships among ideas clear.

2. Problem-solve. Decide which responses you want to use and then rework your draft. Josh made these changes in response to suggestions by one peer reader.

Grammar
─TIP─
If you quote a phrase or line from a published source, remember to enclose it in quotation marks. If the words flow as part of the sentence, you do not need to set them off with commas.

ONE STUDENT'S PROCESS

Housman's tragedy is the tragedy of fleeting fame.

The speaker in Housman's poem claims to find consolation in the runner's death by pointing out that fame
does not last. "Smart lad, to slip betimes away/From
fields where glory does not stay." In spite of these
words, the speaker's sorrow at the death of a great
young athlete comes through.

Flick's fate presents a different kind of tragedy.

Flick, the former star, is now the fellow who pumps
gas and dribbles inner tubes "as a gag." He has become
a pitiful figure to the people of his town, but as the
speaker of the poem points out, most people *of us* remember
him anyway. In other words, Flick Webb has neither
died nor outlived his fame. Instead, he has become an
adult whose life is a waste and a disappointment to
everyone who remembers the potential he showed in
high school.

*The runner will not see his records being broken or endure the silence that follows
the cheers.*

I don't understand what you're getting at here.

This shift is kind of abrupt.

I didn't realize this until I read your essay.

3. Proofread your work.   After you have made the changes you decide to implement and you are satisfied with the content and style
of your essay, proofread it for errors in grammar, spelling, and punctuation. Writing that emphasizes comparison and contrast often uses
subordinate clauses as transitional devices. Remember that such
phrases cannot stand alone. Join them to independent clauses and
provide proper punctuation.

GRAMMAR A N D WRITING

Punctuating Subordinate Clauses

A phrase that begins with words such as *while* or *although* is typically a subordinate clause and is often used in writing that compares. If the subordinate clause comes before the independent clause, use a comma to separate the two parts. Usually, if it follows the independent clause, no comma is needed.

BEFORE: Although he was once a basketball player, he was now just pumping gas.

FOLLOWING: He was now just pumping gas although he was once a basketball player.

See Grammar Handbook 32, pages 612–613 for additional help with this problem.

PUBLISH AND PRESENT

- **Present your essay as an oral report.** If your essay compares items that you can easily transport, bring them to class and use them as visual aids. Bring in other relevant visual aids, such as slides or photos (for example, of two vacation spots) to enhance your presentation.

- **Submit your essay to a school publication.** For example, submit your work to the school literary magazine or to the school newspaper.

- **Send your essay to the local newspaper.** If you are comparing or contrasting items of interest to your community at large—such as political candidates or various recycling plans—you might send your essay to your local paper as a letter to the editor.

- **Read your essays in small groups.** Then select representative essays to read aloud to the whole class.

- **Save your work in your writing portfolio.** Compare this essay with something you wrote several months ago. Did you use more subordinate clauses in your comparison-and-contrast essay? What other differences in your writing style can you detect?

Grammar
—TIP—

Titles of poems are enclosed in quotation marks. Titles of books and plays are underlined or italicized.

HANDBOOKS

FOR HELP & PRACTICE

Oral Reports, pp. 497–498

The Aftermath

Josh Secora

Introduces items to be compared and contrasted

States thesis

"To an Athlete Dying Young" by A. E. Housman and "Ex-Basketball Player" by John Updike are two poems about athletes who have made their mark in particular sports. The poems focus on what happens to the athletes after their moment of glory, and they both mourn the fleeting nature of success and fame. Yet the differences between the two poems may be as significant as the similarities.

Uses quotations from both poems to show similarities

Housman's runner and Updike's basketball player have both enjoyed applause. Housman's track star won a big race for his town, and his fans carried him joyously through the streets; "Man and Boy stood cheering by,/ And home we brought you shoulder-high." Similarly, Updike's Flick Webb was "the best," scoring in one season "three hundred ninety points,/A county record still."

Shows a clear transition to the discussion of differences

There is, however, a crucial difference between the two athletes and between the two poems. Housman's runner dies before his athletic feats are overshadowed by those of others.

> Now you will not swell the rout
> Of lads that wore their honors out
> Runners whom renown outran
> And the name died before the man.

In contrast, Flick Webb survives his glory years, but never lives up to the expectations set by his high school successes. Now he "just sells gas,/Checks oil, and changes flats." His only cheers come from "bright applauding tiers/of Necco Wafers, Nibs, and Juju Beads" on the shelves at the local luncheonette. Thus, both stories are tragic, but in different ways.

Housman's tragedy is the tragedy of fleeting fame. The speaker in Housman's poem claims to find consolation in the runner's death by pointing out that fame does not last. "Smart lad, to slip betimes away/From fields where glory does not stay." The runner will not see his record being broken or endure the silence that follows the cheers. In spite of these words, the speaker's sorrow at the death of a great young athlete comes through.

Flick's fate presents a different kind of tragedy. Flick, the former star, is now the fellow who pumps gas and dribbles inner tubes "as a gag." He has become a pitiful figure to the people of his town, but as the speaker of the poem points out, "most of us remember anyway." In other words, Flick Webb has neither died nor outlived his fame. Instead, he has become an adult whose life is a disappointment to everyone who remembers the potential he showed in high school.

Both poems present curious messages about fame and glory. Housman recognizes that his runner did not get the chance to really enjoy his fame, but on the other hand, he did not see his fame fade, either. Updike points out that the memories of fame may linger, but people must continually create their own lives and are responsible for their own shattered dreams.

Elaborates on distinctive features of each poem

Presents an effective conclusion that summarizes the main points of the comparison

Comparison
and Contrast   **131**

The stock market crash of 1987 reminded people of the crash of 1929.

FOR YOUR
PORTFOLIO

WRITER TO WRITER

Learn, compare, collect the facts!

Ivan Petrovich Pavlov, Russian scientist and author

1. Reflect on your writing. Now that you have completed your own essay of comparison and contrast, think about the process you followed. Ask yourself the questions below and record your answers in your journal, or attach the page containing your answers to your essay.

• What did you discover about your topic from examining the similarities and differences between the two items?
• What would you do differently the next time you set out to compare or contrast two items?
• What parts of the process that you used in this piece of writing might you use in another piece of writing?
• What did you like best about the piece you wrote? Thinking back, what aspect of the writing process led you to achieve this result?

2. Apply your skills. Try one or more of the following activities.

• **Cross curricular** Write a paper comparing an interesting event currently in the news to a similar event in the past. For example, you might compare a current war, election campaign, epidemic, or protest movement to one that took place earlier in history.
• **Literature** Did you ever read a book you liked and then see a movie or television show made from that book? Write an essay comparing the book and the movie, or the book and the television show.
• **General** What advice do you have for your fellow consumers? Write a consumer report comparing two products. For example, you could compare styles of clothes, athletic shoes, stereo equipment, or even foods.
• **Related assignments** Follow the suggestions on pages 136–142 to write a definition and an extended analogy.

On the Lightside

SPELL BOUND

When I look up something in the dictionary, it's never where I look for it.

The dictionary has been a particular disappointment to me as a basic reference work, and the fact that it's usually more my fault than the dictionary's doesn't make it any easier on me. Sometimes I can't come close enough to knowing how to spell a word to find it; other times the word just doesn't seem to be anywhere in the dictionary. I can't for the life of me figure out where they hide some of the words I want to look up. They must be in there someplace.

"Wait! Wait!. . . Cancel that, I guess it says 'helf.'"

Other times I want more information about a word than the dictionary is prepared to give me. I don't want to know how to spell a word or what it means. I want to know how to use it. I want to know how to make it possessive and whether I double the final consonant when I add -ing to it. And as often as I've written it, I always forget what you do to make a word that ends in s possessive. "The Detroit News' editor"? "The Detroit Newses editor"? I suppose the Detroit News's editors know, but I never remember and the dictionary is no help.

I have at least twenty words that I look up ten times a year. I didn't know how to spell them in high school, and I still don't. Is it "further" or "farther" if I'm talking about distance? I always go to the dictionary for further details. I have several dictionaries, and I avoid the one farthest from me. Furthest from me? I am even nervous about some words I should have mastered in grade school. I know when to use "compliment" instead of "complement," when to use "stationery" and not "stationary," and "principle" not "principal"; but I always pause just an instant to make sure.

You'd think someone who has made a living all his life writing words on paper would know how to spell everything. I'm not a bad enough speller to be interesting, but there are still some words I look up in the dictionary because I'm too embarrassed to ask anyone how they're spelled. I've probably looked up "embarrassed" nine times within the last few years, and I often check to make sure there aren't two s's in "occasion." "Ocassion" strikes me as a more natural way to spell the word.

Andrew A. Rooney

Definition

THE RIGHT STUFF

by Tom Wolfe

What is your definition of "justice"? How do you define "good taste"? What is the meaning of "maturity"? A definition sets boundaries around a word, phrase, object, or idea. Whether it explains an idea within a piece of writing or serves as the purpose for an entire essay, presenting a definition is a very straightforward way of explaining an unfamiliar concept.

In *The Right Stuff*, Tom Wolfe defines a term he invented. As you learn what "the right stuff" is, notice how the writer uses a mixture of description and analysis.

A young man might go into military flight training believing that he was entering some sort of technical school in which he was simply going to acquire a certain set of skills. Instead, he found himself all at once enclosed in a fraternity . . . the world was divided into those who had it and those who did not. This quality, this it, was never named . . . [The idea] seemed to be that a man should have the ability to go up in a hurtling piece of machinery and put his hide on the line and then have the moxie, the reflexes, the experience, the coolness, to pull it back in the last yawning moment—and then to go up again the next day, and the next day, and every next day. . . . A career of flying was like climbing one of those ancient Babylonian pyramids made up of a dizzy progression of steps and ledges . . . and the idea was to prove at every foot of the way up that pyramid that you were one of the elected and anointed ones who had the right stuff. . . .

Think AND Respond

Tom Wolfe has defined a quality for which there was previously no name. After reading his essay, do you feel you understand what "the right stuff" is? How does Wolfe use description, analysis, and comparison in his definition? How would you go about trying to define such an abstract idea?

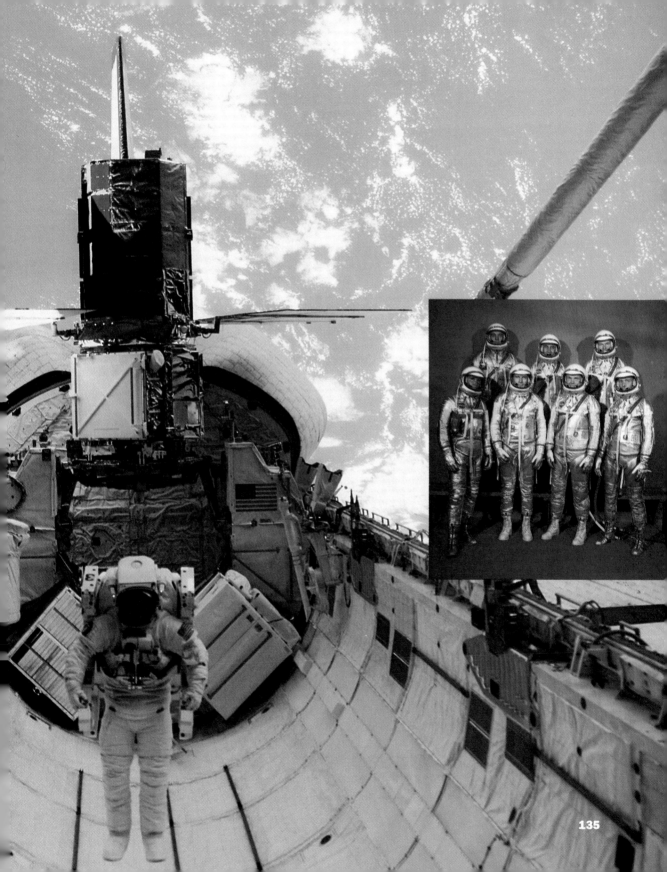

INVITATION
—— TO ——
Write

Tom Wolfe defines a term used to describe the qualities that some military pilots possess. Using a variety of details, define a term, object, or idea so that your readers gain a clear understanding of it.

In the guided assignment, the writer used a comparison to introduce a new idea. Often, you will use another more comprehensive type of writing—the definition—for this purpose and to classify ideas you wish to explain. In an informal definition, you might treat your topic personally or with humor.

PLANNING YOUR DEFINITION

HANDBOOKS
FOR HELP & PRACTICE

Elaboration,
pp. 364–369
Conclusions,
pp. 386–390
Reference Works,
pp. 490–495

1. Develop a list of subjects and choose one.   Consider terms you might understand more fully by developing a definition. For example, you might define "blank verse" for English class or "federalism" for American history. Scan the newspaper for unfamiliar concepts. Also explore popular expressions, such as the meaning of being "in."

2. Explore your subject in many ways.   Dictionaries and encyclopedias provide basic information. Also try experimenting with comparisons, similes, metaphors, and examples. Tom Wolfe, for instance, defines "the right stuff" by giving several examples of actions that demonstrate this quality. Putting the subject in a larger class allows you to examine the features that make it similar to or differenct from others in that class.

DRAFTING A DEFINITION

1. Write an introduction.   A good beginning presents your subject in a way that makes your reader want to learn more. Consider beginning with a teaser, a question, or an example.

For instance, a definition of "virtual reality" might begin, "Picture yourself walking along a Martian landscape, viewing the canals all without leaving your home. Thanks to a new technology called virtual reality, such an experience could be yours."

 Writer's Choice Will you write a formal, objective definition or a more subjective, personal one?

2. Elaborate on the characteristics. Discuss the characteristics of your subject, moving from general to specific or from familiar to unfamiliar. You might also devote one paragraph to each part of your subject. In any case support your point with vivid descriptions, personal experiences, and comparisons. For example, Tom Wolfe shows how having "the right stuff" is like working one's way up the steep side of a pyramid and what it is like to "put his hide on the line." If you use abstract or technical terms, give clear examples.

3. Write a conclusion. Close with a summary of your definition, a generalization about the important qualities of your subject, or a final illustration that puts your definition in perspective.

REVIEWING YOUR WRITING

1. Read and evaluate your definition. Have you achieved your goal? Is your definition clear? Are your examples and comparisons pertinent to the subject? Are your details organized effectively?

2. Have a reader restate the definition. Is the definition clear to the reader? If not, how could you clarify it?

3. Revise your definition. Do you need further elaboration? Should you add examples or eliminate irrelevant information? Could altering your word choice help you to fulfill your purpose?

PUBLISHING AND PRESENTING

- **Present your definition orally.** Begin with a daily "FYI" (for your information) session in your classroom. Have a different person present a definition each day.
- **Create a class encyclopedia or dictionary.** Group definitions according to topic. Include pictures.

Analogy

Have you ever tried to make a point or explain an idea but been at a loss for the right words? You may have found yourself saying, "Well, look, it's like. . . ." When you use these words, you are making an analogy.

An analogy is a comparison that uses similarities between two essentially different subjects in order to clarify an idea or make a point. An analogy can also be used to add humor or call attention to an otherwise ordinary topic.

In the following excerpt, the writer uses an analogy to explain the importance of apologies. As you read, decide whether you think the analogy helps the writer make her point.

LOVE MEANS ALWAYS HAVING TO SAY YOU'RE SORRY

by Kathleen Thompson

Making an apology is like fixing a flat tire. It's hard, dirty work, but you have to do it sometimes if you want to get anywhere.

Suppose you're tooling along with a new boyfriend. You're having a great time. You're moving into high gear. Everything's running smoothly. That's when you have a blowout. It happens every time. It's a law of nature.

Maybe you told a friend something he said—something he thought was personal. Maybe you didn't pay enough attention to him at a party. Maybe you told him his nose resembled a kumquat, never thinking it would bother him. Just as there are lots of ways to end up with a flat tire, there are lots of ways to get into trouble with someone you like.

You may be tempted to ignore it and see if you can get by. This is like driving on a flat tire. You may be able to get along for a while, but the ride will be increasingly bumpy. Almost before you know it, your teeth will be sounding like maracas. When you finally can't go any farther, the tire will have been cut to ribbons and your wheel rim will be a perfect octagon. Both will be long past fixing.

With a friend, if you try to keep going without admitting you made a mistake and apologizing, you'll find that things don't run smoothly. There will be little problems every day. He'll start sniping, tossing nasty little comments your way. You'll snap back. The course of true love will be running far from smooth. And by the time you're forced to deal with the situation, your relationship will be hanging in shreds, like the tire.

So it makes sense to fix the flat when it happens. Apologize to your friend as soon as you realize there's a problem. Both of these will make your life temporarily more difficult. And both of them will end up making things run more smoothly.

Think AND Respond

What similarities does the writer point out between riding on a flat tire and ignoring a problem with a friend? How did the use of her analogy affect your enjoyment and understanding as you read the article? How could you use analogies to clarify ideas in your own writing?

INVITATION TO Write

Kathleen Thompson used the analogy of riding on a flat tire to explain the dangers of not addressing problems that arise in a relationship. Now, write an analogy that will help you explain one situation or process in terms of another.

When you make an analogy, you are comparing the various qualities of one thing with the corresponding qualities of another. In expository writing, you can use analogies to help you explain a process or provide an insight about a situation or event.

PLANNING YOUR ANALOGY

HANDBOOKS

FOR HELP & PRACTICE

Exploring Ideas, pp. 330–332
Coherence, pp. 376–385

1. Think about the uses for analogies. Analogies can be used in expository writing as well as in more imaginative pieces of writing. If you decide to use an analogy in a science or history report, for example, you might use it to explain a difficult or abstract idea in terms of something more familiar. If you choose to use an analogy in a creative piece, your analogy can serve as the subject of an entire essay (as it is in the selection on the preceding page), a poem, or a song lyric. An analogy can also be used as the basis for a passage in a longer work, a piece of description in a novel, for example.

2. Choose a subject. In an expository piece, the subject to be explained in terms of an analogy might be a complex issue, such as an environmental problem, or a process, such as a chemical reaction. For a creative piece, choose a subject about which you wish to express your personal thoughts and feelings.

3. Choose an analogy that illuminates your subject. To get ideas, free associate by allowing thoughts to drift through your mind and link up with other thoughts. Consider the qualities of your main subject and look for another subject with some comparable characteristics. What associations do you think lead Kathleen Thompson to compare a poor relationship to a flat tire?

4. Consider your audience. Since an analogy explains something unfamiliar by comparing it to something known, make sure your readers are familiar with the known object.

5. Evaluate your analogy in terms of your purpose. Remember that your two subjects must share enough similar qualities to establish a reasonable and helpful comparison. For example, a round of labor negotiations might be effectively compared to a game of tennis in order to make a point in an expository paper. However, comparing a presidential campaign to a beauty contest would be useful only if your purpose was to criticize or satirize rather than to inform or define.

 Writer's Choice Will you treat your subject seriously, or do you wish to be humorous?

WRITING YOUR ANALOGY

1. Explore your ideas. You can begin by making two lists in which you write down the corresponding qualities of both subjects. Listing allows you to do much of your thinking "up front" before composing your draft. You might also draft immediately, thinking as you write about the similarities between your two subjects. Begin with a sentence such as "Gossip is like a plague." Then see where the points of comparison take you.

2. Clarify your purpose. What point will you make? The writer of the excerpt you read used an analogy to provide an insight about human relationships. She also used humor to accomplish her purpose. Will your purpose be to inform, persuade, or entertain?

3. Shape your material. You might cover the elements of the comparison one at a time or you could completely describe one subject and then show how the second subject is similar.

4. Elaborate on each point. Use specific details or examples to strengthen your analogy. Kathleen Thompson compares delaying an apology to driving along on a flat tire until it is "cut to ribbons" and the "wheel will be a perfect octagon."

5. End by summarizing the points of your analogy. Conclude by clearly expressing the purpose of your analogy. Your conclusion might be a strong, final insight or a recommendation to the reader.

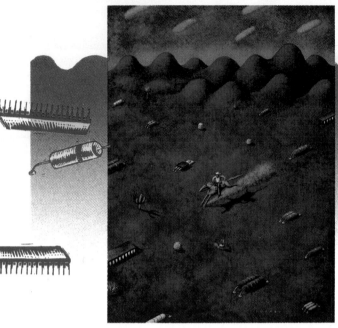

A pony-express rider traveling through a silicone prairie environment suggests the speed of electronic mail.

Writing
─TIP─

Use concrete, visually appealing details to support the power of your comparison.

R EVIEWING YOUR WRITING

1. Read and evaluate your analogy. Is the purpose of your analogy clear? Are the individual points of your comparison convincing? Has the main point of your analogy been lost among the less important points of comparison? Are your examples and details specific and sufficient in number?

2. Have a classmate read your analogy. Ask your classmate to summarize the main points of your analogy. Is the point of your analogy clear to your classmate? Is your classmate's summary consistent with the purpose of your analogy?

P UBLISHING AND PRESENTING

- **Present your analogy orally.** An analogy can be very useful in a report for almost any school subject. Deliver your report orally to the class and answer any questions that your audience may have.
- **Publish your analogy.** If you have written a poem or story, offer it to your school newspaper or literary magazine.
- **Perform your analogy.** If you have written a song lyric, ask a musician friend to set it to music and perform it with him or her.

Sentence

Varying Present Participial Phrases

As you know, present participial phrases can end a sentence. They can also begin one, and they can be placed in the middle, between a subject and a verb. Whatever their position, these phrases add detail and provide variety.

MODELS

1. (Opener) <u>Avoiding one another's eyes</u>, Tom and Lily stood up.

   Joan Aiken, "Searching for Summer"

   s
2. (S-V Split) The withered moon, <u>shining on his face</u>,

   v

   awakened him.   **John Steinbeck, "Flight"**

3. (Closer) The old professor looked up at the assistant, <u>fumbling fretfully with a pile of papers</u>.

   Dorothy Canfield, "The Heyday of the Blood"

Punctuation Note: Present participial phrases are set off by commas.

A. Unscrambling Sentences First, identify the present participial phrase in each set of sentence parts. Then unscramble each sentence and write it out, adding commas as needed. Some sets of sentence parts can be unscrambled in more than one way; if yours makes sense, it is acceptable.

Important: To practice each of the three positions, use each at least once.

1. a. was the first ashore
   b. Professor Kazan
   c. wearing a spotlessly white tropical suit and a wide-brimmed hat

   Arthur C. Clarke, *Dolphin Island*

2. a. was a little bothered by it
   b. watching the pony stop and start and trot and gallop
   c. Jody's father

   John Steinbeck, *The Red Pony*

3. a. came in and whispered with Jake and Lou
   b. two heavy-set men
   c. perspiring through their summer suits

   Robert Lipsyte, *The Contender*

4. a. standing in the shadows
   b. with the bright window behind him
   c. he blazed with sunburned health

   John Knowles, *A Separate Peace*

B. Combining Sentences Two or more present participial phrases may occur in a series within a sentence. The series usually ends a sentence, but it may also start one or come between the subject and the verb.

In this exercise, the first sentence in each set is the base sentence. Change the other sentences in the set into present participial phrases. Then insert the present participial phrases into the base sentence, making a series. In each, place your series where it makes most sense. Punctuate correctly.

> ***Example*** Sometimes a gaggle of them came to the Store. They were filling the whole room. They were chasing out the air. They were even changing the well-known scents.
>
> ***Result*** Sometimes a gaggle of them came to the Store, filling the whole room, chasing out the air, even changing the well-known scents.
>
> **Maya Angelou, *I Know Why the Caged Bird Sings***

1. The magician patted the hand. He was holding it quietly with a thumb on its blue veins. He was waiting for life to revive. **T. H. White, *The Book of Merlyn***

2. We wandered about the stock exhibit. We were gazing at the monstrous oven. We were hanging over the railings where the prize pigs loved to scratch their backs. **Dorothy Canfield, "The Heyday of the Blood"**

3. He spent a day in idleness. He was sitting in the mouth of his cave. He was gazing up at the farther peaks on which there were still patches of snow. **J. M. Coetzee, "Life and Times of Michael K"**

4. We caught two bass. We were hauling them briskly as though they were mackerel. We were pulling them over the side of the boat in a businesslike manner without any landing net. We were stunning them with a blow on the back of the head. **E. B. White, "Once More to the Lake"**

C. Imitating Sentences The models contain present participial phrases, either singly or in series. Imitate each model, in structure but not content. *Important:* Imitate as many sentence parts as possible, not just the underlined participial phrases.

1. Walking down a church aisle between hundreds of people, I had a feeling of eyes on me. **Carl Sandburg, "Fair and Circus Days"**

2. Year after year, learning to be quiet, Michael K sat on a blanket, watching his mother polish other people's floors. **J. M. Coetzee, "Life and Times of Michael K"**

3. Trembling, he'd push himself up, <u>turning first red, then a soft purple</u>, and finally collapse back onto the bed like an old worn-out doll.

James Hurst, "The Scarlet Ibis"

4. <u>Walking forward, watching the bull's feet</u>, he saw successively his eyes, his wet muzzle, and the wide, forward-pointing spread of his horns.

Ernest Hemingway, "The Undefeated"

D. Expanding Sentences Complete each sentence by adding a present participial series at the end. Your series should start with the underlined words, and the content you choose should blend well with the rest of the sentence. Punctuate correctly. After you have written your sentences, compare them with the originals on page 311.

1. He sat on a bench here, <u>watching</u>. . . , <u>thinking</u>. . .

Bernard Malamud, "A Summer's Reading"

2. Jan trotted about in a circle, <u>slapping</u>. . . and <u>pounding</u>. . .

Elliott Merrick, "Without Words"

3. Then Mama began to cry and ran over to him, <u>hugging</u>. . . and <u>kissing</u>. . .

James Hurst, "The Scarlet Ibis"

4. He walked to the corner of the lot, then back again, <u>studying</u>. . . , <u>frowning</u> and <u>scratching</u>. . .

Harper Lee, *To Kill a Mockingbird*

5. And so we went to the station, across the meadow, <u>taking</u>. . . , <u>trying</u>. . .

Gerda Weissmann Klein, *All But My Life*

Application Use the sentence below as the beginning of a paragraph that will be part of a story. As you write the rest of the paragraph, use present participial phrases, singly and in series. Vary their positions in your sentences. Notice how they add detail and variety.

> Jade Snow had grown up reading Confucius, learning to embroider and cook rice, developing a taste for steamed fish and bean sprouts, tea, and herbs, and she thought of her parents as people to be obeyed.
>
> **Jade Snow Wong, *Fifth Chinese Daughter***

Grammar Refresher When a participial phrase is placed incorrectly in a sentence, the result can be a misplaced or dangling modifier. For information about avoiding this common error, see Handbook 32, page 597.

Sketchbook

The artist Christo is known for dramatically wrapping objects, land forms, buildings, and other structures in a variety of materials. What does wrapping something conceal? What does it reveal? What would *you* like to wrap?

Additional Sketches

Write an outrageous excuse. Support it with as many preposterous reasons as possible.

Look at the night sky. Speculate about what is going on "out there."

Informative
Exposition: Analysis

Guided Assignment
CAUSE AND EFFECT

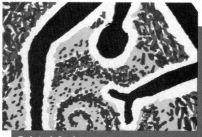

Related Assignment
MYTH

Related Assignment
HYPOTHESIS

An artist drawing a person might first sketch the head, then the torso, then the legs, and so on. A math student solving a long, complicated problem might first break it down into smaller parts and then solve each part. Breaking something down into its parts is called **analysis**.

In the next three assignments, you will practice different ways to apply the skill of analysis to your writing. In the guided assignment, you will write an analysis of a cause-and-effect relationship. Then, in the related assignments, you will apply your understanding of cause and effect to write an imaginative myth and a scientific hypothesis.

Cause and Effect

Guided
ASSIGNMENT

FROM

THE WATER IS WIDE

BY PAT CONROY

When something important happens in life, we usually want to know why. By analyzing causes and effects, we can understand the world better, learn from mistakes, and even make improvements.

In the following excerpt, Pat Conroy analyzes what went wrong to destroy life on the island of Yamacraw, off the coast of South Carolina. As you read, notice how one primary cause sets off a chain of effects that leads to the end of a way of life.

[Yamacraw] is not a large island, nor an important one, but it represents an era and a segment of history that is rapidly dying in America. The people of the island have changed very little since the Emancipation Proclamation. Indeed, many of them have never heard of this proclamation. They love their island with genuine affection but have watched the young people move to the city, to the lands far away and far removed from Yamacraw. The island is dying, and the people know it.

In the parable of Yamacraw there was a time when the black people supported themselves well. . . . Each morning the strong young men would take to their bateaux and search the shores and inlets for the large clusters of oysters, which the women and old men in the factory shucked into large jars. Yamacraw oysters were world famous . . . and the oyster factories operating on the island provided a substantial living for all the people. Everyone worked and everyone made money. Then a villain appeared. It was an industrial factory situated on a knoll above the Savannah River many miles away from Yamacraw. The villain spewed its excrement into the river, infected the creeks, and as silently as the pull of the

148

tides, the filth crept to the shores of Yamacraw. As every good health inspector knows, the unfortunate consumer who lets an infected oyster slide down his throat is flirting with hepatitis. . . . Soon after this, little white signs were placed by the oyster banks forbidding anyone to gather the oysters. Ten thousand oysters were now as worthless as grains of sand. . . .

Since a factory is soulless and faceless, it could not be moved to understand the destruction its coming had wrought. When the oysters became contaminated, the island's only industry folded almost immediately. The great migration began. A steady flow of people faced with starvation moved toward the cities. They left in search of jobs. . . . Over 300 people left the island. They left reluctantly, but left permanently and returned only on sporadic visits to pay homage to the relatives too old or too stubborn to leave. As the oysters died, so did the people.

Think AND Respond

What does Pat Conroy say caused the waters around Yamacraw to become polluted? According to Conroy's analysis, what effects did the pollution have on the island's way of life? What do you think was Conroy's goal in analyzing the chain of events on Yamacraw? How could you use a cause-and-effect analysis to explore a problem or situation?

INVITATION
— TO —
Write

You have read Pat Conroy's account of how industrial pollution changed a small island. Now explain a cause-and-effect relationship that you think is important or interesting.

What caused the energy crisis of the 1970's? What are the effects of weightlessness on astronauts? When you explain why something happened or exists, or when you examine the results of an action or condition, you are using cause-and-effect analysis. Cause-and-effect writing involves more than simply explaining events that occur one after another. One event must actually *cause* another to happen. For example, a newspaper report that examines the damage caused by a hurricane is an example of cause-and-effect writing. A newspaper report that traces the path a hurricane followed, however, merely shows a sequence.

PREWRITE AND EXPLORE

HANDBOOKS
FOR HELP & PRACTICE

Thinking Creatively,
pp. 471–474
Reference Works,
pp. 490–494

1. Begin exploring ideas. What cause-and-effect relationships interest you? The following activities can help you to explore some possibilities. Try one or more of these activities.

Exploratory Activities

• **Observing and researching** Look around you at the natural world. Identify some phenomenon in nature that you would like to understand more fully. Ask yourself, "What causes that?" See if you can find some answers to your questions in books and magazines about nature or science.

• **Browsing (history)** Choose a historical event or current event that interests you. The event can be as ancient as the fall of Rome or as recent as the latest headlines. Do some research to find out what caused the event to occur and what its consequences were (or will be).

- **Reflecting**   Working with a group of classmates, think about the successful people around you. These may be adults who are successful in their jobs, students who are successful in school, athletes who are successful in their sports, or any people at all who seem well-adjusted and happy. Ask yourselves, "What secrets do they have that make them successful? Are there any factors that they have in common? What might be the causes of their success?"

- **Predicting**   Think about the decisions you might have to make about your own life. For example, will you want to get married? Will you want to have children? Will you want to go to college, or junior college, or a technical school? What career will you choose? Select an issue, and list all the possible decisions you could make. Then freewrite about the effects each choice might have on your future.

- **Reading literature**   Look through some favorite short stories, such as "The Cask of Amontillado" by Edgar Allan Poe or "Blues Ain't No Mocking Bird" by Toni Cade Bambara. Think about each story, and ask yourself the following questions: What causes the central conflict in the story's plot? What are the effects of this conflict? Why do the characters behave as they do? How does the behavior of each character affect other characters?

 Writer's Choice   You can choose one effect and spend most of your time investigating its causes, or you can choose one cause and spend most of your time investigating its effects. The choice is up to you.

2. Choose a topic.   Freewrite on a few of the ideas you discovered through the exploratory activities to find out which one appeals to you most. You also might consult your journal, "Apply Your Skills" on page 161, or the ideas you experimented with in the Sketchbook on page 146 to find a topic. Then you may wish to discuss your ideas with a group of classmates. Share your freewriting, and then brainstorm to see what types of causes and effects you can identify relating to each idea.

COMPUTER
TIP

Grolier's Academic American Encyclopedia, **available on CD ROM and from database services, has entries for historical events, including timetables that show sequences of causes and effects.**

Writing
TIP

You might want to write a humorous essay about a wildly improbable series of causes and effects. For an example of this kind of writing, see James Thurber's "The Night the Bed Fell."

3. Clarify your purpose. Ask yourself what purpose you would like your writing to serve. Sometimes people write about cause and effect as an end in itself, just to explain what makes something happen. At other times, people use cause and effect in their writing to achieve some additional purpose, such as to persuade people to think or act in a certain way or to offer a solution to a problem. In the opening excerpt, for example, Pat Conroy wanted to do more than simply analyze the events that occurred on one small island. He wanted to alert people to the disastrous effects of pollution and perhaps persuade them to do something about it.

4. Identify your specific goals. In addition to your general purpose for writing, ask yourself if there are any specific personal goals you would like to accomplish. For example, a newspaper article recounting the findings of a new theory about the extinction of the dinosaurs sparked one student's interest in dinosaurs. Eduardo decided to write a summary of various extinction theories for a research paper he was planning to write later in the year. Throughout this assignment, you will follow Eduardo's process in writing a cause-and-effect paper.

5. Choose a form. As you think about different purposes and audiences for your writing, also think about different forms that it might take. A piece of persuasive writing that analyzes causes and effects might take the form of a speech or of a letter to the editor of a newspaper. A humorous or informational piece about cause and effect might make a good magazine article. An analysis of causes and effects in a work of literature might take the form of a critical review. Some cause-and-effect essays might make good reports for history or science classes.

6. Identify your audience. Think about who your audience is, what they already know about the topic, and what they need to know. In some cases your audience may already be familiar with the cause and may need to have the effect explained. In other cases the situation may be reversed. The effect may be clear, but the cause may be uncertain. Concentrate on providing your audience with the information that they need.

7. Gather supporting information. The way in which you gather information for your analysis will depend a great deal on the subject you are writing about. You might gather information by observing, by doing library research, by interviewing an expert or authority, by studying the details of a story, or simply by thinking back on your

PROBLEM
S O L V I N G

What form should I use?

Writing
— TIP —

To find out what your readers already know and what they want to know about your topic, discuss the topic with several of them before you begin drafting.

own experiences. You might also need to use your imagination if you are speculating about causes or effects. The following are some points to keep in mind as you gather your information:

- Remember that events may have multiple causes or multiple effects. Pat Conroy explained the series of effects that resulted when a factory was built on Yamacraw Island.
- Remember that causes and effects are sometimes connected, as in a chain. In a cause-and-effect chain, a cause creates an effect. That effect becomes the cause of another effect, and so on. Eduardo took notes on one extinction theory by making a chart of causes and effects.

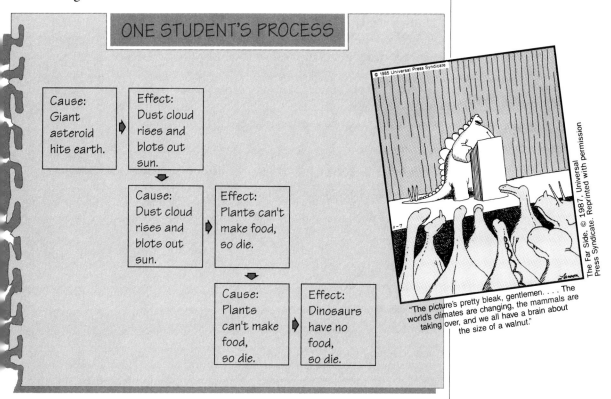

ONE STUDENT'S PROCESS

Cause: Giant asteroid hits earth. → Effect: Dust cloud rises and blots out sun.

Cause: Dust cloud rises and blots out sun. → Effect: Plants can't make food, so die.

Cause: Plants can't make food, so die. → Effect: Dinosaurs have no food, so die.

"The picture's pretty bleak, gentlemen. . . . The world's climates are changing, the mammals are taking over, and we all have a brain about the size of a walnut."

The Far Side. © 1987, Universal Press Syndicate. Reprinted with permission

© 1985 Universal Press Syndicate

8. Avoid fallacies of cause and effect. Don't assume that a single cause always leads to a single effect. One action may result in a variety of effects, or several actions may be required to cause one effect. Also, do not assume that a cause-and-effect relationship exists simply because one event follows another. For example, if five students become ill after gym class, you could incorrectly assume that gym was to blame. In reality the students had been exposed to the flu virus. (See Handbook 24, pages 469–470 for more information on logical fallacies.)

HANDBOOKS
FOR HELP & PRACTICE

Elaboration,
pp. 364–369

PROBLEM
S O L V I N G

How should I organize my essay?

D RAFT AND DISCOVER

1. Examine your information. Look over the information you have gathered. Consider which details would be most meaningful to your audience and most useful in accomplishing your purpose. Decide whether you need to gather more information or have enough with which to begin writing. Remember that at any point in the drafting stage you can stop to gather more information.

2. Organize your writing. The way you organize your material depends on the types of details you will be presenting. Cause-and-effect writing generally follows one of two patterns of organization. In the **cause-to-effect pattern,** you state the cause first and then proceed to the effect. In the **effect-to-cause pattern,** you begin with the effect and then examine what caused it. The following are some common ways of using these organizational patterns:

Cause-to-Effect Patterns		Effect-to-Cause Patterns	
A	**B**	**A**	**B**
Introduction	Introduction	Introduction	Introduction
Cause	Cause 1	Effect	Effect 1
Effect 1	Cause 2	Cause 1	Effect 2
Effect 2	Cause 3, etc.	Cause 2	Effect 3, etc.
Effect 3, etc.	Effect	Cause 3, etc.	Cause
Conclusion	Conclusion	Conclusion	Conclusion

If your subject is a "chain" of causes and effects in which one thing causes another, which causes another, and so on, simply write about each event in turn, pointing out how each is connected to the one that precedes it and the one that follows it. Pat Conroy used this type of organization in the opening excerpt.

Writer's Choice You may choose to include a chart or diagram in your essay to help explain the cause-and-effect relationship to your readers.

3. Begin drafting. Although cause-and-effect writing needs to be structured, it does not have to be dry. As Pat Conroy's essay shows, cause-and-effect writing can make use of powerful images and a carefully crafted mood or tone. Experiment with different approaches as you draft.

4. Elaborate on ideas. As you work on subsequent drafts of your writing, you may find it appropriate to elaborate on some of the details that you have presented. Some strategies you might use to develop specific ideas in your writing include the following:

PROBLEM SOLVING

How can I elaborate on my ideas?

Strategies

- **Description** Create sensory images by using words of sight, sound, touch, taste, or smell to paint a vivid picture for the reader. Also use strong verbs, as Pat Conroy did when he wrote "The villain spewed its excrement into the river, infected the creeks, and as silently as the pull of the tides, the filth crept to the shores of Yamacraw."

- **Narration** Often the clearest way to show a cause-and-effect relationship is to narrate a series of events that demonstrate the relationship. Pat Conroy's narration of events that happened on one particular island provides a powerful example of the destructive effect of pollution.

Eduardo, the student who wanted to write about why dinosaurs became extinct, decided to begin his draft by writing a paragraph based on his notes about the asteroid theory. He tried to trace the chain of causes and effects in one paragraph and to make the relationship between events clear.

ONE STUDENT'S PROCESS

Some scientists believe that an astronomical catastrophe caused the dinosaurs to die out suddenly. According to this theory, a giant asteroid hit the earth about 65 million years ago. As a result, a tremendous dust cloud was created that cut off sunlight to the earth for months. Because plants depend on sunlight for photosynthesis, much of the plant life on earth was destroyed. The destruction of plant life caused the death of, first, the plant-eating dinosaurs and, later, the flesh-eating dinosaurs who fed on plant eaters.

5. Take a break. After you have a good start on your draft, or perhaps after your first or second draft is finished, you might want to take a break. Put the writing aside for a few hours or an entire day. Then you will be able to take a fresh look at it. When you return to your work, ask yourself questions like these, or share your work with peer readers.

Questions for Yourself

- Are all the cause-and-effect relationships I've written about clear? Will readers be able to tell what are the causes and what are the effects?

- Have I presented information in a lively, interesting fashion? Have I avoided sounding like an old textbook?

- Are there any important causes or effects that I haven't presented? Should I add these or would the additional information distract from my main point?

- Have I fulfilled any other purposes that I had in addition to explaining cause-and-effect relationships?

- Have I avoided oversimplifying the cause-and-effect relationship?

Questions for Your Peer Readers

- Can you tell me what you liked most about my piece? What parts work best? Why?

- What parts of my essay seemed to work less well? Can you tell me why?

- Can you summarize the main cause-and-effect relationships that I wrote about? Is there anything I could do to make these clearer or more vivid or lively?

- Is there anything in my paper that you didn't understand? Can you tell me how to make it clearer?

- Are there important parts of my subject that I didn't deal with?

- Do you agree with my analysis? Is there anything that you would add or delete?

R E V I S E   Y O U R   W R I T I N G

1. Evaluate your responses. Review your own thoughts and the responses of your peer readers. As you get ready to revise your work, keep in mind that cause-and-effect analyses generally display the following characteristics.

HANDBOOKS
FOR HELP & PRACTICE

**Coherence,
pp. 376–385
Thinking Critically,
pp. 468–470**

Cause and Effect   **157**

Standards for Evaluation

An effective cause-and-effect analysis . . .

- clearly states the cause-and-effect relationship being examined.
- shows clear relationships between causes and effects.
- arranges details logically and uses transitional words to clarify order.
- demonstrates a clear sense of audience through the use of appropriate language and choice of details.

2. Problem-solve. Decide which responses you want to use and then rework your draft. Eduardo made the following changes in response to suggestions by one peer reader. He also decided to think about adding the paragraphs his peer reader suggested for the final draft of his essay.

ONE STUDENT'S PROCESS

I like how mysterious the beginning sounds.

Say what the two theories are.

Be more specific.

How did physical changes in the earth cause the dinosaur to die?

Milliuns of year's ago the world's most powerful
,the dinosaurs,
creatures vanished from the face of the earth. Why? For
: a gradua
years scientists have debated two main explanations. To-
climate change or a sudden astronomical catastrophe.
day each new fossil find is examined closely by rival

scientists to find clues to support their theries.
, scientists who claim that changes in the earth occur slowly,
Gradualists say that at the end of the Cretaceous pe-
, more than 65 million years ago,   a
riod the geogerphy of earth begun to change. Ocean
ra   ; as a result, the climate
levels gradually dropped, and mountains rose. The dino-

saurs died.   of the earth became cooler, and seasonal differences
increased. Consequently, many new plants developed that were leafless in winter.
Plant-eating dinosaurs were severely affected because they could no longer find
food. As plant-eating animals declined, carnivores, or flesh-eating dinosaurs,
who normally hunted plant eaters, also suffered.

3. Proofread your work. Incorporate all your changes and look for errors in grammar, punctuation, and spelling. Correct these mistakes so that readers will not be distracted by them. Make a clean, final copy of your essay.

Grammar

—TIP—

In most cases, use commas to set off transitional words and phrases, such as *as a result, therefore,* and *consequently.*

LINKING
GRAMMAR ᴀɴᴅ WRITING
Writing Compound Sentences

Using compound sentences in which the clauses are linked by a semicolon can be an effective way to explain cause-and-effect relationships. You can often place the clause stating the cause before the semicolon and the clause stating the effect after the semicolon. Immediately after the semicolon you can use a transition such as *consequently* or *as a result* to show the relationship between the ideas.

The climate changed; consequently, many plants died.

See Grammar Handbook 32, pages 619–620 for more help with compound sentences.

▶UBLISH AND PRESENT

- **Share your paper with a teacher in another class.** If you wrote an analysis of a topic in science, history, or literature, share your work with your teacher in that subject.

- **Prepare a lesson to teach your class about your topic.** Use visual aids such as photographs or slides to reinforce your main ideas.

- **Invent a game based on what you have learned.** Pool information with other students to make a quiz game similar to Jeopardy! or Trivial Pursuit, creating such categories as history, nature, and literature. If several students wrote predictions about the effects on actions in your own futures, turn these predictions into your own version of The Game of Life.

- **Share essays in class.** In a small group, read your essays aloud. Then select one or two to read aloud to the class. Discuss the qualities of these essays.

- **Save your work in your writing portfolio.**

HANDBOOKS

FOR HELP & PRACTICE

**Sharing Completed Writing,
pp. 418–419**

The Great Dinosaur Mystery

Eduardo Rodriguez

Clearly states the
cause-and-effect
relationship being
examined—the
disappearance of
dinosaurs

Millions of years ago, the world's most powerful creatures, the dinosaurs, vanished from the face of the
earth. Why? For years scientists have debated two main
explanations: a gradual climate change and a sudden
astronomical catastrophe. Today each new fossil find is
examined closely by rival scientists to find clues supporting their own theories.

Arranges details
logically and uses
transitional words to
clarify order

Gradualists, scientists who believe that changes in
the earth occur slowly, say that at the end of the Cretaceous period, more than 65 million years ago, the
geography of earth began to change. Ocean levels gradually dropped, and mountains rose; as a result, the
climate of earth became cooler, and seasonal differences
increased. Consequently, many new plants developed that
were leafless in winter. Plant-eating dinosaurs were severely affected because they could no longer find food.

Presents several
causes explaining
an effect

As plant-eating dinosaurs declined, carnivorous, or
flesh-eating, dinosaurs also suffered. Meanwhile, small,
fur-covered mammals with brief lifespans were able to
adapt more quickly and competed boldly for scarce resources. Eventually, the dinosaurs died out completely.

Other scientists believe that an astronomical catastrophe caused the dinosaurs to die out suddenly.
According to this theory, a giant asteroid hit the earth
at the end of the Cretaceous period. As a result, a tremendous dust cloud was created that cut off sunlight to
the earth for months. Because plants depend on sunlight
for photosynthesis, much of the plant life on earth was
destroyed. As in the gradualists' theory, the destruction
of plant life eventually caused the death of both plant-
eating and flesh-eating dinosaurs.

Draws a conclusion
based on the cause-
and-effect relationship

The mystery of exactly what caused the extinction of
dinosaurs may never be solved completely. But the latest
theories provide a fascinating glimpse of the scientific
method at work as today's scientists compete to track
down clues and find the best explanations of dramatic
changes in the earth's past.

WRITER TO WRITER

The important thing is not to stop questioning. Curiosity has its own reason for existing. One cannot help but be in awe when he contemplates the mysteries of . . . life, of the marvelous structure of reality. It is enough if one tries merely to comprehend a little of this mystery every day.

Albert Einstein, scientist

1. Reflect on your writing process.   Now that you have completed your cause-and-effect analysis and read several others, think about the process you followed. Ask yourself the questions below and record your answers in your writing log.

- What did you learn about explaining causes and effects that you might use in your writing in the future?
- In the course of your writing, did you make any diagrams or charts? If so, how did these help you?
- What comments by peer readers do you remember most vividly? Which ones will you keep in mind for future writing?

2. Apply your skills.   Try one or more of the following.

- **Cross curricular**   One area of science in which cause-and-effect analysis is especially important is health and medicine. Write an article for the fitness section of a newspaper or magazine. Explain the cause-effect relationship between some type of behavior that leads to good health or bad health.
- **Literature**   Read several different versions of the legend of King Arthur and write an analysis of some aspect of Arthur's rise to power or the destruction of Camelot.
- **General**   Make a "Tell Me Why" booklet for children, explaining the causes of events in history or in the natural world. Base the booklet on pieces written by your class, but edit the writing to make it appropriate for a younger audience.
- **Related assignments**   Follow the suggestions on pages 164–172 to write a myth or a hypothesis.

FOR YOUR
PORTFOLIO

Myth

As a child, did you ever make up an imaginative story to explain a natural phenomenon like thunder? Throughout history, various cultures have used stories like this to explain beliefs, customs, or happenings in nature. Such stories are called myths.

The following selection from "Arap Sang and the Cranes," a story based on an African myth, offers a fanciful explan-ation of why vultures have bald heads. As you read, look for both the human and the super-human qualities of the characters in this myth.

from

ARAP SANG AND THE CRANES

African Folk Tale

RETOLD BY HUMPHREY HARMAN

Arap Sang was a great chief and more than half a god, for in the days when he lived great chiefs were always a little mixed up with the gods. One day he was walking on the plain, admiring the cattle.

It was hot. The rains had not yet come. The ground was almost bare of grass and as hard as stone. . . .

The sun beat down on Arap Sang's bald head. (He was sensitive about this and didn't like it mentioned.) And he thought, "I'm feeling things more than I used to."

And then he came across a vulture sitting in the crook of a tree, his wings hanging down and his eyes on the lookout.

"Vulture," said Arap Sang, "I'm hot, and the sun is making my head ache. You have there a fine pair of broad wings. I'd be most grateful if you'd spread them out and let me enjoy a patch of shade."

"Why?" croaked Vulture. He had indigestion. Vultures usually have indigestion; it's the things they eat.

"Why?" said Arap Sang mildly. . . . "Because it wouldn't be much trouble to you. Because it's pleasant and good to help people." . . .

"Oh, go home, Baldy, and stop bothering people; it's hot."

Arap Sang straightened himself up, and his eyes flashed. He wasn't half a god for nothing; and when he was angry, he could be a rather terrifying person. And he was very angry now. It was that remark about his lack of hair. . . .

"Vulture," he said, "you're cruel, and you're selfish. I shan't forget what you've said, and you won't either. NOW GET OUT!"

Arap Sang was so impressive that Vulture got up awkwardly and flapped off. . . .

Presently Vulture met an acquaintance of his. (Vultures don't have friends; they just have acquaintances.) They perched together on the same bough. Vulture took a close look at his companion and then another, and what he saw was so funny that it cheered him up.

"He, he!" he giggled. "What's happened to you? Met with an accident? You're bald."

The other vulture looked sour, but at the same time you felt she might be pleased about something.

"That's good, coming from you," she said. "What have you been up to? You haven't got a feather on you above the shoulders."

Then they both felt their heads with consternation. It was quite true. They were bald, both of them; and so was every other vulture, the whole family, right down to this very day.

Which goes to show that if you can't be ordinarily pleasant to people, at least it's not wise to go insulting great chiefs who are half gods.

Think AND Respond

How is this story similar to other myths you have read? How is it different? Do you think the writer's decision to use humor adds to or detracts from the tale? Why? If you were to explain an aspect of nature, such as why roses smell sweet, what imaginative explanations could you make?

163

INVITATION
— TO —
Write

The myth of Arap Sang gives an imaginative explanation of why vultures are bald. Write your own myth in which you tell a story that explains some aspect of nature, society, or human behavior.

Like songs and stories, myths are an important part of a culture's oral tradition. They also represent a universal human need to give shape and meaning to the world around us. By means of a story, myths try to explain the causes of natural processes or common human experiences, such as the rising of the sun or the presence of evil in the world.

When you write your own myth, remember that myths are, to an extent, imaginative stories of cause and effect. However, they are also narratives with all the basic story elements: characters, a plot involving conflict, a setting, dialogue, and a theme. The characters in myths often have qualities beyond ordinary human abilities, and the themes frequently offer advice on how to live morally or wisely.

PREPARING A MYTH

HANDBOOKS
FOR HELP & PRACTICE

Thinking Creatively,
pp. 471–474
Unity/Coherence,
pp. 371–385
Adequate Detail,
pp. 405–406

1. Review familiar myths. With others, retell such stories as the kidnapping of Persephone, or the tale of Narcissus. Discuss similarities in the characters and plot.

2. Choose an event or situation. Observe and ask questions about ordinary things you see in nature: plants, animals, landforms, or the weather. Why is the sky blue? Why does slicing onions bring tears to the eyes? Why do roses have thorns? Why is the neck of a giraffe so long? Also consider aspects of human behavior. For instance, why do we nod our heads when we mean yes and shake them back and forth for no? When did jealousy begin? Write a list of possible topics for a myth and select one.

Horizontal Helment Mask (kyponyungo), Marion Stratton Gould Fund, 70.22. Memorial Art Gallery, Rochester, NY

3. Play with imaginative cause-and-effect relationships. Set aside scientific facts and use your imagination. Let your mind free-associate for unusual connections between ideas. How can you connect an everyday effect with a fanciful cause? Rose thorns might be explained as soldiers transformed by a hero to protect his beloved, who has been magically turned into a rose. Remember that the purpose of your myth is both to explain something and relate a story in an entertaining manner to the reader.

4. Create a hero or heroine. Myths usually involve the actions of heroes or gods. Arap Sang is both "a great chief and more than half a god." He clearly has human needs when he complains of being hot, but he also has the extraordinary power to make all vultures bald. Choose some qualities that will make your hero special, such as courage, strength, or goodness. Also give your character some powers or qualities not possessed by ordinary humans.

5. Sketch out ideas. Using a cluster map or time line, jot down preliminary ideas for plot, characters, and setting. You might also include notes on the theme you wish to illustrate; for example, the rewards of kindness or the value of hard work.

Writer's Choice You can follow tradition and set your myth in ancient times, or you can create a modern myth, setting the story in recent years to explain a modern fad or trend.

Writing
——**TIP**——
Consider using figurative language to express comparisons of your central character with ordinary mortals.

1. Choose a format or style. The writer of the Arap Sang myth chose to use a style and type of language that reminds the reader of fables and fairy tales. He also chose a light, informal tone. Experiment with various approaches in your draft.

2. Introduce your hero or heroine. One good way to start your myth is with a description of the main character. Describe physical details such as hair color, height, or clothing, as well as nonphysical traits such as cleverness, jealousy, or absent-mindedness. Also be sure to establish the extraordinary or superhuman qualities of your hero. These powers, however, need not be revealed right away. Part of the enjoyment readers receive from the Arap Sang myth arises from the fact that the reader doesn't find out what it means to be "half a god" until near the end of the story.

3. Establish the setting. Use specific descriptive details to create the place in which your story takes place, especially if, as in this selection from "Arap Sang and the Cranes," the setting is an important element of the story. In that myth, concrete details are used to establish the setting as a dry, hot plain without grass and hard as stone. These details prepare the reader for the presence of the vulture and for Arap Sang's request.

4. Develop the situation. The body of your myth should explain the problem your hero or heroine encounters. Often this involves a conflict between two characters, such as the quarrel between Arap Sang and the vulture. However, your character may simply be unhappy with a situation and decide to change it. Remember to develop your story in an imaginative manner that will entertain as well as instruct your readers.

5. Add dialogue. Use colorful dialogue in your myth to make characters come alive in your readers' minds. Dialogue enables you to show, rather than just tell about, the important qualities and traits of your hero or heroine. It is also a lively way to present conflict between your characters.

6. Create an ending for your myth. Write an ending that reveals the outcome of the conflict and shows the reader that the results, like the vulture's bald head, are still visible today. You may also want to convey directly a moral or lesson about life. For example, the model myth ends with a warning to be pleasant to others.

1. Read and evaluate your myth. Your myth should proceed logically, even if the events are fanciful. The other elements of the myth should also be well developed. For example, are the hero and other characters vivid? Is the dialogue consistent with the characters' personalities? Is the conflict or situation clearly defined?

2. Share your myth with some friends. Does your myth capture your friends' interest and entertain them? Are the events described in the myth clear? Is the ending satisfying? If not, ask for suggestions for improving your myth.

3. Revise your myth. Do you need to strengthen the beginning, middle, or ending? Do you need to add concrete details to make your characters or setting more vivid? Is there irrelevant information that must be removed? Should you add dialogue?

The story of a hero rescuing a fair maiden from a monster is a myth found in many cultures.

PUBLISHING AND PRESENTING

- **Organize reading of myths.** As a class, share your myths orally, or invite another class or a group of children to hear your myths.
- **Create a collection of myths.** Make a class book of students' myths. Gather related myths into chapters and include illustrations for each myth.

Hypothesis

WHY YOU FEEL CRUMMY WHEN YOU'RE SICK

by Robert M. Sapolsky

Like most people, you've probably learned about, observed, or experienced something that made you wonder "Why?" If you pursued your curiosity, you might have tried to answer your own question by thinking of a hypothesis, or possible explanation for your question. A hypothesis must be tested in order to be proven true or false.

Notice how, instead of just complaining about feeling sick, the researcher mentioned in the following article developed a hypothesis to explain his symptoms. As you read, see how this hypothesis was tested experimentally.

Recently, in preparation for a trip to the tropics, I received a dreadful number of inoculations. As I sat in the clinic after the shots, shifting from cheek to cheek in discomfort, the nurse explained that the vaccines—especially the one for typhoid— could make me feel a bit ill. And, sure enough, by nightfall I felt crummy. . . .

An extraordinary array of illnesses makes us feel crummy in this way. Mostly we just want to sleep. Our joints ache, and we feel cold and feverish. . . . We lose interest in food; if the illness persists, we lose weight even if we force ourselves to eat. And we look like [garbage]. . . .

These symptoms don't just happen; a quite complex system of responses brings them about—and, it seems, for very sound reasons. . . . Clearly, the body works very actively to bring these symptoms about. [But how could one prove that fever is beneficial when a person is ill?]

The easiest way to demonstrate the benefits of feverishness would be to infect laboratory animals with something that typically causes a fever and see how they fare when the fever is blocked. . . . Matthew Kluger, a physiologist at the University of Michigan Medical School, did one of the most supremely clever studies that I have ever heard of. He studied lizards— which are, of course, cold-blooded—placing them in a terrarium that was hot at one end, cold at the other, and had a smooth temperature gradient in between.

When healthy, the lizards settled down at the point in the gradient where their body temperature would stabilize at 98.6 degrees. But when Kluger infected them with a bacterium, they chose to become feverish—they moved up the gradient to a point where their temperature would rise a few degrees. When Kluger prevented the infected lizards from moving to the hotter end of the terrarium, they were less likely to survive the infection. Running a fever, he concluded, helped.

Think AND Respond

What hypothesis does the experiment described in this article test? Did you find the explanation easy to understand? What techniques did the writer use to keep the article lively and interesting? Do you have a hypothesis to explain something you've observed? How could you test your hypothesis?

INVITATION
—TO—
Write

Robert Sapolsky put his mind to work when his body exhibited signs of illness and suggested a hypothesis to explain one of his symptoms. Write a hypothesis to explain a natural or social phenomenon you have observed, and suggest how your hypothesis could be tested.

Writing a hypothesis is one way of examining causes and effects. You observe the effects—the unpleasant symptoms of an illness, for example—and work backward to propose the "why," or cause. People in many fields—in astronomy, medicine, sports, sociology, and psychology—formulate and test hypotheses to try to explain phenomena they have observed. You too have formed hypotheses when you searched for reasons why your best friend was in a bad mood, what made your sports team lose the championship, or why the tire on your bike went flat.

FORMULATING A HYPOTHESIS

HANDBOOKS

FOR HELP & PRACTICE

Thinking Creatively, pp. 471–474

Thinking Critically, pp. 468–470

1. Ask a question about some situation you've observed or experienced. Think about the physical world around you. Observe human behavior and customs. You might notice that dogs howl when emergency vehicles pass by with their sirens blaring; that some people chatter incessantly at total strangers seated next to them on airplanes; that many people feel depressed or cranky when the weather is gray and drizzly. List situations or behaviors like these that have puzzled you or that you've wondered about. Try some creative questioning to probe the subject you're considering. Ask "why" or "what if." For example, while thinking about his own illness and wondering about its symptoms, Robert Sapolsky asked, "What if a cold-blooded animal, which cannot run a fever, gets an infection?"

2. Form a hypothesis. The simplest and most effective way to form a hypothesis that explains your subject is to propose a variety of answers to the questions you asked. Do some focused freewriting about your subject. Why do dogs howl? Perhaps the sound of the siren hurts their ears. Maybe the frequency or pitch of the sound prompts the howling response. Could it be that they are just attempting to imitate the sound they hear? Why do some airline passengers chatter at their fellow fliers? Maybe talking lessens their nervousness. Perhaps they're just friendly folks, or curious, or downright nosey. After you've listed a number of answers, evaluate your responses. You might try ranking your responses from most to least likely. The most likely response is a good hypothesis to test.

3. Think of a suitable way of testing your hypothesis. First look for existing research to verify your hypothesis. Sapolsky, for example, found that a study had already been done that tested his hypothesis. You may want to use related studies or articles as tests of your hypothesis.

A formal test of your hypothesis would involve setting up an experiment to verify your conclusions. For example, you could test a hypothesis about the relationship between a dog's howl and a siren's pitch by observing the dog's reactions to different sirens.

A formal experiment might be difficult to arrange if human behavior is your subject. In that case, you can test your hypothesis by observing general behavior. Do airline passengers seem fidgety, shifting around in their seats, tapping their fingers on the armrests, playing with a piece of jewelry? You might also question people you know who fly frequently and who often talk to their fellow passengers. Ask them why they do it.

A parody of Pavlov's dog.

4. Draw conclusions. After you've tested your hypothesis, draw conclusions from your test. Is your original hypothesis correct? Do you have to modify it in any way? Does your hypothesis need to be reworded or discarded in light of your test?

DRAFTING YOUR HYPOTHESIS

1. Arrange your material in logical order. First present the questions that led to your experiment, describing your observations in detail. Like Sapolsky, you might also describe how you arrived at your hypothesis. Then state your hypothesis and explain it if necessary. Finally, indicate how it was tested, or describe and compare relevant tests other people have done. If you do the test yourself, describe the experiment and its results.

 Writer's Choice Do you want to write your hypothesis as a personal narrative, like the model, or as a more formal report of an experiment? A report may be more appropriate if you've actually tested the hypothesis.

2. Discuss the implications of your hypothesis. Think of other applications of your hypothesis and make some predictions. Kluger, for example, concluded that running a fever helped animals to survive infections. If you found that people talk on airplanes because they're nervous, you might generalize that chattering is one response to nervousness.

REVIEWING YOUR WRITING

1. Evaluate your hypothesis. Make sure your hypothesis is valid and that you have identified a true cause-and-effect relationship. Pretend that you know only the hypothesis and have never observed the phenomenon you described. Based on your past experiences, does the hypothesis make sense?

2. Show your writing to some friends. Ask them to focus on the logical aspects of your hypothesis. Does it really explain the phenomenon? Has any other possible cause for the phenomenon been overlooked? Have you explained your observations, your hypothesis and its implications, and your predictions clearly? Have you fully described your experiment or the studies and articles you found?

PUBLISHING AND PRESENTING

- **Make an oral presentation.** Present your work to your science or social science class. Invite discussion of its ideas, methods and conclusions.
- **Create a classroom magazine.** Collect classmates' hypothesis papers to create a scientific journal. Use magazines such as *Scientific American, National Wildlife,* and *Smithsonian* as models.
- **Hold a round-table discussion.** Exchange hypothesis papers with classmates, and challenge each other to find alternative hypotheses and tests for the phenomenon presented in each paper. Then hold a round-table discussion and, if you wish, choose one or two phenomena to investigate further as a group.

Sentence

Using Past Participial Phrases

Experienced writers use past participial phrases to add descriptive detail to their sentences. These phrases usually begin with a past participle, a verb form generally ending in *-ed* and used as a modifier. Past participial phrases may occur anywhere in a sentence, at the beginning, in the middle, or at the end.

MODELS

1. (Opener)   <u>Rolled in his blanket and their caribou robe</u>, he had the best sleep yet.
   Elliott Merrick, "Without Words"

2. (S-V Split)   His nose and ears, <u>nipped by the wind</u>, thawed painfully in the even warmth of the house.   **Elizabeth Bowen, "Foothold"**

3. (Closer)   I pushed through the brass-framed glass doors into the tiny lobby, <u>paved with freshly mopped, permanently dirty tile</u>.
   Jack Finney, "Of Missing Persons"

Punctuation Note: Past participial phrases are set off by commas.

A. Combining Sentences   In each set, change the second sentence into a past participial phrase. Then insert the phrase into the first sentence near the word it describes. Use each of the three positions (opener, S-V split, and closer) at least once.

> **Example**   Angel's face bobbed up, mocking him. Angel's face was framed in the headguard.
>
> **Result**   Angel's face, framed in the headguard, bobbed up, mocking him.   **Robert Lipsyte, *The Contender***

1. Five or six pieces of apparatus arrived. The pieces were followed by a battalion chief.   **James Thurber, "Snapshot of a Dog"**

2. Its walls had been lined with human remains. The human remains were piled to the vault overhead in the fashion of the great catacombs of Paris.

   Edgar Allan Poe, "The Cask of Amontillado"

3. Our illegal radio was broadcasting the news. The radio was turned too low to be intelligible. **John Knowles, _A Separate Peace_**

4. Suddenly a great wolf started from somewhere and galloped along the edge of the canyon. The wolf was outlined black and clear by the setting sun.

   Elinor Steward, _Letters of a Woman Homesteader_

5. The old fire truck was being pushed from town by a crowd of men. The fire truck was killed by the cold. **Harper Lee, _To Kill a Mockingbird_**

6. Nearly fifty people greeted Nancy Belle. The people were gathered in the big parlor upstairs at the hotel. **Conrad Richter, "Early Marriage"**

7. The cup from which her aunt had drunk her last cup of tea lay beside the sink. The cup was washed and long since drained dry.

   Shirley Jackson, "The Little House"

8. He had driven his great train across the land ten thousand times. The train had been loaded with its weight of lives.

   Thomas Wolfe, "The Far and the Near"

B. Imitating Sentences Write a sentence imitating the structure of each model, but using your own words. Note that some past participles do not end with *-ed;* instead, they take whatever form the verb takes when used with *have:* for example, fallen, gone, lost.

   Important: Imitate as many sentence parts as possible, not just the underlined past participial phrases. Punctuate correctly.

1. Changed, I headed back through the mud. **John Knowles, _A Separate Peace_**

2. He saw the two women, startled, duck behind their sled.

   Elliott Merrick, "Without Words"

3. Her hair, braided and wrapped around her head, made an ash-blonde crown.

   John Steinbeck, _The Grapes of Wrath_

4. They were diggers in clay, transformed by lantern light into a race of giants.

   Edmund Ware, "An Underground Episode"

5. The scientific weeds, seen from close up, looked straggly and gnarled.

   Anne Tyler, "With All Flags Flying"

C. Expanding Sentences   Finish each sentence by completing the past participial phrase. Use content that blends with the rest of the sentence. Then compare your sentences with the originals on page 312.

1. Out on the playground, C.T. was standing in a swing, gently swaying to and fro, surrounded . . .   **Mary Elizabeth Vroman, "See How They Run"**

2. Amazed . . . , I understood everything as never before.
   Alphonse Daudet, "The Last Lesson"

3. Presently the dawn began to break, and the sky to the east grew yellow and red, slashed . . .   **Winston S. Churchill, "I Escape from the Boers"**

4. Brought . . . , the pickers would step out of the backs of trucks and fold down, dirt-disappointed, to the ground.
   Maya Angelou, *I Know Why the Caged Bird Sings*

5. A little house, perched . . . , appeared black in the distance.
   Joseph Conrad, *Tales of Unrest*

6. Sometimes I found little pools of idle water, walled . . .
   Peter Abrahams, *Tell Freedom*

7. I was typing some paragraph from some shoe newspaper, fascinated . . .
   Dorothy Uhnak, *Policewoman*

8. Harriet had watched them, fastened . . . , stumble down the road toward the Deep South.   **Henrietta Buckmaster, *Women Who Shaped History***

Application   First, change each underlined sentence into a past participial phrase. Then insert each of these phrases into the sentence before it. Vary the positions of the phrases, and punctuate correctly.

At dawn, without waking anyone, I crept out. I was dressed in my swimsuit and nylon jacket. On the porch, I retrieved my surfboard, put on my sandals, and headed for the beach. I saw the surf. It was illuminated by the first rays of the sun. The waves were high and just right. They were tossed and pulled by the tide and the wind. I ran toward the water. The crash of the waves, the cries of the seagulls were like music. It was played for me in a symphony of sunshine and sea.

Grammar Refresher   The model sentences in this lesson contain past participial phrases. For more on past participles and participial phrases, see Handbook 32, pages 595–596.

Sketchbook

Anxieties are concerns about uncertainties in the future. What concerns do you have? Is there a particular problem that you think needs to be solved? Is there something you can do to ease your anxiety?

©1983 Washington Post Writers Group. Reprinted with permission

Additional Sketches

What would the perfect friend be like? Describe his or her characteristics.

What is the most significant injustice you see in your daily life? How could people put an end to it?

Informative Exposition: Synthesis

Guided Assignment
PROBLEM AND SOLUTION

Related Assignment
ADVICE ESSAY

Related Assignment
GROUP DISCUSSION

Great achievements—artistic masterpieces, new inventions, creative solutions to long-standing problems—don't just happen. They are made possible by our ability to take our experiences, prior knowledge, and new information, analyze them and combine, or **synthesize,** them to make something entirely new. In this workshop, you will learn how to synthesize ideas, experiences, and information. In the guided assignment, you will examine the aspects of a problem in order to find solutions. In the related assignments, you will employ synthesis in order to give advice and explore issues with a group of people.

ASSIGNMENT

Problem and Solution

LETTER **F**ROM **M**EXICO **C**ITY

We all face problems in our personal lives, our jobs, and at school. By putting our thoughts on paper, we can get a grip on any tough situation. We can also examine the problems around us, big and small, and try to find solutions.

Journalist Alma Guillermoprieto wrote a magazine article exploring a problem facing many large urban areas throughout the world. As you read this excerpt, notice how she uses facts and anecdotes to introduce the problem.

Garbage has become an obsession for the inhabitants of Mexico City, spawning any number of fantastic stories, all of them true. There is, for example, the story of the open-air garbage dumps that spontaneously ignited one day in July, spreading fire and toxic fumes over acres of refuse stacked twenty yards high. . . .

Then, there are the rats. . . . The fact is that once started on the subject most city residents can come up with giant-rat stories of their own, and few are more thoroughly documented than the one told by Iván Restrepo, a genial scholar of garbage who directs a government-financed institute for ecological research called the Centro de Ecodesarrollo. Five years ago, in Chapultepec, the city's most popular public park, Restrepo and his center mounted an exhibit on the subject of garbage. A tent, designed by an artist, had a long, dark entrance, filled with giant illustrations of microbes and garbage-related pests, from which the public emerged into "the world of garbage." One of the exhibits, Restrepo said, was "the most gigantic rat we could find.". . .

If *capitalinos*—the residents of Mexico City—flock to an exhibit on garbage featuring a giant rat, it is because the subject is never very far from their minds. The problem of waste disposal may be only one of the critical aspects of the city's ongoing public-services emergency, but it is certainly among the most visible. One of the world's three largest urban conglomerates, the city never had a proper service infrastructure to begin with and has been growing too much too fast for too many years. . . . By the year 2000, if current trends persist, the urban area will be home to twenty million souls,

**BY
ALMA
GUILLERMOPRIETO**

all clamoring for services that are already strained to the breaking point in some areas and nonexistent in others.

Not only are services dangerously insufficient but there is almost no way to expand them. Water is now piped in from as far as fifty-five miles away. Ringed by mountains, the urban area is also gasping for fresh air. . . . Visibility has improved markedly since late last year, when the government passed a law restricting circulation of a fifth of the city's 2.5 million vehicles each weekday, but, because public transport is also in an awful state, car owners are now buying spare vehicles to use on the day their regular cars aren't allowed out. The poor, who can't afford any car at all, can spend as much as four hours a day travelling between the outlying shantytowns and their urban workplaces: the metro system, which has seventy miles of track and provides more than four million rides a day, serves only a small part of the Federal District, which covers some five hundred and seventy-nine square miles, and the same is true of the crowded, aging buses that spew their fumes along the city's uncharming streets. . . . And the deep-drainage system—nine miles of cavernous tunnels and thousands of miles of pipes, hailed as an engineering marvel when it was inaugurated, barely fifteen years ago—is now hopelessly overloaded, as anyone knows who saw the sewers backing up during each of this summer's downpours.

Bad as the city's public-service difficulties are, most of them appear to have fairly straightforward solutions: build more subways, install more phones. Not trash. The question is not how to put more of anything in but how to reduce the sheer bulk of what exists. The poor, who constitute the vast majority of [the] population, have lately produced almost as much waste as the rich; eager initiates into the world of junk consumerism, they find some consolation for their fate in the First World's plastic-encased gew-gaws. And although the city has so far heroically managed to keep more or less abreast of the growing tonnage of waste, cleanup-service problems merely have their beginning in the dumps. Here Mexico's First and Third Worlds meet and fester. Rats are the least of it. There is pollution and, above all, the tangle of human misery and political intrigue represented by a peculiar sector of Mexico's body politic—the thousands of *pepenadores* [garbage pickers], and their leaders, who stand in the way of neat solutions.

Think AND *Respond*

What is the main problem Alma Guillermoprieto addresses? How does she present the problem? Why is this problem difficult to solve? Guillermoprieto explores a problem that concerns many cities; what is a problem that concerns you?

INVITATION
— TO —
Write

Alma Guillermoprieto explored a serious problem facing Mexico City. Choose a problem you're deeply interested in, and use the suggestions below to write an editorial, proposal, or letter that defines it, examines its causes, and explores possible solutions.

You can find problem-solution writing in the editorial sections of newspapers and magazines, in proposals that officials and businesspeople write in order to launch their ideas, and even in personal letters between friends and relatives. The specific form a piece of problem-solution writing takes depends on the writer's purpose, the identity of the audience, and the specific nature of the problem.

PREWRITE AND EXPLORE

HANDBOOKS
FOR HELP & PRACTICE

Personal Techniques,
pp. 322–324
Other Techniques,
pp. 327–329
Thinking Creatively,
pp. 471–474

1. Begin exploring problems.   What are the problems that concern you most at home, at school, in your community, or in the world? Use these activities to discover writing ideas.

Exploratory Activities

- **Brainstorm**   Without censoring yourself, write down things that bother you. You might make three columns: world problems, community problems, and home problems.
- **Problem poll**   Take an opinion poll in which you ask people these or similar questions: "What problem worries you most in the world today?" or "What problems do you as a high school student face these days?"
- **Listing: What's in the news?**   Alma Guillermoprieto's magazine article told about the garbage problem in Mexico City. Read today's newspaper or a recent news magazine. List all the problems you read about in it that seemed interesting and important to you. Then freewrite about one or more ideas you find intriguing.

- **Reading literature** In his autobiographical account of growing up, *Barrio Boy,* Ernesto Galaraza writes about the problem of becoming Americanized without giving up his Mexican heritage. Think about the problems raised in other works you have read. How were the problems resolved?

Once you have completed some of the Exploratory Activities, discuss with your classmates the problems you have identified. Share topic ideas as well as thoughts about how you might explore various problems.

One student, Lucy, found a topic through freewriting about a personal experience in her journal. You will follow her process in developing her problem-solution essay throughout this assignment.

ONE STUDENT'S PROCESS

Last weekend there was a fire in our apartment. Luckily it was a small fire because we were standing outside and my mom thought there was something burning in the kitchen. We ran inside and Mom grabbed the newspaper that was burning on the stove and threw it into the sink. It was the first time that Grandma's forgetting things had gotten dangerous, though in a way it is also dangerous that Grandma forgets to eat during the day when no one else is home. She had left the stove on and by accident had put the newspaper down on a burner. She didn't notice it burning. Even if she had noticed the fire, she might not have gotten to it quickly enough because of her hip. We're worried about Grandma because she's home by herself during the day.

In the early 20th century, many women in the United States were determined to gain the right to vote; after years of demonstrating, they finally achieved that right in 1920.

2. Select a problem you wish to explore. Choose from the ideas that came to you as a result of your exploratory activities, or look to your journal or writing portfolio for an idea that seems particularly important or interesting to you personally. You may also find a topic in "Apply Your Skills" on page 189 or in the ideas you experimented with in the Sketchbook on page 176.

3. Determine your purpose. Are you most interested in drawing attention to the problem so that others can become involved in it? Are you mainly interested in a specific solution you are proposing? Perhaps you simply want to examine the problem to find out more about it. Thinking about your purpose will help you focus your research and organize your paper.

4. Identify your audience. Depending on your topic, you might write an editorial for the school newspaper, a letter to the editor of a magazine, a letter to a parent, a proposal to a government or business organization, or an essay for some other audience.

5. Examine the problem carefully. To explore your topic, discuss the problem or potential solutions with your classmates. Also consider the following questions. You may wish to do freewrites on ones you feel are particularly important or promising.

PROBLEM
S O L V I N G

How can I explore the problems and solutions related to my topic?

Exploring the Problem

1. What is the problem?
2. Why should the reader care about the problem?
3. What is the extent of the problem?
4. What are the causes of the problem?
5. What are the effects of the problem?
6. Is the problem getting worse? How do I know?

Exploring the Solution (or Solutions)

1. Is there an ideal solution?
2. Is this solution feasible? Why?
3. What are other possible solutions?
4. What are the merits and drawbacks of these solutions?
5. Which solutions are significant enough to be included in your composition?

HANDBOOKS
FOR HELP & PRACTICE

Introductions,
pp. 352–355
Elaboration,
pp. 364–369
Conclusions,
pp. 386–389

DRAFT AND DISCOVER

1. Begin drafting. At first, don't be too concerned about form or completeness. However, one way to organize your draft is to follow this pattern:

1. Identify the problem.
2. Explain why the reader should care about the problem.
3. Give a full explanation of the problem, including examples.

4. Give a full explanation of the solution (or solutions), including examples. Address any concerns or objections that might be raised.
5. Conclude by telling what action is needed to implement the solution, or what the next step in finding a solution should be.

2. Elaborate on ideas. As you write, you may want to expand on some of the points you are making. Consider using one or more of these strategies.

Strategies

- **Description and definition** Use these strategies to identify the specific qualities of the problem.
- **Narration** Recounting a story or incident can illustrate the problem and gain reader interest. Notice how Guillermoprieto used an anecdote about a garbage exhibit to draw attention to the problem.
- **Cause and effect** This form of analysis enables you to identify the source of a problem and explain its effects, or to explain the effects that would result if a solution were implemented.

Trevor's Campaign for the homeless was founded by Trevor Ferrell in 1983, when he was 11.

**How can I
evaluate my
draft?**

3. Take a break. After you finish the draft, put it away for a day or at least an hour. When you come back to your writing, sit back and read it aloud. Make notes on what you want to add, delete, or change or on questions you want to ask your peer readers.

R E V I E W   Y O U R   W R I T I N G

Questions for Yourself
• Have I adequately explained what the problem is?

• Can I add details that would clarify the problem?

• What more would I like to find out about the problem or the solution I've proposed? Is there someone I would like to talk to on the subject?

Questions for Your Peer Readers
• What statements or arguments did you find memorable?

• Can you summarize the problem I've discussed and the solution I identify?

• Do you have any objections to my description of the problem? How might I address those objections?

• Do you have any objections to my proposed solution? How might I address those objections?

R EVISE   YOUR   WRITING

HANDBOOKS

FOR HELP & PRACTICE

**Peer Response,
pp. 398–401
Sharing Writing in
Progress,
pp. 417–418**

1. Evaluate your responses. Review your own thoughts and think about the responses of your peers. Keep in mind that problem-solution essays generally demonstrate certain basic qualities.

Standards for Evaluation
An effective problem-solution essay . . .

• identifies the problem clearly and makes the reader understand the significance of the problem.
• explores the causes and effects of the problem.
• examines potential solutions to the problem.
• uses language, details, and examples appropriate to the audience.

2. Problem-solve. After deciding which responses you want to use, rework your draft. Lucy made these changes in response to a peer's comment that her essay might appeal to a broader audience if she used a more objective, rather than personal, approach.

ONE STUDENT'S PROCESS

However, to some acquainted with the opposite problem—the problem of caring

We were picking up my little brother from Day Care

for preschool children— is

when the solution came to me. It's obvious. This is what

is

we need for Grandma, a kind of day care center for her.

healthy senior citizens who don't have a place to go

She isn't sick. She just needs someone around during

the day. That way Grandma would have someone to

make sure she's alright.

The center would be warm, friendly and profes-

sionally staffed. Companionship could be available in the

form of a peer group.

There would be friends to talk to, classes to take, books and other entertainment activities, a facility for lunch and snacks, and a place to nap.

I like your message but in order to be taken seriously, try a less informal tone.

You need to convince readers that it's their problem too.

How would this work?

Problem and
Solution   **185**

**Set off an intro-
ductory preposi-
tional phrase with
a comma.**

3. Proofread your work. Make a clean copy, and correct any errors in spelling, grammar, usage, and punctuation. Change any words or phrases that seem awkward. Also make sure your essay includes the material you wanted it to include, in the order you had planned, and that it answers objections.

LINKING
GRAMMAR **AND** WRITING
Personal Pronouns

Personal pronouns such as *she, he, we, they,* and *I* can make your prose flow more smoothly by avoiding repetition of nouns. Be sure that every pronoun refers clearly to a specific noun.

PROBLEM: It wasn't the first time that Grandma's forgetting things had gotten dangerous. At other times, Grandma has forgotten to eat while alone during the day.

CORRECTED: It wasn't the first time that Grandma's forgetting things had gotten dangerous. At other times, she has forgotten to eat while alone during the day.

See Grammar Handbook 30, pp. 527–529, for additional help.

PUBLISH AND PRESENT

- **Make a class anthology.** Arrange the class's writing into categories for a booklet called "Solutions to common problems."
- **Share your proposal.** Locate an organization or government department that deals with the problem you've discussed. Send your writing to the organization along with a letter explaining your purpose.
- **Submit your essay to a periodical.** Try your school or community newspaper or magazine. You could submit your writing as an article or a letter to the editor.
- **Read your essay aloud to your family or friends.** Use the reading as the basis for a discussion of the problem.
- **Save your work in your writing portfolio.**

HANDBOOKS
FOR HELP & PRACTICE

**Sharing Completed
Writing,
pp. 418–419**

Day-Care Centers for Senior Citizens

Lucy Smith

Last week there was a fire in our apartment. My mom, my little brother, and I were standing outside when Mom suddenly shouted, "I smell smoke!" She turned and ran inside, just in time to put out the newspaper that Grandma had accidentally placed on a lit burner of the stove. Grandma was sitting in the living room, reading a magazine.

If a similar fire had happened while she was alone, she might not have been able to put out the flames before they spread. It wasn't the first time that Grandma's forgetting things had gotten dangerous, either. At other times, she has forgotten to eat while alone during the day. By the time we get home, she is quite weak.

This isn't just one family's problem; it's a problem faced by every family in America with elderly members. Even active, healthy people in their seventies or eighties may need someone around the house. Otherwise, they may not be able to get help in case of injury, and they may not receive proper nutrition. In addition, the boredom and loneliness suffered by old people can be a very real health hazard not only for themselves but for those who love them.

Ironically, people who are too healthy and independent to enter rest homes are the ones most likely to suffer from this problem. Most of them can't afford a full-time companion—and wouldn't want one, anyway. Independent elderly people want companionship, not nursing by strangers taking charge of their lives for them.

Uses an example that involves the audience

Identifies the problem and shows why the reader should be concerned

Problem and Solution

187

Finding good living situations for older people has gotten harder in this era of working couples. Few families can spare an adult to take care of retired relatives. Another cause of the problem is a more positive one: people live longer nowadays. This means that more families, for longer periods of time, will face the problem of providing a good life for their oldest members.

Proposes a workable solution

However, to someone acquainted with the opposite problem—the problem of caring for preschool children—the solution seems obvious. What we need are day-care centers for healthy senior citizens who don't have a place to go during the day. The centers should be warm, friendly, and professionally staffed. Companionship would be available in the form of a peer group. There would be friends to talk to, classes to take, books and other entertainment activities, a facility for lunch and snacks, and a place to nap. No one would go hungry because of forgetting to eat or because of feeling too tired to prepare a meal.

Addresses possible concerns

One possible objection to this plan is that such a center might not be as happy and cheerful in practice as in theory. This danger can be avoided by giving attention to the individual needs of the people attending the center. For instance, some people like conversation and others prefer to read or watch television. A caring staff and a wide range of activities can make the center comfortable for all.

Summarizes the problems and solution forcefully

Day care will benefit those "in-between" senior citizens who need some help but can do most things for themselves. It would provide dignified care for people, and that word "dignified" is perhaps what's most important.

WRITER TO WRITER

A writer's problem does not change . . . It is always how to write truly and, having found what is true, to project it in such a way that it becomes a part of the experience of the person who reads it.

Ernest Hemingway

1. Reflect on your writing. Now that you have read a problem-solution essay by Alma Guillermoprieto and one by a student, and have completed one of your own, ask yourself the following questions about the process involved. Write your responses in your journal, or attach them to your essay as an afterword.

- Did anything surprise you as you were working? Did you find information or observations you hadn't known before?
- Did your views on the problem develop or change as you worked on the essay? If so, how?
- Did your ideas for organizing the writing change during the writing process? If so, how? How might you use this experience in planning future problem-solution essays?

2. Apply your skills. Try one or more of the following activities.

- **Cross-curricular** Think back to a problem you have faced in studying any of your other subjects this year. Write an essay proposing a solution to your study problem.
- **Literature** Think of a character you have particularly liked in any work you have read this year. What problem did that character face? How did he or she face it? Write an essay, or a letter to the author or to the character, proposing a solution of your own.
- **General** Identify a problem facing your school or community, and write a proposal that tells your plan for solving it.
- **Related assignments** Follow the suggestions on pages 192–200 to write an advice column or conduct a group discussion.

FOR YOUR
PORTFOLIO

Problem and
Solution   **189**

Advice Essay

The Pursuit of

POPULARITY

by Carol Weston

Everyone loves to give advice. Ann Landers counsels people in love and people in trouble. Automobile experts offer advice about cars. Financial experts help with investments, and medical experts discuss health care. You yourself may advise a friend on how to get a date or pass a test. In this essay, Carol Weston offers high-school students a balanced view on the quest for popularity.

As you read, notice how Weston uses her own experiences to back up her advice that students recognize the price of popularity.

The word *popularity* hardly exists in college. There are many groups of friends, and no one thinks about which is "cool" or in or right or best. Yet you're not in college, and being popular may matter to you now.

It mattered to me. For a long time, all I wanted was to be popular. No such luck. The twins and their chic circle did me the favor of talking to me, but I was never important to them. Wanting in and not getting in was lousy for my ego, but thank heavens Judy talked some sense into my head.

"What's so great about the twins?" she wanted to know.

"They're popular," seemed like a pretty feeble answer, but I ran it by her anyway.

"The masses look up to them. Big deal! They may be perfectly wonderful, but they've never been wonderful to you. With all the nice people out there, I can't believe you're hung up on them. Will it damage your reputation if you are seen with less popular people? Will it injure your image? I swear, Carol, sometimes your values make me ill."

At this point, I'd usually want to tell her to can it. But Judy was a genuine friend who knew me thoroughly and liked me anyway. And she had a point. Since the popular crowd wasn't spending time worrying about me, it was pretty crazy for me to spend time worrying about them.

If you are popular, congratulations. If not, relish your close friends and try not to care about the others. It may help to realize that popularity has a flip side. Sure it must be fun to be a trend-setting center of attention. But some popular [students] feel cramped by their clique.

Melissa, a college friend, told me about the disadvantages of her high school popularity. She said she felt terrible when she won the class election because she knew her opponent cared more about school issues. "And I hated when my clique got into shoplifting. I didn't want to steal, but I felt I had to—like I'd lose popularity points if I didn't. There were sides of me the girls never knew. Since they liked me because I was funny, I felt I always had to be 'on.' If I was depressed, I couldn't cry. Sometimes it was as if I didn't have any friends." Melissa sighed. "I'd be lying if I said I didn't enjoy feeling liked and important. But it made the transition to college hard. No one here knew they were supposed to bow down to me. I was one more lowly freshman. Except I was full of myself."

A clique can be a crutch. Members feel secure, but they're taking their identity from the group and letting group values mold their characters rather than becoming unique individuals.

Although you may not be as popular as other[s] in your class, your friendships may include a closeness that the popular [students] have not found. And you are learning to be more self-reliant than [classmates] who cling to a group for support.

Think and Respond

What is the purpose of Carol Weston's essay? Why do you suppose she uses anecdotes from her own life to illustrate her advice? Does Weston's essay remind you of any similar issues affecting teenagers about which you might offer advice?

INVITATION
— TO —
Write

Carol Weston advises her teenage readers not to worry too much about being popular in high school. Now write your own essay offering advice about a subject you know well.

Like other types of problem-solution writing, advice essays are forums for discussing problems and offering solutions or for sharing helpful information. Sometimes, advice essays are also persuasive—intended to convince the readers to alter their behavior or attitudes or take some other course of action. Newspapers and magazines often offer their readers advice on a variety of subjects from romance to homemaking to finance.

PREPARING TO OFFER ADVICE

HANDBOOKS
FOR HELP & PRACTICE

**Writing Variables,
pp. 317–321**
**Personal Techniques,
pp. 322–324**
**Organization,
pp. 342–349**

1. Explore your areas of expertise. To give effective advice, you have to feel confident about your knowledge or experiences of certain subjects. What subjects do you know enough about to offer helpful information to others? You might choose a field of study, such as computer programming, or a recreational pursuit, such as basketball. Or, as in Carol Weston's essay, you might choose an aspect of everyday life that personally affects you and your friends. Whatever subject you choose, be sure you feel truly qualified to offer advice about it. You wouldn't want to offer advice about preparing for and surviving a cross-country bike trip unless you had made such a trip yourself.

2. Consider your readers. Whom will you be addressing? What type of information and details will make your advice most meaningful to them? The examples and anecdotes Carol Weston used, for example, were clearly targeted at high-school students. Had she been addressing politicians on the issue of popularity, she would have chosen different examples to develop her advice. List some characteristics of your audience. Keep these qualities in mind as you write.

3. What specific problem do you want to address? Carol Weston's area of expertise was popularity in general, but she zeroed in on a particular aspect of that subject—how important or unimportant it is to be popular in high school. To help you focus your thinking, write down your area of expertise, and then jot down a variety of questions about it. One of these questions should help you focus on a specific kind of advice you want to offer.

 Writer's Choice Will your essay simply offer helpful information, or will you try to persuade your readers to alter their behavior or attitudes in some way?

4. Develop your advice. What are the main points you want to make? What type of details, examples, anecdotes, and other general information will you offer to support each point? You may also wish to supplement your advice with the advice of experts. Consider interviewing an authority on the subject or exploring what information your library can offer.

DRAFTING YOUR ADVICE ESSAY

1. Select a format. As you begin drafting, experiment with different formats. Will you open with a question and then supply an answer, like a newspaper advice columnist? Will you begin with an anecdote that illustrates the problem you want to address and then offer advice on how to solve it? Will your essay be reflective, illustrated primarily with details from your own life as is Carol Weston's? All of these are effective formats for offering advice or helpful information.

Fenollosa-Weld Collection. Courtesy, Museum of Fine Arts, Boston

Confucius at the Apricot Altar and His Two Disciples, 17th c. (Detail)

2. Organize your information. If you have chosen a question-answer format, you will want to classify the information you've collected into two general categories—the problem and the solution—and then present the information in that order.

The solution part of your information, whether part of a problem-solution format or a general-essay format, might be presented as a step-by-step process organized in one of the following ways: order of importance, order of complexity, or order of familiarity. Carol Weston, for example, chose a general-essay format and organized her information in the order of familiarity: first she discussed her own experiences, then she talked about the experiences of a friend, and finally she generalized her discussion to include all high-school students.

3. Include interesting examples. Well-developed examples can personalize your advice and make it more helpful to your readers. Use examples that are targeted to your specific audience.

REVIEWING YOUR WRITING

1. Evaluate your advice. Reread your essay and think about your advice. If you've posed a question, does your advice answer the question thoroughly? Is your advice helpful? Is your advice targeted at your particular audience? If your purpose is to persuade, is your advice convincing enough?

2. Present your credentials. Be sure your audience understands that you have the necessary expertise to offer advice on your subject or that you've consulted experts in the field. Document your credentials and those of any expert whose information you use.

PUBLISHING AND PRESENTING

- **Join the professionals.** Submit your advice to the school or community newspaper as a sample of a column you might like to write on a regular basis.
- **Share your essay with the class.** Hold an advice-writers' round table in which you and your classmates read your essays to one another. Follow each reading with a question-and-answer session.

On the Lightside

GOBBLEDYGOOK

Instructions in "gobbledygook"—pompous, wordy, convoluted language—can make the performance of simple tasks nearly impossible. What tasks do these instructions describe?

Initiating SUPA VESTA Ignition

1. Grip the outer sleeve firmly in the left hand with the box's longer axis running diagonally.
2. With the right thumb slide out the inner reticule. STOP IMMEDIATELY if the box is upside down.
3. Use the right thumb and forefinger to extract one SUPA VESTA and hold with the blue combustible knob outermost.
4. Return the reticule with the left-hand index finger. Twist the box through 90° to expose one of the special abrasive strips.
5. Place the blue combustible knob on the near end of the abrasive strip. Slide the knob along the strip.

For the necessary acceleration, begin with the right wrist cocked inwards and let it unwind briskly but naturally. (DO NOT FORCE at this point.) When the knob has covered not less than half *and not more than four-sevenths* of the strip, flick it forward, simultaneously imparting a contrary motion to the box by a free-flowing torque of the left elbow.

Your SUPA VESTA should now be alight.   **G. H. Harris**

Answer: lighting a match

Avoiding Discalceation

Place Foot M (found at base of leg T) into shoe P. (Warning; Confusing M and N may result in acute pain and ultimately deformity.) Grasp ends A and B of lace R. Pass end A over end B, then loop under. Pull A and B tightly. Take end B (in former position of end A) and, wrapping round right thumb H, form loop pinched between left-hand fingers C and D (illustrated). Take end A (in former postion of end B), loop over and under loop held by C and D. Pull both loops gently. If result does not satisfy, do *not* tug ends A or B. Merely take scissors X (not included) and cut vigorously at point Z.

Answer: tying shoelaces

Simon Rose

**from *Peacocks and Commas:
The Best of the Spectator
Competitions***

Group Discussion

STRUGGLING
FOR SANITY

by Anastasia Toufexis

Some problems can best be worked out with the help of others. In such cases, a group discussion can clarify the problem, uncover a possible solution, and develop a plan of action.

The following magazine article discusses the pressures facing many teenagers today. As you read, think about the concerns you and your classmates face, and about how you cope with these concerns.

The dozen telephone lines at the cramped office of Talkline/Kids Line in Elk Grove Village, Ill., ring softly every few minutes. Some of the youthful callers seem at first to be vulgar pranksters, out to make mischief with inane jokes and naughty language. But soon the voices on the line—by turns wistful, angry, sad, desperate—start to spill a stream of distress. Some divulge their struggles with alcohol . . . and their worries about school. . . . Others tell of their feelings of boredom and loneliness. . . . What connects them all, says Nancy Helmick, director of the two hot lines, is a sense of "disconnectedness."

Such calls attest to the intense psychological and emotional turmoil many American children are experiencing. It is a problem that was not even recognized until just a decade ago. Says Dr. Lewis Judd, director of the National Institute of Mental Health: "There had been a myth that childhood is a happy time and kids are happy-go-lucky, but no age range is immune from experiencing mental disorders.". . .

What is causing so much mental anguish? The sad truth is that a growing number of American youngsters have home lives that are hostile to healthy emotional growth. Psyches are extremely fragile and must be nourished from birth. Everyone starts out life with a basic anxiety about survival. An attentive parent contains that stress by making the youngster feel secure and loved. . . .

As children mature within the shelter of the family, they develop what psychologists call a sense of self. They acquire sensitivities and skills that lead them to believe they can cope independently. "People develop through a chain," observes Dr. Carol West, a child psychotherapist in Beverly Hills. "There has to be stability, a consistent idea of who you are."

The instability that is becoming the hallmark of today's families breeds in children insecurity rather than pride, doubts instead of confidence. Many youngsters feel guilty about broken marriages, torn between parents and

households, and worried about family finances. Remarriage can intensify the strains. Children may feel abandoned and excluded as they plunge into rivalries with stepparents and stepsiblings or are forced to adjust to new homes and new schools. Children from troubled homes used to be able to find a psychological anchor in societal institutions. But no longer. The churches, schools and neighborhoods that provided emotional stability by transmitting shared traditions and values have collapsed along with the family.

Such disarray hurts children from all classes; wealth may in fact make it harder for some children to cope. Says Hal Klor, a guidance counselor at Chicago's Lincoln Park High School: "The kids born into a project, they handle it. But the middle-class kids. All of a sudden—a divorce, loss of job, status. Boom. Depression.". . .

At the same time, family and society are expecting more from kids than ever before. Parental pressure to make good grades, get into college and qualify for the team can be daunting. Moreover, kids are increasingly functioning as junior adults in many homes, taking on the responsibility of caring for younger siblings or ailing grandparents. And youngsters' own desires—to be accepted and popular with their peers, especially—only add to the strain.

Children express the panic and anxiety they feel in myriad ways: in massive weight gains or losses, in nightmares and disturbed sleep, in fatigue or listlessness, in poor grades or truancy, in continual arguing or fighting, in drinking, . . . in reckless driving or . . . promiscuity, in stealing and mugging. . . .

Despite the urgency of the problems, only 1 in 5 children who need therapy receives it; poor minority youngsters get the least care. Treatment is expensive, and even those with money and insurance find it hard to afford. But another reason is that too often the signals of distress are missed or put down to normal mischief.

Treatment relies on therapeutic drugs, reward and punishment, and especially counseling—not just of the youngster but of the entire family. The goal is to instill in the children a feeling of self-worth and to teach them discipline and responsibility. Parents, meanwhile, are taught how to provide emotional support, assert authority and set limits . . .

As necessary and beneficial as treatment may be, it makes better sense to prevent emotional turmoil among youngsters by improving the environment they live in. Most important, parents must spend more time with sons and daughters and give them the attention and love they need. To do less will guarantee that ever more children will be struggling for sanity.

Think AND Respond

What types of problems does the author identify? What are the causes of these problems? What possible solutions does she suggest? What problems do you see around you? What suggestions could you and your classmates make to deal with these problems?

INVITATION
—TO—
Write

As Anastasia Toufexis points out, teenagers must cope with a variety of emotional pressures. Organize a group discussion to examine ways to deal with the pressures you or your peers face. After the discussion, write a summary of the discussion or develop an action plan proposing solutions.

A group discussion is an organized and focused way to brainstorm. It can be especially helpful when you are trying to find solutions to a complex problem. By taking part in a problem-solving group, you can develop more potential solutions than you could on your own. In addition, a group discussion can lead to a comprehensive plan to solve the problem, and the group itself can act together to put the plan, or parts of it, into action.

ORGANIZING A GROUP DISCUSSION

HANDBOOKS
FOR HELP & PRACTICE

Community of Writers,
pp. 5–7
Other Techniques,
pp. 327–329
Oral Reports,
pp. 497–498

1. Form your group. Choose people for your discussion who are concerned about the issue. Look to include people who may take a variety of viewpoints. You might, for example, want to ask a school counselor to participate in the group or act as an advisor.

2. Become familiar with your subject. Before holding your discussion, each member should take some time to explore the subject. Freewrite about your feelings or experiences, or conduct some research to familiarize yourself with the subject, gather facts and statistics, or support a point of view.

CONDUCTING THE DISCUSSION

1. Assemble your group. Select a moderator, who leads the discussion and maintains order, and a secretary, who takes notes during discussion or tape records it and later transcribes the tape.

2. State your subject and purpose. The moderator of your group should introduce the problem and make sure that everyone in the group agrees on the purpose of your discussion. For example, will this be primarily an information-gathering, mutual-support, or action-oriented group? A discussion on the stresses facing teenagers could focus on trying to identify major causes, or on producing suggestions for how to cope, or on taking action such as setting up a telephone help line—among other possibilities.

3. Define key terms. Misunderstandings can be avoided if the group spends time discussing the meanings of key terms and concepts. For example, if your group were to consider feelings of depression, the group members should make sure they agree on what they mean by the term *depression*. Confusion about how words are being used can result in "false disagreements."

4. Manage the discussion. The moderator should encourage all participants to take part and also request that only one person speak at a time. He or she should remind participants to support their statements and opinions with facts, examples, or references to authorities on the subject. Each participant is responsible for listening attentively when another person is speaking and taking notes on key points.

5. Come to a consensus. Frequently, a discussion group will divide into two opposing sides. If the group members become too involved in defending their own positions, each side may be able to see only its own point of view. In that case, ask individuals to take turns restating ideas in different words. This may help you pinpoint false disagreements. Then explore alternatives and possible compromises to find a solution that is satisfactory to everyone. If participants become too emotional, or if more authoritative information is needed, you may want to postpone the development of a plan of action in favor of more study and discussion.

6. Develop an action plan. The eventual result of your discussion may be a plan of action, a step-by-step outline of how you could solve the problem or a part of it. Try to come up with practical ideas, such as an educational program carried out with posters and brochures, or letters to persons in positions of authority, or a fund-raising event.

7. Summarize the discussion. The moderator should end the discussion with a brief summary of key points and group decisions.

D RAFTING YOUR SUMMARY OR ACTION PLAN

1. Draft a summary. Begin with a statement of the problem and, if appropriate, its causes. Summarize the views of the group and possible solutions and their merits. State the decisions reached by the group and the reasons for them.

 Writer's Choice You may choose to summarize the entire discussion to provide a basis for further exploration. Or you may write only about the eventual action plan recommended by the group.

2. Describe a plan of action. Briefly state the problem. Then state the action decided upon by the group and describe the steps proposed for implementing the solution.

Writing
—TIP—

A flowchart or other graphic aid can be useful in describing an action plan.

R EVIEWING YOUR WRITING

1. Check for clarity. Have you presented a clear description of the problem, the views of the group, and of the action plan?

2. Have other group members read your summary. Ask them if you have been fair to all points of view and included all the important points of the summary or action plan.

P UBLISHING AND PRESENTING

- **Submit a copy of your summary or action plan to a person in authority who could help you execute the plan.**
- **Submit your summary or action plan in a letter to the editor of your school or local paper.**

Sentence

Using Appositive Phrases

Effective writers often use appositive phrases to create concise definitions and explanations in their sentences. These phrases contain an appositive, a noun or pronoun that defines another noun or pronoun in the same sentence.

MODELS

1. (Opener) A tall, rawhide man in an unbuttoned, sagging vest, he was visibly embarrassed by any furnishings that suggested refinement.
   Conrad Richter, "Early Marriage"

2. (S-V Split) One of these dogs, the best one, had disappeared.   **Fred Gipson, Old Yeller**

3. (Closer) Halfway there he heard the sound he dreaded, the hollow, rasping cough of a horse.   **John Steinbeck, The Red Pony**

Punctuation Note: Appositive phrases are set off by commas.

A. Unscrambling Sentences   Find the appositive phrase in each set. Then unscramble and write the sentence, inserting the appositive phrase where it makes the most sense. Use each position (opener, S-V split, closer) at least once. Set off appositive phrases with commas.

Example
   a. a dilapidated baby carriage
   b. out into the garden
   c. together we guide our buggy
   d. and into a grove of pecan trees

Result   Together we guide our buggy, a dilapidated baby carriage, out into the garden and into a grove of pecan trees.
   Truman Capote, "A Christmas Memory"

1. a. for the snake
   b. a pretty little tan-and-coral rattlesnake from Baja
   c. he felt sorry
      Frank Bonham, *Chief*

2. a. in the neighborhood
   b. their pool was perhaps the oldest
   c. a fieldstone rectangle fed by a brook
      John Cheever, "The Swimmer"

3. a. when they came in
   b. was licking a black crayon and marking prices on soap-flake boxes
   c. the youngest brother
   d. Ben
      Robert Lipsyte, *The Contender*

4. a. an old man with a white mustache
   b. the writer
   c. had some difficulty in getting into bed
      Sherwood Anderson, *Winesburg, Ohio*

5. a. a slight boy with his father's blue eyes
   b. even when he shot a stray duck on the tank
   c. he seldom made a fuss over anything
   d. or when they braked down the last cedar hill into Santa Fe with all the open doors of the plaza shops in sight
      Conrad Richter, "Early Marriage"

6. a. spent the last hours before our parting
   b. keeping to himself and avoiding me
   c. Poppa
   d. moving aimlessly about the yard
   e. a good quiet man
      Gordon Parks, "My Mother's Dream for Me"

B. Imitating Sentences Write a sentence imitating the structure of each model, but using your own words.

   Important: Imitate as many of the sentence parts as possible, not just the underlined appositive phrases. Use commas as needed.

   Example   One of these dogs, <u>the best one</u>, had disappeared.   **Fred Gipson, *Old Yeller***

   Student Sentence   Three of those plums, the ripe ones, were eaten.

1. <u>The third of eleven brothers and sisters</u>, Harriet was a moody, willful child.
   Langston Hughes, "Road to Freedom"

2. The judge, <u>an old, bowlegged fellow in a pale blue sweater</u>, had stopped examining the animals and was reading over some notes he had taken on the back of a dirty envelope.   **Jessamyn West, "The Lesson"**

3. She arose, dressed quickly, and hurried to the house of Mr. Nakamoto, <u>the head of her Neighborhood Association</u>, and asked him what to do.
                                        John Hersey, *Hiroshima*

4. Mrs. Halloran, <u>a stout woman with white hair and a serene face</u>, was reading the *Times*.   **John Cheever, "The Swimmer"**

5. Hour after hour he stood there, silent, motionless, <u>a shadow carved in ebony and moonlight</u>.   **James V. Marshall, *Walkabout***

C. Expanding Sentences   Finish the sentences by completing the appositive phrases or series in each. The words that the appositive phrases should identify are underlined, and the first word of each appositive phrase is provided. Use content that fits the sentence. Then compare your answers with the originals on page 312.

1. From under the counter he brought out a heavy stamping <u>machine</u>, the . . .   **Jack Finney, "Of Missing Persons"**

2. In our clenched fists we held <u>our working cards</u> from the shop, the . . .   **Gerda Weissmann Klein, *All But My Life***

3. The <u>land</u> that lay stretched out before him became of vast significance, a . . .   **Sherwood Anderson, *Winesburg, Ohio***

4. The <u>tree</u> was tremendous, an . . .   **John Knowles, *A Separate Peace***

5. He heard <u>every little sound</u> of the gathering night, the . . . the . . . the . . . and the . . .   **John Steinbeck, *The Pearl***

Application   Write a paragraph in which you explain how the parts of a fairly simple gadget (such as an eggbeater or a zipper) work together. Use appositive phrases as you identify and describe each part. Notice how these phrases allow you to create concise definitions and explanations.

Grammar Refresher   The model sentences in this lesson contain appositive phrases. For more information about appositives and appositive phrases, see Handbook 32, pages 589–592. For information about punctuating these phrases, see Handbook 39, page 789.

Sketchbook

"I can't believe that," said Alice.

"Can't you?" the Queen said in a pitying tone. "Try again; draw a long breath, and shut your eyes."

Alice laughed. "There's no use trying," she said; "one can't believe impossible things."

"I dare say you haven't had much practice," said the Queen. "When I was your age I always did it for half an hour a day. Why, sometimes I've believed as many as six impossible things before breakfast."

Lewis Carroll
THROUGH THE LOOKING GLASS

Follow the Queen's advice. What impossible things can you believe? What impossible things would you like to believe?

Additional Sketches

Write the dialogue of a conversation between yourself and someone you disagree with. Start by saying what you think, then write what the other person might say, and so on.

Where do you go for advice?

Persuasion

Guided Assignment
CONTROVERSIAL ISSUE

Related Assignment
PERSUASIVE SPEECH

Related Assignment
EDITORIAL

How is an advertising copywriter like a boy who asks a girl to the prom? What does a newspaper editorial have in common with a friendly debate about what television show to watch? What does a politician making a speech share with a parent who is trying to talk you into mowing the lawn?

In all these examples, someone uses words to try to persuade another person to take action, whether it's the action of mowing the lawn, voting for a candidate, or going on a date. In this workshop you will learn to use words persuasively by writing a convincing argument on a controversial issue. Then you will proceed to write a persuasive speech and an editorial.

205

from "The Publisher Could Have Said

'DON'T PRINT THIS'"

by Patrick Marshall

Do school administrators have the right to censor student news stories they consider unsuitable? There are at least two sides to this and every other issue. Often, emotion rather than reason controls people's views. One thing seems certain: if everyone knew how to present arguments clearly and reasonably, controversies would probably be resolved more easily. As you read Patrick Marshall's argument about the controversial issue of censoring student newspapers, notice what strategies he uses to support his point of view.

Newspaper columnists work fast. Sometimes too fast. Only the day after the Supreme Court affirmed a school principal's right to determine what articles went into the school newspaper, the news wires were loaded with commentary articles decrying the decision as an infringement on students' right of free speech. . . . It's a little disheartening that those who depend on the 1st Amendment apparently don't know the difference between free speech and a free press. . . .

In ruling that school officials have broad powers to censor school newspapers, the court did nothing to abridge students' free speech right. . . . A student has no more "right" to put an article in a newspaper produced with school funds at school facilities than an adult citizen has to write an article and demand that it be published on the front page of the local newspaper. Newspaper columnists who condemn the court's decision as an infringement of students' rights should consider that their own columns are published not under some guaranteed right, but because the publishers of their newspapers allow them to be published. The government can't yank a column, but the publisher can. . . .

The government is prevented from abridging freedom of the press; but it is not required to provide a press to any citizen who desires one, nor are schools required to provide the means for students to produce newspapers. . . .

Finally, student journalists who find the constraints imposed by their principal/publisher too confining are free to start their own newspaper. Students at one high school in San Mateo, Calif., recently did just that. . . .

Newspaper columnists, and the public, are right to be concerned, even outraged, when a principal censors a responsible article in a school newspaper. But asking the courts to revise the Constitution isn't the best response.

Think AND Respond

What argument does Marshall use to win his audience over to his point of view? Notice how he presents both sides, but then quickly makes his opinion on the issue clear. Did you think of any responses to his argument as you read? Do you feel satisfied with his argument, or does he make you angry? What are your own views on this issue or a related issue?

INVITATION
—TO—
Write

Patrick Marshall expressed his side of the school journalism controversy in strong, well-thought-out terms. Now select a controversial issue that intrigues you or angers you or nags at you, and present your point of view as convincingly as you can.

No one can escape controversy—perhaps we'd be bored if we could —but coping with controversy by learning from it and persuading others is possible. Dealing with controversial issues requires more than a readiness to debate and attack an opponent's position. You must also examine your own assumptions, test the assumptions of your opponents, find evidence for your side, and build a case on that evidence using the rules of logic and persuasion. All of this preparation can be difficult and time-consuming, but it can also be exciting and rewarding especially if the issue you choose is one you really care about.

▶ PREWRITE AND EXPLORE

HANDBOOKS
FOR HELP & PRACTICE

Personal Techniques, pp. 322–324

Other Techniques, pp. 327–329

Thinking Critically, pp. 468–470

1. Find an Issue. The world is full of controversies. The best ones to write about are ones in which you have a strong interest, a personal stake. To help you focus on a topic about which you have strong feelings, try some of the following activities.

Exploratory Activities

• **Newspaper search** Get together with two or three classmates to conduct a newspaper search. Cull through issues of your local newspaper for the past week or so, looking for news articles, editorials, feature stories, letters to the editor, and political cartoons about controversial subjects. Which newspaper articles and cartoons interest you or rouse your emotions? Which make you angry?

- **Opinion poll** Interview at least five students and five adults, asking each person a single question: What, in your opinion, is the most controversial issue of the day?
- **Personal issues** Jot down the subjects of arguments you've had recently with friends, family members, teachers, or others. Some of them might also be controversial issues for a wider audience.
- **Fill-in-the-blanks** Think of as many ways as you can to fill in the blanks in the following question: "Should _____ be allowed to _____ ?" (A good word to fill in the first blank is *I*.)
- **Building on a prior controversy** As you read Patrick Marshall's essay on school journalism, did it trigger your thoughts on any related issues connected to free speech or to student life? Focus on one for your own essay.
- **Reading literature** Literature is usually about conflict, and conflict can become controversy if it goes beyond the private lives of the characters. For example, in Lorraine Hansberry's *A Raisin in the Sun,* Ruth and Walter Younger are involved in a controversy over whether African Americans ought to embrace their African heritage. Choose a work of literature you read this year that raised an issue you cared about, and write about that aspect of the work.

COMPUTER TIP

With a partner, adapt the fill-in-the-blanks technique to the word processor. One partner types out new questions containing blanks. The other fills in the blanks.

2. Choose an issue that interests you. Then evaluate it. Ask yourself the following start-up questions.

- Do other people consider this a controversy? You don't want to argue a point no one disagrees with, so make sure the controversy is real.
- Is the controversy manageable in a paper? You might very well avoid some classic controversies such as the death penalty just because you feel you couldn't do them justice in the time you have. If you are really interested in a large, complicated topic, try focusing on just one aspect of the controversy.

3. Explore your opinion by doing a quick freewrite. Joel decided to answer Patrick Marshall with a plea for freedom in student journalism. He began exploring his ideas through freewriting. Throughout this assignment, you will follow Joel's process as he writes about this controversial issue.

Freedom of the press is guaranteed by the first amendment--supposedly! But at schools all over this country, student reporters and editors are finding out that principals can overrule the Bill of Rights. Should school administrators be allowed to censor student newspapers? Absolutely not! We're not talking about printing sick jokes here, or obscene stories. We're talking about stories on drugs, suicide, and gangs. School administrators are banning these stories because they don't think they're suitable for a school newspaper. When they do this, they make a joke out of the newspaper.

4. Examine your assumptions. Look over your freewriting, and think more critically about your position. One way to do this is to make a tree diagram. Start by stating your stance on the issue as a tree's trunk. Then sketch out the branches by listing as many reasons as you can to support your statement. Try to group related supporting statements on the same branch. Finally, for the roots, examine all the statements you have written so far, and see if you can list the basic assumptions that support your position. These assumptions will help to add focus to your writing. Study the tree diagram that Joel made for his topic.

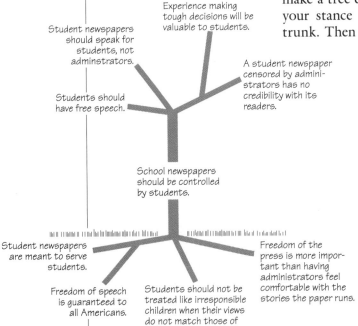

Experience making tough decisions will be valuable to students.

Student newspapers should speak for students, not administrators.

A student newspaper censored by administrators has no credibility with its readers.

Students should have free speech.

School newspapers should be controlled by students.

Student newspapers are meant to serve students.

Freedom of speech is guaranteed to all Americans.

Students should not be treated like irresponsible children when their views do not match those of administrators.

Freedom of the press is more important than having administrators feel comfortable with the stories the paper runs.

Writer's Choice After examining your position more closely, are you confident you can support it in a persuasive essay, or do you want to consider changing your position or even finding a new issue?

5. Examine the opposing viewpoint. It's important to understand your opposition's position in order to answer the arguments against you. Readers who disagree with you will be more likely to consider your point of view if they see that you have considered theirs. Readers who aren't sure what to think may find your consideration of both sides of the issues very persuasive.

You might draw your opposition's stand on the issue as a tree trunk, just as you did your own. Joel found the following roots and branches in Patrick Marshall's essay.

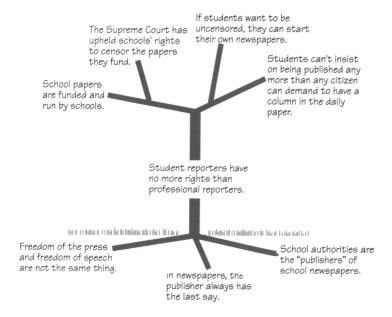

The Supreme Court has upheld schools' rights to censor the papers they fund.

If students want to be uncensored, they can start their own newspapers.

Students can't insist on being published any more than any citizen can demand to have a column in the daily paper.

School papers are funded and run by schools.

Student reporters have no more rights than professional reporters.

Freedom of the press and freedom of speech are not the same thing.

In newspapers, the publisher always has the last say.

School authorities are the "publishers" of school newspapers.

PROBLEM
S O L V I N G

How can I anticipate and explore opposing viewpoints?

To argue against censorship, Joel needs to anticipate and counter a number of persuasive arguments such as those presented by Marshall. To see what opponents you may have, get your classmates to help you brainstorm all possible arguments against your position, no matter how wild. Afterward, evaluate the assumptions underlying those arguments, and discuss ways of countering them.

6. Identify your purpose and your audience. Often, in controversial writing, your purpose involves changing people's minds. In order to change people's minds, it's important to know who they are, what information they need, and what approach will work best with them. For instance, do they already agree with you and simply need to be persuaded to take action, do they disagree with you, or are they neutral? Do they know as much as you about the issue, or less, or more? By gauging your audience's needs, you can more easily write in a way that "speaks" to them.

7. Consider different forms. Writing about controversial issues can take many forms, including letters to editors, speeches, articles, advertisements, editorials, and direct mail solicitations. You don't have to limit yourself to an essay just because that is the form Patrick Marshall and Joel Goldman chose. Consider which form is best for you, given your particular issue, audience, and personal interests.

8. Research your topic. In order to support your position and counter opposing ideas, you'll probably need to find more information than you already have. When gathering evidence, look for:

- **Facts**   Find statements that can be proven true, such as statistics.
- **Examples**   Gather statements about single instances that illustrate your point.
- **Anecdotes**   Recount brief stories that illustrate your position.
- **Observations**   Give accounts of events that you or other people have actually witnessed.
- **Authoritative opinions**   Include points of view expressed by persons thought to have special knowledge of the issue.

Writing
TIP

Are there experts in your own community whom you can interview about the topic?

1. Begin your draft. You've searched out evidence to support your side; now you're ready to put it on the page. In the course of drafting, you'll probably refine and clarify your ideas on the issue, strengthening some arguments and discarding others. Throughout the process, keep in mind your major goal: getting the reader on your side.

You might want to use one of the two following patterns as a basic guide to organizing your draft.

HANDBOOKS

FOR HELP & PRACTICE

Thesis Statements,
pp. 355–356
Unity/Coherence,
pp. 371–385
Concluding a
Persuasive Essay,
p. 390
Denotation/
Connotation,
p. 424
Thinking Critically,
pp. 468–470

Organizational Patterns

1	2
Define the issue.	Define the issue.
State your position.	State both sides.
Support your position.	Give your opinion.
Note the arguments of the other side.	Support your opinion by comparing the two
Present your counter-arguments.	points of view and answering opposing arguments.

2. Elaborate on ideas. Patrick Marshall compared and contrasted student reporters with professional reporters, and school principals with newspaper publishers. What strategies can you use to develop your position? Reread the section "Research Your Topic," on the preceding page. Then consider the following ways of developing your findings into arguments.

PROBLEM
SOLVING

How can I
elaborate on
my ideas?

- **Definition** Different people may define the same issue in different ways. Some readers may not have any accurate definition of the issue in mind at all. A clear statement of what is at stake in the issue, as you see it, is a crucial first step toward bringing readers over to your view.

- **Comparison and contrast** You may want to compare and contrast your facts and authoritative opinions with the opposition's. You might also bring up examples for comparison and contrast, as Marshall brought up the example of commercial newspapers and compared them with school newspapers.

- **Cause and effect** This strategy is effective for drawing attention to the causes of a problem or to the effects that could result if your position is ignored.
- **Problem and solution** You may wish to use this strategy to propose a solution to a problem and then persuasively support your proposal.

In his essay on school newspapers, Joel began by defining the problem. He also made his tone more formal than in his earlier freewrite in order to appeal effectively to an audience that included school administrators and parents.

ONE STUDENT'S PROCESS

The Bill of Rights guarantees our right to freedom of the press—unless we happen to be students. More and more principals are currently censoring articles in student newspapers, and the courts are upholding their right to do it.

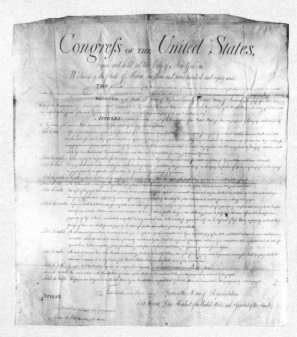

3. Use persuasive language effectively. Your position should be based on well-supported facts, but you can draw attention to your position by using persuasive language. Choose words that precisely convey your position and your emotions. Keep in mind the connotations attached to words. For example, you might say a researcher *discovered* a new vaccine, or he *stumbled upon* a new vaccine. *Discovered* has a positive connotation, while *stumbled upon* has a negative connotation. However, don't let emotional appeals substitute for sound reasoning. Check your writing for common errors in reasoning such as logical fallacies. (For more information on logical fallacies, see Writing Handbook 24 "Thinking Strategies for Writing," pages 468–470.)

4. Test your arguments. When you have a fairly complete draft, share it with some classmates. Use some of the following suggestions to test your ideas and your presentation.

Response Experiment

- **Graphic response** Have your readers make a tree sketch of your draft, labeling roots, branches, and trunk. Does it resemble your sketch? This may tell you whether the argument you intended is the one you actually made.
- **Collect objections** Give one reader permission to attack anything in your draft on any grounds whatsoever. Get another reader to help you sort out which objections make sense and how you can fix weak areas.
- **Believing and doubting** Ask your readers to list two reasons for believing your argument, and two for doubting it.
- **Test for feeling** Ask readers how your argument made them feel. Were they convinced? If not, don't try to argue them to your side. Listen to them, and work on erasing their doubts in a later draft.
- **Test for tact** Ask readers whether there were any places in your draft where they felt you were talking down to the audience or sneering at your opposition. Negative approaches can work against you.
- **Test for strength** Have readers search for places where you had a basically strong point to make, but did not give it its due. You may have said too little—or too much—about it, or used weak or loaded language.

PROBLEM
S O L V I N G

How can I
test my
arguments
on readers?

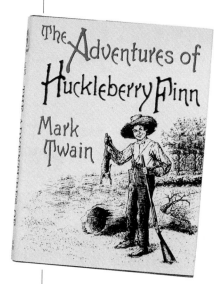

The casual life and careless grammar of Twain's character, Huck Finn, prompted the Concord, MA public library to ban the novel in 1885.

Controversial
Issue   **215**

Writer's Choice After testing your arguments, do you wish to add any additional points or modify your position in any way?

5. Review your writing. Take a break, then use questions such as the following to find the strengths and weaknesses of your draft.

R E V I E W   Y O U R   W R I T I N G

Questions for Yourself

- Did I say what I wanted to say, or did I get sidetracked into pursuing some other goal?
- Did I meet the opposition's objections, or did I simply state my own case and pretend there was no other side?
- If this were someone else's paper, would I be convinced?

Questions for Your Peer Readers

- Which of my arguments did you find most convincing? Which did you find least convincing?
- Can you think of additional arguments to support my point of view?
- Are there arguments against my point of view that I haven't considered?

REVISE   YOUR   WRITING

HANDBOOKS
FOR HELP & PRACTICE

Self-Assessment, p. 397
Peer Response, pp. 398–401

1. Evaluate your responses. Review your own reactions to your draft as well as those of your peers. Also keep in mind the following characteristics of writing on controversies.

Standards for Evaluation

An effective persuasive essay . . .

- defines the issue clearly in the introduction.
- sets forth the two sides of the issue and states the author's position.
- anticipates and answers possible challenges.
- uses persuasive language effectively and precisely.
- avoids faulty logic.

- Supports the author's views with facts, examples, authoritative opinions, and other appropriate details.
- Uses language appropriate for the audience.

2. Problem-solve. Decide which responses will help you improve your draft. Joel made the changes below in response to his peer readers' reactions.

ONE STUDENT'S PROCESS

Principles who censor stories aren't "protecting" students, they are merely making necessary information harder to get. Student editors and reporters need to write what their audience needs to know.

als (above Principles)

from unpleasant issues;

know that they can

about   they feel

If there is a drug problem in their school, for example, they ought to be able to confront it openly. The only thing that's accomplished by not confronting the problem in the school newspaper is that the school newspaper will seem out of touch with reality. Writing about controversial issues will give students a valuable lesson in freedom and responsibility.

Good, but do reporters always know what their readers need?

I agree with you. Can you say something to back up your point?

Avoid the tempta-
tion to use too
many exclamation
points when writ-
ing about contro-
versial issues.

3. Proofread your work. Make a clean copy of your work, then check it for errors in grammar, usage, and mechanics. Also, make sure that your language is strong and vivid but that it is not unfairly loaded against your opposition.

LINKING
GRAMMAR ▪AND▪ WRITING
Using Vivid Verbs

Vivid action verbs create a more forceful argument. Verbs that are too general or weak water down the impact of your arguments.

PROBLEM: Do students *do* this extracurricular activity in order to learn how to *be* obedient?

REVISED: Do student journalists *sign up for* this extracurricular activity in order to learn how to *knuckle under* to authority?

See Style Handbook 18, "Enriching Your Language," pages 424–432, for more help with this problem.

PUBLISH AND PRESENT

- **Deliver your paper as a speech.** Rather than reading it straight from the page, adapt it as an informal talk. Accompany your talk with photographs, videotapes, statistical charts, diagrams—whatever visual materials you can find to support your arguments.
- **Conduct a panel discussion or debate on your topic.** Work with others in your class who have written on similar topics. If some classmates have taken the opposing side, so much the better for your debate.
- **Turn your paper into a pamphlet.** Distribute copies to classmates, friends, and relatives. You may want to illustrate the pamphlet with a memorable political cartoon.
- **Adapt your paper into a letter.** If you wrote about a controversy in your community, mail copies of the letter to influential decision-makers in your community.
- **Save your work in your writing portfolio.**

School Newspapers
Should Be Uncensored!

Joel Goldman

The Bill of Rights guarantees our right to freedom of the press—unless we happen to be students. More and more principals are currently censoring articles in student newspapers, and the courts are upholding their right to do it.

My view is this: as long as the material in a student newspaper is neither obscene nor libelous, its editors and writers should be the only ones who decide its contents. In recent cases, school administrators suppressed articles not for being obscene or libelous but merely for being about controversial subjects that made the administrators uncomfortable. In the famous Hazelwood, Missouri, case and other cases, censored articles were about such topics as divorce, drugs, and gangs. This is not only wrong; it's harmful to students as American citizens. One of the most important life-lessons we can learn at school is how to discuss issues in a free society. How can we do this if school administrators won't even let us mention certain issues? Principals who censor these stories aren't "protecting" students from unpleasant issues; they are merely making necessary information harder to get.

Student editors and reporters need to know that they can write about what they feel their audience needs to know. If there is a drug problem in their school, for example, they ought to be able to confront it openly. The only thing that's accomplished by not confronting the problem in the school newspaper is that the school newspaper will seem out of touch with reality. Writing about controversial subjects will give students a valuable lesson in freedom and responsibility.

Defines the issue

States author's position

Gives specific examples

Controversial Issue   **219**

Supporters of school administrators' rights of censorship, like Patrick Marshall, think that student reporters have no more right than other reporters to have their stories printed. The censorship, they say, teaches students about the reality of the publishing world, where the publisher holds the power. For example, if a reporter for <u>The New York Times</u> wants to write an article on gangs, he can't demand that his publisher print it. The publisher may just not think the subject is newsworthy at the moment.

My reply is, should school newspapers follow the same corporate pattern? Do student journalists sign up for this difficult and rewarding extracurricular activity in order to learn how to knuckle under to higher-ups? When we're adults, will we be more professional newspaper reporters, more powerful thinkers, and more responsible Americans because of our experience hearing the principal tell us, "You can't write that"?

Learning the value of freedom of speech and press is more important than learning what power corporate heads sometimes have. It's exactly the kind of lesson that parents pay the schools to teach their children. We learn about it in social studies. We should be allowed to practice it in real life.

Mr. Marshall and others want to teach students that power belongs to the people who own newspapers. My position is that we, the students and our parents, are the ones who own the school newspaper. It is funded with tax money or tuition. The principal has no financial investment in the school paper; therefore he or she is not its publisher. By Patrick Marshall's own logic, we deserve the power to control our newspaper's contents. Administrators should have a great deal of control over what is taught in their schools, but not over what students can decently say. The first journalism lesson students must learn is that they can have the power to express themselves freely.

Sets forth opposition's position

Replies to opposition's challenges

Appeals to audience

Uses persuasive logic and language

WRITER TO WRITER

We are not descended from fearful men, not from men who feared to write, to speak, to associate, and to defend causes which were, for the moment, unpopular.

Edward R. Murrow, journalist and broadcaster

Edward R. Murrow, one of the world's most respected journalists.

1. Reflect on your writing. When you are ready to submit your paper or place it in your writing portfolio, attach an "afterword" commenting on what you have learned from the process of completing your piece of persuasive writing. Think particularly about the following questions.

- How has your work on this paper influenced your thinking about your topic?
- Did you find a conflict between your desire to win an argument and your responsibility to inform your reader? If so, how did you resolve the conflict?
- If you were to rewrite your paper now, how would you argue differently?
- How do you feel about your use of persuasive language? Did you use it ethically?

2. Apply your skills. Try one or more writing activities in the following areas.

FOR YOUR
PORTFOLIO

- **Current events** Find a political cartoon that takes a strong stand on a controversial issue. Newspapers and news magazines are a good source of such cartoons. Then write a letter to the editor of your local newspaper supporting one side of the issue depicted in the cartoon.
- **Literature** Select a short story or novel you have recently read, and consider alternative ways in which it might end. In a brief essay, present an argument showing why a particular alternative ending would be preferable to the actual ending. You could also explain why the author's ending is the most effective one possible.

Related ASSIGNMENT

Persuasive Speech

SPEECH

★ ★ ★ ★ ★ ★ ★ ★ ★ ★ ★

by Chen Mingyuan,
April 23, 1989

For a brief period in 1989, the Chinese Democracy Movement focused world attention on China. Ignoring government threats, students took to the streets to demonstrate for freedom, democracy, and reform of the government. Ultimately the movement was crushed, but the impassioned writings and speeches of many students and professors have been saved.

A Chinese professor gave the following speech at a student rally. As you read, notice the techniques he uses to draw attention to his heartfelt message.

★

My name is Chen Mingyuan. I would like to say that I did not come here for personal fame and gain, absolutely not. If there is someone in the audience who would like to report me to the authorities you may take my name right to the Public Security Bureau. . . . I would also like to say that I did not come here to "spread evil words and delude the masses"; neither did I come with "ulterior motives." But the government, the news agencies, and our China Central Television station have already prepared these "caps" [political labels] and are dangling them over us. . . . Under such circumstances, many people are made afraid; many keep in mind that there are parents and children to worry about, that they have a job, that they earn barely enough each day to meet daily expenses, that if they get thrown into jail how are they going to survive. . . . I have never spoken in public before an audience this large, but today I feel I must step up to speak, for I can't bear it any longer. . . .

Whenever I mention

★

"freedom," some people react as though the word "freedom" is taboo. Some say that "freedom" is a bad word; some others say that it ought to be avoided altogether. . . . But I feel that "freedom" is the most beautiful word in the world. Do I have to leave it to the possession of someone else? Why can not our great country and great people possess such a beautiful word?

Yes, it's true that we are poor, we are backward, we are unenlightened, we pass our days in hardship. But we do have this one ideal—freedom and democracy! Indeed, until the end of this century, until the end of my days and my children's days, we will live our lives impoverished, . . . But we have a one source of pride— that we have struggled for freedom and democracy!

It's not possible that this government will give us wealth. It's not possible that it will allow everybody to get rich. . . . But there is one thing that the government can do . . . to win over the people's hearts—give us our democratic rights! Give

★

us freedom! And not lump us together with reactionaries! He who opposes freedom is a reactionary.

In addition, there's the issue of education, about which we have talked and talked until our tongues bled. Why can't we have education given top priority in the finances of the government? Up to now, the government has behaved in the manner of squeezing tooth paste, and today our educational funds are no match for those of any other country in the world. The government has been crying that "we must reform," that "we must make China prosperous." But why is there always so little to spend on education? . . . Because the government is always trying to explain about this or that difficulty: our industry is in difficulty, our agriculture is in difficulty. . . . Even building houses for the provincial governors and county magistrates is very difficult. We have difficulty buying cars. But I think there is one thing that is not difficult at all—confiscating the unlawfully gained properties

★

of the "profiteering lords," and putting them to use in education.

My fellow students, I feel very excited and inspired. Our country has problems, all too many. However, I feel what I've so far said are the basic things we must demand.

I suggest, my fellow students, that we organize investigation committees, that we act as the masters of our country and investigate corruption in our government. In the meantime, we will praise those government officials who are men and women of honesty and integrity, officials who work for the people, even though honesty and integrity are the basic requirements for a government official and perhaps deserve no special praise. . . .

Down with bureaucracy! Promote education! . . . Increase significantly funds for education! Long live democracy! Long live the People's Republic of China! Long live freedom! Long live freedom! . . .

Think AND Respond

What audience is Chen Mingyuan addressing? How does he support his points? How does he address the arguments of the other side? What action does he want his audience to take? What topic or issue do you feel strongly enough about to get up and deliver a persuasive speech?

INVITATION TO Write

Chen Mingyan believes that freedom and democracy are necessary for all, and he tries to persuade his audience to take part in keeping corruption out of government. Now write your own speech, persuading others to believe as you do about an issue or cause.

In a persuasive speech, as in editorials and essays on controversial issues, you take a position and then support it. Like editorials and essays, a persuasive speech must include facts and reasoned arguments that back up the author's opinions. However, speeches have a special characteristic: they are intended to be spoken before an audience, whether at a rally, in a classroom, or in an auditorium. Because a live audience is more likely than a reader to be distracted, a speaker must make an extra effort to capture and keep the listeners' attention long enough to make his or her point.

PLANNING A PERSUASIVE SPEECH

HANDBOOKS
FOR HELP & PRACTICE

Thinking Critically, pp. 468–470
Concluding Persuasive Essay, p. 390
Denotation/ Connotation, p. 424
Oral Reports, pp. 497–498
Types of Advertising Appeals, pp. 514–516

1. Choose a subject. It is evident from Chen Mingyan's speech that he strongly believes the people have the right to demand freedom and investigate corruption. Pick an issue about which you have strong feelings. Look in newspapers for stories that provoke you. Brainstorm with friends to find issues in your school or community. Then write a statement that sums up your opinion. Be clear about your position; the rest of the speech will then flow more easily.

2. Research your subject. Find information that will support your position. Begin by discussing the issue with other concerned individuals. If your subject is a current issue, *The Readers' Guide to Periodical Literature* is another good source. Consider using other valuable sources of information, such as reference books and interviews with experts or eyewitnesses.

M.A.D.D. (Mothers Against Drunk Driving) was a forerunner of S.A.D.D. (Students Against Drunk Drivers).

Poster titled "Too much fun isn't always a pretty picture. Party safe."

3. List as many reasons as possible. It helps to write them in full sentences, such as "The school should establish a branch of SADD (Students Against Drunk Drivers) because local police report an increase in alcohol consumption among students in this community" or "Government student loan programs should continue because they make higher education accessible to students from low-income families." Then gather the strongest supporting information you can for each reason. Hard facts and specific examples are usually most effective. Remember that you are trying to persuade people who have not yet formed an opinion, or people whose opinion is opposed to yours.

4. Consider the arguments of the other side. If you don't address opposing concerns, you are likely to hurt your own argument.

WRITING A PERSUASIVE SPEECH

1. Open with a clear statement of the issue. No matter how you choose to engage your audience—anecdotes, statistics, quotations—establish your topic in the first few sentences of your speech. You can state the topic as a question, such as "Should student parking be provided by high schools?" or in a direct statement. After Chen Mingyan explained why he was addressing the audience, he made statements about how some people react to the word *freedom*. Then he stated, "But I feel that 'freedom' is the most beautiful word in the world." Chen Mingyan continued with questions that state the issue: "Do I have to leave it to the possession of someone else? Why can not our great country and great people possess such a beautiful word?"

 Writer's Choice Many positions can be stated either negatively or positively. Saying that you are against something can have a powerful impact. A positive solution to a problem, on the other hand, can lead to direct action.

2. Choose an effective organization. Would a cause-effect format for your speech suit your subject? Would order of importance allow you to position your strongest arguments so that they have the greatest impact?

3. Present your supporting points clearly and logically. Because persuasive speeches often deal with emotionally charged subjects, it is easy to get carried away. State what you think in a logical manner that appeals to the minds, as well as to the emotions, of your audience. Use loaded language sparingly, if at all. (For more help in preparing and organizing a persuasive argument, see the Guided Assignment in this Workshop.)

4. Sum up your position. After you have presented and supported your points, restate your original position. It will now carry with it the strengths of your arguments. Add a call to action, if appropriate, so that your audience feels they can take part in accomplishing or improving something.

5. Rework your ideas for oral presentation. Address your listeners directly. Use the pronoun *you* or *we* to help your listeners feel that they must somehow respond to your speech. Take advantage of sound devices as well. For example, alliteration or the repetition of key points can be very effective. Notice how Chen Mingyan repeatedly used "long live . . ." at the end of his speech. Finally, consider the use of flip charts or other visual aids.

6. Practice your speech aloud. Look for words and phrases to stress. Pause before or after key points. Use gestures occasionally for emphasis. Above all, practice maintaining eye contact with your audience to help keep their attention. Address people in all parts of the room, including those sitting in the back or at the far sides, so that everybody will feel important to the speaker.

1. Read your speech to one or more listeners. Ask them to respond to the content, organization, and presentation.

2. Ask for reactions to your style and tone. Remember that slang is offensive to some audiences and that jargon may make your speech hard to understand. Also, an objective and reasonable tone may be more effective than an angry or indignant one.

3. Check your language and timing. Are any of your sentences too long, or are some words difficult to pronounce? Ask your listeners if your language could be more colorful or persuasive in some places. Then rephrase, or substitute a stronger verb or a more colorful adjective. Time your speech to make sure it is not too long.

PUBLISHING AND PRESENTING

- **Give an oral presentation.** Deliver your speech at a rally or a school council meeting where the issue is being discussed.
- **Enter a speech contest.** Consult with your speech teacher about entering the next speech tournament.

Editorial

AWAY WITH BIG-TIME ATHLETICS

by Roger M. Williams

Many American universities are known more for the teams they field than for the education they impart. Each year they pour hundreds of thousands of dollars apiece into athletic programs whose success is measured in games won and dollars earned—standards that bear no relation to the business of education and offer nothing to the vast majority of students.

The waste of resources is not the only lamentable result of the over-emphasis of intercollegiate athletics. The skewing of values is at least as damaging. Everyone involved in the big-time system—players, coaches, alumni and other boosters, school officials, trustees, even legislators—is persuaded that a good football team is a mark of the real worth of an educational institution. Some of the most successful coaches elevate that bizarre notion to a sort of philosophy. Woody Hayes [the late coach at Ohio State] said that the most important part of a young man's college education is the football he plays.

One of the easiest ways to start an argument is to voice an opinion on a controversial issue such as nuclear power or flag burning. The editors and publishers of newspapers and magazines invite this kind of heated debate every day. They write editorials, the statements of opinion that appear on special editorial pages.

In this editorial, Roger Williams challenges the worth of college athletic programs. As you read, look for a clear statement of opinion. What examples does Williams use to support his ideas?

Everyone knows something about the excess of recruiting high-school players and something about the other trappings of the big-time system: the athletic dormitory and training table, where the "jocks" . . . are segregated in the interests of conformity and control; the "brain coaches" hired to keep athletes [in] school; the full scholarships . . . worth several thousand dollars apiece, that big-time schools can give to [hundreds] of athletes each year. . . .

What few people realize is that these are only the visible workings of a system that feeds on higher education and diverts it from its true purposes. The solution, therefore, is not to deliver slaps on the wrist to the most zealous recruiters, as the NCAA often does, or to make modest reductions in the permissible number of athletic scholarships. . . . The solution is to banish big-time athletics from American colleges and universities.

Think AND Respond

What does the author think ought to be done about intercollegiate athletics? How does he support his opinion? Do you agree or disagree with him? Why? Suppose you were the editor of your school newspaper. What issue would you choose to discuss on your editorial page?

INVITATION
—TO—
Write

The editorial on the nature of college athletic programs expressed a strong opinion. Now write your own editorial on an issue about which you feel strongly.

A good editorial is persuasive writing at its best: convincing and written with confidence and power. An editorial is convincing when the writer's opinions are supported with verifiable facts and thoughtful arguments. However, even a thoughtful argument may lack the power to convince the reader if the writer does not truly believe in his or her point of view, or feel strongly about the issue at hand.

PLANNING YOUR EDITORIAL

HANDBOOKS
FOR HELP & PRACTICE

Organization,
pp. 342–349
Reference Works,
pp. 490–495
Concluding
Persuasive Essay,
p. 390
Word Choice,
pp. 402–404

1. Choose an issue. What issue in your school or community needs public discussion, demands action, or simply annoys you? The issue may involve after-school programs or safe conditions at a busy intersection. Perhaps you are concerned about a state, national, or international issue, such as victim's rights or threats to free speech. Write down as many issues as come to mind. Then choose an issue about which you deeply care as the topic for an editorial.

2. Take a stand on the issue. Express your belief in a clear, brief statement. The purpose of your editorial will be to persuade your readers of the opinion summarized in this statement.

3. Collect your data. Freewrite or cluster to discover what you already know about your subject, then do some research. Your opinion will be more convincing if it is based on well-documented facts. Your local library and newspapers are good sources for information. Statistics—dollar amounts and population figures, for example—and quotes from involved parties are often useful. Notice how Williams uses a statement made by a prominent coach and refers, in general terms, to the amount of money spent on college sports.

Writer's Choice You may begin to change your opinion when you know more of the facts. If this happens, go ahead! After all, you will only be able to write an effective editorial if you believe in what you say.

4. Make an outline. It will help you focus on your key point, figure out how to develop your argument, and then progress to a satisfactory solution. A simple outline of Williams's editorial would show (a) a clear statement of his position on sports in higher education, (b) the main points to be covered and the facts and quotes to support them, and (c) a proposed response or solution.

W RITING YOUR EDITORIAL

1. Keep your purpose in mind. Use your outline to help you stick to the issue and to include facts and quotes that support your points.

2. Organize your ideas effectively. You can start with a clear statement of your opinion, or you may want to present the facts first and then reveal your convictions.

Writing
—TIP—
As you write, keep your readers in mind so that you can include details that will have meaning for them.

Many students successfully balance athletics and studies.

3. Choose words carefully. Make a forceful statement of your opinion without using words so emotionally charged that readers will react with anger rather than thought. However, a skillful writer can deliberately use strong language to persuade the reader by overstating the case. Williams uses such words as—"bizarre," "lamentable," and "excess" to highlight the absurdly high priority he believes athletics are given in colleges and universities.

4. Take extra care with your conclusion. You may want to end your editorial by restating—in different words—the main idea expressed in your introduction. Check to see that your conclusion is consistent with the main points of your editorial and does not introduce any new or unrelated information.

REVIEWING YOUR WRITING

1. Be sure your information is correct. Double check the accuracy of the facts you've used. Verify the sources of quoted material.

2. Revise your draft. Read your editorial aloud to yourself. Ask others to read it. Does it flow? Is it convincing? Even if the information you provide acknowledges other sides of the issue, make sure that your own point of view remains clear.

PUBLISHING AND PRESENTING

- **Put it in print.** Submit your editorial to your school newspaper for publication.
- **Use your editorial to promote change.** Rally support for your solution to the issue by initiating a petition or a letter-writing campaign.

Editorials express ideas through images as well as words.

Oliphant © 1972. Universal Press Syndicate. Printed with permission. All rights reserved

Sentence

Using Absolute Phrases

Absolute phrases provide a concise way to combine related ideas in one sentence. Many of these phrases modify nouns or pronouns. Others modify no specific word but add material related to the whole sentence (as in model 3).

MODELS

1. (Short)   The boy watched, <u>his eyes bulging in the dark</u>.
   Edmund Ware, "An Underground Episode"

2. (Medium) Alfred trailed a few steps behind, <u>a strange new excitement bubbling in his stomach</u>.
   Robert Lipsyte, *The Contender*

3. (Long)   Like giants they toiled, <u>days flashing on the heels of days like dreams as they heaped the treasure up</u>.
   Jack London, *The Call of the Wild*

Most absolute phrases resemble sentences missing the *to be* part of the verb. To identify an absolute phrase, use this test: If you can turn the phrase into a sentence by adding a form of *to be* (such as *is, are, was,* or *were*), the phrase is an absolute.

Example   1. His eyes *were* bulging in the dark.
2. A strange new excitement *was* bubbling in his stomach.
3. Days *were* flashing on the heels of days like dreams as they heaped the treasure up.

Punctuation Note: Absolute phrases are set off by commas.

A. Combining Sentences   First, remove *was* or *were* from the second sentence in each set, creating an absolute phrase. Then use a comma to join the phrase to the end of the first sentence.

Example   My brother came to my side. His eyes were drawn by the blazing straw.

Result   My brother came to my side, his eyes drawn by the blazing straw.
Richard Wright, *Native Son*

1. He was an old man. His long matted beard and hair were gray to nearly white.   **Walter Van Tilburg Clark, "The Portable Phonograph"**

2. He returned, shuddering, five minutes later. His arms were soaked and red to the elbows.   **Ray Bradbury, "A Sound of Thunder"**

3. I looked across to a lighted case of Chinese design which held delicate-looking statues of horses and birds, small vases and bowls. Each was set upon a carved wooden base.   **Ralph Ellison, *Invisible Man***

4. I could hear him crashing down the hill toward the sea. The frightening laughter was echoing back.   **Theodore Taylor, *The Cay***

5. Two little girls were clinging together against the wall. Their voices were inhumanly high as they shrieked.   **Leslie Morris, "Three Shots for Charlie Beston"**

6. She slid back the roof of the cockpit once again. Her nose was wrinkling at the rankness of the dripping morass encircling them.
            Alan Dean Foster, "Splinter of the Mind's Eye"

7. The dogs were standing on the wire fence in dappled rows. Their voices were lifted in greeting.   **Borden Deal, "The Christmas Hunt"**

8. The motorcycle on the sidewalk speeded up and skidded obliquely into a plate-glass window. The front wheel was buckling and climbing the brick base beneath the window.   **Frank Rooney, "Cyclist's Raid"**

B. Imitating Sentences Write a sentence imitating the structure of each model, but using your own words.
Important: Imitate as many of the sentence parts as possible, not just the underlined absolute phrases. Use correct punctuation.

> ***Example***   About the bones, the ants were ebbing away,
> <u>their pincers full of meat.</u>
>   **Doris Lessing, "A Sunrise on the Veld"**

> ***Student Sentence***   Inside the house, the walls were caving in, their timbers powdery with decay.

1. There she'd find me, bent over a picture, <u>the brush between my toes.</u>
            Christy Brown, *My Left Foot*

2. Freddy Malins clambered in after her and spent a long time settling her on the seat, <u>Mr. Browne helping him with advice.</u>   **James Joyce, "The Dead"**

3. He trudged with his hands and tight fists in his pockets, <u>his head to the wind and the rain.</u>   **Walter Edmonds, "Water Never Hurt a Man"**

4. Once, Barnes tried to duck the jab and stumbled, <u>his unprotected face bobbing up six inches from Alfred's right fist.</u> **Robert Lipsyte, *The Contender***

5. We rowed along the shore, <u>the barman holding the line in his hand and giving it occasional jerks forward.</u> **Ernest Hemingway, *A Farewell to Arms***

C. Expanding Sentences Complete each absolute phrase, using content that fits the rest of the sentence. Then compare your sentences with the originals on page 312.

1. A water snake slipped along on the pool, its head. . . .
John Steinbeck, *Of Mice and Men*

2. I said nothing, my mind. . . . **John Knowles, *A Separate Peace***

3. This was what I feared when I lifted the dark-green shade: I feared a face outside the window, dead eyes. . . . **Mary Gordon, *Final Payments***

4. As he looked, the bull gathered itself together and charged, its. . . .
Ernest Hemingway, "The Undefeated"

5. Mr. Nathan Radley was standing inside his gate, a shotgun. . . .
Harper Lee, *To Kill a Mockingbird*

Application The abridged paragraph below from "The Eighty-Yard Run" by Irving Shaw describes a football player, nicknamed "Darling," running for a touchdown. Add absolute phrases that start with the underlined words. Then compare your paragraph with the original on page 313.

(1) The pass was high and wide and Darling jumped for it. (2) The center floated by, <u>his hands</u>. . . . (3) He had ten yards in the clear and picked up speed, watching the other backs heading him off toward the sideline, <u>the men</u> . . . , <u>the blockers</u>. . . . (4) He smiled a little to himself as he ran, <u>his knees</u> . . . , <u>his hips</u>. . . . (5) The first halfback came at him, and he fed him his leg, then swung at the last moment, took the shock of the man's shoulder without breaking stride, ran through him, <u>his cleats</u>. . . . (6) There was only the safety man now, coming warily at him, <u>his arms</u> . . . , <u>hands</u>. . . . (7) Darling tucked the ball in, <u>his legs</u> . . . , <u>knees</u> . . . , <u>all two hundred pounds</u> . . . . (8) He pivoted away, keeping the arm locked, dropping the safety man as he ran easily toward the goal line, with the drumming of cleats diminishing behind him.

Grammar Refresher Model sentences in this lesson contain nonessential phrases. For more on essential and nonessential phrases, see Handbook 32, pages 590 and 596.

Sketchbook

Sunday Afternoon on the Island of La Grande Jatte, by Georges Seurat

The Grande Jatte is an island in the Seine just outside Paris. In Seurat's day, it was a park that attracted city residents seeking recreation and relaxation. Over the past several decades, many attempts have been made to explain the meaning of this great composition. For some, it shows the middle class at leisure; for others, it reveals, through its groups and details, social tensions of modern city dwellers. Ironically, the Art Institute's most famous painting remains one of its most enigmatic.

MASTER PAINTINGS IN THE
ART INSTITUTE OF CHICAGO

What do you see when you look at something?

Additional Sketches
What was the best live performance you ever saw?

What actor would you choose to play you in the movie of your life? Why?

Writing About Literature

INTERPRETIVE ESSAY

INTERPRETING ART

DIRECTOR'S NOTES

You've had a great deal of experience at interpretation. All your life, you've interpreted people's actions and words in order to find what they meant for you—love, hate, anger, fear, hope. Interpreting literary texts is a more specialized form of this same process. You read a poem or story, you watch a movie or play; then you explore the experience. You sort out your feelings and test your understanding in order to gain a deeper appreciation. In the next three assignments, you will practice rereading and interpreting literary texts. You'll write an interpretive essay on a literary work of your choice, then go on to interpret works of visual and dramatic art.

A FIRE-TRUCK

BY RICHARD WILBUR

The title of
the poem you will now
read is "A Fire-Truck,"
and the poem itself is
indeed a description of
a fire-truck racing to a
fire. But is that all it is
about? Read the poem,
then read it a second
or third time, and ask
yourself if the poet is
doing a good deal more.
Try interpreting the
poem—that is, under-
standing it—as a work
that has as much to
do with your response
to it as it does with
an object or scene
it describes.

Right down to the shocked street with a siren-blast
That sends all else skittering to the curb,
Redness, brass, ladders and hats hurl past,
   Blurring to sheer verb,

Shift at the corner into uproarious gear
And make it around the turn in a squall of traction,
The headlong bell maintaining sure and clear,
   Thought is degraded action!

Beautiful, heavy, unweary, loud, obvious thing!
I stand here purged of nuance,[1] my mind a blank.
All I was brooding upon has taken wing,
   And I have you to thank.

As you howl beyond hearing I carry you into my mind,
Ladders and brass and all, there to admire
Your phoenix-red[2] simplicity, enshrined
   In that not extinguished fire.

[1] nuance: subtle variation in color or meaning
[2] phoenix: mythical bird that consumes itself in flames every
500 years, then rises anew from its own ashes

INVITATION TO *Write*

As you have seen, Richard Wilbur's seemingly simple poem may be interpreted as having more than one level of meaning. Choose a poem, play, story, novel, or essay that is sufficiently difficult to require interpretation. Write an essay that presents your interpretation of the text.

Reading a piece of literature often demands that you do more than understand the obvious or literal meaning of the words. You may find that you are puzzled about how to make sense of what you are reading. Or perhaps the text is easy to read, yet you feel that it is saying something more significant than it appears to say. You may need to reread and think about a text more deeply in order to **interpret** it—to figure out meanings that may not be apparent at first glance. Your pleasure and interest as a reader can be enhanced by rereading a text and reflecting on questions of interpretation.

PREWRITE AND EXPLORE

HANDBOOKS
FOR HELP & PRACTICE

Writing Techniques,
pp. 324–326
Thinking Critically,
pp. 468–470
Reading Skills,
pp. 476–477

1. Choose a piece of literature to explore. You may wish to choose a poem or story you are studying, or another piece you find challenging. You might also consider exploring "A Fire Truck" or one of these selections: poems "Loo-Wit" by Wendy Rose or "We Are Many" by Pablo Neruda, and short stories "Rules of the Game" by Amy Tan or "A Very Old Man with Enormous Wings" by Gabriel Garcia Márquez.

2. Keep a reading log. Record your questions, interpretive comments, and responses as you read and reread the text. Pay particular attention to recording the changes that take place in your understanding as you read it the first time and then reread it.

For each entry in your log, make sure you show what text or part of a text you are writing about. Then record your response—which may be a feeling, a thought, a question, a memory of something the

Ruby, an elephant at the Phoenix Zoo, is a recognized artist. She painted *Fire Truck* after seeing a fire engine and its blue-clad rescue team in action.

text reminds you of, or an interpretive comment. Don't feel you have to make judgments; just respond. Whatever you happen to think, feel, or wonder is an appropriate response.

Sometimes, however, the specific elements of the literature might intrigue you. For example, if you are reading a poem, you may find yourself responding to such features as its speaker, content, theme, mood, form, or language (including figures of speech). As you read a work of fiction, you may ask questions about characters, setting, point of view, theme, or style. A play may be characterized by any of these features, but in reading or seeing a play you may also find yourself responding to its dialogue, staging, costumes, or acting.

3. Freewrite. At the end of each reading or rereading of the entire text, freewrite for five or ten minutes. Explain your most current understanding of the text.

4. Rate your understanding. At the end of each reading, record your degree of understanding on a ten-point scale, with a rating of 0 meaning "no understanding" and a rating of 10 meaning "perfect understanding." Use a rough-drawn scale like this:

no understanding   perfect understanding
0 ———————————— 5 ———————————— 10

COMPUTER TIP

To get started free-writing, input the most interesting words or phrases from the text onto your screen. Below them, input the first words and phrases that enter your mind as you look at the selected words.

Writer's Choice Instead of using a reading log to record and examine your reading process, you might simply read the text several times, writing out a rough interpretive commentary after each reading.

Sheri's entries in her reading log show her understanding of "A Fire Truck" changed over several readings. Throughout this assignment, you will follow Sheri's process in writing an interpretation of the poem.

ONE STUDENT'S PROCESS

1st reading. The poem seems fairly simple in parts, but some of it I can't understand. It's basically about a fire engine going to a fire and the poet or speaker watching the red color, hearing the siren blasting, the bell ringing, etc. I don't know what else to write, unless I read the poem again. So I'll do that now.

Rating from readings 1 & 2:

```
                      x
 |------------|------------|
 0            5           10
```

3rd reading. Let me go through it again, stanza by stanza, saying what's going on and the things I don't understand:

Stanza 1: easy except line 4, "Blurring to sheer verb"

Stanza 2: The truck shifts gears at the corner. I didn't notice that before. What's "squall of traction"? Oh! I know. It's the squeal of the tires taking the corner. Pretty neat. But what about line 8, "Thought is degraded action!"?

Stanza 3: My mind's a blank here. In lines 10-12, why does his mind go blank when he sees a fire engine? Does it mean the siren overpowers anything he was thinking before he saw the fire engine? Is his mind blank because of the size and power of the engine? Is "you" the fire engine?

Last stanza. I can't make sense of the last lines, "En- shrined/ In that not extinguished fire." A shrine is a place of worship. Does he worship the fire? Did he set the fire? I understand this poem less now than I did before I read it so many times!

How come the hardest lines in the poem are the short lines at the end of each stanza? Are the lines shorter to give them a special emphasis? Do those lines have the most to say? I don't think I like this poem.

Rating from reading 3:

```
                                 x
              ┌──────────────────────────────┐
              0               5              10
```

4th reading. I met with my group after my third reading and found that most people had the same problems I did.

We all had problems with "purged of nuance." Does that mean his mind is cleared of subtle shades of meanings, of fine points of relationships? Now he is thinking only of bright, bold things.

Our discussion helped me understand how the third stanza shows the speaker thanking the fire engine for distracting him (with its physical beauty and "obvious" noise, etc.) from his brooding thoughts. The speaker's mind goes blank be- cause he stops worrying and just looks at and listens to the fire engine. I still don't understand it completely, but I like the poem a lot better.

Rating after 4th
or 5th reading:

```
                                    x
              ┌──────────────────────────────┐
              0               5              10
```

Last reading (5th or 6th). What problems still bother me?

Stanza 1: I guess now I understand "blurring to sheer verb."
A verb is a word of action. A firetruck rushes past so fast it
blurs, like on a film. A verb is a word of action, so a firetruck
is pure, fast action.

Stanzas 2 & 3: The big problem here is the line "Thought is
degraded action!" Why is it degraded and not just different
from action? Maybe because it keeps people from acting. In
the third stanza the speaker says he's standing there
"brooding" and he thanks the firetruck for taking his mind off
his worries. So brooding—worrying—is something like
degraded action because it keeps you from doing anything.
Seeing the firetruck, his thoughts "take wing"—fly away. He
is "purged," purified, cleaned of his brooding and now his
mind is a blank.

Stanza 4: In his mind he now has the sights and sounds of
the fire engine. They are like an unextinguished fire in his
mind. The images in his mind are also like the phoenix that is
reborn from its own ashes. I don't get that exactly. But I feel
pretty good about my understanding of most of the poem.
It's a lot more complex than it looked at first.

Rating from 5th reading: 0   5   10

5. Explore your understanding. After you have responded to the
text a few times, meet with one or two other readers who have been
working on the same text. Discuss the difficulties you are finding in
the text and some possible solutions. Then try a few more readings
on your own, continuing to make log entries or commentaries. Try
some of these activities to explore your text.

Exploratory Activities

- **The story of your reading** Read over all your log entries and commentaries and then write for ten minutes, telling the story of your reading. Explain your progress and problems in understanding the text. Focus especially on the most difficult problems you had to deal with and on the questions you still have.

PROBLEM S O L V I N G

How can I explore my understanding of the piece of literature I have chosen?

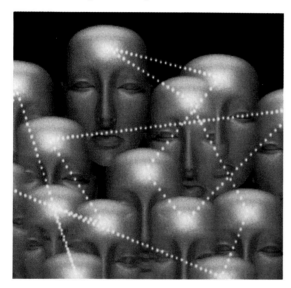

- **Collaborative problem-solving** With a partner or a group of other students, read aloud to each other your stories of your reading and your unresolved problems or questions. Try to answer each other's questions and resolve the remaining problems. Identify clearly the problems you are collectively unable to solve. Those problems might be taken up in a discussion with the whole class or explored further in interpretive essays. Keep notes in your log on problems and solutions.
- **The most important line** What line or short passage in your selected text is the most important one to you? Write out that passage and do ten minutes of freewriting about it.
- **An unresolved problem** Select one of the problems that you and your classmates have not been able to resolve satisfactorily and explore it in writing. Clarify the problem. Explore solutions.

6. Review your reading. Look back at your reading log and your freewriting experiments. Jot down the points that seem most interesting or important to you. What topics for an essay do they suggest to you? Freewrite on a few ideas.

Writing
—TIP—

7. Choose a topic for an interpretive essay. You might choose to focus on the whole text or on only one part or passage. You might also find that one of the freewriting exercises you have already completed will make a good start for a first draft.

8. Identify your purpose. Some interpretive essays are written to offer readers a more insightful view of the text than they had before. Others clear up interpretive problems or questions readers might have experienced. Be careful, however, that you don't turn your essay into a mere catalog of translations of difficult lines or phrases.

9. Identify your audience. How familiar are your readers with the text you are interpreting? If they don't know the text very well or have not read it recently, you will probably want to begin your essay with a fairly detailed summary of the text, reminding readers of what happens, who the characters are, and so on. Even readers who are very familiar with a text (like your teacher) appreciate some information describing it.

1. Begin your first draft. A good way to start is to try to get through an entire first draft in a rush, as if you were freewriting it. When you get stuck, don't pause long; just leave a blank or a note for yourself and go on writing. If you change your mind as you're writing, don't go back to change the first part of your emerging essay. You'll have time to change it later.

2. Write a thesis statement. Try to begin your essay with a thesis statement in which you present your main point—the point that all the rest of your essay will need to support. If you need help getting started, try the following beginning: "On a first reading of _____, a reader is likely to think it's a simple story (or poem) about _____. However, additional readings reveal details and meanings that make it a more complicated and interesting work of literature."

Sheri wrote the following thesis statement, and later incorporated it into the first paragraph of her essay.

ONE STUDENT'S PROCESS

Richard Wilbur's poem "A Fire Truck" seems at first to be about seeing a firetruck rush out of a fire station, screech around the corner, and zoom off to a fire in a blur of speed with a clanging bell and a wailing siren. After several additional readings, however, it becomes clear that the poem tells more about the speaker than about the truck.

3. Elaborate on ideas. The following strategies can help you develop your writing.

Strategies

- **Description** Recreate the characters, setting, or mood of the text by including descriptive details.
- **Comparison and contrast** Compare aspects of the text with other texts. Also, compare your initial thoughts about the text with your thoughts after later readings.

HANDBOOKS

FOR HELP & PRACTICE

Organization,
pp. 342–349
Thesis Statement,
pp. 355–356
Source Materials,
pp. 481–484

Writing
TIP

Instead of starting with a blank page, start with one of the prewriting exercises you have already completed, such as the story of your reading.

• **Paraphrase and summary** Explain key passages in your own words. Be sure to include a brief summary of the entire text.

• **Quotation** Quote passages that are essential to your understanding of the text or particulary well stated.

4. Organize your draft. Many interpretations can be presented by using a problem-solution structure, beginning with a problem in understanding a text and then developing a solution; or a narrative structure in which you present an account of your initial reading of a text and then discuss the interpretation that emerged from rereadings; or an argumentative structure in which you begin by stating your interpretation as a thesis and then offer supporting evidence.

5. Reread and reflect. After completing your draft, put it aside for a day or so. Then reread it and ask the following questions.

R E V I E W   Y O U R   W R I T I N G

Questions for Yourself

• Did I identify the text and tell the reader enough about the work to make sense of my interpretation?

• Is my essay organized around a single main point?

• Are there relevant parts of the text I'm still not clear about? Do I need to reread it again?

• Have I acknowledged plausible alternative interpretations?

Questions for Your Peer Readers

• Have I given you a clear idea of the contents and facts of the text?

• Can you say back to me what my main point is?

• Have I provided you with sufficient evidence and support to explain my interpretation?

• Is my interpretation convincing? If not, is it because of lack of supporting evidence or faulty logic?

• Is there anything you'd like to hear more about—or less?

• Are there places where my essay is confusing to you?

• What did my essay contribute to your understanding of the text?

REVISE YOUR WRITING

1. Evaluate your responses. Review your thoughts and the responses of your peers. Also keep in mind that a well-written interpretation of literature usually displays certain qualities.

Standards for Evaluation

An effective interpretive essay . . .

- identifies the work by title and author and briefly describes its contents.
- presents a plausible, well-organized interpretation of the text or an aspect of it.
- supports its interpretation with evidence and with details and quotations from the text.
- addresses problems in interpreting the text and shares the author's difficulties and successes in resolving them.

2. Problem-solve. Decide which of your own thoughts and of your peers' responses you want to use. Then rework your draft.

Sheri made the following changes to strive for a clearer interpretation of the line *"Thought is degraded action!"*

HANDBOOKS

FOR HELP & PRACTICE

Peer Response,
pp. 398–401
Word Choice,
pp. 402–404
Quotation Marks,
pp. 825–826

ONE STUDENT'S PROCESS

I interpret this to mean that thinking is a poor substitute for action or that life becomes diminished when we spend our time thinking instead of acting. This fits in with another important idea. That ~~the~~ idea is that the poem is about how the speaker escapes from his brooding. Does he trade in his thoughts for action?

Yes, in the sense that he writes a poem. But writing poetry is a very thought-oriented action. Perhaps the poet gives up his old, worried brooding for a more creative kind of thought. Being a poet, however, he can never entirely escape his own mind.

> Good point! I couldn't figure out what he meant.

> I'm confused. How is poetry action?

3. Proofread your work. Make a clean copy, incorporate your changes and correct errors in grammar, usage, and mechanics.

Grammar
—TIP—

When you include a lengthy quotation (8 type lines or longer) in an essay, set it off from the rest of the paragraph, indent it from the left, and do *not* enclose it in quotation marks.

LINKING
GRAMMAR A N D WRITING
Quoting Literary Texts

Make sure all quotations from literary texts are exact and set off with quotation marks. When quoting more than one line of poetry, put a slash between lines of the poem.

PROBLEM: He admires "its phoenix-red simplicity" enshrined in that not extinguished fire.

REVISED: He admires its "phoenix-red simplicity, enshrined/ In that not extinguished fire."

See Grammar Handbook 41, pages 825–826, for more help with this problem.

The Phoenix is a legendary symbol of immortality that renews itself by fire.

PUBLISH AND PRESENT

- **Start a writing support group.** Share your interpretive essay with other members of the group.
- **Create an anthology.** Collect related essays in an anthology for future students to consult.
- **Submit your work to a literary magazine.** Try to get your essay published in the school literary magazine or newspaper.
- **Save your work in your writing portfolio.**

HANDBOOKS
FOR HELP & PRACTICE

Sharing Completed Writing, pp. 418–419

The Two Dramas in Richard Wilbur's "A Fire-Truck"

Shari Dann

Richard Wilbur's poem "A Fire-Truck" seems at first to be about seeing a firetruck rush out of a fire station, screech around the corner, and zoom off to a fire in a blur of speed with a clanging bell and a wailing siren. After several additional readings, however, it becomes clear that the poem tells more about the speaker than about the truck.

I first realized that the poem was more than a description of a fire engine when I looked closely at the short lines that end each stanza. Their shortness and their placement emphasize that these are important lines. The line ending the second stanza is even printed in italics for greater emphasis. The third stanza of the poem seems (after its first line) hardly to be about the fire engine at all, yet it ends with the speaker saying to the firetruck, "I have you to thank." What does he thank the truck for?

The answer is that he thanks the firetruck for what its noise and color and speed do for him. They relieve him of the thoughts and worries that filled his mind before he saw the "Beautiful, heavy, unweary, loud, obvious thing" (line 9). He says in the third stanza that his mind is now "a blank," and that he is "purged of nuance," or cleaned out ("purged") of his old thoughts about subtle differences. He says that "All I was brooding on has taken wing," which means that his sad thoughts or worries have flown away.

I think this shows that in Richard Wilbur's poem two dramas are taking place at once. One is the drama of the fire with the firetruck rushing to the rescue.

Identifies and briefly describes the work

Addresses problems in the text and successfully resolves them

Presents a plausible well-organized interpretation

Interpretive
Essay   **251**

The other drama is in the speaker's mind, where the rushing firetruck also comes to the rescue. In the second drama the firetruck rescues the speaker from his own brooding thoughts and from the unhappiness that comes with too much worrying.

Uses language appropriate for the audience

The line that may be the most important and difficult in the poem is the one italicized for emphasis: *"Thought is degraded action!"* I interpret this to mean that thinking is a poor substitute for action or that life becomes diminished when we spend our time thinking instead of acting. This fits in with the idea that the poem is about how the speaker escapes from his brooding through the sights and sounds of the firetruck. Does he trade in his thoughts for action? Yes, in the sense that he writes a poem. But writing poetry is a very thought-oriented action. Perhaps the poet gives up his old, worried brooding for a more creative kind of thought.

Supports its interpretation with details and quotations from the text

The difficult last stanza says that after the speaker can't hear the firetruck anymore, he carries it in his mind, where he admires its "phoenix-red simplicity, enshrined/In that not extinguished fire." I think that the "not extinguished fire" is the speaker's own mind, which is always burning with thoughts. In that fire, the boldness and simplicity of the firetruck are enshrined as a "beautiful . . . unweary . . . obvious" contrast to the speaker's usual thoughts, which are probably often ugly, weary, and subtle. The "enshrined" image of the firetruck is almost a holy icon for him. "Phoenix-red" suggests that the truck has helped new, fresh thoughts be born out of the ashes of the speaker's old worries. This supports the way I have been interpreting the poem, but makes it even more dramatic and religious. The italicized line, then, fits with the rest of the poem because the speaker has changed his "degraded" thoughts into a higher, active type of thought—poetry.

WRITER TO WRITER

In a very real sense, the writer writes in order to teach himself, to understand himself, to satisfy himself; the publishing of his ideas, though it brings gratifications, is a curious anticlimax.

Alfred Kazin, literary critic

1. Reflect on your writing. Write a brief (up to one page) introduction to your essay in which you tell your reader what you think you accomplished as a reader and writer in producing the essay and what you now think of the essay you produced. Comment, too, if space allows, on which activities of the writing workshop contributed most to your progress as a reader and writer and what contributed least. Share these introductions with classmates and discuss them in class. Attach your introduction to your paper when you submit it to your teacher or put it in your writing portfolio.

2. Apply your skills. Try one or more of the following activities.

- **Cross curricular** Select an historical event or act of an important historical figure and consider possible ways to interpret the event. What did it "mean" in its time? What does it mean from a contemporary perspective?
- **General** The real meanings in political cartoons or even comic strips are not always immediately clear. Choose a cartoon, examine it closely, and write an essay discussing your response to it.
- **General** A photograph represents a moment frozen in time. Browse through some books of famous photographs. Select one and write an interpretation of what you see. Include both an objective interpretation (what you can actually see) and a subjective interpretation (the hidden or implied meaning).
- **Related assignments** Follow the suggestions on pages 256–264 to write an interpretation of art or director's notes on a play.

◀ FOR YOUR
PORTFOLIO ▮

Interpretive
Essay   **253**

Interpreting Art

The Persistence of Memory,
by Salvador Dali, oil on canvas.
Salvador Dali Museum, St. Petersburg, Florida

Painters, writers, composers, and other artists usually have a purpose or vision in mind when they create a work of art. However, the artist also strives to create something that will allow an individual to respond to the work in a personal way. That response may take a variety of forms. It may produce an emotional reaction, stir memories or associations, or raise questions about what is going on in the work or why the artist chose a certain technique.

As you study this painting by Salvador Dali, how do you interpret his famous soft watches? What meaning do you draw from his other images?

Think A N D Respond

What response to his painting do you think Dali wanted to evoke in the viewer? What kind of images did he choose to include? Consider your first reaction to the painting. What do the timepieces suggest to you? What do you make of the rest of the landscape? What images or ideas would you focus on in writing an essay about this painting?

255

INVITATION
— TO —
Write

Now that you've studied the Dali painting and thought about its effects on you, write your interpretation of some work of art—a painting, sculpture, or piece of music—that interests you.

Interpreting art is a very personal matter. Your ideas about a painting, sculpture, or piece of music don't have to match the artist's purpose or intention. For example, you and a friend may interpret the same sculpture in completely different ways. You may hear altogether different values in a piece of music than your parents do. Discovering accepted standards of evaluation is not necessary at this time. What counts is honest observation and reaction.

PLANNING AN INTERPRETATION

HANDBOOKS
FOR HELP & PRACTICE

Personal
Techniques,
pp. 322–324
Other Techniques,
pp. 327–329
Unity/Coherence,
pp. 371–385
Adequate Detail,
pp. 405–406

1. Choose a work of art to interpret. You may use either the Dali painting or some other work—another painting or a drawing, photograph, sculpture, song, or symphony. You may already have a favorite work in mind, or you may wish to explore something unfamiliar. Browse through recordings and art books at the library. A work that makes you think—that raises some questions—will give you the most to say. The limp watches in Dali's painting, for example, are much more open to interpretation than a very naturalistic landscape or even a famous portrait. If possible, experience the work of art in person. Go to a museum, gallery, or concert hall where you can see or hear the work itself.

2. Record your reactions and observations. Once you have chosen a subject, really study it. One way to make sure that you are observing carefully is to ask yourself questions. For example, if there are people in a painting or photograph, ask who they are. Are they rich or poor? Is the setting rural or urban, contemporary or historical? What are the people doing or what is happening to them? What do they seem to be feeling?

Ask yourself how the work makes you feel. Does the Dali painting, for example, make you uneasy? Amused? Angry? Upset? If this odd landscape were real and actually in front of you, how would you feel? Would you like to be in such a situation? Make notes of your answers, and then ask yourself what images in the work evoked your feelings and led you to your conclusions.

 Writer's Choice You may want to enrich your own responses by discussing the work with a friend or reading about the artist's life, or you may choose to keep yourself free from other people's ideas and reactions.

DRAFTING AN INTERPRETATION

1. Begin with a description of the work. Your reader may never have seen or heard of the work. So, in addition to identifying the subject by title and artist, describe the work clearly enough so that your reader can follow your points. Add details as you write. Use colorful language and create specific images for your reader. With the Dali painting, for example, you might start by describing the landscape—the sky, the cliffs, the tree—and the colors. Then you might explain the unexpected elements—the limp timepieces, the geometrical platforms, the peculiar shape just below center.

You might discuss a piece of music in terms of the emotional quality of the performance, its rhythms and melodic themes, or perhaps the most prominent instruments.

2. Discuss your reactions to the work. Begin with a sentence or two that presents what you think is most important about the work and why you think so. Then use details from the work to support your idea. For example, you might begin a discussion of the Dali painting by saying, "Dali's painting is like a startling dream in which time and space melt and change. If I woke up in this landscape, I would feel that nothing was understandable or reliable." You would then describe the soft watches and geometrical shapes to support your idea.

3. Write a conclusion. Summarize your reactions in a few sentences, including the significance of the work for you personally. State what you learned about yourself by examining your reaction to the work, for example, or summarize your new understanding of the artist or the work.

Writing
TIP
Don't try to say too much or make too many points. Limit yourself to one main focus.

Carnaval, by Haitian
Emilano di Cavalcanti

REVIEWING YOUR WRITING

1. Go back to the work of art. Check your writing against the original work. Have you failed to mention any important aspects?

2. Check your organization and detail. Make sure your writing is clearly structured and that you have supported your ideas with details from the work. Can your writing be made more interesting, colorful, or accurate?

3. Evaluate your conclusion. Have you ended with a clear restatement of your main idea?

4. Use a peer reader. Ask a friend to read your interpretation and give you feedback based on your specific questions.

PUBLISHING AND PRESENTING

- **Submit your interpretation to your school or community newspaper.** A subject familiar to readers is best, such as a sculpture on the courthouse lawn.
- **Bring a reproduction or recording of the work to class.** Share your interpretation with your classmates, or lead a discussion involving possible alternative interpretations.
- **Arrange a debate or round-table discussion.** If you and a classmate have interpreted and evaluated the same work, discuss and defend your own interpretation while taking account of the reactions of the other participants.

On the Lightside

ESPERANTO

One hundred years ago a young Polish man dedicated his life to using language to bring the people of the world together. Ludwig Zamenhof grew up in Bialystock, Poland, a city made up of people from diverse racial and cultural backgrounds who spoke many different languages. Zamenhof believed that many of the disagreements among people could be eliminated if everyone spoke a common language. So he invented one.

Zamenhof devised a new language made up of root words from many European languages. To promote his invention, he wrote about it extensively under the pen name Doktoro Esperanto, which means "Dr. Hopeful" in the new language. Soon, the language became known as Esperanto. It uses a twenty-eight-letter alphabet, and each letter has only one sound (unlike English, in which vowels and some consonants can have several different sounds). It has only sixteen rules of grammar to remember and, unlike English, there are no exceptions to the rules. See if you can translate the following Esperanto sentence:

La inteligenta persono lernas la interlingvon Esperanto rapide kaj facile.

Zamenhof's followers continue to promote Esperanto as an aide to international understanding. In addition, as the sentence above explains, "the intelligent person learns the international language Esperanto quickly and easily."

Related ASSIGNMENT

Director's Notes

Notes for

MATEWAN

by John Sayles

One of the most important people in the production of any drama is the director. He or she is responsible for creating an interpretation of the work and communicating that vision to the actors.

Directors often write notes explaining their ideas. John Sayles wrote these notes while preparing to direct *Matewan*, a movie about a strike at an Appalachian coal mine in the 1920's. The character Hickey works for the company that is trying to end the strike. The information in Sayles's notes was used by the actor who played Hickey in the film.

As you read, imagine that you will be acting the role of Hickey and think about how these notes might help you portray the character.

This is a character sheet, a [few thoughts] that I'd either mail to the actors in advance or give to them when they got to West Virginia. Since we didn't have time for rehearsal before shooting, these were meant to help the actors think about their characters and to be the basis for further discussions we might have.

Hickey

A few thoughts on the character of Hickey. Hickey is someone who volunteered for service in [World War I], probably out of boredom, and was older than most of the cannon-fodder he found around him in the trenches. He was in some heavy, grisly hand-to-hand combat . . . and his mind has not returned from the place where it's kill-or-be-killed. Hickey feeds on violence, or at least the atmosphere of violence, and everything he does is to control and shape that atmosphere. When he meets someone new he immedi-ately starts to push to see if they'll push back and how much—he's constantly filing informa-tion for future conflict. He wants people to be afraid of him, realizing that intimidation is often more effective than actual violence. He realizes he is a foreigner in a guerrilla conflict—anyone, man, woman or child, could shoot him in the back at any time. . . . Hickey has a dog-eat-dog world view and wants to be the big dog. Violence is a sickness with him. . . .

Think AND Respond

What was John Sayles's purpose for writing these notes? Would these notes help you if you were preparing to play the role of Hickey? What else might you like to know about Hickey? If you were directing a production of a play, what might you say to help the actors play their parts? What would you say in program notes for the theater audience?

INVITATION
TO
Write

You have read film director John Sayles's notes about one character in his movie. Now write director's notes for a play, movie, or television program you are familiar with—or one you would like to create.

Any works that are performed, and not just read—plays, films, TV shows, and even music videos—must be interpreted by a director. The script usually includes basic stage or camera directions, but the director must consider what the work means as a whole and how to get that meaning across to the audience. One of the ways the director does this is by helping the actors develop their characters. The director offers insight into the personalities of the characters and suggests specific ways for the actors to speak and move. The director also works with other professionals to decide how scenes should be staged and what costumes, sets, and lighting should be used.

DEVELOPING DIRECTOR'S NOTES

HANDBOOKS
FOR HELP & PRACTICE

Limiting a Topic,
pp. 340–341
Elaboration,
pp. 364–369
Reference Works,
pp. 490–494
Other Information
Sources,
pp. 495–496

1. Choose a work.   Think of a play, movie, or TV show that really interested you. Consider also works you have read: *A Raisin in the Sun, Marty,* or *Julius Caesar,* for example. In addition to reading and studying these works in class, you may be able to see a staged, filmed, or videotaped production.

2. Explore the work.   Try freewriting about your personal vision of the whole work and its individual aspects, such as theme, character, setting, costuming, and casting. Consider, for example, whether you think the work should be presented in a realistic way, or perhaps be set in an imaginary country or distant time period. Should the approach be humorous or serious? Mr. Sayles's vision of the *Matewan* story was serious and realistic, and his final film looks and feels almost like a documentary.

Writer's Choice Will your notes explore your overall vision of the work or focus on one aspect, such as one character or the costumes or setting? If you focus on one aspect, it may be helpful to work out in your mind how that aspect fits into a larger vision.

3. Focus your writing. Decide on a specific topic and the direction you want to take with that topic. Write down your ideas and do any research you may need to flesh out your topic. In writing about costumes for *A Raisin in the Sun,* for example, you might start by noting what the script says about each character's clothing. Then in order to fill in necessary details you could do some research on the fashions of the 1950's.

4. Identify your audience. As the director, you may wish to address your notes to all the actors and designers, or to a smaller group, such as the actors only, or maybe to a single individual, such as the lighting designer. You also may choose to share your overall vision of the play with the theater audience by writing notes that will appear in the program.

A Raisin in the Sun concerns a black family's dream of leaving the ghetto.

WRITING DIRECTOR'S NOTES

1. Draft your notes. Begin putting your ideas on paper. Director's notes are generally presented in a straightforward informational style. However, consider your audience when deciding how much information to include. Program notes are usually only a few paragraphs, but notes for actors and designers require more detail and explanation and may be several pages long. Remember Mr. Sayles's statement that his notes "were meant to help the actors think about their characters and to be the basis for further discussions." Notes for the lighting designer, however, would be aimed at helping him or her think about the mood and atmosphere and how the lighting might enhance these elements.

2. Elaborate on your ideas. The interpretation skills presented in the guided assignment can help you clarify and develop your ideas. Mr. Sayles's notes about Hickey are based on his interpretation of Hickey's character and function in the plot. They also reflect his observation and understanding of how people behave. Descriptive details, examples, and quotations from the work are good types of elaboration. In writing about a film or TV show, you might also want to discuss technical directions for camera setups and angles from such teleplays as *Marty.*

Alfred Hitchcock's individual style of directing makes his movies distinctive. Illustration by Don Brennan

Writing
—TIP—

If appropriate, quote from the work or draw rough sketches to help the actors or designer see what you want.

R EVIEWING YOUR WRITING

1. Look again at the work you chose.   Does your interpretation of the work make sense? Are there additional points you need to cover? Do you need to broaden or narrow your focus? Should you rethink your interpretation?

2. Ask a friend to respond to your director's notes.   Does he or she find your notes clear and complete? Have you said too much? Too little?

P UBLISHING AND PRESENTING

- **Discuss your notes with your "cast."**   Ask classmates to read the work you've chosen together with your notes. Assign them each a role (technician, actor) and begin to develop a production.
- **Stage or videotape a scene from the work you chose.**   Use your director's notes as a guide. You also might sketch several costumes or a set design.
- **Submit your director's notes to fulfill an assignment.**   Consult with your teacher about using your notes as a writing assignment on a dramatic work.

Sentence

Varying the Position of Absolute Phrases

You have seen that absolute phrases provide a concise and emphatic way to join related ideas in sentences. These phrases occur in many positions in the sentences of professional writers: at the beginning (opener), between subject and verb (S-V split), and at the end (closer). If you need to review absolute phrases before continuing, study pages 233–235.

MODELS

1. (Opener)   The sharp edges gone, he continued to work with the leaf, pulling off half-inch-wide strips and laying them in a pile.
   Robb White, *Deathwatch*

                        s
2. (S-V Split)   Miss Hearne, her face burning, hardly
                        v
   listened to these words.
   Brian Moore, *The Lonely Passion of Judith Hearne*

3. (Closer)   She walked along slowly, scuffing her heels, her face wearing the expression of a person surfeited with food.
   Jane Bowles, "A Stick of Green Candy"

Punctuation Note: Absolute phrases are set off by commas.

A. Unscrambling Sentences   First identify the absolute phrase in each set. Then write out the sentence, using commas as needed. Some sets can be unscrambled in several ways; be sure your version makes sense. Use each position (opener, S-V split, closer) at least once. Punctuate correctly.

Example   a. a heap of boys
               b. their hiking lunches half devoured
               c. daring each other in shrieky whispers
               d. there they stood in the dead city

Result   There they stood in the dead city, a heap of boys, their hiking lunches half devoured, daring each other in shrieky whispers.
   Ray Bradbury, *The Martian Chronicles*

Alternate: <u>Their hiking lunches half devoured</u>, there they stood in the dead city, a heap of boys, daring each other in shrieky whispers.

1. a. his hands full of tops and marbles, old dusty kites and junk collected through the years
   b. and a moment later he appeared
   c. there were sounds of sweeping and cleaning out

   Ray Bradbury,
   The Martian Chronicles

2. a. high in the air
   b. his hands thrust in his short jacket pockets
   c. stood staring out to sea
   d. a little figure

   Katherine Mansfield,
   "The Voyage"

3. a. she got up in an apologetic sort of way
   b. her teeth chattering
   c. at last
   d. and moved toward the better protected rear of the car as she went on a palpable search for hot pipes

   Henry Syndor Harrison,
   "Miss Hinch"

4. a. toward his home
   b. now, in the waning daylight
   c. his arms swinging as he moved onto the unpaved road
   d. he turned into Glover Street

   Norman Katlov,
   "The Torn Invitation"

B. Combining Sentences Sometimes absolute phrases occur in a series of two or more within a sentence. The effect can be strong and dramatic. In the sets below, change each sentence after the first into an absolute phrase. Then insert the absolute phrases into the first sentence as a series. Insert your series in whichever of the three positions (opener, S-V split, closer) makes the most sense.

Punctuation Note: Series of absolute phrases are set off by commas.

1. He caught the lantern and ran outside into the gale, and he saw Gabilan weakly shambling away into the darkness. Gabilan's head was down. Gabilan's legs were working slowly and mechanically. **John Steinbeck, _The Red Pony_**

2. It ran, leaving prints six inches deep wherever it settled its weight. Its pelvic bones were crushing aside trees and bushes. Its taloned feet were clawing damp earth. **Ray Bradbury, "A Sound of Thunder"**

3. Father lay crumped up on the stone floor of the pantry, clad just in his vest and trousers. His face was down. His arms were twisted at a curious angle. **Christy Brown, _Down All the Days_**

4. A hill began to rise before them, and up it the horse sped. His breath was whirring and rattling in his throat. But his strength was still unspent.

Esther Forbes, "Break-Neck Hill"

5. In the long mirror across the room, she saw herself. Her hair was hanging wild. Her long bare legs were scratched. Her broadly smiling face was dirt-streaked. Her torn skirt was dangling. Her dog was laughing up at her.

Dorothy Canfield Fisher, *The Apprentice*

C. Imitating Sentences Imitate the structure of each model, using your own words.

1. Men, <u>their caps pulled down, their collars turned up</u>, swung by.

Katherine Mansfield, "The Voyage"

2. He joined the laughter this time, <u>his belt creaking</u>, and <u>the perspiration standing out all over his face</u>. **Evan Conell, Jr., "The Condor and the Guests"**

3. He stood watching the approaching locomotive, <u>his teeth chattering, his lips drawn away from them in a frightened smile</u>. **Willa Cather, "Paul's Case"**

4. <u>His feet sinking in the soft nap of the carpet, his hand in one pocket clutching the money</u>, he felt as if he could squeal or laugh out loud.

Theodore Dreiser, *An American Tragedy*

5. Turning, <u>his shoulder pressing against the wall</u>, he moved until he was standing sideways, <u>his feet together on the narrow ledge, his side hugging the wall</u>, as he faced the wide opening of the V. **Robb White, *Deathwatch***

Application Use one of the sentences below to start a paragraph that could be part of a story. Make up the rest of the paragraph, including several sentences containing absolute phrases. Vary the positions of these phrases. Write an absolute phrase series to lend power to the last sentence of your paragraph. Use commas correctly.

1. A beautiful animal, it lay in the position of a marble lion, its head toward a man sitting on an upturned bucket outside the cage. **Frank Bonham, *Chief***

2. In the far corner the man was still asleep, snoring slightly on the intaking breath, his head back against the wall. **Ernest Hemingway, "The Undefeated"**

Grammar Refresher For information on other types of phrases and their placement within sentences, see Handbook 32, pages 586–603.

Sketchbook

The future of these majestic birds, California condors, is in doubt. Less than thirty of them survive today in the United States. Every year, pieces of our heritage disappear. What else is disappearing? Why?

Additional Sketches

If you could live in any period in history, what period would you choose?

What souvenirs would you bring back from a trip to the moon?

Reports

Guided Assignment

RESEARCH REPORT

Related Assignment

SATURATION REPORT

New York, Night, by Georgia O'Keefe (detail)

Halfway through the game, you hear the sportscaster say, "The last time a left-handed pitcher hit a grand slam was twenty years ago." *The man sounds like he has been to every baseball game ever played!* you think in amazement. Actually, a researcher working behind the scenes dug up that fact while the game was in progress.

Research is a way of tapping into the wealth of knowledge that has been accumulating throughout the world since the invention of writing. In this workshop, you will use research to gather information from various sources for use in writing a research report and a saturation report.

Research Report

FROM
CALIFORNIA'S REVENGE

BY ANN FINKBEINER

When you research a topic, you have the opportunity to discover fresh insights about even familiar subjects. For example, you probably know that many earthquakes have occurred in California, but are you aware of the destructive quakes that have shaken other parts of the country? Writer Ann Finkbeiner decided to research this subject for a magazine article. As you read this excerpt, notice the types of sources, both current and historical, that she consulted. The skills she used in developing this article are the same skills needed in creating a research paper.

The earthquake that struck near Santa Cruz on October 17, 1989, killed 62 people and was felt over 66,000 square miles. But most of San Francisco and large parts of Santa Cruz itself were unscathed. The earthquake that struck Charleston [South Carolina] on August 31, 1886, flattened the city. Few buildings went untouched. Nearby dams burst, and the floods washed trains off their tracks. In a town of 50,000, as many as 110 people died. The quake cracked walls in Chicago, 750 miles away; it was felt over an area of 1.5 million square miles, from Massachusetts to Wisconsin to Bermuda. . . .

Charleston's quake was not the strongest ever to strike east of the Rocky Mountains. In December 1811 and January and February 1812 the area around the Mississippi River town of New Madrid, Missouri, was rocked by three earthquakes, the description of which is a series of superlatives.

John Bradbury, a Scottish naturalist who was traveling down the Mississippi to collect plant specimens when the first quake occurred, wrote that the sound was "equal to the loudest thunder but more hollow and vibrating." Other sources reported geysers of sand and black water shooting into the air as high as trees, leaving behind craters 5 to 30 feet wide. The ground rolled in waves several feet high, knocking people down. Collapsing riverbanks changed the Mississippi's course and even created new lakes; one of them, Reelfoot Lake, now covers 18,000 acres 20 feet deep and is littered with the trunks of drowned cypress trees. "All nature," wrote Bradbury, "seemed running into chaos."

Not only were the New Madrid earthquakes strong—judging from their effects they were probably between magnitudes 8 and 9—but their reach was unparalleled. They cracked sidewalks in Charleston and collapsed scaffolding around the Capitol in Washington. They damaged well-constructed buildings over an area of 235,000 square miles, 20 times the area damaged by the San Francisco quake of 1906 (a magnitude 8.3). People felt the shaking over perhaps 4 million square miles, the largest area ever affected by any recorded quake. . . .

Other eastern earthquakes, although not as spectacular, have been strong enough to cause damage. In 1929 a 7.2 quake on the coast of Newfoundland set off a large underwater landslide and triggered a tsunami that killed 27 people. The Charlevoix region, northeast of the city of Quebec along the St. Lawrence River, has had five

earthquakes over the past 330 years that were magnitude 6 or greater; the most recent one, a magnitude 7 in 1925, was felt strongly as far away as New York City.

New York itself is not immune: in 1985 a magnitude 4 quake, centered just north of the city in Westchester County, woke up people throughout the area. Although it didn't do much else, it was an unsettling reminder. The fault that triggered it is one of a family of intersecting faults, some of which extend directly under Manhattan; among them are faults under 125th Street and 145th Street, as well as several under the East River. "For years now I've been beating the drum that seismicity isn't dead around New York," says geologist Charles Merguerian of Hofstra University, who has trekked into subway and water tunnels to map the city's hidden faults. "The mechanism may be different from the one in California, but it warrants concern."

All told, since the late seventeenth century eastern North America has had 16 earthquakes larger than magnitude 6 and several hundred larger than magnitude 4. (Each step up in magnitude increases an earthquake's strength by ten times, so magnitude 6 is 100 times stronger than magnitude 4.) Although Charlevoix and New Madrid are now the most seismically active areas—they feel minor tremors on a regular basis—quakes have occurred in many other parts of the East. The past century happens to have been comparatively quiet, which is why there is a lack of public concern.

Think AND Respond

What types of details did Finkbeiner discover during her research? What new insights about earthquakes does her report give you? What ideas does her report give you for subjects you could research?

INVITATION
—TO—
Write

Ann Finkbeiner researched and wrote a fact-filled report on earthquakes in North America. Gather information about a subject that interests you and write a short research report about it.

Any question that piques your interest can be a starting point for a research report. For example, you may find yourself wondering: What is the weather like on Venus? How do dogs communicate? What is the future of video games? If you ask a question that is rich in possibilities, you probably won't find the answer in any one place. Writing a research report is like gathering the pieces of a puzzle. You might find one piece in a book, another in a magazine article, and another in an interview with someone. As with any puzzle that is put together for the very first time, your finished report may create a picture no one has ever seen before.

PREWRITE AND EXPLORE

HANDBOOKS
FOR HELP & PRACTICE

**Exploring Ideas,
pp. 330–332
Limiting a Topic,
pp. 340–341
Thesis Statements,
pp. 355–356**

1. Look for ideas.   Since you will gather a great deal of new information in writing a research report, think of a topic you already want to know more about. Even if you have no choice about the general subject, you may be able to find an interesting aspect to focus on. For example, if you like mysteries, and you are asked to write a history paper about early settlers in America, you could focus on the disappearance of the Roanoke settlement around 1590. One or more of these activities may help you generate ideas.

Exploratory Activities

- **Listing** If your broad subject was not assigned, list all the subjects you thought about today or recently. These can include news events, subjects you study in school, ideas from your reading, and special interests you would like to pursue.

- **Clustering** To find a unique angle on an assigned subject, or to focus on any broad area of interest, work with a group of friends to create a cluster diagram. Write the subject in the center of a piece of paper and circle it. Outside the circle, write any related ideas that come to mind. Circle these ideas and draw lines connecting them to the central subject. Branch out from each of the related ideas in the same way.
- **Knowledge Inventory** Ann Finkbeiner's work on likely earthquake locations cast new light on a subject we might have thought we knew about. List what you already know about your assigned subject or broad area of interest from your own experience, your reading, your classes, and other sources. Then list questions you would like to answer about your subject and types of information you could gather to answer them.
- **Exploring everyday items** Look at the items around you now and ask yourself such questions as Who invented it? Where did it come from? What is it made of? If you have no answers, you may have located a topic for your research report.
- **Reading literature** Think of literary works you have read that are based on historical figures or events, such as Shakespeare's *Julius Caesar*. What ideas for historical research do these works suggest to you?

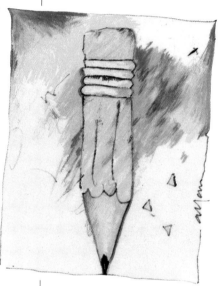

2. Choose a specific topic. If you haven't yet found a subject for your report, check the "Apply Your Skills" section on page 294 or the Sketchbook on page 268 for more ideas. Doing some preliminary reading on the most promising topics can help you make a decision and narrow a topic to a manageable size for a short report. Skim relevant articles in encyclopedias and specialized dictionaries and scan the tables of contents and indexes of books on your general subject to see how the topic can be divided into smaller parts.

One student, Jenna Lind, had been fascinated by lasers ever since she saw a demonstration at a museum. To narrow this broad subject, she did some preliminary research and found that lasers are used in a variety of fields. She made the cluster diagram on the next page to show her findings and to help her choose a report topic. Throughout this workshop, you will follow the process Jenna used in researching and writing her research report.

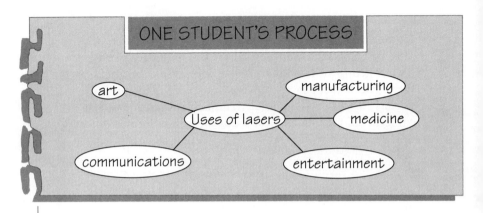

ONE STUDENT'S PROCESS

art — Uses of lasers — manufacturing
Uses of lasers — medicine
communications — entertainment

Since Jenna was interested in a career as a surgeon, she decided to focus on how lasers are used in medicine.

3. Determine the purpose of your report. Finding a purpose—a reason for writing—can help keep you focused during your writing process. It may even help you find a unique approach to your topic. Also think about your personal goals, or what you hope to accomplish by researching and writing your report.

The chart below lists examples of purposes and report topics.

ONE STUDENT'S PROCESS

Purpose of Report	_Example of Topic_
To inform the audience	The medical uses of lasers: an overview
To examine cause and effect	How has the discovery of lasers changed medicine?
To compare and contrast	Laser surgery versus more traditional methods
To analyze the topic	Are lasers a "miracle cure?"

Writer's Choice You can set your general purpose and specific goals now or wait until you have done more research. Either way, keep in mind that you can always modify your goals and purposes later in the process.

4. Write a statement of controlling purpose. Before you begin researching your topic, write a **statement of controlling purpose** that briefly tells what you think your paper will be about. This statement will help you stay on the right track as you look for suitable sources of information about your topic. Your statement of controlling purpose will also help you glean the most useful, relevant information from those sources.

Keep in mind, however, that your statement of controlling purpose is flexible at this stage of your writing process. You may find that you want to change your topic or purpose during your research. For example, instead of analyzing your subject, you may decide to compare and contrast it with something else. In that case, you will need to revise your statement of controlling purpose. After you've completed your research, you will use your statement of controlling purpose as the basis of your thesis statement.

Once Jenna had limited her topic to that of lasers in medicine, she knew what information she needed to cover in her report. Here is her statement of controlling purpose.

ONE STUDENT'S PROCESS

I will define laser technology, review the history of lasers in the field of medicine, and describe the many ways doctors in various specialties are using lasers to heal the sick.

RESEARCH YOUR TOPIC

1. Prepare research questions. Gathering information is perhaps the most important part of writing a research report. Nothing—not even good writing—can save a poorly researched report. Therefore, focus your information hunt by making a list of questions you want your research to answer. Add more questions to your list as you learn about your topic.

Jenna's list of questions is shown on the next page. Notice that all her questions relate in some way to her controlling purpose.

HANDBOOKS
FOR HELP & PRACTICE

Study and Research Skills,
pp. 475–481

Source Materials,
pp. 481–484

The Library and Other Informational Sources,
pp. 486–496

Outline Form,
pp. 846–847

- What is a laser?
- How was the laser developed?
- How do lasers work?

- What can lasers do?
- What are some of the medical uses of lasers?
- Are lasers a new "miracle cure"?

PROBLEM SOLVING

What resources are most appropriate for my topic?

2. Use the resources of your school and local libraries. Begin your research by looking for books and magazine and newspaper articles on your specific topic. Your library's card or computer catalog lists the titles of books you'll want to examine. Also look up your subject in a magazine index, such as the *Readers' Guide to Periodical Literature,* or a newspaper index, such as the *New York Times Index.*

3. Evaluate the sources you find. Once you identify sources on your topic, you'll need to examine them and determine their usefulness. Remember, you shouldn't judge a book by its cover, and that goes for magazines and newspapers too. Look inside, and make sure that each source meets certain standards:

- **The author is an authority.** Someone who has written several books or articles on your subject or whose work has been published in a well-respected newspaper or journal may be considered an authority.
- **The source is up-to-date.** In some fields, such as science and medicine, using recently published material is very important.
- **The source is respected.** In general, tabloid newspapers and popular-interest magazines are not suitable sources for a report.

The information you'll find in your library's reference books is nearly always reliable. The chart on the next page lists a variety of references available at your school or local library. Be sure to ask your librarian if he or she can recommend other references on your specific topic.

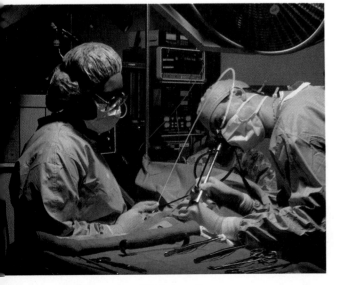

Laser technology has revolutionized the treatment of operable conditions.

Library Reference Materials

Reference	Contents	Examples
Encyclopedias	detailed articles on nearly all subjects	*Encyclopaedia Britannica, The World Book Encyclopedia, Encyclopedia of Computer Science, Dictionary of American History, Harper Encyclopedia of Science*
Almanacs and Yearbooks	up-to-date facts, statistics, and unusual information	*Facts on File, Information Please Almanac*
Atlases	detailed maps and geographical information	*National Geographic Atlas, Times Atlas of the World*
Biographical References	detailed information about the lives of well-known people	*Dictionary of American Biography, Webster's Biographical Dictionary, Dictionary of American Authors*
Vertical File	pamphlets, booklets, catalogs, handbooks, and clippings filed by subject	
Indexes	listings of articles that have appeared in periodicals	*Readers' Guide to Periodical Literature, Social Science Index, Art Index*

COMPUTER TIP

At some libraries you can do a computer search for source materials related to a particular topic. Ask the librarian to show you how to conduct such a search.

Remember that interviewing people who are knowledgeable about your topic can also be an excellent way to gather information. Ann Finkbeiner, for example, interviewed geologists when she researched her report on earthquakes.

4. Make source cards. After you locate potential sources, skim them to decide which ones you might use for your report. If a source seems useful, record complete publication information for the source on a three-by-five-inch index card. You will need this information when you credit the source for ideas in your report and when you create a Works Cited list. Follow the guidelines below when you make source cards.

Research
━TIP━
The list of forms for Works Cited entries on page 287 can help you see what information you should include on source cards for a wider variety of source types.

Guidelines for Source Cards

- **Books** Write the author or editor's complete name, the title, the name and location of the publisher, and the copyright date.
- **Magazines and Newspapers** Write the author's complete name (unless the article is unsigned), the title of the article, the name and date of the magazine or newspaper, and the page number(s) of the article.
- **Encyclopedias** Write the author's complete name (unless the entry is unsigned), the title of the entry, and the name and copyright date of the encyclopedia.

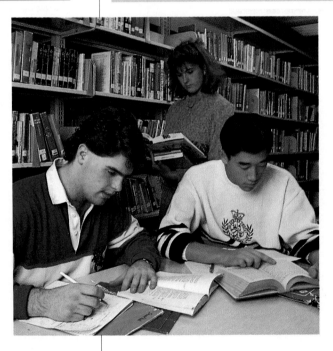

Be sure to number each source in the upper right-hand corner of the card for easy reference during note taking. That way, you can avoid rewriting the title and author in your notes each time you use a source that you will eventually need to credit in your report. Just jot down the source-card number instead. You may also want to include on each source card a library call number and a note about where you found the source, in case you ever need to find it again. Three of Jenna's source cards are shown on the next page.

Source Card for Book

Source number ①

Author   Book title
Bender, Lionel. <u>Lasers in Action</u>.

New York: Bookwright, 1985.
City of publication/Publisher/Copyright date

Location of source   TA1520
Public Library   Library call number   .M38

Source Card for Magazine or Newspaper Article

②

Article title
Cowley, Geoffrey. "Hanging Up the Knife."

<u>Newsweek</u> 12 Feb. 1990: 83–87.
Name and date of publication/Page number(s)

Public Library

Source Card for Encyclopedia Entry

③

Entry title
De Maria, Anthony J. "Laser." <u>The World</u>

<u>Book Encyclopedia</u>. 1993 ed.
Encyclopedia title/Copyright date

School Library

5. Take notes from your sources. As you review your sources, look for information that suits your purpose and that answers your research questions. When you find material you want to remember and include in your report, take notes, using one or more of the following techniques.

- **Quotation** Copy from the original text word for word, including all punctuation. Use quotation marks to signal the beginning and the end of the quotation. Use this method when you think the author's own words would best support a point you want to make in your report.
- **Paraphrase** Restate material in your own words. A paraphrase captures both the main ideas and the supporting details of an original passage. Use this method when your notes need to be very detailed.
- **Summary** In your own words, record only the main idea of a passage. Use this method when you need to remember a general idea.

Research TIP

Notice that the order and the punctuation of the information on these source cards matches the format of the same information in entries A, F, and I on page 287. If you use the correct formats on your source cards, it will be easy to copy the information into your Works Cited list when your report is complete.

The following guidelines can help you take notes efficiently.

Guidelines for Note Taking

- Use a separate four-by-six-inch index card for each quotation or piece of information. At the top of each card, write a brief heading that summarizes the main idea of the note. Later, you can group your cards according to their main ideas and arrange them into a logical order to help you create your draft.

- In the upper right-hand corner of each note card, write the number of the corresponding source card.

- At the bottom of each note card, indicate whether the material is a quotation, a paraphrase, a summary, or an idea of your own. This will help you to remember whether the idea needs to be credited to a source.

- At the end of each note, write the number of the page on which you found the material in your source. You'll need the page number to give credit to the source if you use the information in your report; you may also need it to verify a fact or a quotation or to gather more information from the source.

Here is a note card Jenna wrote as she read one of her sources.

Source number

Laser—Definition by Example   Main idea

A laser is a device that strengthens light, producing an extremely intense beam of light—so strong it can burn a hole in a diamond or travel to the moon and back. Also very precise—can cut through skin of a tomato without touching the meat. 83 Page number

(Paraphrase) Type of note

6. Write a thesis statement.   Once you complete your research, you'll be ready to write a thesis statement that expresses the main idea you will develop in your report and that tells what you will accomplish in your writing. A thesis statement may also indicate the organizational pattern you will follow and reflect your tone and point of view. You may wish to use your statement of controlling purpose as the basis of your thesis statement.

Remember Jenna's controlling purpose:

> I will define laser technology, review the history of lasers in the field of medicine, and describe the many ways doctors in various specialties are using lasers to heal the sick.

This statement was especially effective in helping Jenna to focus her research and to find information that suited her purpose. However, Jenna knew that her thesis statement should be part of an opening paragraph that would both interest her readers and provide a general introduction to the topic. Here is the thesis statement Jenna wrote to provide a focus for her draft.

> Lasers have had perhaps their most important and most dramatic effects in the field of medicine.

When Jenna drafted her introduction, she revised her thesis statement again. If you read the opening paragraph of her report on page 289, you'll see that she reordered her statement and added an important transition to make her ideas flow smoothly.

7. Begin organizing your information. First review your note cards and sort them into groups. The information on the cards in each group should be related in some way. For example, Jenna put her cards about each of the medical uses of lasers into separate groups. As you sort your cards, you may find that some of them contain information that no longer suits your purpose or that doesn't fit in with the other material you gathered. Set those cards aside; you may not need them when you draft your paper.

8. Make a working outline. An outline is a plan for the order in which you'll present your information. First put your groups of related note cards into an order that flows logically from one group to the next. Then write your outline. The main ideas and supporting details in your note cards can provide headings and subheadings for your outline. Remember that your working outline is only a plan you can follow as you write; you are always free to change your mind—and your plan—as you draft your report. Guidelines for standard outline form, as well as models of both sentence and topic outlines, can be found in the Appendix, pages 846–847.

Part of Jenna's topic outline is shown on the next page. Notice that she plans to provide general information about lasers in the beginning of her report before she details their medical uses.

Writing
——**TIP**——

A thesis statement tells the main idea of a piece of writing in the same way that a topic sentence tells the main idea of a paragraph.

Writing
——**TIP**——

Before you make a standard outline, try using a graphic organizer, such as a cluster diagram, a time line, or a tree diagram, to help you see how your information and your ideas are related.

ONE STUDENT'S PROCESS

Lasers and Medicine

Introduction—lasers' effects in the field of medicine

I. Origin of laser technology

II. Description of laser
   A. What it is
   B. Why it works
   C. How it works

III. Medical uses of lasers
   A. First medical uses of lasers
      1. Eye surgery
      2. Skin discoloration
   B. Surgeon's scalpel
   C. Heart and circulatory diseases

DRAFT AND DISCOVER

HANDBOOKS
FOR HELP & PRACTICE

Organization,
pp. 342–349

Elaboration,
pp. 364–369

Unity and Coherence,
pp. 371–385

Conclusions,
pp. 386–390

Incorporating Source Materials,
pp. 481–484

1. Begin writing. Start setting your ideas down on paper, using your outline as a guide. Remember, however, that you don't have to begin with the introduction or draft the sections of your paper in the order that they appear in the outline. You can begin wherever you feel most comfortable. Just make sure that you write one or more paragraphs for each of the headings in your outline and that you put the sections in order before you review your writing and revise your draft.

Writer's Choice If your note cards don't have all the information you need for a section of your report, you may either stop drafting and do more research or go on to another section of your outline and do more research later.

2. Share your own ideas and interpretations. Writing a report means more than restating the information you find in a number of sources. It means making inferences, analyzing and interpreting evidence, synthesizing material, and drawing a reasonable conclusion. Therefore, use the facts, examples, and other evidence you've gathered to back up your own ideas.

3. Avoid plagiarism. You need to tell your readers where you got the information—the direct quotations, paraphrases, and summaries—you include in your report. If you do not credit, or document, your sources, you will be committing **plagiarism,** the dishonest presentation of someone else's ideas as your own. The only material you do not need to credit is common knowledge—information that many people have—and your own unique thoughts and ideas.

4. Document your sources. Check with your teacher to see whether you should credit your sources by means of footnotes, endnotes, or parenthetical documentation. Parenthetical documentation is the most common way of crediting sources in the body of a paper. When you use parenthetical documentation, you put enough information about a source in parentheses so that a reader can find the full source listing on the Works Cited page. Usually, the parenthetical note includes a reference to the title or author of a source and the page number. Follow these guidelines for parenthetical documentation; you can consult Jenna's final draft on pages 289–293 for examples.

PROBLEM SOLVING

How can I acknowledge the sources I use?

Guidelines for Parenthetical Documentation

- **Work by one author**   Put the author's last name and the page reference in parentheses: (Lieberman 25–28). If you mention the author's name in the sentence, put only the page reference in parentheses: (25–28).

- **Work by more than one author**   Put the authors' last names and the page reference in parentheses: (Lobin and Wilk 15). If a source has more than three authors, give the first author's last name followed by *et al.* and the page reference: (Fishbeck et al. 122).

- **Work with no author given**   Give the title (or a shortened version of it) and the page reference: ("Laser Pioneers" 19).

- **One of two or more works by the same author**   Give the author's last name, the title or a shortened version, and the page reference: (Louis, Light Show 201).

- **Two or more works cited at the same place**   Use a semicolon to separate the entries: (Chaffin 33; Levenson 98).

5. Double-check the structure of your report. Your report should open with an interesting introduction that will grab readers' attention. Depending on your subject, a fascinating fact or short narrative may be effective. Your introduction may also include a thesis statement that reveals the main purpose of your report.

The body of your report should develop your thesis and present your information in a series of logically organized paragraphs. Chronological order often works for historical information or for steps in a process. Order of importance, order of impression, and comparison and contrast are other organizational techniques you might use.

Your report should close with a conclusion that summarizes your research and leaves your readers with a lasting impression. As part of your conclusion, you might even restate your thesis in different words.

6. Set your draft aside. Take a break for a day or two to distance yourself from your work. Then reread your draft and share it with a classmate. The following questions can guide your review.

REVIEW YOUR WRITING

Questions for Yourself

- Have I written a thesis statement and developed it in the body of my report?

- Have I included all the information I want to present? Have I included any information that doesn't suit my purpose? What should I add or delete?

- Are all my facts and quotations accurate? Have I documented my sources correctly?

- How can I organize my material more effectively?

- Have I met the requirements of this assignment?

- What did you like most about my report? What did you like least?
- Which parts of my report did you find most interesting or most surprising?
- What did you learn from my report that you didn't know before?
- Which parts of my report—if any—did you find difficult to understand? What confused you about these parts?
- What do you need more information about? What parts do you think I should leave out?
- Did the introduction capture your interest? Did the conclusion leave you satisfied?

R EVISE YOUR WRITING

1. Evaluate your responses. Review your own thoughts about your report and the comments and responses of those who read it. What changes do you want to make? Keep in mind that a well-written research report usually has the following characteristics.

Standards for Evaluation

An effective research report . . .

- begins with a compelling introduction, including a thesis statement that clearly states the report's topic and purpose.
- develops the topic logically in the body, using specific details.
- contains only accurate and relevant facts.
- weaves information from a variety of sources into a coherent whole.
- documents its sources clearly and correctly.
- uses exact quotations from sources effectively but sparingly to support ideas.
- reads smoothly and logically from beginning to end, using transitional devices to clarify the relationships among different ideas.
- includes an effective conclusion.

HANDBOOKS

FOR HELP & PRACTICE

Revision,
pp. 391–396

Self-Assessment
and Peer Response,
pp. 397–401

Achieving Clarity,
pp. 402–407

2. Problem-solve. When you've decided what changes you want to make, rework your draft. Jenna made the following changes after she received feedback from a peer reader.

You really seem to know your subject well! This is really interesting.

The detailed explanation is good, but I don't under-stand some of your terms. Photons? Coherently?

Can you make the contrast with ordinary light more clear?

The information about Star Wars is interesting, but does it belong in your report?

The laser works as follows. The atoms in a specially prepared substance are excited by an outside energy source. As the atoms begin to lose energy, they ~~shoot out~~ _emit_ photons, _or units of light energy_. The photon from one atom stimulates another atom to give off an identical photon. This process continues until a number of photons are proceeding _—that is, in the same direction and at the same wavelength_ coherently. This coherent pattern of photons is what makes laser light so intense. Ordinary light goes off _is incoherent: it_ in a number of different directions at many differ-ent wave lengths. The coherent laser light bounces between two mirrors in the laser, gaining tremendous power, the light released is thus a single intense beam. ~~That is how a laser works.~~ (De Maria 85; Jacob 37). ~~The Jedi knights in the movie Star Wars fought with lasers, their "lightsabers."~~

3. Prepare a Works Cited list. The last page of your report should be a Works Cited list that gives complete publication infor-mation for each source you actually used and documented in your report. Gather the appropriate source cards and alphabetize them by the author's last name or by the first word in the article title if no author is given. Then use the information to create a Works Cited list. The samples on the next page show what information to include and what spacing and punctuation to use. Also use Jenna's Works Cited list on page 293 as a model.

Models for Works Cited Entries

A. Book with one author

Ackerman, Diane.   <u>A Natural History of the Senses</u>.   New York: Random, 1990.

B. Book with two authors

Commager, Henry S., and Raymond H. Muessig.   <u>The Study and Teaching of History</u>.   Columbus: Merrill, 1980.

C. Book with an editor, but no single author

Carpenter, Humphrey, ed.   <u>The Letters of J.R.R. Tolkien</u>.   Boston: Houghton, 1981.

D. A poem, a short story, an essay, or a chapter in a collection of works by one author

Angelou, Maya.   "Remembering."   <u>Poems</u>.   New York: Bantam, 1986.   11.

E. A poem, a short story, an essay, or a chapter in a collection of works by several authors

Welty, Eudora.   "The Corner Store."   <u>Prose Models</u>.   Ed. Gerald Levin.   San Diego: Harcourt, 1984.   20–22.

F. An article in a magazine

Batten, Mary.   "Life Spans."   <u>Science Digest</u> Feb. 1984: 46–51.

G. An article in a newspaper

James, Noah.   "The Comedian Everyone Loves to Hate." <u>New York Times</u> 22 Jan. 1984, sec. 2: 23.

H. An editorial in a newspaper

"A Case for Leniency."   Editorial.   <u>Chicago Tribune</u> 10 Dec. 1993, sec. 1: 26.

I. An encyclopedia article

"Laser."   <u>Encyclopaedia Britannica: Micropaedia</u>.   1993 ed.

If the article is signed, put the author's name—last name first—before the article's title.

J. An interview

Barber, Theodore.   Personal interview.   29 Nov. 1992.

4. Proofread your report. Reread your final draft slowly and carefully and correct any errors you might have made in grammar, spelling, and mechanics. Also be sure to proofread any direct quotations against your note cards or against the original sources if you have them on hand. Then make a clean final copy of your report, following the Modern Language Association's guidelines for manuscript preparation, listed below.

MLA Manuscript Guidelines

- **Typing or printing** Type your final draft on a typewriter, or if you are using a word processor, print out a letter-quality copy. Do not justify the lines. If you have to write your final copy by hand, use dark blue or black ink and make sure your handwriting is neat and legible. Use only one side of the paper.

- **Paper** Use 8½-by-11-inch, white, nonerasable paper.

- **Margins** Except for page numbers, leave one-inch margins on all sides of the paper. Indent the first line of each paragraph five spaces from the left margin. Indent set-off quotations (those of more than four lines) ten spaces from the left margin. Do not indent long quotations from the right.

- **Spacing** The entire paper—including the heading and title on the first page, the body of the paper, quotations, and the Works Cited list—should be double-spaced.

- **Heading and title** One inch from the top of the first page and flush with the left margin, type your name, your teacher's name, the course name, and the date on separate lines. Below this heading, center the title on the page. Do not underline the title or put it in quotation marks, and do not use all capital letters.

- **Page numbers** Number all pages consecutively in the upper right-hand corner, one-half inch from the top. You may type your last name before the page number to identify your work in case a page is misplaced.

---

5. Share your report with others, then save it in your portfolio. Try giving an oral presentation of your report. You might include visual aids—such as illustrations, models, photographs, or graphs—to make your presentation more lively. You might also tell your audience about your research process.

Jenna Lind
Ms. Nathan
English II
14 May 1994

Lasers and Medicine: A Bright Ray of Hope

One morning in 1951, as physicist Charles H. Townes sat on a park bench, he had an idea—a practical way to obtain a very powerful form of energy from molecules. This energy, Townes believed, would be useful in scientific research, allowing extremely accurate measurement and analysis (153). Townes's discovery was more earthshaking than he realized. It provided the basis for the laser, a device that today has an amazing variety of applications in such fields as manufacturing, communications, and entertainment. It is in the field of medicine, however, that lasers have had perhaps their most important and most dramatic effects.

A laser, most simply defined, is a device that produces an extremely intense beam of light. The beam is so strong that it can burn a hole in a diamond or travel as far as the moon (De Maria 83). Yet it can be controlled with precision. In fact, it can cut through the skin of a tomato without touching the meat.

How does the laser produce such a powerful beam? All substances are made up of atoms and molecules, which possess energy. The addition of more energy from an outside source "excites" or adds energy to atoms and molecules. When the energy source is removed, the substance's atoms and molecules become less "excited" and give off their excess energy (Jacobs 37). This process is known as stimulated emission. Townes discovered how to use this stimulated emission to produce intense energy beams in the form of microwaves. His device

Includes strong introduction with striking anecdote

Provides a clear thesis statement

Clearly defines laser

Uses question as transition

Provides necessary definition of scientific term

was called a maser, from the first letters of the words microwave amplification by stimulated emission of radiation (Hecht and Teresi 50–51). In 1960, physicist Theodore Maiman constructed the first laser, which produces light rather than microwaves.

The laser works as follows. The atoms in a specially prepared substance are excited by an outside energy source. As the atoms begin to lose energy, they emit photons, or units of light energy. The photon from one atom stimulates another atom to give off an identical photon. This process continues until a number of photons are proceeding coherently—that is, in the same direction and at the same wavelength. This coherent pattern of photons is what makes laser light so intense. Ordinary light is incoherent: it goes off in a number of different directions at many different wavelengths. The coherent laser light bounces between two mirrors in the laser, gaining tremendous power. The light released is thus a single intense beam (De Maria 85; Jacobs 37).

One of the first medical applications of a laser beam was for surgery on the retina of the eye. In 1963, two doctors sent a laser beam through the transparent cornea of a patient's eye to repair a detached retina. The heat from the beam welded the retina to the back of the eyeball. The operation was a success and the patient felt no pain (Maurer 1–2). Laser eye surgery has become commonplace.

Also among the first to use lasers were dermatologists, or skin doctors. With lasers, doctors can "erase" deep-red birthmarks and unwanted tattoos. More recently, dermatologists have used lasers to speed up the healing of wounds (Hecht and Teresi 73–75).

When a laser is attached to a special arm, it can

be used as a surgeon's scalpel. A surgeon can burn away only surface tissues by using a less intense focus. Since human cells are poor conductors of heat, surrounding tissues remain undamaged. Surgeons can also make deep incisions by focusing the beam to a fine point; in fact, the beam can be focused finely enough to vaporize a single cell (Hecht and Teresi 65). The laser is a "bloodless scalpel," sealing all blood vessels that are smaller than 0.02 inch (0.5 mm). It is also fast and gives no contact pressure. Thus, compared to the conventional scalpel, the laser reduces the trauma that accompanies surgery.

The major value of laser surgery, however, lies in doctors' ability to perform delicate operations within the body in sensitive areas that are rich in blood vessels. For this reason, the laser has been a valuable tool in the treatment of heart and circulatory problems and in cases of internal bleeding.

Presents information logically—in order of increasing importance

One common heart and circulatory problem is plaque, a fatty deposit that clogs arteries and restricts blood flow. A buildup of plaque can cause a stroke or heart attack. Laser surgeons are working on a process in which they thread a tube into the clogged blood vessel and vaporize the plaque with a laser (Adler 14–15).

Defines terms

In a similar manner, doctors can stop internal bleeding. The patient swallows a tube known as an endoscope, which contains optical fibers. These fibers allow the surgeon to see along the length of the tube. Next, the surgeon seals the bleeding vessels with a laser beam (Hecht and Teresi 71–72).

Uses transition words

Provides descriptions of processes

Recently surgeons have combined a laser with a laparoscope, a tiny medical telescope that can be inserted into the body like a needle. The laparoscope is attached to a video camera, which projects a greatly magnified image of the patient's tissues on a video monitor. The surgeon can perform extremely delicate surgery, using this enlarged image, without opening up the patient's body. The new procedure, called video-laseroscopy, is currently used mainly for reproductive and abdominal surgery; but doctors feel its use will widen in years to come (Cowley 58–59).

The field of dentistry is also benefiting from laser technology. Dental surgeons are using lasers to vaporize damaged tooth material with amazing accuracy (Bender 22). In addition, orthodontists are able to precisely measure the effects of braces on the position of teeth by using holograms—three-dimensional photographs made by lasers (Hecht and Teresi 78–79).

Even some acupuncturists have begun using lasers. Traditionally, acupuncturists have treated illnesses by stimulating specific points in the body with needles. But some acupuncturists are finding lasers to be faster, cleaner, and less painful than needles. There are reports from China that laser treatment has relieved asthma symptoms in 72 percent of the patients treated (Hecht and Teresi 75–76).

Lasers, it seems, have miraculous capabilities in the field of medicine. Yet, many doctors and writers try to keep this relatively new technology in perspective, calling it "a new hope" with "bright promise." Many insist that it is not the "cure-all" it seems to be (Hecht and Teresi 62, 79). Nevertheless, even Charles H. Townes is amazed at the medical applications resulting from his idea in the park in 1951 (155). The future looks bright, however. "The applications of lasers seem limited only by the imagination of scientists and engineers" (Jacobs 38).

Makes references to introduction in a conclusion that summarizes implications of the research

Works Cited

Adler, Valerie. "Beyond Balloons: Lasers and Drill Bits Bust Plaque." <u>American Health</u> Mar. 1988: 14–15.

Bender, Lionel. <u>Lasers in Action</u>. New York: Bookwright, 1985.

Cowley, Geoffrey. "Hanging Up the Knife." <u>Newsweek</u> 12 Feb. 1990: 58–59.

De Maria, Anthony J. "Laser." <u>The World Book Encyclopedia</u>. 1993 ed.

Hecht, Jeff, and Dick Teresi. <u>Laser: Supertool of the 1980s</u>. New Haven: Ticknor, 1982.

Jacobs, Madeline. "The Light Fantastic: Lasers Brighten the Future." <u>The Futurist</u> Dec. 1985: 36–39.

Maurer, Allan. <u>Lasers: Light Wave of the Future</u>. New York: Arco, 1982.

Townes, Charles H. "Harnessing Light." <u>Science 84</u> Nov. 1984: 153–55.

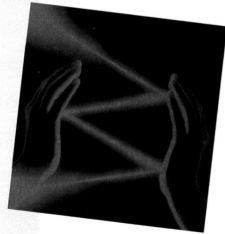

Woman with a Guitar,
by Pablo Ruiz y
Picasso. 1881–1973

WRITER TO WRITER

My first draft is generally a jumble of all my ideas on a given subject. In my next draft I choose those ideas that are most important and pertinent to each other. From there on it is simply a matter of refining the paper.

**Adam Shoughnessey, student
Watertown, Massachusetts**

1. Reflect on your writing. Now that you have completed a research report and read several others, think about the writing process you went through. Ask yourself questions such as these.

- How was the process of writing a research report different from that of writing other kinds of pieces? What would I do differently the next time I write a research report?
- What techniques did I discover while writing this paper that I could use in other kinds of writing?
- How does my research report differ from other pieces I have written in terms of voice, tone, and style? How does it differ from pieces written by other students? What elements of other writers' styles would I like to make a part of my own style?
- What would I now say characterizes a good research report?

2. Apply your skills. Try one or more of the following activities.

- **Cross-curricular** Imagine yourself applying for the job you most want in the world. Prepare for your interview by doing some research. Collect information that will help you impress the interviewer.
- **Literature** Look into the background of a favorite book. Under what circumstances did the author write it? How did the book reflect the author's life? Were some of the characters based on real people? Who were they? How did the book reflect events and ideas of the times?
- **Related assignment** Follow the suggestions on pages 295-296 to write a saturation report.

INVITATION
—TO—
Write

Write a saturation report about a topic you know well or can study in depth.

Related
ASSIGNMENT

▼

> New York is a city of things unnoticed. It is a city with cats sleeping under parked cars, two stone armadillos crawling up St. Patrick's Cathedral, and thousands of ants creeping on top of the Empire State Building. The ants probably were carried up there by winds or birds, but nobody knows for sure. . . .
>
> New York is a city for eccentrics and a center for odd bits of information. New Yorkers blink twenty-eight times a minute, but forty when tense. Most popcorn chewers at Yankee Stadium stop chewing momentarily just before the pitch. . . .
>
> **Gay Talese, "New York Is a City of Things Unnoticed"**

LITERARY
M O D E L

So begins a magazine article focusing on the odd and unusual aspects of life in New York City that caught the attention of Gay Talese during his years as a newspaper reporter. It is an example of a **saturation report,** a type of research in which you "saturate" yourself with your topic and write about it in depth. Saturation reports appear frequently in newspapers and magazines.

WRITING A SATURATION
REPORT

1. Choose a topic. Find a person, place, group, or other subject in which you would like to "saturate" yourself. For example, you might try to recount a day in the life of a person, describe an interesting or unusual place, or capture in words an event you witness.

HANDBOOKS
FOR HELP & PRACTICE

Personal Techniques, pp. 322–324

Georgia O'Keeffe (American, 1887– 1986). *New York, Night* 1928–29.

2. Research your topic. Saturation reports involve many of the same skills as writing a research report. However, a saturation report usually requires you to gather information from personal experiences, observations, and interviews, as well as from written sources. Get to know your subject in depth. Look for telling details that seem to characterize your subject.

3. Choose your approach. You may use a more conversational tone for a saturation report, and your style can be more personal. If your report is based heavily on personal experience or observation, you might choose to write in the first person, with yourself as a participant in the narrative. Also consider using techniques of fiction—such as creating scenes, developing characters, and using dialogue—to present your information in the form of a story.

4. Write your report. Since a saturation report is less formal than a research report, you may wish to consider presenting your information as a series of scenes or sketches. You may also consider presenting the information as a narrative. When you paraphrase or quote material directly, identify the source in the text rather than in a parenthetical note. A list of Works Cited is not required.

5. Publish your report. Consider submitting your report to the school newspaper, or to a general-interest newspaper or magazine. Contact the editor of the feature section for information about the publication's requirements.

Sentence

Reviewing Sentence Composing Skills

In the preceding sentence composing exercises, you have studied how professional writers use inverted sentence order, participial phrases, appositive phrases, and absolute phrases to add emphasis and provide variety in their writing.

Skill 1: Using Inverted Sentence Order (pages 83–85)

>   v   s
> Outside, upon this lawn, <u>stood</u> an iron <u>deer</u>.
> **Ray Bradbury, *The Martian Chronicles***

Skill 2: Using Present Participial Phrases (pages 113–115)

> Just before supper Miguel came into the kitchen, <u>stamping the bits of dirty snow from his overshoes</u>.   **Durango Mendoza, "The Passing"**

Skill 3: Varying Present Participial Phrases (pages 143–145)

> (Opener)   <u>Avoiding one another's eyes</u>, Tom and Lily stood up.
> **Joan Aiken, "Searching for Summer"**

>   s   v
> (S–V Split) The withered moon, <u>shining on his face</u>, awakened him.
> **John Steinbeck, "Flight"**

Skill 4: Using Past Participial Phrases (pages 173–175)

> I pushed through the brass-framed doors into the tiny lobby, <u>paved with freshly mopped, permanently dirty tile</u>.
> **Jack Finney, "Of Missing Persons"**

Skill 5: Using Appositive Phrases (pages 201–203)

> <u>A tall, rawhide man in an unbuttoned, sagging vest</u>, he was visibly embarrassed by any furnishings that suggested refinement.
> **Conrad Richter, "Early Marriage"**

Skill 6: Using Absolute Phrases (pages 233–235)

> The boy watched, <u>his eyes bulging in the dark</u>.
> **Edmund Ware, "An Underground Episode"**

Skill 7: Varying Absolute Phrases (pages 265–267)

(Opener)   <u>The sharp edges gone</u>, he continued to work with the leaf, pulling off half-inch-wide strips and laying them in a pile.   **Robb White, *Deathwatch***

$$\overset{s}{} \qquad\qquad\qquad\qquad \overset{v}{}$$

(S-V Split) Miss Hearne, <u>her face burning</u>, hardly listened to these words.   **Brian Moore, *The Lonely Passion of Judith Hearne***

A. Imitating Sentences   Each model below illustrates one or more of the seven sentence composing skills. Using your own words, write a sentence that imitates the structure of each model sentence.

Important: Imitate as many of the sentence parts as possible, not just the underlined part. Punctuate correctly.

1. On a tarnished gilt easel before the fireplace <u>stood</u> a crayon <u>portrait</u> of Miss Emily's father.   **William Faulkner, "A Rose for Emily"**

2. <u>Frozen with caution</u>, she looked under the edge of her sunbonnet and saw a tall man reading aloud an advertisement to a companion.
   Henrietta Buckmaster, "Harriet Tubman"

3. The bull, <u>hypnotized by the cloth</u>, followed, hooking his horns past Chamaco's kneecaps.   **Richard Wright, "Pagan Spain"**

4. In the half-dark under his eyelids <u>appeared</u> the girl's <u>face</u>.
   Mario Vargas Llosa, "Sunday, Sunday"

5. That summer, <u>the summer of 1918</u>, was blighted.
   James Hurst, "The Scarlet Ibis"

6. It was a short walk from the hotel to the house where we turned in, <u>the tallest I had ever seen</u>.   **Ernesto Galarza, *Barrio Boy***

7. Between the two sections <u>was</u> a <u>fence</u>, also of blond wood.
   Tom Wolfe, *Bonfire of the Vanities*

8. Nearly fifty people, <u>gathered in the big parlor upstairs at the hotel</u>, greeted Nancy Belle.   **Conrad Richter, "Early Marriage"**

9. Alfred trailed a few steps behind, <u>a strange new excitement bubbling in his stomach</u>.   **Robert Lipsyte, *The Contender***

10. Holding to the rock with his hands to keep the weight off his feet, Ben moved back behind the outcrop and slowly let himself down again.
Robb White, *Deathwatch*

11. The sun, gilded with the yellow cast of autumn, still burned fiercely, but the dark green woods through which we passed were shady and cool.
James Hurst, "The Scarlet Ibis"

12. The heat, the noise, the strangeness—none of these daunted Nellie.
Iris Noble, "Nellie Bly—Woman Reporter"

13. Sometimes I found little pools of idle water, walled off by stones from the flow.
Peter Abrahams, "Joseph"

14. Beside the desk, in a dark blue dress sat Ariadne, looking somber and beautiful.
Harry Mark Petrakis, "The Wooing of Ariadne"

15. My log is gone for sure, I think—but in fact, I discover later, it holds, rammed between growing trees.
Annie Dillard, "Flood"

16. There was a girl beside me, hands folded on her purse.
Jack Finney, "Of Missing Persons"

17. Then I came to a man sitting on the ground, a deep-chested man with a face that had quiet on it and wouldn't bawl at you.
Carl Sandburg, "Fair and Circus Days"

18. Standing straight and awkward in her full-skirted red cotton dress, Jade Snow was caught by surprise and without words.
Jade Snow Wong, *Fifth Chinese Daughter*

19. The twig, crushed in her hand, smelled like some store in Santa Fe.
Conrad Richter, "Early Marriage"

20. In another corner was a stand, holding books with thick leather bindings, leaning and lying on each other.
Aharon Megged, "The Name"

21. Across a narrow little office sat a young black man in work clothes, his wife beside him, holding their little girl in her lap.
Jack Finney, "Of Missing Persons"

22. The market, a large open square with wooden houses on two sides, some containing first-floor shops, was crowded with peasant carts with grains, vegetables, wood, hides, and whatnot.
Bernard Malamud, *The Fixer*

23. There they all were now, the cream of the school, the lights and leaders of the senior class, with their high I.Q.'s and expensive shoes, as Brinker had said, pasting each other with snowballs.   **John Knowles, _A Separate Peace_**

24. And there was a man of around fifty, his face averted from the rest of us, staring out into the rain at passing pedestrians.
    Jack Finney, "Of Missing Persons"

25. It was good to sit there in Charley's kitchen, my coat and tie flung over a chair, surrounded by soul food and love.
    Eugenia Collier, "Sweet Potato Pie"

26. A woman stood on her back step, arms folded, waiting.
    Doris Lessing, "The Summer Before Dark"

27. Many fishermen were around the skiff, looking at what was lashed beside it, and one was in the water, his trousers rolled up, measuring the skeleton with a length of line.   **Ernest Hemingway, _The Old Man and the Sea_**

28. Now I spotted it, the address in the 200 block, an old, pseudo-modernized office building, tired, outdated, refusing to admit it but unable to hide it.   **Jack Finney, "Of Missing Persons"**

29. The male fish always let the female fish feed first, and the hooked fish, the female, made a wild, panic-stricken, despairing fight that soon exhausted her, and all the time the male had stayed with her, crossing the line and circling with her on the surface.
    Ernest Hemingway, _The Old Man and the Sea_

30. Chief stood in the middle of it, blank-faced, in a blue pullover shirt and flared wash-and-wear pants, a beaded headband drawn down on his brow.
    Frank Bonham, _Chief_

31. Every mile he stopped and listened, mouth open, holding his breath.
    Jack Finney, "Of Missing Persons"

32. He rocked his head in his hands, bewildered and hating this mental tangle.
    Elliott Merrick, "Without Words"

33. Her head was bent, with a line of light round the hair from a clump of electric candles on the wall above; she was looking into the fire, her arms stretched out, resting her finger-tips on the mantelpiece between the delicate china.   **Elizabeth Bowen, "Foothold"**

34. Blindly his right hand flew over the ledge, <u>his fingers dancing across it,</u> <u>reaching, feeling, searching until his body began to drop, scraping,</u> down again, and he caught the edge with his right hand and stopped falling.

Robb White, *Deathwatch*

35. The younger man burst out in exclamations, <u>waving his thin, nervous,</u> <u>knotted fingers, his face twitching as he spoke.</u>

Dorothy Canfield, "The Heyday of the Blood"

36. The companions followed the shady woodroad, <u>the cow taking slow steps,</u> <u>and the child very fast ones.</u>　　**Sarah Orne Jewett, "A White Heron"**

37. The older professor looked up at the assistant, <u>fumbling fretfully with a</u> <u>pile of papers.</u>　　**Dorothy Canfield, "The Heyday of the Blood"**

38. <u>Being the youngest and therefore the most likely to err,</u> I was plopped between my father and my mother on the long wooden bench.

Eugenia Collier, "Sweet Potato Pie"

39. <u>Below him spread</u> the river, <u>ice-locked between the hills.</u>

Elliott Merrick, "Without Words"

40. Mama Torres, <u>a lean, dry woman with ancient eyes,</u> had ruled the farm for ten years, ever since her husband tripped over a stone in the field one day and fell full length on a rattlesnake.　　**John Steinbeck, "Flight"**

B. Identifying Sentence Composing Skills　For each sentence in Exercise A, *identify the skill or skills illustrated by the underlined parts: inverted sentence order, present participial phrase, past participial phrase, appositive phrase, absolute phrase.*

Application　Without using models or writing imitations, compose seven original sentences, each illustrating one of the seven sentence composing skills covered in this review lesson. You may write seven unrelated sentences, or you may include the seven sentences in a piece of writing you are currently working on.

Sketchbook

MRS. JOHNSON
PALM READER
CARD READING   **ADVISOR**

What's your fortune?

Additional Sketches

What is your earliest memory of writing? Tell all you can.

Write a postcard to someone you miss, telling (him, her) how you feel.

Writing for Assessment

Guided Assignment

ESSAYS IN OTHER SUBJECTS

How would you analyze the qualities of inert gases for a chemistry test? How would you define the Pythagorean theorem for a geometry exam? How would you explain the causes of the French Revolution in your world history class? In all the courses you take, you are called on to use your thinking and writing skills. The strategies you have studied in the preceding workshops can help you write essay question answers that are clear, logical, and to the point.

Essays in Other Subjects

THE TRANSPORTATION REVOLUTION

from *Links Across Time and Place: A World History*

The business changes caused by the Industrial Revolution made better transportation necessary. Large quantities of raw materials required transport to factories. Finished products had to be transported to markets.

Road Construction. During the 1700's, roads often were nothing more than deeply rutted dirt trails. Wagons got stuck in the mud when it rained, and their drivers and passengers choked on dust during dry weather. In 1815, John McAdam, a Scottish engineer, brought road construction into the industrial age.

McAdam proposed putting layers of small stones directly on a hard, leveled bed of earth. This surface was called a macadam road after John McAdam. Traffic over the road compacted the stones and created a fairly smooth surface. Roads were constructed rapidly, and by 1825 England had nearly 4,000 miles of them newly prepared.

Canals Connect Waterways. Even over better roads, raw materials and finished products moved slowly and in limited amounts. Great Britain, however, had an extensive network of navigable rivers. On river highways, goods could be transported in large quantities, quickly and cheaply. To expand navigable waterways, the British began to deepen and widen rivers and streams by dredging.

Then, in 1759, the Duke of Bridgewater improved the transportation of his coal. He had a canal dug from his coal mine to the factory city of Manchester, 7 miles away. Using the canal, he could deliver more coal faster than before. Then he could reduce the price of his coal by 50 percent and still make a profit.

Although the Chinese opened the Grand Canal in 605, canals were not common in England until the 1800's. Canal building caught on, and by 1830 Great Britain had nearly 3,200 miles of canals. France, other western European countries, and the United States also expanded their water networks.

The Steam Engine Improves Transportation. Although canals made transportation within a country cheaper, they did nothing to improve trade over the expanding global community. Sailing ships still dominated trade routes. Steam-powered ships soon improved trans-Atlantic trade.

An American, Robert Fulton, adapted Watt's steam engine to power ships. In 1807, his steamboat, the *Clermont,* began regular trips on the Hudson River between New York City and Albany. In 1838, a British sidewheeler, *Sirius,* became the first ship to cross the Atlantic using only steam power. In 1840, Samuel Cunard and two partners established steamship mail service between Britain and the United States.

Steam power successfully applied to shipping was next applied to land transportation. A British engineer, George Stephenson, was one inventor of a locomotive, a steam engine that ran on tracks. In 1830, an engine, the *Rocket,* pulled a string of rail cars from Liverpool to Manchester. At 29 miles per hour, it won a prize for speed.

By the middle of the 1800's, every country in Europe was building railways. More than 20,000 miles of track crisscrossed the continent in 1850. Railroad construction stimulated economic growth. Railroads provided fast, cheap transportation for both passengers and large quantities of goods. As the boom in railroad building spread, so did the demand for iron and laborers.

Think AND *Respond*

What points would you discuss if you were asked to compare land and water transportation in Great Britain? What facts could you cite to explain the effects of improved transportation?

INVITATION
— TO —
Write

Here is an example of the type of essay question you might find on one of your tests. "Analyze the major changes in transportation during Great Britain's Industrial Revolution."

Whenever you take a test, you should consider the special requirements of the subject area. For example, writing about the sciences often requires you to present facts objectively and make deductions based on concrete evidence. On the other hand, writing about the social sciences and literature often calls for a greater emphasis on interpretation or subjective reactions. For tests in all subject areas, however, you can improve your performance by knowing what is expected of you and carefully planning your responses.

PREWRITE AND EXPLORE

HANDBOOKS
FOR HELP & PRACTICE

Thesis Statements, pp. 355–356
Thinking Critically, pp. 468–470
Reading Skills, pp. 476–477

1. Preview the test. To answer test questions effectively, you need to analyze both the individual questions and the test as a whole. To get an overview of what you are expected to do, look over the entire test and read all the directions and questions before you start answering any of them. Then budget your time. Allow the greatest amount of time for the questions that are worth the most points. Answer easier questions first to give you a sense of accomplishment, but be careful to spend only the time you've allotted on them.

2. Analyze the questions. Read the questions carefully and determine exactly what each question is asking. Find the key words, such as *analyze, evaluate, synthesize, apply, compare, contrast, describe, discuss, explain, interpret,* and *summarize.* These are important cues that will help you determine the specific thinking and writing skills you need to use. The following sample essay questions provide a guide to some key words, their meanings, and strategies for answering each type of question.

Sample Essay Questions and Writing Strategies

Question: *Analyze* the composition of Earth's atmosphere and the function of each element.

Strategy: In order to analyze something, break it down into its parts and explain how each part contributes to the whole. To answer this essay question, you need to discuss the most important gases in the atmosphere one at a time, explaining how each is important to life on Earth.

Question: *Compare and contrast* the goals of W.E.B. Du Bois and Booker T. Washington.

Strategy: To compare and contrast, you need to explore both similarities and differences. Here, you could initially discuss what goals these two black leaders shared. Then you could discuss goals on which they disagreed.

Question: *Explain* the origins of the Korean War.

Strategy: Most essay questions ask you to explain something, even when *explain* isn't in the question. An explanation requires that you make a problem, relationship, process, or term clear and understandable. Use examples, facts, quotations, and reasons to help support your explanation.

Question: *Define* the various types of triangles.

Strategy: To define, list the distinguishing characteristics of the subject or describe it exactly. Here, your first sentence might define a triangle and identify the different types. The following sentences could define each type. Note that for some essay questions, it is appropriate to give a formal definition; for others, you can provide examples, synonyms, or make comparisons.

Question: *Interpret* the line "And miles to go before I sleep" in Robert Frost's poem "Stopping by Woods on a Snowy Evening."

Strategy: To interpret something, you need to give your opinion of what it means and support your opinion with reasons and details. Here, use specific details from the rest of the poem for support.

Question: *Summarize* the plot of the play *A Raisin in the Sun*.

Strategy: Summarizing requires that you present a condensed version of a story or process. Concentrate on the major events or main points of the topic, but be careful not to leave out too much. One part should lead to the next, so that your reader will be able to see how the story or process was presented. Specific details, illustrations, or elaborations should not be included in your summary.

PROBLEM SOLVING

What strategy does this essay question require?

Peanuts cartoon reprinted by permission of USF, Inc.

Essays in
Other Subjects   **307**

Writing
—TIP—

Use the note-taking method with which you are most comfortable. Cluster maps and tree diagrams are good ways to recall and generate ideas.

Question: *Discuss* how transportation changed during Great Britain's Industrial Revolution.

Strategy: When you are asked to discuss, you need to make a general statement and support it with facts and details.

3. Begin planning your answer. Some students like to take notes in a modified outline form. Others find it helpful to jot down words and phrases quickly without worrying about logical order. Then they organize their notes by numbering them. Remember, you have little or no time to revise the answers to essay questions, so plan carefully. One student, Casey Franklin, made these notes as he prepared to answer the question about transportation changes during Great Britain's Industrial Revolution.

ONE STUDENT'S PROCESS

- railroad (the *Rocket*)   3
- new roads constructed   1
- canals built (3,000 miles)   2
- steamships   4

4. Develop a thesis statement. A good thesis statement should set a goal for your answer and keep you on track as you write. It should contain your main idea and show that you understand the question. You can sometimes begin by restating the question, adding to it as appropriate to set the goals for your essay. Casey composed the thesis statement shown below by restating and expanding on the essay question.

ONE STUDENT'S PROCESS

Great Britain's Industrial Revolution brought about improvements in four areas of transportation: roads, canals, railroads, and steamships.

DRAFT AND DISCOVER

1. Meet the question head-on. Start with your thesis statement, and then support it with facts, examples, and other details. Refer to your outline or notes as you write to help you stay on track. A good answer is not padded with information that is unnecessary or irrelevant.

2. Move smoothly from one idea to the next. Use your prewriting notes to guide your writing, but don't be afraid to include any new ideas that occur to you. Use transitions to move from one point to another.

3. Provide a strong conclusion. Your conclusion should restate your thesis in light of the evidence you have presented.

HANDBOOKS

FOR HELP & PRACTICE

**Coherence,
pp. 376–385
Conclusions,
pp. 386–390**

REVIEW YOUR WRITING

Questions for Yourself

- Does my response directly answer the question?
- Have I covered all the points I intended to?
- Do I need to include more facts or details?
- Does my conclusion restate my main point?
- Is my essay accurate, neat, and legible?

REVISE YOUR WRITING

1. Reread each question. Since your time is limited, you will have to work quickly to revise your essay. You will not have enough time to make major revisions, but you should reread each question and answer, making sure that you have understood and responded to the key words.

2. Add ideas that come to mind. See if there is anything in your prewriting notes that you would like to include, and add any other ideas that support or clarify your main points.

3. Proofread your work. Correct errors in grammar and mechanics. Use proofreading symbols neatly to mark any changes, making sure that your essay is easy to read.

HANDBOOKS

FOR HELP & PRACTICE

**Self-Assessment,
p. 397**

Thesis statement

First main point

Second main point

Third main point

Fourth main point

Conclusion

Great Britain's Industrial Revolution brought about improvements in four areas of transportation: roads, canals, railroads, and steamships.

In 1815, John McAdam devised a method of constructing smooth and durable roads. As a result, roads were constructed rapidly throughout Great Britain. Around this time, canal building became common, and by 1830 Great Britain had more than 3,000 miles of canals. The canals connected various waterways and made it easier to ship materials and products by boat.

In 1830, a locomotive called the *Rocket* pulled a string of rail cars from Liverpool to Manchester. Before long, railroads connected the nation. In the middle part of the century, steamships also became commonplace. They made it possible to transport all kinds of goods quickly and safely over great distances, across England and across the oceans of the world.

Improved roads, canals, steamships, and railroads made it easier and faster to reach nearly all parts of Great Britain and many other parts of the world.

APPLY YOUR SKILL

Try writing your own essay test questions. Use any of the key words listed on page 306 to write three questions on material you are studying in your other classes. Then, for one of the questions, write a thesis statement and a plan for your answer—a modified outline or list of major points you would include.

Sentence

Authors' Expansions

You have used your sentence composing skills to complete sentences begun by professional writers. Now look at the sentences they wrote. What qualities do your sentences share? What differences do you see? Whose sentences do you prefer?

Using Present Participial Phrases, Exercise D, page 115

1. I spent as much time as I could alone in our room, trying to empty my mind of every thought, to forget where I was, even who I was.

2. I dream I'm flying over a sandy beach in the early morning, touching the leaves of the trees as I fly by.

3. For a long while we just stood there, looking down at the profound and fleshless grin.

4. Jem threw open the gate and sped to the side of the house, slapped it with his palm and ran back past us, not waiting to see if his foray was successful.

5. James had a library book on rocks, and they spent days just wandering around the park, filling their pockets with little rocks that matched the pictures in the book.

6. Black clouds began to gather in the southwest, and he began watching them, trying to pull the oars a little faster.

Varying Present Participial Phrases, Exercise D, page 145

1. He sat on a bench here, watching the leafy trees and the flowers blooming on the inside of the railing, thinking of a better life for himself.

2. Jan trotted about in a circle, slapping his mittens together and pounding the toes that were aching in his moccasins.

3. Then Mama began to cry and ran over to him, hugging him and kissing him.

4. He walked to the corner of the lot, then back again, studying the simple terrain as if deciding how to best effect an entry, frowning and scratching his head.

5. And so we went to the station, across the meadow, taking the longer way, trying to be together as long as possible.

Using Past Participial Phrases, Exercise C, page 175

1. Out on the playground, C.T. was standing in a swing, gently swaying to and fro, surrounded by a group of admiring youngsters.

2. Amazed at the simplicity of it all, I understood everything as never before.

3. Presently the dawn began to break, and the sky to the east grew yellow and red, slashed across with heavy black clouds.

4. Brought back to the Store, the pickers would step out of the backs of trucks and fold down, dirt-disappointed, to the ground.

5. A little house, perched on high piles, appeared black in the distance.

6. Sometimes I found little pools of idle water, walled off by stones from the flow.

7. I was typing some paragraph from some shoe newspaper, fascinated by the weirdness of the machine.

8. Harriet had watched them, fastened together with chains, stumble down the road toward the Deep South.

Using Appositive Phrases, Exercise C, page 203

1. From under the counter he brought out a heavy stamping machine, the kind you see in railway ticket offices.

2. In our clenched fists we held our working cards from the shop, the sacred cards that we thought meant security.

3. The land that lay stretched out before him became of vast significance, a place peopled by his fancy with a new race of men sprung from himself.

4. The tree was tremendous, an irate, steely black steeple beside the river.

5. He heard every little sound of the gathering night, the sleepy complaint of settling birds, the love agony of cats, the strike and withdrawal of little waves on the beach, and the simple hiss of distance.

Using Absolute Phrases, Exercise C, page 235

1. A water snake slipped along on the pool, its head held up like a little periscope.

2. I said nothing, my mind exploring the new dimension of isolation around me.

3. This was what I feared when I lifted the dark-green shade: I feared a face outside the window, dead eyes looking in at me as I pulled out of sleep.

4. As he looked, the bull gathered itself together and charged, its eyes on the horse's chest.

5. Mr. Nathan Radley was standing inside his gate, a shotgun broken across his arm.

Using Absolute Phrases, Application, page 235

(1) The pass was high and wide and Darling jumped for it. (2) The center floated by, *his hands desperately brushing Darling's knee as Darling picked his feet up high and delicately ran over a blocker and an opposing linesman in a jumble on the ground near the scrimmage line.* (3) He had ten yards in the clear and picked up speed, watching the other backs heading him off toward the sideline, *the men closing in on him, the blockers fighting for position.* (4) He smiled a little to himself as he ran, *his knees pumping high, his hips twisting in the almost girlish run of a back in a broken field.* (5) The first halfback came at him, and he fed him his leg, then swung at the last moment, took the shock of the man's shoulder without breaking stride, ran through him, *his cleats biting securely into the turf.* (6) There was only the safety man now, coming warily at him, *his arms crooked, hands spread.* (7) Darling tucked the ball in, *his legs pounding, knees high, all two hundred pounds bunched into controlled attack.* (8) He pivoted away, keeping the arm locked, dropping the safety man as he ran easily toward the goal line, with the drumming of cleats diminishing behind him.

Du Nord, by Stanton MacDonald-Wright, 1958

Writing Handbook

Sketchbook

I'm not aware of too many things
I know what I know if you know what I mean
philosophy is a walk on the slippery rocks
religion is a light in the fog.

Edie Brickell
"WHAT I AM"

What do you know?

Additional Sketches

What are your goals: for the world, for the next ten years, for the next year, for this month, for today?

Have you ever experienced stage fright? Tell the story or imagine what it would be like.

Understanding the Writing Activity

Every writer approaches writing differently. For example, you may begin a writing assignment by sitting outside under a tree and daydreaming, while your best friend may find it impossible to concentrate on writing unless she is sitting at her desk with her computer in front of her. No matter how differently writers work, however, they all need to consider the following writing variables: **topic, purpose, personal goals, audience, form,** and **voice.**

IDENTIFYING YOUR
WRITING VARIABLES

There is no "right" time to consider each writing variable. You may make decisions about some variables before you begin writing. Other decisions you may put off until later in the writing process. Furthermore, you can change your mind about any variable at any point in the process.

Finding a Topic

One piece of proverbial wisdom about writing is that people should write about what they know. However, knowing a lot about your topic beforehand is not essential. Sometimes it's more fun to explore a topic you don't know anything about but would *like* to learn more about. If you have a choice, it's usually best to start with a topic that you really enjoy and think is important. If you are interested in a topic and have something important to say about it, chances are that your readers will also be interested.

WRITER TO WRITER

My advice to other student writers would be to write about things that they feel strongly about or that make them happy.

**Tamiha Smith, student,
Northfield, Illinois**

The amount of freedom you have to choose your topic varies greatly among writing assignments. Sometimes the topic may be provided by your teacher. In such a situation, however, you can usually make the topic your own by finding some angle or aspect of it that particularly interests you. For example, suppose you were asked to write a report on television news for a journalism class. If technology interests you, you might want to write about how special effects are created for news programs. If you are more interested in the human side of the news, you might prefer to write about the dangers faced by television journalists reporting live from the sites of natural disasters.

Establishing a Purpose

One way to focus your ideas for a piece of writing is to think about your purpose, or reason for writing. Common purposes for writing include **to express yourself, to entertain, to inform, to describe, to analyze,** and **to persuade.**

Sometimes a piece of writing has only one main purpose. For example, the purpose of an article discussing the development of sailing ships would be to inform. Other pieces of writing have more than one purpose. For instance, a student who writes about her first experiences in a sailboat might want to express her feelings about the experiences and also to persuade other students to try the sport.

As you think about the purpose of your writing, ask yourself these questions:

- What do I want to accomplish in this piece of writing?
- What effect do I want my writing to have on readers?

Here is what one student wrote when considering his purpose for writing a personal narrative about learning to sail:

> I want to entertain people with some of the humorous mistakes I made when I was learning to sail. I also want to inform them that anyone can learn this skill.

Statement of Controlling Purpose Explaining what you want to accomplish in a piece of writing is called writing a **statement of controlling purpose.** Such a statement is used to help you focus your writing and does not appear in the finished piece of writing.

Writing
—**TIP**—

Graphic devices can help you explore what you know and feel about a topic.

S T U D E N T
M O D E L

The following are some statements of controlling purpose for various types of writing.

- **Writing that defines** The purpose of this essay is to define the word *democracy* and to give examples of democracy in action in our Student Council.
- **Writing that shows cause and effect** The purpose of this report is to explain the major causes of poor photographs, including overexposure, underexposure, and poor composition.
- **Writing that describes** The purpose of this travel article is to describe the city of New Orleans, its atmosphere, points of interest, and restaurants.
- **Writing that persuades** The purpose of this letter to the editor is to persuade my classmates to respect cultural differences in our school.
- **Writing that analyzes** The purpose of this flowchart is to analyze, or examine part by part, the process of four-color printing.

Determining Your Personal Goals

In addition to determining your general purpose for writing, you must also consider your personal goals—what you would like to accomplish in this specific piece of writing. For example, a student whose controlling purpose is to explain how he learned to sail might have a personal goal of reminiscing about his older brother, who taught him sailing. A personal goal for writing about your hobby might be to make friends with people who share your interest. Being clear about your personal goals can give you—and your readers—a greater sense of involvement in your writing.

Considering Your Audience

Writing is a form of communication, and most pieces of writing are written *to* someone. That person can be real or imaginary, living or dead, or even just yourself. The audience for your writing can influence all the other writing variables, including what you write about, the form your writing takes, the information you include, and the language you use. Analyze your audience by asking questions such as these:

- What information do my readers need? What facts do they already know? What is their attitude toward this subject?
- What parts of my subject will my readers find most interesting? Should I expand these parts?

- What part of my subject might be uninteresting to my readers? Can I present this information in a more interesting way, or should I delete it?
- How should I "talk" to this audience to really reach them?

The student who wanted to write about learning to sail wrote this brief analysis of his audience and their needs:

> Many of my readers won't be familiar with sailing at all, so I'll be sure to define terms I usually take for granted. I also want my audience to know they don't have to be rich to sail. Many outdoor clubs give lessons and make boats available at very low cost.

If your audience does not have a natural interest in the subject, you may need to capture their attention. You might present a report in an unusual format, as a news report, for example, or from an unusual viewpoint, perhaps that of an invisible bystander.

Choosing a Form

Form is the type of writing in which you express your ideas. For example, someone who wanted to write about learning to sail might decide to write a short story, a personal narrative, an expository essay, a letter, a magazine article, or a poem. The form of your writing is often the first variable you know, but sometimes you may not decide what form to use until *after* you have explored your topic and thought about possible purposes and audiences for your work. Among the many forms that a piece of writing can take are those listed in the following chart.

advertisement	classified ad	lab report	poem
anecdote	dialogue	lecture	press release
biography	essay	legend	proposal
book review	fable	magazine article	questionnaire
brochure	freewriting	memorandum	report
business letter	history	myth	short story
campaign speech	instructions	news report	speech
cartoon	joke	parable	summary
catalog	journal entry	play	TV script

Thinking About Voice

Imagine you had to make two telephone calls this afternoon, one to your best friend and the other to an employer who was hiring workers your age. How might your tone of voice and use of language change from one call to the next? In the same way, different kinds of writing require different voices. When you write an essay about a personal experience, for example, you might use a voice that is very close to your own informal speaking voice. In contrast, when you write a formal report, you probably will want to use an objective, authoritative voice.

Role-playing a Speaker In some types of writing, you may even want to imagine that a character other than yourself is doing the "talking." When writing a report on mystery writers, for example, you could imagine that a great fictional detective, such as Sherlock Holmes, is evaluating today's mystery writers. When writing a humorous essay, you might imagine that your narrator has the personality of your favorite comedian.

All six of the writing variables are interrelated, and changing one may mean rethinking others. Try to keep an open, experimental attitude as you write.

Practice Your Skills

A. Imagine that your teacher has asked you to write an informative, entertaining piece of writing on some aspect of the future. Complete all of the following activities in any order.

- Brainstorm some specific aspects of the future you might enjoy writing about, and choose one.
- Write a statement of controlling purpose for your topic, and list two personal goals for writing.
- Choose an audience for your writing, and write a brief paragraph analyzing its special needs, interests, and attitudes.
- List three possible forms for your writing. Choose one.
- Consider what voice will best suit your purpose and your audience, and imagine a character other than yourself who will do the talking in your piece. Write a paragraph describing this speaker.

B. Now imagine that you will rewrite your work for a very different audience. Write a paragraph analyzing the needs of that audience and explaining what other writing variables you might change.

COMPUTER TIP

You may want to try writing the same piece in different voices and save each variation in a different file on the same computer disk. Save all the files until you decide which version you prefer.

Finding Ideas for Writing

Years ago the biologist Otto Loewi speculated that messages in the body were carried between nerve cells by a chemical. However, he had no way of testing his theory. One night, while he was asleep, Loewi dreamed of an experiment that would prove whether his theory was correct. He woke up, went to his laboratory, and did the experiment. The experiment worked and Loewi won a Nobel Prize.

Ideas come from the strangest places. As Otto Loewi's story shows, great ideas sometimes come from dreams. At other times, they result from using conscious techniques to stimulate creative thinking. Consider the following techniques that other writers have used to generate writing ideas.

PERSONAL TECHNIQUES

You can generate ideas by focusing your attention on the world around you and the world inside your head. Some focusing techniques include recalling and reflecting, observing, imaging, conducting a knowledge inventory, and using trigger words.

Recalling and Reflecting Thousands of memories stored in your brain can be raw materials for new writing ideas. You can tap these ideas by recalling and reflecting.

When you **recall** something, you simply think back on it, trying to create an image in your mind. People find it easiest to recall something if they close their eyes and concentrate on one sensory aspect of the thing—a sound, a color, or a smell, for example. One student who wanted to tap childhood memories experimented with recalling articles of clothing that he wore as a child. He remembered wearing a loose, billowing red shirt and running across a field with the shirt flapping in the wind. It seemed at the time that he could run forever.

When you **reflect** on something you have recalled, you ask yourself questions about its significance. You associate your recollections with present-day experiences and observations in order to come up with writing ideas. The student who remembered running with his shirt flapping in the breeze reflected on his memory and decided the scene could represent the carefree innocence and freedom of his childhood. He chose to write about how people can hold on to some of these childhood feelings as they get older.

Observing Paying close attention to, or **observing,** your environment means using your senses to gather information. Observing means more than merely looking; it means becoming aware of what makes each person, place, thing, or situation special. For example, if you need descriptive details for characters in a story you are writing, you might try thinking about people you know. You might also try "people watching" in a public place such as a restaurant or park. Zero in on features and mannerisms that might suggest ideas for fictional characters. As you observe, your senses will help you focus. Take notes on all that you perceive—or imagine you perceive—by seeing, hearing, touching, tasting, or smelling. The following are some qualities that you can observe using your senses.

Sight	size	shape	color	age
Hearing	loudness	pitch	rhythm	pleasantness
Touch	temperature	hardness	texture	shape
Taste	sweetness	saltiness	sourness	bitterness
Smell	sweetness	spiciness	sourness	freshness

Imaging In addition to calling up pictures from your past, you can also bring to mind pictures of things that you've never seen before. Calling up pictures in your mind is called **imaging.** Creating imaginary images can be a great deal of fun because you are free to think about absolutely anything. For example, suppose that you want to write a short story set in the distant future. You might begin by creating a mental image of an imaginary setting. Close your eyes and see what details come to mind. Keep a pencil and paper ready and jot down the details.

W R I T E R   T O   W R I T E R

Some men see things as they are and say, "Why?" I dream things that never were and say, "Why not?"

Robert Kennedy, politician

Conducting a Knowledge Inventory Don't underestimate how much you already know. You have a vast amount of knowledge about the world stored in your mind—facts, figures, impressions, feelings, and images. When you first begin considering a subject for writing, it is a good idea to think about what you already know about the subject. You can do this by conducting a **knowledge inventory.** On the following page are some questions you might ask.

1. What do I already know about _____ ?
2. Have I ever seen or experienced _____ ? What did it look or feel like? What impressions did it leave?
3. How do other people seem to regard _____ ?
4. What have I read about _____ ? Where?
5. What movies or TV shows have I seen about _____ ?
6. What unusual things have I noticed about _____ ?
7. What questions would I like answered about _____ ?

Using Trigger Words One way to jolt your imagination is to use **trigger words.** The best trigger words are those that stimulate emotional associations, questions, memories, or fantasies. The following words may trigger some associations for you: *danger, flying, hungry, celebration, baseball, mystery, sweet.* When you're really stuck for writing ideas, you can simply flip through a dictionary and look at words at random. Think about the feelings, images, and experiences you associate with these words until an idea for writing occurs to you.

WRITING TECHNIQUES

You can use several informal writing techniques to help you explore ideas. These techniques include listing, freewriting, writing dialogue, and using a journal.

Listing Making a list of details you have observed, imagined, or remembered is a good way to begin exploring a writing topic. Here is a part of a list for a description of an elderly man a student saw on a bus.

over six feet tall	peacock blue shirt
husky, broad chest	booming voice, loud laugh
jacket buttons straining	sitting in rear of bus
thick, blue-veined hands	hale and hearty
white hair, ruddy face	talkative
bright green pants	not prosperous looking
plaid jacket	clothes worn out; hole in shoe

Freewriting The purpose of **freewriting** is to allow your thoughts to flow freely as you explore ideas for writing. Because freewriting is for your eyes only, you don't have to worry about the way other people might judge what you write. You can relax and explore ideas for the fun of it. To use freewriting, follow these steps.

1. Think of an idea you want to explore. Start with any picture, experience, or word that's in your mind.
2. Write whatever comes to mind as you think about your idea. Let your thoughts flow freely without stopping to evaluate them. Continue writing for ten minutes. If you get stuck, keep your pen or pencil moving by doodling until you get another idea.
3. Don't worry about using complete sentences or proper spelling and punctuation.

The student who made the list about the old man on the bus decided to do some freewriting about him after studying her list. Here is part of what she wrote.

> He didn't look as if he had any money, but he seemed happy. Maybe he's the kind of person who finds joy in simple things. He could probably teach other people how to appreciate life. What a great character for a story!

Sometimes it's hard to keep yourself from trying to control or shape the thoughts you put down as you freewrite. If you find yourself tempted to hold back or interrupt the flow of ideas by stopping to make corrections, you might try invisible writing. This is a technique for recording your thoughts without analyzing them. You can experiment with invisible writing by using an inkless pen and carbon paper (you can read what you've written later) or with a computer (you dim the screen as you write).

Writing Dialogue   Writers use **dialogue** in both fiction and nonfiction to add variety and a feeling of authenticity to their writing. Dialogue, though, can also be useful as a device for finding out what you're thinking. For example, you can hold a "conversation" with yourself about a controversial issue. Writing down this kind of imaginary dialogue can be especially useful in persuasive writing or argument, when you want to examine as many points of view as possible.

When using dialogue to explore ideas, try to relax and "listen" to your own mind. For example, if you were having an internal dialogue about your future, one part of you might say, "I'll never figure out what I want to do with my life!" Then another voice might answer, "Of course, you will. You know how hard you work when you find something you really like to do, like building things." The first voice might then say, "Oh, yes. Remember when I built that model boat from scratch? Maybe I'll research careers in design or engineering."

Using a Journal Some of your best writing can be done in a journal, a notebook in which you write regularly. Your journal can fulfill a variety of needs. It can be a diary—a private narrative account of your life over a period of time. It can also serve as a sourcebook of writing ideas, containing your impressions, observations, reactions, and feelings. If you write in your journal faithfully, it can become a "growth chart" of your progress, both as a writer and as a person.

Some writers set aside a particular time each day for journal writing. Others carry their journals with them and write whenever inspiration strikes. Most writers find it helpful to date their journal entries for future reference. You might want to divide one journal into sections or to keep separate notebooks for different purposes.

For example, you could have separate sections or notebooks for observations, quotations, questions to follow up on, daily diary entries, writing ideas, and so on.

Here is an example of a student's journal entry:

> Today when I was doing my laps, I felt like a swimming machine. My arms were pistons, rising and falling in rhythm. I ripped through the water, hardly aware of who I was. It was just me and the blue water and the empty sky. Afterward, I clung to the pool edge, breathing hard. It was like waking from a dream.

Tarzan contemplates another entry.

SHARING TECHNIQUES

Even though writing is usually thought of as a solitary activity, writers can benefit from sharing ideas with each other. Other people can provide a valuable perspective, especially at the beginning of the writing process when you are trying to generate ideas. Some sharing techniques you can use to discover ideas for writing are brainstorming, discussion, and idea exchange.

Brainstorming Like freewriting, **brainstorming** is a technique that allows you to follow your thoughts wherever they lead. Brainstorming can be done alone, but it is most productive when it involves conversation with other people. When brainstorming, pose a question or bring up a subject and let everyone talk about it freely, saying whatever comes to mind. Appoint a recorder to jot down every idea. The only rule for brainstorming is that every idea deserves a fair hearing, no matter how unrelated it might seem at first. Brainstorming is often used as a way of finding creative solutions to problems.

Discussion Whereas the purpose of brainstorming is to generate as many ideas as possible, the purpose of **discussion**—with a friend, parent, or group of people—is to explore a few ideas in depth. For example, if a group of students brainstormed a list of ideas for solving a problem in your school, they might then discuss the pros and cons of the two best solutions and assign group members to write about each proposal. Try discussion when you want to consider several points of view on a topic.

Idea Exchange Writers often exchange ideas with each other. Such an exchange helps each writer to test the strength of his or her thinking. It also stimulates new ideas. Just as our own minds can create new ideas out of combinations of old ones, people can often come up with new ideas by combining their thoughts with the thoughts of other people.

OTHER TECHNIQUES

Many other creative thinking techniques can help you generate ideas for writing topics. Some of these techniques include questioning, browsing, gleaning, keeping a clip file, and using graphic devices.

Questioning One of the best techniques for generating writing ideas is **questioning.** Creative questioning helps you to look at the world in a fresh light. To use this technique, ask yourself questions that begin with the words "What if?" For example, suppose you were examining an everyday item such as a paper cup. Using creative questioning, you might ask yourself, "What if this were made of another material?" or "What if I changed the shape of this item?" or even "What if I combined this with another item in order to create something different?" Creative questions are limited only by your imagination.

Writing
—TIP—

A good time to talk over ideas with another writer is when you get stuck and aren't sure how to proceed. Another writer can often see possibilities you may have overlooked.

Finding Ideas   **327**

Another common questioning technique is to ask action questions, ones that begin with *who, what, where, when, why,* or *how.* If you are planning a newspaper article, a story plot, an election campaign, a television commercial, or any idea that involves action, questions such as these allow you to investigate an idea in depth.

1. **What?** What happened? What is it? What does it mean?
2. **Who?** Who is responsible? Who else is involved?
3. **Where?** Where does it happen? Where can I get information?
4. **When?** When does it happen? When will it change?
5. **Why?** Why does it happen? Why should people care?
6. **How?** How does it work? How can we change it?

Browsing Casually leafing through material can be a good way to stimulate your mind to generate ideas. **Browsing** relaxes your mind because you don't have to struggle to retrieve ideas from your memory. As you flip through source materials, ideas may simply "jump off the page." Those ideas may stimulate your imagination or memory and trigger new ideas.

Suppose, for example, that you want to write a biographical essay but you're having trouble choosing a subject. You might pick up a copy of *Bartlett's Familiar Quotations* in your library. As you browse through quotations by famous people, you may run across a statement that intrigues you. Then you can explore information about the person who made that statement to see if he or she might be a worthwhile subject.

If you're not sure which book to flip through, you can simply browse through the bookshelves in the library or bookstore until you see a title in your particular area of interest that seems a likely source of ideas. In a library, you might find good sources in the reference section, the periodicals department, or in sections that contain books in such subject areas as social science, philosophy, history, or the arts.

Gleaning If you pay attention to what is going on around you, you may find ideas in unexpected places. **Gleaning** is the gathering of bits and pieces of information for the purpose of formulating writing ideas. During each waking moment—and in some sleeping moments—you are bombarded with possible ideas. Learn to glean those that might prove valuable. Become a collector of interesting sights, sensations, words, and thoughts. Savor and examine the items in your collection, and pursue as writing topics those ideas that hold the greatest promise.

COMPUTER TIP

Using a computerized card catalog in your library is an efficient way to browse for books on a particular topic. Ask your librarian to help you learn how to use this service.

Suppose, for example, you are trying to think of a story idea. Your mother has asked you to walk to the grocery store after school to pick up some milk. On the way, you see a police officer standing by a tired-looking horse, talking softly to it and feeding it a carrot. You start to consider a story idea about a horse and a mounted police officer who have to part company after working together for many years. Later, waiting in line at the checkout, you read some ridiculous headlines in tabloid newspapers and wonder who wrote the articles and what really happened to the people the articles are about. In one short trip, you have collected two possible story ideas.

Keeping a clip file   As you browse through magazines and newspapers at home, looking for ideas, you may come across an article that you want to keep for future reference. If you're sure no one else needs that article, you can clip it out and save it in a file folder called a **clip file.** Better yet, you can photocopy the material to avoid tearing up the original. As you continue to collect articles, you may even want to file them by subject.

Be sure to write the name and date of the newspaper or magazine on the article if the information is not printed there. That way, if you choose to quote something in your writing, you can give credit to the source. It's also important to know when the article was written since you may not use it for months or even years to come.

Using graphic devices   Another excellent way to explore ideas is to use graphic devices such as time lines and cluster maps. See pages 330–332 for a detailed discussion of graphic devices.

Practice Your Skills

A. Recall a time when you felt very happy and reflect on it. Freewrite in your journal for ten minutes about that time.

B. Find a photograph of a person, place, or thing that intrigues you. Make a list of descriptive details about the subject in the picture. Then make up a series of action questions or "what if?" questions about the person, place, or thing.

C. In a group, brainstorm as many associations as you can for the word *disaster*. Later, discuss which associations might make good ideas for a personal narrative or short story.

D. Browse through a news magazine to find several current issues that concern you. Have a dialogue with yourself to sort out your feelings on one of these issues. Record the dialogue in your journal.

WRITING
H A N D B O O K
3

Using Graphic Devices for Writing

Although language is the medium in which writers express their ideas, many find that picturing their thoughts graphically helps them clarify their thinking. Useful graphic devices can be divided, roughly, into two main types. Some are useful for finding and elaborating on ideas—for gathering information about a topic, for focusing a topic, or for uncovering specific details related to a topic. Other graphic devices are valuable for organizing ideas.

DEVICES FOR
EXPLORING IDEAS

Graphic devices that you can use to help you explore ideas include observation charts, pro-and-con charts, and cluster diagrams.

Observation Charts You can use **observation charts** to record information you gather through your five senses. To make an observation chart, simply list the five senses as column or row headings. Below each heading, list what you see, hear, taste, touch, or smell.

**Observation Chart
The Primate House**

Sight	Sound	
Fat orangutans	Squalls	
Scampering spider monkey	Screeches	
Chimp eating bananas	People saying dumb things to the monkeys	
Baboons with red and blue faces	Head baboon keeps others in line with his calls	

Touch	Taste	Smell
Iron fence	Peanuts	Stench of the spider monkey cage
Branches of trees	Cotton candy	Odor of rotting vegetables

Pro-and-Con Charts   You can explore the positive or negative aspects of an idea or course of action by using a **pro-and-con chart.** Just list the alternative courses of action as row headings and the words *Pro* and *Con* as column headings and categorize your ideas accordingly.

Pro-and-Con Chart

Question: Should I study painting or business when I go to college?

	Pro	Con
Study Painting	It's something I love. I'm good at it. I've had a lot of experience. I would be able to pursue my dream of becoming a famous painter. I might be able to teach art in high school.	College is expensive; as a painter I might have a hard time repaying my college loans. The life of a painter is difficult; it's hard to get showings in galleries or jobs in university art departments.
Study Business	I would be able to go into my uncle's business. This would please my parents very much.	I'm not particularly interested in business. I don't know much about business.

Cluster Diagrams If you have a general writing idea and want to elaborate on it, you can use several types of cluster diagrams to generate additional ideas that are associated with it. Two common types are **cluster maps** (or **webs**) and **tree diagrams** (or **spider maps**). To make a cluster map, write your main idea or topic in the middle of a sheet of paper and circle it. Then, mentally explore that idea and list any ideas you can think of that are related to it. Write these related ideas near the main idea, circle them, and connect them to the main idea with lines. Next, think about the related ideas, and write down ideas you associate with each. Continue in this way until you have a web-like chart full of interrelated ideas.

Cluster Map

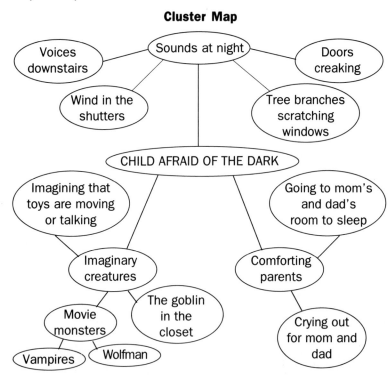

A **tree diagram,** or **spider map,** is a type of clustering that can help you break a topic or idea into its parts. You write the main idea or topic at the bottom or top of a piece of paper. Then you think of subordinate ideas, and write these below or above your main idea, connecting them with lines that serve as "branches" of the tree. Then, just as when clustering, you write down further ideas subordinated to your previous ideas as they occur to you and again connect them with lines.

DEVICES FOR
ORGANIZING IDEAS

Graphic devices for organizing ideas include time lines, category charts, comparison-and-contrast charts and Venn diagrams, flow charts, analysis frames, and inductive-reasoning frames.

Time Lines A **time line** is used to organize information in chronological order. To make a time line, draw a line and place times or dates along it and write in the corresponding events.

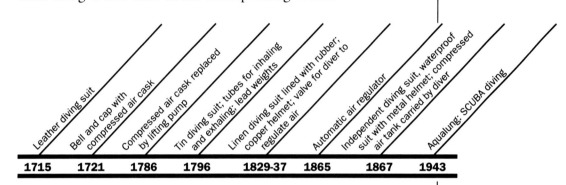

| 1715 | 1721 | 1786 | 1796 | 1829-37 | 1865 | 1867 | 1943 |

Category Charts A **category chart** is used to classify objects or ideas according to their characteristics or membership in a group.

Category Chart	**Deciduous**	**Evergreen Trees**
Characteristics	Leaves change color in fall/Shed leaves in winter	Leaves stay green throughout year/Do not lose leaves
Examples	aspen, beech, birch, chestnut, dogwood, elm, hawthorn, hickory, locust, magnolia, maple, mulberry, oak, pecan, persimmon, poplar, sassafras, sumac, sycamore, walnut, willow	cedar, cypress, fir, pine, redwood, spruce, yew

Comparison-and-Contrast Charts and Venn Diagrams Two other graphic aids—**comparison-and-contrast charts** and **Venn diagrams**—can help you organize ideas in terms of their similarities and differences. The easiest way to construct a comparison-and-contrast chart is to present the objects or ideas to be compared in the title of the chart and then summarize the results of your comparison in columns marked *Similarities* and *Differences*.

Comparison-and-Contrast Chart
Jazz vs. Rock 'n' roll

Similarities	Differences
Both use many of the same instruments—drums, guitars, electric basses, sometimes acoustic or electric pianos, synthesizers Both have roots in blues and gospel music Both originated in American South	Some differences in instruments used; jazz makes more use of horns, for example Lots of improvisation in jazz; much less in rock 'n' roll Jazz influenced by big-band music, swing, be-bop; rock 'n' roll influenced by country and western music

Louis Armstrong, legendary jazz musician, and Elvis Presley, rock 'n' roll great

An alternate way of exploring similarities and differences graphically is by using a **Venn diagram.** This graphic is particularly helpful in visualizing ideas both as a whole and in relation to other ideas. To use a Venn diagram, draw intersecting circles—one for each idea you are comparing, and list their common characteristics in the intersecting region and their distinguishing traits outside this area.

Venn Diagram

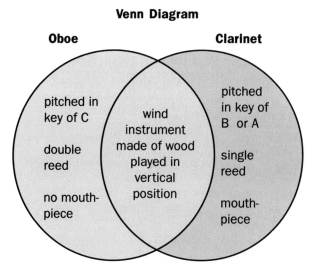

Oboe / Clarinet

pitched in key of C

double reed

no mouth-piece

wind instrument made of wood played in vertical position

pitched in key of B or A

single reed

mouth-piece

Flow Charts A **flow chart** shows the stages in a process or the steps necessary to complete an activity. These steps or stages are listed in the order in which they occur and connected by arrows that indicate the direction of movement.

Flow of Goods in the Food Industry

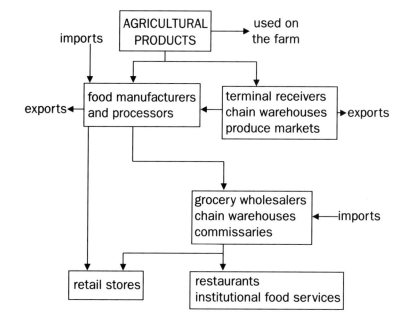

Analysis Frames You can use an **analysis frame** to break down a subject into its component parts. The simplest way to construct an analysis frame is to write your subject at the top of the chart, then list its parts as column headings and finally summarize the characteristics of the parts under their respective column heads.

Grand Canyon Looking North, Sept. 1982 Photographic collage, 45 × 99 ½ edition of 15. ©David Hockney

Analysis Frame
Summer Camp

Sports	Crafts	Other Activities
Hiking and backpacking	Macramé	Singing around campfire
Canoeing	Basket-weaving	Group discussions
Swimming	Painting	Nature walks and instruction
Rock climbing	Music lessons	
Horseback riding		
Tennis		

Inductive-Reasoning Frames An **inductive-reasoning frame** is used to show **inductions**—or conclusions you can draw from specific facts. To make an inductive-reasoning frame, you simply make a numbered list of the specific facts and then draw an arrow to the conclusion that can be drawn from the facts.

Inductive-Reasoning Frame

Fact 1:	Zaire declared its independence in June of 1960.
Fact 2:	Somalia declared its independence in July of 1960.
Fact 3:	Dahomey, Ivory Coast, Chad, Congo Brazzaville, Gabon, and Senegal declared their independence in August of 1960.
Fact 4:	Mali declared its independence in September of 1960.
Fact 5:	Nigeria declared its independence in October of 1960.
Fact 6:	Sierra Leone declared its independence in April of 1961.

▼

Conclusion:	The year between June of 1960 and June of 1961 saw a great birth of freedom and independence for African peoples.

Practice Your Skills

Use a graphic device to help you find, elaborate, or organize ideas about three of the following topics.

- the experience of a picnic at the beach or a sports event
- the advantages and disadvantages of exercise classes and individual fitness routines
- ideas related to one of the following topics: music, athletics, mass media, environmental resources, the arts, weather
- family life today vs. family life a generation ago
- how to locate a business telephone number in a phone book
- the types of mass transportation
- the conclusions you can draw about people's lifestyles based on the groceries they buy

Focusing a Topic

Almost every writer sometimes has trouble thinking of a topic to write about. To deal with this problem, you can start by thinking of a broad subject that interests you. Then you can limit that subject step by step until you have brought a specific topic into focus.

ASSESSING YOUR WRITING SITUATION

Two factors may affect how you focus and limit your topic: the length of your piece and the amount of detail you want to include.

Length

In some kinds of writing you don't need to worry about length. For example, when writing for enjoyment you can explore your topic freely, stopping when you feel "all written out." Sometimes, however, you need to keep your manuscript to a set length.

Suppose, for example, that a student magazine has asked you to write an essay about outer space and the editor has allotted three pages for your piece. If you exceed that length, your article will have to be trimmed. You probably have more to say about outer space as a whole than would fit in three pages. To make the most of the space available, therefore, you will have to focus on one aspect of the subject.

You might choose, for example, to discuss outer space explorations. Once you start working on your piece, you may find you need to limit your topic further. You may then decide to focus on one particular space voyage instead of on space exploration in general.

You could, however, limit the same topic in other ways. Instead of focusing on exploration, you could discuss physical conditions in outer space. If this topic is too broad, you could narrow your focus to one physical condition, such as temperature.

Detail

Focusing your topic affects the amount and kind of detail you can include in your writing. If you are trying to cover a very broad topic in a limited space, you will most likely be able to make only very general statements. If you write the same number of words about a more limited topic, you can include a number of specific details. Suppose, for example, that you were asked to write a paper on some subject related to America before the coming of Europeans. Possible topics include:

Very general topic	America before the coming of Europeans
General topic	The Great Plains before the coming of Europeans
More specific topic	The buffalo of the Great Plains
Very specific topic	A buffalo legend of the Kiowa Indians of the Great Plains

Of course, you could write a three-page paper about any of these topics. However, if you choose the first topic, you would have to write very generally. You wouldn't have room to include much detail. If you choose the last topic, on the other hand, you could include a great deal of detail.

Only you can decide how narrowly to focus your topic. Keep in mind, however, that general statements often make dull reading. If you focus your topic just enough to match the space available, you can pack your writing with specific and concrete details—the kind that tend to capture and sustain your reader's interest.

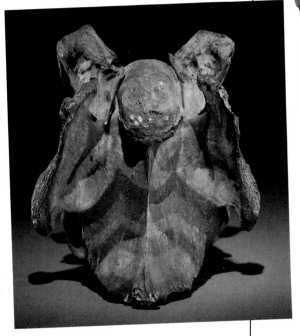

The Plains Indians use a whole buffalo skull (above) and the individual vertebrae (left) as ritual objects.

Focusing a Topic   **339**

If you decide to limit your topic, several strategies can help you. These strategies include questioning, brainstorming, and the use of graphic devices.

Questioning

Asking questions about your topic can help you come up with a list of aspects you might focus on. Keeping the words *who, what, where, when, why,* and *how* in mind as you think about your topic can help you ask appropriate questions.

For example, if you want to write about a specific aspect of Antarctica, you might ask questions like these:

> Who has explored Antarctica?
> What kind of wildlife lives in Antarctica?
> Where are the major landmarks in Antarctica located?
> When did people first establish settlements in Antarctica?
> Why are scientists interested in Antarctica?
> How have explorers managed to survive the weather in
>   Antarctica?

Suppose the last question catches your interest. As you look for the answer, you may find yourself zeroing in on one aspect of the question, such as protective clothing worn by Antarctic explorers. You may limit your topic further by asking other questions related to your original question, such as "Who makes the clothing?" This would make a sharply focused topic for a short report.

Brainstorming

Brainstorming is another way to focus a topic. Working with a partner or in a small group, each person mentions whatever he or she can think of about a given subject. When you brainstorm, don't stop to judge or discuss ideas; just jot them down and keep the ideas flowing. If you brainstorm about Antarctica, for example, you might end up with a list of ideas such as these: *penguins, 1990 Expedition, scientific laboratory in Antarctica, use of Husky dogs in Antarctic exploration,* and *first explorers.*

Any item on this list could trigger a focused topic for an essay related to Antarctica. If you choose one of these ideas and start working on your paper, you might decide to focus your topic even further. For example, suppose you start researching the use of

Writing
TIP
When you've answered one question, use the questions again on the answer to generate more ideas.

Huskies in Antarctic travel. You might learn of the great friendship that frequently develops between explorers and their dogs, and decide to focus specifically on that relationship. This procedure of brainstorming and researching will help you explore and limit your topic to fit the requirements of the composition.

Using Graphic Devices

A graphic device such as a chart, map, or cluster can also provide a way to focus a topic. For example, a cluster map on the subject of Antarctica might look like this:

Cluster Map

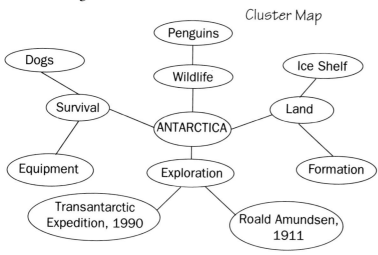

Notice that the topics become more specific as you move farther from the center of the cluster. By continuing to add items to the diagram, you increase your chance of finding a focused topic that interests you. (See also page 332.)

Practice Your Skills

Read the list of subjects below. For each subject, think of a specific topic you could cover effectively in a five-page paper. Use questioning, brainstorming, or clustering to find your topics. Then use the same strategies to come up with a different topic related to each subject.

Cooking	Disasters
Winter sports	Games
Literature	Friends

Organizing Your Writing

W R I T E R   T O   W R I T E R

The author's deepest pride, as I have experienced it, is not his incidental wisdom, but his ability to keep an organized mass of images moving forward, to feel life engendering itself under his hands.

John Updike, novelist

As John Updike suggests, any good piece of writing comes alive to the extent that it brings order out of chaos. Some writers can never begin writing without an organizational plan. Others do exploratory writing and drafting first, leaving the business of working out a suitable plan for later; they plan "after the fact," in a sense.

You will probably use a different organizational approach for different types of writing. Sometimes you will organize your thoughts early in the writing process; this approach works best when you already know most of the main points you want to make. However, if your ideas are still evolving, you can let your organization evolve with them.

Whatever approach you choose, at some point you will want to formulate a specific summary statement listing the main points you want to make. You will also want to prepare an informal outline for your paper, either before you begin your rough draft or after you finish.

Writing TIP

Planning your main ideas and supporting details in a chart can help you see the relationships among them.

TYPES OF ORGANIZATION

The organization of any piece of writing should emerge naturally from the material itself. There are a number of common organizational patterns you will want to consider as you work.

Main Idea and Supporting Details One useful way of organizing your writing is by supporting a main idea with details. Notice the specific details Charles Gallenkamp uses to support the main idea in the following paragraph.

> Unknown to the Spaniards [the first Europeans to view the Maya ruins] they were witnessing the final glimmer of far greater glories. At least two thousand years earlier, the Maya had emerged from shadowy origins to begin a steady climb toward what eventually became a civilization characterized by monumental architecture, superlative works of art, thriving trade networks, a system of writing and mathematics, a highly accurate calendar, a substantial body of astrological knowledge, and a powerful elite class who ruled over huge cities— all of which comprised one of the most original expressions of human ingenuity ever known.
>
> **Charles Gallenkamp, *Maya: The Riddle and Rediscovery of a Lost Civilization***

When writing this paragraph, Gallenkamp may have worked from an informal outline such as the following.

> Maya built a glorious civilization
> —monumental architecture
> —great works of art
> —system of writing and mathematics
> —calendar and astrological knowledge
> —system of government, huge cities

Chronological Order   When using chronological order, you organize events in the order of occurrence, as the following passage from the biography of a snake-handler, Grace Wiley, illustrates. Notice how the transitions *when, then, next, final,* and *at last* clarify the order of events.

> When Grace approached a wild cobra, she moved her hand back and forth just outside the snake's range. The cobra would then strike angrily until he became tired. Then he was reluctant to strike again. Grace's next move was to raise her hand over the snake's hood and bring it down slowly. Because of his method of rearing, a cobra cannot strike directly upward, and Grace could actually touch the top of the snake's head. . . .
>
> Then came the final touch. Grace would put her open palm toward the snake. At last the cobra was able to hit her.
>
> **Danniel P. Mannix, *Woman Without Fear***

You can vary strict chronological order by beginning with the last event, then describing the events that led up to it. Another variation is called **flashback**—jumping temporarily back in time, then back to the present. Yet another way is called **foreshadowing**—giving hints about events that will occur later in the story.

Spatial Order When using spatial organization, you present ideas in order of their physical position—from top to bottom, left to right, or background to foreground—as seen from a particular vantage point. For example, you might describe a concert from the back of the auditorium, or from the stage, looking out at the audience. Or you could describe both the stage and audience from a catwalk above. Your vantage point determines the details you will include.

The numbers below show how a writer might arrange ideas in spatial order for a report on the Snowbird climb of Mt. Everest.

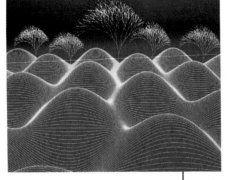

2. The Khambu Icefall, a jagged glacier with deep crevasses, between Base Camp and the supply depot at 19,300 feet

5. Final encampment at 26,000 feet on South Col (a gap between peaks, used as a pass). Teams will attempt to reach the summit from here

3. A high altitude base at 21,500 feet, with living quarters, a mess tent, and a full-time cook

1. Base Camp at 18,000 feet, a sprawling, rocky tent city, shared with climbing teams from France and Austria

4. A camp at 23,500 feet on the face of Lhotse, a peak near Everest, from which climbers can reach the South Col

In a narrative, you might present a character's observations as he or she makes them. That kind of spatial order is known as **order of impression.** In the following paragraph, Stephen Crane describes a Civil War army barrack through the eyes of a soldier lying on his bunk.

LITERARY
M O D E L

He lay down on a wide bunk that stretched across the end of the room. In the other end, cracker boxes were made to serve as furniture. They were grouped about the fireplace. A picture from an illustrated weekly was upon the log walls, and three rifles were paralleled on pegs. Equipment hung on handy projections, and some tin dishes lay upon a small pile of firewood. . . .

Stephen Crane, *The Red Badge of Courage*

Organization by Degree To organize details by degree, choose a quality that all the details share. For example, suppose you had to evaluate these fund-raising ideas.

> —Hold a dance in the gym and charge admission.
> —Mail letters to the community asking for contributions.
> —Hold a student arts-and-crafts sale.

You could evaluate the ideas by judging each more or less practical, more or less time-consuming, or more or less likely to raise enough money.

Almost any quality can be used for organizing by degree; however, two especially common qualities are **importance** and **familiarity.** In both cases, you could arrange details either from most to least or from least to most of the quality. Note how the following paragraph builds background for an unfamiliar term by beginning with the familiar experience of watching a movie.

As you think about the last movie you saw, you may recall a series of images, much like images you see in real life. But a movie is actually a rapid succession of photographs. What fools you is a characteristic of your eye called *persistence of vision*. Any image you see stays in your mind—in your eye—for a fraction of a second. Because of this delay in the human mind and eye, movies can create the illusion of continuing motion, a phenomenon know as the *cinematic effect*.

Running is an example of continuous action and coordination.

Comparison-and-Contrast Order Sometimes you will want to explore the similarities and differences of ideas or objects by comparing and contrasting them.

Suppose, for example, that you want to report on Dr. Paul Ekman's research on two kinds of smiles—genuine smiles and those that mask unpleasant feelings. Before beginning to write, you might organize your ideas in a chart such as this.

Both	True Smiles	False Smiles
produced to show pleasure	cheeks move up	cheeks may move up but not as much
	no furrow between eyebrows	furrow between eyebrows
corners of mouth curve up	crow's-feet form	no crow's feet
	skin around eyebrows droops	no drooping skin around eyebrows

You could present this information in several ways. For example, you might discuss all the characteristics of true smiles first, then all the characteristics of false ones. You also might discuss all the similarities first, and then all the differences. Still another possibility would be to compare and contrast each characteristic of the two kinds of smiles.

Cause-and-Effect Order Organizing events that are linked causally can show how two or several events are connected. Consider how the following complex cause-and-effect chain links heavy rains to the failure of sardine fishing in Egypt.

STUDENT
M O D E L

Every spring, heavy rains fell near the source of the Nile River in Egypt, causing the river to swell and flood each summer. This flooding created a fertile strip of land in the desert, which allowed farmers to plant one crop every fall—but only one. This limitation, in turn, led to the building of the giant Aswan Dam, which provided water year-round and stopped the flooding. The end of flooding reduced the flow of tiny plants to the sea, depriving sardines of their food supply and leading to the collapse of Egypt's sardine industry.

Classification Classifying means grouping items by the presence or absence of certain characteristics. For example, biologists classify animals into vertebrates (those with backbones) and invertebrates (those without backbones). These are the steps for classifying ideas.

1. Identify the quality that you want to use as a principle for classifying (such as presence or absence of a backbone).
2. Group the items based on whether or not they have the identified quality (such as invertebrates and vertebrates).

Suppose that you wanted to write an introduction to the section in the school yearbook on sports teams and athletic clubs. You might classify the material into team and individual sports and use a chart such this one to organize your ideas before writing.

Team Sports	Individual Sports
baseball	skiing
basketball	tennis
football	track and field
soccer	swimming

COMBINING TYPES OF ORGANIZATION

Fiction and drama are usually organized chronologically. Other types of writing, however, may require different organizational strategies for different parts. Consider these notes for an essay on Impressionism (a style of painting).

COMPARISON-CONTRAST ORGANIZATION

Paragraph One: Define "Impressionism"
—Like realism, presents recognizable objects (boats, trees, etc.)
—Unlike realism, objects are not clearly outlined; often misty or vague
—Realism shows things as they might appear to everyone; Impressionism shows an individual artist's impression

CHRONOLOGICAL ORGANIZATION

Paragraph Two: Brief history of Impressionism
—Word comes from Claude Monet's painting, titled *Impression: Sunrise* (1872)
—Impressionist artists at work in early 1870's included Claude Monet, Auguste Renoir, Camille Pissarro, and Alfred Sisley; all tried to capture on canvas their impressions of rapidly changing light and atmosphere
—First major exhibit of impressionist works, Paris, 1874; works by Cezanne, Degas, Gauguin, Cassatt

Writing TIP

Begin a file of writing samples (photocopies, not clippings) from newspapers, magazines, and books that you think are effective. Label each by the type of organization used.

SPATIAL ORGANIZATION
Paragraph Three: Analysis of sample Impressionist paintings
—Monet's *Water Lilies, Giverny* (1907), a good example
—Bottom foreground shows patches of lily pads on water
—Middle area all pond, with light shimmering off it
—Background more pond w/water lilies & light receding

Combining Types of Organization Within a Paragraph In the sample outlined above, each paragraph of a multi-paragraph essay used a single method of organization. Sometimes, however, you may need to vary your method organization *within* a paragraph to make your ideas flow smoothly. As you read the following paragraph, consider how each sentence is related to the ones that precede and follow it.

LITERARY
M O D E L

In mid-October the miracle occurred. Rhyader was in his enclosure, feeding his birds. A gray northeast wind was blowing and the land was sighing beneath the incoming tide. Above the sea and the wind noises, he heard a clear, high note. He turned his eyes upward to the evening sky in time to see first an infinite speck, then a black-and-white pinioned dream that circled the lighthouse once, and finally a reality that dropped to earth in the pen and came waddling forward importantly to be fed, as though she had never been away. It was the snow goose. There was no mistaking her. Tears of joy came to Rhyader's eyes.

Paul Gallico, "The Snow Goose"

This paragraph combines spatial and chronological order effectively because every sentence presents a single idea that follows logically from the one that precedes and leads logically to the next.

Practice Your Skills

A. Classify the following animals in two ways. Write each method on a sheet of paper, and beneath the description of the method, group the creatures according to that method.

eagle	domestic cat	wolf	loon
grizzly bear	sparrow	mole	duck
shark	snake	bass	jellyfish
dog	canary	rabbit	whale

B. Arrange these facts on the history of New Zealand chronologically.

As an independent nation, fought in both World War I and World War II on the side of Allies

Maoris prevented the landing of a Dutch navigator, first European to view New Zealand

Niue, 400 miles west, became self-governing in 1974

Britain declared New Zealand a colony and began organizing settlements

British Captain James Cook explored coast of New Zealand during the eighteenth century

In 1965 Cook Islands became self-governing

Colony finally became a dominion—independent member of the British Commonwealth

Maoris, Polynesians from the eastern Pacific, were the first inhabitants of New Zealand

C. Suggest a possible way of organizing each piece of writing described below, and explain the reasons for your choice.

1. a short story about a boy's reunion with his father after a long separation
2. a persuasive essay giving reasons why more nuclear power plants should (or should not) be built
3. a short essay for children explaining the differences between alligators and crocodiles
4. a magazine article for children on how to build and fly an old-fashioned Chinese dragon kite
5. an essay for your biology class on the different types of creatures found on the beaches between Maine and North Carolina

Maori art, New Zealand

Organizing
Your Writing   **349**

Drafting as Exploration

Drafting is the process of getting your ideas on paper, of exploration and discovery. Like the artist Jackson Pollock throwing pails of paint on a canvas, you can simply spill your ideas onto the page and then explore their implications. When drafting, you don't have to "get it right" the first time, or even the second or third time.

DISCOVERIES WHILE DRAFTING

Drafting can produce exciting insights and discoveries.

1. You ask questions that are worth researching. While drafting a letter to the editor of the local paper to protest the use of chimpanzees in animal research, Marion wrote, "Chimpanzees look so human." Her sentence made her stop and ask, "How much like humans are chimps?" She researched and found that chimpanzee and human chromosomes are 98 percent identical!

2. You discover new ideas. For an essay for his social science class, Phil was assigned to discuss a problem in society and recommend a solution. He chose to write about the climbing rate of high school dropouts. After researching, he stated in his draft, "Dropouts see no reason to go to school." As he continued writing, ideas occurred to him for motivating turned-off students to stay in school.

3. You gain self-knowledge. Carlos was asked to write a personal essay on what makes a place a "home." He was homesick for Mexico yet felt that he belonged in the United States as well. While freewriting he wrote, "I want to go back and I want to stay—I don't know which place is my 'home.'" In trying to explain his confusion, Carlos began to understand his feelings better.

WRITER TO WRITER

If I am lucky, I will find the answers in me that I never knew were in me.

Stephen Elsasser, student
Cedar Rapids, Iowa

You can start drafting anywhere. You can begin with the conclusion and "write backward," plunge into the middle and work both ways, or begin with the introduction. Only you can determine which method suits you or your specific writing activities. For example, whereas Jackson Pollock used a "see-how-it-falls" approach to artistic creation, Albrecht Dürer divided his drawings into squares, finishing one at a time. Had these artists tried to use each other's methods they might not have produced their best work. Similarly, successful writers range from very adventuresome to very careful drafters, each using the approach that suits him or her best.

Adventuresome Drafts An adventuresome draft is a kind of free-writing. It works well when you have a few ideas or the germ of a story you haven't thought through. You just write to see where your ideas lead, forgetting about organizational and grammatical "rules." Novelist John Steinbeck worked this way.

Careful Drafts In writing a careful draft, you begin with a plan—an outline, detailed notes, or notecards. You can start writing anywhere, but you polish each part before moving on. Novelist F. Scott Fitzgerald often used this drafting method.

Intermediate Drafts Most writers use a drafting method that combines elements of each extreme. For example, you may make a few prewriting notes or have a general plan in mind. As you write, however, you discover new ideas and follow their lead. **Bridge building** is a good way to write this type of draft. You start with a few key ideas and then discover and create the connections among them.

Drafting and Revision

Revising as You Draft Because drafting is a process of discovery, it often involves a certain amount of revision. Some writers incorporate new ideas and work out difficulties as they arise. Others quickly get down an entire draft and revise later. Feel free to revise as much as you like during drafting.

Drafting When You Can't Revise When you are writing under pressure, for essay tests or news stories, for example, you will not have time to revise your draft. You need to plan before you write by briefly outlining your main ideas. Cover essential points first in your draft and add details in subsequent paragraphs.

COMPUTER TIP

When revising your work, save your original draft on disk and experiment with changes in a new document. Then you can always return to your original version.

Beginning a Draft

Putting your first words on paper can be the most difficult part of your writing process. Remember, though, a draft doesn't have to be perfect the first time, or even the second or third time. Relax. Have some fun with your writing. Eventually, you will discover an approach that feels comfortable, and the ideas will begin to flow.

There are several common ways of beginning a draft. You can start by writing an introduction, by writing a thesis statement and topic sentences, or by simply writing any part of the draft for which you already have some ideas or information.

STARTING ANYWHERE

You might find it easier to start with some part of your paper other than the beginning. Try starting by writing about any idea that seems important to you or that is somewhat developed in your mind. A thought you wrote down in your sourcebook, an idea you got from a prewriting activity, or the results of a discussion you had while sharing can inspire you. Once you get started, you may see that the process of putting words on paper leads you to ideas you didn't even know you had. When you have written a portion of your draft this way, you can stop and determine how to introduce and conclude what you have composed.

WRITING AN INTRODUCTION

Writing
—**TIP**—

In writing an introduction, think about aspects of your topic that interest you. Then try to convey them to your readers.

Wherever you start writing your draft, you eventually will have to write the beginning, or **introduction.** An introduction usually serves two purposes—it catches the reader's attention, and it either suggests the main idea or states it directly. Some introductions begin with specific examples and conclude with a general statement. Other introductions begin with a general statement. Stating the main idea in your introduction makes it easier for the reader to understand what you are trying to analyze, describe, or prove.

Introductions vary in length, from one or two sentences to a whole paragraph for a longer piece of writing. However, not every piece of writing needs an introduction. If you are writing a story, for example, you may find that a formal introduction would clash with the tone or structure of your narrative.

Catch the Reader's Interest

The introduction is your first opportunity to catch your reader's interest. How can you achieve that? Experienced writers often use one of the following methods.

Include Startling or Interesting Facts

Begin with a statement that will surprise, disturb, or startle your readers, making them want to find out more. Reflect on aspects of the topic that caught your interest in the first place and determine if one event or fact will have the same impact on your readers.

It happened quickly. First there were 60 million, roaming the prairies and plains, blanketing whole valleys almost shoulder to shoulder for miles, the greatest abundance of any species of large mammal that modern humankind ever had the privilege to behold. And then, in 1889, there were (by one informed estimate) just 541 bison surviving throughout all the United States.

David Quammen, "The Last Bison"

Provide a Vivid, Detailed Description A dramatic, suspenseful, or mysterious description of an event or personality can both catch your readers' interest and provide an image that will aid their understanding of the topic.

It has a body of bronze and wings made from razor blades, and it behaves so much like a bee that it can convince real ones to leave their hive in search of nectar. It's a robot built by Danish and American researchers who study how bees communicate.

Scientific American

Ask a Question   Sometimes you may wish to intrigue your readers by putting your main idea in the form of a question.

What do six months of cramped quarters, zero-g [zero-gravity] toilets, and squeeze-bottle food do to your mind? The prospect of astronauts living on the space station has NASA studying the question in earnest for the first time.

Washington Post Health

Present an Anecdote   Could you relate a story that would make your reader smile or nod in recognition? A brief, sometimes amusing, retelling of an event is called an **anecdote.**

The land rover hurtled and lurched across the East African bush, alternately chasing and being chased by a huge, black rhinoceros. John Wayne leaned out of the open vehicle and nonchalantly lassoed the beast, reeling it in as if it were no more powerful than a small fish. A few scenes later, the film *Hatari* ended, the houselights in the New Jersey theater came on, and an impressionable 9-year-old boy made a career decision: drop plans to attend law school and go chase rhinos in Africa instead.

Eric Dinerstein, *Smithsonian*

Begin with a Quotation   A quotation can provide a sense of informality, action, or immediacy to your introduction.

"It's easy," they said. "Nothing to it. Wearing snowshoes is just like walking," they said. But with my face two inches above the snow, my feet twisted above my head, and my body wedged between two willows in minus 20° weather on an island in the frozen Yukon River, it did not seem all that easy.

Brad Reynolds, *National Geographic*

Address the Reader Directly   In this strategy, you "speak" directly to the readers as you introduce your topic.

> Imagine a summer day, 15,000 years ago. On a coastline along the North Pacific, where the Bering Sea will eventually rise to separate Siberia from Alaska, a group of men and women are butchering seals.
>
> **"Indelible Imprint of the Ice Age"**

Take a Stand If you begin your composition by taking a stand on a controversial issue, a reader may become interested because he or she strongly agrees or disagrees with your point of view.

> There *is* life on other planets. Communications from extraterrestrials have come to us in many forms. Midwestern farmers, southern blue-collar workers, Massachusetts bankers—even the government—have seen evidence of the existence of other life forms in the universe.

WRITE THESIS STATEMENTS AND TOPIC SENTENCES

If you are writing a formal essay or report, you may want to begin your writing by drafting a thesis statement and topic sentences. These statements sum up the ideas you will support and develop. They not only help you structure your writing, but also help your readers understand it.

Thesis Statements A **thesis statement** contains the main idea of a paper, essay, or report. It is most often a single sentence, but it can be split into two or more sentences. In addition to focusing your topic and explaining how you will treat it, a thesis statement may suggest a pattern of organization and reveal the tone.

To begin an essay for your social studies class on how cities grow and change, you might draft the following thesis statement:

> As a city grows, it starts to face several major problems: how to move people efficiently from one place to another, how to dispose of waste safely, and how to preserve the character of traditional city neighborhoods.

This thesis statement serves several purposes: it tells what the subject of the essay will be, it suggests the organization of the essay, and it establishes an impersonal, informative tone.

Topic Sentences After you have come up with a thesis statement, you can develop your ideas in separate paragraphs. Many writers state the main idea of each paragraph in a **topic sentence.** Main ideas for the essay on how cities change might be expressed in the following topic sentences:

> **Topic Sentence 1.** As cities grow, plans must be made for roads, more parking areas, and greater access to public transportation.
>
> **Topic Sentence 2.** Growing populations produce more waste, which leads to problems in providing environmentally sound disposal.
>
> **Topic Sentence 3.** Preservation of a city's neighborhoods and historic buildings is vital to maintaining the city's character.

Practice Your Skills

A. Choose any one of the topics below and gather some ideas about it. Then either write a thesis statement and two or three topic sentences that could serve as starting points for a draft, or write a paragraph that could go anywhere in your paper.

> The history of dolls, toys, or a specific toy
> The process of making a mummy
> The world's largest animals
> The history of a particular clothing style or a current fad

B. Choose one of the following introductory paragraphs. Using what you have learned in this handbook and the suggestions given, rewrite the paragraph to make it more interesting.

1. I've learned a lot about owning and caring for a pet. I've found it's not always fun. And I've learned that it's a special feeling to have a pet that's all your own. (Suggestion: Tell an anecdote about pet ownership or find a quotation about affection or responsibility.)
2. It's much easier and more interesting to get the news on television than by reading the newspaper or listening to the radio. The nightly news tells you everything you need to know in thirty minutes. (Suggestion: Listen to a TV news show. Write down an interesting "headline" or flash. Use it to open your essay.)

Hong Kong is one of the world's most crowded cities.

Drafting Paragraphs and Longer Writing

W R I T E R T O W R I T E R

When you indent for a new paragraph, it's like a singer taking a breath or a painter dipping the brush in a new color.

Amy Rosanbalm, student
Hillsboro, Oregon

WHAT IS A PARAGRAPH?

How do you know when it's time to start a new paragraph—to take the "breath" that Amy Rosanbalm spoke about? A paragraph is a group of sentences that belong together because they form a natural unit of meaning. Indent when your sentences begin to cluster around another idea. A well-made paragraph has unity, coherence, and elaboration.

Unity A paragraph is unified when all its sentences support a single main idea. Usually, the main idea is expressed in a **topic sentence,** which can appear anywhere in a paragraph. It can also be implied rather than directly stated. This is especially common in stories. In such paragraphs, unity is achieved when each sentence works toward the creation of a specific effect.

Coherence A paragraph is coherent when all the sentences relate clearly and logically to one another. In most coherent paragraphs, transitional devices are used to link sentences. Coherent paragraphs can be organized in a number of ways, such as chronologically, spatially, by cause and effect, by comparison and contrast, and by order of importance. (See "Organizing Your Writing," pages 342–349.)

Elaboration A paragraph is well-elaborated when the main idea is effectively supported by details that develop the idea of the stated or implied topic sentence or the incident or object being described. (See "Elaboration," pages 364–369.)

Paragraphs with Topic Sentences

As you continue to develop your own writing skills, you will become more and more aware of the importance of unity, coherence, and elaboration in creating effective paragraphs. The paragraph below begins with a topic sentence that states the main idea. Notice how Dylan Thomas uses elaboration in developing the main idea and achieves unity and coherence.

The magic in a poem is always accidental. No poet would labor intensively upon the intricate craft of poetry unless he hoped that, suddenly, the accident of magic would occur. . . . The miraculous thing about miracles is that they do sometimes happen. And the best poem is that whose worked-upon unmagical passages come closest . . . to those moments of magical accident.

Dylan Thomas, "On Poetry"

The paragraph is unified because all its sentences relate to the main idea of accidental magic in poetry. It is coherent because it presents a series of points about poetic magic that all lead sensibly to one another. Finally, because Dylan Thomas adequately developed the main idea of poetic magic, the paragraph displays effective elaboration.

Paragraphs Without Topic Sentences

Not all paragraphs have a topic sentence. The topic sentence may be stated in a previous paragraph, it may be stated in a paragraph that follows, or it may never be stated at all. Many narrative paragraphs, for instance, do not contain topic sentences. Instead, each sentence presents a bit of description or an event. The whole series of sentences presents a single incident or effect.

The following paragraph has a single idea: that almost everyone has heard Muzak and almost everyone dislikes it. All the sentences in the paragraph relate to that idea. Nevertheless, no one sentence in the paragraph states this topic. In other words, this paragraph has an **implied topic sentence.**

▼

Everyone, except for a few aliens from distant galaxies, has heard Muzak. It plays, of course, on elevators. Many people associate it with the pleasures of being held captive in the dentist's chair or waiting, ear squashed to the telephone, on hold. Others consider it a form of unregulated air pollution, stupefyingly bland and toxically pervasive, as calming a sound as the grinding drone of garbage compactors. Only the pop artist Andy Warhol professed to love Muzak. But then, Warhol also said he would really rather be a robot.

Jeanne McDermott, "Muzak Is the Music We Hear but Don't Listen To"

PROFESSIONAL
M O D E L

Even though there is no topic sentence, the sentences in this paragraph all deal with a single topic and present a logical sequence of ideas. In a logical sequence, each idea builds on the ideas presented before it and leads logically to the ones that come after it. For example, in the paragraph above, Jeanne McDermott first introduces the subject of Muzak by reminding us of how pervasive it is in our society. She then goes on to tell how most people feel about Muzak, and she ends with a wry comment about Andy Warhol. The paragraph forms a chain of ideas that fit together neatly.

Writing
━TIP━

Even when you draft a paragraph without a topic sentence, it is helpful to write a rough topic sentence in your notes.

FROM PARAGRAPHS TO LONGER WRITING

Most paragraphs do not stand alone, but are part of a longer piece of writing—a group of related paragraphs that develop a single idea or theme. As a building block, a paragraph can serve two basic functions: structural or developmental. You should try to mix these two functions effectively in your writing.

Structural Paragraphs

The structural paragraphs in a longer piece of writing provide the framework of the piece—they help join the parts of the work together and move the reader from one idea to the next. Such a paragraph may introduce the work, provide a transition between ideas, or conclude the work. You are probably conscious of introductions and conclusions as you read, but are you equally aware of transitional paragraphs such as the following?

> You would think such an experience would have unnerved the young actor. Instead, it served to prepare him for his next big challenge.

This paragraph refers to an episode described earlier in the piece and sets the stage for one to follow. In other words, it links two other paragraphs. Try using transitional paragraphs like this in your own writing.

Developmental Paragraphs

Developmental paragraphs present or develop an idea. They may define, describe, narrate, classify, analyze, explain a process, or combine two or more of these purposes. A longer piece of writing usually requires a mix of these types of paragraphs to adequately develop its topic.

Paragraphs That Define and Classify When you define a particular term or a special concept, you discuss it in detail, distinguishing it from similar terms or concepts. When you classify, you provide categories into which something or someone can be placed. The following paragraph begins by providing a functional definition of comedy. Then it goes on to classify it into two major categories— physical comedy and verbal humor.

For me, comedy is whatever makes people laugh. Many comedians rely on physical comedy, or slapstick, such as the classic banana peel on the sidewalk. Other comedians rely on verbal humor—on making us laugh with words. The kind of verbal comedy that appeals to me most is the one-liner—the short, tart quip that usually relies on giving a surprising twist to our expectations.

Paragraphs That Narrate and Describe In a narrative paragraph, you tell all or part of a story. In a descriptive paragraph, you share with the reader observations you made with your five senses. In the paragraph below, Willa Cather tells the story of a snowfall in words that vividly appeal to the senses.

The first snowfall came early in December. I remember how the world looked from our sitting room window as I dressed behind the stove that morning: the low sky was like a sheet of metal; the blond cornfields had faded out into ghostliness at last; the little pond was stiff under its willow bushes.

Willa Cather, *My Antonia*

Paragraphs That Analyze In a paragraph of analysis, you break a complex topic down into smaller parts and examine each part. Often, analysis takes the form of comparison or contrast, in which you discuss the similarities or differences between two or more related items. The paragraph below analyzes a child's development through a before-and-after contrast.

In some ways the transition from two to three is the most crucial of a person's life. At the beginning, he has a vocabulary so small you could list all the words, and he can only say one of them at a time; at the end, he's discoursing and debating. . . . At the beginning, you worry that any mistake in discipline might misshape his future personality; at the end, he already has a personality which you don't have any power to change.

Richard Cohen, *Say You Want Me*

Paragraphs That Explain a Process In this type of paragraph, you explain the steps that go into a process, using chronological order to make the steps easy to follow.

▼

> Sit close to the model or object which you intend to draw and lean forward in your chair. Focus your eyes on some point —any point will do—along the contour of the model. Place the point of your pencil on the paper. Imagine that your pencil point is touching the model instead of the paper. Without taking your eyes off the model, wait until you are convinced that your pencil is touching that point on the model upon which your eyes are fastened.
>
> **Kimon Nikolaïdes, *The Natural Way To Draw***

Practice Your Skills

A. Identify the topic sentence of each paragraph below, or if there is no topic sentence, tell what the implied topic of the paragraph is. Then identify the elements that make each paragraph unified, coherent, and well-elaborated.

1. Back east they name towns Willow Springs and Elmhurst and Appleville. Out here, where willows, elms, and apples will not grow, there's a town name Greasewood and another named Cocklebur, and another named Hackberry. That's the honest truth, you see. Yucca, Arizona. It doesn't sound as pretty as Willow Springs, but it's the truth; no willows, lots of yuccas.

   Charles Kuralt

2. While most anti-fur groups work by moral persuasion, a few animal activists have adopted extreme, even criminal tactics to advance their cause. In New York City they have sprayed coats with paint. On Fur-Free Friday several fur shops were vandalized in Miami and Fort Lauderdale. In Europe anti-fur commandos have even attacked fur wearers to gain attention.

   J.D. Reed, "The Furor Over Wearing Furs"

3. The old man wore the simplest cottons, faded from long use and countless washings. His skin was as parched and brown as the slopes above his high pasture in Baltistan's Karakoram Range. Only the old man's eyes, twinkling like diamonds behind thick glasses, hinted that this was no ordinary farmer.

   Galen Rowell and Barbara Cushman Rowell

B. Read each of the following paragraphs, and state its possible developmental function or functions in a longer piece of writing.

1. The whole world is in flood, the land as well as the water. Water streams down the trunks of trees, drips from hat-brims, courses across roads. The whole earth seems to slide like sand down a chute; water pouring over the least slope leaves the grass flattened, silver side up, pointing downstream. Everywhere windfall and flotsam twigs and leafy boughs, wood from woodpiles, bottles, and saturated straw spatter the ground or streak it in curving windrows. . . .

    Annie Dillard, "Flood"

2. This [idea of partisanship] is a harmless attitude in sporting contests, but I think it represents a widespread human tendency . . . . There is no psychological challenge or excitement in remaining neutral; lack of partisanship is boring compared to the fervor of cheering for a favorite. Taking sides gives one a feeling of *belonging,* which is evidently one of the most forceful drives of the human animal. . . . No matter how much "individualism" we may preach philosophically, in emotional terms we have a deep need to identify ourselves with some specific goal.

    Sydney J. Harris, *Clearing the Ground*

3. Love is the bridge that leads from the *I* sense to the *We,* and there is a paradox about personal love. Love of another individual opens a new relation between the personality and the world. The lover responds in a new way to nature and may even write poetry. Love is affirmation; it motivates the *yes* responses and the sense of wider communication. Love casts out fear, and in the security of this togetherness we find contentment, courage. We no longer fear the age-old haunting questions: "Who am I?" "Where am I going?"—and having cast out fear, we can be honest and charitable.

    Carson McCullers, "The Mortgaged Heart"

4. Plant the common small white bush bean about the first of June, in rows three feet by eighteen inches apart, being careful to select fresh round and unmixed seed. First look out for worms, and supply vacancies by planting anew. Then look out for woodchucks, if it is an exposed place, for they will nibble off the earliest tender leaves. . . . But above all harvest as early as possible, if you would escape frosts and have a fair and salable crop; you may save much loss by this means.

    Henry David Thoreau, *Walden*

Elaboration: Developing Your Ideas

Finding a writing idea is a major part of your writing process. However, an idea is only a skeleton. At some time during the writing process, you will need to flesh out that skeleton by developing your main ideas in detail. The process of working out the details of an idea is called **elaboration.**

Finding details to develop a main idea is usually easier than initially coming up with the idea, because you know the key points, events, or concepts you need to support. To develop a main idea, you can use any of the personal, writing, sharing, or graphic techniques for finding ideas described in Writing Handbooks 2 and 3 (pages 322–337). For example, consider the following situations:

- You are writing a report on hunger in India. One of your main ideas is that famine is much less common in India today than it was twenty years ago. To support this main idea, you need to find some facts or statistics about famine in India in the 1960's, 1970's, and 1980's.
- You are writing a short story about a female rodeo rider. You want to begin with a scene that will grab the attention of your readers, and you have come up with the idea of starting with an incident in which a rodeo rider is thrown from a bull. To support this main idea, you need to find sensory details that can be used to describe the experience of riding a bull.

You would probably want to conduct research to locate facts and statistics on famine in India, while interviewing, discussion, and listing would be helpful sources of details about riding a bull.

What types of details should you use to develop your main ideas? The answer depends on the type of idea you wish to develop. To support an opinion, you may wish to use facts and statistics, or you may decide to quote an authority. To present a great many specific facts in a brief space, you might use a chart, a table, or some other kind of graphic aid. To describe a person, place, or thing, you would want to use sensory details. To illustrate a point, you can describe an incident. To clarify a point, you can provide examples.

Facts and Statistics A **fact** is a statement that can be proved either by the use of reference materials or by first-hand observation. **Statistics** are facts expressed in numbers. Notice in the following article how the writer used facts and statistics to develop the main idea.

> According to Earth's first complete wilderness inventory, a third of the planet's land mass remains unchanged by humans. That's approximately 18 million square miles, but only a fifth of it is legally protected. The bulk of the world's wilderness— 41 percent—lies in the barren polar regions. Some of it extends into northern Canada, Alaska, and the Soviet Union. A much smaller tract snakes through Tibet, Afghanistan, Saudi Arabia, and Africa. North America is the wildest of the settled continents, with over 37 percent wilderness. Europe is the tamest, with less than three percent of its land left untouched.
>
> **AMBIO, "How Wild Is the World?"**

COMPUTER TIP

A computer data bank can be a good source for facts and statistics.

PROFESSIONAL
M O D E L

Among the Sierra Nevada Mountains, California, 1868, by Albert Bierstadt

Sensory Details Often you develop an idea by including relevant details that appeal to your reader's senses of sight, smell, taste, touch, or hearing. Which senses does the author appeal to in the following paragraph?

> From every hill slope came the trickle of running water, the music of unseen fountains. All things were thawing, bending, snapping. The Yukon was straining to break loose from the ice that bound it down. It ate away from beneath; the sun ate from above. Air-holes formed, fissures sprang and spread apart, while thin sections of ice fell through bodily into the river. And amid all this bursting, rending, throbbing of awakening life, under the blazing sun and through the soft-sighing breezes, like wayfarers to death, staggered the two men, the woman, and the huskies.
>
> **Jack London, *The Call of the Wild***

Anecdotes One way to make a point is to tell an anecdote—an incident or single event that is interesting or significant. In the following paragraph the writer uses an anecdote to elaborate on his main idea.

> Show-business tradition holds that whatever happens, "the show must go on." Often performers are called upon to make enormous sacrifices to achieve this end. For example, once flutist James Galway was performing in an outdoor concert at Ravinia, just north of Chicago. At one point in the show, when Galway opened his mouth to take a breath, a large bug flew into it. For a moment, he stopped playing and considered what he might do. Then realizing that the show must go on, he took a great gulp and continued with his playing.
>
> **Bob Shepherd, "The Show Must Go On"**

Specific Examples Sometimes you can support or explain a main idea with one or more specific examples. Examples can also help you define a new or unusual term you are using. In the following example, the journalist Russell Baker begins an article on illegal copying by providing his readers two examples of this kind of activity.

> Copying machines are revolutionizing the way we live. With recording tape plugged into the radio, a person can now create a private musical library far more cheaply than by buying records. With print duplicators, a fetching piece of writing can be quickly reproduced and circulated among hundreds of acquaintances without the expense of paying the writer for his labor.
>
> **Russell Baker**

Quotations   Quotations can be used for many purposes. You can quote an expert to lend authority to a point that you've already made. You can also use quotations to introduce new ideas or details. The quotation in the following passage does both.

> The propulsion systems featured in *Star Trek* and *Star Wars* can surpass the speed of light, which many researchers dismiss as impossible. But the McDonnell Douglas engineers still wonder. "Maybe it will be like breaking through the sound barrier," Runge muses. "The faster you go, the harder it gets and the greater the drag until you break through; then it gets easier."
>
> **Dennis Meredith, "The Planet of Origin: Hollywood"**

PROFESSIONAL
M O D E L

Opinions   There are many types of opinions. Some of the most common are judgments and predictions. One way to select and organize opinions is by comparing and contrasting them. The following paragraph is organized by presenting a judgment and then supporting it with facts and predictions.

> The United States is in trouble due to falling interest in and knowledge of science. For the past two decades, the number of college students choosing to pursue science and mathematics has declined steadily. Today, more than half of the graduate students in the United States are from other countries. If this trend continues, there will not be enough trained scientists and technical people in the United States to meet the challenges of the twenty-first century.

STUDENT
M O D E L

Elaboration   **367**

Graphic Aids Another way to present supporting information in your writing is visually using graphic aids. Common graphic aids include bar graphs, pie charts, maps, tables, and time lines. For example, suppose that you were writing a report on the changes in the labor force in the United States over the last century. An encyclopedia included the following statistics in tabular form. You could present this information clearly and concisely in your report in the form of a graph, calculating and plotting statistics for the total labor force to give the graph more impact.

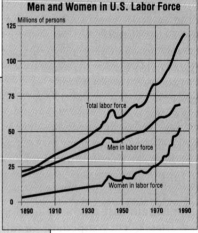

Men and Women in U.S. Labor Force

Men and Women in U.S. Labor Force

Year	Men in labor force	Male % of labor force	Women in labor force	Female % of labor force
1890	18,129,000	83%	3,704,000	17%
1900	22,641,000	82%	4,999,000	18%
1910	*	*	*	*
1920	32,053,000	80%	8,229,000	20%
1930	37,008,000	78%	10,396,000	22%
1940	42,020,000	75%	14,160,000	25%
1950	45,446,000	71%	18,412,000	29%
1960	48,870,000	68%	23,272,000	32%
1970	54,343,000	63%	31,560,000	37%
1980	62,088,000	58%	44,733,000	42%
1985	65,967,000	56%	51,200,000	44%
1986	66,973,000	56%	52,568,000	44%

* Not available
Source: U.S. Bureau of Statistics

Practice Your Skills

A. Choose three of the following main ideas. To support or develop each statement you select, either follow the suggestions in parentheses or choose some other approach for finding new details and ideas.

1. Children's television programs are often violent. (*Suggestion:* Use clustering, observation, brainstorming, or discussion to find specific examples.)
2. The time of year often affects the way people think and act. (*Suggestion:* Use freewriting about the effect of the seasons on your own life to come up with one or more incidents you can use to develop this idea.)
3. The United States is a land of many varied cultures. (*Suggestion:* Use your own knowledge, information from a group discussion, or information from library research to gather examples, facts, and statistics.)
4. Playing a musical instrument can help you understand and appreciate music. (*Suggestion:* Use freewriting, brainstorming, or discussion to gather details. You may wish to give specific examples. You also may wish to quote one of your classmates.)

B. Choose one of the following sets of directions and create a graphic aid that might be used in a report. Use reference works such as atlases, encyclopedias, or almanacs as necessary. Be sure your graphic is easy to understand. If necessary, include a key so that readers can interpret the information.

1. Imagine that you are working for your school librarian. The librarian has asked you to write a brief guide for other students on how to use the library. Create a floor plan as a graphic aid to be used in your guide.
2. The four largest oceans in the world are the Pacific, which covers 64 million square miles; the Atlantic, which covers 32 million square miles; the Indian, which covers 28 million square miles; and the Arctic, which covers 5 million square miles. Create a table or a bar graph to represent this information.
3. Imagine that you are writing a brief biography of your favorite author. Make a time line showing major events in his or her life, including publication of his or her books.
4. Create a graphic that shows the relative heights of the five tallest buildings in the world. Include the height of each building in feet or stories and the location of each structure. Remember to give your graphic a title.

GULLAH

About 250,000 people living on the islands off the southeastern coast of the United States awake to *dayclean*, not dawn. There, *tek e foot enn 'e han* means "to hurry away." *Onrabel e mout*, which literally means "unravel his mouth," is the way to describe someone who talks a lot. The people on these islands speak Gullah, an English dialect that blends English vocabulary with West African grammar and intonations.

Gullah is an example of the type of language that develops when people from different cultures struggle to communicate. Its roots go back to the sixteenth century, when Africans who spoke hundreds of different local languages were captured by the slave traders. Since the Africans and the traders did not speak a common language, they developed a "pidgin" that combined aspects of their various languages. Pidgin English became the language of the slave ships. It continued to evolve on the plantations of the

Bather. Louis LeBlanc (1954). Oil. Permanent art collection; Texas Southern University.

South and began to disappear when slavery ended. However, Gullah has survived, primarily because it is spoken in island communities that have remained relatively isolated for much of the past century.

Unity and Coherence

Reading good writing is effortless because the writer's ideas flow smoothly and logically from one another. This smooth flow is due to two factors—unity and coherence. Writing has **unity** when all the details support the main idea; it has **coherence** when all the ideas are connected logically to one another.

Unity and coherence are characteristics of both paragraphs and longer pieces of writing. Techniques for achieving them in paragraphs can easily be transferred to whole compositions.

UNITY IN PARAGRAPHS

All good writing is characterized by unity. In a unified paragraph, all the sentences relate to the main idea of the paragraph, whether that idea is stated or implied. You can achieve unity in your paragraphs in several ways.

Topic Sentence and Supporting Details

One way to create a unified paragraph is to write a clear, concise topic sentence that states the main idea of the paragraph. Then support that idea with details in all the other sentences. A topic sentence is often most effective at the beginning of a paragraph. However, it may also appear later in the paragraph or at the end to summarize or reinforce the main idea presented. In the following model, the topic sentence falls at the beginning of the paragraph. The rest of the sentences provide the specific details, elaborating on the main idea.

> When archaeologists of the future excavate our landfills, they will discover information about our society that we would probably rather keep secret. For example, they'll see that people in our era were wasteful, throwing away broken appliances and machines instead of fixing them. They'll see that people threw away soiled diapers instead of washing and reusing cotton ones. Archaeologists of the future will also see that people in our society were lazy. We continued to throw away recyclable goods long after recycling became possible in our communities.

S T U D E N T
M O D E L

Separate Paragraphs for Separate Ideas   Each paragraph you write should concern a single idea. A paragraph will not be unified if more than one main idea is discussed. Therefore, analyze each paragraph during revision and create new paragraphs wherever necessary. Notice that the writer of the model below inserted a paragraph break to avoid having two main ideas in the same paragraph.

Seasickness, or motion sickness, results when your brain receives conflicting messages from the eyes and the organs of balance in the inner ear. These organs do not always correctly report to the brain the motions of the body. For example, when you're on a boat, your balance organs may tell your brain that your body is going up, while your eyes tell your brain that your body is going down. The brain mistakenly interprets the mixed signals as a sign that the body has been poisoned. Then it triggers a response of nausea and vomiting to rid the body of the poison. ¶ You can avoid or reduce the effects of seasickness, however, by keeping your brain from receiving conflicting signals. To do this, hold your head still—for example, by bracing it on a headrest. Second, stare straight ahead, fixing your eyes on the distant horizon. In addition, before you travel you can take medication that helps to prevent seasickness.

Implied Main Idea

Not every paragraph has to contain a topic sentence to be unified. You can also achieve unity by writing a series of sentences related to an idea that is implied, but not stated directly. For example, in the following paragraph, all the sentences help support a single main idea—that old-fashioned bicycle gears are being replaced by safer, easier-to-use pushbutton gears. However, no single sentence expresses this idea.

Changing gears on a ten-speed can be difficult and danger-ous. A rider has to look away from the road to see and adjust the shift levers. If a cyclist tries to change gears while standing up to climb a hill, the chain—and the rider—can slip. "Gear fear" is the main reason that "so many of the ten-speeds that were bought in the cycling boom of the 70's are hanging in gar-ages," says Fred Zahradnik, technical editor of *Bicycling* maga-zine. "But with new index shifting systems . . . ," he explains, "you just push the button, hear it click, and you're in gear."

Linda Williams, "Reinventing the Wheel"

Logical Progression of Ideas

You can also write a unified paragraph in which the main idea is neither stated nor implied by presenting ideas in a logical sequence. Notice the logical progression of ideas in the following paragraph from weird-looking people, to rich, to those who are both.

In the first place, we have more weird-looking people in New York City than can be found in any other American city. Also, more rich people. We have so many rich people that I once came to the conclusion that other cities were sending us the rich people they wanted to get rid of. . . . Some of the weird-looking people and some of the rich people are the same peo-ple. Why would a rich person want to look weird? As we New Yorkers like to say, Go know.

Calvin Trillin, "What Makes New Yorkers Tick"

Related Details

Unity is particularly important in descriptions. A good description creates a complete picture or impression in your reader's imagination by presenting details that vividly support that impression. Consider the following paragraph from an article about the 1989 San Francisco earthquake.

I prowled the Marina, past water crews restoring the area's sixty-six broken mains, past streams of evacuees towing wheeled suitcases full of clothes. I saw houses that were intact but had partially sunk into the soil. Beside them I found small volcano-shaped piles of sand, signs that the shaking had liquefied the soil, allowing the building to settle.

National Geographic

San Francisco
Earthquake, 1989

Notice the words and phrases that support the image of the aftermath of a disaster: *prowled, broken, evacuees towing wheeled suitcases, sunk into the soil, volcano-shaped piles of sand, shaking, liquefied.* If the narrator had used words such as *orderly* and *smiling,* the unity of the descriptive image would have been destroyed.

UNITY IN LONGER PIECES OF WRITING

The same techniques you use in creating paragraph unity work for creating unity in longer pieces of writing. To ensure that an essay or a research paper has unity, make sure that each paragraph is related to your main idea and that all your supporting details in fact support that idea as well as the main idea of the paragraph in which they appear. For example, suppose a classmate had written the following persuasive essay about the positive aspects of school uniforms and had given it to you for your response. What would you say about the unity of the piece?

▼

S T U D E N T
· · · · · · · · · · · · · ·
M O D E L

Say "school uniforms," and most students will respond, "Ugh!" However, I think that wearing a uniform to school every day would make things a lot easier for everyone. First, uniforms would eliminate the anxiety students currently feel about their clothes. Are my clothes new enough, fashionable enough, the right color, the right brand? We wouldn't have to worry any more about how our classmates felt about our clothes. We would all be equal.

There is an economic benefit as well. We would all save a lot of money by not having to buy fashionable clothes to wear to school. True, buying more than one uniform can be expensive, but buying many individual outfits for each season is even more so.

Finally, think of all the time we would save by not having to decide what to wear each day. Maybe some teen-agers like staring bleakly into their closets while the clock ticks ahead, or trying on shirt after shirt to match their pants, but I'd rather have more time for breakfast.

You would probably respond that the essay is unified, because each paragraph is related to the main idea and the supporting details support those ideas.

Practice Your Skills

Revise the following paragraphs to improve their unity.

1. One should never attempt weight lifting without first consulting a doctor or getting some coaching from an experienced weight lifter. If these steps are not taken first, you can easily injure yourself. If you don't lift properly, with a spotter to help you, you can drop weights on your feet or chest, crushing them. You should also be careful about dropping objects in a pool where people are swimming. If you try to lift too much weight too quickly, you can easily break a bone, tear a tendon or ligament, dislocate a joint, or cause other physical trauma. People with high blood pressure should stay away from certain types of weight lifting because of the danger of fainting and subsequent injury. Weight lifting can help you to build a firm, toned body and to improve your aerobic fitness.

Writing
━━ **TIP** ━━

One way to check for unity in longer writing is to summarize each paragraph in one sentence and see if each sentence relates to the main idea.

2. A dense, white fog rolled through the darkened woods. Above, through the gnarled limbs of the trees, one could see the silver moon, gliding in and out of dark clouds. There were lots of apple trees, the kind that produce those delicious McIntoshes. The woods were eerily silent, except for the occasional crack of a twig. When an owl hooted, we jumped out of our skins. We were alone and afraid.

3. For much of the fifth century B.C., Athens was dominated by Pericles. As leader of the popular party, he worked to make his city the most outstanding in Greece. Pericles loved a cultured and intelligent woman named Aspasia. Gossip claimed that she influenced his policies to a degree unusual in Athens, where upper-class women were kept secluded. Pericles tried to extend Athenian power by foreign conquest and to beautify the city by an ambitious program of public works.

COHERENCE IN PARAGRAPHS

Even if your writing is unified, the ideas must flow smoothly, or the paragraph will not be coherent. To achieve coherence, you must present your ideas in a logical sequence—chronologically or spatially; by cause and effect or comparison and contrast; or by order of importance, degree, or familiarity. (For more information, see "Types of Organization," pages 342–347.) Here are two techniques for making the relationships among your ideas clear:

- Include transitions to show how ideas are related.
- Use word chains—pronouns, synonyms, and repeated words—to show that statements made in separate sentences refer to the same things.

Transitional Devices

Transitional devices play a key role in achieving coherence both within and between paragraphs. Without transitions, readers sometimes have difficulty determining the relationships among ideas.

Some of the most common transitions show temporal or spatial relationships. Other transitions show relations of degree, comparison and contrast, or cause and effect, or provide additional information.

Time or Sequence When telling a story or describing a process that involves a temporal sequence of events, you can connect ideas with words and phrases such as the following:

Transitions That Show Temporal Relationships

after	preceding	finally
next	then	during
before	again	every time
the next day	while	soon
always	meanwhile	simultaneously
first	second	at the beginning
at that time	last	at the same time

Simultaneously all three went for the ball and the coconut-like sound of their heads colliding secretly delighted the bird.

Notice how temporal transitions were used to connect ideas in the following paragraph.

When I was four I wanted to be a garbageman. I loved the rattling of the cans and the whir of the compressor; I thought that all of New York's trash might be squeezed into a single, capacious truck. *Then*, when I was five, my father took me to see the Tyrannosaurus at the American Museum of Natural History. *As* we stood in front of the beast, a man sneezed; I gulped and prepared to utter my *Shema Yisrael* [a prayer]. But the animal stood immobile in all its bony grandeur, and *as* we left, I announced that I would be a paleontologist *when* I grew up.

Stephen J. Gould, *The Panda's Thumb*

PROFESSIONAL
M O D E L

Space When writing a visual description, consider using the following words that show spatial relationships to connect your ideas.

Transitions That Show Spatial Relationships

behind	in back of	on the left of
to the right of	in front of	above
below	over	under
around	beneath	down
up	here	there
on top of	through	in the center
at the bottom of	inside	outside

Note how the spatial transitions used in the following paragraph help you not only to connect ideas but also to visualize the scene.

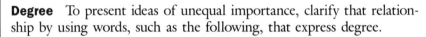

Deep inside the huge limestone cave was a pipe organ made of stalactites and stalagmites. We stood *in the middle* of the cavern. The giant natural pipe organ was *all around* us. When the organist began to play "Shenandoah," we heard the beautiful tune ringing from *above*, from *below*, and from *the most distant corners* of the cavern.

Degree To present ideas of unequal importance, clarify that relationship by using words, such as the following, that express degree.

Transitions That Show Degree

first	second	mainly
more important	most important	best
less important	least important	worst

The paragraph on the next page shows how transitions of degree can be used to rank ideas. As you read, notice that the transitions *first, second,* and *third* show chronological relationships as well as degrees of importance.

If a fire starts, the _most important_ thing to remember is—don't panic. Everyone should leave the building immediately. If you see smoke, it's _best_ to get down and crawl toward the nearest door, because smoke rises. Feel the door before going through it to see if it's hot. If your clothing catches fire, the _main_ thing to remember is this simple process: stop, drop, and roll. _First_, stop where you are; _second_, drop to the floor; _third_, roll around until you've extinguished the flames. Don't panic and run because the flames may spread if you do that. The _least important_ thing to do in a fire is to save your belongings. Human life is the _most important_ consideration.

Comparison and Contrast Some of the following transition words may be useful when you are comparing and contrasting ideas.

Transitions That Show Comparison

as	than	similarly
in the same way	likewise	also
either . . . or	neither . . . nor	like

Transitions That Show Contrast

yet	but	however
unlike	in contrast	instead
on the other hand	on the contrary	nevertheless

Unity and
Coherence   **379**

Note how the transitions of comparison and contrast in the following paragraph help reveal similarities and differences.

Two twentieth-century women stand out in the history of physical fitness, _but_ for entirely different reasons. They were Adelle Davis and Babe Didrickson Zaharias. Adelle Davis had a firm _but_ practical approach to health, _in sharp contrast_ to the ideas of food faddists. She said of such extremists, "Frankly, I often wonder what such persons plan to do with health in case they acquire it." Babe Didrickson Zaharias, _on the other hand_, was not a nutritionist _but_ the finest female athlete in modern times. In her battle with cancer, she said, "I _not only_ wasn't going to let it kill me, I wasn't even going to let it put me on the shelf."

Cause and Effect   When you are writing about a cause-and-effect relationship, you can use some of the following transitions to help clarify that relationship and to make your writing coherent.

Transitions That Show Cause and Effect

because	therefore	so
consequently	as a result	for
accordingly	thus	if . . . then
since	due to	for this reason
owing to	although	so that

In the following paragraph, note how transitions of cause and effect help explain the writer's proposal for legislative reform that would remedy a source of political conflict.

▼

The founding fathers made no mention of political parties in the U.S. Constitution. *As a result*, this document is of little help in solving problems that arise from the existence of parties. The political party of the President often loses seats in Congress in the elections held between presidential elections. *Because* of this, the Congress and the executive branch are often in political conflict. Some have suggested that, to remedy the source of conflict, the President and Congress should run for office simultaneously and should hold office for four-year terms. Others have suggested that *in order to* create political harmony in Washington, we should have a parliamentary system. *As a consequence* of such a system, our legislative branch would be elected along with the executive branch, eliminating one source of conflict.

Other Relationships Transitions make your writing coherent by alerting your reader to what is coming next. In addition to the uses already discussed, transitions can be used to signal that an example is coming up, that the material following the transition is being emphasized, or that additional information or an explanation is being given.

Transitions That Introduce Examples

as	for example	for instance
like	such as	to illustrate
that is	namely	in particular

Transitions That Signal Emphasis

indeed	in fact	certainly

Transitions That Signal More Information

in addition	besides	furthermore
moreover	also	as well as

Notice as you read the following paragraph how the transitions alert you to examples and additional information needed for a clear understanding of the subject.

Consumer Reports rates products according to various characteristics so that consumers can choose among the products. *In other words*, the magazine lists products in order of their quality. *For example*, sandwich and storage bags are rated from 1 to 5 on measures *such as* price, cost per bag, closure, moisture retention, bursting resistance, and puncture resistance. *In addition*, the writers and editors of *Consumer Reports* bracket brands that they consider about equal in quality and rank them according to price.

Word Chains

Another way you can achieve coherence in your writing is by using a pronoun or synonym for a word or phrase you used earlier. Occasionally, you might also want to reiterate a word or phrase to create an emotional effect.

Pronouns Using pronouns can help you achieve both coherence and economy in your writing. Notice how the writer of the following passage used pronouns to convey his message simply and clearly.

Adding an engine to a flying machine gives *it* the power to dispense with winds and air currents that govern the flight of unpowered craft such as balloons and gliders. In order to steer an airplane, a system of flaps is used. *These* act just like the rudder of a boat. *They* deflect the air flow and turn or tilt the airplane so that *it* rotates around *its* center of gravity, which in all airplanes lies between the wings.

David Macaulay, *The Way Things Work*

Synonyms and Near-Synonyms In addition to using pronouns to achieve coherence, you can substitute words that indicate the same thing. In the following paragraph, a single fish is mentioned several times, but many different terms, including synonyms, near-synonyms, and pronouns, are used to refer to that same fish.

And then, in 1938, a trawler fishing off the coast of South Africa brought up _a very strange fish_. _It was large, nearly two metres long, with powerful jaws and heavy armoured scales._ After _the catch_ had been landed at East London, the curator of the small local museum, Miss Courtney-Latimer, came down to look _it_ over. She noticed _this peculiar fish_ and although she was not a fish specialist, she became convinced that _it_ was of great importance. She wrote to Professor J.B.L. Smith, . . . describing _it_ briefly . . . _It_ was a gutted _specimen_ that he eventually saw. In spite of this, and the fact that _it_ was so large, he recognized _it_ immediately. . . . He named _it_ Latimeria and informed an astonished world that _a creature_ thought to have been extinct for 70 million years was still alive.

David Attenborough, Life on Earth

Repeated Words In descriptive or persuasive writing, you might consider repeating a word or phrase several times in a passage for emphasis or to create a mood. Repetition of words is also used in speeches, where the human voice can give several different tones to the same word or phrase. Note how this device helps build the emotional impact of the final paragraph of the "Gettysburg Address."

But, in a larger sense, _we can not_ dedicate—_we can not consecrate_—_we can not_ hallow—this ground. The brave men, living and dead, who struggled here, have _consecrated_ it, far above our poor power to add or detract. The world will little note, nor long remember _what we say here_, but it can never forget _what they did here. It is for us the living_, rather, _to be dedicated_ here to the unfinished work which they who fought here have thus far so nobly advanced. _It is rather for us to be here dedicated_ to the great task remaining before us—that from these honored dead we take increased _devotion_ to that cause for which they gave the last full measure of _devotion_— that we here highly resolve that these dead shall not have died in vain; that this nation, under God, shall have a new birth of freedom—and that government _of the people, by the people, for the people_, shall not perish from the earth.

Abraham Lincoln, "Gettysburg Address"

WRITER TO WRITER

I don't use tricks for writing. I just try to keep the paper interesting and keep it flowing.

Mike Hultberg, student
Seattle, Washington

The paragraphs in a longer piece of writing also should flow smoothly from one another and be logically connected. The same devices that you can draw on to achieve coherence in a paragraph—logical pattern of organization, transitions, and word chains—also work to create coherence in longer works. Note how chronological organization and the use of repetition of words, pronouns, and synonyms help make the following narrative passage coherent.

PROFESSIONAL
MODEL

The total mass of living things on Earth is estimated to be about seventeen billion billion tons. This is only about 1/300 the mass of the atmosphere, and only 1/70,000 the mass of the ocean. Nevertheless, the biosphere is so active chemically that it is responsible for much of the environment about us. For instance, it is thanks to the green plants that the air is full of free oxygen. Also, the great layers of limestone produced by corals make up large atolls and long reefs.

On the other hand, the biosphere is extraordinarily fragile and even small changes in temperature or the addition of small quantities of poisons could change it drastically or wipe it out altogether. Man himself has been putting great strains on the biosphere in recent years and this is of growing concern. . . .

Isaac Asimov, *More Words of Science*

Practice Your Skills

A. Revise the following paragraphs to increase their coherence.

1. They are always encouraging you to do well. Parents, grandparents, aunts, and uncles all seem to pay more attention to you. There are

many advantages to being a family's firstborn child. It's no wonder that more than half our presidents have been firstborns. This gives the firstborn child a lot of self-confidence and a belief that he or she will be taken seriously.

2. Dense forests covered most of its 11,000-foot splendor. Matching the whiteness of the peak was one isolated, billowy cloud that created a sharp contrast with the clear blue western-Canadian sky. Above the timberline was the snowy-white peak—the purest white I had ever seen. There stood the mountain, regally dwarfing all the others in the range.

B. The following letter to the editor is made up of several short paragraphs. To improve its coherence, add transitional words or phrases to connect the paragraphs, as suggested in parentheses.

Next Tuesday the town council will be voting on whether to make school facilities available to the Parks and Recreation Department during the summer. I would like to raise my voice in support of a yes vote on this proposal. (Add a transition that indicates the writer is about to give reasons for voting yes.)

(Add a transition indicating that this paragraph will deal with the first reason.) Opening the grounds of the schools to public events such as concerts and outdoor theater will help the town raise revenues through concessions and a share in ticket sales. These are certainly less painful ways to raise revenues than through increased taxes.

(Add a transition indicating that the writer considers this next reason to be more important.) Making school grounds available for summertime activities will give young people a place to go so that they won't have to hang around on street corners or in shopping malls. Of particular importance in this regard would be opening up the schools' athletic facilities for use in the summer.

(Add a transition indicating that the writer considers the following reason the most important one.) Holding summertime concerts, theater, and athletic events on school grounds will help foster a sense of community. It will bring neighbors together for positive experiences.

(Add a transition indicating that this is the conclusion.) We can't lose by voting yes on the proposal. Funds from the concessions and ticket sales will more than offset the cost of maintaining the facilities for summer use, and many positive effects will be felt throughout the community.

Writing a Conclusion

Every experience—from a film to a tennis match—has to end. To be satisfying to your readers, your writing also needs a conclusion, one that leaves them with a sense that your ideas have been developed completely—that all that should be said has been said. Although every conclusion differs, in general, a good conclusion displays the following characteristics:

- follows logically from the rest of the piece of writing
- does not introduce new, unrelated material
- leaves the reader with something to think about

COMMON TYPES OF CONCLUSIONS

Writing
— **TIP** —

When restating or summarizing, try to use different words, and present your idea from a different angle.

Every conclusion should develop naturally from what has preceded it. Therefore, each conclusion has to be unique. However, there are some commonly used techniques that can provide you with a general direction. These techniques include restating the central idea, summarizing the ideas developed in the body paragraphs, generalizing about the information given, making a prediction, asking a question, or presenting a quotation or an anecdote that summarizes the main idea. Some conclusions combine two or more of these methods.

Restating the Central Idea   One way to end a piece of writing is by returning to your central idea and restating it in a new way. The following is the conclusion from a humorous piece about the importance of feet.

PROFESSIONAL
· · · · · · · · · · · · · · · · ·
M O D E L

▼

Feet have gotten a dirty deal over the years. . . . We ought to give them a better break, and the women walking to work in sneakers or running shoes are taking a big step in that direction. If I wore a hat, I'd take it off to them.

Andrew A. Rooney

Summarizing the Ideas of the Body Paragraphs   When you are presenting a great deal of information, making a series of points, or describing a process, you might conclude by recapping the main ideas of your paragraphs. Begin with a sentence that summarizes your piece of writing as a whole. Then, in each of the following sentences, restate the idea of one of your body paragraphs.

▼

Keeping a journal, then, can do a lot more than simply improve your writing. Like a hot bath or a long walk, making a journal entry can be a soothing ritual, a break from the rest of your hectic daily life. It can also be a way to identify problems in your life and possible solutions to them. Finally, writing in your journal can help you live more fully—to notice things, to savor and remember them.

Generalizing About the Information Given Another method for concluding involves making a general statement that ties together information presented in the rest of the work. When you generalize about something, you make a broad or all-inclusive statement about it.

▼

He felt that the natural world held whatever hopes remain for the recuperation of our perennially injured spirits. Which is why it's important that his pictures are reminders of that world's frailty as well as its vigor. They are emblems of a shared intuition—that as the wilderness contracts, our hearts shrink with it.
   Richard Lacayo, "The Man Who Captured the Earth's Beauty."

Making a Prediction Often a writer will end on a note of hope, gloom, or suspense by making a prediction.

▼

In the streets of Eastern Europe this year, a different revolutionary tradition has replaced the old one. With its respect for nonviolence and the rule of law, and even a degree of forgiveness for those who have abused power, it is in the tradition of Thoreau, Gandhi, Martin Luther King, Jr., and Lech Walesa. If that spirit is sustained, this year's events, unlike those of 1848, could lead to the establishment of stable, durable and peaceful democracies.
   Michael Mandelbaum, "In Europe, History Repeats Itself"

Asking a Question One way to leave your readers thinking is by ending with a question that makes them reconsider the ideas you have presented. You might even ask more than one.

> Can the Okefenokee survive? The sound of the swamp . . . overwhelms a man's thoughts on that question. But it reminds us that in the end, nature does not play by man's rules.
>
> **Bob Dotson**

You can also end your paper with a quotation that expresses your key point, or with an **anecdote,** or brief story, that ties your material together.

CONCLUSIONS FOR NARRATIVES

A **narrative** is a story. It can be imaginary, as is a short story, or real, as is a newspaper account. You can draw on a number of types of conclusions that are particularly suited for any narratives.

Ending with the Last Event Some stories end simply with the final incident in a series of events. This is particularly common in newspaper and magazine articles.

> The woman kept her silence for all those years. Hearing her secret, the police searched the place that she pointed out. Bulldozers were used. So were tools that can find hidden metal. But they did no good. The police found nothing. If anything, the missing crown jewels of Ireland were more of a mystery than ever.
>
> **Thomas G. Gunning, *Strange Mysteries***

Ending with a Climactic Event At the heart of a story is often a conflict. At the moment of greatest tension in the main conflict, the climax of a story occurs. Occasionally, stories end at this moment or with another climactic moment that follows shortly after. In the following passage, Edgar Allan Poe narrates a deranged murderer's climactic confession.

> "Villains!" I shrieked, "dissemble no more! I admit the deed!—tear up the planks!—here, here!—it is the beating of his hideous heart!"
>
> **Edgar Allan Poe, "The Tell-Tale Heart"**

Ending with a Resolution   Most often, a story ends with an episode or thought that occurs after the climactic event. This can be a last look at the central character or a final way of expressing the theme.

The following lighthearted conclusion ends a story about a man who has finally given up a horrible thought that has possessed him—robbing his neighbor. He has just slipped stolen money into an envelope and returned it, without being detected, to the neighbor he has robbed. The humorous ending shows that all is well again.

At the climactic ending of the movie *King Kong*, the gorilla climbs the Empire State Building.

> As I walked away from the house, a police car drew up beside me, and a patrolman I know cranked down the window and asked, "What are you doing out at this time of night, Mr. Hake?"
>
> "I'm walking the dog," I said cheerfully. There was no dog in sight, but they didn't look. "Here, Toby! Here, Toby! Here, Toby! *Good dog!*" I called, and off I went, whistling merrily in the dark.
>
> **John Cheever, "The Housebreaker of Shady Hill"**

Writing
A Conclusion   **389**

You can conclude a persuasive essay with your final argument, a restatement of your thesis, or a summary of your main points. As many do, you may want to end with a call for a specific action.

PROFESSIONAL
M O D E L

▼

If we are really to move toward our linked goals of saving forests and reducing the solid-waste stream, we must push for greater use of post-consumer material in *all* recycled papers.

Douglas Scott

Practice Your Skills

A. What method was used to conclude each of these paragraphs?

1. Could the Mounties be wrong? Was there a village near far-off Lake Anjikini that disappeared? If there wasn't, how did the story of the disappearances get started? And if it's just a story, why do magazines and books keep on printing it as though it really happened?

Thomas Gunning, *Strange Mysteries*

2. In almost every type of biological research, the microscope plays a fundamental role. By allowing the exploration of a once-hidden world, the microscope has contributed immeasurably to our understanding of the earth's life forms. **Modern Biology Investigators**

3. The band went on playing. Some of the people thought Lily was on the train, and some swore she wasn't. Everybody cheered, though, and a straw hat was thrown into the telephone wires.

Eudora Welty, "Lily Daw and the Three Ladles"

B. Read the following plot summary. It might be fiction or nonfiction. Briefly describe how you might end it with the last event, with a call for action, with a restatement, with a question, with a resolution, and with a generalization.

> Peter is from a poor family. His parents have sacrificed for years to pay for piano lessons for him. Their sacrifices pay off. He wins a piano competition and an offer to make his debut with the Cleveland Orchestra. Then, two months before his debut, as he is walking home from school, he is shot in a random act of violence. An ambulance rushes him to the hospital.

Understanding Revision

Few writers, not even experienced professionals such as Aldous Huxley, get everything right the first time. Revising is your chance to create a finished product.

Revision can occur at any point in the writing process. You can revise after you finish your first draft, making revision a separate writing stage. You can revise as you draft, reworking each part before you move on to the next. You can even revise before you draft, changing your prewriting notes or your writing plan before committing words to paper. However you go about it, revision can be an exciting process of finding new ideas and new ways of presenting them.

TYPES OF REVISION

When you revise, there are basically three kinds of changes you can make. You can change the content of your draft, adding new ideas, elaborating on old ones, or deleting ideas altogether; you can restructure it, making changes in organization; or you can correct the draft, fixing errors in grammar, usage, and mechanics. As you revise, you may find yourself making all three of these types of changes at the same time. You may also find it useful to revise a piece of writing several times, concentrating on each type of revision separately.

Rethinking Content

Rethinking the content of your writing is the most important aspect of revision. You may want to do this before you look at anything else. If your content changes, so will its structure and mechanics. Consider the following questions as you revise for content.

Focus on content as you read the following draft.

Bicycles help reduce the traffic problems of Hong Kong.

For me, bikes are mainly a way of having fun and getting exercise. Many people commute to work on bikes. Around the world the number of bicycles is much greater than the number of automobiles. By the 1890's the bicycle wasn't just a way to get around, it became a pastime. A craze. *The Thing to Do!!!* Today we have skateboards and rollerblades. I doubt if they will last as long as the bicycle, whether it's a touring bike or a mountain bike. The modern bicycle goes back to france and england. In the late 18th Century the bicycle consisted of two wheels. Connected by wood that the rider sat or balanced on, it had no pedals. Feet on the ground moved the early bike. In 1816 this was improved, by the invention of stearing. The front wheel could be turned, by a handle. In the 1880's the safety bike appeared, pedals moved its front wheel. In 1879, a major improvement: the Chain! By the 1890's there were lamps, bells, and—something very useful—breaks.

Some problems you might notice include the following:

- It lacks a clear focus—a single sentence that states the main idea.
- It lacks unity—the paragraph includes several ideas unrelated to the main idea.

Think about how you might go about revising the content of this draft. You might start by writing a topic sentence to clarify the purpose of the paragraph. Then you could delete unnecessary, unrelated ideas, such as the statements about skateboards and rollerblades. You might make additional changes in content—such as adding details—to further clarify the ideas.

Reworking Structure

When you revise writing for structure, evaluate it based on the following criteria and make any changes necessary.

Checklist for Reworking Structure

- Is my writing unified—are all the ideas related directly to my focus or main idea?

- Does the organization make the relationships among ideas clear?

- Is my writing coherent—is the flow of sentences and paragraphs smooth and logical?

Forms of logical order you might use include chronological, spatial, cause-and-effect, comparison-and-contrast, and order of degree or importance. Once you've chosen the order for your ideas, you can link the sentences containing them with transitional words. Such words include *now, instead, then,* and *finally.* Also look for places where sentences can be combined to eliminate unnecessary repetition. Notice that the ideas in the draft on page 392 are not presented chronologically.

Refining Mechanics—Proofreading

When you **proofread,** look for and correct errors in grammar, usage, spelling, and mechanics. Ask yourself the following questions as you revise your writing.

Checklist for Refining Mechanics

- Have I used punctuation marks and capitalization correctly?
- Have I used a dictionary to check the spellings of unfamiliar words?
- Have I corrected all run-ons and sentence fragments and checked end marks?
- Have I used all parts of speech correctly?

The **proofreading and revising marks** shown below can be used to show any type of change the writer decides to make, from major changes, such as reorganization of content, to minor revisions, such as spelling corrections.

Proofreading and Revising Marks

^ Add a letter or word	⁀ Close up
⊙ Add a period	¶ Begin a new paragraph
≡ Capitalize a letter	^ Add a comma
/ Make a capital letter lowercase	∼ Transpose the position of letters or words
— or ℯ Delete letters or words	

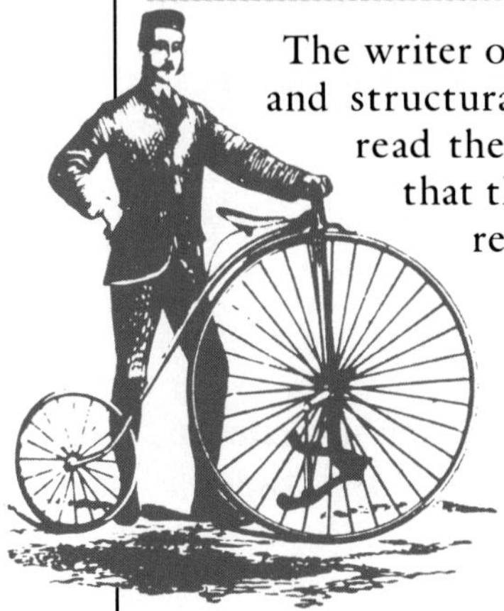

The writer of the paragraph about bicycles made content and structural changes on the word processor. As you read the hard copy shown on the next page, notice that the focus of the paper was strengthened, unrelated ideas were deleted, necessary information was added, and the logical connection among ideas was clarified. The writer then proofread the copy for errors in mechanics, usage, and grammar using the proofreading and revising marks shown above.

¶ Today there are songs about skateboards on the radio, but in our great-great-grandparents' time they sang "A Bicycle Built for Two." Bicycling became a craze at the turn of the century, when a series of improvements changed it from a crude, unsafe machine to a faster, safer, recreational means of transportation. ¶ The modern bicylce goes back to late 18th Century france and england; at first it consisted of two wheels connected by a wooden bar that the rider sat or balanced on. It had no pedals; the rider walked the early bike along the ground. The invention of stearing in 1816 meant that the front wheeled could be turned, by a handle. In 1879, a *another* major improvement: the Chain. *appeared* Then, in the 1880's the safety bike appeared with pedals that moved its front wheel. Finally, by the 1890's there were lamps, bells, and something very useful—breaks. *brakes.* Now the bicycle wasn't just a way to get around, instead, it became a pastime. ¶ In the 20th century, automobiles took over as America's favorite way of commuting. But around the world bicycles still outnumber cars. In my opinion, only the bicycle combines fun, exercise, and a practical, independant way to get to my after-school job on time.

"Bone Shaker" bikes were so named because of their rough riding quality.

Practice Your Skills

A. Go back to the revised version of the sample paragraph used in this lesson. Working in a small group, discuss ways that the paragraph could be revised yet again to improve it even more. Incorporate some of those ideas into a draft of your own.

B. Choose one of the following paragraphs and revise it. Share your revised paragraph in a small group. Study the different ways group members revised each paragraph. Remember that there is no one right revision, except in matters of mechanics.

Pearl Buck died on March 6, 1973, after a long life of many accomplishments. She spent her youth in China. The daughter of missionaries. She became a misionary herself and wrote extensively about her chinese experiences. Won the 1938 Noble Prize for literature. In 1931 published her most famous novel; The Good Earth. Also wrote biographys, in 1936, of her mother and father. Through out her life, contributed to lots of charitable causes. Including helping retarded kids and orphans from Asia. Altogether, she wrote over eighty works. A truly remarkable woman!

One of the most mysterious of all plants is the mandrake. Its scientific name is *Mandragora officinarum*. Though traditionally used in folk medicine, the mandrake is poisonous. The thick root of the plant is shaped like a human body. Sort of. Therefore, during the middle ages people thought that the mandrak had magical powers. They believed for example, that the plant would cry out in pain. Unless it was picked at special times. Such as at midnight during the full moon. I'd believe it too if I was around then. People in the Middle Ages used the plant in all kinds of potions and remedies. The so-called "deadly nightshade" is a plant related to the mandrake. Before there was modern medicine, people knew a lot about plants and herbs that had healing powers. Even today, about half of our medicines come from plants.

C. Rewrite the following sentences on your own paper. Make the corrections the proofreading marks indicate are needed.

The brain has fasinated people for centuries, scientists have only recently begun to discover how it works. Although the brain wieghs only three and a half pounds it controls who we are and how we percieve our World.

In ancient times, the mandrake root was considered the most evil plant in the world of herbs.

Self-Assessment and Peer Response

If you have tried to evaluate your own writing, you know it is hard to be impartial. However, some self-assessment strategies can help.

STRATEGIES FOR SELF-ASSESSMENT

Read Aloud   When you read your work to yourself, your mind may unintentionally slide by errors or awkward phrasing. You may even read what you *intended* to write rather than what you actually *did* write. Reading your work aloud enables you to hear your words as if they were someone else's. Also, reading aloud can give you a sense of the rhythm and flow of your writing.

WRITER TO WRITER

If I feel that I must "fix" something, then I judge that part [against] my original intention.

Michelle Sobarnia, student
Northfield, Illinois

Read from the Audience's Point of View   Try to think as your audience would think in reading your writing. Ask yourself what questions they might ask, what they would find interesting, what they might like to know more about.

Outline Your Writing   Many writers make an outline when planning their work, but you can also make an outline after you complete your writing to check the structure of your piece. Your outline can show you if there are gaps in your basic structure, development, or reasoning.

Use Revision Checklists   You can use the Revision Checklists in Writing Handbook 12 on pages 392–394 to check your writing for problems with content, form, sentence structure, grammar, usage, and mechanics.

As your peers, or equals, your classmates share many of your interests and life experiences. This shared experience often enables them to see your writing sympathetically, but objectively. They can read your work for the pure pleasure of seeing what you have to say, and also can share their responses.

Questioning Your Peer Readers

Here are six useful ways to get peers to respond freely and honestly to your writing.

Sharing Say to your reader, "Please listen. Don't respond. Just let me read this to you." Sharing is especially useful when your piece is at an early stage or you're not ready to hear comments.

Pointing Say to your reader, "Point to some specific things in my writing that you liked, that worked for you, or that stuck in your mind." Build on these positive aspects of your writing.

Replying Ask your reader, "What are your ideas on this topic? Where do you agree or disagree with me? What do you want to hear more about? Talk to me about what I've said."

Because good writers often disagree about the best way to express an idea, you may feel more comfortable having readers respond to your ideas rather than to how you have expressed them. Different readers will respond differently to your ideas, giving you helpful information about their interests and prior knowledge of your topic. You can add this information as you draft and revise.

Summarizing   Say to your reader, "Tell me what you hear. Help me see what my words actually say. What do you hear as the main idea in my essay or the main feeling or theme in my story? What other ideas or themes do you hear?" There are two benefits from such questioning: You find out whether your words really say what you think they say, and you get new ideas to enrich your writing.

Responding to Specific Features   Say to your reader, "There are certain aspects of my piece that I want specific help on. Please tell me about. . . ." (Point to one or more features of your piece.)

Watching "Movies of the Reader's Mind"   Say to your reader, "Please tell me what was actually going on in your mind—moment to moment—as you were reading my piece." This kind of response gives you the most immediate reactions of your reader.

Readers sometimes need help going beyond general comments such as "I liked it" or "I didn't get too interested." You can help your reader respond more specifically if you stop in the middle of reading your piece aloud, and ask, "What are you thinking or feeling now?" You can do the same thing if your peer is reading your written work silently. Just ask him or her to stop reading at the bottom of every page or after each paragraph, and write you a note about what's happening in his or her mind at that moment.

Incorporating Responses to Your Writing

Each reader has a unique perspective and a unique response to your writing. However, only you know what you are trying to express. Therefore, don't feel tyrannized by your readers' reactions. Listen to all the different responses, consider them, and then make up your own mind. Trust yourself to make the final decisions about your writing. Some specific ways you can use peers' responses are:

- to help you clarify what you want to say
- to see what works in your writing
- to extend your ideas
- to gain perspective or distance
- to help you organize and clarify your ideas

Responding to Others' Writing

The most important rule for responding to other people's writing is to be constructive. Phrase your criticisms in positive, useful ways, trying to suggest actual steps that the writer might take to improve the piece. Avoid simply making vague negative statements. For example, instead of saying, "This description really doesn't do anything for me," you might say, "Maybe your description of the triathlon could be made more specific by a metaphor or some vivid imagery."

You can respond to another student's writing in the same ways that you might ask people to respond to your writing: by sharing, pointing, replying, summarizing, responding to specific features, and running movies of your mind.

Even Shakespeare may have benefitted from the responses of his peers.

Practice Your Skills

A. Read the negative comments on the following page about a piece of writing. Discuss with your classmates how the same points might be made more constructively.

Negative	And what's this here? How do you expect anyone to know what you're trying to describe in this part?
Constructive	I had trouble understanding what you were describing here. Maybe you could help me out by adding more details—some specific sights and sounds, for example.

1. This scene is boring. Everyone just talks and talks. There's no action in it at all.
2. You obviously didn't bother to proofread. Look at all these spelling errors.
3. The beginning was great, but it doesn't have an ending. I mean, it just stops, as if you ran out of ideas.
4. You sure didn't prove your point to me. There's not a shred of evidence here to support your opinion.
5. You jump from one idea to another without any attempt to connect them. The whole thing's confused—a mess.

B. Read the following piece of student writing. It has many fine qualities, but like most writing, it can be improved. In a small group, practice responding to this piece in each of the six ways described in this handbook. Then, if your teacher directs you to do so, revise the piece of writing based on the comments made in your group.

A reporter once asked Dr. Zeus, the cartoonist, how he decided to go into his unusual type of work. Dr. Zeus answered by telling a story. When he was a child, Zeus had an art teacher who ridiculed him and told him he would never be able to draw. So, he became a cartoonist just to prove that teacher wrong.

There is an important message for all of us in Dr. Zeus's story. Don't give up on your dreams just because of other people's criticisms. Sometimes people can be cruel or insensitive, and everyone therefore needs to learn, sometimes, how to ignore what other people say about stuff that you do and all and just do it, you know?

The playright Christopher Frye once wrote that making fun of the work of a beginning writer is like making fun of an acorn for not being an oak. When people write or paint or do anything else creative, they are doing something brave, and they ought to be encouraged. Not discouraged. When people are encouraged, they develop their potenshul. It doesn't happen overnight but eventually the tiny acorn does become the mighty oak—if its given the right conditions in which to grow. Like becoming an actress or a singer or a football player or a scientist or anything else that a person might dream about.

Achieving Clarity

Because the purpose of writing is to communicate, at some point in your writing process you will need to consider whether your writing accomplishes that purpose. Ask yourself if you have expressed your ideas as clearly and succinctly as possible and if your readers will understand your message.

If your own review of your work or a peer reader's comments suggest a need for clarification, you can apply a few simple strategies. These include choosing your words carefully, including adequate detail, and paragraphing correctly.

WORD CHOICE

One way to clarify your writing is to choose your words carefully. Proper word choice, or **diction,** involves identifying words that say precisely what you mean.

Using a Dictionary and Thesaurus

If you are unsure about the meaning of a word, you can verify its definition in a dictionary. Then you can be certain the word precisely conveys your intended meaning. You can also look up your word in the thesaurus, which groups words with similar meanings, if you want to be sure that you have chosen the most appropriate word, given the context of your sentence. For example, suppose you have written the following sentence:

Rio de Janeiro is a *community* on the eastern coast of Brazil.

In responding to this sentence, a peer reader may have told you that *community* sounded strange to her. If you check the denotative meaning listed in a dictionary—a group of people living together— you will find that you have used the word correctly. In a thesaurus, however, you will find related words with connotations that may make your meaning clearer. For example, a thesaurus entry might look like this:

community: borough, burgh, city, colony, district, group, metropolis, settlement, town, township, tribe, village

You might realize that *metropolis,* with its connotations of size, importance, and bustling activity, better expresses your ideas. Then you could revise your sentence accordingly.

Selecting Specific Words

In the previous example, notice that the word *metropolis* is much more specific than the word *community*. A **specific** word, such as *metropolis,* refers to one thing or one kind of thing. A **general** word, such as *community,* names a category, which may include different members.

Choosing Specific Nouns   Nouns are specific when they refer to individual or particular things. In this example, the word *instruments* is not specific:

> The madrigal group was accompanied by musicians on medieval
> *instruments*.

Using specific nouns communicates more information to the reader.

> The madrigal group was accompanied by musicians on record-
> ers and lutes.

Choosing Specific Verbs   Because verbs convey action, they contribute greatly to the clarity and vigor of your writing. Compare the verbs used in the sentences that follow:

> The angry mob *threw* tomatoes.
> The angry mob *hurled* tomatoes.

In this example, the word *hurled* expresses the speed and anger with which the tomatoes were thrown. Therefore, it is more effective in helping to convey the anger of the mob.

Choosing Specific Modifiers   The words you choose to modify nouns and verbs should be specific as well. Some writers lose effectiveness by using vague or "empty" modifiers, such as those listed on the next page. These words do nothing more than express approval or disapproval, leaving the reader to wonder about the extent of the like or dislike and why the writer or character feels that way.

Achieving Clarity   **403**

Empty Modifiers

good	boring	really	very	nice
awesome	exciting	great	fine	fun
super	totally	pretty	awful	cute
interesting	fantastic	wonderful	terrible	bad

Consider the following example:

Empty Modifier   The peppers tasted *bad*.
Specific Modifiers   The peppers tasted *unripe* and *bitter*.

Notice that the empty modifier has been replaced with **sensory details**—words that refer to things that can be sensed by sight, touch, taste, hearing, or smell. However, you should be cautious about overusing modifiers. A vivid modifier is no substitute for a specific noun or a strong verb.

Modifier   The antelopes *stood motionless,* gazing at each other.
Strong Verb   The antelopes *froze,* gazing at each other.

Practice Your Skills

Rewrite each of the sentences below to achieve clarity. In sentences 1–6, concentrate on replacing weak verbs. In sentences 7–12, concentrate on replacing general and vague nouns and modifiers. Remember to use words that appeal to the senses.

1. What Tony said to Claire was an insult.
2. She got out of bed when the alarm went off.
3. He made his way through the crowd.
4. The child ran to the corner.
5. When her supervisor walked in, Susie quickly put the money in her desk drawer.
6. Night comes suddenly as day leaves.
7. His parents were happy about the report card.
8. Kim complained that the class was long and boring.
9. When George Bush walked onto the platform, it was an awesome moment.
10. That exciting event brought an end to the day's activities.
11. My new job is pretty nice, especially compared to the last one, which was terrible.
12. Those big trees in California were totally fantastic, and we had fun seeing them.

ADEQUATE DETAIL

Being specific is important, but, alone, it does not ensure the clarity of your writing. You also must provide sufficient detailed information to support your ideas so your reader knows exactly what you mean.

When you write, be sure to think about the questions your readers might ask and to provide the details that answer those questions.

Inadequate Detail	That vacation turned out to be the best one ever.
Reader's Questions	Why was it the best vacation? What did you do? What was special about it?
Adequate Detail	Our family camping trip to Thatcher State Park in August was our best vacation ever. We hiked and rock climbed, spent long days at the swimming pool, and learned how to make and tend a campfire. We even saw two rattlesnakes and a bald eagle! But best of all we shared our good times with new friends who camped next to us.

The second example includes sentences that tell where the vacation took place, what specifically happened, and why it turned out to be so enjoyable.

In the following passage, which tells why fresh air can be dangerous when sleeping during the wintertime, what specific words and details help to make the writing clear?

▼

> The body slows down during sleep, the heart beats less rapidly, and blood pressure, pulse, and breathing rates all decline. Cold air entering though open windows makes it more difficult for our slowed-down systems to retain body heat and maintain a proper temperature.
>
> **Hal Linden,** *FYI*

PROFESSIONAL
M O D E L

Specific verbs in this passage include *beats, decline, and retain.* Specific nouns include *blood pressure, pulse,* and *body heat.* The writer lists details to illustrate all the changes that occur in the body during sleep, giving the reader a clear picture of what happens.

Showing Action Through Detail

Which of the following passages helps you better understand what lunchtime is like at Riley's Place?

Telling   Riley's Place is a loud and busy restaurant at lunchtime.

Showing   Waiters banged dishes onto bare metal tables; knives and forks clattered together; customers shouted above the din. It was lunchtime at Riley's Place, and there wasn't a seat in the house.

In the second passage you can see the scene; the writer enables you to experience the loudness and bustle of Riley's Place. The second passage is clearer than the first because it *shows* the action. It doesn't simply mention or tell about it. Whenever possible, try to fill your writing with action-packed passages that help your readers visualize what you are writing about.

P A R A G R A P H I N G

When you organize your writing into groups of related ideas, or paragraphs, you make it easier for your reader to follow and understand what you are saying. You can form paragraphs in two different ways: by gathering ideas and sorting them into paragraphs as you write, or by writing your first draft without worrying about paragraphs, and then forming them as you revise.

Follow these guidelines when you are paragraphing your work.

Paragraphing Nonfiction

- **Study your draft for appropriate paragraph breaks.** When a new idea is introduced or you change topics, you should probably start a new paragraph.

- **Think about the order of your paragraphs.** Do they follow a logical order? Do they need to be rearranged?

- **Look for paragraphs that present too many ideas.** Break these long paragraphs up into shorter units.

- **Watch for unnecessary or unrelated ideas in a paragraph.** Consider deleting them or moving them elsewhere.

- **Be sure your paragraphs include transitions that make the order of your ideas clear.** Add transitions if necessary.

Paragraphing Fiction

- **Notice changes in setting, time, and plot or action.** Create a new paragraph to clarify each change.
- **Notice your dialogue.** Create a new paragraph when the speaker changes.
- **Notice shifts in voice and point of view.** Be sure these shifts are intentional. If they are, create paragraphs where the shifts occur. If the shifts are unintentional, eliminate them or provide enough information to clarify them.

Practice Your Skills

A. Revise the following paragraphs to make them clearer and more effective. To do so, choose specific words. Also add detail where it is needed and, where possible, show rather than tell.

1. All during that very long car ride we thought about what the house might be like. Then finally we saw it. It was old and in rather bad shape. Still, there was the sea, just beyond the house, and the wide beach.
2. Watching fish swim in an aquarium can be good for you. Studies have shown that it makes your blood pressure drop. In addition, many people enjoy the variety of shapes and colors in an aquarium.

B. Read the following passage. Then rewrite it, creating new paragraphs where necessary, adding transitions, and moving or deleting irrelevant ideas.

Connie Young, professional bicycle racer

> All evening, Randy worked to fix the bike. It was in terrible shape, the spokes bent and twisted, the frame dented, the chain broken. Dinnertime came and went, with only a visit from her mother to tell Randy it was getting late. "Aren't you hungry, honey?" Mrs. Tallin said, startling Randy with her unexpected presence. "No, Mom. I've got to get this finished. The race is tomorrow!" A plate of spaghetti magically appeared on the workbench a few moments later, and Randy did pause to take a bite or two, but she got right back to work. How her scraped knees hurt! How could she have been so stupid as to miss the stop sign at the bottom of Acre Drive? She'd ridden there a hundred times before. Now the race she'd been training for these past months seemed beyond her reach.

Achieving Clarity **407**

Improving Your Sentences

Revising sentences is your chance to display your individuality and sense of style. In particular, you can look for and eliminate empty, stringy, overloaded, and padded sentences from your drafts. You can also improve the clarity of your writing by ensuring that subject-verb relationships are clear and sentence parts are parallel.

R EVISING EMPTY SENTENCES

One way to improve your writing is to eliminate empty sentences. Empty sentences repeat ideas you have already expressed or make assertions without supporting them.

Eliminating Repeated Ideas To eliminate repeated ideas, you can omit repetitious words or combine groups of sentences that contain related ideas.

Repetitive	Sandy is a volunteer, and she gets no money for her work.
Strategy	The word *volunteer* and the phrase *gets no money for her work* express the same idea. Omit the second clause.
Revised	Sandy is a volunteer.

Repetitive	My friends took a plane. They took the plane last year. The plane was going to Rome. It was hijacked. It was forced to land. It landed in a desert.
Strategy	Combine related ideas and sentences.
Revised	Last year, the plane my friends took to Rome was hijacked and forced to land in a desert.

Sometimes a writer may try to prove a statement by repeating it in other words. This is called *circular reasoning*. To avoid circular reasoning, make sure you provide support for your statements.

Repetitive	I like kayaking because it is my favorite sport.
Strategy	Give a good reason for liking kayaking.
Revised	I like kayaking because it challenges me physically and mentally.

Correcting Unsupported Statements Your writing will frustrate your readers if you give no reasons, facts, or examples to support your opinions.

In the following paragraph, which sentence makes you wonder why?

> The exploration of space began in the 1960's. Yet, piloted and unpiloted space vehicles have already investigated the moon and several planets. Although some people think that this activity should stop, I believe it should continue.

The writer offers no explanation for believing that space exploration should continue. One way to satisfy the reader's desire to know why would be to add reasons:

> Space exploration satisfies a human longing to investigate the unknown. Furthermore, space explorers might discover new supplies of resources that are becoming scarce on Earth.

Use the guidelines below to correct unsupported statements.

- Look for statements that will make the reader ask, "Why?"
- Provide facts, reasons, and examples to support your claims. If you cannot support a claim, omit the sentence.
- Add transitional words and phrases for clarity and coherence.

Practice Your Skills

A. Revise the following sentences by omitting repeated ideas or combining sentences to avoid repetition.

1. Maria is a talented guitarist. She plays the guitar with an exceptional amount of skill.
2. Hawaii is an enjoyable vacation spot, and it is my favorite place to visit.
3. Max decided that owning a car was too expensive because it was costing him so much to keep.
4. It was early Tuesday morning. Rachel got a telephone call. The call was surprising. It came from a disc jockey named Boppo Lewis. He has a radio show in San Francisco.

B. Revise the following statements by adding reasons, facts, or examples to support the claims. (Use reference materials as needed.)

1. Some of Shakespeare's most popular plays were comedies.
2. As President of the United States, Abraham Lincoln faced many difficult problems.
3. Earth has a natural satellite called the moon. However, Earth is not the only planet that is orbited by satellites.
4. I believe that the Great Depression, which lasted from 1929 to the beginning of World War II, was the most difficult time Americans have faced in the twentieth century.

TIGHTENING STRINGY AND OVERLOADED SENTENCES

Both stringy and overloaded sentences confuse readers because they do not convey information clearly and concisely. In a **stringy sentence,** ideas are loosely connected with *and*'s, obscuring the relationships between the ideas. An **overloaded sentence,** on the other hand, contains too much information. Following are some ways to correct stringy and overloaded sentences.

Reconstruction #20, by
Lucas Samaras, 1977

Collection of the Denver Art Museum

Connecting Ideas Clearly Making sure that each of your sentences expresses only one idea and that the sentences are connected logically can help you eliminate both stringiness and overloading.

Stringy My brother and I had a fight, and he insulted my friend, and we were really angry, and we both yelled a lot, and he made a joke, and I laughed and the fight was over.

This sentence presents too many ideas, and the *and*'s do not show the relationships among ideas. First, look at the separate parts:

My brother and I had a fight.	He made a joke.
He insulted my friend.	I laughed.
We were really angry.	The fight was over.
We both yelled a lot.	

How do the ideas connect? What is the order of events? Are there cause-and-effect relationships?

Strategy	Show relationships by replacing *and*'s, where appropriate, with transitional words (*because, then, but, later, after,* and *so,* for example). Create two sentences. Here is one possible revision.
Revised	My brother and I had a fight *because* he insulted my friend. We were really angry, *so* we both yelled a lot. *Later,* he made a joke, and I laughed. *After that,* the fight was over.
Stringy	My sister started doing aerobics and swimming, and she really felt better about herself, and she was cheerful, energetic, and calm, and the exercise helped her forget her anxiety.
Broken down	My sister started doing aerobics and swimming. She really felt better about herself. She was cheerful, energetic, and calm. The exercise helped her forget her anxiety.
Revised	*After* my sister started doing aerobics and swimming, she really felt better about herself. She was cheerful, energetic, and calm, *because* the exercise helped her forget her anxiety.
Overloaded	Sarah accepted the gold medal, but she had a sober look on her face, and then the band played the national anthem, while tears slid down her cheeks.
Strategy	Make two sentences, describing the separate actions.
Revised	Sarah had a sober look on her face as she accepted the gold medal. As the band played the national anthem, tears slid down her cheeks.

Avoiding Overuse of Modifiers   Sometimes a writer uses too many modifiers, creating an overloaded sentence.

Overloaded	The guitar is a beautiful member of a proud family of stringed instruments with a long, romantic, and wonderful tradition of helping ordinary people express their deepest emotions and tell fascinating and exciting stories about their lives.
Strategy	Remove unnecessary modifiers, leaving just enough to give the description color and life.
Revised	The guitar belongs to a family of stringed instruments with a long, romantic tradition of helping people express their emotions and tell their stories.

The techniques summarized below will help you revise stringy and overloaded sentences.

- Divide each sentence into two or more simpler phrases, clauses, or sentences.
- Use sentence-combining techniques that you have learned whenever possible.
- Reduce the number of *and*'s and other conjunctions.
- Use transitional words such as *when, first, as, although, finally, however, but, then,* and *because* to show the logical connections between ideas.

Practice Your Skills

Revise the following stringy or overloaded sentences using the techniques described above.

1. Every morning, he raised the shade in his bedroom, and he looked out the window, and he would fervently hope to see his lost dog playing in the yard.
2. We flew to Kennedy Airport in New York, and we wanted to make sure to get to the wedding on time, and our luggage was lost, and we had to spend three hours waiting for it to arrive.
3. Racehorses in the Northern Hemisphere have their official birthday on January first, and in the Southern Hemisphere, racehorses have their official birthday on August first, and a colt born on December thirty-first would be counted one year old at birth in Connecticut, and he would be six months old at birth in Argentina.
4. Becky thought she wanted to be a nurse, and she thought this as a young girl, and she changed her mind in high school, and she decided to become a doctor instead.
5. English has a huge vocabulary, and this makes it difficult to learn, and its nouns do not have gender and so people do not need to remember different forms for adjectives.

CORRECTING PADDED SENTENCES

A **padded sentence** contains unnecessary words and phrases that can bury your meaning. To revise a padded sentence, remove unnecessary words or substitute a more economical expression.

Reducing or Eliminating Wordy Phrases Notice how each of the following wordy phrases can be stated more directly.

"Fact" Expressions	**Reduced**
because of the fact that	because, since
on account of the fact that	because, since
in spite of the fact that	although
the fact of the matter is	(Just say it!)

"What" Expressions	**Reduced**
what I want is	I want
what I mean is	(Just say it!)
what I want to say is	(Just say it!)
what I believe is	(Just say it!)

Other Expressions to Avoid

the point is	the thing is	it happens that
the reason is	being that	personally, I think

Notice how reducing wordy phrases improves the following padded sentences.

Padded Don can't come to the phone because *of the fact that* he's in the shower.

Revised Don can't come to the phone because he's in the shower.

Padded *What I want to say is* we want to go to the National Football League playoffs.

Revised We want to go to the National Football League playoffs.

Reducing Wordy Clauses A clause is a group of words that contains a subject and a verb. Often, clauses beginning with *who is, that is,* or *which is* can be simplified or reduced to phrases:

Lengthy Marilyn, *who is* the captain of the soccer team, scored seven goals in yesterday's game.

Revised Marilyn, the captain of the soccer team, scored seven goals in yesterday's game.

Lengthy The goose *that is* in Barbara's yard attacks all her visitors.

Revised The goose in Barbara's yard attacks all her visitors.

Remember these techniques when you revise padded sentences.

• Omit words and phrases that do not contribute to the meaning of a sentence.

• Remember that clauses beginning with *who, that,* and *which* can often be simplified.

Practice Your Skills

Revise the following sentences to eliminate padding.

1. What I mean is that Olga sprained her ankle seriously and cannot dance tonight.
2. Dana left work early on account of the fact that he lost one of his contact lenses.
3. It was obvious that he could not climb the rope that hung down the mountainside.
4. What I think is that the jazz festival was crowded but the musicians were very entertaining.
5. Due to the fact that it was snowing heavily, we decided to postpone our tennis game.
6. The fact of the matter is that the treasurer of the organization stole funds entrusted to him.

KEEPING SENTENCE PARTS TOGETHER

When you check your draft, make sure that related sentence parts, such as subject and verb, verb and object, and parts of compound verbs, are not separated. Notice how placing related sentence parts together makes these sentences less choppy and confusing.

Awkward	*Margo,* after calling the police department, *went* next door to her neighbor's house.
Better	After calling the police department, Margo went next door to her neighbor's house.
Awkward	*I will,* when I save enough money, *buy* an acoustic guitar with twelve strings.
Better	When I save enough money, I will buy an acoustic guitar with twelve strings.
Awkward	With meals I drink, depending on the time of day and how I feel, either milk or cola.
Better	With meals I drink either milk or cola, depending on the time of day and how I feel.

These steps will help you keep sentence parts together.

- Find the "bare bones" of the sentence—the subject, the verb, and the object.
- If the connection among the subject, verb, and object is unclear, look for ways to position them closer together.

Practice Your Skills

Revise each sentence below, following these steps: Read the sentence carefully. Think about how you can bring the subject, verb, and object closer together. Then rewrite the sentence.

1. Darlene, no matter how hard we tried to convince her, would not change her mind about the date of the hike.
2. Dina's parents volunteer, for the holiday season, their time at a shelter for the homeless.
3. Student chefs, traveling all over the world as apprentices, learn from some of the greatest gourmets.
4. I traveled after I graduated from school, across the continental United States.
5. The ancient Greeks never, even when they were waging bloody civil war, forgot their common heritage.

MAKING SENTENCE PARTS PARALLEL

Words or groups of words that function similarly in a sentence should also have similar, or parallel, structure. When you revise your writing, look for opportunities to make sentence parts parallel:

Awkward   In their award-winning routine, Jack and Anita skated *with precision* and *using graceful movement.*

In this sentence, each italicized word group modifies the verb *skated*. Because both word groups perform a similar function, they should be parallel in structure. When they are made parallel, the sentence becomes clearer and more graceful.

Parallel   In their award-winning routine, Jack and Anita skated *precisely* and *gracefully.*

Parallel   In their award-winning routine, Jack and Anita skated *with precision* and *with grace.*

To correct errors in parallelism, look for sentence parts that function in a similar way in the sentence and cast them in a similar form. Often these sentence parts are modifiers of verbs, or objects

Improving
Sentences   **415**

of prepositions. Notice how the following problems with parallelism have been solved, and try to determine the function of each italicized part of the sentence.

Faulty	Everyone needs *sympathy* and *to be noticed*. (noun and infinitive; both are objects of the verb *needs*)
Revised	Everyone needs *sympathy* and *attention*. (two nouns)
Faulty	Students sometimes have to choose between *studying for school* and *to relax with their friends*. (gerund phrase and infinitive phrase; both are objects of the preposition *between*)
Revised	Students sometimes have to choose between *studying for school* and *relaxing with their friends*. (two gerund phrases)
Faulty	We will go *to the San Diego Zoo* and then *the restaurant*. (prepositional phrase and noun; both are adverbial phrases modifying the verb *go*)
Revised	We will go *to the San Diego Zoo* and then *to the restaurant*. (two prepositional phrases)

W R I T E R   T O   W R I T E R

I fix things that do not flow smoothly or that break the rhythm of the paper.

Stacia Graham, student
Seattle, Washington

Practice Your Skills

Read the following sentences and identify the problems with parallelism. Rewrite each sentence making sentence parts parallel.

1. Theresa made a choice between taking ballet lessons and to play on the softball team.
2. At Camp Edgewater you will learn surviving in the wilderness and how to canoe down the Black River.
3. We all want to enjoy the holiday and visiting with friends we have not seen for a while.
4. Students attend school for nine months and are vacationing or working for three months.
5. Yusi wanted a sweater for her birthday and to travel to her cousin Lee's house in southern California.

Sharing and Publishing

Writing is usually a social activity, a way to communicate with other people. As you develop a piece of writing, you are instinctively reaching out toward a public, even toward a publication.

You can share your work at any time during the writing process. By sharing work in progress—by asking others to comment on your topic, notes, outline, or drafts—you can gain insights that will help you shape your final piece. After many revisions and discussions you will feel comfortable about sharing with a wider audience.

W R I T E R   T O   W R I T E R

It took me fifteen years to discover that I had no talent for writing, but I couldn't give it up because, by that time, I was too famous.

Robert Benchley, essayist and humorist

SHARING YOUR WRITING
IN PROGRESS

All writers have some apprehension about sharing an unfinished, or even a finished, piece of writing. If you're nervous about sharing your writing, show it first to the people you trust most, such as friends and relatives. If you wish, meet privately with your teacher or one classmate. Later, you may feel ready to meet with a group.

Ways to Share Your Writing

- Discuss your notes, outline, or draft.
- Have the other person read and respond to your work on your word processor or in the margins of your paper.
- Have a writer's conference with your teacher.
- Meet with other writers from your class and discuss methods of carrying out your assignments.

Writing
── **TIP** ──
You might want to share an informal outline with your readers so they can see clearly the places where you may need to delete or add information.

It is helpful if you prepare a list of questions to ask the person who is responding to your work. For example, "What questions come to your mind as you read my piece?" or "Why do you think I chose this topic?"

SHARING YOUR COMPLETED WRITING

A finished piece of writing is something to be proud of, a present to give to people. However, since you may not be sure how they'll receive it, you might want to form a writing exchange group first and share your writing with others who want to share theirs, too. Ask your fellow writers to exchange their work with you and share ideas, keeping the following points in mind:

- Provide a list of questions for others to respond to.
- Be supportive and constructive in your responses.

Specific strategies for questioning your peers and for providing helpful responses include sharing, pointing, replying, summarizing, responding to specific features, and watching movies of the reader's mind. These strategies are discussed in detail in "Strategies for Peer Response," pages 398–401.

Methods of Self-Publishing

- Use a photocopy machine to make copies or to make a transparency for an overhead projector.
- Save your work on a computer diskette and share it.
- Present your work orally.
- Send your work in a letter to a friend or relative.
- Use a file folder to make a writing portfolio.
- Make your writing part of a poster or a collage that can be displayed at your school or local library.
- Share a cassette recording of your work.
- Create a book, magazine, or newspaper with your own sketches or cover design.

Ideas for Conventional Publishing

- Write for your school newspaper or literary magazine.
- Submit an article to the newsletter or magazine of a local group such as the YMCA.
- Submit your article to a specialized magazine.
- Write a letter to the editor of a newspaper.
- Present your work orally, in skits or plays.
- Get a copy of *Writer's Market* or *Market Guide for Young Writers* at a local bookstore or library.
- Enter a national or local writing contest.

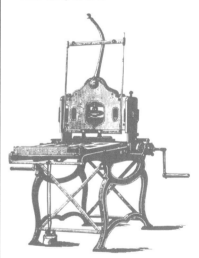

Jean Mielot, 15th century scholar, copying a manuscript in his scriptorium.

Practice Your Skills

A. Go to your school or public library and find the names of at least three magazines or literary contests that accept works by young people. *The Writer's Market, Market Guide for Young Writers,* and magazines for young people are good sources of information.

B. With your class, discuss imaginative ways you might publish or share each of the following:

1. a skit about your school's basketball team
2. a persuasive letter arguing that tobacco ads should be banned
3. a poem that sums up your relationship with a relative
4. a humorous tale about a school production of *Oklahoma!* at which everything went wrong

Developing Your Voice and Style

Every speaker and writer has a unique way of using language—his or her individual **voice.** What gives a person's voice its uniqueness is the language choices that he or she makes. Think about a time when you spoke out effectively about something you believe in or were excited about. Maybe you even surprised yourself with your own strength and confidence. What did you sound like? What were the characteristics of the language you chose? You can learn to recognize the distinct qualities of your own voice by analyzing your language choices when you are speaking out comfortably and confidently.

THE COMPONENTS OF VOICE

Just as you have a distinct speaking voice, you also have a distinct writing voice. The uniqueness of that voice—your style—is determined by the words you use and the way you put them together. For example, you and your best friend would describe a concert by your favorite rock group very differently, even if you both felt similarly about it. This is because you each have an individual style.

WRITER TO WRITER

I don't think that style is consciously arrived at, any more than one arrives at the color of one's eyes. After all, your style *is* you.

Truman Capote, writer of fiction and nonfiction

The elements of style that make up your personal writing voice include sentence structure, diction, and tone.

Sentence Structure Writers vary widely in the types of sentences they use. Some writers, such as James Joyce, are known for using very long sentences. This technique can be almost hypnotic, making you feel as if you are overhearing the thought processes of a character. Most writers use a variety of sentence types, depending on the effect they want to achieve. In the following passage, notice how Henry James used two long sentences to build tension.

Writing
—TIP—

As you plan your writing, think about your purpose and audience, and ask yourself, "How do I want to speak to these people?"

> The story had held us, round the fire, sufficiently breathless, but except the obvious remark that it was gruesome, as, on Christmas Eve in an old house, a strange tale should essentially be, I remember no comment uttered till somebody happened to say that it was the only case he had met in which such a visitation had fallen on a child. The case, I may mention, was that of an apparition in just such an old house as had gathered us for the occasion—an appearance, of a dreadful kind, to a little boy sleeping in the room with his mother and waking her up in the terror of it; waking her not to dissipate his dread and soothe him to sleep again, but to encounter also, herself, before she had succeeded in doing so, the same sight that had shaken him.
>
> **Henry James, *The Turn of the Screw***

Diction   A writer's **diction,** or word choice, can be generally concrete or abstract, formal or informal.

Concrete words name or describe things you can see, hear, smell, touch, or taste, such as *popcorn* and *sour*. Abstract words name things that cannot be perceived through the senses. *Peace* and *brave* are examples.

Formal diction is dignified and often serious. It is appropriate when you are writing a report or a business letter. Informal diction, which is casual and conversational, is appropriate when you are speaking or writing a letter to a friend or dialogue for a story or a poem.

Notice how J. D. Salinger used concrete, informal diction to create a very real, accessible character.

> The funny thing is, though, I was sort of thinking of something else while I shot the bull. I live in New York, and I was thinking about the lagoon in Central Park, down near Central Park South. I was wondering if it would be frozen over when I got home, and if it was, where did the ducks go. I was wondering where the ducks went when the lagoon got all icy and frozen over. I wondered if some guy came in a truck and took them away to a zoo or something. Or if they just flew away.
>
> **J. D. Salinger, *The Catcher in the Rye***

Tone The emotional effect a piece of writing conveys is its **tone.** For example, the tone of a mystery story may be frightening or suspenseful; the tone of a letter to the editor of a newspaper may be angry or congratulatory. Tone in writing is created by both sentence structure and diction. In the following passage, notice how short sentences and informal diction contribute to the humorous tone.

▼

> You don't know about me without you have read a book by the name of The Adventures of Tom Sawyer; but that ain't no matter. That book was made by Mr. Mark Twain, and he told the truth, mainly. There was things which he stretched, but mainly he told the truth. That is nothing. I never seen anybody but lied one time or another, without it was Aunt Polly, or the widow, or maybe Mary.
>
> **Mark Twain, *The Adventures of Huckleberry Finn***

W AYS TO DEVELOP
YOUR VOICE

Marian Anderson, first African-American soloist to sing with the Metropolitan Opera of New York City

When your language flows freely and seems comfortable to you, you are writing in your own natural voice. However, as you grow and develop as a writer, your voice will change and mature. At this point in your life, it's a good idea to experiment with different voices—try them out the way you might try out several different styles of clothing until you find the one that fits you best. To track how your writing voice develops over time, keep a writing portfolio of all your written work.

Sometimes you may be asked to write in a way that makes you feel uncomfortable—for example, in a way that is more formal than your usual diction and tone. When this happens, you might try writing your first draft as though it were addressed to a friend, using your natural voice. Then, after you have produced a draft that presents your ideas, you can revise the voice to make it more formal.

For information on using various types of language for various purposes, see "Varieties of Language," pages 428–432.

Imitating Other Writers' Voices One way to experiment with different voices is to imitate other writers' voices. Simply choose a writer whose work you really enjoy. Read several works by the author, and study a few paragraphs in detail. Then try to write paragraphs of your own that sound similar to those of the writer. Analyze the elements of the writer's diction and tone that make his or her voice unique, and try to reproduce those characteristics in your own writing.

Practice Your Skills

A. Read the following passages from works of fiction. Then write a brief note explaining what kind of person might be speaking in each case. Note the aspects of sentence structure, diction, and tone that make each voice unique.

1.   Every morning I lay on the floor in the front parlor watching her door. The blind was pulled down to within an inch of the sash so that I could not be seen. When she came out on the doorstep my heart leaped. I ran to the hall, seized my books and followed her. I kept her brown figure always in my eye and, when we came near the point at which our ways diverged, I quickened my pace and passed her. This happened morning after morning. I had never spoken to her, except for a few casual words, and yet her name was like a summons to all my foolish blood.   **James Joyce, "Araby"**

2.   But after I had got them out and shut the door and turned off the light it wasn't any good. It was like saying good-bye to a statue. After a while I went out and left the hospital and walked back to the hotel in the rain.   **Ernest Hemingway, A Farewell to Arms**

3.   It is a truth universally acknowledged that a single man in possession of a good fortune must be in want of a wife.
      However little known the feelings or views of such a man may be on first entering a neighborhood, this truth is so well fixed in the minds of the surrounding families that he is considered as the rightful property of someone or other of their daughters.
                                       Jane Austen, Pride and Prejudice

B. Choose any two of the passages in the preceding exercise, and write paragraphs of your own in which you imitate each writer's voice. That is, write paragraphs in which you try, as much as possible, to sound like the voices in the models. Afterward, reflect on your writing experience. How did the pieces of writing that you produced differ from your usual writing? Were they better? Worse? Did you learn anything about voice that you might use in the future? Any new techniques or tricks? If so, what were they? How might you apply them in your writing.

Enriching Your Language

The English language has a larger vocabulary than any other language—more than 600,000 words you can choose from. The impact of your writing depends largely on the choices you make.

DENOTATION AND CONNOTATION

The basic characteristic of the words you use is their meaning. There are two types of meaning—denotation and connotation. The **denotation** of a word is its dictionary meaning. For example, the following words all have the denotation "meal": *banquet, feast, potluck,* and *supper.* However, these words would be used in different situations because of the different associations people have with them—their **connotations.** For example, the word *feast,* in addition to having the denotation "meal," also has connotations of elaborateness and bounty.

A writer or speaker can shape the attitude of an audience by choosing words with specific connotations. Persuasive writing is especially dependent on the connotations of words. Consider how differently you react to the two sentences below.

> Fleming *discovered* the miracle of penicillin.
> Fleming *stumbled on* the miracle of penicillin.

If you were arguing that Fleming was simply lucky, you might take advantage of the accidental connotations of *stumbled on* and write the second sentence. If, on the other hand, you wanted to persuade your audience that Fleming played a fundamental role in the discovery, you would probably write the first sentence.

Be particularly aware of negative connotations.

CONCRETE AND ABSTRACT LANGUAGE

In addition to choosing words that convey precise meaning, you can use language with varying degrees of concreteness. **Concrete words** describe things that can be seen, heard, smelled, touched, or tasted. **Abstract words** refer to conditions, qualities, emotions, and other concepts that cannot be perceived directly through the senses.

Although abstract words are perfectly valid and often useful, replacing them with concrete ones will generally make your writing more vivid. In the following example, notice how when you revise a sentence to make it more concrete, you *show* instead of *tell*.

Abstract   She felt very happy.

Concrete   A large smile spread across her face. Her eyes narrowed and crinkled upward, and she broke into song.

LITERAL AND FIGURATIVE LANGUAGE

Another decision you make in choosing your language is how direct and literal it is. **Literal language** is matter-of-fact and to the point, and the words mean precisely what they say. In contrast, **figurative language** is poetic and imaginative. It speaks of things as though they were other than they are, shocking us into new insights.

Types of Figurative Language

Frequently used types of figurative language include simile, metaphor, and personification. These types of figurative language are also known as *figures of speech,* because they paint a vivid visual image in words.

Simile A **simile** is a sentence or phrase using words such as *like* or *as* that reveals similarities in very different things. In the following lines, notice how one poet used a simile to compare the fall of an eagle to another phenomenon of nature.

He watches from his mountain walls,
And like a thunderbolt he falls.

          Alfred, Lord Tennyson, "The Eagle"

Metaphor A **metaphor** is a phrase or sentence that speaks of one thing as though it were something else, suggesting a comparison between the two things but not stating it directly. This implied comparison is often very powerful because it surprises the reader.

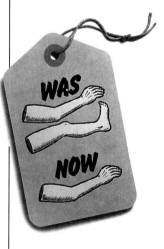

LITERARY
M O D E L

Hold fast to dreams
For if dreams die
Life is a broken-winged bird
That cannot fly.

Langston Hughes, "Dreams"

In these lines, the implied comparison is that life without dreams, like the broken-winged bird, is earthbound and unable to fulfill its nature.

What comparison is suggested in this fanciful rush-hour scene?

Personification A figure of speech in which an animal, a thing, or an idea is given human characteristics is called **personification.** Notice that in the first example below, the personification is a metaphor. The second example is a simile.

> The teakettle ordered us back to the kitchen.
> The dog stood like an arresting officer, ready to read us our rights.

W R I T E R   T O   W R I T E R

The best thing I have ever written was a poem that expressed my feelings about nature. I used lots of colors and metaphors to make it as real as possible.

Stephanie Tubbs, student
Tuscaloosa, Alabama

SOUND DEVICES

You can capitalize on the sounds of words, as well as their meaning, to give depth and interest to your writing. The chart below defines various sound devices and illustrates them with examples from Edgar Allan Poe's "The Bells."

Device	Definition	Example
Repetition	Repeated words and phrases	From the <u>bells</u>, <u>bells</u>, <u>bells</u>, <u>bells</u>, <u>bells</u>, <u>bells</u>, <u>bells</u>—
Rhyme	Repeated sounds, usually at the end of a line	How it <u>swells</u>! How it <u>dwells</u> On the Future!—how it <u>tells</u> Of the rapture that <u>impels</u>
Rhythm	Pattern of stressed and unstressed syllables	While the <u>stars</u> that over<u>sprinkle</u> All the <u>hea</u>vens, seem to <u>twin</u>kle With a <u>crys</u>talline de<u>light</u>; Keeping <u>time</u>, <u>time</u>, <u>time</u>, In a sort of <u>Ru</u>nic <u>rhyme</u>,
Onomatopoeia	Using a word or phrase that imitates a sound	From the <u>jingling</u> and the <u>tinkling</u> of the bells.
Alliteration	Repeating beginning consonant sounds	What a <u>t</u>ale of <u>t</u>error, now, their <u>t</u>urbulency <u>t</u>ells!
Consonance	Repeating internal consonant sounds	In a clamo<u>r</u>ous appealing to the me<u>r</u>cy of the fi<u>r</u>e,
Assonance	Repeating vowel sounds	From the m<u>o</u>lten-g<u>o</u>lden n<u>o</u>tes,

Writing
—TIP—

Practice Your Skills

Revise the following paragraph to make it more interesting and vivid. Replace abstract words with concrete words; also replace any words whose connotations are inappropriate. Consider using figurative language or sound devices to make the writing richer and more vivid.

Springfield, Illinois, is a wondrous place to visit. It is crammed full with memories of Abraham Lincoln. Lincoln lived in that metropolis for a myriad of years, in his very own words, "passing from a young to an old man." There is where the one and only home he ever had is. It is really quite nice. Additionally, his law rooms are there. His final resting place is a big draw for tourists.

VARIETIES OF LANGUAGE

One decision you make about your writing is the level of language that you will use. **Standard English** is language that follows the rules and guidelines for proper usage. This textbook, for example, is written in standard English. Language that does not follow conventional rules of grammar, spelling, and punctuation is called **nonstandard English.**

Standard English may be divided into two varieties, formal and informal. **Formal English** is language that is appropriate in serious, dignified, or ceremonial circumstances, and is often intended for an audience of specialists. Use formal English in writing reports, serious essays, business letters, and professional documents and in speaking for formal presentations, speeches, debates, or interviews.

Informal English is the comfortable but correct language you use in everyday situations to audiences of your friends and peers. Also known as **colloquial English,** it is the language of informal talks as well as the written language of most newspapers and magazine articles. Appropriate uses of informal English include writing intended for a general audience, friendly letters, conversations, and dialogue in literature.

The language you will use in most writing will fall somewhere between formal and informal English. It is important that you not mix extremely formal with extremely informal language, however, because that creates mixed messages that can jar your readers. Sometimes, however, such a mixture can be used to achieve a humorous effect.

The following chart compares the characteristics of formal and informal English.

	Formal	Informal
Tone	Serious, reserved, academic, ceremonial	Personal, friendly, casual
Vocabulary	May use longer or less common words; avoids clipped words and contractions	Uses simpler words; often uses clipped words and contractions
Mechanics	Uses correct grammar, spelling, and punctuation	Uses correct grammar, spelling, and punctuation
Organization	Longer, carefully constructed sentences	Conversational; sentence length varies

Vocabulary Variations

As a writer, you can choose from many types of vocabulary. These include idioms, clichés, slang, jargon, and euphemisms. You must use these types of vocabulary selectively, however, because each is appropriate only in certain situations.

Idioms An **idiom** is an expression that has a different meaning from the sum of the meanings of the individual words. For example, if you heard someone say that painting a house is "a piece of cake," you would know that the actual meaning of the expression has nothing to do with cake. Rather, the speaker meant that the task is easy. Other examples of idioms include the following:

Gregory *put his foot in his mouth.*
The team was *pushing its luck.*
Marianne researched her family's *coat of arms.*

You can use idioms appropriately in all informal situations, but you should generally avoid them in formal writing and speaking.

"Coat of Arms"

Clichés Expressions that have been so overused that they have lost their impact are called **clichés.** Many commonly used idioms become clichés, such as "time is money," "bored to death," and "as cold as ice." Clichés are common in speech and are often useful in writing as a kind of shorthand. However, excessive use of clichés can make it seem as though you don't have anything original to say. Instead, try to use fresh, new expressions and comparisons that stir your readers to think and feel.

"Time is Money"

Slang Newly coined words and expressions as well as established words and phrases that have taken on new, specialized meanings make up the type of vocabulary called **slang.** Often a slang word is first used by people who share a special interest or are in the same age group, and its use then spreads to larger segments of the population. Slang usually seems colorful and interesting when it is first used, and sometimes it even becomes accepted in general use. For example, the words *carpetbagger, hobo,* and *killjoy* began as slang. However, slang terms can fade away quickly and often do. For example, how frequently do you hear the terms *far out* or *groovy* nowadays? Many dictionaries include usage labels that indicate whether a word or phrase is considered an idiom or slang. These labels are usually placed in front of the meaning of the slang word or expression.

Slang can be helpful in creating realistic or lively dialogue in a play or short story, and is sometimes useful in conversations and informal letters. It is inappropriate, however, in a classroom discussion, in a business letter, or in any formal speaking or writing situation.

Jargon The specialized vocabulary used by people who engage in a particular activity is known as **jargon.** For example, the jargon of business includes words and phrases such as *insider trading, leveraged buyout,* and *proxy battle.* The jargon of computers includes *floppy, peripheral, down time,* and *disk crash.* Jargon words should be used only when no other acceptable terms are available, or when you are writing for an audience of specialists. If you find it necessary to use jargon in other types of writing, make sure that you define the terms when you introduce them.

Euphemisms The term **euphemism** describes expressions that are less harsh, and allegedly more polite and acceptable, than the words or ideas for which they stand. For example, *senior citizens* has fewer negative connotations, for most people, than *old people.*

Sometimes, you may want to use a euphemism for the sake of courtesy. However, euphemisms may be used in an attempt to disguise or misrepresent a situation to serve political purposes. For example, terrorists might say they "detained" a member of the press when, in fact, they have kidnapped the person. An oppressive government might say it "resettled" a population when, in fact, it forced people out of their homes and put them in camps. Using euphemisms in this way is dishonest and manipulative.

Look for both courteous and deceptive euphemisms in newspaper and magazine articles and in radio and television broadcasts. Try to avoid using deceptive euphemisms in your own writing.

Dialects

If you visit some other English-speaking country or a different part of your own country, you will notice that people speak English differently. The varieties of a language that are used in different places and by different groups of people are called **dialects.**

There is no one "correct" dialect. However, when writing or speaking to a general audience, especially in a formal situation, it is usually best to use standard English, which is widely understood. Use of dialect is often appropriate in a short story or play in which you want to use distinct speech patterns to identify a character as coming from a particular region or social group.

Various Types of Language in Writing

When you write, you need to decide what kinds of language are appropriate for the occasion. The guidelines that follow are designed to help you choose among the varieties of language.

- Always identify and keep in mind both the situation and the audience.
- Use formal language for formal occasions, such as speeches or written reports.
- Use informal language for personal writing and for less formal occasions and audiences.
- Do not mix extremely formal language with extremely informal language.
- Use idioms only in informal writing or in dialogue.
- Avoid excessive use of clichés.
- Use slang only with your peers, in dialogue, or in very informal writing.

Writing
TIP

If you want to use a certain dialect in your writing, see if you can make or find a recording of people speaking in that dialect.

- Avoid jargon except in situations where you can expect your audience to understand it.
- Beware of euphemisms. If it is more polite to say *deceased* than *dead,* do so. However, do not use euphemisms to cover up the truth.
- Use a nonstandard dialect when it is appropriate to the situation, as in dialogue in a short story, but not in formal speaking and writing.

Practice Your Skills

A. The following passage contains different varieties of language. First, rewrite the passage in formal English as if it were part of a science report on astronomers. Then rewrite the passage for inclusion in a letter to a friend who shares your interest in telescopes and stargazing and is considering studying to be an astronomer.

> Astronomers are guys who spend their lives doing weird things like shining the light of distant stars through a spectrograph. This instrument separates the light into individual wavelengths that form a rainbowlike spectrum for each object that is way, way out there in space somewhere. After studying these spectra, scientists can figure out lots of interesting things, like what stuff stars are made out of and how far away the stars are and how fast those stars are traveling through space. They can then put it all together and figure out how old the stars are. Given the value of such scientific information, one can conclude that sometimes things that look really neat are also extremely useful.

B. The following passage contains mixed levels of language, slang, clichés, and jargon. First, rewrite the passage in the form that would be appropriate for a newsletter to the Student Filmgoers' Club. Then rewrite the passage as if it were a paragraph in a formal report on Western films.

> Let me tell you, in the last scene of the movie, everything goes wacko. The star foregoes his prior Western equestrian pursuits and accedes to the ingenue's matrimonial ambitions. The whole movie looks like it was shot in 16 mm. and has a *film noir* feel to it that is highly inappropriate to its shallow premise. It's hard to imagine that in this day and age folks will shell out a big wad of cash to see such mediocre performances and such a mundane plot. Take my word for it film fanatics; you can miss this bomb.

On the Lightside

PALINDROMES

Language buffs have devoted uncounted hours to inventing new *palindromes*—words or phrases that are identical whether read left-to-right or right-to-left.

Because they were reputedly invented by Sotades, a Greek poet of the third century B.C., palindromes are sometimes called *sotadics.* Short ones are easy to find: "deed," "eye," "kayak," "level," and "noon." The longest such word in English, "redivider," falls short of the longest known palindromic word, *saippuakauppias,* a fifteen-letter Finnish word meaning "soap seller."

The challenge of finding palindromic words pales before the complexity of creating palindromic sentences or stories. Humorists have even described the first conversation as an exchange of palindromes:

He: "Madam, I'm Adam."
She: "Eve."

Once they grow longer than about fifty letters, palindromes usually make little sense, although Penelope

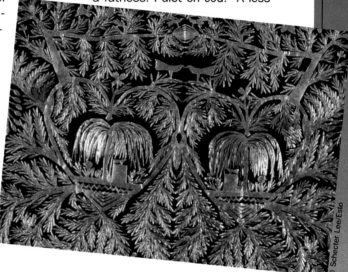

A visual palindrome?
Mourning Picture, cut from gilt foil.
Pennsylvania-German

© Schecter Lee/Esto

Gilliatt used fifty-one to say: "Doc, note I dissent. A fast never prevents a fatness. I diet on cod." A less ambitious writer mused, "Was it a car or a cat I saw?"

John Taylor probably created the first English palindromic sentence in the seventeenth century: "Lewd did I live & evil I did dwel." Napoleon Bonaparte is associated with one of the most famous: "Able was I ere I saw Elba," while history also comes alive in a palindrome attributed to Leigh Mercer: "A man, a plan, a canal—Panama."

Creating Sentence Variety

If variety is the spice of life, sentence variety is the spice of good writing. Give your writing vitality by varying the types, beginnings, and structures of sentences.

TYPES OF SENTENCES

You can choose from four types of sentences.

- A **simple sentence** has one independent clause.

  Mars is a cold, lifeless planet with a thin atmosphere.

- A **compound sentence** has two or more independent clauses.

  Mars is a cold, lifeless planet, but it has a thin atmosphere.

- A **complex sentence** has one independent clause and one or more subordinate clauses.

  Mars is a cold, lifeless planet that has a thin atmosphere.

- A **compound-complex sentence** has two or more independent clauses and one or more subordinate clauses.

  As scientists have discovered, Mars is a cold, lifeless planet, but because it has a thin atmosphere, speculation about Martian life persists.

You can vary your writing by using different types of sentences. For example, how might you improve the following paragraph?

> The merry-go-round, or carousel, has a long history. The merry-go-round comes from Arabia. The merry-go-round is based on a game played with horses. The horses went around in a circle. The game was called "Little War." (The Spanish word for "little war" is *carosella. Carousel* is another name for a merry-go-round.) The Crusaders saw this game being played. They brought the game back to Europe. The game in Europe was played with decorated horses, bows, musicians, and a central pole. The first carousel ride was invented in 1680.

Note how varying the sentences makes it more interesting.

> Did you know that the merry-go-round, or carousel, has a remarkable history? The idea for the merry-go-round is based on an Arabian game in which horses went around in a circle. Called "Little War," this game was brought to Europe by the

Crusaders. There, it was called *carosella,* which is the Spanish word for "little war." The Spanish word is, of course, the source of our word *carousel.* Decorated horses, bows, musicians, and a central pole eventually became part of this game. Finally, the game took the form of a ride when the first merry-go-round was invented in 1680.

SENTENCE COMPOSITION

You can vary the composition of your sentences by altering their beginnings, length, or structure.

Sentence Beginnings As you can see in the previous example, one way to vary sentences is to vary their beginnings. Many writers begin their sentences with *the, he, she, it,* and other articles, nouns, and pronouns. These words are not likely to capture your readers' interest. Instead, try introducing your sentences with other parts of speech—including verbs, verb forms, adverbs, and prepositions.

Sentence Length and Structure Varying the length and structure of your sentences is another way of adding variety and richness to your writing. Long, complex sentences can be especially effective when used in combination with short, simple sentences.

Simple	A Harvard research team recently studied learning. Their report advocated using two simple instructional methods. They suggested using small study groups and frequent tests. These methods cause students to learn significantly more.
Complex	According to a Harvard research team's recent study on learning, students learn significantly more when teachers use small study groups and frequent, short tests.

Creating Sentence
Variety

GRAMMATICAL VOICE

As a writer, you can choose from two grammatical voices—
active and passive—to vary your sentences. You use the *active*
voice to emphasize the doer of the action.

Active   The quarterback and the wide receiver practiced passes
Voice   before the game on Sunday.

The action of this sentence is expressed by the verb *practiced*. The performers of the action are the quarterback and the
wide receiver.

The **passive** voice removes the focus from the doer of the action. The performer of the action
is either not named or is named in
a phrase that follows the verb. For
example, the action in the following sentences is expressed by the
verb *were practiced*.

Passes were practiced by the quarterback and the wide receiver before the game on Sunday. (Doers
of the action are named after the
verb.)

Passes were practiced before the
game on Sunday. (Doers of the
action are not named.)

Sentences in the active voice are
more direct and use fewer words than those in the passive voice
and clarify who is doing the action. They have a more immediate

impact on the reader. Therefore, you should strive to use active sentences as much as possible. Use the passive voice, however, when you want to emphasize the person or thing being acted upon or when the person or thing performing the action is unknown.

Passive Voice	The ball literally *was plucked* from the air by the split end. (Doer is named after the verb.)
Passive Voice	The game was canceled due to the blizzard. (Doer is not known.)

Practice Your Skills

A. Rewrite the following paragraphs to increase the variety of the sentences. Vary the sentence beginnings, types, and structures. Also feel free to combine sentences and to move sentence parts around to make the paragraphs more interesting.

1.   The edges of nickels and pennies are smooth. The edges of dimes and quarters are ridged. You may not know why this is so. It is because dimes and quarters were once made out of silver. The silver was worth more than ten cents or twenty-five cents. Some outlaws would scrape the edges of coins to make chips. They would then sell the chips for cash. The government decided to serrate the edges of silver coins. These edges could not be chipped away so easily.

2.   Hector saw something black. It was bobbing up and down in the water. It didn't seem to be moving. He swam over to it. It was a metal drum. It was floating. Hector hauled it to the shore. He then called the authorities. Some police and some government people showed up. The drum was almost empty. It had been filled with a dangerous chemical. The chemical was dry-cleaning solvent. The drum had been dumped illegally in the lake.

B.   Rewrite the following paragraph. Change the passive voice to the active voice in each case where the emphasis should be placed on the performer of the action.

Do you know why some movies are called *blockbusters?* Are blocks busted by movies? Actually, it is likely that the word *blockbuster* was first used by pilots during World War II. What was meant by *blockbuster* was a large aerial bomb. It was thought of as any bomb big enough to destroy a whole city block. The word was later picked up by people in show business. It was used by show business people to mean "a huge success."

Writing
TIP

If your writing sounds weak or awkward, check to see whether you have overused the passive voice.

Combining Sentences

Too many short sentences can make your writing choppy and unclear. You can often find ways of combining short related sentences to make your writing smoother, livelier, and clearer.

COMBINING SENTENCES AND SENTENCE PARTS

You can combine sentences that express related ideas of equal importance by using a comma and a conjunction. A **conjunction** is a word—such as *and, but,* or *or*—that connects words or groups of words.

If the ideas are similar, use a comma and the conjunction *and* to connect them.

Separate Sentences	London is the capital of England. *Madrid is the capital of Spain.*
Combined Sentence	London is the capital of England, and *Madrid is the capital of Spain.*

Similar ideas can also be joined by a semicolon.

Separate Sentences	The doctor is performing surgery. *She cannot see any more patients today.*
Combined Sentence	The doctor is performing surgery; *she cannot see any more patients today.*

If the ideas contrast, use a comma and the conjunction *but*.

Separate Sentences	The wild ponies of Chincoteague gallop fast. *They tire fairly quickly.*
Combined Sentence	The wild ponies of Chincoteague gallop fast, but *they tire fairly quickly.*

If there is a choice between two ideas, use a comma and the conjunction *or*.

Separate Sentences	You can take the bus to the concert. *We can walk to the concert together.*
Combined Sentence	You can take the bus to the concert, or *we can walk to the concert together.*

Sometimes the ideas expressed by two sentences are so closely related that some words in the first sentence are repeated, or replaced by synonyms, in the second sentence. You can combine sentences like these by eliminating the words that are repeated.

Compare the following sentences. Notice how combining sentences differs from combining sentence parts. You use a comma when combining sentences, because you are joining two independent clauses. You don't need a comma when combining sentence parts, because you have only added a phrase to the original sentence.

| Combined Sentences | Dolphins travel in family groups, and *they communicate with clicks and whistles.* |
| Combined Sentence Parts | Dolphins travel in family groups and *communicate with clicks and whistles.* |

Practice Your Skills

Combine each pair of sentences. Use the word or punctuation mark given in parentheses and eliminate any underlined words.

1. Death Valley in California is a true desert. Many plants and animals thrive there. (*,but*)
2. The dinosaurs disappeared about sixty-five million years ago. Scientists cannot explain why. (semicolon)
3. The jet streaked down the runway. The jet rose gracefully into the air. (*and*)
4. A few spiders are poisonous. Most spiders are harmless. (*,but*)
5. Visitors to China can walk along the top of the Great Wall. Tourists can also explore the Forbidden City. (*or*)

ADDING WORDS TO
SENTENCES

Sometimes two sentences contain related ideas that are not equally important. You may be able to incorporate a key word from one sentence into the other to create a more effective single sentence.

Inserting Words Without Change Often, you can add a key word from one sentence to another sentence without changing the form of the word. However, you must place the word near the person, thing, or action the word describes.

| Separate Sentences | The meteor was *brilliant*. The meteor raced across the eastern sky. |
| Combined Sentence | The *brilliant* meteor raced across the eastern sky. |

You can combine more than two sentences if one of the sentences states a main idea and each of the others adds just one important detail. You may need to use a comma or the conjunction *and*.

Separate Sentences	The earthquake created a tidal wave. The wave was *gigantic*. The wave was *fast-moving*.
Combined Sentence	The earthquake created a *gigantic, fast-moving* tidal wave.

Inserting Words with Changes   Sometimes you must change the form of a word before you can add it to another sentence. The most common changes involve adding endings such as *-y, -ed, -ing,* or *-ly*.

Separate Sentences	They spotted the lion near the wildebeest herd. The lion *slept*.
Combined Sentence	They spotted the *sleeping* lion near the wildebeest herd.

Separate Sentences	The mayor greeted the visitors. Her greeting was *pleasant*.
Combined Sentence	The mayor greeted the visitors *pleasantly*.

Practice Your Skills

Combine the following sentences. In sentences 1–5, eliminate the underlined words and use the word ending or punctuation mark in parentheses. In sentences 6–10, decide which combining techniques to use.

1. A snake slithered under the door. The snake was long. It was speckled. (,)
2. The soup was full of vegetables, noodles, and savory broth. Steam rose from the soup. (-*y*)
3. She showed us her gold medal. She was proud. (-*ly*)
4. The fans leaped to their feet. The fans cheered. (-*ing*)
5. The vase is very valuable. It has a crack. (-*ed*)
6. The poodle next door sleeps on pillows. The pillows are silk. That poodle is pampered.
7. The employee stood at the door of the office. He seemed hesitant to enter.
8. An army of ants moved silently through the jungle. The army moved steadily.
9. The deer ran from the hunter. The deer had a wound.
10. The raccoons come to our back door. They are hungry. They come daily.

In some cases, you may find that a group of words from one sentence can be used in another sentence. Combining sentences in this way will often create more concise, stronger writing.

Inserting Word Groups Without Changes   You can sometimes insert a group of words into another sentence without changing their form. When you revise, place the words close to the person, thing or action they describe.

Separate Sentences	A family moved in next door. They are *from Vietnam.*
Combined Sentence	A family *from Vietnam* moved in next door.

Inserting Appositive Phrases   Sometimes you can combine two sentences by making a group of words from one of the sentences into an **appositive phrase.** An appositive phrase is a group of words that renames a noun and is usually set off by commas.

Separate Sentences	The sunflower may grow from 3 to 10 feet (1 to 3 meters) tall. The sunflower is *a tall plant known for its showy yellow flowers.*
Combined Sentence	The sunflower, *a tall plant known for its showy yellow flowers,* may grow from 3 to 10 feet (1 to 3 meters) tall.

Inserting Word Groups with Changes When you add a group of words to a sentence, you may have to change the form of one of the words by adding *-ing* or *-ed*. As the following examples demonstrate, more than one group of words may be added to a sentence in this way.

Separate Sentences	Everyone in the boat got seasick when the storm hit. The boat had a *round bottom.*
Combined Sentence	Everyone in the *round-bottomed* boat got seasick when the storm hit.
Separate Sentences	The man burst into the room. He *smiled broadly.* He *shouted the news of the victory to anyone who would listen.*
Combined Sentence	The man burst into the room, *smiling broadly and shouting the news of the victory to anyone who would listen.*

Practice Your Skills

Combine the following sentences. In sentences 1–5, eliminate the underlined words and add the word part or punctuation in parentheses. In sentences 6–10, you can decide how to combine the sentences.

1. The firefighter rushed into the burning house. <u>She</u> hesitated just a moment at the door. (comma and *-ing*)
2. Flight 933 is now expected to depart for Chicago. <u>It should depart</u> at approximately 9:45 P.M.
3. In 1565, Spaniards in Florida founded St. Augustine. <u>It was</u> the first permanent European settlement in America. (comma)
4. The acting mayor called an emergency meeting of the village council. <u>He had</u> concerns about the pollution of the harbor. (*-ed* and commas)
5. The people of the town are anxiously watching the raging forest fire. <u>The fire</u> creeps slowly toward their homes. (*-ing*)
6. A gym teacher invented the game of basketball. His name was James Naismith.
7. Carla joined a skydiving club that meets every Saturday morning. Carla is my cousin.
8. If you want to taste something delicious, try a tangelo. This fruit is a cross between a grapefruit and a tangerine.
9. Joel visited the memorial to the Holocaust victims. It is in Israel. He visited it with his aunt and uncle.
10. We crossed over the deep canyon on a bridge the Indians built. The bridge swayed. The Indians had built it with thick vines.

COMBINING WITH *WHO, WHICH, OR THAT*

As you revise, you can eliminate repetition by using the introductory words *who, which,* or *that* to combine sentences.

Inserting Word Groups with *Who* You can use the word *who* to add related details about a person or group of persons to a sentence.

Separate Sentences	To be successful, a candidate needs supporters. The supporters must *be willing to work long and hard for victory.*
Combined Sentence	To be successful, a candidate needs supporters who *are willing to work long and hard for victory.*
Separate Sentences	William Golding won the Nobel Prize for literature in 1983. *He is best known for the novel* <u>The Lord of the Flies</u>.
Combined Sentence	William Golding, *who is best known for the novel* <u>The Lord of the Flies</u>, won the Nobel Prize for literature in 1983.

Notice that in the first example, the added details tell what kind of supporters a candidate needs. These details are essential to the meaning of the sentence, so no commas are needed. In the second example, the added details are not essential to identifying William Golding, so they are set off with commas.

Inserting Word Groups with *That* or *Which* You can use *that* or *which* to add related details to a sentence when those details refer to things.

Separate Sentences	I like any movie. The movie must *make me laugh hard.*
Combined Sentence	I like any movie *that makes me laugh hard.*
Separate Sentences	The Taj Mahal took twenty years to build. The Taj Mahal *is in India.*
Combined Sentence	The Taj Mahal, *which is in India,* took twenty years to build.

In the first example, the added details are necessary to the meaning of the sentence, so *that* is used. The related details in the second example are not essential to the main idea of the sentence, so *which* is used, and the details are set off with commas.

Practice Your Skills

Combine each pair of sentences. In sentences 1–7, eliminate the underlined words and use the word and/or punctuation mark in parentheses. In sentences 8–15, decide for yourself how to use *who, which,* or *that* and commas to combine the sentences.

1. Here is the novel. Jim said we should read <u>it</u>. (*that*)
2. Scotland Yard is a part of the London police force. <u>Scotland Yard</u> is not in Scotland. (*which* and commas)
3. A dentist in Italy pulled over seventy thousand teeth in thirty-six years! <u>He</u> grew up with my father. (*who* and commas)
4. The firefighter is courageous. <u>That firefighter</u> rescued two young children from a burning house. (*who*)
5. The first movie theater was called a nickelodeon. <u>This theater</u> seated ninety-two people. (*which* and commas)
6. In the attic, Richard discovered a crate full of diaries. <u>The diaries</u> had been kept by his grandparents. (*that*)
7. Many computer systems use a dot-matrix printer. <u>It</u> forms letters made of many tiny dots. (*which* and comma)
8. The old legend mentioned a griffin. The griffin is a mythological beast with the head and wings of an eagle and the body of a lion.
9. William Blake introduced Romanticism into British art. He was a great poet and illustrator.
10. Track lighting is adjustable. Track lighting can throw a beam of light anywhere in a room.
11. Samuel Johnson wrote an entire dictionary by himself in only eight years. Johnson lived in England during the 1700's.
12. The diamond tiara is priceless. The queen wears it.
13. The players were the honored guests at a citywide celebration. The players won the world soccer championship.
14. A house in California has 2,000 doors, 10,000 windows, and stairways leading nowhere. It may be the weirdest building on earth.
15. The white roses were gorgeous. You sent them to me for graduation.

USING SUBORDINATING CONJUNCTIONS

Sometimes, in two sentences that contain related ideas, one idea is less important than, or subordinate to, the other. As you revise, you can combine the two sentences by using certain words to show the relationship between two ideas. These words—including *when, because,* and *although*—are called subordinating conjunctions. These conjunctions and the relationships they indicate are shown in the following chart.

Relationship	Subordinating Conjuctions
Time	when, after, before, until, while, as long as, as soon as,
Cause	because, as, since
Condition	although, though, unless, if, whether (or not), considering (that)

Separate Sentences	The cabin attendants started serving dinner. *The captain of the jet turned off the seat-belt sign.*
Combined Sentence	The cabin attendants started serving dinner *when the captain of the jet turned off the seat-belt sign.*
Separate Sentences	All the lights in the city are out. *Lightning struck the main electrical power plant.*
Combined Sentence	All the lights in the city are out *because lightning struck the main electrical power plant.*
Separate Sentences	We enjoyed Hawaii. *Rain fell every day.*
Combined Sentence	We enjoyed Hawaii *although rain fell every day.*

To emphasize a subordinate idea, place it at the beginning of the combined sentence, set off by a comma.

> *Although rain fell every day,* we enjoyed Hawaii.

Faulty subordination occurs when you state the main idea in the subordinate clause.

Faulty	Since the workout was too strenuous for me, the aerobics class was an hour and a half long.
Revised	Since the aerobics class was an hour and a half long, the workout was too strenuous for me.

Writing TIP

Using subordinating conjunctions to show relationships between your ideas will help you create coherence in your writing.

Reptiles. 1943,
by M.C.Escher

©1990 M.C. Escher Heirs/Cordon Art – Baarn – Holland

Practice Your Skills

Combine or revise the following pairs of sentences. In sentences 1–5, use the word in parentheses. In sentences 6–10, you can decide whether to use a subordinate clause and, if needed, a comma or a semicolon.

1. We bought the Escher book. It was fascinating. (*because*)
2. The crowd on both sides of the street cheered loudly. The President's car rolled by. (*while*)
3. The hikers kept going up the Grand Canyon trail. They were very tired. (*although*)
4. Al canceled his date. He had the flu. (*because*)
5. The ski lift was closed. There was no snow. (*since*)
6. Our dog always howls. The moon is full.
7. Chinese pandas are highly valued. They are becoming rare in the wild.
8. Few people agreed with Galileo. He explained that Earth was not at the center of the universe.
9. Iguanas can outwit their enemies. They blend in with their environment.
10. In Columbus's time, people used spices to preserve food. Refrigeration had not been invented yet.

Point of View

Suppose the President of the United States visited your school. The next day everyone would be talking about it—and everyone would have something different to say. If your principal met *Air Force One* at the airport and rode to school in the President's limousine, he or she would have one story to tell. If you sat in the auditorium and heard the President speak, you would have another story to tell. These stories would differ largely because of the point of view from which they were experienced.

USING POINT OF VIEW IN WRITING

You may already know the term *point of view* from studying literature. Simply stated, point of view is the perspective, or angle, from which a piece of writing is told.

- Writing told by a speaker who refers to himself or herself as "I" or "me" is told from the **first-person point of view.**
- Writing in which the speaker does not mention himself or herself but addresses the reader as "you" is told from the **second-person point of view.**
- A piece of writing in which the speaker does not mention himself or herself and in which people are referred to as "he," "she," or "they" is told from the **third-person point of view.**

Perhaps the best way to understand point of view is to look at examples of how different points of view are used in fiction and in nonfiction.

Point of View in Fiction

Fictional narration is generally presented from the first- or third-person point of view.

First-Person Point of View   In a story told from the first-person point of view, the narrator is a character in the story and shares his or her own experiences, attitudes, and opinions. The following paragraph comes from a classic detective novel told from the first-person point of view. The narrator, a private eye, tells about searching for clues.

I went over where the car had stood and got a fountain pen flash unclipped from my pocket and poked the little light down at the ground. The soil was red loam, very hard in dry weather, but the weather was not bone dry. There was a little fog in the air, and enough of the moisture had settled on the surface of the ground to show where the car had stood. I could see, very faint, the tread marks of the heavy ten-ply Vogue tires. I put the light on them and bent over. . . . They went straight ahead for a dozen feet, then swung over to the left. They didn't turn. They went towards the gap at the left hand end of the white barricade. Then I lost them.

Raymond Chandler, *Farewell My Lovely*

A story told from the first-person point of view generally reveals a great deal about who the narrator is and how he or she thinks and acts. In the paragraph above, for example, we learn how observant and careful the narrator is.

Third-Person Point of View In a story told from the third-person point of view, the narrator does not participate in the story, but rather relates events as an all-knowing, or omniscient, observer. The following passage is narrated from the third-person point of view. As you read, notice how the narrator recedes into the background, focusing attention on the characters, setting, and action.

A light kindled in the sky, a blaze of yellow fire behind dark barriers. Pippin cowered back, afraid for a moment, wondering into what dreadful country Gandalf was bearing him. He rubbed his eyes, and then he saw that it was the moon rising above the eastern shadows, now almost at the full. So the night was not yet old and for hours the dark journey would go on. He stirred and spoke.

"Where are we, Gandalf?" he asked.

"In the realm of Gondor," the wizard answered. "The land of Anórien is still passing by."

There was a silence again for a while. Then, "What is that?" cried Pippin suddenly, clutching at Gandalf's cloak. "Look! Fire, red fire! Are there dragons in this land?"

J. R. R. Tolkein, *The Return of the King*

Point of View in Nonfiction

Writers of nonfiction can choose either the first-, third-, or second-person point of view, depending on their purpose, audience, and writing goals.

First-Person Point of View A nonfiction work written from the first-person point of view tends to be **subjective,** presenting the feelings, beliefs, observations, and experiences of a single person— the "I" who is speaking. Keep in mind when you are evaluating information that a first-person narrator interprets and shapes events. The following passage describes an encounter with a great white shark. Notice how the first-person point of view lends immediacy and credibility to the account.

> I felt hopeless and sick with fear as the shark was coming closer. I'm gone, I'm gone, I thought as I kicked at the head as hard as I could. I felt my right fin just touch the shark. I had not allowed that underwater everything appears a third closer. Just a foot away, the giant mouth opened and swallowed the eight-inch nylon buoy I was towing on 40 feet of strong nylon ski rope.
>
> The shark swam out of view as I took a couple of breaths of air. My brain was screaming in fear. I felt no pain. The fear of being eaten alive and the intensity of the moment overrides the feelings of pain.
>
> The rope tied to my weight belt suddenly went tight and now I was pulled through the water faster and faster, spinning and turning. . . . I couldn't get free. Deeper down I was towed. I needed air—I must breathe! My head was going very fuzzy and with all hope gone I was about to take a great gulp—even if it was water—when SNAP, the line parted. I was free!
>
> **Rodney Fox**

PROFESSIONAL
M O D E L

Third-Person Point of View In nonfiction, use the third-person point of view if you want your writing to be **objective,** that is, factual and free of personal opinion and judgment. However, keep in mind when evaluating nonfiction writing that third-person writing can appear objective but actually be colored by the writer's attitudes. The following paragraph about the Eskimos is an example of objective third-person writing. Notice that the author offers no opinion or judgment on the information she presents.

▼

The Eskimos described everyone other than themselves as Kasdlunas. They called themselves Inuit—which simply means "the people." For centuries, since they never saw anyone else, they believed they were the only human beings in the world.

Marle Herbert, _The Snow People_

Second-Person Point of View In using the second-person point of view, the writer can address the reader directly without mentioning himself or herself. This point of view is used mainly to give instructions or directions. Here is an example from a computer manual of writing done in the second-person point of view.

PROFESSIONAL
M O D E L

▼

Save early and often: Once you've given your document a name, if you continue working on it, make a habit of choosing the Save command from the File menu about every 15 minutes or so. (It's a good thing to do while you're waiting for your next inspiration.)

Apple® Computer

Notice that this selection addresses the reader as "you" and gives instructions for saving a computer file.

VARYING YOUR POINT
OF VIEW

Many people find it useful to experiment with different points of view during drafting. Suppose, for example, that you have chosen to write a formal essay for a biology class on snakes because you are both fascinated and horrified by them. You might begin drafting by writing your own thoughts about snakes in the first-person. You can then rewrite your material from the third-person point of view and glean facts from other sources.

Practice Your Skills

A. Read the following paragraphs and tell from what point of view each is written. Discuss with your classmates the differences between the two paragraphs. Which is the most factual, or objective?

I think Mr. Brown has a point.

Wishful Thinking ©1987 David Sipress   SIPRESS

Which is the most personal, or subjective? Which point of view is most appropriate for objective nonfiction writing? For subjective nonfiction writing?

> There were 640 reported incidents of bikes colliding with pedestrians in New York City last year, up from 339 in 1981. Three New York City pedestrians were killed by cyclists in 1986, while nine bikers were killed by motorists.
>
> **Frank Trippet, "Scaring the Public to Death"**

> A recent story in *Time* said that nine bicyclists were killed by motorists in New York City in 1986. I'm surprised that the number wasn't higher. Bike riders are careless commuters; they don't follow the rules of the road, and I wish my community would ban them altogether.
>
> **Kelly Janowicz, student**

B. Think of an event that can be considered from several different points of view—for example, a touchdown pass in a football game as viewed by the quarterback, by a sports reporter, by the fans of the home team or the visiting team, or by the football itself. Describe your scenario in a paragraph, using the point of view of your choice.

C. Choose some event in your life that you feel strongly about to use for an eyewitness report. Write two paragraphs about the event, one subjective and emotionally charged, and one objective, factual, and unemotional. What are the differences between the two paragraphs? Did rewriting the material in an objective form give you a different view of the event? Did you learn anything about yourself, your feelings, or the event by thinking about it objectively?

Writing Dialogue

One way to make your writing more vivid is by using dialogue —actual conversations—to show, rather than tell, what characters are doing and feeling.

U SES OF DIALOGUE

You may think of dialogue as a component of only short stories and novels. However, dialogue can be used effectively in all types of writing, including drama, poetry, and nonfiction.

Using Dialogue in Fiction

Most works of fiction include two different types of writing: narration, which gives an account of events, and dialogue, which presents the characters' own words. When used well, dialogue can reveal much information about both characters and events in fiction.

Dialogue to Reveal Character As you read the following, note what the dialogue reveals not only about Shane, a stranger, but also about the narrator's parents, who are discussing him.

LITERARY
· · · · · · · · · · · · ·
M O D E L

▼

"Wasn't it peculiar," I heard mother say, "how he wouldn't talk about himself?"

"Peculiar?" said father. "Well, yes. In a way."

"Everything about him is peculiar." Mother sounded as if she was stirred up and interested. "I never saw a man quite like him before."

"You wouldn't have. Not where you come from. He's a special brand we sometimes get out here in the grass country. I've come across a few. A bad one's poison. A good one's straight grain clear through."

Jack Shaefer, *Shane*

This dialogue not only establishes that Shane is special and a bit mysterious but also reveals the parents' characters—the mother sheltered, but very curious; and the father, quietly self-confident. Notice how colorful Western expressions, such as "straight grain clear through," add realism to the dialogue.

Dialogue to Present Events Dialogue often functions in fiction to advance the plot or reveal background information. In this passage from the opening pages of *Shane,* the narrator's father and Shane discuss a rancher named Fletcher. The author uses their dialogue to introduce the basic conflict of the novel.

▼

"Sure his [Fletcher's] outfit sprawls over most of the valley and it looks big. But he's got range rights on a lot more acres than he has cows and he won't even have those acres as more homesteaders move in. . . . He thinks we small fellows are nothing but a nuisance."

"You are," said Shane mildly. "From his point of view, you are."

"Yes, I guess you're right. I'll have to admit that. Those of us here now would make it tough for him if he wanted to use the range behind us on this side of the river as he used to. Worse still, we block off part of the river. . . . He's been grumbling about that off and on ever since we've been here."

Jack Shaefer, *Shane*

Notice how the author clarifies who is speaking. The exact words of each speaker are in quotation marks. Each time the speaker changes, the author begins a new paragraph. Speaker tags, such as "said Shane," also let readers know who is speaking and, sometimes, how the words are being spoken.

Using Dialogue in Plays and Skits

Plays and skits consist almost entirely of dialogue, so it must clearly reveal both characters and events. As you read the following passage, consider how the dialogue reveals the individuals' characters and their relationship to one another. How does the dialect, such as the use of *you* instead of *you're,* of *ain't* instead of *isn't,* and of double negatives, help develop the characters? Also notice how the dialogue is presented—without quotation marks. This is one of several ways to punctuate dialogue in plays.

Writing
━ TIP ━

Remember that overuse of unusual spelling to reflect dialect can detract from the power of your writing.

WALTER: I want so many things that they are driving me kind of crazy . . . Mama—look at me.

MAMA: I'm looking at you. You a good-looking boy. You got a job, a nice wife, a fine boy, and—

WALTER: A job. (Looks at her) Mama, a job? I open and close car doors all day long, I drive a man around in his limousine and I say, "Yes, sir; no, sir; very good, sir; shall I take the Drive, sir?" Mama, that ain't no kind of job . . . that ain't nothing at all. (Very quietly) Mama, I don't know if I can make you understand.

Lorraine Hansberry, *A Raisin in the Sun*

Using Dialogue in Nonfiction

Dialogue is often used in autobiographies, biographies, and non-fiction newspaper or magazine articles. In such contexts, the writer must make sure that the dialogue accurately reports what the people actually said.

Notice how succinctly this excerpt reveals an important aspect of President Truman's character.

We would come to a framed copy of that issue of the *Chicago Tribune* that on November 2, 1948, had the headline DEWEY DEFEATS TRUMAN. . . .

I said, "Mr. President, were you really able to go to sleep that night without knowing for sure whether you'd won the election?"

"Of course," said the President. "I knew I was going to win. Never had the slightest doubt about it. Besides, it was all over but the shouting. What would have been the point in not getting a good night's sleep?"

Merle Miller, *Plain Speaking*

Authors of nonfiction also sometimes re-create dialogue that might have taken place to give a historical event more immediacy. Such dialogue should be based on known information about the lives and characters of the individuals involved, as well as the speech and language of the time.

Guidelines for Writing Dialogue

- Select verbs for your speaker's tags or stage directions that describe the speaker's emotion or tone of voice. Whispers, shouts, sighs, giggles, and gasps can be used to reveal a character's feelings and state of mind.

- Create a dialogue that reveals your characters' personalities and social status. One way to do this is to use special forms of language, such as dialect or slang.

- Make the dialogue sound like real speech. Remember that people speak differently in formal and informal situations and that they often use incomplete sentences and contractions.

- In a play, use stage directions to convey tone of voice, facial expressions, body language, and details about the speaker's actions or appearance.

WRITER TO WRITER

If you are using dialogue—say it aloud as you write it. Only then will it have the sound of speech.

John Steinbeck, novelist

Novelist John
Steinbeck, 1952

Practice Your Skills

A. Rewrite the following passage to make it clear which character is speaking. Remember to use speaker's tags with appropriate verbs.

> I say, is anyone here to give service? Oh, I'll be with you directly. Ya seem to be in a mighty big hurry. It's just that my plane leaves at seven, and if I don't leave now I can't be sure of making my flight. Well, if that's all that's bothern' ya, ya can relax right now. The roads are closed. It don't seem likely that you'll be goin' anywheres tonight.

B. Choose a scene such as telephoning to tell your parents you have just had an accident while driving and write a realistic dialogue for a short story. Then rewrite the dialogue as a scene for a play, including stage directions.

Strengthening Your Vocabulary

One of the best investments you can make in your future is to work on building your vocabulary now. Two strategies that you can use for building your vocabulary are inferring word meanings from context and analyzing word parts.

W R I T E R   T O   W R I T E R

I would try to emphasize the importance of reading to student writers everywhere. By reading anything, your vocabulary is made larger and your skills strengthened.

Laurie McEachern, student
Jackson, Mississippi

INFERRING WORD MEANINGS FROM CONTEXT

What should you do when you are reading and you come across an unfamiliar word? You can turn to your dictionary, or you can try to figure out the meaning of the word on your own.

Diplomacy (dĭ-plō´mə·sė) 1, the art of negotiation between peoples. 2, artful management in dealing with others. 3, tact.

Often you can find clues to the meaning of a word by thinking about its **context,** the sentence or group of sentences in which the word appears. In some cases you may have to reflect on the entire passage and **infer,** or draw a conclusion about, the meaning.

Inferring Meaning Through Key Words Several types of context clues may help you determine the meaning of an unfamiliar word. These types of clues include definition and restatement, example, comparison, contrast, and cause-and-effect clues, and often are signaled by key words. Learning to recognize these clues can help improve your reading comprehension.

Type of Context Clue	*Key Words*	
Definition and Restatement		
The writer places the meaning of the unfamiliar word directly after the word itself.	which is that is or	in other words also known as also called
Example		
The writer follows an unfamiliar word with an example of it.	like such as other this these	including for example for instance especially these include
Comparison		
The writer provides clues to the meaning of an unfamiliar word by drawing a comparison using other, more familiar terms.	like as also related likewise	in the same way resembling similar to identical similarly
Contrast		
The writer provides clues to the meaning of an unfamiliar word by discussing it in contrast to something familiar.	but unlike however different	on the other hand on the contrary in contrast to dissimilar
Cause and Effect		
The writer may state a cause in unfamiliar terms but state the effect in familiar terms.	because since when	consequently therefore as a result

Example	Meaning
Metal can be made more flexible by *annealing,* which is a process of heating followed by slow cooling.	The definition of *annealing* is given directly following the words *which is.*
The university had several excellent *entomologists* on its staff. These included Dr. Tower, a specialist on flying insects, and Dr. Mistri, an expert on ants.	Although the word *entomologist* is not directly defined, the two examples suggest that an entomologist is a person who studies insects.
The *dirigible,* like a huge balloon, floated above the stadium with an advertising banner streaming out behind it.	Although the context does not fully reveal what a *dirigible* is, the comparison allows you to visualize what it might look like and leads you to conclude that a dirigible is a balloon-like aircraft.
Zinc is a naturally occurring element. *Einsteinium,* however, is not.	From the contrast developed in the two sentences, you know that *einsteinium* is an element. You also know that einsteinium does not occur naturally. You can infer that einsteinium is an artificially produced element.

Inferring Meaning from General Context Often you will have to infer the meaning of a word from the main idea or supporting details of an entire paragraph. In the following paragraph, notice how the details help you infer the meaning of *eclectic.*

> You have only to turn on your radio to see how eclectic America's musical tastes are. At any time of the day you are sure to find jazz, show tunes, country and western songs, and several varieties of rock. A twist of the dial may bring you "easy listening" music or a string quartet.

Since the idea is supported by details showing a wide variety of music, *eclectic* must have a meaning that is close to "widely varied."

Practice Your Skills

A. Use context clues to select the best definition for the italicized word in each passage below. Write the letter of the best definition.

1. Because the school's halls were so *labyrinthine,* Mr. Bolenger drew a detailed map to help new students find their way.
   - a. long
   - b. like a maze
   - c. narrow
   - d. brightly decorated
2. After several crushing defeats, Wally started to lose his *zeal* for playing basketball.
   - a. curiosity
   - b. patience
   - c. funds
   - d. enthusiasm
3. Benjamin Franklin is noted for his *aphorisms*—short statements expressing wise observations.
   - a. criticisms
   - b. jokes
   - c. sayings
   - d. amendments
4. Amid the remaining *flotsam* from the wrecked ship, rescue workers found only some timber and a single sailor's cap.
   - a. floating debris
   - b. water
   - c. nets
   - d. sailors
5. Although the shopkeeper claimed the painting of Washington was *bona fide,* there was something about it that seemed unauthentic.
   - a. fake
   - b. exotic
   - c. modern
   - d. genuine

B. Read each passage, noting the main idea and supporting details. Then write the letter that represents the best definition of the word in italics.

1. Rock music is *ubiquitous* these days. Not only do we hear it on television and radio, but also in cars, elevators, and stores.
   - a. soothing
   - b. everywhere
   - c. modern
   - d. loud
2. Many creatures undergo a complete *metamorphosis.* The butterfly, for example, begins life as a caterpillar and then changes into its adult form. The frog begins life as a tadpole and only later develops the shape and habits of the adult.
   - a. awakening
   - b. examination
   - c. life
   - d. transformation
3. Ancient Sumeria was a *hagiocracy.* All important decisions were made by priests. They passed laws, settled disputes, and collected taxes.
   - a. country ruled by force
   - b. country ruled by religious leaders
   - c. city
   - d. nation

Writing
——**TIP**——

When using a new word in your writing, look it up in the dictionary to make sure you've used it correctly.

4. Black lung disease is *endemic* among coal miners in the Welsh mountains. The disease is also found among coal miners in the Appalachian mountains.
   a. growing
   b. native to a region
   c. preventable
   d. originating in a rural area
5. Carlotta and I both read the passage several times very carefully. Nevertheless, her *exegesis* differed from mine largely because the author did not clarify what he meant by "courage."
   a. book
   b. interpretation
   c. author
   d. assignment

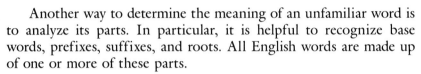

ANALYZING WORD PARTS

Another way to determine the meaning of an unfamiliar word is to analyze its parts. In particular, it is helpful to recognize base words, prefixes, suffixes, and roots. All English words are made up of one or more of these parts.

Base Words Complete words to which a prefix and/or suffix may be added to form new words are **base words.** *Real* is an example of a base word. Here are three words that can be formed from *real*. Can you think of others?

> really   realism   unreal

Each of these words retains the meaning of *real;* however, the meaning is changed somewhat by the parts that are added. Once you know the meaning of these word parts, you can arrive at the meaning of the entire word.

Prefixes A **prefix** is a word part that is added to the beginning of another word or word part.

Now analyze how the two new words below are formed by adding prefixes to the same base word.

Prefix	+	Base Word	=	New Word
intra	+	state	=	intrastate
inter	+	state	=	interstate

The prefix *intra-* means "within." Once you know this, you can infer that *intrastate* means "within a state." The prefix *inter-* means "between." Once you know this, you can infer that *interstate* means "between states."

All prefixes have one or more meanings. The prefixes in the following chart have only one meaning.

Inconvenience stores

Prefixes That Have a Single Meaning

Prefix	Meaning	Example
bene-	good	benediction
circum-	around	circumnavigate
contra-	opposed	contrapositive
equi-	equal	equidistant
extra-	outside	extraordinary
hemi-	half	hemisphere
hyper-	over, above	hypercritical
inter-	between, among	international
intra-	within	intracellular
intro-	into	introversion
mal-	bad	maltreat
mid-	halfway	midday
mis-	wrong	misspell
non-	not	nonworking
pre-	before	predawn
retro-	backward, behind	retrorocket
sub-	under, below	subway

Subway, 1959, by Robert Goodnough

Many prefixes have more than one meaning. Some of these are shown in the following chart.

COMPUTER TIP

If you use a spell-check program, remember that it does not verify correct use of prefixes and suffixes.

Prefixes That Have More Than One Meaning

Prefix	Meaning	Example
ab-, a-	not	abnormal
	away	absent
	up, out	arise
ad-	motion toward	adjoin
	nearness to	administer
ante-	before, prior to	antedate
	in front of	anteroom
anti-	against	anticensorship
	prevents, cures	antitoxin
	opposite, reverse	antimatter
de-	away from, off	derail
	down	degrade
	reverse action of	defrost
dis-	lack of	distrust
	not	dishonest
	away	displace
il-, im-, in,	not	immature
	in, into	insight
pro-	in favor of	prolabor
	forward, ahead	proactive
re-	again	replant
	back	repay
semi-	half	semicircle
	twice in a period	semiannual
	partly	semiconscious
super-	over and above	superhuman
	very large	supertanker
trans-	across	transatlantic
	beyond	transplant

Suffixes A **suffix** is a word part that is added to the end of another word or word part. Each suffix has its own meaning or meanings.

Noun Suffixes **Noun suffixes** are added to base words to form nouns. The following charts show you suffixes for forming two kinds of nouns.

Noun Suffixes That Mean "One Who Does Something"

Suffix	Example
-ant	commandant, occupant
-eer, -ier	auctioneer, puppeteer, cashier
-er, -or	manager, counselor
-ist	geologist, theorist, geneticist
-ician	beautician, statistician

Noun Suffixes That Form Abstract Words

Suffix	Example
-ance, -ence	vigilance, independence
-ation, -ition	imagination, proposition
-dom	freedom, kingdom
-hood	brotherhood, womanhood
-ice	cowardice, prejudice
-ism	realism, federalism
-ment	commitment, encouragement
-ness	fondness, sickness
-ship	ownership, worship
-ity, -ty	sincerity, frailty

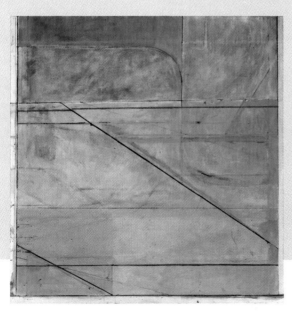

Mr. & Mrs. Robert B. McLain Collection, Newport Beach, CA

Ocean Park No. 114, 1979, by Richard Diebenkorn. Oil on canvas, 81 × 81 inches

Adjective Suffixes Other suffixes, called **adjective suffixes,** are added to base words to form **adjectives**—words that are used to modify nouns and pronouns. Some common adjective suffixes are listed in the following chart.

Adjective Suffixes

Suffix	Meaning	Example
-able	able to	readable
-acious	full of	spacious
-al	relating to	rental
-ant	relating to	triumphant
-ful	full of	wonderful
-ible	able to	convertible
-ic	pertaining to; like	heroic
-ical	pertaining to	economical
-ish	relating to	stylish
-ive	pertaining to	descriptive
-less	without	senseless
-like	like	lifelike
-most	at the extreme	topmost
-ous	full of	furious
-ular	pertaining to	cellular

Verb Suffixes Base words can be changed to verbs by adding **verb suffixes.** Often, these base words are nouns or adjectives.

The chart below lists four common verb suffixes.

Verb Suffixes

Suffix	Meaning	Example
-ate	to make	activate
-en	to become	lengthen
-fy	to make	simplify
-ize	to become	crystallize

Adverb Suffixes The addition of **adverb suffixes** changes base words to adverbs—words that modify verbs, adjectives, or other adverbs. The following chart lists the most common adverb suffixes.

Practice Your Skills

A. For each of the following words, draw lines to separate the word into its parts—prefix, base, and suffix. Determine the meaning of the prefix and suffix. Then, by adding the meanings of the prefix and suffix to the base word, write the meaning of each complete word. Use a dictionary to check your answers.

> **Example**   un/avoid/able = not able to be avoided

1. disclaimer
2. presupposition
3. noncommittal
4. disillusionment
5. prearrangement
6. superstructure
7. neoclassical
8. prematurely
9. misinformation
10. inexactitude

B. In each of the following sentences, fill in the blank by adding a suffix to the base word in parentheses.

> **Example**   At the village water station, engineers added chemicals to _____ (pure) the water. <u>purify</u>

1. Elena's strongest asset was her _____ (thorough).
2. The embezzler returned at night to _____ (false) the bank records.
3. "Take back that _____ (slander) remark!" demanded Helen.
4. After five days of _____ (exhaust) searching, the rescue team found the missing spelunker.
5. The most spectacular view in North America was the _____ (culminate) and reward of their three-day climb to the top of Mt. McKinley.
6. Dr. Benson is one of the _____ (fore) authorities in the field of microbiology.
7. Captain Ahab in Herman Melville's *Moby Dick* is one of the most fascinating of all _____ (fiction) characters.
8. Ike wore a coat and tie, but there was no need for _____ (formal).

Another way to develop your vocabulary is to become familiar with roots. A **root** is the part of a word that contains its basic meaning. Unlike a base word, a root cannot stand alone. Many roots originally came from Greek or Latin.

Useful Greek Roots

Root	Meaning	Example
anthrop	human	anthropology
aster, astr	star	asterisk
auto	self, alone	automobile
bibl	book	bibliography
bi, bio	life	biology
chron	time	chronology
crac, crat	govern	democracy
dem	people	epidemic
dyn	power, force	dynamite
gen	birth, race	generation
geo	earth	geoscience
graph	write	paragraph
gram	write	grammar
helio	sun	helium
hydr	water	hydrogen
log	word, reason	dialogue
logy	study of	geology
metr, meter	measure	barometer
neo	new	neophyte
nom, nym	name, word, order	economic
ortho	straight, correct	orthodontist
pan	all, entire	panorama
phil	love	philosopher
phobia	fear	claustrophobia
phon	sound	phonograph
psych	mind, soul	psychology
scope	see	telescope
soph	wise, wisdom	sophisticated
tele	far, distant	television
theo	god	theology
therm	heat	thermometer

Useful Latin Roots

Root	Meaning	Example
capt	take, hold, seize	capture, captive
cede, ceed, cess	go, yield, give, away	recession, proceed
cred	believe	credit, creed
dic, dict	speak, say, tell	dictate, dictionary
duc, duct	lead	induce, conductor
fac, fec	do, make	factory, defect
ject	throw, hurl	eject, inject
junct	join	junction, conjunction
mit, miss	send	admit, dismiss
pon, pos, posit	place, put	component, deposit
port	carry	porter, portable
scrib, script	write	scribble, description
spec	look, see	spectacle, spectator
ten	stretch, hold	tendon, tenant
tract	pull, move	tractor, retract
vid, vis	see	video, vista
voc, vok	call	vocation, invoke
volv	roll	revolve, involve

Practice Your Skills

A. Each of the following words contains two or more Greek roots. Give the meanings of these roots. Then define the word based on the meaning of its parts. Check your definition using a dictionary.

1. bibliophile
2. demography
3. autobiography
4. astrology
5. astronomy
6. philosophy
7. metronome
8. geothermal
9. autocratic
10. bibliophobia
11. psychobiology
12. telegraph
13. chronometer
14. hydrology
15. orthography

B. Listed below are several different word families. Identify the Latin root for each. Then add two other words to each family.

1. credence
   creditor
2. procession
   secede
3. specimen
   introspection
4. remit
   commit
5. diction
   predict
6. repose
   position
7. export
   portable
8. conduct
   reduce
9. vision
   visual
10. reject
    dejected
11. evolve
    revolving
12. tension
    tenet

Thinking Strategies for Writing

The major activity in writing is not putting words on paper. It is playing with ideas in your head. Writing is really just thinking made visible. You will use two major types of thinking skills in writing—critical and creative. Critical thinking skills include evaluating ideas and identifying logical fallacies. Creative thinking skills include making inferences and solving problems.

THINKING CRITICALLY

What might you be like if you believed everything you heard or read? If you have trouble imagining such a possibility, it's because you know how to think critically about the things people tell you. You've already had a lot of practice at weighing ideas and deciding what they are worth.

Evaluating Ideas

No writing idea is good or bad in itself. The value of an idea is its effectiveness in helping you accomplish your goals. When you evaluate an idea for writing, ask yourself these questions:

- Does the idea involve an accurate reflection of the world? (In other words, is it true?)
- Is the idea well supported by evidence?
- Will the idea help me to accomplish what I want to accomplish?

Suppose you are writing an article for your school newspaper. Your purpose is to convince your fellow students to organize a recycling project. You do some thinking and some preliminary research, and you come up with the following list of points to make. These are:

1. There are five billion people on our planet.
2. Garbage is a tremendous problem.
3. The planet will be drowned in garbage if we don't do something.
4. We need to find ways to understand other cultures.
5. We can get a nickel refund on each bottle or can we return to the store.

Assume that each idea on the list reflects a true statement. There are still two other tests to apply to each one. First, which ideas must be supported by evidence? You'll probably decide that items 2 and 3 should be backed up by evidence. That decision tells you what kind of research you'll need to do for your article.

The next test for evaluating the ideas on your list is to ask, "Which of these ideas will help me accomplish my purpose? Are any of them unrelated to my purpose?"

Remember, your purpose is to convince students to recycle. One item on the list—number 4—is not related to that purpose. Therefore, you can dispense with it before you begin writing.

Remember, though, not to be too critical of your ideas early in the writing process. A good time to evaluate ideas carefully is when you are revising. Remember, too, that ideas aren't the only things you'll be evaluating during your writing process. Strategies, forms of organization, points of view, word choices, and entire drafts are all evaluated in the course of writing and rewriting. See "Understanding Revision," pages 391–396.

Identifying Logical Fallacies

An important criterion for evaluating ideas is the reasoning behind them. Identifying errors in reasoning—*logical fallacies*—can help you recognize misleading or false ideas; it can also keep you

It's easier to rec-
ognize logical fal-
lacies in other
people's arguments
than in your own.
When you revise your
writing, think very
carefully about each
of the arguments
you have used.
Also, have a peer
reader respond to
your work.

from making these errors in your own thinking and writing. The following chart explains some common logical fallacies.

Logical Fallacy	Example
Overgeneralization: A statement so broad that it can be easily disproved. (Overgeneralizations are often signaled by words such as *everyone, no one, always, never, best* or *worst.*)	The weather report is always wrong.
Circular reasoning: An attempt to prove a statement by repeating it in different words, rather than providing evidence.	Vegetables are healthful foods because they're good for you.
Either/or fallacy: A presentation of only two alternatives, when others exist.	Either we win this game or our team is washed up for good.
Single-cause fallacy: A claim that something is the sole cause of some effect, when actually there are multiple causes.	Cancer is caused by smog.
Cause-by-association fallacy: A claim that something causes something else simply because the two can be found together.	Japan is rainy. The Japanese live longer than Americans. Therefore, living in a rainy climate makes people live longer.

Practice Your Skills

Consider the following five statements. What kind of fallacy is illustrated in each? Discuss how to make each statement logical.

1. Students who do poorly on examinations simply don't study enough.
2. Biology is more interesting than geology because life science is much more fascinating than earth science.
3. Every time I plan a picnic, it rains.
4. You either love math or you hate it.
5. The best students I know study before dinner every night. Therefore, studying before dinner results in good grades.

Gathering ideas and evaluating them are skills that are basic not only to writing, but to all human activities. However, you want to be more than a storage place for other people's ideas. You want to go beyond them to ideas and creations that are uniquely yours, to ask "What does this mean?" or "Where does this lead?" You need to go beyond the facts, to see new connections and meanings. Then you can become the research scientist with the new discovery or the moviemaker with the startling vision.

Making Inferences

Drawing **inferences,** or conclusions based on facts, is such a normal activity that you probably don't realize how often you do it. For example, suppose you ride a bus every morning and there are usually ten or more people at the stop with you. You arrive five minutes late, and you find no one waiting. You would probably make an **inference** that you have missed your regular bus. An inference like this is often automatic—you reach a conclusion without being aware of your thinking process. However, the ability both to make inferences consciously and to present your inferences to a reader can help you in planning a piece of writing.

Guidelines for Making Inferences and Drawing Conclusions

- **Study** the facts you have collected or observed.

- **Compare** the information with what you already know and have previously observed.

- **Think** about how all the information might fit together. Look for similarities and differences.

- **Infer** or draw conclusions from the facts and the way you have put them together.

When you are gathering information for a piece of writing, don't simply stop with the facts you gather. Instead, think about those facts and how they are related. See if it is possible to draw inferences, or conclusions, based on those facts. Never be afraid to think things through on your own.

Making inferences is important in writing because it:

- allows you to see beyond the mere facts when observing or researching.
- can help you shape an argument for persuasive writing.
- can make your writing more subtle by letting your readers draw their own conclusions from the information that you provide.

For example, suppose you want to write an article persuading readers that exploration of other planets is a worthwhile goal. You might first study the history of space flight and its accomplishments. You could compare the views of experts who favor further exploration with those who think we should solve problems on earth first. You would then think about how to fit their differing views together. For example, you could cite space-related discoveries that have improved life on earth, such as solid-state electronic devices. Then you might make the inference that past space flights have led to useful, though unpredictable, discoveries, so future ones will, too.

Practice Your Skills

Imagine that you are looking for an idea for a report for your art class. You run across the following information in a newspaper article.

- In 1989, a painting by Vincent van Gogh sold for over 50 million dollars.
- In 1990, a painting by Pierre Auguste Renoir sold for over 70 million dollars.
- Also in 1990, another painting by van Gogh sold for over 80 million dollars.

Write two inferences you might draw from these facts. Then write a thesis statement that you might use for your report.

Solving Problems

Probably the most important application of creative thinking is in solving problems. In writing, problem solving can take the form of writing about problems and solutions—either real or fictitious—or of solving problems of how best to express an idea or organize a paper. When solving writing problems—or any other sort of problems—there are some general strategies you can use.

Guidelines for Problem Solving

Make sure you understand the problem.

- **State the problem.**   Stating a problem as clearly as you can is a major step toward solving it.

- **Analyze and ask questions about the problem.**   Analyzing involves breaking something down into its parts. Asking yourself questions about the parts of a problem is likely to lead you to a better understanding of the problem as a whole.

Use one or more of these problem-solving strategies.

- **The past-experience method**   Think of similar problems you've solved in the past. Evaluate your past solutions to see if they can help you solve the new problem.

- **The simplification method**   Identify the central core of the problem. Solve the core problem first. Then concentrate on the details.

- **The divide-and-conquer method**   Don't try to solve a complicated problem all at once. Instead, divide it into parts and solve the parts one at a time.

- **The "what-if" method**   Imagine things being different from what they are, using "what-if" questions to stimulate your imagination. This will often lead you to a creative solution that you might not otherwise have seen.

- **The pros-and-cons method**   Write each possible solution at the top of a column. Then, below each solution, write the headings "Pros" and "Cons." List the reasons for and against each solution. Then concentrate only on solutions whose pros outweigh their cons.

- **The trial-and-error method**   List all the possible solutions you can think of. Then look at each solution and imagine what its consequences are. Eliminate the solutions that are completely unworkable. Then try the others, one at a time, starting with the one that looks most likely.

- **The collaborative method**   Involve friends, classmates, relatives, and teachers in your problem-solving process. Apply the solution and evaluate the results.

Knowing how it could change the lives of canines everywhere, the dog scientists struggled diligently to understand the Doorknob Principle.

Here is an example of the use of the past-experience method of solving a writing problem. Suppose you are writing a report on the events in Lexington, Massachusetts, on the morning of April 19, 1775. You want to write a lively introduction to your paper. You remember once starting a sports story by quoting the words of an eyewitness to the big game. You think that perhaps someone who was present when the British soldiers fired on the colonial minutemen might have written about his experience. You decide to look for such an account and use that person's words to begin your paper.

Practice Your Skills

In a small group, discuss each of the following problems and their possible solutions.

1. A peer reader says that your eight-paragraph paper contains too much information and is hard to follow. How might you use the divide-and-conquer method to solve this problem?
2. You have three ideas for an introduction. How might you use the trial-and-error method to decide which introduction to use in your final draft?
3. You are trying to come up with an idea for a science fiction story. Use the "what-if" method to get ideas about how the future will be different from today.
4. You are writing a persuasive composition, such as a letter to the editor. How might you use the pros-and-cons method to organize information for your composition?

Developing Study and Research Skills

Fulfilling your many responsibilities at school is a real challenge, and you may often have wished that you could squeeze a few more hours out of the day. You can't hold back the clock, but you can learn techniques to help you manage your time and study more efficiently in the time that you have.

MANAGING YOUR TIME

Imagine that your time is a bank account with limited resources. Regularly ask yourself, "Is this activity worth spending my time resources on?" Here are two useful exercises for managing your time.

1. Evaluate your present use of time. For three days, keep a record of how you spend your time. You may make a chart for each day to log your time and activities. Study the results, noting the time-wasting activities and areas that deserve more time.

2. Prepare a realistic study schedule. Construct a schedule to guide you as you do your school assignments. Divide the assignments into smaller stages, making sure to allot enough time for each stage.

WRITER TO WRITER

According to the circumstances of the time . . . I have allotted myself so many pages a week. . . . There has ever been the record before me, and a week passed with an insufficient number of pages has been a blister to my eye, and a month so disgraced would have been a sorrow to my heart.

Anthony Trollope, British novelist

3. Understand the directions before beginning an assignment. Don't waste time doing a project incorrectly. If the instructions are written, read them carefully and completely before starting your assignment. Look for key words describing what you must do, such as *explain, research, memorize, write,* and *review.*

4. Study efficiently. Tackle the harder assignments first, while your mind is fresh. If one form of study gets monotonous, switch to another form—for example, switch from writing to reading. Give yourself regular study breaks.

Practice Your Skills

Read the instructions for the following assignment. Then plan how to complete the assignment in the time allowed.

> Prepare a detailed report on one emerging nation in Eastern Europe. Review the nation's history in the nineteenth and twentieth centuries and explain the recent changes that have occurred. Draw a map locating your country in Europe. Your report will be presented orally to the class in three weeks.

IMPROVING YOUR
READING SKILLS

Another way to manage your study time more efficiently is to maximize your skills for reading various types of material. For example, novels, textbook chapters, and graphic aids require different types and rates of reading.

Reading Techniques

Not all written material should be read in the same way. Sometimes you will want to **skim** material to get a general idea of what it contains. By moving your eyes quickly over the text, glancing at headings, topic sentences, highlighted phrases, and graphic aids, you can preview material before in-depth study. You can also skim to decide whether material will be useful to you as a reference or source of information for a writing project.

Other times you will want to **scan** material looking for a specific piece of information. When you scan, look for key words and phrases that indicate you are coming close to the information you are seeking.

Some material, such as textbooks, requires **slow and careful reading.** This technique involves taking notes, asking questions, identifying main ideas and relationships among ideas, and drawing inferences, or conclusions. Follow these steps.

1. Preview. Previewing means skimming the material to get a general idea of its contents using the following steps:

    a. Read the first two paragraphs.
    b. Read the first sentence of each succeeding paragraph.
    c. Read the last two paragraphs.
    d. Read any material in special type or in graphics.

2. Take notes as you read. Writing notes will engage more of your attention as you read and increase the likelihood that you will remember the material.

3. Predict. As you read, make guesses, or predictions, about what will come next in your reading. Predicting is especially beneficial when you're reading literature.

4. Question. Before reading, make a list of questions that you would expect to have answered as you read the piece. Write down the answers to these questions as you find them. As you read, add new questions to your notes. Raise unanswered questions in class discussions or in a teacher conference.

5. Identify main ideas. Main ideas often appear as the topic sentences of paragraphs or in introductory or concluding paragraphs. Jot down main ideas in your notes.

6. Identify relationships. Look for relationships among main ideas and supporting details. Be aware of the order of events as you read, looking for cause-and-effect relationships, comparisons, contrasts, and classifications.

7. Make inferences. When you draw a conclusion based on something you have observed, you are making an inference. Note important inferences in your learning log.

8. Respond with your own ideas and opinions. Jot down your ideas and opinions about the material as you read. Think critically, challenging the author and considering possible exceptions and different points of view.

9. Review what you have read. Review your notes. You may choose to organize them by making separate lists containing questions and answers about the reading, main ideas, key terms and their definitions, and ideas and opinions for later use.

10. Summarize and paraphrase. When you restate something in your own words, you are more likely to remember it. These techniques are discussed in detail on page 482.

Note taking in class will reinforce your learning. It engages more of your attention than simply listening or observing. Follow these guidelines.

Guidelines for Taking Notes

- Take notes on all important information. This includes lecture material, lab material, and useful comments from other students.
- Look and listen for key words. Phrases such as *most important, for these reasons, for example,* and *to review* signal material of particular importance.
- Attend to nonverbal cues from your teacher. Notice the teacher's gestures and expressions; they sometimes indicate material of particular importance.
- Keep your notes in one place.
- Do not write down every word. Use the modified outline form described below.
- Go back over your notes as soon as you can. Add words and phrases to make your notes clear.

Note-taking Techniques

Two techniques that can significantly improve your note-taking efficiency are using a modified outline form and using a list of abbreviations.

Modified Outline Form   In a modified outline, you write down the main ideas flush with the left margin of your paper. Then you write related details beneath the main ideas, indenting them and preceding them with dashes. Write the title, or main topic, at the top of the first page. For example, if a biology lesson deals with the parts of a cell, you would write "Parts of a Cell" at the top of your page. The first main point might be about the cell wall and cell membrane. Write this point to the left of your paper and then write each detail under that idea by indenting it and preceding it with a dash. Write the date at the top of each page of notes.

See Appendix pages 846–847 for more information about outlines.

Symbols and Abbreviations   Develop a list of symbols and abbreviations for words that you use frequently in your notes. These will help you increase your note-taking speed. Common abbreviations and symbols include + or & for *and,* *w/* for *with,* *def* for *definition,* and *Amer* for *America.*

Learning Logs

Another way that you can build on your study skills through writing is by using a learning log. In a learning log you use your own questions to help you assimilate what you are learning and clarify concepts that are confusing or complex. The following is a list of questions to consider in your learning log:

1. What have I learned?
2. What is another way to say this?
3. What applications does this have?
4. What is a related idea?
5. What don't I understand?
6. Where can I go with this idea?
7. I wonder why . . . ?
8. What would happen if . . . ?
9. What can I do to learn more about this?
10. One interesting part of this idea is . . .

The following is an excerpt from a student's learning log.

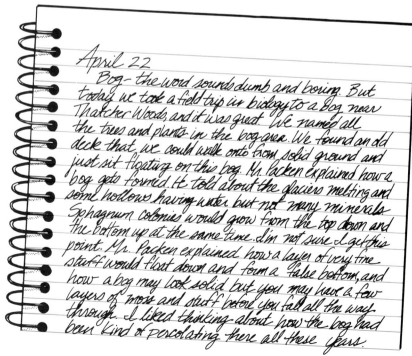

April 22
Bog - the word sounds dumb and boring. But today we took a field trip in biology to a bog near Thatcher Woods, and it was great. We named all the trees and plants in the bog area. We found an old deck that we could walk onto from solid ground and just sit floating on this bog. Mr. Packen explained how a bog gets formed. He told about the glaciers melting and some hollows having water but not many minerals. Sphagnum colonies would grow from the top down and the bottom up at the same time. I'm not sure I get this point. Mr. Packen explained how a layer of very fine stuff would float down and form a false bottom, and how a bog may look solid but you may have a few layers of moss and stuff before you fall all the way through. I liked thinking about how the bog had been kind of percolating there all these years.

Writing
TIP

Different abbreviations will be suitable for different subjects. Keep a list of abbreviations for each class in the front of your notebook for that class.

MEMORIZING

Researchers say that most of us forget at least 25 percent of what we learn by the end of the day we learn it. But researchers have also discovered that much can be done to improve memory. The following are some strategies for memorization.

1. Read and repeat the information out loud.

2. Write down the information.

3. Make connections between facts.

4. Use memory games. Rhymes are especially good for helping you to remember historical dates. For example, consider the following: "In 1941, Pearl Harbor faced the gun."

5. Develop strategies of your own. Use any device that helps you remember, such as the following:

- **Relate the memory to some other information that you know.** One student remembered that 1789 was the year the French Revolution began by thinking of the number on his football jersey (17) and the number of his street (89th).
- **Use mnemonics.** A mnemonic is a memory device. One common mnemonic is using the first letters of words in a rhyme or sentence to stand for the first letters of what you want to remember. For example, in biology you might learn the mnemonic *King Philip Came Over From Germany Slowly* to help you remember the classifications kingdom, phylum, class, order, family, genus, and species.
- **Count items.** If you know that there are seven countries in Central America, but you have thought of only six on a test, you will remember that you need to search your mind to find one final piece of information.

Practice Your Skills

Following is an excerpt about Viking ships. Follow the directions one at a time and answer the questions.

1. Skim the article on the next page. What is the most important clue about the general topic?

2. Scan the article. How many oarsmen sailed on Viking ships? Would this article be a good source for a report on modern ship-building techniques? Why or why not?

3. Now read the article carefully. What is the main idea in the first paragraph? What is the main idea in the second paragraph? What is the main idea in the third paragraph?

Vikings: Sea Rovers and Their Ships

Viking ships were by far the best of the period, made to handle easily and to cleave the water swiftly. The men who sailed in them were both fearless and physically tough.

Without the help of even a crude drawing, depending on skilled hand and eye alone, the shipbuilder fashioned the shell and then fitted ribs to the planking. Low in the middle, and sweeping up at either end, the craft was propelled by a single, square sail and, as a rule, from twenty-eight to forty oarsmen.

The beautiful dragon ships were intricately carved, with a dragon rearing up from the stem post. The longships, however, were the most powerful war vessels. Rows of shields hung over the gunwales, handy in case of attack. Longships rarely had decks, but if a storm arose, tents might be set up at the stern. Merchant vessels were similar to the longships except that they were rather drab and carried no shields.

Helen Hynson Merrick, *Sweden*

INCORPORATING SOURCE
MATERIALS IN YOUR WRITING

Often when you do research for a writing project, you will find that you want to use someone else's ideas or words. Most of the great ideas in human history have been the result of one person combining and building on other people's ideas in a new way.

There are three ways to incorporate material from a source:

- direct quotation
- indirect quotation, or paraphrase
- summary

Direct Quotation

Exact repetition of someone's words is an effective way of incorporating ideas in your writing. Choose your quotations carefully, however; they should be to the point and preferably from people who are recognized authorities. Be sure always to cite quotations accurately and to attribute the quotation to the person who said it.

Paraphrase

Repetition of someone else's statement using your own words is known as a **paraphrase.** This technique is very useful because it enables you to save direct quotations for especially important or well-stated material. Paraphrasing also helps you understand the ideas you are restating. Most paraphrases are approximately the same length as the original material.

Guidelines for Paraphrasing

- Locate the main idea.
- List the supporting details.
- Determine the tone.
- Rework the vocabulary. You can either rewrite each sentence of the original in your own words, or make a list of all the ideas in the source and then write original sentences containing these ideas.
- Credit the authors whose ideas you use.

Summary

A **summary,** like a paraphrase, presents someone else's ideas in different words. Unlike a paraphrase, however, a summary reduces a long passage to its essential ideas.

Guidelines for Writing Summaries

- Look for the topic sentence or the main ideas. Write these down in your own words.
- Look for answers to questions, solutions to problems, and conclusions drawn from the information presented. Jot these down.
- Look for key facts, statistics, and words. Make a list of these.
- Reduce material by eliminating unnecessary details.
- Now write a summary in your own words using your notes. Look back at the original passage to check your summary.

Avoiding Plagiarism

When you use someone else's words or ideas in your writing without saying where you got them, you are guilty of **plagiarism.** Your readers may think the material is yours, when in fact you took it from someone else. Material you copy directly from your sources can be easy to spot, since the vocabulary or the style and tone will be different from your own. You can avoid plagiarism by documenting, or giving references for, all the information you take from your sources and use in your writing.

How do you know when to tell your readers that your material came from another source? Follow these guidelines:

- **Document all direct quotations.** Make sure that you have copied each quotation word for word and that the punctuation is the same as in the original.
- **Document information you've paraphrased or summarized.** This includes all ideas and expressions that you adapted from your sources.
- **Do not document common knowledge.** Information is considered common knowledge if it can be found in several different sources or if it is knowledge that many people have.

Documenting Your Sources in Text If you're writing a persuasive essay, for example, and you want to back up your point of view with a quotation from, a paraphrase of, or a summary of another source, you may credit that source in your text. Simply include the author's name in the sentence preceding the material. For example, you can write "According to Civil War photographer Mathew Brady, . . ." or "As Ulysses S. Grant wrote in his *Personal Memoirs,* . . ."

Company E, 4th U.S. Colored Infantry, at Fort Lincoln

For a more formal piece of writing—such as a research report—in which you use paraphrases of, summaries of, and quotations from a number of sources, you'll need to both document your sources in the text and assemble a Works Cited list that provides complete publication information for each of your sources. In the text of your report, you may document your sources in one of three ways: with footnotes, endnotes, or parenthetical references. Check with your teacher to see which of these methods is preferred. See "Research Report," pages 278–280 and 283, for more information about documenting your sources with parenthetical references and creating a Works Cited list.

Practice Your Skills

A. Read and paraphrase the following quotation.

> Here in Mahone Bay, about 40 miles southwest of Halifax, Nova Scotia, I am at the site of the most intensive treasure hunt in history, a hunt that has lasted 193 years, cost millions of dollars and killed six men. The [reason] for it all is a narrow, water-filled shaft called the Money Pit—and what may be hidden in its muddy depths. To date, not one penny of treasure has been recovered. Nor does anyone know what might be buried here, who buried it, or why. The island stubbornly refuses to yield anything but the most tantalizing and infuriatingly ambiguous clues.
>
> **Douglas Preston, "The Mysterious Money Pit"**

B. Read and summarize the following passage.

> A number of scientists believe that plastic is the most far-reaching, man-made threat facing many marine species, annually killing or maiming tens of thousands of seabirds, seals, sea lions and sea otters, and hundreds of whales, dolphins, porpoises and sea turtles. . . .
>
> Plastic's devastating effect on an entire population of marine animals was first observed in the late 1970s. The victims were the northern fur seals of the Pribilof Islands, which are located in the Bering Sea west of Alaska. Scientists from the National Marine Mammal Laboratory (NMML—a division of the National Marine Fisheries Service) found that, beginning in 1976, the seal population was declining at a rate of 4 to 6 percent annually. They concluded that plastic entanglement was killing up to 40,000 seals a year.
>
> **Michael Weisskopf, "In the Sea, Slow Death by Plastic"**

On the Lightside

WHAT'S COOKING?

Cookbooks are more than mere collections of recipes and household hints. They help shape the way we talk about food, and they have added the names of common dishes and cooking terms to the language.

The first American cookbook, published in 1796, was written by Amelia Simmons, and it was a standard part of American kitchens for the following thirty years. It was the first book to include recipes for such American dishes as cranberry sauce and pumpkin pie, and the first to use American terms such as *molasses* instead of the British *treacle, biscuits* instead of *scones,* and *cookies* instead of *biscuits.* During the 1820's and 1830's, many new cooking terms and names for American

dishes, such as *chowder, succotash,* and *buckwheat cakes,* were added to the language.

Perhaps the most influential cookbook writer was Fannie Farmer. The cookbook she wrote in 1896 is still in use. In addition, she revolutionized kitchen terminology, replacing vague terms, such as *pinch* or *dash,* with her system of level measurement. Terms such as *level teaspoon, measuring cup,* and *oven thermometer* were brought into the language through Fannie Farmer's cookbook.

The Library and Other Informational Sources

Life today is very different from life at any other time, mainly due to the availability of information. Learning how to use libraries and other modern information sources will help you find the specific information you need for almost any purpose.

CLASSIFICATION OF LIBRARY MATERIALS

Libraries are rich resource centers that contain information in many media, including magazines, pamphlets, journals, clippings, computer software, audiotapes, videotapes, records, films, filmstrips, compact discs, microfilm, and microfiche.

Sections of the Library

Most libraries organize their materials similarly, as detailed in the following pages. The librarian can explain the specific organization of your library and can help you locate information quickly.

Stacks Stacks are the large bookshelves where the fiction and non-fiction books available for borrowing are shelved. No reference books are kept in the stacks. In most small libraries, the patrons have access to the stacks.

Search Tools: Catalogs and Indexes The card catalog or computer catalog lists the resources available in the library and is arranged alphabetically by author, title, and subject.

References Reference materials—works containing factual information—include dictionaries, encyclopedias, almanacs, yearbooks, and atlases. These resources are usually shelved in a separate area and must remain in the library.

Periodicals The periodicals section of a library generally contains current issues of magazines and newspapers. This area may be part of the reference section. The librarian can provide older magazines and newspapers and indexes to their contents, such as the *Readers' Guide to Periodical Literature*.

In the animal self-help section.

Special Sections Many libraries have special sections for local history books, books for young readers, and nonprint materials such as records, art reproductions, videocassettes, and filmstrips. Some also provide study areas where computers and typewriters can be used.

The Classification of Books

Understanding the classification and arrangement of books in a library will enable you to find the resources you need quickly and efficiently.

Fiction Novels and short-story collections are arranged alphabetically by the author's last name in a section of the stacks labeled *Fiction*. Multiple works by the same author are arranged alphabetically by title. The fiction section may be further grouped into classifications such as mystery or science fiction.

Nonfiction Works of nonfiction generally are classified by either the Dewey Decimal System or the Library of Congress Classification. The **Dewey Decimal System,** which is named for its originator, Melvil Dewey, classifies all books by number in ten major categories:

000-099	General Works	encyclopedias, bibliographies
100-199	Philosophy	psychology, ethics
200-299	Religion	the Bible, theology, mythology
300-399	Social Science	government, education, law
400-499	Language	languages, grammars, dictionaries
500-599	Science	mathematics, chemistry, biology
600-699	Technology	medicine, cooking, inventions
700-799	The Arts	music, painting, theater, sports
800-899	Literature	poetry, plays, essays
900-999	History	biography, travel, geography

Each major subject area is divided into subcategories. For example, a book on circuses is categorized broadly under the arts (700–799) and specifically under public performances (791).

Library shelves are prominently marked with the Dewey Decimal numbers. Within each section, books are arranged alphabetically by the author's last name.

Biographies may be identified by a *B* on their spine. Biographies and autobiographies are shelved differently in different libraries. Check with the librarian to find out their location in your library. Reference books are shelved separately and are marked with an *R* on the spine.

Instead of the Dewey Decimal System, some libraries use the **Library of Congress Classification,** or **LC,** to classify their materials. The LC system uses twenty-one broad categories designated by letters of the alphabet:

A	General Works	**M**	Music
B	Philosophy, Psychology, Religion	**N**	Fine Arts
		P	Language and Literature
C-F	History		
E-F	American History	**Q**	Science
G	Geography, Anthropology, Recreation	**R**	Medicine
		S	Agriculture
H	Social Sciences	**T**	Technology
J	Political Science	**U**	Military Science
K	Law	**V**	Naval Science
L	Education	**Z**	Bibliography and Library Science

Within these broad categories, subcategories are identified by a second letter.

Every library catalogs its books and nonprint sources. To determine whether your library has a particular book and where to find it, use the computer or the card catalog.

The Card Catalog

The **card catalog** is a cabinet of drawers or file trays containing alphabetically arranged cards. There are three different kinds of catalog cards: subject, author, and title cards. Each card carries a classification or **call number**—the Dewey Decimal number or LC letter code for the book—in the upper left-hand corner. On some cards an additional letter code indicates that a book is kept in one of the special sections of the library. Such codes include *R* or *REF,* reference; *J* or *JUV,* juvenile; *B* or *BIO,* biography; *SC,* short-story collection; and *SF,* science fiction. Call numbers help you locate where a book is shelved.

Types of Cards All three types of catalog cards—subject, author, and title cards—include this information, arranged differently: subject, author, title, publisher, publication date, and catalog number. A book can be located using any of the three card indexes.

Catalogs also include **cross-reference cards,** which read *See* or *See also.* "See" cards refer you to other subject headings in the catalog. For example, a subject card on *movies* may read

"See *Moving pictures*," indicating that the library lists books on movies under the heading *Moving pictures*.

"See also" cards refer you to other closely related subjects. For example, a subject card on *moving pictures* may read "See also *Film criticism*."

Computerized Catalogs   Many libraries offer a computerized catalog system that allows you to use a computer terminal to search for a book by author, title, or subject. Ask your librarian how to operate your library's system. The computerized catalog allows you to search more quickly and over a wider field of sources than does the card catalog. Often it includes several libraries or branches and even tells whether a book is on the shelves or checked out.

Additional Catalog Information   Both card catalogs and computerized catalogs provide important information about each book in their inventory. Both systems usually list the number of pages in a book as well as a notation indicating whether the book has illustrations, maps, tables, or other similar features. In addition, some catalogs provide a brief description of the book.

Library of Congress, Main Reading Room

Alternate Headings If you have difficulty finding information on a topic, or if you have exhausted all the sources readily available, think about broader or narrower topics than the subject you are researching.

For example, information for a report on *offshore drilling* might also be found in articles or books about *petroleum* or *energy sources*. Ask the librarian for suggestions of such alternate headings.

Locating Other Materials in the Library Materials other than books are arranged differently in different libraries. Many libraries have special rooms set aside for audiovisual materials, magazines, newspapers, manuscripts, or rare books. Large libraries often have information stored on microfilm or microfiche. To locate such materials in your library, check with the librarian.

USING REFERENCE WORKS

Once you have located the reference section in your library, you can use the works you find there at any time in your writing process. Here are just a few of the ways reference works can help you.

- To find an idea to write about
- To research an idea you already have
- To learn facts or details to make your writing more vivid, specific, and interesting
- To survey the opinions of authorities on your subject

Types of Reference Works

There are thousands of reference works available to you. The following describes a few of them.

Dictionaries The many varieties of dictionaries include school, college, and unabridged editions, as well as specialized dictionaries of topics such as medical terms, mythology, music, American history, and animal life. Dictionaries are resources for much information about words in addition to spelling and meaning. Each entry in a dictionary contains the following:

- pronunciation
- syllabication
- parts of speech
- definitions
- plural forms and irregular verb forms
- derived words, or words formed by adding suffixes and prefixes

In addition, some dictionaries also provide the following information:

- **homographs**—words that are spelled alike but have different meanings
- **etymologies**—word histories
- **synonyms**—words that are similar in meaning
- **antonyms**—words that are opposite in meaning
- **usage labels**—designations, such as *archaic, colloquial,* or *slang,* that describe the context in which it is appropriate to use a word
- **field labels**—designations, such as *architecture, sports,* or *grammar,* that describe the area of human endeavor in which a word is used
- **cross references**—citations that direct you to places where more information can be found

Study the following dictionary entry to familiarize yourself with its parts.

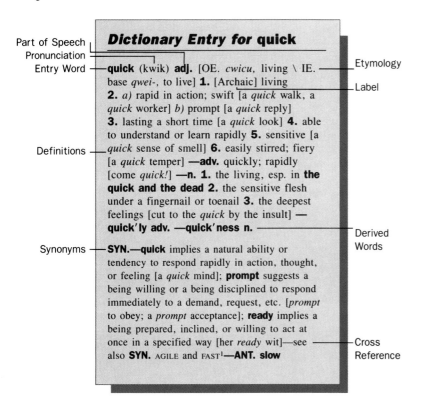

Part of Speech
Pronunciation
Entry Word

Dictionary Entry for quick

quick (kwik) **adj.** [OE. *cwicu,* living \ IE. base *qwei-,* to live] **1.** [Archaic] living **2.** *a)* rapid in action; swift [a *quick* walk, a *quick* worker] *b)* prompt [a *quick* reply] **3.** lasting a short time [a *quick* look] **4.** able to understand or learn rapidly **5.** sensitive [a *quick* sense of smell] **6.** easily stirred; fiery [a *quick* temper] —**adv.** quickly; rapidly [come *quick!*] —**n. 1.** the living, esp. in **the quick and the dead 2.** the sensitive flesh under a fingernail or toenail **3.** the deepest feelings [cut to the *quick* by the insult] — **quick′ly adv. —quick′ness n.**

SYN.—quick implies a natural ability or tendency to respond rapidly in action, thought, or feeling [a *quick* mind]; **prompt** suggests a being willing or a being disciplined to respond immediately to a demand, request, etc. [*prompt* to obey; a *prompt* acceptance]; **ready** implies a being prepared, inclined, or willing to act at once in a specified way [her *ready* wit]—see also **SYN.** AGILE and FAST[1]**—ANT. slow**

Etymology
Label
Definitions
Derived Words
Synonyms
Cross Reference

Thesauruses A thesaurus is a special dictionary of synonyms and antonyms. You can use a thesaurus to find a word whose connotations precisely convey your meaning.

Some thesauruses are arranged alphabetically by entry word, like dictionaries. Others group entries in broad conceptual categories and provide an index or a special usage guide.

Study the following thesaurus entry to see what kinds of information are included.

Thesaurus Entry for *equivalent*

equivalent *adj.* **1** *A dime is equivalent to ten pennies:* equal, the same as, comparable, commensurate with, tantamount, corresponding, correspondent, correlative; even, one and the same, of a piece. **—n. 2** *That dress cost the equivalent of a week's salary:* equal amount, comparable sum; correspondent, peer, counterpart, parallel, match. **Ant. 1** unequal, dissimilar, incomparable, incommensurate, different.

Penny Machines, by
Wayne Thiebaud, 1961

> The element of discovery takes place, in nonfiction, not during the writing but during the research.
>
> **Joan Didion, novelist and essayist**

Joan Didion

Encyclopedias Encyclopedias are collections of articles on a wide variety of subjects. They are usually alphabetically arranged and consist of several volumes. Some encyclopedias cover general knowledge. Others, such as the *Encyclopedia of Science and Technology* or *Grzimek's Animal Encyclopedia,* deal with specialized subjects. At least one encyclopedia, *Grolier's Academic American Encyclopedia,* is available to computer users on compact disc or from commercial computer networks such as CompuServe and America OnLine.

Encyclopedias are extremely useful resources when you are searching for a brief overview of a subject. Written by experts, each article presents a summary or the main or key points about a topic.

Almanacs and Yearbooks For up-to-date facts, statistics, and information on current events, space exploration, population, sports, and many other fields, consult an almanac or yearbook.

Almanacs and yearbooks such as the *Information Please Almanac, Atlas, and Yearbook* can serve as good sources of ideas for topics, since they contain information on hundreds of timely and historical subjects.

Biographical References Biographical articles can be found in biographical dictionaries, encyclopedias, specialized biographical indexes, and *Who's Who.* You may wish to start the search for information on a person by looking at a general biographical reference work such as *Webster's Biographical Dictionary.*

Literary Reference Books If you are looking for a line of poetry, a famous quotation, or the name of a character from a specific literary work, you can consult several sources, including *Bartlett's Familiar Quotations, Granger's Index to Poetry,* or one of the Oxford companions to literature.

Vertical Files Many libraries offer current information in the form of pamphlets, booklets, government publications, and clippings on a wide variety of subjects. These are housed in the **vertical file.**

The Library and
Other Sources   **493**

Atlases Atlases are books of maps that also contain interesting data on a number of subjects, including population, temperatures, oceans, and place names. Additionally, there are many historical atlases that document the changing political borders throughout history.

The Readers' Guide to Periodical Literature The *Readers' Guide* is a directory of articles from magazines. Articles are listed alphabetically by subject and author. The *Guide* is published monthly, and the monthly issues are bound together into yearly collections. Current issues of the *Guide* list recent articles from two hundred different magazines.

The following is part of a sample page from the *Readers' Guide*. Notice the arrangement of the entries and the information each conveys.

OWLS
Gambits and skirmishes [spotted owls and old-growth timber] L. Line. il *Audubon* 92:4 My '90
Food and feeding
Restoring owls and other biological boondoggles. T. Williams, il *Audubon* 92:30-2 + My '90
OXIDATION, PHYSIOLOGICAL
Transcriptional regulator of oxidative stress-inducible genes: direct activation by oxidation. G. Storz and others. bibl f il *Science* 248:189-94 Ap 13 '90
OXYGEN
See also
Ozone
Isotopes
The Ice Age bones of contention. R. A. Kerr. *Science* 248:32 Ap 6 '90
OXYGEN, LIQUID *See* Liquid oxygen
OZONE
1989 Antarctic ozone loss severe. B. Hogan. *The Conservationist* 44:55 My/Je '90
Atmosphere of uncertainty [businesses dependent on CFCs affected by amended Clean Air Act] D. Erickson. il *Scientific American* 262:77-8 Ap '90
Indication of increasing solar ultraviolet-B radiation flux in alpine regions. M. Blumthaler and W. Ambach. bibl f il *Science* 248:206-8 Ap 13 '90
Ultraviolet levels climb in Swiss Alps [research by Mario Blumthaler and Walter Ambach] R. Monastersky. *Science News* 137:228 Ap 14 '90

Periodicals and Newspapers   For current information on your subject, consult the *Readers' Guide to Periodical Literature* and current magazines, journals, and newspapers. Libraries usually display recent issues of newspapers, magazines, and journals on open racks for easy reference. Back issues of magazines and journals are usually stored in stacks, in bound volumes, or on microforms.

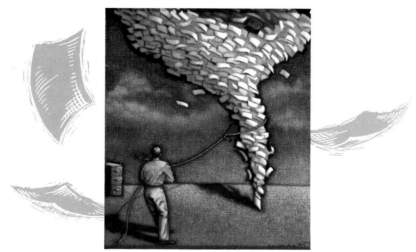

Microforms   Microforms are small photographs of printed pages. They are stored on filmstrips called **microfilm** and on film cards called **microfiche.** Ask the librarian to demonstrate the machine used for viewing microforms.

OTHER SOURCES OF INFORMATION

Writers use other sources of information in addition to libraries and reference works. Three major resources are experts, government agencies, and computer services.

Experts   Consider interviewing experts in the subject that you are researching. Experts can be found in your own circle of relatives and acquaintances, at schools and universities, in businesses, and on the staffs of local museums.

Government Agencies   The government funds many projects, including programs in education, health, natural resources, scientific research, international development, and agriculture. The General

Services Administration Consumer Information Center, a federal agency, distributes this information compiled by the government to the public. By writing to the following address, you can receive a catalog listing over one hundred free or inexpensive government pamphlets on various subjects: Consumer Information Catalog, P.O. Box 100, Pueblo, CO 81002.

Your local government agencies at the town hall and the mayor's office can give you information on local issues. State government agencies, such as the state board of education, the department of natural resources, or the tourism bureau, can provide information about your state.

Many large public and university libraries have special sections containing government publications, which the librarian can explain.

Computer Services If you have access to a computer and a modem, you can make use of a computer information service. A modem allows you to hook your computer up to a telephone line. You can then dial an information service and use on-line encyclopedias or gather information on topics such as current events, travel, sports, and weather.

Practice Your Skills

A. Draw a map or floor plan of your school library and one of your local library. Label the sections mentioned in this lesson. How are the libraries similar? How do they differ? What special sections does your local library contain?

B. Find a title, author, call number, and publication date for a book in each of the categories described below. Use the catalog system that is available in your library.

> collection of American poetry
> book on World War I
> collection of fine-art reproductions
> book by Lewis Carroll

C. Think of a topic you are now studying in social studies, history, civics, or government. Then use your library to list examples of the following types of resources that might provide additional information about that topic.

> specialized encyclopedias   dictionaries
> biographical references   indexes
> magazine articles   government pamphlets

Making Oral Presentations

Making an oral presentation—from a report on your club's fund-raising drive to a dramatic reading—is a way of sharing ideas more directly with an audience than is possible in written work.

PRESENTING ORAL REPORTS

An **oral report** is a presentation of factual information to an audience. In addition to collecting and organizing the facts you will present, you must choose a method of delivery for your report. Here are four possibilities.

1. The Manuscript Method You read a written report to your audience word for word, glancing up to make eye contact. You may find it difficult to keep your audience's attention using this method of presentation.

2. The Memorization Method You memorize and recite a report you have written.

3. The Extemporaneous Method You compose the report in rough form, but determine the exact words as you speak, using an outline or note cards as prompts.

4. The Impromptu Method You talk "off the top of your head" with no prepared draft, outline, or note cards. This method is appropriate only for brief reports that require no research or preparation and is often used as a response in a meeting or debate.

No matter what method of delivery you use for your oral presentation, your manner and appearance communicate as much as your words. To maximize the impact of your message, keep the following points in mind.

- Dress appropriately for the audience and the occasion.
- Maintain a relaxed posture, neither slouching nor rigid.
- Channel stage fright into enthusiasm for your presentation.
- Speak directly to your audience, enunciating clearly.

An effective oral presentation involves both verbal and nonverbal elements. These are listed in the chart on the following page, along with guidelines on incorporating them effectively in your presentation.

COMPUTER
TIP

You can use a word processor to help you memorize your oral report by highlighting important points using italics, boldface, capital letters, or underscoring.

Verbal Elements

Pitch: highness or lowness of the voice
Intonation: rise and fall in pitch
Volume: loudness or softness of the voice
Stress: emphasis created by increasing volume
Rate: speed with which a person talks
Articulation: clarity of pronunciation
Pronunciation: sounds of spoken words
Pausing: silence between syllables or words
Tone: emotional quality of the voice

Nonverbal Elements

Eye contact: looking into the eyes of members of the audience
Gestures: expressive movements of the hands
Facial expressions: showing feelings in use of facial features
Movement: motions such as waving the arms or pacing
Posture: vertical positioning of the body
Visual aids: graphics such as posters, charts, and slides
Audio aids: sounds recorded for a presentation
Note cards or script: written speaker's prompts

Coretta Scott King, widow of the Reverend Martin Luther King, Jr., is a great spokesperson for civil rights.

Guidelines for Oral Presentations

Speak at a comfortable, average pitch.
Speak loudly enough to be heard.
Place extra stress on important words or phrases.
Speak at a moderate rate.
Slightly exaggerate your articulation.
Prepare the correct pronunciation of troublesome words.
Pause at important points so your audience can respond.
Vary your tone to reflect content and create dramatic effect.
Scan the audience. Try to make eye contact with each person.
Avoid overuse of dramatic gestures. Use gestures sparingly.
Use facial expression for emphasis.
Use movement to support your message. Avoid excessive or
    nervous movements.
Make readable visual aids that clarify what you are saying.
Make sure the equipment works and the volume is appropriate.
Organize prompts in the order of use beforehand.

PRESENTING ORAL INTERPRETATIONS

Oral interpretation is the presentation of a literary work to an audience. Create a **cutting**—the selection—in one of two ways:

1. Choose part or all of one piece of literature. Make sure your cutting has a clear beginning and end.
2. Choose several small selections of literature and tie them together with transitions. The selections must share a common element such as theme, form, tone, or author.

Notice how the writer provided an introduction and a transitional passage to link these two literary excerpts that share a common theme—horses. Ellipses (. . .) indicate where cuts were made.

Introduction: There are many ways to group people—male and female, young and old. I myself divide the world into people who love horses and people who don't. Mark Twain didn't.

First Selection: "In Honolulu I said I preferred a safe horse to a fast one. I asked for . . . one with no spirit whatsoever. . . . They showed me an animal who looked as if he wanted to lean up against something and think, so I chose him.

"He . . . went along peaceably enough, but absorbed in meditation. This began to worry me. I said to myself, this horse is planning some outrage. . . . The more the thing preyed on my mind, the more uneasy I got. Finally I dismounted to see if there was anything wild in his eye. I can't tell you what a relief it was to find he was only asleep."

Transition: No, Twain didn't care much for horses, but he had never been a little girl pretending to be a horse as May Swenson had been, as she wrote in "The Centaur":

Second Selection: My hair flopped to the side
like the mane of a horse in the wind.

My forelock swung in my eyes,
my neck arched and I snorted.
I shied and skittered and reared,

stopped and raised my knees
pawed at the ground and quivered . . .

and swished through the dust again.
I was the horse and the rider.

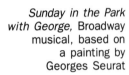

Sunday in the Park with George, Broadway musical, based on a painting by Georges Seurat

Practicing and Delivering Your Oral Interpretation After you prepare your cutting, follow these steps in preparing to present it.

• Memorize your presentation.
• Experiment with voice, tone, gestures, and body language.
• Rehearse before a mirror, with a tape recorder, or before an audience of friends or relatives.

When you are ready to deliver your oral interpretation, review the Guidelines for Oral Presentations on page 498.

Practice Your Skills

A. Use one of the following topics or one of your own to prepare an oral report to present to your class.

• Unusual occupations
• Five ways to lose a friend
• Will TV, video, and computers end printed media?
• Testing cosmetics and household products on animals
• Are star athletes in professional sports overpaid?

B. Refer to the Guidelines for Oral Presentations in the chart on page 498 to evaluate your classmates' oral reports. Incorporate these elements in your own reports.

C. Choose an excerpt from literature such as "A Child's Christmas in Wales." Discuss how you would present it for oral interpretation.

Assessment

How can you measure what someone knows? It's not an easy task. Teachers try in many different ways to assess your mastery of the material you have been studying. One approach they use frequently is the classroom test, which can take several forms. In addition, school administrators use standardized tests to measure your general educational achievement.

CLASSROOM TESTS

The following chart contains some helpful tips and strategies on how to answer the types of questions you regularly encounter on classroom tests. There are several different types of classroom test questions. Each type of test question has its own special characteristics. Therefore, you should use a different strategy for answering each type of question.

Strategies for Answering Common Types of Test Questions

Multiple Choice
1. Read all the choices before deciding on your answer.
2. Eliminate incorrect answers.
3. Choose the most complete and accurate answer.
4. Look for words such as *always, never,* and *only.* These words often indicate incorrect answers.
5. Consider carefully choices such as *none* or *all of the above.*

True/False
1. The whole statement is false if any part of it is false.
2. Absolute words (*all, never*) often make a statement false.
3. Qualifying words (*probably, usually, sometimes*) often make a statement true.

Matching
1. Note whether the number of items in each column is equal and how many times each item can or must be used.
2. Read all items in both columns before pairing any of them.
3. Match easy items first, crossing them out as they are used (unless items are to be used more than once).
4. Keep in mind that if you change one answer, you may have to change several others in related questions.

Completion (Fill-in-the-Blank)
1. Use specific, not general, information.
2. Be sure your wording fully answers the question.
3. Be sure your answer fits grammatically in the sentence.
4. Write legibly. Check for and correct mechanical errors.

Short Answer
1. Answer in complete sentences.
2. Answer all parts of the question. Be specific.
3. Check grammar, spelling, punctuation, and capitalization.

Essay
1. Be sure you understand what each question asks you to do.
2. Make a modified outline of the major points and the supporting details you want to cover. Write your essay.
3. Carefully proofread your essay and make corrections.

STANDARDIZED TESTS

A standardized test measures your performance against that of many other people who take the same test. The Scholastic Aptitude Test (SAT) and the American College Testing examination (ACT) are two tests designed to evaluate how well prepared you are to do college-level work. Both tests offer a preliminary version that may be taken for practice, the PSAT and the P-ACT Plus.

You can prepare for these tests by studying the types of questions they contain and by developing the skills that they measure: vocabulary, reading, computation, critical thinking, and English usage. The following pages give examples of the types of questions in these tests.

Antonym Questions

Antonym questions ask you to choose a word that is most nearly opposite in meaning to the given word.

> EULOGIZE: (A) praise   (B) support   (C) undermine
>
> (D) usurp   (E) malign

To answer an antonym question, use the following strategies:

1. Find a word that is opposite in meaning. Do not be thrown off by synonyms. In the sample above, choice *A* is a synonym.
2. Decide whether the given word is positive or negative, and then eliminate all the choices that are in the same category as the given

word. *Eulogize* has a positive connotation. Therefore, choices *A* and *B* can be eliminated. The correct answer is *E*.

3. Many words have more than one meaning. Think about a word's various meanings as you look for the antonym.
4. If you don't know a word's meaning, try to analyze its parts.

Practice Your Skills

Write the letter of the word that is most nearly opposite in meaning to the given word.

1. AMBIGUITY: (A) clarity   (B) luxuriousness (C) injustice
                  (D) distress   (E) extravagance
2. DECRY: (A) condemn (B) change   (C) praise
                  (D) criticize   (E) depend
3. ABHOR: (A) challenge (B) settle   (C) chide
                  (D) admire   (E) encourage
4. TOLERATE: (A) uphold   (B) forbid   (C) utilize
                  (D) maintain (E) accept
5. BELLIGERENT: (A) animated (B) bland   (C) jovial
                  (D) fervent   (E) peaceable
6. NOXIOUS: (A) diffuse   (B) unique   (C) beneficial
                  (D) latent   (E) static

Analogy Questions

Analogy questions give you two words that are related in some way. You need to determine this relationship and find another pair of words that are related in the same way. Read an analogy question like this: *stanza* is to *poem* as . . . .

STANZA:POEM ::   (A) movie:script   (B) novel:chapter
     (C) story:writer   (D) song:melody   (E) act:play

Follow these strategies in answering analogy questions:

1. Establish the relationship of the given pair of words by creating a sentence that shows their relationship.

     A *stanza* is a section of a *poem*.

2. Find the pair of words among the answer choices that could logically replace the given pair in your sentence:

     An *act* is a section of a *play*.

3. Recognize the types of relationships that can be expressed in analogies. Several are listed in the following table.

Types of Analogies	**Example**
cause to effect	virus:cold
part to whole	finger:hand
object to purpose	car:transportation
action to object	dribble:basketball
item to category	salamander:amphibian
type to characteristic	owl:nocturnal
word to synonym	antipathy:aversion
word to antonym	antipathy:attraction
object to its material	shoe:leather
worker to product	composer:symphony
worker to tool	carpenter:hammer
time sequence	sunrise:sunset

Practice Your Skills

Select the lettered pair that best expresses a relationship similar to the one expressed in the original pair.

1. TEACHER:SCHOOL ::
   - (A) nurse:hospital
   - (B) traveler:journey
   - (C) lawyer:library
   - (D) artist:painting
   - (E) soldier:uniform
2. HURRICANE:DAMAGE ::
   - (A) contamination:sickness
   - (B) wind:storm
   - (C) memory:forgetfulness
   - (D) campfire:kindling
   - (E) ocean:current
3. TRIVIAL:INSIGNIFICANT ::
   - (A) malicious:random
   - (B) site:design
   - (C) invigorating:exhilirating
   - (D) irrational:reasonable
   - (E) irritable:agreeable
4. BREAKFAST:SUPPER ::
   - (A) banquet:meal
   - (B) appetizer:dessert
   - (C) fruit:cheese
   - (D) lunch:sandwich
   - (E) preparation:completion

In 1989, Hurricane Hugo devastated the Eastern Seaboard.

Sentence Completion Questions

A sentence completion question is a sentence with words missing. In answering such a question, select the word or words that best complete the sentence.

Age did not _____ but actually _____ this artist's output.

   (A) renew . . . furthered   (B) decrease . . . increased
   (C) publicize . . . secluded   (D) slow . . . slacked
   (E) lengthen . . . narrowed

To answer completion questions, use these strategies:

1. Read the sentence carefully, noting key words or phrases. Words that signal contrast (*but, however*), similarity (*and, another*), or cause and effect (*because, as a result*) give clues to the relationships expressed in the sentence. For example, the word *but* in the question above is a clue that the answer will contain words with opposite meanings. Thus, the correct answer is *B: decrease . . . increased*.
2. Try each of the choices. Eliminate choices that make no sense, are grammatically incorrect, or contradict some part of the sentence.
3. Look for grammatical clues in the sentence. Does the space call for a verb, an adjective, a noun? Should the word be plural? If it is a verb, which tense is required?

Practice Your Skills

Choose the words that best complete the following sentences.

1. The novel is written in a _____ style that is _____ to read; however, the story that unfolds is so exciting that the reader willingly struggles with the elaborate sentences and formal diction.
    (A) humorous . . . stilted   (B) lofty . . . difficult
    (C) complex . . . easy   (D) profound . . . inspiring
    (E) terse . . . impossible
2. Although she had never taken a single _____ lesson, Dionne could sing a song _____ at first sight.
    (A) piano . . . shakily   (B) skiing . . . confidently
    (C) solo . . . along   (D) voice . . . beautifully
    (E) music . . . adequately
3. Elizabeth was _____ ; she absolutely refused to speak against her friend.
    (A) hesitant   (B) adamant
    (C) disloyal   (D) uncaring
    (E) easygoing
4. We are not told the nature of the illness, but we _____ from the patient's pallor and the large number of medicines on the nightstand that the illness has been lengthy and serious.
    (A) infer   (B) deliberate
    (C) decide   (D) imply
    (E) elucidate

Reading Comprehension Questions

Reading comprehension questions assess your ability to interpret written material. You may be asked to do one of the following tasks:

1. Pick out the central idea.
2. Recall a specific detail.
3. Draw a conclusion from the information given.
4. Determine the meaning of a word.
5. Identify the mood of the passage.
6. Determine specific techniques that the writer has used.

Use these strategies in answering reading comprehension questions:

1. Before you read the passage, read the questions that follow it.
2. Read all the choices before you select an answer.
3. Choose the best answer based on the material in the passage.
4. Note the writer's ideas, reasoning, tone, and style.

Practice Your Skills

Read the following passages and choose the best answer for each question.

Passage 1: Today, all bats fly at night, and it is likely that this was always the case, since the birds had already laid claim to the day. To do so, however, the bats had to develop an efficient navigational system. It is based on ultrasounds like those made by shrews and other primitive insectivores. The bats use the ultrasounds for sonar, an extremely sophisticated method of echolocation. This is similar in principle to radar; but radar employs radio waves, whereas sonar uses sound waves. A bat flying by sonar emits sound waves of between 50,000 and 200,000 vibrations per second. It sends out these sounds in short bursts, like clicks, twenty or thirty times every second. On the basis of the echo each sound makes, the bat is able to judge the position of obstacles as well as of moving prey.

1. The best title for this passage would be
    (A) Creatures of the Night
    (B) Sonar Location Systems
    (C) The Bat's Navigational System
    (D) Hearing of the Bat
2. The major difference between sonar and radar is
    (A) the fact that radar is used for radios
    (B) the type of wave that each uses
    (C) the number of vibrations per second
    (D) the use of sonar for navigation

3. The passage mentions all these facts about bats *except* that they
   - (A) fly at night
   - (B) locate and capture food while flying
   - (C) have extremely acute hearing
   - (D) are the only mammals that truly fly

Passage 2: After his seventh birthday the Sioux boy never addressed his blood mother or sister directly again, speaking to them only through a third person. When he showed signs of coming manhood, he was prepared for his pubertal fasting by men close to the family, including some wise and holy ones. . . . When he was ready, the boy was escorted to some far, barren hill and left there in a breechclout and moccasins against the sun of the day, the cold of the night, without food or water. The ordeal was to strip away every superficiality, all the things of the flesh, to prepare for a dreaming, a vision from the Powers. Usually by the third or fourth day, the youth had dreamed and was brought down, gaunt and weak. He was given a few drops of water at a time and some food, but slowly, and after he was restored a little and bathed and feasted, his advisors and the holy man tried to interpret the vision that was to guide him in this manhood he was now entering.

Mari Sandoz, *These Were the Sioux*

1. The author treats her subject with
   - (A) respect and honesty   (B) scientific detachment
   - (C) active dislike   (D) affectionate good humor
2. It can be inferred that during the preparation the boy was
   - (A) treated with dignity and respect by the men
   - (B) largely ignored by the tribe
   - (C) given a great deal of advice by his parents
   - (D) looked upon as a hero and given many gifts
   - (E) often reduced to tears and entreaty
3. The main topic of the passage is
   - (A) the exclusion of women in the Sioux rituals
   - (B) the cruelty of Sioux toward their adolescents
   - (C) the Sioux theory about dreaming
   - (D) the Sioux manhood ritual
   - (E) the customs of the Sioux
4. The author states that the youth's fasting ritual
   - (A) took place before his seventh birthday
   - (B) lasted no more than three days
   - (C) was intended to strip away superficial things of the flesh
   - (D) allowed the boy water but no food
   - (E) was initiated by holy men and women of the tribe

Grammar, Usage, and Mechanics Questions

Standard English usage questions require you to identify errors, such as incorrect verb tenses, improper agreement between pronouns and antecedents, lack of parallel structure, incorrect use of idioms, and improper word choice. In each sentence, four words or phrases are underlined and lettered. Choose the one underlined part that needs to be corrected. If the sentence contains no error, choose answer *E,* labeled "No error."

Her remarks <u>were</u> startling; <u>their affect</u> on the audience
$\qquad\qquad$**A**$\qquad\qquad\qquad$**B**
<u>was</u> <u>immediately</u> apparent. <u>No error</u>
C$\quad$**D**$\qquad\qquad\qquad$**E**

Use these strategies in answering grammar, usage, and mechanics questions.

1. Read the entire sentence through completely.
2. Check to see that its parts are in agreement: Does the subject agree with its verb? Do pronouns agree with their antecedents? Are all the verbs in the correct tense?
3. Check the grammatical construction of the sentence. In particular, look for improper parallelism.
4. Look for misuse of modifiers and other words. Note any improper word choice. In the sample question, for example, *affect* has been used incorrectly; the proper word is *effect.*
5. Remember, the error occurs in an *underlined* part of the sentence.

Practice Your Skills

Write the letter of the underlined part that must be changed to make the following sentence correct. If there is no error, write *E.*

1. As the <u>plot unfolds</u>, the reader of this story <u>come to</u> fear the cruel
$\qquad\qquad$**A**$\qquad\qquad\qquad\qquad\qquad\qquad$**B**
Madame Defarge <u>and, finally,</u> to pity <u>her</u>. <u>No error</u>
$\qquad\qquad\qquad$**C**$\qquad\qquad\qquad$**D**$\quad$**E**

2. Eager <u>to express</u> <u>there</u> appreciation, the cast <u>presented the director</u>
$\qquad\qquad$**A**$\qquad$**B**$\qquad\qquad\qquad\qquad\qquad$**C**
<u>with</u> a bouquet of roses, <u>while</u> the audience applauded tumultuously.
D
<u>No error</u>
E

3. When you <u>drive on icy roads</u>, remember to drive <u>slowly, to</u> apply the
$\qquad\qquad$**A**$\qquad\qquad\qquad\qquad\qquad\qquad$**B**
<u>brakes by using short</u> pumping motions, and <u>you turn</u> in the direc-
C$\qquad\qquad\qquad\qquad\qquad\qquad\qquad$**D**
tion of a skid. <u>No error</u>
$\qquad\qquad\qquad$**E**

4. Although naturalists <u>have studied</u> migration for years, the inner
A
  <u>mechanism that</u> prompts the migratory bird and <u>holds it on course</u>
B   **C**
  for thousands of miles <u>remains</u> a mystery. <u>No error</u>
D   **E**

5. <u>Not only</u> had both <u>sides sustained</u> heavy casualties, <u>but</u> neither <u>can</u>
A   **B**   **C**
  <u>claim</u> a clear-cut victory for itself. <u>No error</u>
D   **E**

6. Although the crisis <u>was</u> considered <u>grave, the</u> President refused to
A   **B**
  <u>lie</u> the blame on <u>Congress</u>. <u>No error</u>
C   **D**   **E**

7. <u>"Never!"</u> he cried. "You may think me a <u>fool, but</u> I shall never <u>betray</u>
A   **B**   **C**
  my <u>allegiance</u> to the Confederacy." <u>No error</u>
D   **E**

Sentence Correction Questions These items test your ability to correct, rather than just recognize, an error in a sentence. In a sentence correction question, the underlined portion of the sentence contains an element that is wordy, unclear, awkwardly phrased, ambiguous, or illogical. Below the sentence are five versions of the underlined part. You evaluate the sentence and its underlined part and then choose the best version. If you think the sentence is correct as written, choose *A,* which repeats the original.

> More efficient, cost-effective solar power would be a great boon, since its source is readily available <u>and the sun is a virtually inexhaustible supply.</u>

    (A) and the sun is a virtually inexhaustible supply
    (B) and its supply is virtually inexhaustible.
    (C) and the sun being a virtually inexhaustible supply.
    (D) because of its inexhaustible supply.
    (E) and since it is an inexhaustible supply.

To answer sentence correction questions, use these strategies:

1. Keep in mind that only the underlined portion of the sentence can change. Identify the error in the underlined portion first before you look at the choices.
2. Pay careful attention to grammar, punctuation, and word choice. In the example above, the underlined clause is not parallel to the clause that comes before it. "Its source is readily available" should be followed by a clause worded in a similar manner. Choice *B,* "and its supply is virtually inexhaustible," has a parallel structure and is, therefore, the correct answer.

Practice Your Skills

Select the answer that, when used to replace the underlined words, produces the most effective sentence. Select *A* if the original sentence needs no revision.

1. Beyond the dunes, angry <u>clouds that seethed</u> on the horizon, like smoke above the flames of waves.
   - (A) clouds that seethed
   - (B) clouds, which seethed
   - (C) clouds, seething
   - (D) clouds seethed
   - (E) clouds, which were seething

2. A bad accident occurred at the busy intersection, injuring several <u>people, and a traffic light was put up.</u>
   - (A) people, and a traffic light was put up
   - (B) people. The result is that a traffic light was put up
   - (C) people. As a result, a traffic light was put up
   - (D) people, then a traffic light was put up
   - (E) people, a traffic light was put up

3. California was declared a territory of the United States <u>on August 15, 1848, it was admitted to the Union</u> in September 1850.
   - (A) on August 15, 1848, it was admitted to the Union
   - (B) on August 15, 1848; but it was admitted to the Union
   - (C) on August 15, 1848; nonetheless, it was admitted to the Union
   - (D) on August 15, 1848, then it was admitted to the Union
   - (E) on August 15, 1848. It was admitted to the Union

4. The fort, <u>built in the tenth century,</u> is now a tourist attraction.
   - (A) built in the tenth century
   - (B) it was built in the tenth century
   - (C) being built in the tenth century
   - (D) that was built in the tenth century
   - (E) was built in the tenth century and

5. Far from ending space travel, the shuttle accident actually increased the determination of NASA to face the dangers, <u>meet new challenges, and expanding the frontiers of exploration.</u>
   - (A) meet new challenges, and expanding the frontiers of exploration
   - (B) meet new challenges, expanding the frontiers of exploration
   - (C) meeting new challenges meanwhile expanding the frontiers of exploration
   - (D) meet new challenges, and expand the frontiers of exploration
   - (E) so that challenges are met and frontiers are expanding

Mass Communication and Advertising

Today, even the most remote corners of the world are part of a global community. For example, in a Third-World village where there may be no other modern conveniences—no indoor plumbing, no electricity, no refrigeration—there often is a television set, run by a generator, bringing in news of the outside world.

Our century has seen an explosion in methods for communicating with great numbers of people over vast distances. Consider the types of communication, or media, utilized every day: satellite communications, computer networks, video and audio cassette tapes, compact discs, facsimile (fax) machines, newspapers, cellular telephones, television, and magazines. Many of the electronic media did not exist twenty years ago, and except for the print media, none existed a hundred years ago.

Media that are used to communicate with large numbers, or masses, of people are called **mass media.** The act of communicating with a large number of people is called **mass communication.** The modern explosion in media technologies has had major consequences on society. One important consequence is that the world has become smaller. Wherever you are, you can learn almost instantly what is going on in any other place on the globe. Another important consequence of modern mass communication is **mass persuasion** —the ability to influence millions of people to think or act in certain ways. The persuasive power of the mass media is most evident in the field of advertising.

ELEMENTS OF ADVERTISING CLAIMS

Most Americans encounter hundreds of ads every day—in magazines and newspapers, on billboards, on product packages, and, of course, on television—promoting products, services, and political candidates.

Purposes of Advertising

Every advertisement seeks to persuade or influence. A given advertisement can have either of two specific purposes.

- to inform without emotional appeals
- to persuade using emotional appeals, with or without conveying any information

Learning to distinguish information from persuasive techniques can help you make sound decisions. Imagine an ad for a bicycle helmet. If the ad uses words like "tough outer surface," "highly shock absorbent," and "vents help circulate air," you will have received information about the helmet's safety and comfort.

Advertising and Prices

With certain advertising, especially informational ads, the product's price is highlighted. Terms such as the following can make the price sound like a bargain, but can actually be misleading.

- "List price" The list price is the price suggested by the manufacturer. Sometimes a product is advertised as selling at "list price." However, list price is not necessarily a bargain. Many products are intended to sell for less than the list price.
- "Originally" A price that is listed as originally $24.99, now only $21.99 could mean that at one time the product sold at $24.99. Consider that the product may have been overpriced to begin with, or it may have been replaced by a better model.
- "Below manufacturer's cost" An item marked this way may seem like a bargain, but find out why the manufacturer is willing to take a loss. The product may be poorly designed, it may not have a guarantee, or spare parts may be impossible to obtain.

Misleading Claims About Similar Products

Many seemingly different products are actually similar both in price and quality. For example, laboratory tests show that all gasoline brands with the same octane rating perform equally well in car engines. Many brands of blue jeans are indistinguishable without their designer labels. Generic food products and even medicines often differ from their name-brand counterparts only in their packaging and price. Read labels carefully to see if you're getting extra quality when you pay a higher price.

Since many products are essentially similar, advertisers use carefully selected words and images to enhance their product's appeal.

Weasel Words Qualifiers such as *almost, nearly,* and *close to* give the advertiser a convenient "out." For example, a shampoo that leaves your hair "feeling like never before" could actually make your hair feel worse without contradicting the claim in the ad. See "Weasel Words," page 517.

Purr and Snarl Words Ad writers consciously use words with strong positive or negative connotations to sway your feelings. Purr words have positive connotations. Words such as *golden, mother, home,* and *success* trigger pleasant thoughts and help create a favorable impression of a product or service.

Snarl words, which carry negative connotations, attempt to sway you away from something else and toward the product. In the phrase "prevents ugly blemishes," the word *ugly* helps trigger a negative reaction, not to the product itself, but to the situation that the product claims to remedy.

Comparatives/Superlatives Words such as *better, best, more,* and *most* are used often in ads, and you should be aware of what they really represent. According to accepted advertising standards, many similar products can say they are "the best," even though more than one "best" is a logical impossibility. The fact that a product is labeled "the best" tells nothing about its quality. Similarly, an ad in which one car goes farther than another on one tank of gas may simply show that this car has a larger gas tank than does the other car.

Be aware of the relevant questions that are often masked by comparative and superlative wording in ads. Consider what facts are given to substantiate the claim, what the product is being compared with, and who made the comparison.

Unidentified Terms "The sportswear with polypropylene!" The name of the fabric sounds impressive, but what exactly is "polypropylene"? Ad writers realize that scientific-sounding terms impress people. An ad may tell you that the special ingredient YK7 makes Brand Z better than Brand X. If you aren't told what the ingredient is, ignore the ingredient in your purchase decision.

Unfinished Claims These are statements such as "50 percent more pain reliever" and "Nine out of ten doctors recommend. . . ." These claims are "unfinished" because not all of the information is given. You might ask "50 percent more pain reliever than what?" or you might wonder "How many doctors were surveyed?"

Writing
TIP

When you read or write an advertisement, consider the effect of words and phrases that carry strong positive or negative connotations.

Implied Ideas   In a television commercial for a popular breakfast cereal, you are told that the cereal is "part of a complete, balanced breakfast." The announcer deliberately places the emphasis on "complete, balanced breakfast" and de-emphasizes "part of." As a result, the commercial implies that the cereal is *all* you need for a balanced breakfast. To prevent being accused of falsehood, the advertiser pictures orange juice, milk, and toast with the advertised cereal.

Types of Advertising Appeals

Advertisers use a variety of appeals to persuade you to buy their products. Here are some commonly used advertising appeals.

Emotional Appeals   These appeals take advantage of the fact that people have certain universal needs and desires. Most people want health and happiness for themselves and their families. They want to be more physically attractive and to be popular. Advertising slogans such as "Is your family getting enough fiber?" and "Why not be your most beautiful?" appeal to consumers' basic desires. Statements in ads addressed to the product itself, such as "You make me feel fresh" and "Look what you've done for us!" also appeal to emotions by making people think the product cares about them.

Appeals to Authority   These appeals are based on trust in authorities. A testimonial from an expert, such as an auto mechanic's endorsement of a motor oil, may suggest that the product is effective. However, not only do experts often disagree, but the "expert" may only be an actor or actress hired to play the part. In one commercial, the "expert" introduced himself by saying, "I'm not a doctor, but I played one on TV."

Appeals to Reason   Some ads present facts about the product and urge you, as a reasonable consumer, to make the smart choice. Be careful to note what information has been provided. Is it relevant? Is it documented? Have any details been omitted? Are the claims unique?

Also, watch for ads with circular reasoning—"People like Cloud Nine ice cream because they really enjoy it." Ads such as this one try to substitute repetition for logical support of a claim. See "Thinking Strategies for Writing," pages 468–474, for information on identifying such logical fallacies.

Appeals by Association Appeals by association include bandwagon, snob appeal, false testimonials, and transfer. **Bandwagon appeals** encourage you to be part of the crowd and to be like everyone else. Statements such as "Everyone loves Can-Do Computers!" appeal to the common desire to be like other people.

In the 1950s hula hoop manufacturers obviously used the bandwagon appeal effectively.

Ads based on **snob appeal** use a variation on this strategy. They work because sometimes, rather than being like everyone else, you want to be a member of a select group. Ads such as the following suggest that if you buy the item, you can be one of a chosen few: "Dare to be different: Chew Cauliflower gum."

Another kind of appeal by association is the **false testimonial.** Many companies hire celebrities to endorse their products, hoping that people will buy products because of an identification with the celebrity. Of course, a celebrity doing a testimonial often works in a field unrelated to the product. For example, someone who longs to be an Olympic gymnast will not get any closer to that goal by buying flashlight batteries promoted by an Olympic gymnast.

Another appeal by association is called **transfer.** A soft-drink ad might show a group of happy people enjoying a day at the beach, splashing in the cool water. The advertisers hope that consumers will associate the coolness of the water and the vitality of the group with the soft drink. The aim is for the positive feelings evoked by the images to be transferred to the product.

Practice Your Skills

A. Complete the following activities as a class or in a small group.

1. Think about ads for political candidates. In what ways are these ads similar to ads for products? What do advertisers mean when they speak of "packaging" a candidate? What standard advertising techniques do ads for political candidates often use?
2. Think of a major event in the past, such as the Civil War. How might it have been different if television had existed then?
3. According to recent studies, the average American watches over six hours of television a day. What effect might this amount of television watching have on our habits as consumers?
4. In the United States there are many laws governing the use of the media. Here are examples.

> laws that limit the number of different media that one person or group can control in a single area
> laws that require television and radio stations to allow challengers for political office equal time with incumbents

Think about each of these kinds of laws. What protection do they offer to the public against the power of the media?

B. Follow the directions for each numbered item below.

1. Identify the advertising technique used in each of the following slogans.

> Now that you've reached the top, you deserve a Wexter.
> Put Z4000 in your tank. The gas with gusto.
> Six out of seven professional mechanics use Black Gold on their own cars.
> *Everyone* loves Claude's stone-washed jeans.
> When Ty Wyoming isn't wearing a football uniform, he wears Saddle cologne.
> Now you can earn up to $100 in one day!
> Roots shampoo may cost more, but I'm worth it.
> Rice Chunks has more of what you eat a cereal for.

2. Write two advertisements for your favorite tape or compact disc. In one, use no emotional appeals, and in the other, use at least one of the appeals discussed in this handbook.

On the Lightside

WEASEL WORDS

Think about the following advertising claims. As you read, notice the italicized modifier used in each one.

Sudsos leaves dishes *virtually* spotless. (Since *virtually* means "practically," Sudso leaves spots on dishes.)

The FAR SIDE Cartoon by Gary Larsen reprinted by permission of Chronicle Features. San Francisco, California

© Chronicle Features. 1981

Krumbles potato chips are made with 100 percent *natural* ingredients. (What would be *unnatural* ingredients?)

Tum-Eez relieves *simple* indigestion. (What if your indigestion is not *simple*?)

Virtually, natural, and *simple* are examples of **weasel words**—words that seem forthright, but are evasive. Advertising slogans and political rhetoric are frequently accused of being filled with weasel words. The term was coined at the turn of the century by political commentator Stewart Chaplin. He was annoyed with the way politicians often used qualifying words that seemed to add emphasis but in fact made statements weaker. "Why, weasel words are words that suck the life out of the words next to them, just as a weasel sucks the egg and leaves the shell," he said.

Chaplin's phrase became popular in 1916, when it was used by Theodore Roosevelt to describe misleading political statements. Today, weasel words may be used so that they have no meaning at all. Weasel words allow the user to weasel out of commitment.

Chair with Books, Vivienne Flesher

Grammar and Usage Handbook

Skills

Directions In each of the following sentences, one, two, or none of the underlined sections may be incorrect. Look for errors of grammar, usage, punctuation, spelling, and capitalization. On your paper, write the number of the sentence, the letter of each incorrect underlined section, and the correction. If the sentence contains no errors, write E.

Example   Literacy Volunteers of America <u>are</u> an organization
                                A   B
<u>dedicated</u> to helping people <u>learn to read.</u> <u>No error</u>
   C   D   E

Answer   B—is

---

1. <u>Robert</u> <u>mispelled</u> the word <u>*mischievous,*</u> thinking that the *e* came before the *i.*
    A   B   C   D
<u>No error</u>
  E

2. <u>Enjoying the unusual activity of tooth decoration.</u> <u>The Maya Indians made sharp points</u>
                  A   B
<u>in their front teeth.</u> <u>Then they drilled holes in them.</u> <u>They filled the holes with jewels.</u>
                                 C   D
<u>No error</u>
  E

3. An ichthyologist <u>is a person</u> <u>which studies fish,</u> especially <u>their</u> <u>structure and</u>
                  A   B   C   D
<u>classification.</u> <u>No error</u>
            E

4. <u>When you store numbers in a calculator,</u> <u>the memory unit</u> <u>holds</u> the codes for the keys
                  A   B   C
<u>that have been pressed.</u> <u>No error</u>
     D   E

5. <u>Marie Curie discovered two new elements.</u> <u>She named the first one polonium, the other</u>
                A   B
one she named radium. <u>When she was only thirty-six years old.</u> <u>she received the Nobel</u>
                                     C   D
<u>Prize for her work.</u> <u>No error</u>
               E

6. <u>Michelangelo</u> <u>painted</u> <u>*The Last Supper,*</u> and the ceiling of the Sistine Chapel <u>was also</u>
    A   B   C   D
<u>painted by him.</u> <u>No error</u>
            E

7. <u>The city of Chicago</u> <u>lays</u> on the <u>shore</u> of <u>Lake Michigan.</u> <u>No error</u>
        A   B   C   D   E

8. A <u>low steady</u> thumping sound, <u>like the beating of a heart,</u> seemed to fill the room as
      A   **B**
   <u>we was reading</u> the final page of <u>Poe's</u> "The Tell-Tale Heart." <u>No error</u>
       C   **D**   **E**

9. <u>During the Great Depression,</u> thousands of people <u>appealed directly</u> to <u>Franklin and</u>
          A   **B**   **C**
   <u>Eleanor Roosevelt,</u> and <u>in their letters they ask for help.</u> <u>No error</u>
                 D   **E**

10. <u>Tom Wolfe had wrote</u> <u>a series of notes</u> <u>that he was unable to make into a story,</u>
       A   **B**   **C**
   so his editor published the notes, <u>and critics called them</u> "the new journalism."
                               D
   <u>No error</u>
    E

11. Telescopes <u>have counted</u> over <u>7,500</u> pieces of <u>man-made</u> <u>junk, this includes dead</u>
            A   **B**   **C**   **D**
   <u>satellites circling</u> the earth. <u>No error</u>
                   E

12. When the machines are turned <u>on make</u> sure that <u>each</u> of the workers <u>have</u> safety
                     A   **B**   **C**
   <u>goggles</u> on. <u>No error</u>
    D   **E**

13. <u>When you sneeze,</u> the air <u>travels</u> <u>at a rate of</u> approximately <u>one hundred miles per hour.</u>
      A   **B**   **C**   **D**
   <u>No error</u>
    E

14. A flea <u>don't</u> have <u>wings, but</u> it can jump distances <u>that are up to</u> one hundred times <u>its</u>
          A   **B**   **C**   **D**
   own height. <u>No error</u>
             E

15. The <u>surprise</u> birthday party <u>made</u> Susan feel <u>more happier</u> <u>than she had ever been.</u>
      A   **B**   **C**   **D**
   <u>No error</u>
    E

16. <u>The Mother</u> in <u>"The Rocking-Horse Winner"</u> <u>feels badly</u> at the end of the story
      A   **B**   **C**
   <u>when the tragedy occurs.</u> <u>No error</u>
          D   **E**

17. <u>If you and me</u> visit a local chapter of the <u>Red Cross,</u> we can <u>recieve</u> information on
      A   **B**   **C**
   working with the bloodmobile, the Special <u>Olympics, and</u> the adopt-a-grandparent
                                      D
   program. <u>No error</u>
          E

18. In the United States and Canada, the problems of protecting natural resources and
    A   B
    wildlife prevail, and they are constantly alert for possible threats to wild species.
    C   D
    No error
    E

19. One of the Bengal tigers were out of the cage sunning itself on an outcropping of rock.
    A   B   C   D
    No error
    E

20. Maria inquired whether *Lawrence of Arabia* is on the movie channel tonight? No error
    A   B   C   D   E

21. Although most postage stamps printed in the United States are rectangular, Many
    A   B   C
    countries issue stamps that have odd shapes such as banana and pineapple shapes!
    D
    No error
    E

22. The principal by which a lawn sprinkler works is relatively simple, water enters the
    A   B   C
    sprinkler forcing the mechanism to turn. No error
    D   E

23. In a recent issue of "Runner's World" magazine, the editors stated, "A person cannot
    A   B   C
    really be fit without exercise". No error
    D   E

24. After World War II, there was a severe shortage of suitable, affordable housing in the
    A   B   C   D
    United States. No error
    E

25. Deep in this woods there are wolves, owls, and deer, Ive never seen one of them.
    A   B   C   D
    No error
    E

Sketchbook

> Oh Lord! It's hard to be humble
> When you're perfect in every way.
>
> Mac Davis

What are *you* good at? Explain in two or three paragraphs what you think is your best trait or talent. How has it helped you in life? Don't be shy, but do be honest. Vary sentence structure and use descriptive modifiers.

Additional Sketches

Do you know a good ghost story? In a few paragraphs, briefly narrate a ghost story that you have heard or that you have invented. Remember that part of what makes a ghost story scary and suspenseful is the selective use of detail.

Did you know that 92,000 Americans have reservations with Pan American Airlines for a trip to the moon? Imagine that you were on such a trip. What would the experience be like? Write one or more paragraphs in which you describe your voyage. To make your description more interesting, use all four kinds of sentences.

The Parts of Speech

NOUNS

Certain words in English are used as labels to name persons, places, things, and ideas.

A noun is a word that names a person, place, thing, or idea.

Persons	Edith Hamilton, author, friend, Caesar
Places	Athens, city, mall, Shea Stadium
Things	book, cassette, soccer, announcement
Ideas	happiness, democracy, sympathy, success

Concrete and Abstract Nouns

A **concrete noun** names something that can be seen, heard, smelled, touched, or tasted: *book, thunder, perfume, soup.*

An **abstract noun** names something that cannot be perceived through the five senses: *belief, joy, strictness, efficiency.*

Concrete Nouns	Abstract Nouns
Golden Gate Bridge	talent
fireworks	bravery
silk	friendship
smoke	peace
sofa	comfort

Common and Proper Nouns

A **common noun** is a general name for a person, place, thing, or idea. It is a name that is common to an entire group: *teacher, city, song.*

A **proper noun** is the name of a particular person, place, thing, or idea: *Ms. Sullivan, Detroit, "This Land Is Your Land."*

As you can see in the following examples, a proper noun always begins with a capital letter and may consist of more than one word.

Common Nouns	Proper Nouns
country	Costa Rica
valley	Star Valley
state	Wyoming
union	United Mine Workers
actor	Emilio Estevez
building	Lincoln Center

Compound Nouns

A **compound noun** contains two or more shorter words that may be written as one word, as separate words, or with hyphens.

One Word	Separate Words	With Hyphens
foodstuff	disc jockey	brother-in-law
grandmother	Virginia Woolf	rock-and-roll

Collective Nouns

A **collective noun** is a singular noun that refers to a group of people or things.

colony   team   family   herd   audience   council

Colony of bees

Practice Your Skills

A. CONCEPT CHECK

Nouns For each sentence write each noun and identify it as either *Concrete* or *Abstract*. Then write whether the noun is *Common* or *Proper*. Finally, if it is a compound noun or a collective noun, write *Compound* or *Collective*.

1. Moss Hart was a successful playwright known for his wit.
2. He wrote many of his most successful plays with a collaborator.
3. Along with George S. Kaufman, this legendary writer created several plays that combined humor with satire.
4. Kaufman and Hart enjoyed their first success in 1930 with *Once in a Lifetime,* a production about the movies.

5. They based many of their plays on the experiences of their friends, such as Alexander Woollcott and Harpo Marx.
6. This celebrated writing team won the Pulitzer Prize for drama in 1937 for their comedy *You Can't Take It With You.*
7. By himself, Hart wrote the stories for a number of musical comedies, one of which had music by Irving Berlin and another of which had music by Kurt Weill.
8. Also, Moss Hart wrote screenplays for several motion pictures, including *Gentleman's Agreement.*
9. *Gentleman's Agreement* addressed the subject of antisemitic feelings and received the Academy Award in 1947 as best picture of the year.
10. In 1956, Hart won the Antoinette Perry Award for directing *My Fair Lady.*
11. Moss Hart detailed his fascinating life in the theater and movies in his 1959 autobiography, *Act One.*
12. *Act One* quickly became a best seller.
13. Many aspiring writers drew hope from his story.
14. Ranging from amateur theater to Broadway to Hollywood, his career was truly illustrious.
15. Certainly, he received the adoration of audiences everywhere.

B. APPLICATION IN LITERATURE

Types of Nouns Write each italicized noun and identify it by type: *Concrete, Abstract, Compound, Collective.* Some nouns will fit more than one category.

> (1) I was . . . disappointed to find the *shades* still drawn and the *family* fast asleep when I unlocked the door and stepped into the *apartment.* (2) I stood in the *doorway* of the kitchen . . . and gazed at the sleeping *figure* of my *brother* on the *daybed* in the *dining room,* and beyond it at the closed door of the one *bedroom* where my *parents* slept. (3) The frayed *carpet* on the floor was the carpet I had crawled over before I could walk. (4) Each *flower* in the badly faded and worn *design* was sharply etched in my *mind.* (5) Each *piece* of furniture in the cramped dim room seemed mildewed with a thousand double-edged *memories.* (6) The *ghosts* of a thousand leaden *meals* hovered over the dining-room table. (7) The dust of countless black-hearted days clung to every *crevice* of the squalid ugly furniture I had known since *childhood.* (8) To walk out of it forever . . . would give *meaning* to the *wonder* of what had happened to me, make *success* tangible, decisive.

Moss Hart, *Act One*

PRONOUNS

To avoid unnecessary repetition, pronouns are often used to replace nouns. Pronouns can be used in the identical ways that nouns are used.

A pronoun is a word used in place of a noun or another pronoun.

The noun for which a pronoun stands and to which it refers is its **antecedent.**

> *Karen* repaired *her* broken bicycle. (*Karen* is the antecedent of the pronoun *her.*)

Sometimes the antecedent of a pronoun appears in a preceding sentence.

> *Switzerland* has many exports. *Its* cheeses and cuckoo clocks are popular around the world. (*Switzerland* is the antecedent of the pronoun *its.*)

There are seven kinds of pronouns: personal pronouns, reflexive pronouns, intensive pronouns, demonstrative pronouns, indefinite pronouns, interrogative pronouns, and relative pronouns. On the pages that follow, you will learn to identify these pronouns. (For problems in pronoun usage, see Handbook 36.)

Personal Pronouns

Personal pronouns are pronouns that change form to express person, number, and gender.

Person   Pronouns that identify the person speaking are said to be in the **first person.** Pronouns that identify the person being spoken to are in the **second person.** Pronouns that identify the person or thing being spoken about are in the **third person.**

Number   Pronouns that refer to one person, one place, one thing, or one idea are **singular** in number. Pronouns that refer to more than one are **plural** in number.

Singular   The *plant* has lost *its* leaves. (The singular pronoun *its* refers to the singular antecedent *plant.*)
Plural   The *plants* have lost *their* leaves. (The plural pronoun *their* refers to the plural antecedent *plants.*)

Writing
—**TIP**—
When you proof-read your work, always check that pronouns agree in person, number, and gender with their antecedents.

The Parts
of Speech   **527**

This chart shows the person and number of personal pronouns.

Personal Pronouns			
	First Person	**Second Person**	**Third Person**
Singular	I, me (my, mine)	you (your, yours)	he, him (his) she, her (her, hers) it (its)
Plural	we, us (our, ours)	you (your, yours)	they, them (their, theirs)

Gender Pronouns that refer to males are in the **masculine gender.** Pronouns that refer to females are in the **feminine gender.** Pronouns that refer to things are in the **neuter gender.**

Although the neuter pronoun *it* refers to things, the female pronouns *she, her,* and *hers* are sometimes used to refer to countries, ships, and airplanes. Animals may be referred to by *it* and *its* or by *he, him, his, she, her,* and *hers.*

Possessive pronouns are special forms of personal pronouns that show ownership or belonging. In the chart above, the possessive forms are in parentheses.

> The road map is *his.* (ownership)
> *Our* family likes to travel. (belonging)

The possessive pronouns *mine, yours, his, hers, its, ours,* and *theirs* are used like other pronouns to replace nouns. The possessive pronouns *my, your, his, her, its, our,* and *their* are used as modifiers. Notice that *his* and *its* appear in both groups.

> This horse is *mine.* (used like other pronouns)
> This is *my* horse. (modifies the noun *horse*)

Practice Your Skills

CONCEPT CHECK

Personal Pronouns Write the personal pronouns in the following dialogue. Then write the antecedent of each pronoun.

1. Elena: Jason, did you know that Mary Shelley wrote *Frankenstein* when she was only eighteen?
2. Jason: Yes. However, I have never actually read the novel.

Writing Theme
Mary Shelley

3. Elena: Mary wrote it shortly after she married Percy Bysshe Shelley. In reality, their courtship was quite scandalous!

4. Jason: Wasn't he the great Romantic poet and author of *Queen Mab* and *Prometheus Unbound*?

5. Elena: Yes. He, Mary, and a group of their writer friends decided each to write a horror story.

6. Jason: Hers surely must have been considered the masterpiece of the group!

7. Elena: We musn't forget that of all science-fiction novels, Mary Shelley's book is considered the first.

8. Jason: You mean I have read so many of them and have not even read the original?

9. Elena: Her book is the only science-fiction novel that truly terrifies me and at the same time makes me think deeply about its themes and ideas.

10. Jason: You win. May I borrow your copy of *Frankenstein* tomorrow?

Reflexive and Intensive Pronouns

Reflexive and intensive pronouns are formed by adding *-self* or *-selves* to certain personal pronouns. Even though the forms of these two kinds of pronouns are identical, they are used in very different ways.

Singular   myself, yourself, himself, herself, itself
Plural   ourselves, yourselves, themselves

Reflexive pronouns reflect an action back upon the subject.

Mother treated *herself* to a microwave oven.

The guests helped *themselves* to the cold buffet.

Intensive pronouns can be used to add emphasis to a noun or a pronoun in the same sentence; however, they are not essential to the meaning of the sentence. If intensive pronouns are removed, the meaning of the sentence does not change.

I *myself* am in charge of the campaign.
Have you written to the mayor *himself*?
We drew up the petition *ourselves*.

Usage Note   Reflexive and intensive pronouns should never be used without antecedents.

Incorrect   Kip asked Sam and *myself* to go the movies.
Correct   Kip asked Sam and *me* to go to the movies.

Self-portrait,
by Diego Rivera

Writing
—TIP—

Only the forms shown are acceptable reflexive or intensive pronouns. *Hisself* and *theirselves* are never correct.

The Parts
of Speech

Narcissus, by Caravaggio,
National Gallery
of Rome

Practice Your Skills

A. CONCEPT CHECK

Reflexive and Intensive Pronouns   Write an appropriate reflexive or intensive pronoun for each sentence. Then write its antecedent and tell whether the pronoun is *Intensive* or *Reflexive.*

1. Even today, in a time of scientific technology, we occasionally find _____ trying to explain what seems unexplainable.
2. Ancient Greeks and Romans satisfied _____ about things they did not understand by creating myths.
3. Their cultures found it quite natural to link all things with divine powers—in fact, with the gods _____ .
4. For example, the origin of the narcissus, a lovely flower that regenerates _____ each spring, is explained in myth.
5. It seems that a handsome youth had rejected many young maidens who considered _____ hopeful candidates for his love.
6. Finally, the Goddess of the Hunt _____ , Diana, heard the prayers of one of the scorned young ladies.
7. When Narcissus saw _____ in a reflecting pool, the curse of Diana made him fall in love with his own image.
8. "I cannot free _____ ," he cried. "Only death can free me."
9. Where his body lay, some nymphs found a beautiful flower growing; they _____ named the flower narcissus.
10. Although you _____ may find this kind of story an entertaining explanation, an abundance of scientific information in today's world enables us to find explanations without resorting to myth.

B. APPLICATION IN WRITING

A Myth   Write a brief modern myth that imaginatively explains an aspect of nature, for example, the origins of lightning. Use a variety of intensive and reflexive pronouns in your myth.

Demonstrative Pronouns

The **demonstrative pronouns** *this, that, these,* and *those* point out persons or things. *This* and *these* point out persons or things that are near in space or time. *That* and *those* point out persons or things that are farther away in space or time. Demonstrative pronouns may come before or after their antecedents.

Before   *These* are the *sneakers* I want.

After   Look at the *trophies. Those* were won by my father.

Indefinite Pronouns

Pronouns that do not refer to a definite person or thing are **indefinite pronouns.** These pronouns often have no antecedents.

> *Someone* returned my keys.
> *Several* have applied, but *few* have been accepted.

Indefinite Pronouns	
Singular	another, anybody, anyone, anything, each, everybody, everyone, everything, much, neither, nobody, no one, nothing, one, somebody, someone, something
Plural	both, few, many, several
Singular or Plural	all, any, more, most, none, some

Interrogative Pronouns

The **interrogative pronouns** *who, whom, whose, which,* and *what* are used to introduce questions.

> *Who* is pitching today?   *What* is the schedule?

Grammar Note   Demonstrative, indefinite, interrogative, and other pronouns can also function as adjectives. See page 543 for examples.

The Parts
of Speech   **531**

Relative Pronouns

A **relative pronoun** relates, or connects, a clause to the word or words it modifies. The noun or pronoun that the clause modifies is the antecedent of the relative pronoun. The relative pronouns are *who, whom, whose, which,* and *that.*

> Show me the *camera that* you bought. (The antecedent of the relative pronoun *that* is *camera.*)
>
> She is the *candidate whom* everyone prefers. (The antecedent of the relative pronoun *whom* is *candidate.*)

Practice Your Skills

A. CONCEPT CHECK

Pronouns   Write the pronouns in each sentence. Then identify each pronoun as *Personal, Reflexive, Intensive, Demonstrative, Indefinite, Interrogative,* or *Relative.*

1. What is the Asian country that consists of over 13,600 islands?
2. It is Indonesia, which is the fifth most populous country.
3. The name Indonesia itself means "Islands of the Indies."
4. This was the area which Christopher Columbus sought.
5. An Indonesian man who ruled the island of Java asked the Dutch to help him fight a rebellion in the 1600's.
6. That was like an invitation to the Dutch to govern the islands; however, in 1949, the Dutch gave up their rule.
7. Many of the islands in Indonesia cover less than one square mile.
8. Several consist of low-lying terrain; most, however, are noted for their mountains and active volcanoes.
9. In fact, one of the volcanoes on the island of Krakatoa erupted violently, destroying much of the island.
10. Indonesians pride themselves on having a distinctive culture.
11. Men and women dress themselves in colorful skirts, or *sarongs.*
12. Tourists who travel to Indonesia discover an exotic land that is full of fascinating contrasts, and they are always enchanted.

B. REVISION SKILL

Using Pronouns   Revise the paragraph on the following page, using the directions provided in parentheses.

> **Example**   *Some* of the world's largest islands are Great Britain, Japan, and Sicily. (Replace the indefinite pronoun with a number.)
>
> *Three* of the world's largest islands are Great Britain, Japan, and Sicily.

(1) Another unique island nation is Madagascar. This country lies in the Indian Ocean southeast of Africa. (Use a relative pronoun to combine two sentences.) (2) The island nation consists of one very large island and many small ones. (Use a demonstrative pronoun to create a transition.) (3) The main island, also named Madagascar, is the fourth largest in the world. (Add an intensive pronoun for emphasis.) (4) Sea pirates, one of *who* was Captain Kidd, used the island as a base in the 1600's. (Correct the relative pronoun.) (5) Some of the inhabitants today are of African descent; *some* are descended from Indonesian settlers. (Vary the indefinite pronoun.) (6) France made *the entire area* of Madagascar a colony in 1896. (Replace the phrase with a single indefinite pronoun.) (7) The nation won independence for *its own people* in 1960. (Replace the phrase with a reflexive pronoun.) (8) Today, Madagascar is the world's greatest producer of vanilla. The vanilla is exported to many countries. (Use a relative pronoun to combine sentences.) (9) Besides this valuable plant with *their* distinctive flavor, the country is also home to rare wildlife. (Correct the personal pronoun.) (10) Lemurs are among the island's unique animals. Lemurs are mammals related to monkeys. (Use a relative pronoun to combine sentences.)

C. APPLICATION IN WRITING

An Informative Paragraph Read the following facts about the island nation of Haiti. Then use these facts to write a short paragraph about Haiti that you think would furnish useful information to elementary-school children. After writing your paragraph, make a list of all the pronouns that you used.

Haiti
— country in the West Indies between Cuba and Puerto Rico
— Columbus established a base in what is now Haiti in 1492
— was one of the richest colonies of France in the seventeenth century
— won independence in 1804 and is the world's oldest African-American republic
— is known for its folk art and crafts in mahogany wood
— is the only French-speaking republic in the Americas
— is now one of the poorest and most densely populated countries in the Western Hemisphere
— almost two-fifths of the population is younger than fifteen years of age

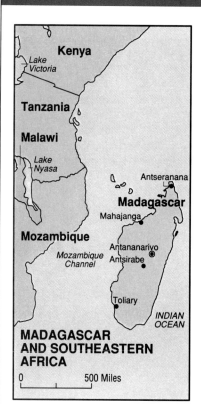

MADAGASCAR AND SOUTHEASTERN AFRICA

0   500 Miles

The Parts
of Speech   **533**

VERBS

A verb is a word that expresses an action, a condition, or a state of being.

There are two main categories of verbs: **action verbs** and **linking verbs.** Other verbs, called **auxiliary verbs,** are sometimes combined with action verbs and linking verbs.

Action Verbs

An **action verb** is a verb that tells what action someone or something is performing. The action may be physical or mental.

Physical Action	We *worked* hard on the fund drive.
Mental Action	Everyone *hoped* for success.

Linking Verbs

A **linking verb** does not express action. Instead, it links the subject of the sentence to a word in the predicate.

> Mr. Kachenko *is* our teacher. (The linking verb *is* links the subject *Mr. Kachenko* to the noun *teacher.*)
> That dog *looks* miserable. (The linking verb *looks* links the subject *dog* to the adjective *miserable.*)

Linking verbs may be divided into two groups.

Types of Linking Verbs

Forms of *To Be*

I *am* happy.

My sister *is* a pharmacist.

They *are* my cousins from Ireland.

Our shoes *were* wet.

Verbs That Express Condition

Everyone *looked* hot.
The tomatoes *grew* tall.

Our cat *seems* intelligent.
The basement *smells* damp.
The music *sounds* loud.

The children *appeared* sleepy.
The audience *became* restless.

The salad *stayed* fresh.
The baby's skin *feels* smooth.
This yogurt *tastes* different.

Sometimes a verb can be a linking verb or an action verb.

Linking Verb	**Action Verb**
The fish *tastes* delicious.	The cook *tastes* the fish.
Everyone *looked* hungry.	He *looked* for some herbs.

Note If you can substitute *is, are, was,* or *were* for a verb, you know it is a linking verb.

The fish *tastes* delicious.	The fish *is* delicious.
Everyone *looked* hungry.	Everyone *was* hungry.

Writing
—**TIP**—
Do not overuse linking verbs. Well-chosen action verbs make writing lively.

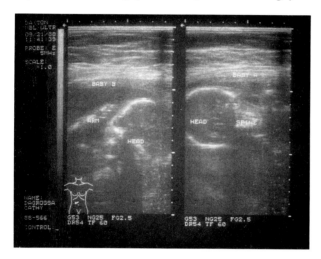

Ultrasound produced this computer-generated image of twins.

Practice Your Skills

CONCEPT CHECK

Action Verbs and Linking Verbs Write the verb in each of the following sentences. Identify each verb according to its kind: *Action Verb* or *Linking Verb.*

Writing Theme
Ultrasound

1. An ultrasound system detects objects with sound waves.
2. It is a system with many practical applications.
3. With ultrasound scanners, doctors look inside the human body.
4. An ultrasound scanner sends sound waves inside the body.
5. A computer then converts the echoes from these waves into electronic signals.
6. An image of the inside of the body appears on a computer screen.
7. The picture on the screen looks fuzzy.
8. However, these pictures are clear enough for diagnostic purposes.
9. Parents seem grateful for ultrasound scanners.
10. They give parents a view of the baby before the child's birth!

The Parts
of Speech

Auxiliary Verbs

An action verb or a linking verb sometimes has one or more **auxiliary verbs,** also called **helping verbs.** The verb that the auxiliary verb helps is the **main verb.** In the following examples, the auxiliary verbs are in italics. The main verbs are in boldface type.

> The skies *should* **brighten** by noon.
> The wind *has been* **blowing** since midnight.

The most common auxiliary verbs are forms of *be, have,* and *do,* as in the following examples.

Be	am, is, are, was, were, be, been, being
Have	have, has, had
Do	do, does, did

Other common auxiliary verbs are listed below.

can	will	shall	may	must
could	would	should	might	

Together the main verb and one or more auxiliary verbs make up a **verb phrase.**

Auxiliary Verb(s)	+	Main Verb	=	Verb Phrase
had		been		had been
have		had		have had
was		doing		was doing
could have		helped		could have helped
might have been		seen		might have been seen
is being		repaired		is being repaired

In the first three examples above, note that the auxiliary verbs *be, have,* and *do* may also be used as main verbs.

Often the auxiliary verb and the main verb are separated by one or more words that are not part of the verb phrase. In the examples that follow, note that the contraction *n't* is not considered part of the verb phrase.

> They certainly *were*n't *being* very helpful.
> We *had* just *left* for the airport.
> My parents *will* never *forget* your kindness.
> *Have* you really *been* to Saudi Arabia?
> *Would*n't rapid action *have helped* you during this disaster?
> The principal *might* not *have been teasing* you.

Practice Your Skills

A. CONCEPT CHECK

Auxiliary Verbs and Main Verbs   Read the following paragraph by author Isak Dinesen. Make two columns on a sheet of paper. Label one column *Auxiliary Verbs* and the other column *Main Verbs*. List the verbs from each sentence in the appropriate column. Some sentences may contain more than one verb phrase.

Writing Theme
Memorable Scenes

(1) The wind in the highlands blows steadily from the north-north-east. . . . (2) Up here it is felt as just the resistance of the air, as the earth throws herself forward into space. (3) The wind runs straight against the Ngong Hills, and the slopes of the hills would be the ideal place for . . . a glider, that would be lifted upwards by the currents, over the mountain top. (4) The clouds, which were traveling with the wind, struck the side of the hill and hung round it, or were caught on the summit and broke into rain. (5) But those that took a higher course and sailed clear of the reef, dissolved to the west of it, over the burning desert of the Rift Valley. (6) Many times I have from my house followed these mighty processions.

Isak Dinesen, *Out of Africa*

B. REVISION SKILL

Using Specific Verbs   Read the following first draft of a description. Rewrite the paragraph, replacing each italicized verb with a more specific verb to create a stronger impression.

(1) Across the bay is the old stone house where I often *go*. (2) It *is* on top of a hill, overlooking the rocky coast. (3) The house *has been* there, unoccupied, for many years. (4) Wooden shutters *are* over the windows. (5) Inside, the gray paint on the walls *is coming off*. (6) Even in summer the air *is* cold. (7) The rain *hits* the shingled roof with great force. (8) This evening dark clouds have *come* in from the ocean, bringing an early twilight. (9) The house looks tired and forlorn, as though it were beginning to give up its valiant effort to *stay around*. (10) Eventually, the ancient walls of this noble dwelling will *go* into the sea.

Writing
— **TIP** —

Use vivid, specific verbs to create a clear image of what you are describing.

The Parts
of Speech   **537**

Transitive and Intransitive Verbs

Action verbs can be either transitive or intransitive. A verb is **transitive** when the action of the verb is directed toward someone or something, called the **object** of the verb.

>   VERB   OBJECT
> Nerve cells *transmit* electrical *impulses* throughout the body. (The action of the verb *transmit* is directed toward the noun *impulses*.)

A verb is **intransitive** when the person or thing doing the acting does not direct its action toward someone or something. That is, a verb is intransitive if it does not have an object. Some action verbs, such as *sleep,* are always intransitive. All linking verbs are intransitive.

>   VERB
> These cells *act* as biological relay stations. (The verb *act* has no object; therefore, it is intransitive.)

>   VERB
> Nerve cells *are* fascinating and complex structures. (*Are* is a linking verb and is therefore intransitive.)

To tell whether an action verb is transitive or intransitive, consider whether the action is directed toward someone or something.

>   VERB   OBJECT
> We *studied* human *anatomy* in biology class. (The verb *studied* is transitive because the action is directed toward the object *anatomy*.)

>   VERB
> We *studied* extensively for several weeks. (The verb *studied* is intransitive; the action is not directed toward an object.)

Note that *extensively* is an adverb, not an object. Do not confuse an adverb that tells *how, when,* or *where* with an object that receives the action of the verb.

Verb or Noun?

Many words may be used as nouns or as verbs. To distinguish between nouns and verbs, decide if the word names a person, place, or thing (noun), or expresses an action or state of being (verb).

> We chipped away at the ice with a *pick*. (noun)
> *Pick* a melon that's not too ripe. (verb)

> Our club is in good *shape* financially. (noun)
> Everyone will *shape* up during spring training. (verb)

Practice Your Skills

A. CONCEPT CHECK

Transitive and Intransitive Verbs   Write the verb or verb phrase in each of the following sentences. Then identify the verb as *Transitive* or *Intransitive*.

Writing Theme
Unusual Sports

1. Have you ever seen a boomerang?
2. A boomerang may be between one and three feet in length.
3. The arms of a boomerang form a bracket, like two sides of a triangle.
4. The surface of one arm shows more curvature than the surface of the other.
5. Because of this shape, the boomerang spins in flight.
6. It will often return to the thrower.
7. Long ago, the Australian aborigines fashioned boomerangs from hard wood.
8. These native people used boomerangs as weapons for hunting and in warfare.
9. Nowadays, boomeranging has developed into a popular sport in Australia.
10. This unusual sport is spreading to other countries as well, such as the United States.

B. APPLICATION IN LITERATURE

Transitive and Intransitive Verbs   Read the following paragraph by a professional writer. Write each verb and verb phrase from the paragraph and identify each verb as *Transitive* or *Intransitive*. Some sentences will have more than one verb or verb phrase. Notice that transitive verbs direct their action toward an object while intransitive verbs can help a writer describe the subject or explain *when, where,* or *how* an action is taking place.

> (1) The ball in jai-alai is harder and heavier than a golf ball and may travel at better than 150 miles per hour. (2) This makes movement of the jai-alai ball the fastest in any sport. . . . (3) The singles game, which is played between two men, follows these lines: The server must bounce the ball once on the floor at the service line. (4) Then he scoops up the ball as it bounces and throws it to the front wall. (5) The ball must return from the wall and land in "fair" territory. (6) Then the opponent must in one motion catch and return the ball to the wall in the wall's "fair" portion. (7) In turn, his return must remain within the boundary of the court.
>
> **Frank G. Menke, *The Encyclopedia of Sports***

C. APPLICATION IN WRITING

Directions Choose one of your favorite sports and write a paragraph of directions for playing it. Assume that you are writing your paragraph for the benefit of an exchange student from a foreign country where this sport is unknown or unfamiliar. In your paragraph, use a variety of both transitive and intransitive verbs.

CHECK POINT

PAGES 524–538

PAGES 524–538

CHECK POINT

A. Write the italicized nouns in the following sentences. Identify each noun as *Concrete, Abstract, Common, Proper, Compound,* or *Collective.* Each noun will fit two or three categories.

> **Example** My *sister-in-law* read a book about theater of the *Orient.*
> sister-in-law—Concrete, Common, Compound
> Orient—Concrete, Proper

1. In *Japan,* attending *plays* is a popular form of *recreation.*
2. Large *audiences* gather to witness *performances* of traditional dramas.
3. One popular *type* of drama is the *no.*
4. These plays developed in the fourteenth *century* from *dances* performed at religious *shrines.*
5. Influenced by the religious *beliefs* of *Buddhism,* these plays were serious treatments of history, legend, and *folk tales.*
6. In these historical dramas, *groups* of actors used *masks* and carefully controlled *movements.*
7. The *Japanese* also crowd into *playhouses* to see kabuki plays.
8. Kabuki plays feature melodramatic plot *concepts* and colorfully stylish *costumes.*
9. These plays borrow theatrical *techniques* from Japanese puppet *shows.*
10. Japanese *theatergoers* of all ages especially admire the spectacular stage *scenery* in these plays.

B. Write the pronouns in these sentences. Identify each pronoun according to its kind: *Personal, Reflexive, Intensive, Demonstrative, Indefinite, Interrogative,* or *Relative.* Some sentences will contain more than one pronoun.

1. Among the crafts of Japan, one of the most beautiful is the popular hobby known as origami.
2. This is a craft that involves folding paper into decorative objects.

3. What are some of the objects made by people who practice origami?
4. They make representations of people, animals, and plants.
5. If you want to create an origami figure, use a piece of paper about ten inches square.
6. Practitioners observe the traditional rules of origami, which forbid cutting or gluing the paper.
7. Most of the figures are made from thin Japanese paper called *washi;* some, however, are made from foil-backed wrapping paper.
8. Origami, like paper itself, probably originated in China.
9. Japanese children, who enjoy art, enjoy this as a pastime.
10. Today, in addition, many of the adults in Japan amuse themselves by creating beautiful origami decorations.

C. Write the verbs and verb phrases in the following sentences. For verb phrases, underline the auxiliary verb once and the main verb twice. Identify each verb as an *Action Verb* or a *Linking Verb* and as a *Transitive Verb* or an *Intransitive Verb*.

1. The traditional sport of kendo has become very popular in Japan.
2. Both men and women may compete in kendo.
3. In a kendo contest, each player uses a bamboo sword, or *shinai.*
4. This weapon can be dangerous.
5. Pads should protect the waist and chest of each player.
6. The costume for kendo also includes a short jacket and a floor-length garment, or *hakama.*
7. Players score points for hits to the body of their opponent.
8. The first player with two points wins.
9. Matches seldom are longer than five minutes.
10. Kendo contests remain a favorite form of recreation in Japan.

ADJECTIVES

Words that change or limit the meanings of other words are called **modifiers.** One kind of modifier is the **adjective.**

An adjective is a word that modifies a noun or a pronoun.

An adjective answers one of the following questions: *Which one? What kind? How many? How much?*

Which One	this, that, these, those
What Kind	huge, new, green, courageous
How Many	few, several, both, ten, most
How Much	more, less, sufficient, plentiful

Position of Adjectives

Adjectives usually appear before the nouns or pronouns that they modify.

Irate passengers have complained about the *dark* windows on the *new* buses.

Sometimes, for variety, a writer will put adjectives in other positions. Compare the following sentences.

The skier, *swift* and *powerful,* outdistanced his rivals.

Swift and *powerful,* the skier outdistanced his rivals.

Articles

The most common adjectives are the articles *a, an,* and *the.* The word *the* is called a **definite article** because it usually refers to a specific person, place, or thing. The words *a* and *an* are called **indefinite articles** because they refer to one of a general group of people, places, things, or ideas.

Use *a* before a word beginning with a consonant sound: *a check, a history paper.* Use *an* before a word beginning with a vowel sound: *an envelope, an hour.*

Proper Adjectives

A **proper adjective** is formed from a proper noun and is always capitalized.

Proper Noun	Proper Adjective
Spain	Spanish
Canada	Canadian
Shakespeare	Shakespearean
Jackson	Jacksonian

Predicate Adjectives

An adjective that follows a linking verb and modifies the subject of the sentence is called a **predicate adjective.** Unlike most adjectives, predicate adjectives are separated from the words they modify.

Some movies seem *endless.*

The pages of the diary were *yellowed* and *brittle.*

Other Parts of Speech as Adjectives

Nouns, pronouns, and certain verb forms sometimes function as adjectives. To understand the function of a word, decide how it is used in a sentence. If a word tells *what kind, which one, how much,* or *how many* about a noun or pronoun, it is functioning as an adjective. The nouns, pronouns, and verb forms below are functioning as adjectives.

Nouns	The Hawaiian dancers wore *grass* skirts.
	Dorothy walked down a yellow *brick* road.
Pronouns	*This* ticket will admit you to the football game. (demonstrative pronoun)
	Marty played *her* new tape at least ten times. (possessive pronoun)
	Many students went on the field trip. (indefinite pronoun)
	We didn't know *which* road to follow. (interrogative pronoun)
Verb Forms	Ellie straightened up her *cluttered* room.
	Rod stirred the soup mix into some *boiling* water.

Practice Your Skills

A. CONCEPT CHECK

Adjectives   Write the words used as adjectives in the following sentences. Do not include articles.

Writing Theme
Bees and Honey

1. Honey has been a valuable substance since earliest times.
2. Most foods that early people ate were tough and bland; honey, in contrast, was smooth, sweet, thick, and delicious.
3. Early people began to gather raw honey when they discovered nests of wild bees.
4. The ancient lore about bees included many superstitions.
5. One myth was that loud noises attract bees, but actually bees have a very poor sense of hearing.
6. A Hittite law of about 300 B.C. established the value of honey.
7. A tub of honey in those days was as valuable as a tub of butter or one sheep.
8. The ancient Chinese and the medieval Europeans were among those who used honey for medicinal purposes, for instance, to cure severe burns and minor cuts.
9. Honey has been eaten for quick energy since the days of the original Greek Olympic games.
10. There are still many people who eat honey for energy, including marathon runners and Arctic explorers.

B. REVISION SKILL

Eliminating Unnecessary Words   Revise the following paragraph by adding a single adjective from the numbered, italicized sentence to the sentence that precedes it.

Example	*Unrevised*	Honeybees live in hives that display a degree of social organization. (1) *This degree of organization is elaborate.*
	Revised	Honeybees live in hives that display an *elaborate* degree of social organization.

Animals have developed many methods of communication. (1) *These methods are marvelous.* For example, scientists have shown that honeybees communicate through a "dance." (2) *The dance is complex.* Scout bees dance on the hive to convey information about the direction and distance of a food source. (3) *This information is precise.* When nectar can be found nearer than about ten yards away, the scouts perform in a pattern. (4) *The pattern they use in this case is circular.* For distances, the scouts use a figure-eight pattern in their dance. (5) *This pattern signals longer distances.* Within the hive, other bees use their antennae to receive signals from the scouts about the direction of the nectar. (6) *The bees possess sensitive antennae.*

C. APPLICATION IN WRITING

Field Notes Naturalists often go out into the wild and observe animals to learn about their behavior. The written observations that naturalists make are called "field notes." Choose an animal that interests you. Then go to a place where you can observe this animal carefully for half an hour. Write down what you observe. Then, based on your field notes, write a descriptive paragraph about the animal's behavior. Use adjectives to describe the animal and its behavior clearly and vividly.

ADVERBS

Another kind of modifier is the **adverb.**

An adverb is a word that modifies a verb, an adjective, or another adverb.

Modifying a Verb	The ship sailed *slowly* out of the harbor.
Modifying an Adjective	We all had a *rather* hectic day of sightseeing in San Francisco.
Modifying an Adverb	The traffic moved *very* quickly.

Adverbs answer the questions *Where? When? How?* or *To what extent?*

Where	We moved the table *outside*.
When	The picnic begins *later*.
How	The storm came *unexpectedly*.
To What Extent	Everyone got *very* wet.

Grammar Note Adverbs that modify adjectives or other adverbs by adding emphasis are called *intensifiers*. These include *too, very, extremely, truly,* and *really.*

Forms of Adverbs

Many adverbs are formed by adding *-ly* to an adjective: *correct, correctly; rapid, rapidly; prompt, promptly; easy, easily.* Some modifiers that end in *-ly,* however, are adjectives: *friendly* dog, *lonely* soldier, *ugly* bruise.

Avoid the overuse of intensifiers. Too many *very*'s and *really*'s can weaken your writing.

The Parts
of Speech

Some common adverbs do not end in *-ly*. These adverbs include the negatives *no, not,* and *never,* and time words such as *soon, later,* and *often*.

Position of Adverbs

An adverb usually follows the verb it modifies.

Their bus arrives *there tomorrow.*

Sometimes, however, an adverb comes before the verb.

Frequently, the bus leaves on time.

The bus *frequently* leaves on time.

Intensifiers or other adverbs that modify adjectives or other adverbs usually come directly before the word they modify.

Ours is a *very* common name.

We worked *extremely* hard on his campaign.

Nouns as Adverbs

Several words that are generally thought of as nouns can also function as adverbs. These adverbs tell *where* and *when*. Look at the following examples.

Noun	Adverb
My *home* is in Tulsa.	She went *home* early. (where)
Tomorrow will be sunny.	I'll study *tomorrow*. (when)
I love the *outdoors*.	We hiked *outdoors*. (where)

Adjective or Adverb?

Words like *fast* and *early* have the same form when used as adjectives or as adverbs. To tell whether a word is an adjective or an adverb, determine which word it modifies. If the word modifies a noun or a pronoun, it is an adjective. If it modifies a verb, an adjective, or another adverb, it is an adverb.

Adjective   My grandmother has always been an *early* riser. (The adjective *early* modifies the noun *riser* and tells *what kind.*)

Adverb   My grandmother rises *early*. (The adverb *early* modifies the verb *rises* and tells *when.*)

Grammar Note Many adverbs are combined with verbs to make idioms. An *idiom* is a group of words whose meaning is different from the literal meanings of the individual words. Some idiomatic verb phrases are *break down, bottle up, check out, fill in, grow up, set up,* and *strike out.*

Practice Your Skills

A. CONCEPT CHECK

Adverbs Read the following selection by a famous Scottish writer. Then find at least fifteen adverbs in the selection and write them on your paper. Analyze the sentence and tell which question each adverb answers: *Where? How? When?* or *To What Extent?* As you read the passage, notice how the adverbs add specific details that make the story vivid.

> (1) "Nicholas, Nicholas!" she screamed, "you are to come out of this at once. (2) It's no use trying to hide there; I can see you all the time."
> (3) Presently the angry repetitions of Nicholas's name gave way to a shriek, and a cry for somebody to come quickly.
> (4) Nicholas shut the book, restored it carefully to its place in a corner, and shook some dust from a neighboring pile of newspapers over it. (5) Then he crept from the room, locked the door, and replaced the key exactly where he had found it.
> (6) His aunt was still calling his name when he sauntered into the front garden.
> (7) "Who's calling?" he asked.
> (8) "Me," came the answer from the other side of the wall. (9) "Didn't you hear me? (10) I've been looking for you in the gooseberry garden, and I've slipped into the rain-water tank. (11) Luckily there's no water in it, but the sides are slippery and I can't get out. (12) Fetch the little ladder from under the cherry tree—"
> (13) "I was told I wasn't to go into the gooseberry garden," said Nicholas promptly.
> (14) "I told you not to, and now I tell you that you may," came the voice from the rain-water tank rather impatiently.
> (15) "Your voice doesn't sound like aunt's," objected Nicholas. (16) "You may be the Evil One tempting me to be disobedient. (17) Aunt often tells me that the Evil One tempts me and that I always yield. (18) This time I'm not going to yield."
>
> **H. H. Munro (Saki),** ***The Lumber Room***

B. REVISION SKILL

Eliminating Unnecessary Adverbs   A word is redundant if it unnecessarily repeats an idea. In the sentence "He shouted loudly," for example, the adverb *loudly* is redundant because the verb *shouted* already communicates the idea of loudness. Read the following paragraph and identify the adverbs. Then make a list of all the adverbs that are redundant.

(1) Everyone in our family was laughing happily on the first day of vacation. (2) We were absolutely convinced that the car trip to Yellowstone would be really enjoyable. (3) However, fifty miles from our destination, I saw my father's face glower angrily in the rearview mirror. (4) He was staring silently at the gas gauge on the dashboard. (5) Then he turned his head quickly and sharply toward my mother, asking her if she had remembered to fill up the tank completely. (6) "Oh," she replied slowly, "that gas gauge has been broken for months. (7) When it's on empty, it means full—and vice versa!" (8) Immediately, we knew that this vacation was going to be a unique experience. (9) If *full* meant "empty" and *empty* meant "full," then the entire vacation would probably run in some kind of reverse order. (10) As soon as we all softly hummed the theme song from *The Twilight Zone,* my father guffawed loudly, and we instinctively relaxed, knowing that his good humor had been restored again.

C. APPLICATION IN WRITING

A Narrative   Write a short narrative about a conflict. In your narrative, use adverbs to describe how the people involved are acting or speaking. You may choose from the lists below of possible conflicts and adverbs, or you may invent your own subject and think up appropriate adverbs for your narrative. Avoid unnecessary adverbs.

Conflicts

a dispute about a call by a referee or umpire
a debate between two candidates for office
a scene at a fence dividing two neighbors' property
an effort to return a purchase at a store
a conversation between an employer and an employee

Adverbs

extremely	loudly	fast	tomorrow
simply	hastily	sensibly	unreasonably
fairly	frequently	there	angrily
thoughtlessly	harshly	critically	gently

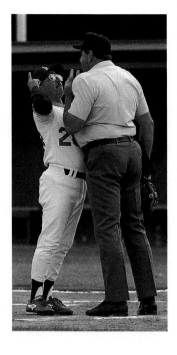

CHECK POINT
PAGES 541–547

A. Write the modifiers in the following sentences and identify the function of each as an *Adjective* or *Adverb*. Then write the word or words that each one modifies. Do not include articles.

1. The city of Bombay has long been recognized as the economic center of India.
2. Diverse and industrious, the people of Bombay are extremely proud of their city's vitality.
3. Bombay has recently become famous as the Hollywood of India.
4. The Indian film industry is the largest in the world.
5. Even more surprisingly, the industry flourishes in a multilingual country with a long history of hardship.
6. Each year, films are made in more Indian languages than you can imagine.
7. Bombay filmmakers frequently use several sets of subtitles for one film.
8. Directors ingeniously match a single film to different soundtracks.
9. Indian films have played a very important role in reviving ancient, mythological traditions.
10. The films are so popular that stars regularly enjoy celebrity status.

B. Find at least six adverbs and six adjectives in the following paragraph and write them on your paper. Do not include articles. Identify the function of each modifier as an adverb or adjective and tell what word it modifies. Notice how a careful choice of modifiers can create a strong, clear description. Remember that some words can function as more than one part of speech.

> (1) After that, he searched the streets for a replacement for the first cat in his life. (2) They were not so easy to find. (3) Even if they were everywhere, especially in the vicinity of the cafes and restaurants where he had his meals and cups of tea, they were by no means inclined to respond to his polite blandishments and enticing calls; they glared at him suspiciously and sprang aside if he came too near. (4) He was abashed to find he was less attractive to them than a life in the harsh streets, but told himself they could not possibly know what comfort, what care waited for them in his little room.
>
> **Anita Desai, *Baumgartner's Bombay***

Bombay is the largest city in India; overcrowding has been one of its most serious problems for years.

The Parts of Speech   **549**

A preposition is a word used to show the relationship between a noun or a pronoun and another word in the sentence.

> Several *of* America's best poets have come *from* New England.
> (The preposition *of* relates the pronoun *Several* to the noun
> *poets;* the preposition *from* relates the verb *have come* to
> the noun *New England.*)

Prepositions often express relationships of location (*by, near*), direction (*to, down*), and association (*of, with*). Look for prepositions that express these relationships in the following list.

Commonly Used Prepositions

about	before	down	of	throughout
above	behind	during	off	to
across	below	except	on	toward
after	beneath	for	onto	under
against	beside	from	out	underneath
along	between	in	outside	until
among	beyond	inside	over	up
around	but	into	past	upon
as	by	like	since	with
at	despite	near	through	within

Usage Note The words *but* and *as* are usually conjunctions. However, *but* is used as a preposition when it means "except." *As* functions as a preposition when it means "in the capacity of."

A **compound preposition** is formed by combining words.

Commonly Used Compound Prepositions

according to	by means of	in place of	on account of
aside from	in addition to	in spite of	out of
because of	in front of	instead of	prior to

Objects of Prepositions

A preposition never appears alone. It is followed by a word or a group of words called the **object of the preposition.**

> The box fell behind the *refrigerator*. (The word *refrigerator* is the object of the preposition *behind*.)
>
> Before *baking a cake,* you should read the recipe carefully. (The group of words *baking a cake* is the object of the preposition *before*.)

A preposition and its object, plus any modifiers, form a **prepositional phrase.**

into the house	because of the icy roads
among her papers	on the northeast corner
near the train tracks	in the year 2000

A preposition may have a **compound object,** that is, more than one object.

> I wrote a letter to my *sister* and her two *children.*
>
> We walked home in spite of the blustery *wind,* the driving *rain,* and the dark *sky.*

Adverb or Preposition?

A number of words may be used either as prepositions or as adverbs. One simple test may help you to tell the difference. A preposition is never used alone. It is always followed by a noun or a pronoun as part of a phrase. If the word is in a phrase, it is probably a preposition. If the word is not followed by an object, it is probably an adverb.

> Sue put on her coat and went *out*. (*Out* is an adverb. It has no object.)
>
> Sue put on her coat and went *out* the door. (*Out* is a preposition. It has an object, *door.*)

> The sundial had been knocked *down*. (adverb)
> The cart rolled *down* the hill. (preposition)

> Will you all please stand *up?* (adverb)
> The mountaineers struggled *up* Pikes Peak. (preposition)

> Our new neighbor dropped *by*. (adverb)
> The students responded *by* raising their hands. (preposition)

For more information on prepositional phrases, see Handbook 32, "Using Phrases and Clauses," pages 586–588.

Practice Your Skills

A. CONCEPT CHECK

Prepositions and Their Objects   Write the prepositions in the following sentences. After each preposition, write its object.

1. Prior to 1689 Russia was a society controlled by nobles.
2. There was little contact with Western Europe.
3. A major problem was the lack of seaports.
4. During this time, Sweden blocked passage to the Atlantic Ocean in the west, while the Ottoman Empire (Turkey) controlled the waterways in the south.
5. When Peter the Great came to power in 1689, he began plans for the introduction of Western culture throughout Russia, the capture of neighboring ports, and the creation of a navy.
6. Peter made extensive trips to Europe, where he observed, studied, and even worked as a carpenter for a shipbuilder.
7. When he returned to Russia, he brought a number of European scientists and craftspeople with him. He also brought European ideas of dress, politics, education, and military training, which he forced upon his subjects.
8. Many of Peter's Western ideas were not popular among the nobility, but this did not stop him.
9. In 1721, four years before his death, Peter captured some Baltic seaports from Sweden and established the Russian navy.
10. Peter also built a new capital called St. Petersburg near the Baltic. He called the town his "window to the world."

B. REVISION SKILL

Sentence Expanding   Read the following biographical paragraph. Then use the list of facts on the following page to revise the paragraph. Revise the paragraph by adding prepositional phrases that answer the questions given in parentheses.

> Mikhail Gorbachev, the Soviet leader, was born (When?) (Where?). When he was a teenager, he worked during the summer (In what capacity?). Gorbachev was educated (Where?). He graduated (When?), having earned a degree in law. After his marriage to a fellow student, Raisa Maksimovna, his rise in Soviet politics was swift: he became a member of the Central Committee (When?), and in 1979 he was elected (What group did he join?). When General Secretary Konstantin Chernenko succumbed to illness in 1985, Gorbachev became the youngest leader (Where?) since Stalin succeeded Lenin in 1924. He rapidly moved to build broad support (What policies?).

Facts About Mikhail Gorbachev

Place of birth: village of Privolnoye in Stavropol province
Date of birth: March 2, 1931
Summer job as a teenager: combine harvester operator
Education: Moscow State University; graduated 1955
Posts held: member of Central Committee (1971), member of
    Politburo (1979), general secretary of Communist Party in
    Soviet Union (1985)
Best-known policies: *glasnost* (openness) and *perestroika*
    (restructuring)

CONJUNCTIONS

Prepositions show relationships between words. Conjunctions connect words or groups of words.

A conjunction is a word that connects words or groups of words.

There are three kinds of conjunctions: coordinating conjunctions, correlative conjunctions, and subordinating conjunctions.

Coordinating Conjunctions

A **coordinating conjunction** is used to connect words or groups of words that have the same function in a sentence.

To keep ideas
clear, use a
comma before a
coordinating con-
junction that con-
nects clauses.

Coordinating Conjunctions						
and	but	or	nor	for	yet	so

Coordinating conjunctions can connect the following:

Nouns	**Rain** *and* **fog** made travel impossible.
Pronouns	This package is for **you** *and* **me.**
Verbs	We **bathed** *and* **groomed** the dog.
Adjectives	Our principal is **strict** *yet* **fair.**
Adverbs	They worked **slowly** *but* **accurately.**
Prepositions	Are you **with** *or* **against** us?

A coordinating conjunction can also connect phrases or independent clauses. Clauses are groups of words containing both a subject and a verb. For a discussion of clauses, see Handbook 32.

Phrases	The fog crept <u>over the water</u> *and* <u>toward the city</u>.
Clauses	<u>They acted human</u>, *yet* <u>their feet were definitely webbed</u>.

The conjunctions *for* and *so* always connect clauses.

<u>We know spring is coming</u>, *for* <u>the river is beginning to thaw</u>.
<u>We needed extra chairs</u>, *so* <u>we borrowed some from Ian</u>.

Nor is used as a coordinating conjunction only when it is preceded by such negative words as *no* or *not*.

The team has *no* coach, *nor* does it have a catcher.

Correlative Conjunctions

Correlative conjunctions are similar to coordinating conjunctions. However, correlative conjunctions are always used in pairs.

Correlative Conjunctions		
both . . . and	neither . . . nor	whether . . . or
either . . . or	not only . . . but (also)	

Both my grandfather *and* my aunt are physicians.
The peaches are *neither* in the refrigerator *nor* on the table.
The lettuce is *not only* wilted *but also* moldy.

Subordinating Conjunctions

A **subordinating conjunction** introduces subordinate clauses—clauses that cannot stand by themselves as complete sentences. A subordinating conjunction joins a subordinate clause to an independent clause—a clause that stands by itself as a complete sentence.

INDEPENDENT ⌐⌐ SUBORDINATE ⌐
A crowd gathers *whenever* there is an accident.
(The subordinating conjunction *whenever* connects the subordinate clause to the independent clause.)

Subordinating conjunctions show relationships including those of time, manner, place, reason, comparison, condition, or purpose.

Subordinating Conjunctions	
Time	after, as, as long as, as soon as, before, since, until, when, whenever, while
Manner	as, as if
Place	where, wherever
Cause or Reason	because, since
Comparison	as, as much as, than
Condition	although, as long as, even if, even though, if, provided that, though, unless, while
Purpose	in order that, so that, that

Conjunctive Adverbs

A **conjunctive adverb** is an adverb that is used to connect clauses that can stand by themselves as sentences.

We were not convinced that this was the correct address; *nevertheless,* we rang the doorbell.

A conjunctive adverb may also be used parenthetically within a sentence.

Michelangelo, *however,* is known as both a sculptor and a painter.

The words most often used as conjunctive adverbs are listed in the chart on the following page.

The Parts
of Speech

Writing Theme
Animals and the Seasons

Conjunctive Adverbs

accordingly	furthermore	nevertheless
also	hence	otherwise
besides	however	still
consequently	indeed	then
finally	moreover	therefore

Practice Your Skills

A. CONCEPT CHECK

Types of Conjunctions Write the conjunctions in the following sentences. Then identify each conjunction according to its kind: *Coordinating Conjunction, Correlative Conjunction, Subordinating Conjunction,* or *Conjunctive Adverb.*

1. Although people often refer to hibernating bears, these animals are not true hibernators.
2. A bear's body temperature rarely falls below 86 degrees Fahrenheit in winter, so it is easily awakened.
3. True hibernators include ground squirrels and hedgehogs.
4. Both hamsters and woodchucks hibernate periodically.
5. These animals enter a deathlike state for five or six months.
6. Also, their body temperature can drop to 34 degrees Fahrenheit.
7. Neither this low temperature nor the animals' slow pulse rate would seem possible.
8. Furthermore, scientists still do not fully understand the causes of hibernation in these small mammals.
9. If ground squirrels are kept indoors at a constant warm temperature, they still lose weight once a year.
10. Accordingly, scientists have inferred the presence of some sort of internal body clock in these squirrels.
11. In addition, scientists have found evidence of "trigger" and "anti-trigger" substances in the bloodstream of hibernators.
12. When squirrels were given a "trigger" substance from woodchucks, the squirrels hibernated.
13. Whether hibernators are asleep or periodically awake, some of their behavior remains puzzling.
14. A hibernating squirrel breathes only once every several minutes; however, its system does not seem to lack oxygen.
15. The puzzles of animal hibernation are fascinating but still largely unsolved.

B. REVISION SKILL

Combining Sentences Write each pair of sentences as one sentence by using the kind of conjunction indicated in parentheses. Delete words as necessary. Use commas and semicolons correctly.

1. Monarch butterflies cover vast distances. They make their annual migrations. (subordinating)
2. In late summer the monarchs leave the eastern United States. They also head south from Canada. (coordinating)
3. Responses to daylight affect the timing of the migration. Magnetic material in the butterflies' bodies may serve as an internal compass. (conjunctive adverb)
4. The route must be unfamiliar to them. The monarchs are less than two months old. (subordinating)
5. The monarchs have never seen their destination. Every year they arrive at one of a handful of sites in central Mexico. (conjunctive adverb)
6. The dense forest cover shelters the monarchs from danger. It also insulates them from cold weather. (correlative)
7. The scientist Fred Urquhart first discovered some of these sites in 1975. The butterflies were wintering. (subordinating)
8. Millions of monarchs clustered in these small areas. Tree branches were bent with the extra weight. (conjunctive adverb)
9. The sites are astounding spectacles of nature. They must be protected for the preservation of these colorful, delicate butterflies. (coordinating)
10. The monarchs are among the most beautiful creatures in the animal world. They are also among the most mysterious of living things. (correlative)

INTERJECTIONS

An interjection is a word or a group of words that expresses feeling or emotion.

An interjection may precede a sentence or appear within a sentence. A strong interjection that precedes a sentence is followed by an exclamation point. A mild interjection or an interjection within a sentence is set off by commas or a comma.

> *Good grief!* Are those your new sneakers?
> His new sneakers, *alas,* were ruined.
> *Well,* what are we going to do now?

Practice Your Skills
CONCEPT CHECK

Interjections   If a sentence contains an interjection, write that interjection on your paper. If it does not, write *None.*

1. "Wow! Isn't it exciting to be here in Paris?"
2. "Yes! Seeing the city from a boat on the river Seine is terrific."
3. "Hey, what's that building over there?"
4. "I think that is the Louvre museum."
5. "Isn't that where they keep the *Mona Lisa,* the famous painting by Leonardo da Vinci?"
6. "Oh, no! I left the guidebook back at the hotel."
7. "Still, maybe we can visit the Louvre after our boat ride."
8. "My goodness, there's Notre Dame cathedral in the distance."
9. "Look! The cathedral looks as if it's on an island."
10. "That island is the oldest part of the glorious city of Paris."

C H E C K   P O I N T
PAGES 550–557

A. Write and identify the adverbs and prepositions in the following sentences. After each adverb, write the word or words it modifies. After each preposition, write its object.

1. Zoos were first established during ancient times.
2. Queen Hatshepsut of Egypt established a zoo around 1500 B.C.
3. When the Spaniards arrived on Mexican shores in 1519, they discovered a very large zoo built by Aztec Indians.
4. Nowadays zoos around the world serve many quite useful purposes.
5. Zoos make people more fully aware of nature's diversity.
6. At zoos visitors see creatures they might never see.
7. In addition, zoos function as wildlife conservation centers.
8. Curators and zoologists systematically collect facts about animals.
9. Within zoos, zoologists often breed endangered species.
10. Two of these species, the European bison and the Hawaiian goose, have recently been saved from extinction and returned to the wild.

B. Write the conjunctions in the following sentences. Identify each conjunction: *Coordinating Conjunction, Correlative Conjunction, Subordinating Conjunction,* or *Conjunctive Adverb.*

1. Zoologists study the behavior and environments of animals.
2. These scientists work both in laboratories and in the field.
3. One world-famous zoologist, George Schaller, came to America from Germany when he was a teenager.

4. The common yet intriguing lizards he caught in the backwoods of Missouri stimulated his interest in animals.
5. After he attended college in Alaska, Schaller carried out fieldwork on the birds of the Colville River.
6. In the early 1960's, Schaller pioneered studies of the mountain gorillas of Africa; then he traveled to India to study tigers.
7. Many observers would have been frightened by these animals, but Schaller always studied them unarmed.
8. Schaller published many studies of endangered species; consequently, he helped focus public attention on wildlife conservation.
9. In 1980, Schaller not only visited China but also became the first Westerner in half a century to view Chinese giant pandas in their native habitat.
10. Because he has contributed so much to our understanding of the animal kingdom, George Schaller has become one of America's most respected zoologists.

C. Identify the part of speech of each italicized word in the sentences below. Then, write a new sentence using the word as indicated in parentheses.

1. The *wildlife* of East Africa is spectacular for beauty and variety. (adjective)
2. Many animal species, however, are *fast* disappearing. (adjective)
3. *Which* animals may not survive? (pronoun)
4. The rhinoceros and the elephant might disappear in the *next* century. (adverb)
5. *In* Kenya and Tanzania, both species are protected. (adverb)
6. A system of national *parks* exists in both of these African countries. (verb)
7. *One* park, the Serengeti in Tanzania, is the size of the state of Connecticut. (pronoun)
8. *This* makes it extremely difficult for officials who must patrol the grounds. (adjective)
9. Rangers *use* aircraft to prevent poaching. (noun)
10. Poachers, however, pursue elephants because of the *value* of their tusks. (verb)
11. *Elephant* tusks are valuable for their ivory. (noun)
12. It is *well* known that poachers kill hundreds of elephants every year. (interjection)
13. *What* is the best solution to this problem? (adjective)
14. Many countries have recently declared a *ban* on ivory imports. (verb)
15. Only if this plan succeeds will the African elephant survive *beyond* the year 2000. (adverb)

The Parts
of Speech   **559**

GRAMMAR
H A N D B O O K
30

Writing Theme
Wonders of the Sky

A. Understanding How Words Are Used Tell whether each italicized word is used as a *Noun, Pronoun, Verb, Adjective, Adverb, Preposition, Conjunction,* or *Interjection.*

1. In *ancient* times, people believed that lightning was a deadly weapon *of* the gods.
2. *Science* proved that lightning is *really* a flow of electricity.
3. *This* flow *occurs* between clouds high above the earth.
4. Clouds *actually* consist of huge numbers of tiny water *droplets.*
5. *Each* of these droplets is *electrically* charged.
6. *If* one cloud comes near another with an opposite charge, an enormous spark *may result.*
7. Such a spark, *or* lightning flash, can happen *within* a cloud, between different clouds, or between *them* and the earth.
8. Sparks between clouds *and* the earth may be eight *miles* long.
9. A single *flash* one mile long contains *enough* electrical current to light one million light bulbs.
10. The temperature of lightning flashes is *greater* than the temperature *on* the surface of the sun.
11. According to legend, *Benjamin Franklin first* demonstrated the connection between lightning and electricity.
12. *He* attached a piece of wire to the top of a silk kite and an *iron* key to the end of the kite string.
13. During a *violent* storm, Franklin put his hand *near* the key and felt a spark travel from it to his finger.
14. *Good grief!* What a dangerous experiment *that* was!
15. *Fortunately,* Franklin was unharmed; however, he built the first lightning rod on the roof of his own house in *Philadelphia.*

B. Recognizing Parts of Speech Determine the part of speech of each italicized word in the following paragraph.

(1) A *monsoon* is a seasonal wind often accompanied *by heavy* rainfall. (2) In Japan, monsoons are *extremely* important because they bring the moisture that nourishes *the* country's rice fields. (3) *Since* the Japanese depend *heavily* on this crop for food—the word "gohan" is used in Japan for both "food" and "rice"—failure of the monsoon to appear has *often* resulted in famine. (4) In other words, the monsoon is both a giver *and* taker of life. (5) In early fall, *it* often brings *typhoons,* Pacific Ocean counterparts to Atlantic hurricanes. (6) These roaring winds *sometimes* churn up *monstrous* tidal waves that wreak havoc *along* the shorelines of the *island* kingdom. (7) Monsoons also bring tremendous amounts of rain *to* the lands that *they* move across. (8) In fact, one *Asian* city receives an average of 240 inches of rain *annually.*

C. Using Words as Different Parts of Speech   Identify the part of speech of the italicized word in each of the following sentences, according to how it is used. Then, write a new sentence using the same word as the part of speech indicated in parentheses.

1. Comets are *some* of the most spectacular wonders of the sky. (adjective)
2. The tail of a comet can be *longer* than the distance from the earth to the sun. (adverb)
3. Comets may have one or *more* tails. (adverb)
4. The head, or nucleus, of a comet probably consists of frozen gases and frozen *water.* (verb)
5. Scientists have used a dirty snowball *as* a comparison for a comet's nucleus. (conjunction)
6. Studies also indicate that comets travel in elliptical, or oval-shaped, orbits *within* the solar system. (adverb)
7. Moreover, *all* of a comet's light comes from the sun. (adjective)
8. Perhaps the *most* famous comet is named after the British astronomer Edmund Halley. (pronoun)
9. Halley correctly predicted the *return* of a great comet in 1682 after a seventy-six-year absence. (verb)
10. Just over three centuries *later,* Halley's comet reappeared on schedule in 1986. (adjective)

D. Identifying Parts of Speech   Identify the part of speech of each of the italicized words in the following sentence pairs.

1. a. The aurora borealis is more commonly known as the northern *lights.*
   b. In this phenomenon, an eerie glow *lights* up the night sky in northern latitudes.
2. a. The aurora is *one* of nature's most impressive sights.
   b. The light often appears in the shape of *one* huge arc.
3. a. You can occasionally see an aurora at *night* in regions such as northern Alaska and Labrador.
   b. The aurora sometimes appears as bright red patches in the *night* sky.
4. a. Violent eruptions of gases *inside* the sun may be related to this phenomenon.
   b. Working in laboratories, scientists have taken bell jars and have created artificial auroras *inside.*
5. a. Research into *this* phenomenon suggests a strong connection between the aurora and the earth's magnetic field.
   b. A corresponding phenomenon also occurs in the Southern Hemisphere; *this* is the aurora australis.

On the Lightside

WHAT IS AND AIN'T GRAMMATICAL

In the excerpt below, humorist Dave Barry reflects upon the importance of English grammar and speculates about its "origins."

I cannot overemphasize the importance of good grammar.

Actually, I could easily overemphasize the importance of good grammar. For example, I could say: "Bad grammar is the leading cause of a slow, painful death in North America," or "Without good grammar, the United States would have lost World War II."

The truth is that grammar is not the most important thing in the world. The Super Bowl is the most important thing in the world. But grammar is still important. For example, suppose you are being interviewed for a job as an airline pilot, and your prospective employer asks you if you have any experience, and you answer: "Well, I ain't never actually flied no actual airplanes or nothing, but I got several pilot-style hats and several friends who I like to talk about airplanes with."

If you answer this way, the prospective employer will immediately realize that you have ended your sentence with a preposition. (What you should have said, of course, is "several friends with who I like to talk about airplanes.") So you will not get the job, because airline pilots have to use good grammar when they get on the intercom and explain to the passengers that, because of high winds, the plane is going to take off several hours late and land in Pierre, South Dakota, instead of Los Angeles.

We did not always have grammar. In medieval England, people said whatever they wanted, without regard to rules, and as a result they sounded like morons. Take the poet Geoffrey Chaucer, who couldn't even spell his first name right. He wrote a large poem called *Canterbury Tales,* in which people from various professions—knight, monk, miller, reever, riveter, eeler, diver, stevedore, spinnaker, etc.—drone on and on like this:

In a somer sesun whon softe
   was the sunne
I kylled a younge birde ande I
   ate it on a bunne.

When Chaucer's poem was published, everybody read it and said: "Good grief, we need some grammar around here." So they formed a Grammar Commission, which developed the parts of speech, the main ones being nouns, verbs, predicants, conjectures, particles, proverbs, adjoiners, coordinates, and rebuttals. Then the commission made up hundreds and hundreds of grammar rules, all of which were strictly enforced.

Dave Barry

The Sentence and Its Parts

THE SENTENCE

Sentences make statements, ask questions, give commands, and show feelings. Each sentence expresses a complete idea. As you learn more about sentences, you will expand on the following definition.

A sentence is a group of words that expresses a complete thought.

When part of an idea is missing from a sentence, the group of words is a **sentence fragment.**

Sentence Fragment	The car's owner. (What about the owner?)
Sentence	The car's owner filed an accident report.
Sentence Fragment	Seemed dull. (Who or what seemed dull?)
Sentence	The movie seemed dull.

You will work more with sentence fragments in Handbook 33.

Practice Your Skills

A. CONCEPT CHECK

Sentence Fragments   Writers sometimes use sentence fragments intentionally. In a taped interview with Studs Terkel, Timuel Black shares his memories of marching to Washington, D.C., with Martin Luther King, Jr., during the civil rights struggle of the 1960's. Note how Black uses sentence fragments to capture the moment.

Study the excerpt. Write whether each numbered item is a sentence or a fragment. Why might Black have used fragments?

> (1) Twenty-four years ago. (2) Hard to believe. (3) The Monument, the reflecting pool, all those people, black, white, King's speech, so pure, so touching. (4) We thought America would be moved by this event. (5) This is going to do it.
> (6) Such a feeling of joy and relief. . . . (7) Reality hit us very quickly, didn't it? . . .
> (8) I realized we had a lot more work to do. . . .
> (9) It would not be honest to say that progress had not been made. (10) Consciousness has been raised by people like Dr. King and events like the march.
>
> **Timuel Black, *The Great Divide***

Writing Theme
Martin Luther King, Jr.

Birmingham, 1963:
Firemen turned hoses on
civil rights demonstrators

B. REVISION SKILL

Sentence Fragments   Following each number are one complete sentence and one or more sentence fragments. Correct each fragment, either by adding words or by combining it with the complete sentence. When you combine sentences, you may need to add a comma, as well as some additional words, to the word groups being joined.

1. Martin Luther King, Jr., was the leader of the American civil rights movement. Winner, in 1964, of the Nobel Peace Prize.
2. King's inspiration was Mahatma Gandhi. Who led the nonviolent protests that led to Indian independence.
3. King led a nonviolent demonstration in Birmingham in 1963. For which he was jailed.
4. In prison, King wrote a famous document. Now known as the *Letter from the Birmingham Jail.*
5. In 1963, with other civil rights leaders. King led the march on Washington.
6. Standing on the steps of the Lincoln Memorial, before thousands of people, King gave a famous address. Referred to as the "I Have a Dream" speech.
7. Because he was fighting nonviolently for justice. King frequently put himself in dangerous situations.
8. King launched a voter-registration drive. In Selma, Alabama, in 1965.
9. Assassinated in Memphis on April 4, 1968. King was mourned by millions.
10. An inspiration to all people struggling for liberty. King is remembered every year on his birthday, a national holiday.

A **declarative sentence** expresses a statement of fact, wish, intent, or feeling. It ends with a period.

> Hulda Crooks climbed Mt. Fugi at the age of ninety-one.
> Everyone wished the balloonist a successful flight.

An **interrogative sentence** asks a question. It always ends with a question mark.

> Why do so many people wear contact lenses?
> Will the Olympic pool be finished on time?

An **imperative sentence** gives a command, request, or direction. It usually ends with a period. If the command or request is strong, an imperative sentence may end with an exclamation point.

> You return that book as soon as possible.
> Follow that car. *or* Follow that car!

An **exclamatory sentence** expresses strong feeling. It always ends with an exclamation point.

> What a great time we had! I won first prize!

Punctuation Note When an exclamatory sentence is preceded by a separate exclamation, either a period or an exclamation mark can be used at the end of the sentence.

> Oh, no! I lost my wallet. *or* Oh, no! I lost it again!

Practice Your Skills

A. CONCEPT CHECK

Types of Sentences The following passage by Iris Noble describes the hiring of the first woman reporter, Nellie Bly, by the pioneering journalist Joseph Pulitzer. The passage contains all four kinds of sentences. The author uses them to vary the dialogue and help convey the feelings of the speaker. Note that the end marks for the sentences are missing. Number your paper from 1 to 15. Identify each sentence according to its kind. Then write the appropriate end mark for each sentence. Be sure to find at least one sentence that can end with an exclamation point.

> (1) Cockerill ushered [Nellie] to the door (2) "You go home now and wait, Miss Bly (3) Leave your address at the desk downstairs as you go out"

Writing
—TIP—

Using a variety of sentence types adds interest to your writing.

Writing Theme
Journalism Yesterday
and Today

The Sentence
and Its Parts

(4) She turned to go (5) Again Joseph Pulitzer did an unprecedented thing (6) "Have you any money (7) Can you wait those few days or perhaps a week"

(8) "Oh . . . I forgot" (9) She told them the story of her lost purse (10) "I can't even pay my rent"

(11) Pulitzer fumbled in his pocket and . . . gave up (12) "Give her a voucher, John (13) Give her twenty-five dollars" (14) Then to Nellie: "This money, this is not a loan; it is an advance on your salary"

(15) She didn't walk downstairs; she floated

Iris Noble, *Nellie Bly: First Woman Reporter*

B. REVISION SKILL

Achieving Sentence Variety   The following draft deals with journalists called muckrakers. These writers have exposed dishonesty and greed among powerful public figures. The draft consists of only declarative sentences. Revise the numbered sentences to add interest through sentence variety by following the directions in parentheses. You may need to change or add words to make the revised sentences read smoothly.

Upton Sinclair, famous muckraker who wrote *The Jungle,* a novel that exposed the horrible conditions in Chicago's meat packing industry

(1) This is a report about muckrakers. (Rewrite as an opening question that engages a reader's interest.) Muckrakers were journalists of the early twentieth century that exposed corruption in politics and business. For example, they told the public about children who were forced to work long hours in inhuman factory environments. (2) The children often had to work sixteen hours a day. (Change to an exclamatory sentence.) The writings of the muckrakers helped make government and business more responsible.

(3) Some people believe that muckraking no longer exists. (Change to an interrogative sentence.) (4) You can look at any newspaper or television news program today. You will see that muckraking is alive and well. (Change sentence 4 to an imperative sentence. Combine it with the next sentence by using *and.*) Journalists today, as in the past, still believe their responsibility is to expose dishonesty and corruption. (5) Some journalists, in fact, think that no part of a politician's personal life should be kept from the public. (Change to an exclamatory sentence.) Others believe a balance should be maintained between the privacy rights of politicians and the public's right to information.

C. APPLICATION IN WRITING

The Profile A profile is a brief, informative description of a particular person's appearance, lifestyle, and accomplishments. Do some research about one of the following journalists. A librarian may be of help in finding biographical reference materials. Write a profile of the journalist. In your profile, vary the types of sentences that you use.

Edward R. Murrow	Ted Koppel	Peter Jennings
Dan Rather	Barbara Walters	Connie Chung

COMPLETE SUBJECTS
AND PREDICATES

A sentence has two parts: a complete subject and a complete predicate. The **complete subject** includes all the words that identify the person, place, thing, or idea that the sentence is about. The **complete predicate** includes all the words that tell what the subject did or what happened to the subject.

Complete Subject	**Complete Predicate**
Children	play.
The children on our block	always play in a nearby park.

Practice Your Skills

A. CONCEPT CHECK

Complete Subjects and Predicates Write the following passage. Underline the complete subject of each sentence once and the complete predicate twice.

(1) The southern edge of Africa served as home for the San people for thousands of years. (2) A hunter-gatherer society, the San coped well with the desertlike conditions of their land. (3) These desert dwellers used ostrich eggs for the storage and transportation of water. (4) The varied diet of the San included tortoise and elephant meat. (5) Large animals such as elephants and hippopotamuses were trapped in pits. (6) Smaller animals were killed with bows and arrows. (7) The San's quiet lifestyle was threatened about two centuries ago. (8) Herders and their herd animals moved into the area. (9) Europeans later hunted and killed many of the San. (10) The heirs of the survivors inhabit remote desert regions today.

The Sentence
and Its Parts **567**

B. DRAFTING SKILL

Sentence Combining   Improve the flow of ideas in the following paragraph by combining each numbered pair of sentences. You may wish to eliminate some words.

> (1) The San are often incorrectly referred to. They are often called "the Bushmen." (2) They produced paintings. The paintings were excellent and complex African paintings. (3) Some of the paintings are in Namibia. Namibia is on the southwest coast of Africa. (4) The earliest paintings are very old. They are over twenty-five thousand years old. (5) The paints were all handmade. They were made of clays, plants, egg whites, blood, and other natural materials.

CHECK POINT
PAGES 563–568

A. Write *Sentence* for each group of words below that is a complete sentence and *Fragment* for each group of words that is a fragment. Rewrite each fragment as a complete sentence, by providing the missing part. Identify the part you added as *Subject or Predicate.*

> **Example**   Dream of traveling to exotic faraway places.
> *Fragment*
> Many people dream of traveling to exotic faraway places.
> *Subject*

1. The beautiful tropical islands of Hawaii.
2. Relax on white sandy beaches.
3. Surfers look forward to riding the perfect wave.
4. Other vacationers want to attend a luau.
5. The Bahamas are visited regularly by cruise ships.
6. Are ideal for snorkling and scuba diving.
7. Like to go deep-sea fishing for marlin.
8. A growing number of tourists enjoy Iceland's glaciers.
9. Ireland, the Emerald Isle.
10. Others travel halfway around the world to New Zealand.
11. Prefer the Galapagos Islands.
12. Great lumbering turtles and strange-looking iguanas.
13. Easter Island, the home of mysterious stone statues.
14. Reputed to be the most beautiful island in the world.
15. My favorite vacation would be exploring the ruins of ancient civilizations on the isle of Crete.

Writing Theme
Exotic Islands

B. Identify each of the following sentences according to its kind: *Declarative, Imperative, Interrogative,* or *Exclamatory.* Indicate the correct end punctuation by writing *Period, Question Mark,* or *Exclamation Point.*

> **Example**   Look up Sri Lanka in the encyclopedia
>   Imperative; Period

1. Sri Lanka is an island country south of India
2. Did you know that Sri Lanka was once known as Ceylon
3. More than five-sixths of the country lies at an altitude of less than 1,000 feet
4. Rising seas threaten to submerge this tiny island
5. Something must be done to keep the waters from rushing over this land of exquisite natural beauty
6. Other problems endanger the country of Sri Lanka
7. How have people altered the forests and animal life of the island
8. Have the forests of Sri Lanka been cut down to make farmland for growing tea, rubber, and coconuts
9. As a result of poaching, the once-plentiful elephant population has fallen to a few hundred
10. The members of the Sri Lanka environmental conservatory demand that the poaching and deforestation be stopped now

SIMPLE SUBJECTS AND PREDICATES

The simple subject is the key word or words in the complete subject.

To find the subject, ask *who* or *what* before the verb.

Holly called yesterday.	**Verb**	called
	Who called?	Holly
	Subject	Holly

The simple subject does not include modifiers. In the examples below, the simple subjects are in italics.

> Every *atom* in the universe has an effect on every other atom.
> The late *Roman Jakobson* could read in twenty-five languages.

Do not confuse the simple subject with other words that appear between the subject and the predicate. In the first example above, the subject is *atom,* not *universe.*

A simple subject made of two or more key words is a **compound subject.** The parts of a compound subject are joined by a conjunction such as *and* or *or.*

> The *Nile,* the *Amazon,* and the *Mississippi* are three of the world's longest rivers.

The simple predicate, also called the *verb,* is the key word or words in the complete predicate.

The verb may be a phrase consisting of more than one word: *had seen, should have seen, was singing, had been singing.* The words making up the verb phrase may be interrupted by a modifier. Such a modifier is not part of the verb. The verbs below are in italics.

> Hair *grows* more quickly in warm climates.
> Two bears *had ransacked* the garbage during the night.
> We *will* not *be going* to the lake this summer.

A **compound verb** is made up of two or more verbs or verb phrases joined by a conjunction.

> The park ranger *found* and *destroyed* the traps.
> The flowers *were swaying* and *dancing* in the breeze.

In this text, the word *subject* will be used to refer to the simple subject of a sentence; the word *verb* will be used to refer to the simple predicate.

Sentence Diagraming For information on diagraming subjects, verbs, and their modifiers, see pages 861–868.

Practice Your Skills

A. CONCEPT CHECK

Simple and Compound Subjects and Predicates Write the simple subject and verb of each of the following sentences. Ignore any modifiers. Underline the subject once and the verb twice. Some sentences contain a compound subject or a compound verb.

> **Examples**   Many Chinese-American immigrants have become famous.
> <u>immigrants</u>   <u>have</u> <u>become</u>
> Their ambition and hard work were rewarded.
> <u>ambition</u>, <u>work</u> <u>were</u> <u>rewarded</u>

1. I. M. Pei is one of the most respected American architects.
2. He came to America from his native China at the age of eighteen.
3. The young Ieoh Ming Pei had been living in the province of Canton.
4. In the United States, he studied architecture at the Massachusetts Institute of Technology and at Harvard.
5. Today almost every book about modern architecture contains his name.
6. Pei's simple geometric buildings have drawn praise from other architects.
7. These structures of steel, granite, and glass have large interior spaces.
8. The well-known architect has designed and built many famous buildings across the country.
9. The John F. Kennedy Library in Boston, the Dallas Symphony Hall, and the east building of the National Gallery of Art in Washington, D.C., were designed by I. M. Pei.
10. These public buildings are regarded as fine examples of modern American architecture.

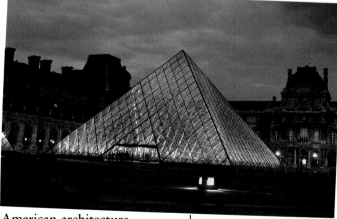

The Pyramid, adjacent to the Louvre, designed by I.M. Pei, Paris, France

B. APPLICATION IN LITERATURE

Simple and Compound Subjects and Predicates Jade Snow Wong, author of *Fifth Chinese Daughter,* is a second-generation Chinese American. Read the following passage from her book. Underline each subject once and each verb twice.

(1) Jade Snow's parents had conceded defeat. . . .
(2) [Now] Jade Snow came and went without any questions.
(3) In spite of her parents' dark predictions, her new freedom in the choice of companions did not result in a rush of undesirables. (4) As a matter of fact, the boys were more concerned with copying her lecture notes than with anything else.

(5) As for Joe, on the evening of Jade Snow's seventeenth birthday, he gave her as a remembrance a sparkling grown-up bracelet. . . . (6) There under the stars he gently tilted her face and gave her her first kiss.

(7) Straight and awkward in her full-skirted red cotton dress, Jade Snow was caught by surprise and without words.
(8) She had been kissed at seventeen . . . a cause for rejoicing.

Jade Snow Wong, *Fifth Chinese Daughter*

C. APPLICATION IN WRITING

The Biographical Report Following are notes for a brief report about the life of Jade Snow Wong. As you can see, the notes are not written as complete sentences. Incorporate the notes into one or two paragraphs. Be sure to write complete sentences. Try to make some of the subjects and verbs compounds.

born in 1922
parents from China
emigrated to San Francisco
only Chinese spoken in her home
worked in tailoring shop in San Francisco
unusual middle name
born during rare California snowfall
first college graduate in her family
chose chemistry as major
one of the first Chinese-American women to become a published author

primarily interested in pottery and ceramics
autobiography, *Fifth Chinese Daughter,* published in 1950
admits her experiences may not be typical
wrote about struggle between Chinese ways and American customs
written in third person because of Chinese habit
second book, *No Chinese Stranger,* published in 1975, a continuation of her life story

In most of the sentences that you read or write, the subject appears before the verb. In some types of sentences, however, this order is not followed.

Subjects in Inverted Sentences

Inverted sentences are those in which a verb or part of a verb phrase is positioned before the subject. Following are the three most common types of inverted sentences.

Questions In most questions, the subject appears between the words that make up the verb phrase. In the examples below, the subject is underlined once and the verb twice.

> Have you called yet?
>
> Are your neighbors moving to Detroit?
>
> Where should we put these boxes?

In most questions beginning with the interrogative words *where, when, why, how,* or *how much,* the subject falls between the parts of the verb. In questions beginning with an interrogative adjective or pronoun, the verb may follow the subject in normal order. Notice how the interrogative words *who* and *what* can function as subjects.

> Which picture fell off the wall?
>
> Who shouted?
>
> What happened?

Writing
— TIP —

You can achieve sentence variety by occasionally inverting the position of the subject.

The Sentence
and Its Parts   **573**

Sentences Beginning with *There* and *Here* When a sentence begins with *there* or *here,* the subject usually follows the verb. Remember that *there* and *here* are never the subjects of a sentence.

> There <u>are</u> my red <u>sneakers</u>.
> Here <u>is</u> your <u>passport</u>.

In the examples above, *there* and *here* are adverbs. They modify the verb and tell *where.* To find the subject, reword the sentence.

> My red <u>sneakers</u> <u>are</u> there. (*Sneakers* is the subject.)
> Your <u>passport</u> <u>is</u> here. (*Passport* is the subject.)

Sometimes, however, *there* is used as an **expletive,** a word that merely helps to get a sentence started. If you can rearrange the sentence and drop the word *there,* you can assume it is an expletive.

> There is Ms. Dobkin's office.
> Ms. Dobkin's <u>office</u> <u>is</u> there. (*There* is an adverb.)
> There were several people in line.
> Several <u>people</u> <u>were</u> in line. (*There* is an expletive.)

Occasionally, a sentence beginning with the adverb *there* or *here* will follow regular subject-verb order.

> Here <u>she</u> <u>comes</u>.
> There <u>he</u> <u>is</u>.

Sentences Inverted for Emphasis For emphasis or variety a speaker or writer may intentionally place the verb before the subject. This technique focuses extra attention on the subject. When used sparingly, this type of sentence adds drama. When it is overused, the result can sound artificial.

Normal Order	A <u>wall</u> of flood water <u>burst</u> through the door.
Inverted Order	Through the door <u>burst</u> a <u>wall</u> of flood water.
Normal Order	An abandoned <u>cottage</u> <u>was</u> at the end of the path.
Inverted Order	At the end of the path <u>was</u> an abandoned <u>cottage</u>.

Finding Subjects in Inverted Sentences One way to find the subject in an inverted sentence is to find the verb first. Then ask *who* or *what* before the verb.

> From the distance came the howl of a timber wolf. (The verb is *came.* What came? Howl came. The subject is *howl.*)

Another way to find the subject is to reorder the sentence. Putting the words in a different order often makes the subject easier to identify.

After the rain <u>came</u> the <u>wind</u>.
The <u>wind</u> <u>came</u> after the rain.

Subjects in Imperative Sentences

The subject of an imperative sentence is always *you*. When the subject is not directly stated, as is usually the case, *you* is understood to be the subject.

<u>You</u> <u>look</u> at these pictures.
(<u>You</u>) <u>Speak</u> to the landlord tomorrow.

Sentence Diagraming For information on diagraming imperative sentences, see page 861.

Practice Your Skills

A. CONCEPT CHECK

Unusually Placed Subjects Write the subject and verb of each of the sentences in the passage below. Underline the subject once and the verb twice.

Writing Theme
Life with Robots

(1) In the future, we will find robots as much a part of our daily lives as automobiles or television sets. (2) Where will robots be utilized? (3) You will find robots in homes, schools, and businesses. (4) What will these mechanical servants do for us? (5) They will perform many of our more tedious tasks.

(6) Here are the only requirements for a basic robot. (7) It needs a computer, of course, and a mechanical arm with claws. (8) Along the arm run cables. (9) Instructions from the computer to the claws are transmitted through these cables. (10) Robots can only follow instructions programmed into their computer "brains."

B. REVISION SKILL

Subjects in Unusual Positions Rewrite the numbered sentences, following the directions given in parentheses. In dialogue, you may need to change a phrase such as *She said* to fit the revised sentence.

(1) A state-of-the-art robot stood at the center of the electronics exhibit. (Invert the sentence.) (2) Several people crowded around it. (Rewrite the sentence to begin with the

expletive *There*.) (3) "The hand can move in any direction," one viewer remarked. (Rewrite the viewer's comment as a question.) (4) Another person said, "The sections of the arm turn around joints." (Rewrite this comment as a question.)

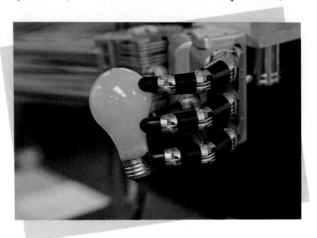

(5) "You should notice the similarity to the parts of a human arm," the science museum guide said. (Rewrite the guide's statement as an imperative sentence.) (6) "You will also notice that the wrist is engineered to move up and down." (Rewrite this statement as an imperative sentence.)

(7) Tools such as paint sprayers and welding torches sat next to the robot. (Invert the sentence.) (8) "Several other examples of tools used by robotic arms on automobile assembly lines are displayed in the exhibit halls," the guide commented. (Rewrite the guide's statement to begin with the expletive *There*.)

(9) "I want to know what kind of system is used to drive the robot's joints," said one viewer. (Rewrite the viewer's statement as a question.)

(10) "An example of an electrohydraulic system used to drive the joints is here," said the guide, pointing to a glass case. (Rewrite the sentence to begin with *Here*.)

C. APPLICATION IN WRITING

The Fantasy Imagine that you could have a robot for a personal companion. This robot could go anywhere with you and do menial tasks. What jobs would you have it do? What would you not want it to do? As you describe your ideal robot companion, create sentence variety by varying the placement of your subjects.

Some sentences, such as *Joan sings,* contain only a subject and a verb. Most sentences, however, require additional words placed after the verb to complete the meaning of the sentence. These additional words are called **complements.**

A complement is a word or a group of words that completes the meaning of the verb.

> Friction produces *heat.* (Produces what? Produces heat. *Heat* completes the meaning of *produces.*)
> The guide showed the *visitors* from Japan some unusual *minerals.* (Showed what to whom? Showed minerals to visitors. *Visitors* and *minerals* complete the meaning of *showed.*)
> Old Faithful is a well-known *geyser.* (Is what? Is a geyser. *Geyser* completes the meaning of *is.*)
> Many volcanoes are *dormant.* (Are what? Are dormant. *Dormant* completes the meaning of *are.*)

Now you will study four different kinds of complements: direct objects, indirect objects, objective complements, and subject complements.

Direct Objects

A **direct object** is a word or group of words that receives the action of an action verb. A direct object answers the question *What?* or *Whom?* about the verb. Verbs that take direct objects are called **transitive verbs.** See page 538 for more information about transitive verbs.

> Everyone knows your *secret.* (Knows what?)
> The fans cheered *Paul Molitar.* (Cheered whom?)

Do not confuse a direct object with an adverb that follows an action verb. A direct object tells *what* or *whom.* An adverb tells *where, when, how,* or *to what extent.*

Direct Object We followed the *trail.* (Followed what?)
Adverb We followed *closely.* (Followed how?)

The direct object may be compound.

> I misplaced my *pad* and *pencil.* (Misplaced what?)
> The officer helped my *sister* and *me.* (Helped whom?)

The Sentence
and Its Parts   **577**

Indirect Objects

An **indirect object** is a word or group of words that tells *to whom* or *for whom* the action of the verb is being performed. A verb has an indirect object only if it also has a direct object. The indirect object always comes before the direct object.

> The book club sent *us* a refund. (Sent a refund to whom?)
> My aunt made *Lisa* a sweater. (Made a sweater for whom?)

The indirect object may be compound.

> Our grandmother taught my *cousin* and *me* Greek.
> Dale handed the *customer* and her *children* menus.

The words *to* and *for* never appear before the indirect object. *To* and *for* are prepositions when they are followed by a noun or pronoun. The noun or pronoun is the object of the preposition.

Indirect Object	The team sent the *coach* a telegram.
Object of a Preposition	The team sent a telegram to the *coach*.

For more information on prepositions, see pages 550–552.

Practice Your Skills

A. CONCEPT CHECK

Direct and Indirect Objects Make three columns labeled *Verb, Indirect Object,* and *Direct Object.* For each sentence, write the verb and its object or objects in the proper columns. If there is no indirect object, write *None.* Some sentences have compound indirect objects or direct objects.

1. The United States put astronauts on the moon on July 20, 1969.
2. The *Apollo XI* spacecraft carried Neil Armstrong, Edwin Aldrin, and Michael Collins into orbit around the moon.
3. Armstrong and Aldrin guided a detached lunar module to the surface of the moon.
4. Collins radioed Armstrong and Aldrin messages and information from the orbiting spacecraft.
5. In response, Armstrong sent Collins his location and findings.
6. On earth, television cameras brought us moment-to-moment coverage of the event.
7. The astronauts planted an American flag on the lunar surface.
8. Speaking for the mission, Armstrong communicated his joy, his wonder, and his pride at their accomplishment.
9. The astronauts did not find animals or plants on the moon.
10. This mission left us no hope of life on the lunar surface.

B. REVISION SKILL

Effective Word Usage   Revise these sentences, following the directions given in parentheses.

1. For centuries, people have studied things in the heavens. (Replace the vague direct object with more specific words.)
2. They made sky maps. They made star charts. (Combine the sentences to form a compound direct object.)
3. People also thought they saw something on the surface of the moon. (Replace the vague direct object with a more specific word or words.)
4. The light and dark areas on the moon looked like a face. (Rewrite the sentence. Change the object of the preposition *like* to a direct object. Use the verb *formed.*)
5. The moon is without air, wind, or water. (Rewrite the sentence. Change the objects of the preposition *without* to direct objects.)
6. The moon has only a black sky and an unchanging surface to offer us. (Make the sentence more direct by using the word *us* as an indirect object and the word *offers* as the main verb.)
7. The moon has a boiling hot, two-week day. It also has a freezing cold, two-week night. (Combine the sentences to form a compound direct object.)
8. Lunar explorers wear spacesuits as protection from the extreme heat and cold. (Make the sentence more direct by turning *Lunar explorers* into a direct object and using *protect* as the main verb.)
9. NASA has given some of these spacesuits to the Smithsonian Institution. (Rewrite the sentence. Make it more direct by replacing one of the prepositional phrases with an indirect object.)
10. You can also see spacesuits at the National Air and Space Museum. In addition, you can see a lunar landing module at the National Air and Space Museum. (Eliminate unnecessary words by combining the sentences to form a compound direct object.)

In Jules Verne's 1865 novel, *From the Earth to the Moon*, travelers journeyed in a capsule shot from a giant cannon.

Objective Complements

An **objective complement** is a word or group of words that follows a direct object and renames or describes that object. Objective complements follow certain verbs and their synonyms: *appoint, call, choose, consider, elect, find, make, keep, name, think.*

An objective complement may be a noun or an adjective.

Noun   Tennis experts consider Steffi Graf a unique *player.*
               (*Player* renames the direct object *Steffi Graf.*)
Adjective   Many even call her *unbeatable.* (*Unbeatable* describes the direct object *her.*)

Practice Your Skills

CONCEPT CHECK

Direct Objects, Indirect Objects, and Objective Complements
Identify each complement in the following sentences according to its kind: *Direct Object, Indirect Object,* or *Objective Complement.*

1. Eleanor of Aquitaine ruled France and England.
2. Marriage made Eleanor the Queen of France in 1137.
3. Later, a divorce separated Eleanor and Louis VII.
4. Later, Eleanor married Henry II of England.
5. The marriage gave Henry control over Eleanor's lands in France.
6. Her lands and his created the Angevin Empire.
7. Quarrels soon rendered Henry and Eleanor hostile to each other.
8. As a result, Henry made Eleanor his prisoner.
9. After Henry's death, her son Richard I appointed her regent of England.
10. Historians have called her regency wise and benevolent.

Subject Complements

A **subject complement** is a complement that follows a linking verb and renames or describes the subject. Subject complements often come after a form of the verb *be*. For a discussion of linking verbs, see pages 534–535. There are two kinds of subject complements: predicate nominatives and predicate adjectives.

Predicate Nominatives A **predicate nominative** is a word or a group of words that follows a linking verb and names or identifies the subject of the sentence. Predicate nominatives can be either **predicate nouns** or **predicate pronouns.**

Predicate Noun	My favorite sport is *football.*
Predicate Pronoun	The winner should have been *she.*

The predicate nominative may be compound.

Benjamin Franklin was a *statesman* and an *inventor.*

Predicate Adjectives A **predicate adjective** is an adjective that follows a linking verb and modifies the subject of the sentence.

Everyone on the team felt *confident* of victory.

The predicate adjective may be compound.

Medieval castles were usually *cold, damp,* and *gloomy.*

Sentence Diagraming For information on diagraming subject complements, see page 863.

Practice Your Skills

A. CONCEPT CHECK

Predicate Nominatives and Predicate Adjectives Write each subject complement in the following sentences and identify it according to its kind: *Predicate Nominative* or *Predicate Adjective*. Ignore modifiers of the subject complements. Remember that a subject complement may be compound.

1. Paul Cézanne was an influential French painter.
2. The creator of this marvelous still life was he.
3. The apples in the painting look ripe and fresh.
4. They appear colorful and unblemished on the canvas.
5. Cézanne's apples are experiments and explorations in shape, line, and color.
6. Their colors are red, yellow, orange, and even blue!
7. Perhaps one of Cézanne's apples would feel strange in your hand.
8. Would that apple be fuzzy?
9. In this painting, the apples appear beautiful but inedible.
10. Would such apples taste strange?

B. DRAFTING SKILL

Using Vivid Language Inexperienced writers sometimes use predicate nominatives and predicate adjectives that are too vague or too informal. Consider the following examples.

Weak   The painter's brush strokes were *great.*
Strong   The painter's brush strokes were *forceful* and *bold.*

Rewrite the following paragraph, replacing the italicized subject complements with predicate nominatives or predicate adjectives that are more formal or more precise.

(1) Paul Klee's drawing "Twittering Machine" is really *good.* (2) It is not a complicated *thing,* but it evokes strong feelings. The work consists of simple lines that portray a machine capable of twittering like a bird. (3) The object at the right of the drawing is an *object* that turns the machine and evidently causes it to twitter. The twittering machine appears to be sculpted of wire. (4) Its sound, therefore, might be rather *weird.* Klee is satirizing the machine age. (5) His twittering machine is deliberately *silly.*

Twittering Machine, 1922 by Paul Klee. Collection, Museum of Modern Art

The Sentence and Its Parts   **581**

A. Identify the italicized words in the sentence as *Subject, Verb, Direct Object, Indirect Object, Objective Complement,* or *Subject Complement.*

1. Zoologists have given the medical *world* exciting news.
2. The canary *possesses* a truly remarkable capability.
3. The brain of an adult bird can regenerate nerve *cells.*
4. Scientists call the ability *neurogenesis.*
5. Careful study of the song patterns of brain damaged canaries produced *evidence* of tissue regeneration.
6. This characteristic may be *dormant* in the human brain.
7. Physicians consider this possibility very *important.*
8. Finding a way to reawaken this potential is the *challenge.*
9. The key *is* identification of certain molecular signals.
10. Then those *signals* must be found in the human brain.

B. Write the following sentences. Underline each subject once and each verb twice. Identify each complement by writing *DO* (*Direct Object*), *IO* (*Indirect Object*), *OC* (*Objective Complement*), *PN* (*Predicate Nominative*), or *PA* (*Predicate Adjective*) over the appropriate word. Not every sentence has a complement.

> **Example**   Not all <u>birds</u> <u><u>raise</u></u> their young in trees.
>   **DO**

1. Birds find the shores of ponds and oceans attractive for nests.
2. They also like fields, underground burrows, and cliffs.
3. Nesting places offer the offspring protection.
4. Nests, burrows, and holes can provide camouflage and easy access to food sources.
5. The tall grasses at the edges of ponds are hiding places and nesting grounds for baby mallard ducks.
6. The floating nest of the female grebe appears safe and tranquil.
7. Belted kingfishers even dig burrows in the banks of ponds.
8. They bring their offspring fish.
9. Desert birds, of course, must hide from the hot sun.
10. The tiny elf owl considers a hole in a cactus home.
11. That hole may have previously been the home of a woodpecker.
12. A stork would consider a chimney-top nest comfortable.
13. The golden eagle reuses the same elaborate nest year after year.
14. The nest is a huge platform of vines, sticks, grasses, and stems.
15. Biologists call the eagle's nest an aerie.

Here and at the end of Handbook 32, you will add to the basic definition of the sentence given on page 563. You now know a sentence is a group of words that (1) expresses a complete thought, (2) contains at least one subject and verb, and (3) may contain a complement.

Practice Your Skills

PROOFREADING SKILL

Complete Sentences Combine the fragments in the following paragraph into complete sentences. Also correct any errors in punctuation, capitalization, or spelling.

Writing Theme
Defending Haiti

Citadelle Henry is one of the largest forts. In the world. It sits atop a jungle peek. On the Caribbean island of haiti. The fort was begun in the early nineteenth Century. By Haitian liberator Jean-Jacques Dessalines. Under his leadership, the slaves of Haiti. Rebelled and defeated they're French masters. The next ruler, King henry Christophe, oversaw most of the Citadelles' construction. King Christophe hoped the forte would protenkt his subjects. From any future European invasions. He wiseley decided that fighting from the Hills. Was the best plan of defence for the island.

Haitian street art

The Sentence
and Its Parts

GRAMMAR
HANDBOOK
31

Writing Theme
People and Places
in History

A. Identifying Complete Sentences Write the word *Sentence* for those groups of words that are complete sentences. Write *Fragment* for those that are not.

1. The first hot-air balloon flight, made by Jacques and Joseph Montgolfier in 1782
2. The first propeller-driven balloon premiered in 1784
3. Madame Thibble, the first woman to make a balloon flight
4. The zeppelin a rigid-frame airship
5. The history of balloons and dirigibles is extensive
6. Nevertheless, aviation was actually born at Kitty Hawk, North Carolina
7. The first heavier-than-air ship, built by the Wright brothers
8. Changing the course of history
9. Making way in 1927 for the first solo transatlantic flight
10. This flight was made by Charles Augustus Lindbergh in his *Spirit of St. Louis*

B. Sentence Composing Rewrite each of the following sentence fragments as a complete sentence.

1. Verrazano, the first European to sail into New York Harbor
2. Henry Hudson exploring the Hudson River in 1609
3. The island of Manhattan
4. Peter Stuyvesant, the last Dutch governor
5. British occupation of the city during the Revolutionary War
6. The largest city in the United States by 1800
7. The Brooklyn Bridge
8. The Statue of Liberty, a gift from the people of France
9. The Empire State Building, completed in 1931
10. The Verrazano-Narrows Bridge, named after the early explorer

C. Finding Subjects and Verbs Write the verb and its subject in each of the following sentences. Some subjects and verbs may be compound.

1. The eruption of a volcano is a spectacular event.
2. History has recorded the eruption of almost five hundred volcanoes.
3. About halfway between Sumatra and Java lies the volcanic island of Krakatoa.
4. Its eruption in 1883 was one of the world's worst disasters.
5. Over nearby islands washed a towering tidal wave.
6. An underwater eruption formed the island of Surtsey.
7. From 1963 to 1967 it grew to more than one square mile.

8. Mount Vesuvius is the only active volcano in Europe.
9. It erupted and buried Pompeii in A.D. 79.
10. Even today archaeologists find remains of ancient Pompeii.
11. Mount Saint Helens is a famous American volcano.
12. It spewed forth a cloud of ashes on May 18, 1980.
13. Startled and stunned, the nation followed the event.
14. Luckily not all active volcanoes do erupt.
15. Mount Baker in Washington, however, has been steaming since October 1976.

D. Identifying the Parts of a Sentence Label six columns *Subject, Verb, Direct Object, Indirect Object, Objective Complement,* and *Subject Complement.* Place those parts of the following sentences in the proper columns. Some sentence parts may be compound.

1. Many historians call Thomas Jefferson the most influential figure in early American history.
2. Jefferson was born in Virginia.
3. His knowledge of law, his political abilities, and his literary talent made him valuable to the revolutionary movement.
4. He and other founding fathers opposed British rule.
5. Jefferson drafted the Declaration of Independence.
6. Many political figures of his day corresponded with Jefferson.
7. He wrote them long, detailed letters.
8. Biographers have collected and published many of his letters.
9. In 1789, voters elected George Washington President.
10. That clearly was one of the most important years in American history.
11. In 1789, George Washington appointed Thomas Jefferson Secretary of State.
12. That same year Washington named Alexander Hamilton Secretary of the Treasury.
13. Jefferson later became governor of Virginia, Vice-President of the United States, and President of the United States.
14. Beyond his obvious political skills, Jefferson's talents were many and varied.
15. For example, historians consider him a pioneer in American architecture.
16. He left the nation several superb homes and public buildings.
17. He designed the University of Virginia and his own home, Monticello.
18. He was also the founder of the University of Virginia.
19. Dumas Malone's detailed biography of Jefferson is outstanding.
20. She gives us his life and times in six large, impressive volumes.

Using Phrases and Clauses

PREPOSITIONAL PHRASES

A **phrase** is a group of related words that does not have a subject and a predicate and that functions in a sentence as a single part of speech. One kind of phrase is a **prepositional phrase.**

A prepositional phrase is a phrase that consists of a preposition, its object, and any modifiers of the object.

> The mockingbird imitates the calls *of other birds.* (*Birds* is the object of the preposition *of.*)

As you learned, the object of a preposition is always a noun, a pronoun, or a group of words used as a noun. A prepositional phrase may have two or more objects joined by a conjunction.

> Deliver the letter *to whoever answers the door.* (The group of words *whoever answers the door* is the object of the preposition *to.*)
>
> A majority of members *of both the House and the Senate* strongly supported the bill. (*House* and *Senate* are the compound objects of the preposition *of.*)

A prepositional phrase is a modifier and functions in a sentence as an adjective or an adverb.

Adjective Phrases

A prepositional phrase that modifies a noun or pronoun is called an **adjective phrase.** An adjective phrase can modify a subject, direct object, indirect object, or predicate nominative. The phrase usually tells *which one* or *what kind* about the word it modifies.

Modifying a Subject	The clock *in the church steeple* struck ten. (*Which* clock?)
Modifying a Direct Object	Kim repaired the shutter *on my camera.* (*Which* shutter?)
Modifying an Indirect Object	Mom gave the family *next door* a plum pudding. (*Which* family?)
Modifying a Predicate Nominative	A marmoset is a monkey *from South America.* (*What kind* of monkey?)

An adjective phrase sometimes modifies the object in another prepositional phrase.

> Several scenes in the documentary *about grizzlies* were frightening. (*Which* documentary?)

Adverb Phrases

A prepositional phrase that functions as an adverb is called an **adverb phrase.** An adverb phrase modifies a verb, an adjective, or another adverb. Like an adverb, an adverb phrase tells *how, when, where,* or *to what extent* about the word it modifies.

Modifying a Verb	The milk spilled *on the floor.* (Spilled *where?*)
Modifying an Adjective	Charles Dickens was very skillful *at characterization.* (Skillful *how?*)
Modifying an Adverb	Autumn color begins soon *after the first frost.* (*How* soon?)

More than one adverb phrase may modify the same word.

> Who rapped *on our door at dawn?* (Both phrases modify *rapped. On our door* tells where. *At dawn* tells when.)

Punctuation Note There are three times when a prepositional phrase at the beginning of a sentence is followed by a comma.

1. If the phrase is followed by a natural pause when read: According to the fire marshal, smoke detectors save lives.
2. After a series of prepositional phrases: After three weeks of heavy rain in April, the fields were wet and muddy.
3. To avoid confusion: Next to the school, houses were being built.

Placement of Prepositional Phrases

A prepositional phrase may come before or after the word it modifies. However, to avoid confusion, place a prepositional phrase close to the word it modifies.

Confusing	Edward explained how to raise earthworms in his report.
Clear	*In his report,* Edward explained how to raise earthworms.

Sentence Diagraming For information on diagraming prepositional phrases, see page 864.

Writing
──TIP──
Use adverb phrases to add details about time, place, or causes.

Practice Your Skills

A. CONCEPT CHECK

Adjective and Adverb Phrases. List the prepositional phrases in the following passage. Tell whether the phrase is used as an *Adjective* or *Adverb*. Notice how the writer uses prepositional phrases to add clarity and interest to the nouns and verbs in the passage.

> (1) The inhabitants of the wall were a mixed lot, and they were divided into day and night workers, the hunters and the hunted. (2) At night the hunters were the toads that lived among the brambles, and the geckos, pale, translucent, with bulging eyes, that lived in the cracks higher up the wall. (3) Their prey was the population of stupid, absent-minded crane-flies that zoomed and barged their way among the leaves; moths of all sizes and shapes . . . fluttered in soft clouds. . . .
>
> **Gerald Durrell, "The World in a Wall"**

B. REVISION SKILL

Sentence Expansion and Combination Use prepositional phrases to make your writing smoother. Revise the following sentences by changing the information in parentheses into an adjective or adverb phrase. Add or delete words as necessary.

> (1) Many mammals have adapted to a harsh way of life. (They live in the desert.) (2) To survive, desert animals store food and get water. (Plants provide water.) (3) (The heat of the day is intense.) Some mammals use water very slowly. (4) Other desert mammals have characteristics that help them hide. (They avoid predators.) (5) Others have adaptations that help them move quickly. (They cross the hot desert sand.) (6) The light color of some animals blends. (It blends with the sand.) (7) Others have fringed toes. (These toes are for quick movement.) (8) Most desert animals are active during the cooler hours, when there is dew. (The dew is on the ground.) (9) Jackrabbits, prairie dogs, and predators live there. (The desert environment is fragile.) (10) A drama unfolds daily between hunters and hunted. (Their environment is stark.)

C. APPLICATION IN WRITING

A Scientific Report One answer to the world's hunger problems may lie in farming the sea. Sea farming, or aquaculture, is the controlled production of fish, shellfish, and marine plants. Imagine that you are a staff member of the first sea farm. Use a variety of prepositional phrases in a paragraph describing your first harvest.

"Now! ... *That* should clear up
a few things around here!"

APPOSITIVES AND APPOSITIVE PHRASES

An appositive is a noun or pronoun that usually follows another noun or pronoun and identifies or explains it.

Balloonist *Julian Nott* is planning an around-the-world flight.
(The appositive *Julian Nott* identifies *balloonist.*)

An appositive phrase consists of an appositive and its modifiers.

Nott's balloon, *a new model with a pressurized gondola,* can ascend seven miles. (The appositive *model* explains the subject *balloon.* The adjective *new* and the adjective phrase *with a pressurized gondola* modify *model.*)

Sometimes the appositive phrase precedes the word it explains.

A noted pilot of her era, Anne Morrow Lindbergh was also a writer of exceptional ability. (The appositive *pilot* explains the subject *Anne Morrow Lindbergh.*)

An appositive may be compound.

Antoine de Saint-Exupéry, a *writer* and an *artist,* began his career in aviation as a mail pilot.

Using Phrases
and Clauses   **589**

An appositive may be essential or nonessential. An **essential appositive** is one that is needed to make the intended meaning of a sentence complete.

> The aviator *Beryl Markham* wrote about her historic transatlantic flight. (Without the appositive, the meaning would not be complete.)

A **nonessential appositive** is one that adds extra information to a sentence in which the meaning is already clear and complete.

> Nevil Norway, *a British pilot,* wrote novels under the name of Nevil Shute.

Sometimes special circumstances affect whether an appositive is essential or nonessential. Consider the example below.

> My nephew Alex just graduated from college.

If the writer has several nephews, and only Alex graduated, then the appositive is essential. Usually, however, an appositive such as the one above would be considered nonessential.

Punctuation Note As shown above, nonessential appositives are set off with commas. Commas are not used with essential appositives.

Sentence Diagraming For information on diagraming appositives and appositive phrases, see page 866.

Practice Your Skills

A. CONCEPT CHECK

Appositives and Appositive Phrases Write the sentences below. Underline each appositive or appositive phrase. Add commas as needed for the nonessential appositives.

1. Sitting Bull's birthplace the Black Hills of South Dakota was known to the Sioux as Paha Sapa.
2. A treaty signed in 1868 granted the Sioux permanent ownership of Paha Sapa their sacred land.
3. In 1872, hundreds of white people came to the area looking for gold the great temptation to adventurers of the day.
4. The dauntless Sioux leader Sitting Bull refused the U.S. government's offers for his tribe's land.
5. The government then sent the famous military leader General George Armstrong Custer to fight Sitting Bull.
6. The warriors of Sitting Bull and his close associate Crazy Horse soundly defeated Custer at the Battle of the Little Bighorn.

Writing
— **TIP** —

Appositives can be used to add detail to a sentence or to streamline your writing.

Pictographic account
of the Battle of the
Little Bighorn.
Drawn by Red Horse,
Miniconjou Dakota Tribe

7. Ironically, in the end Sitting Bull was betrayed by some of his own people a group of Sioux chiefs.
8. In 1888, he opposed further land concessions and made an enemy of the Indian agent James McLaughlin.
9. On December 15, 1890, Sitting Bull and a son Crow Foot were murdered by McLaughlin's Indian police.
10. Two weeks later, Sitting Bull's struggle for Paha Sapa ended at Wounded Knee site of the final massacre of the Sioux.

B. DRAFTING SKILL

Eliminating Unnecessary Words You can use appositive phrases to streamline your writing. Improve the following numbered sentence pairs by combining them. Use each second sentence as an appositive in the first sentence. Eliminate words as necessary and use appropriate punctuation.

> *Example*   Sequoyah conceived the idea for writing the language of the Cherokee. He was an illiterate man.
> Sequoyah, an illiterate man, conceived the idea for writing the language of the Cherokee.

1. A hunting accident led to the development of an eighty-six-symbol alphabet. This was the Cherokee written language.
2. Native Americans had preserved their lore and philosophies by word of mouth for thousands of years. They were the original inhabitants of the Americas.
3. The Cherokee admired the "talking leaf." This was the written language of the European settlers.

Using Phrases
and Clauses

4. Sequoyah was the inventor of the written Cherokee language. Sequoyah had been an admirer of the talking leaf since childhood.
5. Sequoyah gave up many of his normal pursuits when he became partially crippled in a hunting accident. He was a talented silversmith, painter, and warrior.
6. For a period of twelve years after the accident, Sequoyah studied the Cherokee spoken language. The language is a complicated system of individual sounds.
7. At first he tried to use *pictographs*. Pictographs are picture symbols that represent words or sounds.
8. Then Sequoyah adapted the written symbols of three languages to create the Cherokee alphabet. The languages were Greek, Hebrew, and English.
9. Sequoyah's alphabet earned him respect from his people and from his country. His country was the United States.
10. Giant trees in California were named after this giant in American history. The trees are the sequoias.

VERBALS AND VERBAL PHRASES

A **verbal** is a verb form that functions as a noun, an adjective, or an adverb. A **verbal phrase** consists of a verbal, all its modifiers, and all its complements. There are three kinds of verbals: **infinitives, participles,** and **gerunds.**

Infinitives and Infinitive Phrases

An infinitive is a verb form that usually begins with *to* and functions as a noun, an adjective, or an adverb.

Noun	*To leave* was a difficult decision. (subject)
	King Edward did not choose *to rule*. (direct object)
	His choice was *to abdicate*. (predicate nominative)
Adjective	That is the game *to see*. (modifies the noun *game*)
Adverb	Everyone stood *to stretch*. (modifies the verb *stood*)
	Kiwis are unable *to fly*. (modifies the adjective *unable*)

Grammar Note Do not confuse an infinitive (*to* plus a verb form) with a prepositional phrase (*to* plus a noun or pronoun).

An infinitive is often used with one or more auxiliary verbs.

Selma was proud *to have been elected*.

To, which is called "the sign of the infinitive," is sometimes left out of the sentence.

Leon will help you *pack*. (Leon will help you [*to*] *pack*.)

Infinitives used with the following verbs do not usually include *to: dare, help, make, see, hear, let, please, watch.*

An infinitive phrase consists of an infinitive, its modifiers, and its complements.

Infinitives may be modified by adverbs and by adverb phrases.

Firefighters have *to practice daily*. (*Daily* is an adverb modifying *to practice*.)

We packed sandwiches *to eat on the bus*. (*On the bus* is an adverb prepositional phrase modifying *to eat*.)

Since an infinitive is a verb form, it can have complements.

Rita offered *to make everyone pizza*. (*Everyone* is the indirect object of the infinitive *to make; pizza* is the direct object.)

When the infinitive is formed from a linking verb, its complement is a predicate adjective or predicate nominative.

We tried *to look serious*. (*Serious* is a predicate adjective after the infinitive *to look*.)

Like infinitives, infinitive phrases can function as nouns, adjectives, or adverbs.

Noun   *To chase after the dog* would be futile. (subject)

Adjective   Ms. Lawry is the candidate *to watch in this election*.

Adverb   We meet every Friday night *to play Scrabble*.™

Usage Note   Avoid placing a modifier between *to* and the rest of the infinitive. Such a modifier is said to "split the infinitive." A split infinitive usually sounds awkward and should be reworded.

Awkward   The principal hopes to greatly increase our test scores.
Improved   The principal hopes to increase our test scores greatly.

Sentence Diagraming   For information on diagraming infinitives and infinitive phrases, see page 866.

Practice Your Skills

A. CONCEPT CHECK

Infinitive Phrases Write the infinitives and infinitive phrases in the following sentences. Then tell how each infinitive phrase is used in the sentence: as a *Noun,* an *Adjective,* or an *Adverb.*

1. In the eighteenth century, an Arab worker helped discover one of the most famous stones in history, the Rosetta stone.
2. Thinking the oddly shaped black basalt stone was magical, the worker's first impulse was to destroy it.
3. Fortunately, the engineer in charge of the crew became interested in the stone and decided to clean it.
4. On its polished surface were three broad bands of etched writing that proved very difficult to read.
5. To decipher the writing on its surface, scholars examined it carefully.
6. Once they realized that the three messages were the same and that one was written in Greek, scholars were able to read the hieroglyphics.
7. Still, it took over twenty years to unlock the entire Egyptian script.
8. In time, the Rosetta stone was so important it became booty to be fought over by nations warring in Egypt.
9. Meanwhile, many people worked to piece together the puzzling facts and unlock the stone's message.
10. Finally, Jean François Champollion was to get credit for deciphering the hieroglyphics.

The Great Sphinx of Giza, Egypt, was one of the wonders of the ancient world.

B. DRAFTING SKILL

Achieving Sentence Variety Infinitives and infinitive phrases can appear in different positions within sentences. Experiment by rewriting the following sentences according to the instructions in parentheses. In some sentences, the position of the verb will change.

1. Scholars have studied ancient tombs and their contents to unlock the secrets of Egyptian culture. (Move the infinitive phrase to the beginning of the sentence.)
2. Those early tombs, called *mastabas,* were built for preserving the dead kings and queens. (Change the prepositional phrase to an infinitive phrase.)
3. Offerings were placed in the mastabas. (Add an infinitive phrase saying the offerings provided for the needs of the dead.)
4. To be known for the most impressive tomb was King Djoser's desire. (Move the infinitive phrase to the end of the sentence.)
5. He hired the architect Imhotep. Imhotep designed a structure above the mastaba. (Combine the sentences by changing the second sentence to an infinitive phrase.)
6. The structure was the first. (Add an infinitive phrase saying it would be built entirely of stone.)
7. Imhotep had had an innovative idea. The idea was to stack smaller rectangular mastabas on top of one another. (Combine the sentences by changing the second sentence to an infinitive phrase.)
8. The finished structure, the Step Pyramid, became a model for others by copying it and improving it. (Change the final prepositional phrase to an infinitive phrase.)
9. To create the most magnificent pyramid was the goal of Egyptian kings and queens. (Move the infinitive phrase to the end of the sentence.)
10. Pyramids and their contents became the most important source of knowledge about Egyptian culture for scholars. (Add an infinitive phrase saying that scholars study them in modern times.)

Participles and Participial Phrases

A participle is a verb form that functions as an adjective.

Like adjectives, participles modify nouns and pronouns.

Modifying a Noun	The *shaken* passengers talked about their escape. (*Shaken* modifies the noun *passengers.*)
Modifying a Pronoun	*Bored,* everyone soon became restless. (*Bored* modifies the pronoun *everyone.*)

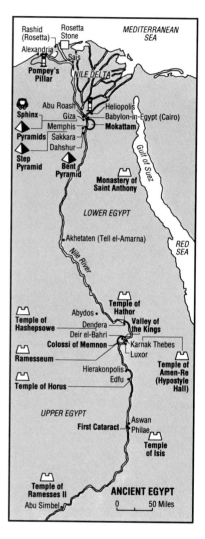

ANCIENT EGYPT

Using Phrases
and Clauses

There are two kinds of participles: **present participles** and **past participles**. Present participles of all verbs end in -*ing*. Past participles have several forms; most end with -*d, -ed, -t,* or -*n*. Handbook 34, pages 650–657, lists irregular verbs and their past participles.

When a present participle or past participle is used with an auxiliary verb to form a verb phrase, it functions as a verb. When it is used as an adjective, it is a verbal.

Verb Phrase	The child on the monkey bars *was laughing*.
Verbal	*Laughing,* the child swung from the monkey bars.

A participle used as an adjective is sometimes used with one or more auxiliary verbs.

> *Having finished,* we turned in our test papers and left.

A participial phrase consists of a participle and its modifiers and complements. Participial phrases function as adjectives.

Since a participle functions as an adjective, it can be modified by adverbs and by adverb phrases.

> *Already soaked by the rain,* I struggled with my umbrella. (In the participial phrase, the participle *soaked* is modified by the adverb *already* and the adverb phrase *by the rain*.)

Since a participle is a verb form, it can have complements.

> *Handing the sailor the navigational charts,* the captain went below. (*Sailor* is the indirect object of the participle *handing; charts* is the direct object.)

Punctuation Note Introductory participles and participial phrases are followed by a comma.

Participial phrases may be essential or nonessential. An **essential participial phrase** is one that is needed to make the meaning of a sentence complete. A **nonessential participial phrase** is one that adds extra meaning to the sentence.

Essential	The puppy *curled up in the corner* is ours. (The participial phrase points out a particular puppy.)
Nonessential	The puppy, *curled up in the corner,* slept. (The participial phrase adds to the description of the puppy.)

Punctuation Note Nonessential participial phrases within a sentence are set off by commas. Commas are not used to set off essential participial phrases.

Misplaced Participles   A participle or participial phrase should be placed as close as possible to the word that it modifies. Otherwise, the meaning of the sentence may not be clear.

Confusing	Holsteins are the most popular cows among dairy farmers *producing the most milk.* (The participial phrase appears to modify *farmers.*)
Clear	*Producing the most milk,* Holsteins are the most popular cows among dairy farmers. (The participial phrase clearly modifies *Holsteins.*)

Dangling Participles   A participle or a participial phrase that does not clearly modify anything in a sentence is called a **dangling participle.** A dangling participle causes confusion because it appears to modify a word that it cannot sensibly modify. Correct a dangling participle by providing a word for the participle to modify.

Confusing	*Peering through the microscope,* several amoebas wiggled across the slide. (Who is peering? The amoebas?)
Clear	Peering through the microscope, the biology student watched several amoebas wiggle across the slide.
Confusing	*Carefully calculating the danger,* the victims were rescued. (The participial phrase has no word to modify.)
Clear	Carefully calculating the danger, the paramedics rescued the victims.

Sentence Diagraming   For information on diagraming participles and participial phrases, see page 866.

Practice Your Skills

A. CONCEPT CHECK

Participles and Participial Phrases   Write the participles and participial phrases in the following sentences. After each participle or participial phrase, write the word that it modifies. (Note: There may be more than one participle or participial phrase in a sentence.)

1. Charmed by the glamorous image of the investigative reporter, many young people decide to enter the crowded field of journalism.
2. Having received their college degrees, they often knock on the doors of overworked city-newspaper editors.
3. In the early 1900's, however, determined young writers did not need a college education to write for the newspapers.
4. For example, having completed his high-school studies, H. L. Mencken was hired at the *Baltimore Morning Herald* at the age of eighteen.

Writing Theme
Journalism Today

5. Standing for thirty-seven nights in the corner of the *Morning Herald*'s city room, he finally got his chance.
6. Mencken, granted a few trial assignments, proved himself.
7. Favorably impressed, the editors of the *Herald* hired him.
8. Advancing up the titled ranks, Mencken became city editor in 1903 and then editor of the *Morning Herald* in 1905.
9. He attacked established beliefs in his column "The Free Lance."
10. The jeering, lively style of the column influenced many other journalists.
11. Reaching his peak of popularity in the 1920's, Mencken jabbed unmercifully at society and at politics.
12. Hated by many of his readers, Mencken satirized America and Americans in magazines and newspapers throughout his career.
13. In their magazine *Smart Set,* Mencken and his coeditor George Jean Nathan promoted promising new writers of fiction.
14. Among the writers benefiting from their encouragement were Sinclair Lewis and Theodore Dreiser.
15. In addition to his biting satire, Mencken was best known for his book *The American Language,* a highly respected work on the English language in America.

B. REVISION SKILL

Using Participles Correctly   The following paragraphs contain misplaced and dangling participles as well as participial sentence fragments. Rewrite any numbered items that have errors. Write *Correct* for sentences that have no errors. Note that some numbered items may be corrected by combining them.

(1) The Associated Press news bureau, or AP, is a nonprofit news-gathering organization. (2) Serving approximately 1,300 newspapers and 5,700 radio and television stations worldwide. (3) Transmitting about 1,000 stories a day, the Associated Press is the central nervous system of the news business. (4) There are over a hundred Associated Press regional offices. (5) Operating across the United States. (6) Employing about 1,500 reporters and photographers, all people who read, watch, or listen to the news benefit from the AP bureau.

(7) When a national news story breaks in a small town, a local AP reporter, or stringer, calls it in to a local Associated Press office; the staff then distributes the story locally and also sends it to the national AP bureau. (8) Providing this information quickly and accurately to its members, local newspapers and television stations are able to report news as it occurs.

(9) Meeting at mid-morning inside the Associated Press Building in New York City, the story summaries received from local offices the previous day are discussed by the editors at the AP central office. (10) Considering such factors as importance and interest, the local stories that will be distributed nationally and internationally are decided on by these editors. (11) Making such decisions, reports in newspapers and on television around the world are strongly influenced by the AP editors. (12) Other important news-gathering services, operated like the AP through networks of local stringers or offices, include United Press International and Reuters.

C. APPLICATION IN WRITING

The News Story   By using verbal phrases, you can add energy and movement to your writing. For example, compare the following descriptions of an accident.

> The truck swerved wildly. It went around a corner. Then it jumped the curb and crashed through a storefront.
> Swerving wildly around a corner, the truck jumped the curb and crashed through a storefront.

Imagine that you are a reporter. You have just covered one of the following events (or one of your choice). Write a brief article that captures the action and contains at least four participial phrases.

a volcanic eruption in Hawaii
a firefighter's rescue of a small girl
a movie crew filming a chase scene through city streets
a bear—having escaped from the zoo—rummages through the local produce market

Gerunds and Gerund Phrases

A gerund is a verb form that ends in *-ing* and functions as a noun.

A gerund can be used in a sentence in almost every way that a noun can be used.

Subject	*Jogging* is not recommended for everyone.
Direct Object	Never cease *dreaming*.
Object of a Preposition	If you swim too soon after *eating,* you may get a muscle cramp.
Predicate Nominative	My favorite Olympic event is *kayaking*.
Appositive	Her new hobby, *skydiving,* sounds dangerous to me.

A gerund phrase consists of a gerund and its modifiers and complements.

Like verbs, gerunds are modified by adverbs and adverb phrases.

> *Running away from a problem* won't solve it. (The adverb *away* and the adverb phrase *from a problem* modify the gerund *running*.)

Unlike a verb, however, a gerund may also be modified by an adjective.

> *Proper lighting on stage* is a necessity for a good performance. (The adjective *proper* and the adverb phrase *on stage* modify *lighting*.)

Since it is a verb form, a gerund may have complements of various kinds.

> *Telling me that story* has certainly changed my outlook. (*Me* is the indirect object of the gerund *telling; story* is the direct object.)
>
> *Being a dancer* requires great discipline. (*Dancer* is the predicate nominative after the gerund *being*.)

Like gerunds, gerund phrases function as nouns.

Subject	*Playing tennis on a tour* is not always fun.
Direct Object	The photographer tried *adjusting the shutter*.
Predicate Nominative	Their biggest mistake was *giving my brother a trombone*.

Object of a Preposition	Read everything carefully before *signing a contract.*
Appositive	On vacation we had one unforgettable experience, *fishing for tarpon.*

Sentence Diagraming   For information on diagraming gerunds and gerund phrases, see page 865.

Practice Your Skills

A. CONCEPT CHECK

Gerunds and Gerund Phrases   Write the gerunds and gerund phrases in the following sentences. Tell whether each is a *Subject, Direct Object, Predicate Nominative, Object of a Preposition,* or *Appositive.* If there is no gerund or gerund phrase, write *None.*

1. Batik, using wax to dye fabric in intricate patterns, is a process that originated in Java.
2. Planning the design is very important, since some areas of the fabric will be colored and some areas will remain plain.
3. Liquid wax, paraffin, or rice paste forms a coating that is painted onto the areas that are not to be dyed.
4. When the fabric is dipped into the dye, the covered areas resist the pigment.
5. After the cloth is dry, the wax can be removed by boiling.
6. The design created by the coating stands out now against the colored background.
7. Two difficult tasks are achieving multiple shades of the same color and introducing a second color.
8. Two shades of one color can be made by protecting the parts that are not to be dyed darker.
9. The fabric is then dipped into the dye again.
10. Repeating the same process with different dye allows a new color to be added.

B. REVISION SKILL

Using Gerunds and Gerund Phrases   Using gerunds and gerund phrases can make your writing more concise. Revise the sentences in the paragraph by following the instructions in parentheses.

> (1) It was very popular to tie-dye clothes in the 1960's and 1970's. (Change the infinitive phrase to a gerund phrase and move it to the beginning of the sentence.) (2) During those years, to wear brightly colored clothes was a fashion trend started by young people known as "hippies." (Change the infinitive phrase to a gerund phrase.) (3) Very few hippies who were

Tubular Indonesian Sarong, c.1900. Dallas Museum of Art, Textile Purchase Fund

Using Phrases and Clauses   **601**

creating tie-dyed wardrobes knew that they were following an ancient process *by which material was printed.* (Change the italicized phrase into a gerund phrase starting with *of.*) (4) This process *in which cloth is dyed by hand* is quite simple. (Change the italicized words into a gerund phrase starting with *of.*) (5) Small portions of material are tied with waxed string and immersed in dye to create colorful patterns. (Change the infinitive phrase to a gerund phrase.)

C H E C K ✔ P O I N T
PAGES 586–602

A. Tell whether each italicized phrase is an *Appositive Phrase,* a *Gerund Phrase,* an *Infinitive Phrase,* or a *Participial Phrase.* When you have finished, write the only italicized phrase that does not contain a prepositional phrase.

1. Few people study etiquette, *a system of rules for social behavior.*
2. In the 1950's, however, behavior *accepted by people in society* was prescribed by Emily Post and Amy Vanderbilt.
3. *Following the rules of good manners* was considered important.
4. *To avoid criticism* caused by committing a social error, people across the United States read Emily Post's books.
5. Amy Vanderbilt, *a successor to Emily Post,* was also an author, a journalist, and a television and radio personality.
6. These two women influenced behavior *ranging from meeting strangers to using the proper silverware.*
7. The etiquette rules *established by society* were enforced by peer pressure.
8. However, as life became more complicated, changes in society caused people *to question the old ideas about etiquette.*
9. *Worrying about the proper fork for salad* seemed frivolous when nuclear war was possible at any moment.
10. In our changed society, columnist Judith Martin, *known to millions as Miss Manners,* teaches etiquette for contemporary life.

B. Write the verbals in the following sentences. Identify each as a *Gerund,* an *Infinitive,* or a *Participle.* Tell whether each gerund is acting as a *Subject, Direct Object,* or *Object of a Preposition.* Tell whether each infinitive is acting as a *Noun, Adjective,* or *Adverb.* Also tell which word each participle is modifying.

1. Cultivated for centuries, the aromatic vanilla plant has a long and fascinating history.

2. To the ancient Aztecs, vanilla was a highly cherished gift from the gods.
3. Considered very precious, vanilla was once reserved for European royalty.
4. Classified as part of the orchid family, the vanilla plant must be pollinated by hand.
5. A plant needs four years to mature before producing beans.
6. Then the skilled workers pollinating the plants don't dare waste any time.
7. Having matured, the plants flower only one day a year.
8. Fertilizing the plants needs to occur between nine and ten in the morning, when the blossoms are completely open; only then will the fertilized flower develop.
9. Pampered like customers in an expensive spa, the beans are then treated to a sunning treatment by day and a sweating session at night.
10. Once it undergoes the processes of drying and sorting, the valuable product goes to market branded with the owner's special mark to protect it from vanilla rustlers.
11. Buyers must also beware of counterfeiters who sprinkle white powder on inferior beans to make them resemble the frosted crystals on the outside of superior beans.
12. Could you dare call vanilla plain again?

C. Application in Literature   Write the phrases in the following passage. Identify each as a *Prepositional Phrase, Participial Phrase, Gerund Phrase,* or *Infinitive Phrase.* Remember that prepositional phrases sometimes appear as modifiers in other types of phrases. Notice how the writer uses a variety of phrase constructions to create an interesting and vivid passage.

> (1) Why he couldn't possibly recognize her. . . . (2) John would be looking for a young woman with a peaked Spanish comb in her hair and the painted fan. (3) Digging post holes changed a woman. (4) Riding country roads in the winter . . . was another thing: sitting up nights with sick horses and sick children . . . [but] it was time to go in and light the lamps. . . . (5) Lighting the lamps had been beautiful. (6) The children huddled up to her and breathed like little calves waiting at the bar in the twilight. (7) Their eyes followed the match and watched the flame rise and settle in a blue curve, then they moved away from her. (8) The lamp was lit. (9) They didn't have to be scared . . . any more. Never, never, never more.
>
> **Katherine Anne Porter, *The Jilting of Granny Weatherall***

A clause is a group of words that contains a subject and a verb.

There are two kinds of clauses: **independent clauses** and **subordinate clauses.**

Independent Clauses

A clause that can stand alone as a sentence is an independent, or main, clause.

The sentence below contains two independent clauses.

> <u>Beethoven</u> gradually <u>became</u> deaf; nevertheless, <u>he</u> <u>continued</u> to compose and conduct great music.

In the example above, the subject of each independent clause has been underlined once, and the verb has been underlined twice. Each clause is capable of standing alone as a sentence, as shown by the following example.

> Beethoven gradually became deaf. He continued to compose and conduct great music.

Subordinate Clauses

A clause that cannot stand alone as a sentence is a subordinate, or dependent, clause.

Both of the clauses that are shown below have a subject and a verb. However, they are not sentences because they do not express complete thoughts.

> If <u>you</u> <u>like</u> houses with a history. (Then what happens?)
> Where <u>George Washington</u> <u>stayed</u> after the surrender at Yorktown. (What about where he stayed?)

To form a sentence, you must combine the subordinate clause with an independent clause.

> SUBORDINATE CLAUSE INDEPENDENT CLAUSE
> If you like houses with a history, you will enjoy a trip through the Hudson Valley.

> INDEPENDENT CLAUSE SUBORDINATE CLAUSE
> We visited the house where George Washington stayed after the surrender at Yorktown.

Do not confuse a subordinate clause with a verbal phrase. A verbal phrase does not have a subject and a verb.

Subordinate Clause	Unknowingly, ancient Egyptians used treatments *that contained penicillin.* (The subject is *that* and the verb is *contained.*)
Verbal Phrases	Unknowingly, ancient Egyptians used treatments *containing penicillin.* (The participial phrase does not have a subject and a verb.)
	The treatments were used *to cure skin ailments.* (The infinitive phrase does not have a subject and a verb.)

The subject of a subordinate clause may be a relative pronoun such as *who, whom, whose, that,* or *which.* In the first example above, *that* is a relative pronoun.

Practice Your Skills

A. CONCEPT CHECK

Independent and Subordinate Clauses Write the italicized group of words in each of the following sentences. Then identify each group as a *Phrase* or a *Clause.* When you identify a group as a clause, tell whether it is an *Independent Clause* or a *Subordinate Clause.*

1. *If you have never snorkeled before,* you are in for an exciting adventure.
2. *Having spent your life on the land,* you have had little experience of the breathtakingly beautiful underwater world.
3. To enjoy this wonderful water sport, you should seek instruction *before you begin snorkeling.*
4. Clear, clean lake or sea water along rocky shores is best for observing underwater life; *there you may see everything from tiny kelp plants to schools of angelfish.*
5. Snorkeling is easy, but *you should familiarize yourself with all the equipment.*
6. For example, there is the snorkel tube, which is a hollow tube *that permits a swimmer to breathe below the surface.*
7. The snorkel tube, *invented during World War II,* was first used on German submarines.
8. Resembling the fins of a seal, *swim fins help propel the snorkeler through the water,* and they give added force to the swimmer's kicks.

Using Phrases
and Clauses   **605**

9. Masks enable snorkelers *to see clearly under water.*
10. Many snorkeling enthusiasts *who travel to seas around the world* insist that snorkeling is the best way to discover the mysteries of underwater life.

B. DRAFTING SKILL

Imitating Sentence Structures   One way to master sentence variety is by imitating the good writing of others. Each of the following sentences is made up of two or three parts, separated by slashes (/). Tell whether each underlined group of words is an *Independent Clause,* a *Subordinate Clause,* or a *Verbal Phrase.* Then write an original sentence that imitates the structure of each numbered sentence.

> **Example**   Windsurfing on the lake near her home, / she developed strong muscles.
> Verbal Phrase / Independent Clause
> Wearing a wet suit, she pushed her sailboard from the shore.

1. To learn windsurfing, / the novice needs a little perseverance.
2. A sailboard is like a surfboard with a sail on it, / and the surfer guides it around on the water.
3. The windsurfer holds onto the bar / attached to the sail; / then she pulls herself and the sail to an upright position.
4. Once a windsurfer is standing, / the person's body acts as a mast.
5. As soon as the sail catches the wind, / the windsurfer can easily steer the sailboard by pulling or pushing the sail bar.
6. To go in a certain direction, / the windsurfer pulls the sail in the opposite direction.
7. Windsurfing is like sailing, / and it is somewhat like waterskiing, / but it is least like surfing.
8. Whereas the surfer depends on the ocean waves for movement, / the windsurfer relies on the speed and direction of the wind.
9. Frequent windsurfing develops balance, / and it improves one's coordination.
10. Envy the windsurfer / who lives close to a lake or the sea / and who can experience the exhilaration of sailing across the water every day.

KINDS OF
SUBORDINATE CLAUSES

There are three kinds of subordinate clauses: **adjective clauses, adverb clauses,** and **noun clauses.**

Adjective Clauses

The single-word adjective, the adjective phrase, and the adjective clause are used in the same way. They modify a noun or a pronoun.

An adjective clause is a subordinate clause that is used as an adjective to modify a noun or a pronoun.

Like adjectives, adjective clauses tell *what kind* or *which one.* An adjective clause is usually placed immediately after the word the clause modifies.

The stamps *that commemorate American locomotives* feature four different models. *(What kind* of stamps?)

That is the wealthy collector *who bought the rare stamp.* (*Which* collector?)

Words Used to Introduce Adjective Clauses Most adjective clauses begin with a relative pronoun: *who, whom, whose, that, which.* A **relative pronoun** relates the clause to the word it modifies. The modified word is the antecedent of the relative pronoun.

Newton, the English scientist, was born the same year *that Galileo, the famous Italian astronomer and physicist, died. (Year* is the antecedent of the relative pronoun *that* and is modified by the entire adjective clause.)

Sometimes the relative pronoun functions in the adjective clause as a subject, a direct object, an object of a preposition, or a modifier.

Subject	Westwater Canyon cuts through rock *that* is two billion years old. (The relative pronoun *that* is the subject of the verb *is* in the adjective clause.)
Direct Object	The artist *whom* I admire most is Mary Cassatt. (The relative pronoun *whom* is the direct object of the verb *admire* in the adjective clause.)

Object of a Preposition	The tourists to *whom* we spoke are from Germany. (The relative pronoun *whom* is the object of the preposition *to* in the adjective clause.)
Modifier	He is the friend *whose* father is an engineer. (The relative pronoun *whose* modifies *father,* the subject of the adjective clause.)

An adjective clause introduced by a relative pronoun is sometimes called a **relative clause.**

Usage Note As you use adjective clauses in description and other writing, be aware that the case of the pronoun, *who* or *whom,* is determined by the use of the pronoun in the adjective clause. *Who* can be used as a subject or predicate nominative within a clause. *Whom* can function as a direct object, indirect object, or object of a preposition.

The **relative adverbs** *after, before, since, when, where,* and *why* may also introduce adjective clauses. Like relative pronouns, relative adverbs relate the clause to the word it modifies. Unlike a relative pronoun, a relative adverb modifies the verb in the adjective clause.

> We visited a workshop *where birch-bark canoes are made by hand.* (The adjective clause modifies the noun *workshop.* The relative adverb *where* modifies the verb *are made* in the adjective clause.)

Sometimes the introductory word in an adjective clause is omitted.

> The trail *the guide indicated* led to a mill. (The relative pronoun *that* is omitted: *that* the guide indicated.)

Essential and Nonessential Adjective Clauses An adjective clause may be essential or nonessential. An **essential adjective clause** is one that is needed to complete the intended meaning of a sentence.

> We asked for a houseplant *that is not overly fond of direct sunlight.* (The clause is needed to complete the meaning of the sentence.)

A **nonessential adjective clause** is one that adds additional information to a sentence in which the meaning is already complete.

> The wax begonia, *which can be red, white, or pink,* blooms all year long. (The clause adds an idea to the sentence.)

That is always used to introduce essential clauses. In formal writing, *which* introduces nonessential clauses. *Who* may be used to introduce essential or nonessential clauses when the antecedent is a person. *Which* is never used to refer to people.

Punctuation Note As shown in the preceding examples, commas are used to set off a nonessential clause from the rest of the sentence. Commas are not used with essential clauses.

Sentence Diagraming For information about diagraming adjective clauses, see page 867.

Practice Your Skills

A. CONCEPT CHECK

Adjective Clauses Write the adjective clauses in the following sentences and the word each modifies. Then underline the relative pronoun or the relative adverb that introduces the clause.

1. The Mayas built a great civilization in the land that people now call Central America.
2. The Mayan empire, which covered 125,000 square miles, spread over mountains, deserts, and rain forests.
3. The ruins of their temples, pyramids, and plazas tell of architects who had great skill in mathematics and engineering.
4. Guatemala, Belize, Honduras, and Mexico are the countries where Mayan ruins can still be seen.
5. Modern archaeologists are amazed by discoveries that the Mayas made.

Gold pendant from the Mixtec civilization, early inhabitants of Oaxaca, Mexico

6. For example, the Mayas invented the concept of zero, which they used for mathematical calculations.
7. One famous site is Chichén Itzá, where the Mayas built many temples and an observatory.
8. With the mathematics that they developed, the astronomers plotted the movements of the sun and the moon.
9. They invented an accurate calendar whose smallest unit of time was a day and whose longest unit was twenty-three billion days!
10. Mayan books that have survived are fascinating.
11. The books, which were written in hieroglyphics, have never been fully translated.
12. Unfortunately, Diego de Landa, a missionary who objected to the Mayan religion, destroyed many Mayan books in 1562.
13. It is the loss of these books that makes translating Mayan hieroglyphics so difficult.
14. Around A.D. 800 the Mayas suddenly disappeared from the cities where they had lived.
15. Archaeologists who have studied the mysterious disappearance of the Mayas still cannot explain it.

B. REVISION SKILL

Combining Sentences Combine each of the following sentence pairs into a sentence with an adjective clause. Remember to punctuate the sentences correctly.

> ***Example*** The Aztecs once lived in the land. We now call the land Mexico.
> The Aztecs once lived in the land that we now call Mexico.

1. The Aztecs were clever architects. They built temples and pyramids.
2. They established their capital in the middle of present-day Mexico. Their capital was called Tenochtitlán.
3. The capital of modern Mexico stands on the ruins of the Aztec capital. The capital of Mexico is Mexico City.
4. Every day, thousands of Aztec merchants gathered at the marketplace. The marketplace was in the center of Tenochtitlán.
5. The Aztecs bought gold, silver, jade, leather, pottery, and perfume in the marketplace. They could also buy food and chocolate drinks.
6. Aztec children went to school. At school they learned crafts, religion, picture writing, astronomy, and history.
7. Neighboring tribes were no match for the Aztecs. The Aztecs were skilled in the arts of war.
8. European explorers of Central America heard rumors. According to these rumors, the Aztecs had vast wealth.

9. In 1519 the Aztec emperor welcomed the European explorer Hernando Cortes. The Aztec emperor was named Montezuma.
10. The Aztec Empire was crushed by this man. Montezuma had befriended this man.

The ruins of Machu Picchu, ancient walled city of the Incas

C. PROOFREADING SKILL

Improve the following paragraph by using adjective clauses to combine some thoughts. Be alert for errors in existing adjective clauses, as well as for other errors in usage or mechanics.

The Incas were a South American indian people. These people ruled one of the largest and richest empires in the americas. Because the Incas did not develop a writing system before the Spanish conquest of thier civilization, archaeological remains provide the major source of information about them.

Historians know a number of interesting facts about the incas. The Incas had special officials to who was given the duty of record keeping. The officials used a *quipu*. The *quipu* was a cord. The cord was tyed with knotted strings of various lengths and colors. Each knotted string represented a calculation. There were also surgeons. These surgeons performed an operation which involved cutting away part of the skull. They held the belief that this would relieve pressure on the brain and let out evil spirits. It often did releive pressure, and many of the patients survived the operation.

Adverb Clauses

An adverb clause is a subordinate clause that is used as an adverb to modify a verb, an adjective, or an adverb.

Modifying a Verb   The sheriff posted the notice *where every-one could see it.*

Modifying an   In cooking class we learned that dough is
Adjective   ready *when it has risen.*

Modifying an Adverb   The jet flew faster *than you can imagine.*

Like adverbs, adverb clauses tell *where, when, why, how,* or *to what extent* about words they modify. Adverb clauses can also explain *under what circumstances.*

> *If demand exceeds supply,* prices will go up. (Go up *under what circumstances?*)

> He lost the debate *because he was not prepared.* (Lost *why?*)

Like verbs, verbals also may be modified by an adverb clause.

Modifying an   Erin wants to visit Ireland *so that she can
Infinitive   kiss the Blarney stone.* (Why?)

Modifying a   Waiting *until the nurse slept,* Juliet drank
Participle   the bitter-tasting potion. (Under what
                         circumstances?)

Modifying a Gerund   Guessing *if you don't know the answer* may
                         help improve your test score. (Under what
                         circumstances?)

Words Used to Introduce Adverb Clauses Adverb clauses begin with subordinating conjunctions. A **subordinating conjunction** relates the clause to the word it modifies.

Time	after, as, as soon as, before, since, until, when, whenever, while
Cause	because, since
Comparison	as, as much as, than
Condition	although, as long as, even though, provided that, unless
Purpose	in order that, so that
Manner	as, as if, as though
Place	where, wherever

Writing
TIP

Writers use subordinating conjunctions to establish a specific relationship between the ideas expressed in a sentence.

Elliptical Clauses *Elliptical* comes from *ellipsis,* which means "omission of a word or words." An **elliptical clause** is an adverb clause from which a word or words have been omitted.

> *When applying for a job,* you should dress appropriately. (The words *you are* have been omitted: when *you are* applying.)
> You seem happier with the results *than I.* (The word *do* has been omitted: than I *do.*)

Punctuation Note An adverb clause at the beginning of a sentence is followed by a comma.

Sentence Diagraming For information about diagraming adverb clauses, see page 867.

Practice Your Skills

A. CONCEPT CHECK

Adverb Clauses and Subordinating Conjunctions Write the adverb clauses in the following sentences. Underline the subordinating conjunction in each clause. After each clause write the word or words that it modifies.

> *Example*   Whenever drought is a problem, people hope
> for rain.
> <u>Whenever</u> drought is a problem, hope

1. Even though it seems difficult or impossible, humans have long tried to make rain.
2. When an ancient rainmaker cast a spell, people could not always count on rain.
3. More recent "pluviologists" have proved no better at the task than the ancient rainmakers were.
4. One rainmaker was almost lynched because he "caused" a twenty-inch rain and washed out a dam.
5. Until Vincent Schaefer had a happy accident, rainmaking remained a hoax.
6. Seeding clouds so that drops of water would form had been tried by many different scientists.
7. Would seeding work if the temperature of the clouds were below freezing?
8. After Schaefer tried out this idea in a series of almost comical experiments with his home freezer, he succeeded.
9. One day, as he was putting a block of dry ice into the freezer, Schaefer exhaled.
10. Soon his improvised laboratory looked as if a miniature snowstorm were in progress.

B. DRAFTING SKILL

Using Adverb Clauses Sometimes you can vary your sentence structure by combining sentences and using adverb clauses. For each sentence or set of sentences below, follow the directions given in parentheses.

1. Deserts are found in two belts to the north and south of the equator. (Add a "where" adverb clause to explain that deserts occur in areas with little rainfall.)
2. Winds carry hot air away from the doldrums at the equator. The air eventually reaches the tropics. (Combine the sentences by using *until.*)
3. The tropics are cooler than the equator. They get less direct sun. (Combine the sentences by using *because.*)
4. Therefore, the air from the equator is cooled. (Add a "when" adverb clause explaining that the cooling of the air occurs on its arrival in the tropics.)
5. The water vapor in cooler air condenses. Rain falls on the tropics. (Combine the sentences by using *because.*)
6. The air passes the tropics. It has already lost much of its moisture. (Combine the sentences by using *when.*)
7. That is why the deserts farther from the equator than the tropics do not receive as much rain. (Expand the sentence by adding the adverb clause *as the tropics do* to complete the comparison.)
8. Similarly, a cold current in the Pacific Ocean causes winds to dry out before they reach the Atacama Desert in South America. The Atacama Desert borders the Pacific Ocean. (Combine the sentences by using *even though.*)
9. The rain does not fall. These areas of the world will remain dry. (Combine the sentences by adding *As long as* to the first sentence.)
10. Nonetheless, these deserts do manage to support life. (Add an adverb clause beginning with *provided that.* In the clause explain that for these deserts to support life, some small yearly amount of rain must fall.)

C. APPLICATION IN WRITING

A Setting Imagine that you are writing a science-fiction story about a torrential downpour that never ends. As you write about the increasingly strange, dangerous, and unexpected occurrences that are part of this ongoing storm, establish the setting by using adverb clauses to tell *where, when, why, how, to what extent,* and *under what circumstances* each event you are describing takes place.

Noun Clauses

A noun clause is a subordinate clause that is used in a sentence as a noun.

A noun clause may be used in any way that a noun is used. Consequently, noun clauses most frequently function as subjects, direct objects, indirect objects, predicate nominatives, and objects of prepositions.

Subject	*Where the hostages are* remains a mystery to the police.
Direct Object	Hoyle believed *that his theory would revolutionize the study of the universe.*
Indirect Object	Give *whoever comes in last* a prize.
Predicate Nominative	My question is *how do I load this computer program?*
Object of a Preposition	We have to limit expenses to *whatever funds are available.*

A noun clause may function as the direct object of a verbal.

Alice tried to decide *if she had been dreaming.* (The noun clause is the direct object of the infinitive *to decide.*)

Henry VIII had no trouble deciding *whether he should remarry.* (The noun clause is the direct object of the gerund *deciding.*)

Words Used to Introduce Noun Clauses   Noun clauses are introduced by pronouns and by subordinating conjunctions.

Pronouns   who, whom, which, what, that, whoever, whomever, whatever

A pronoun that introduces a noun clause may also function as a subject or an object within the clause.

The American Red Cross provides shelter and emergency relief aid for *whoever needs it.* (*Whoever* is the subject of the verb *needs* in the noun clause.)

Subordinating Conjunctions   how, that, when, where, whether, why (For a complete list of subordinating conjunctions, see page 555.)

Notice that some of the same words that introduce noun clauses can also introduce adjective and adverb clauses. To determine whether a clause is functioning as a noun, decide if the clause is doing the job of a noun in the sentence. In the first example on the next page, the clause is a noun clause because it is functioning as a direct object. The clauses in the second and third examples are modifying other words; therefore, they are not functioning as noun clauses.

> The orchestra conductor announced *when the concert would begin.* (Announced *what?* The noun clause is the direct object of the verb *announced.*)
> This is the time of year *when the Canada geese fly over.* (*Which* time? The adjective clause modifies the noun *time.*)
> The engine knocks *when you use low-octane gas.* (Knocks *when?* The adverb clause modifies the verb *knocks.*)

Sometimes the introductory word is omitted from a noun clause.

> The report said *unemployment is at an all-time low.* (The report said *that* unemployment is at an all-time low.)

Sentence Diagraming For information on diagraming noun clauses, see page 867.

Practice Your Skills

A. CONCEPT CHECK

Identifying Noun Clauses Write the noun clauses in the following quotations. Tell how each clause functions in the sentence by writing *Subject, Object of a Verb, Object of a Preposition,* or *Predicate Nominative.*

1. Genius does what it must, and talent does what it can.
   Owen Meredith
2. I regret that I have but one life to give for my country.
   Nathan Hale
3. Don't invent with your mouth what you don't see with a smile.
   Mother Teresa
4. Whoever gossips to you will gossip about you.   **Spanish proverb**
5. The best way to be thankful is to make use of what the gods have given you.   **Anthony Trollope**
6. What is wanted is not more law, but a better public opinion.
   James G. Blaine
7. A Bill of Rights is what the people are entitled to.
   Thomas Jefferson
8. Paradise is where I am.   **Voltaire**
9. Remember that time is money.   **Benjamin Franklin**
10. Whoever does not rise early will never do any good.
    Samuel Johnson

B. DRAFTING SKILL

Using Noun Clauses Create wise sayings by adding clauses from the second column to the sentence parts in the first column. Find the noun clause in each new sentence and write whether it is used as a *Subject, Indirect Object, Direct Object, Object of a Preposition,* or *Predicate Nominative.*

1. you are	whoever wrongs you
2. fights imaginary foes	what talents he or she has
3. give _____ the benefit of the doubt	that their child is the most beautiful one in the world
4. should never be predicted	what you eat
5. it's not whom you know; it is	who you are
6. has no friends	whoever does not help his friends
7. one must do the utmost with	what you feel inside
8. all parents think	whatever lies ahead in life
9. peace of mind is	whoever tilts at windmills
10. don't hide	what people most desire

C. APPLICATION IN WRITING

An Advice Column Suppose that your younger brother or sister—or someone else you know—is spending so much time on sports that his or her grades are slipping. Write an advice column that discusses the consequences of such behavior. Use at least three noun clauses.

C H E C K   P O I N T
PAGES 604–617

A. Write the italicized groups of words in the following sentences. Tell whether each group is a *Phrase* or a *Clause*. Then identify each clause as *Independent* or *Subordinate.*

1. *In the far western Pacific,* just north of the equator, lies a newly formed nation of islands.
2. Actually, *people have lived on the Micronesian islands for a long time.*
3. Basalt temples on the island of Pohnpei show *that there was a civilized society in Micronesia as far back as* A.D. *1300.*
4. *Administered by Europeans and Americans for about 150 years,* the islands have only recently received their independence.
5. *Spaniards claimed the islands in the 1500's,* although they did not interfere with the islanders until the late 1800's.
6. In 1899, Germany bought the islands *to harvest coconut oil there.*

7. The Japanese took control of them around 1920, *after which they settled the islands heavily.*

8. There are four main island chains in Micronesia, and *by 1940 the Japanese made up two-thirds of the population of three of these island chains.*

9. After World War II, Micronesia became a trust territory of the United States, *administered by the United States government.*

10. In 1979, *when the Federated States of Micronesia formed its own constitution,* the nation began its journey back to self-rule.

B. Write the subordinate clauses in the following sentences. Tell whether each is an *Adjective, Adverb,* or *Noun Clause.* For each adjective or adverb clause, tell the word it modifies. Tell whether each noun clause is used as a *Subject, Object of a Verb, Object of a Preposition,* or *Predicate Nominative.*

1. The capital state of the Federated States of Micronesia is Pohnpei Island, which is also the largest island in the FSM.

2. Pohnpei's green, rounded mountains rise gently out of the Pacific as if they were pushed straight up by the waves.

3. Even though the temperature is high throughout the year, rain and the spring trade winds cool the air.

4. There are frequent sudden downpours that nurture lush tropical vegetation.

5. Because their ancestors had built a city of temples, the islanders named their island *Pohnpei,* meaning "on the altar."

6. Who built the basalt temples at Nan Madol, Pohnpei, is a secret no one knows.

7. The temples, which are still used for religious ceremonies, are sacred to the Pohnpeians.

8. Kosrae, which lies to the east of Pohnpei, is the smallest of the four states of the FSM and is shaped like a sleeping woman.

9. In the nineteenth century, European whalers found that they could live comfortably on Kosrae.

10. Truk State, which is a collection of volcanic islands to the west of Pohnpei, is home to one of the largest barrier reefs in the world.

11. Truk is a popular diving spot because beautiful reefs have grown around the World War II ship and plane wrecks in Truk Lagoon.

12. That most of the people of the FSM live in the Truk islands is not surprising.

13. Yap State, where the people still grow taro and breadfruit in their gardens, is the most traditional of all the Micronesian islands.

14. Yap is most famous for its money, since the coins are giant stones up to twelve feet wide.

15. Since this money is so very heavy, it cannot easily be stolen.

THE STRUCTURE OF THE SENTENCE

You have learned that sentences may be classified according to their purpose: declarative, interrogative, imperative, and exclamatory. Sentences may also be classified according to their structure—the number and kinds of clauses they contain. The four kinds of structural sentence classifications are (1) simple, (2) compound, (3) complex, and (4) compound-complex.

Simple Sentences

A simple sentence is a sentence that contains one independent clause and no subordinate clauses.

The candidate is confident.

A simple sentence may have any number of phrases.

The candidate, Mrs. Schulman from Queens, is confident about the outcome of the mayoral race.

The parts of a simple sentence may be compound.

Compound Subject	Both the *Montagues* and the *Capulets* contributed to the feud.
Compound Verb	Someone *had split* the logs and *stacked* the wood in the shed.
Compound Complement	Mark Twain was both a *writer* and an *inventor*.

More than one part of a simple sentence may be compound.

The firefighters and several police officers rushed into the building and warned the tenants of the danger. (simple sentence with a compound subject and a compound verb)

Compound Sentences

A compound sentence is a sentence that has two or more independent clauses that are joined together.

The clauses in a compound sentence may be joined with a comma and a coordinating conjunction: *and, but, nor, or, for, yet.*

Everyone stopped work, **and** the factory became silent.

Writing
—**TIP**—

Short simple sentences give emphasis and create the feeling of action.

The independent clauses may be joined with a semicolon.

> There is no joy in Mudville; Mighty Casey has struck out.

In some compound sentences the clauses may be joined by a semicolon and a conjunctive adverb. (For a list of conjunctive adverbs, see page 556.)

> Our library may be small; **however,** it has an extensive collection of reference books.

Punctuation Note As shown above, a conjunctive adverb is usually preceded by a semicolon and followed by a comma.

Sentence Diagraming For information on diagraming simple and compound sentences, see pages 861–868.

Practice Your Skills

A. CONCEPT CHECK

Identifying Simple Sentences, Compound Sentences, and Compound Sentence Parts Write the following sentences. Label each sentence *Simple* or *Compound.* Underline each subject once and each verb twice. Label compound parts as *Compound Subject, Compound Verb,* or *Compound Complement.*

1. In the United States the game is called checkers, but in England it is called draughts.
2. Antonio Torquemada wrote and published the first book about the game in 1547.
3. In his book Torquemada described the board, the pieces, and the rules.
4. Peter Mallet, of France, wrote another book on checkers in 1668, and he described the origins of the game as mysterious.

La Famiglia del Pittore, by Henri Matisse. The Hermitage, Leningrad, Russia

5. According to Mallet, people throughout the world play checkers; furthermore, the game is probably as old as chess.
6. In England, William Payne and Joshua Sturges both wrote rule books for checkers.
7. A player uses twelve playing pieces on a board with sixty-four squares.
8. One player's pieces are dark; the other player's pieces are light.

Writing Theme
Board Games

9. Dark moves first, and then the players alternate.
10. A skillful player quickly captures the opponents' pieces and wins.

B. REVISION SKILL

Combining Sentences Combine each of the following sentence pairs into either a compound sentence or a simple sentence with a compound subject, compound verb, or compound complement. Add the word *and, but, both,* or *however* to the new sentence when necessary. Use a comma or semicolon to punctuate the new sentence correctly.

1. Checkers is a board game. So is chess.
2. Both are war games. In both, opponents capture each other's pieces.
3. The origins of both games are shrouded in mystery. They both were probably created in Persia or India.
4. The Spaniards of the fifteenth century loved checkers. They also loved chess.
5. The Spaniards first devised the modern rules of the game of chess. They also first described the modern rules of the game of chess.
6. In checkers each player has twelve pieces. In chess each player has sixteen.
7. As in checkers, the pieces in a game of chess are either dark or light. Whatever their actual color, they are referred to as "black" and "white."
8. The rules of checkers are simple. The rules of chess are also simple.
9. The rules of both games are easy. Strategy in chess is much more complex.
10. Unlike checkers, the pieces in chess move in different ways. The king, for example, can move only one space to a nearby square. The queen can move any number of spaces in any direction.

Complex Sentences

The complex sentence consists of one main clause and one or more subordinate clauses.

In a complex sentence, the subordinate clause is used as a noun or as a modifier. If it is used as a modifier, the subordinate clause usually modifies a word in the main clause.

> *When you leave,* shut the door. (Clause modifies *shut.*)
> *If he quits that job,* he will regret it later on. (Clause modifies *will regret.*)

In each preceding example, the main clause can stand as a sentence by itself: *Shut the door. He will regret it later on.*

Writing
—TIP—
Skillful writers use a combination of simple, compound, and complex sentences to engage the reader's interest.

Using Phrases
and Clauses   **621**

The subordinate clauses, however, cannot stand alone because their meaning is incomplete.

> When you leave. . . . (What then?)
> If he quits that job. . . . (What will happen?)

Complex sentences containing noun clauses are somewhat different from those with adjective or adverb clauses. The noun clause is used as a noun within the main clause. The noun clause, in other words, is part of the main clause.

> *What we saw* is impossible! (Noun clause is subject of *is*.)
> Kira is sorry about *what she said*. (Noun clause is object of preposition *about*.)

Usually, as in the examples above, neither the main clause nor the noun clause can stand by itself. Nonetheless, a sentence containing one main clause and noun clause is regarded as a complex sentence.

Sentence Diagraming   For information on diagraming complex sentences, see page 868.

Practice Your Skills

A. CONCEPT CHECK

Simple, Compound, and Complex Sentences   Write the following sentences. Label each sentence *Simple, Compound,* or *Complex.* Underline the subordinate clauses in the complex sentences.

1. Anyone who has come under the spell of a great piece of music may have wondered what inspired the composer.
2. Many contemporary composers deny working from inspiration.
3. According to one, he composes because he can't help it!
4. As a rule, creative artists do not sit around waiting for inspiration.
5. They turn to their creative tasks, and they do their best.
6. Many composers, however, seem to write music as though they had the gift of automatic writing.
7. Mozart and Schubert, two of the most spontaneous composers, seemed to write music with little or no conscious effort.
8. Others started with an idea; they then labored over their work.
9. Beethoven was busy with his *C Minor Symphony* for over five years, and it took Brahms over twenty-five years to write his great symphony.
10. That each composer works in his or her own way is an acknowledged fact.

B. DRAFTING SKILL

Sentence Imitation By imitating the structure of professional writers' sentences, you may improve your own writing. Write each sentence and tell whether it is *Simple, Compound,* or *Complex.* Then break the sentence into its clauses and label each one as a *Main Clause* or a *Subordinate Clause.* Finally, write a sentence of your own that has the same structure.

> *Example*   Musical composition is an art that anyone can enjoy. (Complex Sentence)
> Musical composition is an art (Main Clause) that anyone can enjoy. (Subordinate Clause)
> Written composition is a skill that anyone can learn.

(1) Even if you have never played an instrument, you can compose your own songs. (2) First, you find a piano, and you sit down at it. (3) It doesn't matter if you can't play the piano. (4) You just sit down on the piano bench, and then you strike any of the black keys. (5) You should, however, remember which black key you began with. (6) Then play any of the other black keys in any order and with any rhythm. (7) Finally, come back to the key that you started on. (8) Remarkably, if you play just the black keys, you can't hit any wrong notes! (9) Musicians call the notes on the black keys a "pentatonic scale." (10) Pentatonic scales are great for folk songs, and they are also wonderful for children's melodies.

Compound-Complex Sentences

A compound-complex sentence is a sentence that has two or more independent clauses and one or more subordinate clauses.

In the following examples of compound-complex sentences, the independent clauses are underlined once, and the subordinate clauses are underlined twice.

> The bicycle, which I repaired myself, had better work, for I certainly cannot afford to buy a new one any time soon. (The subordinate clause interrupts the first independent clause.)

> When the ice melted, heavy rains began, and the streets flooded.

Sentence Diagraming For information on diagraming compound-complex sentences, see page 868.

Practice Your Skills

A. CONCEPT CHECK

Simple, Compound, Complex, and Compound-Complex Sentences
Make four columns with the headings *Simple, Compound, Complex,* and *Compound-Complex*. Read the following literary excerpt. List the numbers of the sentences that fit under each heading.

(1) One day after school, twenty-five years ago, several of us were playing with a football in the yard at Randy Shepperton's. (2) Randy was calling signals and handling the ball. (3) Nebraska Crane was kicking it. (4) Augustus Potterham was too clumsy to run or kick or pass, [and] so we put him at center, where all he'd have to do would be to pass the ball back to Randy when he got the signal.

(5) It was late in October and there was a smell of smoke, of leaves, of burning in the air. (6) Nebraska had just kicked to us. (7) It was a good kick too—a high, soaring punt that spiraled out above my head, behind me. (8) I ran back and tried to get it, but it was far and away "over the goal line." (9) It hit the street and bounded back and forth with that peculiarly erratic bounce a football has.

Thomas Wolfe, *The Child Tiger*

B. REVISION SKILL

Achieving Sentence Variety The following paragraph is made up entirely of simple sentences. Rewrite the paragraph, using some compound, complex, and compound-complex sentences to add variety. Follow the directions in parentheses.

(1) American football evolved from the English games of rugby and soccer. (2) Rutgers and Princeton played the first football game in the United States in 1869. (3) Twenty-five people played on each side. (Combine sentences 2 and 3 into a compound sentence separated by a semicolon.) (4) Developments in the game came slowly. (5) Many changes were made by one man, Walter Camp. (6) Camp was a freshman at Yale in 1876. (Combine sentences 5 and 6 into a complex sentence.) (7) He was responsible for many innovations. (8) He decreased team size. (9) He decreased the field size. (Combine sentences 8 and 9 into a simple sentence with a compound object.) (10) He campaigned for the first-down rule. (11) The rule applies in the following situation. (Combine sentences 10 and 11 into a complex sentence.) (12) The offensive team moves fewer than five yards in three downs. (13) At this time, the offensive team must

give up the ball. (Combine sentences 12 and 13 into a complex sentence.) (14) Passing is a key part of the game today. (15) In the nineteenth century, football was a runner's game. (16) Hardly anyone ever passed then. (Combine sentences 14, 15, and 16 into a compound-complex sentence.)

CHECK POINT
PAGES 619–623

A. Write the following sentences. Underline each independent clause once and each subordinate clause twice. Then identify each sentence by kind: *Simple, Compound, Complex,* or *Compound-Complex.* Note that some of the complex sentences have more than one subordinate clause.

Writing Theme
Marine Environments

Kelp Forest,
Monterey Bay Aquarium

1. When David Packard went fishing in Monterey Bay, California, in 1929, he didn't know that he would someday build a unique aquarium and research center on the bay.
2. He was an inventor/researcher, and his two daughters, who were scientists, studied the creatures of Monterey Bay.
3. The family built an aquarium in Cannery Row, which had been made famous in two novels by John Steinbeck.
4. Cannery Row was once a strip of fish factories, but now it is a popular tourist attraction.
5. It is filled with little restaurants and shops.
6. The Monterey Bay Aquarium opened its doors in 1984, and it drew enormous crowds because it was filled with marvelous exhibits.
7. The aquarium features anemones, starfish, and other creatures that live in tide pools.
8. The most unusual exhibit at the aquarium, though, is the Giant Kelp Forest.
9. The kelp grows to enormous heights, and fish swim in and out of it, just as they do in the bay itself.
10. No one had grown kelp on such a large scale before, but this didn't stop the Packards or their research team.
11. A surge tank pushes currents through the twenty-eight-foot tank and keeps the kelp healthy.
12. Water is pumped in from the bay itself so that the fish and other creatures in the aquarium can have a homelike habitat.
13. At another very popular exhibit, the acrobatic feats of a group of California sea otters delight spectators.
14. If you ever visit Monterey, which is on the California coast between San Francisco and Los Angeles, you should certainly make time for a visit to this special place.

Using Phrases
and Clauses   **625**

B. Write the following sentences. Underline each independent clause once and each subordinate clause twice. Then identify each sentence according to its kind: *Simple, Compound, Complex,* or *Compound-Complex.*

1. Aquaculture is the finny future of high-tech fish farming.
2. An Aquacell at the University of Arizona provides an ideal environment for raising fish and other aquatic animals.
3. The fish are raised both as a subject for study and as a food source that is high in yield.
4. Because conditions must be carefully controlled, a computer checks oxygen levels and food consumption, and computer readings are taken each morning.
5. Scientists know more about warm-water species than they do about cold-water fish.
6. Eels are included in the study, but not as a food source.
7. Eels have a terrible feed-conversion ratio; eight pounds of food produces only one pound of eel.
8. Catfish, which outstrip their closest rivals, are the number-one fish in U.S. aquaculture, and their popularity is growing.
9. Paddlefish, which produce fine meat and are an excellent source of eggs for caviar, are also under study.
10. The world has many mouths to feed; perhaps aquaculture holds the answer to the food shortage.

Sturgeon in tanks

Shown growing in tanks, the tilapia fish is a major food source for many countries.

A. Prepositional Phrases and Appositive Phrases Write the prepositional phrases and appositive phrases in every sentence, and label each one. Then tell whether each prepositional phrase is functioning as an *Adjective* or *Adverb*. Remember that an appositive phrase may include a prepositional phrase.

> *Example*   Ramadan, a religious holiday for Muslims, lasts for an entire month.
> a religious holiday for Muslims, Appositive
> for Muslims, Prepositional, Adjective
> for an entire month, Prepositional, Adverb

Writing Theme
Special Days

1. Throughout the world, people have observed holidays for many reasons over the centuries.
2. The word *holiday* comes from the English phrase *holy day*.
3. Many of the traditional holidays around the world were first celebrated for religious reasons.
4. For example, Yom Kippur, a Jewish holiday, is observed by fasting and praying.
5. The Day of Atonement, Yom Kippur is the most solemn day of the Jewish year.
6. For Christians of the Western world, Easter, a major holiday, occurs on the first Sunday after the first full moon following the vernal equinox.
7. Holidays have also been related to cycles of the seasons.
8. On May Day, people in many countries celebrate the beginning of spring.
9. Midsummer Day, a holiday in Europe, is an observance from pre-Christian times.
10. To celebrate Midsummer Day, a holiday with ancient customs, men and women light bonfires on mountain peaks and even dance around them.

B. Identifying Verbal Phrases Write the italicized verbal phrase or phrases in each of the following sentences. Identify each phrase according to its kind: *Participial, Gerund,* or *Infinitive.* Remember that some verbal phrases contain prepositional phrases as complements.

1. The Egyptians were the first people *to celebrate birthdays*.
2. Cleopatra gave a party for Mark Antony on his birthday, *distributing gifts to the other guests instead of to the guest of honor.*
3. *Borrowing from the Egyptians,* the Greeks added the Persians' birthday tradition of *eating sweet cakes.*

4. Greek worshipers of the moon goddess Artemis celebrated her birthday every month by *baking a flour-and-honey cake.*
5. The Romans began *celebrating statesmen's birthdays as national holidays.*
6. In 33 B.C., Romans held parades, circuses, and banquets *celebrating Julius Caesar's birthday.*
7. By the twelfth century, *celebrating a birthday with a party* had become popular for everyone.
8. During the Middle Ages, German parents would honor their children with a birthday celebration *called a "kinderfest."*
9. An elf by the name of "Birthday Man" was said *to bring gifts to the German children.*
10. Today, even adults celebrate by *singing "Happy Birthday."*

C. Identifying Clauses Indicate whether each group of italicized words is an *Independent Clause* or a *Subordinate Clause.* Tell whether each subordinate clause is functioning as an *Adjective, Adverb,* or *Noun.*

1. The calendar we use today, *which begins the year on January 1,* was first established in 46 B.C. by Julius Caesar.
2. Until the Middle Ages, however, *northern Europeans celebrated the new year at the end of March.*
3. Then, in 1594, King Charles IX of France ordered *that the French celebrate the new year on January 1.*
4. When the king did this, *April Fools' Day was born.*
5. If you are wondering why this is so, *the answer is steeped in history and science.*
6. The French did not easily accept the king's command *that they celebrate the new year on the first of January.*
7. *After Charles IX had issued his proclamation,* many of the French continued celebrating at the end of March.
8. On March 25, the constellation Pisces, *which is known as the fish,* is passing the sun.
9. French people identified the sign of the fish with those citizens *who would not obey the king's directive.*
10. *These people would not accept the new holiday;* consequently, other people made fun of them.
11. For example, they invited people *who would not accept the new holiday* to nonexistent parties.
12. Someone *who fell victim to the pranks* was known as a "Fish of April."
13. *It took almost two hundred years,* but eventually, playing pranks on April 1 spread from France to England.

14. *When "April Fish" became "April Fool"* is not clear.
15. Today April Fools' Day is still celebrated in England and America, and *people still observe the day with pranks*.

D. Identifying Sentence Types Identify each of the following sentences as *Simple, Compound, Complex,* or *Compound-Complex.* Then find each subordinate clause and tell whether it is functioning as an *Adjective, Adverb,* or *Noun.*

1. Nearly everyone knows that the Pilgrims held the first Thanksgiving in the fall of 1621, but Americans did not celebrate the holiday regularly until the Civil War.
2. Harvest-time thanksgiving traditions are ancient; for example, the ancient Greek, Roman, and Hebrew cultures all had harvest celebrations.
3. The Pilgrims were thankful when they and their crops survived that first bitter winter in the New World.
4. They celebrated for three days, along with ninety Wampanoag Indian friends.
5. Four women and two girls cooked ducks, geese, lobster, clams, bass, corn, green vegetables, and dried fruit for 146 people.
6. Despite popular belief, the Pilgrims may not have had turkey and definitely did not have pie because they lacked enough flour for pie crusts.
7. George Washington tried to establish Thanksgiving as a national holiday, but many Americans, including Thomas Jefferson, did not feel that the Pilgrims' first harvest was a deeply significant event.
8. Just after the Battle of Gettysburg was fought, President Lincoln proclaimed Thanksgiving, the last Thursday in November, a national holiday.
9. In the 1930's, merchants wanted more selling days between Thanksgiving and Christmas, and the date for Thanksgiving was changed to the third Thursday in November.
10. The change proved unpopular, however, and the date was returned to the original date.

On the Lightside

SOPHOMORE

Each school year, you take a step up the ladder, from freshman to sophomore, to junior, to senior. What is behind those names?

Some of the meanings are obvious. Seniors have reached the highest rung of the educational ladder, and juniors are a step below them. The *fresh* in freshmen shows they are new or inexperienced, so they are at the bottom of the ladder. But what about sophomores?

Sophomores have taken one step up the ladder, but juniors and seniors are quick to tell them they have a long way to go. According to one explanation of the word's origin, so does *sophomore*. Some language experts claim the name comes from the Greek words *sophos,* meaning "wise," and *moros,* meaning "foolish." The combination indicates that sophomores have gained some wisdom, but that they have much more to learn. Taken literally, it means sophomores are "wise fools." Other experts, however, claim the word comes from a form of the Greek word *sophism,* which means "to become wise." So a sophomore is someone who is learning. These experts say it has evolved through such forms as *sophy moors, sophumer,* and *soph mor* before taking on its present form.

Whatever the origin of the word, however, sophomores soon enough leave the controversy behind and move another step up the educational ladder.

Classic "wise fools," the Three Stooges

Writing Complete Sentences

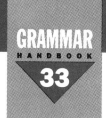

SENTENCE FRAGMENTS

A sentence fragment is a group of words that is only part of a sentence.

Unlike a full sentence that expresses a complete thought and has at least one subject and one verb, a sentence fragment risks confusing a listener or reader because it expresses only part of a thought. It may be missing either the subject or the verb, or both.

Fragment	Will begin at 7:30 A.M. on Saturday, August 15th. (What will begin? The subject is missing.)
Sentence	*The crew race* will begin at 7:30 A.M. on Saturday, August 15th.
Fragment	Eighteen boats in the race around Manhattan Island. (What about the race? The verb is missing.)
Sentence	Eighteen boats *are competing* in the race around Manhattan Island.
Fragment	Under the Brooklyn Bridge. (Who or what is under the bridge? What is happening there?)
Sentence	*The boats will pass* under the Brooklyn Bridge.

In writing, fragments are usually the result of haste or incorrect punctuation.

Fragments as Incomplete Thoughts

You can think much faster than you can write. Many sentence fragments occur, therefore, because your mind has raced ahead of your hand. As a result, you may find yourself writing a second thought before you have completed the first. In other cases you may discover that you have left out a key part of a sentence. Suppose, for example, that you wrote the following passage:

> In 1215 King John was presented with the Magna Carta. His nobles and churchmen forced him to sign the document. Establishing the principle that even the King of England must obey the law.

The third group of words in the paragraph above is not a sentence because it does not express a complete thought. The reader can only guess that you meant to say that the Magna Carta established the principle described.

Practice Your Skills

A. CONCEPT CHECK

Fragments Write *S* for each group of words that is a sentence or *F* for each fragment.

1. Associate many heroes and adventurers with the Old West.
2. Native Americans, cowhands, trappers, and rustlers.
3. For example, there was Kit Carson, a frontiersman and scout.
4. After whom Carson City, Nevada, is named.
5. Many other memorable characters during westward expansion.
6. Chief Joseph, for instance, is remembered as a brave leader of the Nez Percés and champion of Native American rights.
7. In addition, Wild Bill Hickok, a scout, spy, and marshal.
8. Numerous exaggerated tales of his courage and marksmanship.
9. Many legends about these folk heroes sprang up.
10. About Wyatt Earp and Doc Holliday, for example, who participated in the famous shootout at the O.K. Corral.

B. REVISION SKILL

Correcting Unclear Fragments Improve the following paragraph by revising the seven fragments as complete sentences.

(1) Ghost towns all across the country. (2) Pithole, Pennsylvania, one of the most famous. (3) It flourished for ten years. (4) For a time more than twenty thousand people in the town. (5) However, everyone left after the oil dried up. (6) Elsewhere, ghost towns in timber country. (7) Modern ghost towns in the iron-mining regions of Minnesota. (8) The best-known in the mining sections of the West. (9) Houses full of furniture and offices with papers still in the desks. (10) Wherever the resources gave out, there are ghost towns.

Fragments Caused by Incorrect Punctuation

Sentences begin with a capital letter and end with a period, a question mark, or an exclamation point. Many fragments occur because the writer inserts end punctuation and a capital letter too soon.

Fragment	We will leave. *As soon as the dishes are done.*
Sentence	We will leave as soon as the dishes are done.
Fragment	*Before signing the bill.* The President congratulated the cosponsors.
Sentence	Before signing the bill, the President congratulated the cosponsors.

Practice Your Skills

A. CONCEPT CHECK

Fragments Caused by Incorrect Punctuation   Each item below consists of two word groups: a fragment and a sentence. Write each fragment on your paper. Then rewrite each item, using correct punctuation to join the two word groups into one sentence.

1. During the long, hot summer of 1787. The Constitution was drafted in the stuffy statehouse in Philadelphia.
2. Fifty-five representatives from twelve of the newly formed states had convened. To "take into consideration the situation of the United States."
3. All believed in states' rights. But felt they needed unity with the other states as well.
4. Finding a compromise was a persistent problem for the leaders of the convention. James Madison, George Washington, Benjamin Franklin, and Alexander Hamilton.
5. With few guidelines from history. The delegates eventually agreed on the seven articles of the Constitution.
6. In the true spirit of compromise. Everybody got something, but nobody got everything.
7. The Great Compromise overcame a major stumbling block. The conflict between the big states and the little states over the basis of representation in the future Congress.
8. The delegates agreed there would be two houses of Congress. One having two representatives from each state and the other a number of representatives based on each state's population.
9. The delegates also agreed on the three main purposes for the new central government. Making laws, interpreting laws, and carrying out laws.
10. To this day these purposes are served by the federal government's three branches. Commonly known as the Congress, the Supreme Court, and the Presidency.

B. PROOFREADING SKILL

Correcting Fragments   Rewrite the following paragraph, correcting the sentence fragments. Also correct any other errors in punctuation, spelling, and capitalization.

> The new presidency. One of the last important Issues at the Constitutional Convention. The resolution of this issue was largely due to the effort of james Wilson. An Immigrant from Scotland. James Madison had originally proposed that the President should be chosen by Congress. However, Wilson argued.

That the President should draw his strength from a popular election. He would thus be accountabel directly to the people, further guaranteeing a genuine seperation of powers.

The Signing of the Constitution, by H.C. Cristy

PHRASES AND CLAUSES AS FRAGMENTS

Writing
— TIP —
Use fragments to save time while taking study notes.

As you know, a **phrase** is a group of words that does not contain a subject and a verb. A common mistake occurs when a verbal phrase is mistaken for a complete sentence. This error occurs because verbals (gerunds, participles, infinitives) look like verbs and function somewhat like verbs. They are not verbs, however, and cannot be used as such.

The most troublesome verbals are those that end in *-ing,* such as *running* and *searching.* All gerunds and present participles end in *-ing,* and thus are often mistaken for verbs. You will avoid many sentence errors if you remember the following fact:

No word ending in *-ing* can be a complete verb unless it is a one-syllable word like *sing, ring,* or *bring.*

If an *-ing* word is preceded by *is, are, was,* or some other form of *be,* the words together are a verb: *is running, were searching.*

When you discover that a verbal phrase has been used as a fragment, you can correct it in one of two ways. Either add the verbal phrase to an already complete sentence or change the verbal into a verb and use it in a sentence.

The following chart shows how verbal phrases can be rewritten as complete sentences.

Changing Verbal Phrases into Sentences

Participial Phrase — Covered with ice

Sentence — *Covered with ice,* the roads were impassable. (The phrase is added to a sentence.)

Sentence — The roads *were covered with ice.* (A subject is provided and an auxiliary verb is combined with the participle to make a verb phrase.)

Gerund Phrase — Canoeing across the lake

Sentence — I enjoy *canoeing across the lake.* (A subject and verb are added. The gerund becomes a direct object.)

Sentence — *Canoeing across the lake* is risky. (The gerund phrase becomes the subject of the sentence.)

Infinitive Phrase — To see the midnight sun

Sentence — Wendy and I have always wanted *to see the midnight sun.* (A subject and verb are added. The infinitive phrase becomes the direct object.)

Sentence — *To see the midnight sun* must be thrilling. (The infinitive phrase has become the subject.)

Sentence — It must be thrilling *to see the midnight sun.* (The infinitive phrase modifies *thrilling.*)

Prepositional Phrase — At the end of a long day

Sentence — Everyone enjoys relaxing *at the end of a long day.* (The phrase is added to a sentence.)

Sentence — *At the end of a long day,* Sheila takes a brisk walk. (The phrase is added to a sentence.)

Appositive Phrase — One a true story and the other fiction

Sentence — Both books, *one a true story and the other fiction,* were best sellers. (The phrase is added to a sentence.)

Series Fragments

Occasionally, items listed in a series may be so long or so complicated that they are mistaken for a sentence. This is especially true if the series is composed of verbal phrases. Series fragments may lack either a subject or a verb or both.

Fragment	I saw three interesting birds during the hike. *A heron, a hummingbird, and an owl.*
Sentence	I saw three interesting birds during the hike: a heron, a hummingbird, and an owl.
Fragment	Having hoped, having dreamed, and finally having won the trophy.
Sentence	*Having hoped, having dreamed, and finally having won,* Kimo clutched the trophy.

Practice Your Skills

CONCEPT CHECK

Phrase and Series Fragments   Each item below consists of two word groups: a fragment and a sentence. Write each fragment on your paper. Then rewrite each item to eliminate the fragment. You may join the two word groups into one sentence, or you may add words to make the fragment a complete sentence on its own.

1. It is crucial for all living creatures. To hide from predators.
2. Nevertheless, some fish live in open water. Without reefs or plants for shelter.
3. While staying right out in the open. They have found a special way to protect themselves.
4. By traveling in schools, these fish find safety in numbers. Swimming behind or next to each other.
5. As one of hundreds, moving in unison, forming a large mass. Each fish reduces its odds of being singled out by predators.
6. Some fish hide by blending with their background. Even brightly colored ones.
7. Their color and shape act as camouflage. To help them match the seabed, lie flat against some surface, or appear so narrow as to be almost invisible.
8. For example, lying on the ocean floor. The flat, mud-colored flounder is almost indistinguishable from its background.
9. Similarly, a slender trumpetfish is difficult for a predator to spot. Swimming next to a stripe on a much bigger fish.
10. Some fish even have transparent bodies. Among the strangest forms of animal camouflage.

Subordinate Clauses as Fragments

Unlike a phrase, a subordinate clause does have a subject and a verb. However, a subordinate clause does not express a complete thought and cannot be a sentence. Combine a subordinate clause with an independent clause to correct this kind of fragment.

Fragment   As soon as we saw the flames.
Sentence   *As soon as we saw the flames,* we dialed 911.

Another way to correct a fragment that is a subordinate clause is to rewrite the clause as a sentence.

Fragment   Trevor Library, which seemed like a stuffy mausoleum.
Sentence   *Trevor Library seemed like a stuffy mausoleum.*

Fragments in Conversation

Fragments often occur in conversation without harming communication. Tone of voice, gestures, and the presence of each speaker all help to add meaning and keep ideas clear.

Sentence   When is the canceled game going to be played?
Fragment   Probably Thursday.

Professional writers sometimes consciously use fragments when they want to create realistic dialogue, establish a certain mood, or achieve a particular rhythm in their prose.

Practice Your Skills

A. CONCEPT CHECK

Subordinate Clauses as Fragments Write *S* for each group of words that is a sentence or *F* for each fragment. Then rewrite each fragment by adding new material to make it a complete sentence.

Writing Theme
The Great Dust Bowl

1. The term *Dust Bowl* describes the area of the south central United States that suffered severe drought during the 1930's.
2. When a dry region receives less than normal rainfall.
3. Usually, grassland holds moisture in the soil.
4. Because farmers plowed up grassland and destroyed the roots.
5. As the wind blew over the dry, plowed fields.
6. As soon as the roots of the young crops were exposed.
7. Drifting soil covered fences, roads, and some buildings.
8. When the already discouraged farmers surveyed the damage.
9. Although the federal government stepped in to help.
10. Some counties lost up to 60 percent of their population during the period of the Great Dust Bowl.

B. APPLICATION IN LITERATURE

Using Fragments Effectively As you have learned, professional writers sometimes use fragments intentionally. Identify the fragments in the following selection. Then rewrite each fragment as a sentence. Compare your sentences with the originals and suggest why Steinbeck chose to use fragments in this passage. (Notice that the author has also ignored some punctuation and usage rules.)

(1) But most of the families changed and grew quickly into the new life.
(2) And when the sun went down—
(3) Time to look out for a place to stop.
(4) And—there's some tents ahead.
(5) The car pulled off the road and stopped, and because others were there first, certain courtesies were necessary.
(6) And the man, the leader of the family, leaned from the car.
(7) Can we pull up here an' sleep?
(8) Why, sure, be proud to have you.
(9) What State you from?
(10) Come all the way from Arkansas.
(11) They's Arkansas people down that fourth tent.
(12) That so?
(13) And the great question, How's the water?
(14) Well, she don't taste so good, but they's plenty.
(15) Well, thank ya.
(16) No thanks to me.
(17) But the courtesies had to be.

John Steinbeck, *The Grapes of Wrath*

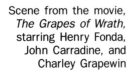

Scene from the movie, *The Grapes of Wrath*, starring Henry Fonda, John Carradine, and Charley Grapewin

C. APPLICATION IN WRITING

A Dialogue Write a dialogue that you imagine taking place between two inhabitants of the Dust Bowl in 1938. Convey their fears about the drought and their awe of the amount of dust covering their homes. Use some fragments to make the dialogue sound natural. Label the fragments you use.

RUN-ON SENTENCES

A run-on sentence is two or more sentences written as though they were one sentence.

In some run-on sentences the writer fails to use an end mark at the end of each sentence.

Run-on   The tide is out now the water is only a foot deep.
Correct   The tide is out. Now the water is only a foot deep.

In other run-on sentences the writer uses a comma instead of an end mark. This error is called the **comma fault** or **comma splice.**

Run-on   Don't worry about my brother Joseph, he can take care of himself.
Correct   Don't worry about my brother Joseph. He can take care of himself.

Correcting Run-on Sentences

There are several ways to correct run-on sentences. In both of the corrections shown above, the run-on sentence has been rewritten as two separate sentences. Sometimes, however, when the ideas expressed are closely related, it is preferable to join them into a single sentence.

You can join the sentences with a comma and a coordinating conjunction to form a compound sentence.

Run-on   The demonstrators were orderly, the mayor willingly listened to their complaints.
Correct   The demonstrators were orderly, **and** the mayor willingly listened to their complaints.

You can form a compound sentence by joining the sentences with a semicolon.

Run-on   The demonstrators were orderly, the mayor willingly listened to their complaints.
Correct   The demonstrators were orderly; the mayor willingly listened to their complaints.

You can also form a compound sentence by joining the sentences with a semicolon and a conjunctive adverb. (See page 556 for a list of conjunctive adverbs.)

Run-on   The demonstrators were orderly, the mayor willingly listened to their complaints.
Correct   The demonstrators were orderly; **consequently,** the mayor willingly listened to their complaints.

Finally, you can join the sentences into one complex sentence by making one of them into a subordinate clause. (See pages 607–618 for a discussion of kinds of subordinate clauses.)

Run-on   The demonstrators were orderly, the mayor willingly listened to their complaints.
Correct   Because the demonstrators were orderly, the mayor willingly listened to their complaints.

Practice Your Skills

A. CONCEPT CHECK

Run-on Sentences   Write *R* for each run-on or *S* for each correctly written sentence. Then use one of the five methods covered in the lesson to correct each run-on. Use each method at least once.

1. During the early 1800's, French painters tended to produce works showing historical, religious, or mythological subjects.
2. Preferring to work in their studios, they seldom depicted scenes of everyday life, timely events were rarely recorded on canvas.
3. These painters used smooth brushwork their paintings show everything in precise detail.
4. In the 1860's, however, a new group of painters emerged in France, eventually they became known as the Impressionists.
5. They believed art should be contemporary, it should not be concerned only with the past.
6. The traditional painters usually painted indoors, the Impressionists often took their easels outside to capture local scenes.
7. They were especially interested in the effects of natural light, they attempted to depict its play on leaves, on flowers, on water.
8. Their brushwork was innovative, too, it was neither smooth nor precisely detailed.
9. Bold colors helped them present new ways of seeing such common sights as a haystack or a field of poppies.
10. At first, many people sneered at this alternative to traditional painting, today Impressionist paintings are eagerly sought by museums and collectors around the world.

B. REVISION SKILL

Avoiding Run-on Sentences Run-ons make writing difficult to read and understand. An important part of revising your work is being sure to eliminate these errors. Identify the run-ons in the following paragraph. Then rewrite the paragraph correctly.

Life-Boat and Manby Apparatus Going off to a Stranded Vessel Making Signal (Blue Lights) of Distress, by Joseph M.W. Turner

(1) Joseph William Turner was one of Britain's greatest painters, he is known for his dazzling paintings of seascapes and storms. (2) When he died in 1851, he willed all of his paintings to his beloved country, England this gesture, although generous, caused the government a great deal of trouble. (3) Turner's family immediately set about to upset the will, claiming that the artist was not of sound mind when he wrote it. (4) Their efforts were unsuccessful Turner's work, finished and unfinished, was delivered to the National Gallery. (5) The gallery, unprepared to accept such a volume of work, stored the canvases in the basement. (6) In 1910, Turner's work was to be displayed it was to hang in the Tate Gallery, an annex of the National Gallery. (7) Instead, the works went from one basement to another. (8) The Thames River overflowed in 1928 many of the canvases were severely damaged. (9) Now, over 140 years after Turner's death, his works hang in a new gallery designed solely to display them finally the conditions of the will are fulfilled.

Writing
—TIP—

In freewriting,
continue writing
nonstop for
several minutes
to generate as
many new ideas
as you can.

Writing Theme
The Grand Canyon

C. APPLICATION IN WRITING

A Response to a Work of Art   Choose a work of art that interests you. Use freewriting to jot down all that you see and think as you look at the work. Do not be concerned about sentence structure and punctuation. Then go back over your freewriting and identify any run-on sentences. Finally, revise your freewriting as a finished response to the work of art.

CHECK ✔ POINT
PAGES 631–641

Rewrite the following fragments and run-ons as complete sentences.

1. The Grand Canyon in Arizona carved out by the Colorado River.
2. It has been called "a spectacle unrivaled on this earth," the canyon is one of the most popular national parks.
3. First recorded exploration in 1540 by Spanish conquistadors.
4. Remained virtually forgotten until two Spanish priests "rediscovered" it in 1776.
5. Thorough exploration, however, did not occur at that time, in 1869 John Wesley Powell studied the canyon by boat.
6. Found numerous ruins of prehistoric cliff-dwelling tribes.
7. Area finally established as a national park in 1919.
8. The canyon ranges in width from four to eighteen miles its greatest depth lies over a mile beneath its rim.
9. Vegetation on the canyon floor is desertlike, at higher elevations evergreen forests grow.
10. Still in the making, constantly changing and growing bigger.
11. Erosion caused by the Colorado River, as well as by rain along the canyon walls, wind, heat, and cold.
12. Tons of sediment carried away by the Colorado River each day.
13. The canyon walls reveal the history of the continent, fossils of ancient marine life, dinosaurs, and even camels and elephants have been discovered at various levels.
14. View from South Rim overwhelming in magnitude and beauty.
15. Today, visitors often explore the canyon on muleback, the mules travel along Bright Angel Trail.
16. The mules safely delivering their riders for more than sixty years.
17. Some restrictions apply, however, riders must be at least twelve years of age and weigh less than two hundred pounds.
18. Other means, such as rafting trips and backpacking.
19. Also scenic auto routes along the rim.
20. Attracts more than a million visitors annually.

A. Correcting Fragments Identify each group of words as a *Sentence* or a *Fragment*. Then rewrite the paragraph, correcting each fragment by joining it to another word group to form a sentence.

(1) Every year, people come from all over America. (2) To gather in the little community of Bean Blossom, Indiana. (3) And take part in the annual Bill Monroe Bluegrass Festival. (4) The festival is a combination of old and new. (5) A celebration of traditional and contemporary bluegrass music. (6) It offers the finest in good old-fashioned, foot-stomping entertainment. (7) Including music by some of the best bluegrass bands in the country. (8) Visitors to the festival stroll up and down several acres of Indiana countryside. (9) Listening to melodies like "Salty Dog" and "*T* for Texas." (10) They can applaud the highly skilled musicians. (11) Who play on instruments ranging from banjos and mandolins. (12) To fiddles, autoharps, and acoustic guitars.

B. Correcting Fragments and Run-on Sentences Identify each group of words as a *Sentence,* a *Fragment,* or a *Run-on.* Then rewrite the paragraph, using a variety of methods to correct the fragments and run-ons.

(1) Theodore Roosevelt, the twenty-sixth President of the United States. (2) He is remembered for his hunting trips, he believed that his most important achievement in public life was his effort to conserve forests and help wildlife. (3) Roosevelt claimed, "The American had but one thought about a tree, and that was to cut it down." (4) In order to preserve the beautiful forests of the United States. (5) Roosevelt created the Forest Service in 1905, he set aside 150 million acres of forest reserves and formed a number of national parks.

(6) The bespectacled New Yorker, who had been a sickly child. (7) He traveled extensively. (8) As a young man who enjoyed riding through the West. (9) Here he saw that much of the wildlife of the country was disappearing. (10) Such as buffalo, wild turkey, and elk. (11) He established wildlife and waterfowl refuges. (12) To protect many endangered species.

(13) However, the animal that Roosevelt did the most to "protect" is the bear, the "Teddy" bear was named after this president when he refused to shoot an old, almost-blind bear while on a hunting trip.

Writing Complete
Sentences

Sketchbook

Searching for a lost expedition in the Amazon jungle, you receive a radio communication. The signal is faint, however, so you can hear only fragments of what one of the explorers is saying. Turn the fragments that follow into a draft of the complete message.

. . . is captain . . . not lost . . . located about three miles northeast of Quizotl . . . ten days . . . cannot move . . . explosion in our camp . . . Julio, of the exploration team . . . most of our party . . . quickly . . . medical supplies and blankets.

Additional Sketches

A local millionaire, sponsoring a contest at your high school, will award ten thousand dollars to the writer of the most entertaining self-description. Describe yourself in a paragraph that contains several predicate nouns and predicate adjectives.

You have been asked to cover an important sporting event. Write an account two paragraphs long. First, describe the setting, competitors, crowd, and general atmosphere. Next, describe the action during the final moments of the event. Choose words (nouns, adjectives, verbs, and adverbs) that create a mood of tension and excitement.

On the Lightside

A CAT IN UNDERWEAR?

As anyone knows who has ever written so much as a letter home to mother, the English language is full of traps and pitfalls. It is harder to write a clear sentence than to keep a clear conscience.

Some time ago, while trying to explain why I thought my neighborhood had that exclusive quality known as ambience, I wrote this sentence. . . .

"A man chasing a cat with a broom in his underwear is ambience by any definition."

Oddly enough, several people evidently misunderstood that simple sentence. . . .

"It was with considerable interest," wrote Bob Byrne, "knowing that you also have long suffered with a back problem, that I read that you keep a broom in your underwear. Is this good?"

The problem seems to be that the reader's understanding is colored or distorted by his own experience. . . . "A gray tomcat with a broom in his underwear is ambience," wrote Mrs. Cecil T. Brown, "in anyone's language. Please call us collect the next time. We will take pictures."

"I do agree," wrote yet another. . . . "Mt. Washington must have ambience—a cat in underwear, indeed! And even more ambient—a cat with a *broom* in his underwear?"

"I have known cats for many years," wrote N.S. Elliott of Hollywood, "but have never seen one wearing underwear. Or outerwear, either, for that matter. Or was it you with the broom in your underwear? If so, why?"

What I would like to do now is to explain exactly what happened that night. . . . We have a new tomcat in the neighborhood, and he had begun to exasperate me beyond the limits of my patience, if not my sanity. He would wait until I had gone to bed, or was about to, then skulk into our yard and crouch in the ivy under my windows to caterwaul his loathsome lovesong.

Among all my virtues, I like to think that tolerance for my fellow creatures is first. But the screech of a . . . tomcat strings me out. So that night, when he did it again, I snapped. I won't go into the ludicrous details.

But if you had been here, you would have seen a man chasing a cat with a broom in his underwear.

As you see, the difficulty of saying exactly what you mean, so that your reader can't fail to understand, is not a common skill, which is why most writing is not so much read as puzzled out.

Jack Smith

Directions In each of the following sentences, one, two, or none of the underlined sections may be incorrect. Look for errors of grammar, usage, punctuation, spelling, and capitalization. On your paper, write the number of the sentence, the letter of each incorrect underlined section, and the correction. If the sentence contains no errors, write E.

> **Example**   Claiming the region for the Dutch. in 1609 Henry Hudson
> <u>A</u>   B   C
> sailed up the river later named for him. No error
>   D   E
>
> **Answer**   A—Claiming the region for the Dutch,

1. Moving at <u>186,000</u> miles per <u>second light</u> takes <u>about eight minutes</u> <u>to travel from the</u>
         A   B   C   D
<u>sun to the earth</u>. <u>No error</u>
            E

2. Over the course of the past <u>seventy-five</u> <u>years many</u> changes <u>have taken place</u> in the game
                             A   B   C
of <u>football. Such as the introduction of the forward pass.</u> <u>No error</u>
                          D   E

3. <u>Melting snow</u> caused floods <u>from the mountains</u> that <u>covered</u> most <u>of the valley</u>.
     A   B   C   D
<u>No error</u>
  E

4. <u>Swinging from branch to branch through the jungle,</u> <u>the naturalists</u> <u>photographed</u> the
                   A   B   C
<u>Orangutan.</u> <u>No error</u>
   D   E

5. <u>Throwing a life saver with a rope attached into the water,</u> the person <u>who</u> fell <u>overborde</u>
                          A   B   C
<u>was saved</u>. <u>No error</u>
    D   E

6. The <u>English</u> teacher showed slides of his visits to Ernest <u>Hemingway's</u> home in Key
     A   B
West, Florida; <u>Mark Twain's</u> home in Hartford, Connecticut; and William Faulkner's
              C
home in <u>Oxford, Mississippi</u>. <u>No error</u>
        D   E

7. <u>Jacques Cartier was a French explorer</u> <u>whom</u> made three trips to <u>the New World</u> and
                  A   B   C
helped to establish fishing and fur trading <u>in Canada</u>. <u>No error</u>
                                     D   E

8. Teddy Roosevelt is one of the presidents <u>to who</u> we owe thanks <u>for protecting many of</u>
   A
   <u>the national parks and forests</u> <u>West</u> of the <u>Mississippi River.</u> <u>No error</u>
   C   D   E

9. New skaters should lace <u>their</u> skates <u>tightly, and</u> <u>they should put a knot</u> a little <u>below the</u>
            A   B   C   D
   <u>ankel</u> to prevent soreness. <u>No error</u>
    E

10. <u>People throughout the world</u> recognize the <u>famous</u> <u>Statue of Liberty,</u> <u>which stands in</u>
       A   B   C   D
    New York Harbor. <u>No error</u>
          E

11. Events <u>which</u> are sometimes considered unlucky <u>include</u> crossing the path of a black
       A   B
    <u>cat walking</u> <u>under</u> a ladder, and talking while riding over a bridge. <u>No error</u>
     C   D   E

12. An editor once <u>discouraged</u> Louisa May Alcott by telling her that <u>no one</u> would ever
         A   B
    buy <u>anything</u> she <u>wrote.</u> <u>No error</u>
      C   D E

13. Many of the Germans and Swedes <u>which</u> <u>imigrated</u> in large numbers during the second
              A   B
    half of the nineteenth <u>century</u> <u>settled</u> in the <u>Midwest.</u> <u>No error</u>
            C   D   E

14. After listening to *The Magic Flute* by <u>Mozart. The</u> young <u>musican was</u> eager <u>to see it</u>
           A   B   C   D
    staged. <u>No error</u>
     E

15. <u>The class reading</u> *A Rose for Miss Emily,* a story about a woman in the <u>South during a</u>
     A   B   C
    time of change. It was a <u>really</u> interesting story. <u>No error</u>
           D   E

16. After his father <u>was imprisoned</u> for <u>debt, the</u> <u>twelve-year-old</u> Charles Dickens <u>went</u> to
         A   B   C   D
    work in a factory. <u>No error</u>
         E

17. If <u>Dracula</u> fails to return <u>to his coffin</u> before <u>morning he</u> <u>dies.</u> <u>No error</u>
     A   B   C   D E

18. When the space telescope needs <u>repairs. The</u> astronauts will travel to <u>it</u> in the <u>space</u>
            A   B   C
    <u>shuttle</u> <u>To do whatever work needs to be done.</u> <u>No error</u>
     D   E

19. Was Guion Stewart Bluford, Jr., the pilot and astronaut, the first African-American
    _____   _____   _____
         A   B   C
    astronaut in space No error
              _____ _____
                 D   E

20. Having suffered, having overcome pover<u>ty, and</u> having overcome <u>prejudice.</u> <u>Richard</u>
                                          A   B   C
    <u>Wright</u> became a <u>powerfull</u> writer. <u>No error</u>
      D   D   E

21. When <u>Christopher Columbus</u> was a young <u>man he</u> was a very good <u>student he</u> learned
                   A   B   C
    three <u>languages and</u> was especially interested in maps. <u>No error</u>
                 D   E

22. Emily Dickinson <u>discouraged by how her first published poems had been changed by the</u>
                                                 A
    <u>editor</u> <u>refused</u> <u>to publish</u> <u>any more poems</u> during her lifetime. <u>No error</u>
       B   C   C   D   E

23. Some people <u>won't</u> do anything <u>without</u> reading their horoscopes <u>first however,</u> other
                  A   B   C
    people consider such behavior <u>ilogical.</u> <u>No error</u>
                                      D   E

24. <u>After the Six Day war ended.</u> Israel <u>had won</u> control of the <u>previously</u> divided city
                  A   B   C
    <u>of jerusalem.</u> <u>No error</u>
         D   E

25. The <u>french</u> impressionists <u>often</u> painted <u>outdoors, they</u> wanted to capture the immediacy
           A   B   C
    of <u>their</u> sensations. <u>No error</u>
          D   E

26. <u>To win the game,</u> <u>confidence and</u> <u>determination</u> <u>are needed.</u> <u>No error</u>
           A   B   C   D   E

27. The French <u>artist</u> Honoré Daumier <u>was</u> imprisoned <u>for six months.</u> <u>Because he drew a</u>
                  A   B   C   D
    caricature of King Louis Philippe. <u>No error</u>
                                           E

28. <u>Executing</u> a flawless <u>pirouette, the</u> <u>ballerina</u> <u>left the audience</u> stunned. <u>No error</u>
          A   B   C   D   E

29. Two <u>famos</u> <u>Americans, who were said to love swimming,</u> <u>were</u> George Washington and
           A   B   C
    <u>Benjamin Franklin.</u> <u>No error</u>
            D   E

30. <u>Editing a dictionary,</u> requires <u>patience, and</u> great <u>attention</u> <u>to detail.</u> <u>No error</u>
             A   B   C   D   E

Using Verbs

THE PRINCIPAL PARTS OF VERBS

Before you study the many forms of verbs, you may want to review some basic facts.

A **verb** is a word that expresses an action, a condition, or a state of being. Verbs are divided into two main categories. **Action verbs** describe a physical or mental action that someone is performing. **Linking verbs** do not express action. Rather, they serve as a link between the subject of the sentence and a word in the predicate that renames or describes the subject. For more information about verbs, see Handbook 30, pages 534–541.

Every verb has many different forms. All of these forms are made from the four **principal parts** of the verb: the **present infinitive** (usually called the **present**), the **present participle,** the **past,** and the **past participle.**

Present	Present Participle	Past	Past Participle
talk	(is) talking	talked	(have) talked
sing	(is) singing	sang	(have) sung
put	(is) putting	put	(have) put
break	(is) breaking	broke	(have) broken

In the examples above, notice that the present participle and the past participle are preceded by auxiliary or helping verbs. As part of a verb phrase, the present participle is used with a form of *be* and the past participle is used with a form of *have.*

> That soprano *will be singing* the role of Aida.
> She *has sung* the role many times.

Also note that the present participle ends with *-ing.* All verbs add *-ing* to the present to form the present participle. The endings of the past and the past participle, however, do change from verb to verb; the past and the past participle may be formed in several ways. These endings determine whether a verb is regular or irregular.

Regular Verbs

A **regular** verb is one to which *-ed* or *-d* is added to the present in order to form the past and the past participle. Most verbs are regular.

Some regular verbs change their spelling slightly when *-ing* or *-ed* is added to the present.

Present	Present Participle	Past	Past Participle
trip	(is) tri**pp**ing	tri**pp**ed	(have) tri**pp**ed
spy	(is) spying	sp**i**ed	(have) sp**i**ed
picnic	(is) picni**ck**ing	picni**ck**ed	(have) picni**ck**ed

Practice Your Skills

CONCEPT CHECK

Principal Parts of Regular Verbs Make four columns in which you list the principal parts of the following regular verbs.

1. grab	6. carry	11. clean
2. expel	7. disappear	12. admit
3. occur	8. regret	13. limit
4. narrate	9. move	14. receive
5. achieve	10. satisfy	15. omit

Irregular Verbs

An **irregular** verb is a verb that does not form the past and past participle by adding *-ed* or *-d* to the present. Irregular verbs form the past and past participle in a variety of ways.

There are approximately sixty commonly used irregular verbs. Because the principal parts of irregular verbs are formed in a variety of ways, you must either memorize these parts or refer to a dictionary. The dictionary will list the principal parts of all irregular verbs. Remembering the parts of irregular verbs will be simpler if you break them down into the five groups that follow.

Group 1 The easiest of the irregular verbs to remember are those that have the same form for the present, the past, and the past participle.

Present	Present Participle	Past	Past Participle
burst	(is) bursting	burst	(have) burst
cost	(is) costing	cost	(have) cost
cut	(is) cutting	cut	(have) cut
hit	(is) hitting	hit	(have) hit
hurt	(is) hurting	hurt	(have) hurt
let	(is) letting	let	(have) let
put	(is) putting	put	(have) put
set	(is) setting	set	(have) set
shut	(is) shutting	shut	(have) shut

Group 2 The irregular verbs in this group have the same form for the past and the past participle.

Present	Present Participle	Past	Past Participle
bring	(is) bringing	brought	(have) brought
catch	(is) catching	caught	(have) caught
fight	(is) fighting	fought	(have) fought
flee	(is) fleeing	fled	(have) fled
fling	(is) flinging	flung	(have) flung
get	(is) getting	got	(have) got
			or gotten
lead	(is) leading	led	(have) led
lend	(is) lending	lent	(have) lent
lose	(is) losing	lost	(have) lost
say	(is) saying	said	(have) said
shine	(is) shining	shone	(have) shone
		or shined	*or* shined
sit	(is) sitting	sat	(have) sat
sting	(is) stinging	stung	(have) stung
swing	(is) swinging	swung	(have) swung
teach	(is) teaching	taught	(have) taught

Writing
—TIP—

In formal writing, it is preferable to use a more precise verb than *got* or *gotten*. Consult a thesaurus for synonyms.

Practice Your Skills

A. CONCEPT CHECK

Principal Parts of Irregular Verbs Write the past or past participle of each verb in parentheses.

1. For over ten years, Mr. Zeitz, the sociology teacher at our high school, has (teach) a unit on modern urban myths.
2. This week he told an urban tall tale about some people who had (catch) baby alligators in Florida swamps.
3. These alligator hunters then (bring) the creatures to New York City, where they sold them as pets.
4. According to the tale, the alligators often (get) loose.
5. Many owners (lose) their pets when they escaped down storm drains.
6. Eventually, years later, the story spread that a sanitation worker (catch) sight of a twenty-five-foot beast in the city sewer system.
7. The worker supposedly (say) of the experience, "It just (sit) there in the middle of the sewer, looking hungry and mean."
8. "Its eyes (shine) like beacons in the dark tunnel."
9. Soon rumors circulated that another city worker almost (lose) his life when he encountered a group of alligators in a large sewer pipe in Queens.

Writing Theme
Tall Tales

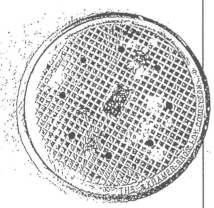

10. As the tale goes, the worker (fight) one of the beasts with his bare hands, narrowly escaping death.
11. Then he (fling) his lunchbox and (hit) the alligator on the nose.
12. Finally, he threw his sandwich at the animal; when it (shut) its jaws over the morsel, the worker (swing) about and (flee).
13. Think of what would have happened if the alligator had (get) the worker in the grip of its death-dealing jaws!
14. If he hadn't distracted the alligator momentarily, it might have (hurt) him badly.
15. The widespread popularity of such stories has (lead) many people to believe such outlandish urban myths.

B. PROOFREADING SKILL

Correcting Verb Forms Rewrite the paragraph, correcting errors in verb forms, spelling, punctuation, and capitalization.

As I sayed to that agriculture expert who came down here from the capitol, the kudzu's not a plant—its a green monster. Now, you may think Im exaggerating, but you should have seen what happened to that agriculture man when he tried to show the farmers around hear how to get rid of this pesky weed. If he had been smart, he would have fleed Instead, that so-called Expert getted out a can of weedkiller. I guess he figgured that plant was just going to lie there while he sprayed it. That old kudzu certainly teached him a lesson! It was a site! The vine catched him, swinged him right off the ground and putted him down in the top of a sycamore tree. well we called the volunteer fire department, and they brung ladders to get him down. When that vine herd the sirens, though, it grabbed him again and flang him up until his head bursted through the underside of a cloud. I guess he would have starved to death if I hadn't lended the fire department my shotgun so they could shoot biscuits up to him. I tell you, that kudzu's mean. So far, everyone that's fighted it has losed.

C. APPLICATION IN WRITING

A Tall Tale A tall tale is a wildly improbable story full of exaggeration and humor. Try writing a tall tale, perhaps one about mosquitoes the size of blue jays. Tell your story as if it happened last week, and use the past tense of some verbs in Groups 1 and 2.

Group 3 The irregular verbs in this group form the past participle by adding *-n* or *-en* to the past.

Present	Present Participle	Past	Past Participle
bear	(is) bearing	bore	(have) borne
beat	(is) beating	beat	(have) beaten
bite	(is) biting	bit	(have) bitten
			or bit
break	(is) breaking	broke	(have) broken
choose	(is) choosing	chose	(have) chosen
freeze	(is) freezing	froze	(have) frozen
speak	(is) speaking	spoke	(have) spoken
steal	(is) stealing	stole	(have) stolen
swear	(is) swearing	swore	(have) sworn
tear	(is) tearing	tore	(have) torn
wear	(is) wearing	wore	(have) worn

Practice Your Skills

A. CONCEPT CHECK

Principal Parts of Irregular Verbs Write the correct past or past participle of each verb in parentheses.

1. Legend has it that Davy Crockett always (wear) deerskin clothing and a coonskin cap.
2. Once, while Davy was napping, a bear (steal) his cap and ran away into the woods.
3. Davy tracked down the bear by following footprints and by looking for places where the bear had (break) twigs and branches as it ran away.
4. When Davy caught up with the bear, he (speak) sternly to it.
5. "I have (wear) that cap for nigh on twenty years now," said Davy, "and I'm not going to let some bear steal it away from me."

6. The bear simply looked at Davy and (bite) down harder on the cap.
7. Davy (swear) that there would be trouble if the bear didn't release the cap immediately.
8. The bear dropped the cap on the ground, but when Davy stooped to pick it up, he saw that the bear had (tear) it down the middle.
9. Davy said to the bear, "Now look what you've done. You have (steal) my cap and have (tear) it. I'll teach you a lesson."
10. The bear (choose) to ignore this comment and took a swipe at Davy.
11. Then the bear (beat) Davy over the head with one massive paw.
12. Davy (break) out in a run and headed back to his camp.
13. Having (bear) all the ill treatment he could take, Davy stripped off his shirt, covered his body with bacon grease, and (steal) back to where that bear was hiding.
14. When Davy found the bear again, he made the bear angry; it chased Davy through the woods and would have (bite) him in two if Davy hadn't jumped into the ice-cold water of the Ohio River.
15. Legend has it that when Davy climbed out of the river on the opposite bank, he was just fine because the bacon grease had kept him warm, but the bear, not having the same protection against the cold, had (freeze) solid as a popsicle.

B. PROOFREADING SKILL

Principal Parts of Verbs   Rewrite the following paragraphs, correcting errors in spelling, punctuation, capitalization, and verb forms.

Like Davy Crockett, Daniel Webster was a real person about whom many far-fetched legends and folk tales were told. Webster represented massachusetts in the senate during the turbulent years before the Civil War. He was famous for having beat many oponents in debate. Supposedly, when he raised his voice against an opponent, he stealed the very soul out of him. According to one author. Webster went fishing one day and simply commanded all the fish to jump out of the River. After hearing the mighty words that Webster had spoke, the fish were so frightened that they obeyed without hezitation.

As a Senator from the North, Webster had swore that he would defend the Union. He refused to see it tore to pieces by the issue of slavery. Once he had chose to become the champion of the Union, he wore himself out in it's defense. Often he busted into fiery speeches on this subject before awe-struck crowds. He is remembered for having bore the banner of the union aloft during a critical period. Thus in both fact and fiction. Webster is a true American hero.

C. APPLICATION IN WRITING

A Legend   A legend is a story passed from generation to generation by word of mouth before being written down. Sometimes a legend may take the form of a folk song. Though often based on historical fact, the characters and details in a legend have usually grown larger than life over the many years of retelling. Choose a familiar hero from American history and write a brief legend or folk song about the person. You may wish to borrow or adapt a traditional tune and supply the lyrics. Be sure your legend or song reveals the figure's larger-than-life qualities. Use at least five of the irregular verbs from the lists on pages 650–653.

Group 4   The irregular verbs in this group change a vowel to form the past and the past participle. The vowel changes from *i* in the present to *a* in the past to *u* in the past participle.

Present	Present Participle	Past	Past Participle
begin	(is) beginning	began	(have) begun
drink	(is) drinking	drank	(have) drunk
ring	(is) ringing	rang	(have) rung
shrink	(is) shrinking	shrank	(have) shrunk
sing	(is) singing	sang	(have) sung
sink	(is) sinking	sank	(have) sunk
spring	(is) springing	sprang	(have) sprung
		or sprung	
swim	(is) swimming	swam	(have) swum

Practice Your Skills

A. CONCEPT CHECK

Principal Parts of Irregular Verbs   Write the correct past or past participle of each verb in parentheses.

1. High on the hill above the beach, the bells of a church (ring) out the hour—six A.M.
2. Another day at Rockport beach has (begin).
3. As daylight broke, the tide slowly (shrink) back from the shore and exposed a row of seaweed high up on the sand.
4. The night before, fiddler crabs had (spring) from their holes in the sand and scurried about the beach.
5. Now, with the rising sun, they (sink) back out of sight.
6. By nine o'clock, sunbathers have (begin) to appear, laden with their beach gear.
7. Before long, they laid out their blankets, set up their chairs, and (swim) in the cool water.

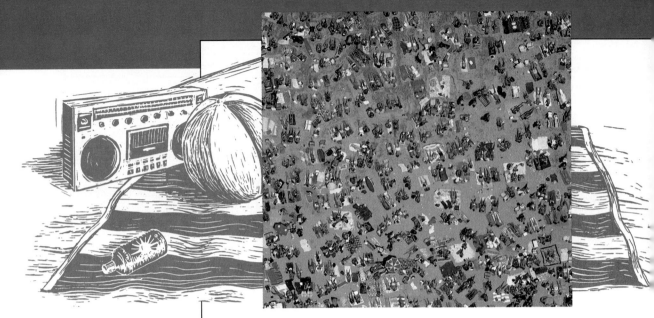

8. After they had (swim), they lay on the beach to tan themselves in the summer sun.

9. By noon, some (begin) to leave the beach to eat in the cafes along the cliff.

10. There they ate fried clams and (drink) milkshakes, which New Englanders call *frappés*.

11. After they had eaten and (drink) their fill, they returned to the shore.

12. One young man, who had brought a guitar to the beach, (sing) a song about sailors and sailing ships.

13. After he had (sing) a few more songs, he put a cup out on the sand to collect coins.

14. By late afternoon, the church bells having (ring) four o'clock, the young man's cup was filled with coins as well as a few bottlecaps.

15. At a little after eight o'clock, the sun had (sink) behind the horizon, the crowd had gone home, and the fiddler crabs emerged again.

B. REVISION SKILL

Checking Verb Forms Most of the following sentences have errors in verb forms. Rewrite the paragraphs correctly, making any other changes you think necessary.

(1) Years ago our family always went to the beach on summer Saturdays. (2) On those days, I springed out of bed without anyone having to pester me to get up. (3) On other days, the alarm clock could have rang for hours and I wouldn't have got up.

(4) Saturdays always begun with a big breakfast. (5) After we ate our eggs and toast and drunk our orange juice, we'd hop into the car. (6) On the way to the beach, the entire family sung songs—the corny songs that families sing together.

(7) Typically, Mom and Dad sunk into their beach chairs while we kids ran around collecting shells and buried one another in the sand. (8) I still have a picture of my sisters and me, with just our heads poking up through the sand, like strange plants that had sprung up in the desert. (9) After we had played and swam, we climbed back into the car—tired, sandy, and tanned—and begun the ride back home.

C. APPLICATION IN WRITING

A Memoir To write a memoir, you need only a memory that you are interested in sharing in writing. Think of some past event that you would like to retell. Then write a brief composition in which you re-create it. Use vivid, specific details. Also try to use at least five verbs from the lists on pages 650–655.

Group 5 The irregular verbs in this group form the past participle from the present—often by adding *-n* or *-en*. In the list below, note the similarity between the present and the past participle forms.

Present	Present Participle	Past	Past Participle
blow	(is) blowing	blew	(have) blown
come	(is) coming	came	(have) come
do	(is) doing	did	(have) done
draw	(is) drawing	drew	(have) drawn
drive	(is) driving	drove	(have) driven
eat	(is) eating	ate	(have) eaten
fall	(is) falling	fell	(have) fallen
give	(is) giving	gave	(have) given
go	(is) going	went	(have) gone
grow	(is) growing	grew	(have) grown
know	(is) knowing	knew	(have) known
ride	(is) riding	rode	(have) ridden
rise	(is) rising	rose	(have) risen
run	(is) running	ran	(have) run
see	(is) seeing	saw	(have) seen
shake	(is) shaking	shook	(have) shaken
slay	(is) slaying	slew	(have) slain
take	(is) taking	took	(have) taken
throw	(is) throwing	threw	(have) thrown
write	(is) writing	wrote	(have) written

Practice Your Skills

A. CONCEPT CHECK

Principal Parts of Irregular Verbs Write the correct past or past participle of each verb in parentheses.

1. Historical records have (give) us some understanding of the causes of floods.
2. Coastal flooding can result from volcanic activity that creates ocean waves, as when the eruption of Krakatoa in 1883 (throw) 4.3 cubic miles of debris into the air.
3. Three thousand miles away, one person (write) that this eruption sounded like the "roar of heavy guns."
4. Eventually, it was discovered that the fifty-foot waves created by the explosion of Krakatoa had (take) more than 36,000 human lives.
5. More recently, torrential rains caused by a cyclone (take) 10,000 lives in the low-lying nation of Bangladesh.
6. To escape the flood, many families (ride) the tops of their houses until the waters subsided.
7. In 1938 many lives were lost to flooding along the Yellow River in China when Chinese troops (blow) up dikes.
8. The soldiers had (blow) up the dikes along the river to stop the advance of invading Japanese troops.
9. The waters rushed beyond the riverbank and (rise) dramatically, flooding hundreds of low-lying villages.
10. The Chinese troops would not have (blow) up the dikes had they (know) what the consequences of this action would be.
11. They had stopped their enemies, but they had also accidentally (slay) over one million of their own people.

An Alaskan coastal town lies ravaged after a 1964 tsunami.

12. In 1960 major floods occurred in Hawaii and Japan after an earthquake (shake) Chile, on South America's west coast.
13. Waves created by the earthquake (run) across the Pacific Ocean at speeds up to five hundred miles per hour.
14. As they neared Hawaii and Japan, they (grow) in size.
15. By the time they crashed ashore, these giant waves, known as tsunamis, had (grow) over a hundred feet high.
16. They (fall) on the coasts with great fury.
17. They (drive) boats onto the beaches and washed away towns.
18. Some of the Japanese who (see) this disaster later (draw) pictures of the enormous tsunamis.
19. Perhaps recalling these famous drawings, the American writer Annie Dillard has (write) that a flood is "like a dragon."
20. Anyone who has (see) the damage that a major flood has (do) would agree with her vivid comparison.

B. PROOFREADING SKILL

Checking Irregular Verb Forms   Proofread the following anecdote, correcting the errors in verb forms, spelling, punctuation, and capitalization.

Young Henry martin was sitting on a large branch that had fell from an old Oak tree. He was watching the waters, of a nearby River, that had rised and were flooding the road. A passing moterist seen the water, slammed on his brakes, swang his car to the side of the rode, and drawed up next to the boy. He stuck his head out the window.

"Has the water became too deep to cross?" he asked.

"No, sir. Go right ahead," Henry replied.

After the motorist had drove partway through the water. his car sunk up to it's hood. He clumb out of the car, swimmed to dry ground, and begun to rant and rave. "Are you crazy? I almost drownded!" he shouted. "You certianly gived me some bad advice you must have knowed the water was too deep to cross."

Young Henry shaked his head in amazment. "That's funny," he said as he putted his hand too inches from the ground. "The water only comed up to hear on the ducks!"

C. APPLICATION IN WRITING

A Report   Choose a recent incident of flooding or one of the floods mentioned in Concept Check A, and do some research on your topic. Then use at least five of the verbs listed on page 657 and write a brief report presenting your findings.

All verbs change form to show the time of the action they express. These changes in form are called **tenses.** English verbs have three simple tenses (present, past, and future) and three perfect tenses (present perfect, past perfect, and future perfect). You can use these tenses to show whether something is happening now, has happened in the past, or will happen in the future. The six tenses are formed by using the principal parts that you have just studied and combining them with auxiliary verbs such as *be* and *have*.

Verb Conjugation

A verb **conjugation** is a list of all the forms used in the six tenses of a verb. A verb conjugation also shows changes in form for the first, second, and third persons in both the singular and plural.

When you study the simple and perfect tenses of verbs on pages 660–663, refer to the conjugation of the regular verb *call* that is shown on the following page.

Using the Simple Tenses

The simple tenses include the **present, past,** and **future** tense.

The Present Tense   To form the present tense, use the first principal part (the present form): *I go, we see.* Add *-s* or *-es* to the present form for the third person singular: *he goes, she sees.*

Use the present tense to show an action that (1) occurs in the present; (2) occurs regularly; or (3) is constant or generally true at any given time.

> There *goes* our bus! (action occurring in present)
> We *attend* band practice every Thursday. (action occurring regularly)
> The heart *pumps* blood. (constant action)

The **historical present tense** is used to tell of some action or condition in the past as though it were occurring in the present.

> The captain *orders,* "Abandon ship!" as the great vessel *lists* dangerously to starboard, its deck ablaze.

In most cases, use the present tense to write about literature.

> In *Macbeth,* William Shakespeare *tells* the story of a Scottish king and his ambitious wife.

Principal Parts

Present	Present Participle	Past	Past Participle
call	(is) calling	called	(have) called

Simple Tenses

	Singular	Plural
Present Tense		
First Person	I call	we call
Second Person	you call	you call
Third Person	he, she, it calls	they call
Past Tense		
First Person	I called	we called
Second Person	you called	you called
Third Person	he, she, it called	they called

Future Tense (*will* or *shall* + the present form)

	Singular	Plural
First Person	I will (shall) call	we will (shall) call
Second Person	you will call	you will call
Third Person	he, she, it will call	they will call

Perfect Tenses

	Singular	Plural

Present Perfect Tense (*has* or *have* + the past participle)

	Singular	Plural
First Person	I have called	we have called
Second Person	you have called	you have called
Third Person	he, she, it has called	they have called

Past Perfect Tense (*had* + the past participle)

	Singular	Plural
First Person	I had called	we had called
Second Person	you had called	you had called
Third Person	he, she, it had called	they had called

Future Perfect Tense (*will have* or *shall have* + the past participle)

	Singular	Plural
First Person	I will (shall) have called	we will (shall) have called
Second Person	you will have called	you will have called
Third Person	he, she, it will have called	they will have called

The Past Tense   To form the past tense of a regular verb, add *-d* or *-ed* to the present form: *you smiled, they laughed.* If the verb is irregular, use the past form listed as one of the principal parts: *she went, we rode, they caught.*

Use the past tense to show an action that was completed in the past.

> Yesterday I *ran* around the reservoir.

The Future Tense   To form the future tense, use the auxiliary verb *will* or *shall* with the present form. *Will* simply indicates future; *shall* usually implies an intention or obligation: I *will stay, we shall stay.*

Use the future tense to express an action that will occur in the future.

> The test *will begin* at nine o'clock.
> I *shall* not *admit* latecomers.

Future time may also be shown by using the present tense in combination with an adverb or phrase that tells time.

> We *pick* up our bus passes next week. (The words *next week* indicate future time.)

Using the Perfect Tenses

The perfect tenses include the **present perfect,** the **past perfect,** and the **future perfect.**

The Present Perfect Tense   To form the present perfect tense, use the auxiliary verb *has* or *have* with the past participle: *you have danced, she has slept.* Use the present perfect tense to show an action (1) that was completed at an indefinite time in the past or (2) that began in the past and continues into the present.

> He *has left* without his books. (action completed at an indefinite time)
> We *have worked* here for ten years. (action continuing into the present)

The Past Perfect Tense   To form the past perfect tense, use the auxiliary verb *had* with the past participle: *I had wondered, we had known.* Use the past perfect tense to show an action in the past that came before another action in the past.

> I *had* already *finished* when you called. (action preceding another past action)

The Future Perfect Tense Form the future perfect tense by using the auxiliary verbs *will have* or *shall have* with the past participle: *you will have eaten.* Use the future perfect tense to show an action in the future that will occur before another future action or time.

> By the time I meet Elena, I *will have bought* her birthday present—a new hat. (action occurring before another future action or time)

Practice Your Skills

A. CONCEPT CHECK

Verb Tenses Write the verb in each of the following sentences and identify its tense.

Writing Theme
Telescopes and
Astronomy

1. Tradition attributes the invention of the telescope to Hans Lippershey of Holland.
2. He supposedly made the first telescope in 1608.
3. In recent years, however, scholars have questioned this traditional belief.
4. By Lippershey's time people had probably known about the principle of the telescope for many years.
5. In the late 1200's, for example, Roger Bacon, the first modern-style scientist, probably knew about telescopes.
6. Nevertheless, the first notable use of a telescope in astronomy occurred in 1609.
7. In that year Galileo Galilei carefully studied the sun, moon, and planets.
8. Within months, he had proved correct the controversial theory of Copernicus (1473–1543).
9. According to this theory, the earth circles the sun, and not the reverse.
10. Since Galileo's time, astronomers have made many other important discoveries with telescopes.
11. Not surprisingly, the telescope has evolved considerably since the 1600's.
12. In 1990, for example, NASA launched the complex Hubble Space Telescope into earth's orbit with great hopes for its performance.
13. Unfortunately, an imperfect lens mars the effectiveness of this telescope.
14. However, even with the flaw, scientists will have an extraordinary view of the universe from this remarkable instrument.
15. With the help of the Hubble telescope and other future technological developments, scientists will probably have answered many of the greatest riddles of modern astronomy by the end of this century.

Correct verb tenses make the order of events clear for your readers.

NASA Hubble Space Telescope transmitting information to Earth stations.

B. REVISION SKILL

Clarifying Sequence   Revise the following paragraphs, changing the italicized verbs to the tenses shown in parentheses. Notice how the changes in tense make the progression of events clearer.

(1) Many scientists *call* the American astronomer Edwin Powell Hubble (1889–1953) one of the greatest astronomers of all time. (present perfect) (2) Appropriately, the space telescope that NASA launched in 1990 *bore* his name. (present) (3) From 1919 until his death, Hubble *had worked* at the Mount Wilson Observatory near Pasadena, California. (past) (4) There, using a new and powerful 100–inch telescope, Hubble *studies* the many cloudlike patches known as nebulae. (past)

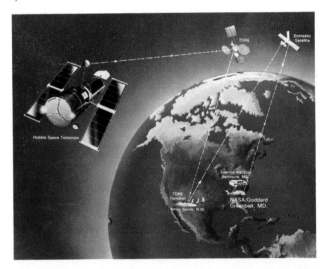

(5) For centuries, many scientists *argued* that nebulae were merely clouds of gas within our own unique galaxy, the Milky Way. (past perfect) (6) A few, however, *had believed* these objects were "island universes," distant galaxies containing millions of stars. (past) (7) In 1925 Hubble *settles* the debate with his report of having seen stars in three nebulae. (past) (8) Moreover, he *has calculated* that these nebulae were situated far beyond our galaxy. (past perfect)

(9) Thanks to Hubble, scientists everywhere now *accepted* as fact that the Milky Way *was* not unique, but one of millions of "island universes." (present) (10) They hope that the space telescope bearing his name *provides* many other startling discoveries about the far reaches of the universe. (future)

PROGRESSIVE AND EMPHATIC VERB FORMS

In addition to the six basic tenses, verbs also have other special forms. These include the progressive and emphatic forms.

Using the Progressive Forms

The **progressive forms** show ongoing action. They are made by using a form of *be* with the present participle; they always end in *-ing*.

> I *am calling*. (present progressive)
> I *was calling*. (past progressive)
> I *will (shall) be calling*. (future progressive)
> I *have been calling*. (present perfect progressive)
> I *had been calling*. (past perfect progressive)
> I *will (shall) have been calling*. (future perfect progressive)

Use the **present progressive** form to show an ongoing action that is taking place now.

> The tenants *are planting* a garden in the courtyard.

The present progressive form can also be used to show future time when the sentence contains an adverb or a phrase, such as *tomorrow* or *next week,* that indicates the future.

> We *are leaving* for Detroit tomorrow.

Use the **past progressive** form to show an ongoing action that took place in the past.

> I *was studying* all morning.

Use the **future progressive** form to show an ongoing action that will take place in the future.

> This summer we *will be visiting* all our relatives.

Use the **present perfect progressive** to show an ongoing action continuing in the present.

> My mother *has been taking* guitar lessons.

Use the **past perfect progressive** to show an ongoing action in the past interrupted by another past action.

> The car *had been running* smoothly until it was sideswiped.

Use the **future perfect progressive** to show a future ongoing action that will have taken place by a stated future time.

> By this time tomorrow, I *will have been wearing* this cast for six weeks.

Using the Emphatic Forms

The present tense and the past tense have **emphatic forms** that give special emphasis or force to the verb. To form the present emphatic, use the auxiliary verb *do* or *does* with the present form of the main verb. To form the past emphatic, use the auxiliary verb *did* with the present form of the main verb.

> They usually *practice* every day. (present)
> They usually *do practice* every day. (present emphatic)
> They really *won* twelve games in a row. (past)
> They really *did win* twelve games in a row. (past emphatic)

Usage Note When the emphatic form is used in negative statements or questions, there is usually no special emphasis intended.

> He *doesn't* usually *forget* his appointments.
> *Do* you *think* this avocado is ripe?

Practice Your Skills

CONCEPT CHECK

Progressive and Emphatic Forms of Verbs Rewrite each of the following sentences, adding the verb form described in parentheses.

1. Mark Wellman _____ his legs in a terrible accident. (past emphatic form of *lost*)
2. However, that _____ not _____ him from pursuing his two great interests—mountain climbing and skiing. (past emphatic form of *stop*)
3. Since his accident, Wellman _____ regularly. (present perfect progressive form of *climb*)
4. Though he _____ people for years, Wellman really raised some eyebrows when he announced his intention to climb Yosemite's El Capitan. (present perfect progressive form of *surprise*)
5. Nevertheless, he _____ this challenging mountain successfully. (past emphatic form of *scale*)
6. In contrast, these days he _____ not _____ in the same way that he skied in the past. (present emphatic form of *ski*)
7. However, he _____ skiing, using a ski sled he designed for handicapped people—the Monoski. (present emphatic form of *enjoy*)

8. Currently Wellman _____ as a park ranger and ski instructor at Yosemite National Park. (present progressive form of *work*)

9. There he _____ ways to help handicapped people to ski. (present perfect progressive form of *find*)

10. When reporters from *Headline News* came to see him, he _____ some handicapped students how to use special needs skiing equipment. (past perfect progressive form of *show*)

11. He _____ how to use the Monoski. (past progressive form of *demonstrate*)

12. The instructors at Yosemite _____ not _____ all the answers for overcoming a handicap. (present emphatic form of *have*)

13. However, they _____ that having a handicap should not prevent a person from enjoying outdoor sports. (present emphatic form of *know*)

14. After a few lessons from Wellman, a handicapped person _____ just like anyone else. (future progressive form of *ski*)

15. Wellman _____ his course for handicapped people the "Adaptive Ski Program." (present progressive form of *call*)

16. Many handicapped youngsters _____ Wellman's program this coming winter. (future progressive form of *attend*)

17. Without doubt, they _____ forward to this experience. (present progressive form of *look*)

18. By spring, each of them _____ down the slopes for several months. (future perfect progressive form of *glide*)

19. Because of the work of people like Wellman, many other handicapped people _____ their dreams. (future progressive form of *realize*)

20. All of this proves that determination _____ the seemingly impossible possible. (present emphatic form of *make*)

Improper Shifts in Tense and Form

Use the same tense to show two or more actions that occur at the same time.

Within a paragraph or between sentences, do not shift tenses unless the meaning calls for a change. Use the same tense for the verbs in most compound sentences and in sentences with a compound predicate.

Incorrect	We *washed* the car, and then we *polish* it.
Correct	We *washed* the car, and then we *polished* it.
Incorrect	Chris *drafts* her letters and *corrected* them.
Correct	Chris *drafts* her letters and *corrects* them.

A shift in tense is not necessarily incorrect. There are times when a writer must use a tense shift to express a logical sequence of events or the relationship of one event to another. For example, to show one action occurring before or after another action, two different tenses are needed.

> Marcus *had solved* (past perfect) the problem before Mr. Weiss *explained* (past) how to do it.
> You *will have heard* (future perfect) the results by the time I *arrive* (present).
> I *see* (present) that you *have* already *finished* (present perfect) the book I *lent* (past) you.

Practice Your Skills

A. CONCEPT CHECK

Shifts in Tense and Form A commonplace book is simply a scrapbook in which you jot down interesting passages that you come across in your reading. The following passages demonstrate how professional writers use the tenses and forms of verbs to lead the reader back and forth through time. Write the tense of each italicized verb. Also tell if the verb is in the progressive or emphatic form. Notice how logically each author shifts tense and form.

1. When enough years *had gone* by to enable us to look back on them, we sometimes *discussed* the events leading to his accident. I *maintain* that the Ewells *started* it all, but Jem, who *was* four years my senior, *said* it *started* long before that. **Harper Lee**
2. I *had been reading* . . . of the Spanish influenza. At first it *was* far off. . . . Then the stories *told* of people dying in California towns we *knew,* and finally the [paper] *began* reporting the spread of the "flu" in our city. **Ernesto Galarza**
3. "Harry, what *are* you *thinking* of?" Mrs. Oliver *asked* me. "*Don't* I *get* any change?" She *was laughing.* **Albert Halper**
4. In true quicksand a trapped pedestrian soon *sinks* to the depth of his knees and *will sink* further if he *stands* still or *struggles* wildly. **Gerard H. Matthes**
5. . . . I *like* to think that the flood *left* them a gift, a consolation prize, so that for years to come they *will be finding* edible mushrooms here and there about the house. . . . **Annie Dillard**
6. I *remember* the last time I *saw* him. It *was* early in September, and I *was sitting* on the gate. . . . **Durango Mendoza**
7. There *was* a commotion in Roaring Camp. It *could* not *have been* a fight, for in 1850 that *was* not novel enough to have called together the entire settlement. **Bret Harte**

8. But part of me is English, for I *love* England with a peculiar, possessing love. I *do possess* something of England.   **Pearl S. Buck**

9. I *said* that writing *is* a craft, not an art, and the man who *runs* away from his craft because he lacks inspiration *is fooling* himself. He *is* also *going* broke.   **William Zinsser**

10. "Oh, I *have had* such a curious dream!" *said* Alice, and she *told* her sister, as well as she could remember them, all these strange Adventures of hers that you *have* just *been reading* about; and when she *had finished,* her sister *kissed* her and said, "It *was* a curious dream, dear, certainly; but now *run* in to tea; it *is getting* late."   **Lewis Carroll**

"The Mad Hatter's Tea Party," illustrated by Sir John Tenniel for Lewis Carroll's *Alice in Wonderland*

B. REVISION SKILL

Making Verb Tenses and Forms Consistent   Revise the following paragraphs to correct any confusing shifts in tense and form.

(1) In the eighteenth and nineteenth centuries, many people kept commonplace books, in which they jot down interesting passages from their reading. (2) Both Benjamin Franklin and Thomas Jefferson were keeping commonplace books and benefited greatly from looking back over them from time to time. (3) They sometimes will quote passages from their books in their own writings.

(4) Today few people keep commonplace books. (5) It was, however, a practice worth reviving. (6) Sometimes writers will be collecting passages for commonplace books over a period of many years. (7) In time, their collections numbered thousands of passages. (8) Then, when they needed a writing idea, the writers simply browse through their commonplace books. (9) The passages often do stir up memories or will jog the imagination. (10) As a source of interesting quotations, a commonplace book had made any writer's work more fun to read.

C. APPLICATION IN WRITING

A Commonplace Book Set aside part of your journal or writer's sketchbook for quotations from your reading. For a week or more, record interesting passages from poems, stories, essays, or news articles along with the author's name and the original source. Then bring your commonplace book to class and share your favorite quotations in a group discussion. Be prepared to talk about the shifts in tense in these passages and why they are made.

CHECK POINT
PAGES 649–670

PAGES 649–670

A. Write the correct past or past participle form of each verb in parentheses.

1. For many months the crew of H.M.S. *Bounty* had (bear) the terrible temper of their captain, William Bligh.
2. Bligh suffered from paranoia, and his crew had (know) him to burst into rages.
3. Eventually, on April 28, 1789, the *Bounty's* crew (rise) up against him.
4. Fletcher Christian, the master's mate, (lead) the mutiny.
5. The actions of the mutineers had almost (cost) Bligh his life.
6. However, despite all that Bligh had (do), Fletcher Christian allowed him to live.
7. The mutineers (put) Bligh and eighteen crew members adrift in a small boat and then (set) sail for Tahiti with Christian at the helm of the *Bounty*.
8. Although Bligh had been overthrown, the mutineers had not (beat) him.
9. A brilliant navigator, Bligh assumed command of the small boat and (begin) a voyage of nearly four thousand miles that eventually (bring) him safely to the island of Timor.
10. Meanwhile, Christian (take) the *Bounty* first to Tahiti and then to Pitcairn, a small uninhabited island in the South Pacific.
11. After the mutineers had (get) their supplies off the *Bounty,* they burned the ship and (sink) its remains offshore.
12. If some passing ship (see) the *Bounty* off Pitcairn, the mutineers' whereabouts might be reported.
13. They had not (break) the law and committed a capital offense only to be discovered now.
14. At first the mutineers lived happily on Pitcairn, along with some South Pacific islanders who had joined them in Tahiti, but soon ill fortune (come) to the tiny colony.

Writing Theme
Aquatic Mishaps

15. The South Pacific islanders (rise) up against Fletcher Christian and (slay) him.
16. Then the Englishmen and the male islanders (fight) one another until only four of the men were left.
17. Of these, one died of asthma, one was killed in a brawl, and another, who (drink) excessively, leapt off a cliff.
18. Of all the men who had (throw) in their lot with Christian, only one man survived, along with a handful of women and children.
19. This small group (grow) slowly over the years, until today Pitcairn's population numbers about five dozen descendants of the *Bounty*'s crew.
20. In 1932 Charles Nordhoff and James Norman Hall (write) a novel based on these historical events, called *Mutiny on the Bounty*.

Charles Laughton as Captain Bligh, and Clark Gable as Mr. Christian in the movie *Mutiny on the Bounty*

B. Write the correct past or past participle form of each verb in parentheses.

1. On May 30, 1889, the dam of the South Fork Reservoir at Conemaugh Lake, about twelve miles east of Johnstown, Pennsylvania, (burst) due to heavy rains.
2. The owners of the dam had been warned about its flawed construction, but they had (choose) to ignore the warnings.
3. Due to the torrential rains in the last week of May, the Conemaugh River had already (rise) over its banks.
4. On the morning of May 30, messengers on horseback (ride) through the valley warning people that the dam could go.
5. At three o'clock came the awful cry, "The dam has (break)!"
6. People have (say) that they could hear the roar of the cataract for miles as it tumbled down the valley.
7. A wall of water forty feet high and a half mile wide (tear) through the valley.
8. The flood (bear) locomotives along like leaves.
9. It (fling) giant trees and boulders into the air.
10. It (take) with it bridges, houses, and hundreds of human lives.
11. In seven minutes the flood and the mountain of wreckage reached Johnstown, where it (hit) the Pennsy Bridge.
12. The bridge resisted the impact, but the wreckage (catch) fire.
13. Many townspeople had (flee) in time.
14. However, over two thousand people (lose) their lives.
15. It (cost) over ten million dollars to repair the damage caused by the Johnstown Flood.

The Gulf Stream,
by Winslow Homer,
1899. The Metropolitan
Museum of Art, Wolfe
Fund, 1906. Catherine
Lorillard Wolfe Collection

C. Identify the tense of each italicized verb in the following sentences.

1. For many years Rodney Fox, along with his colleague Eugenie Clark, *has studied* the great white shark.
2. This shark, which *grows* to over twenty-one feet in length, often *prowls* Australia's coast.
3. In 1963, Fox's interest in sharks almost *cost* him his life.
4. He *was fishing* with a spear gun in the same waters where he *had* often *studied* shark behavior.
5. Suddenly, a great white shark *appeared* and *closed* its enormous jaws around Fox's chest and back.
6. "What can I do?" Fox *thought*. "I *have* no weapon to defend myself. I *will* surely *die*."
7. By chance, he *broke* free and, after wrestling with the shark, *swam* to the surface.
8. By the year 2000, Australia *will have used* shark nets for over six decades to protect its coastal waters, but anyone swimming beyond their protection *risks* being attacked as Fox *was*.
9. Recently, researchers *have invented* a shark-proof diving suit made of thousands of interlocking steel rings.
10. These scientists *hope* that by the end of the decade their invention *will have saved* many lives.

D. Rewrite the following paragraph to correct any improper shifts in tense.

(1) On November 5, 1872, the United States brig *Mary Celeste* sails from New York City. (2) As well-wishers waved goodbye, they do not know that they would never see Captain Briggs, his wife, daughters, and crew again. (3) When a British craft spotted the ship a month later, the *Mary Celeste* does not respond to any signals. (4) The British crew will board, only to find the ship deserted. (5) There were no signs of a struggle; however, the lifeboat is missing, and a piece of line is dangling from the stern. (6) To this day, nobody knew what caused the captain, his family, and the crew to abandon the *Mary Celeste*.

E. Make three columns labeled *Progressive, Emphatic,* or *Neither.* Then list all the verbs used in the following paragraphs in the appropriate columns.

(1) Mermaids do exist! (2) Some of them are even living in Florida! (3) You probably do not believe this. (4) In one sense, however, it is quite true. (5) Sailors have been sighting manatees in Florida's coastal waters for centuries. (6) In earlier times, sailors mistook the manatees for mermaids. (7) Of course, these sailors certainly did have active imaginations. (8) In reality, manatees are aquatic mammals with a bristly snout, flippers, and a large, mermaidlike tail.

(9) Today, manatees are fighting for survival. (10) Unfortunately, speedboats have been killing these slow and gentle creatures. (11) The propellers wound the manatees, and they do sometimes die from such injuries.

(12) Conservationists have been studying the situation. (13) They are hoping for a solution to the problem. (14) If they do find an answer, manatees will be living in Florida's waters long into the future. (15) Like the sailors of earlier times, the tourists of tomorrow will tell the folks back home that they have seen mermaids.

Writing
——TIP——

A passive-voice verb can eliminate the use of "you" in formal writing: You control a marionette with strings. A marionette is controlled with strings.

You have already seen that verbs can take on many forms—the emphatic forms, the progressive forms, and the forms of the various tenses. The verbs change depending upon the purposes for which they are used. In addition to these common changes in verb form, there are other, more subtle forms that verbs can take. Writers use these verb forms to achieve special purposes.

Using the Active and Passive Voice

The **voice** of a verb tells whether the subject performs or receives the action of the verb. When the subject performs the action expressed by the verb, the verb is in the **active voice.** When the subject receives the action, the verb is in the **passive voice.** To form the passive voice, use a form of *be* with the past participle of the main verb.

Active Voice	The quarterback intentionally *threw* the ball out of bounds. (The subject *quarterback* performs the action of *throwing*.)
Passive Voice	The ball *was* intentionally *thrown* out of bounds by the quarterback. (The subject *ball* receives the action of being *thrown*.)
Active Voice	Dana *was cooking* dinner. (*Dana* performs the action of *cooking*.)
Passive Voice	Dinner *was being cooked* by Dana. (*Dinner* receives the action of being *cooked*.)

Notice that the verbs in the active voice above are transitive verbs; they have direct objects. When the verbs are changed from the active to the passive voice, the direct object becomes the subject; the subject becomes the object of a prepositional phrase introduced with *by*. Only transitive verbs can change from active to passive. Intransitive verbs and linking verbs do not have direct objects. Therefore they cannot be in the passive voice because there is no word to become the subject.

Using Voice in Writing

In the passive voice, the subject does not act; it receives the action. Therefore, the active voice is usually more lively and more precise than the passive voice. For this reason, you should avoid writing long passages in the passive voice. You should also avoid mixing the passive and active voice in the same sentence or in related sentences.

On the other hand, do not hesitate to use the passive voice when you want to emphasize the person or thing receiving the action or when the person or thing performing the action is unknown.

> The performers *were given* a standing ovation. (The persons receiving the action are emphasized.)
> The concert *has been canceled* without notice. (The person performing the action is not known.)

Practice Your Skills

A. CONCEPT CHECK

Active and Passive Voice Write the verbs in the following sentences. Then identify each verb according to its voice: *Active* or *Passive*. Finally, if a sentence can be made more direct by rewriting it in the active voice, do so.

1. Abraham Lincoln was born in a log cabin in Hardin County, Kentucky, in February of 1809.
2. His grandfather had been killed at a young age.
3. As a result, little education was received by Lincoln's father, Thomas.
4. The loss of their farm drove the Lincolns to Indiana in 1816.
5. Then, two years later, at age nine, Abe lost his mother, Nancy Hanks, to illness.
6. His younger brother, Thomas, was also lost to illness by him.
7. In 1819, Lincoln's father married Sarah Bush Johnston.
8. Nine years later, another tragedy—the death of Lincoln's older sister, Sarah—was caused by complications during childbirth.
9. In Lincoln's adult years, four sons were born to his wife, Mary Todd Lincoln.
10. However, only one of these children, Robert, lived to adulthood.
11. After Lincoln's election to the presidency, the Union was torn in two by the secession of the Southern states.
12. Lincoln was deeply saddened by this turn of events.
13. A great toll was also taken on Lincoln by the loss of young lives during the Civil War.
14. Nevertheless, he met these tragedies with courage and perseverance.
15. Because of his strength of character, Lincoln is considered the greatest of American presidents by many historians.

Writing Theme
Abraham Lincoln

B. REVISION SKILL

Achieving Directness   Revise the following paragraph. Where appropriate, change verbs in the passive voice to active voice and make any other changes that might improve the description.

(1) On the night of April 14, 1865, the play *Our American Cousin* was seen by President Lincoln at Ford's Theater. (2) The play was watched by the President and his wife from a special box. (3) The man who crept up behind him could be seen by no one. (4) The pistol was fired by him before anyone could protect the President. (5) The President's head was hit by the bullet, causing him to fall forward. (6) Down from the box jumped the man, breaking his leg; however, escape was still managed by him. (7) A Latin phrase, *Sic semper tyrannis!* meaning "Thus always to tyrants!", was supposedly shouted by the assassin as he fled. (8) The man, an actor and Southern sympathizer by the name of John Wilkes Booth, was later caught and shot.

Understanding and Using Mood

The **mood** of a verb is the manner in which a verb expresses an idea. In English there are three moods: the indicative, the imperative, and the subjunctive. The **indicative mood,** which you use most of the time, states a fact or asks a question.

Indicative Mood   The beautiful killer whales *were captured* in Puget Sound.
Have you ever *seen* a herd of orca whales?

The **imperative mood** is used to give a command or make a request. This mood has only one tense (the present) and only one person (the second).

Imperative Mood   *Look* at this brochure about Big Sur, California. Please *show* it to your teacher.

The **subjunctive mood** is used (1) to express a wish or a condition that is doubtful or contrary to fact or (2) to express a command or request after the word *that*.

Subjunctive Mood   I wish I *were* king. (expressing a wish)
If I *were* you, I would write that letter. (expressing a condition contrary to fact)
He asked that the books *be returned* promptly. (expressing a command or request after *that*)
We insisted that Fred *paint* the fence green. (expressing a command or request after *that*)

The forms of the subjunctive mood are identical to those of the indicative mood, with the following exceptions:

1. The *s* is omitted from the verb in the third-person singular.

Indicative   He *uses* safety belts.
Subjunctive   We asked that he *use* safety belts.

2. The present tense of the verb *to be* is always *be*.

     Andrew asked that the order *be* canceled.

3. The past tense of the verb *to be* is always *were*.

     If she *were* President, she would advocate programs to provide
       increased employment.

Usage Note   The subjunctive mood is used primarily in formal writing.

Practice Your Skills

CONCEPT CHECK

Mood of Verbs   Read the following fable. Then list the ten italicized verbs and identify the mood of each.

Writing Theme
Fables

(1) Long ago, two kings, Ludwig and Roy, *held* a summit meeting. (2) Ludwig asked that he *be recognized* as the most powerful king in the world. Roy laughed. "You cannot be the most powerful king," said Roy. (3) "If you *were* the most powerful king, then you would have powerful wizards at your command. Your wizards are weak and incompetent."

(4) "I would watch my tongue, if I *were* you," said Ludwig. "And what makes you think that my wizards are weak?"

"Well," said Roy, "I'll give you an example. My wizards can make frogs and lizards appear out of thin air. (5) *Watch* this."

At Roy's command, his wizards made lizards and frogs appear at Ludwig's feet.

"That's nothing," said Ludwig. "My wizards can do that." And Ludwig called his wizards before him. (6) When they arrived, he commanded them, saying, "*Make* me a frog."

(7) The wizards *looked* puzzled and frightened. "Make me a frog!" Ludwig repeated, beginning to fume with rage.

(8) He kept insisting that his wizards *obey* him. (9) Finally, Ludwig's wizards *waved* their magic wands and *turned* him into a frog.

Ludwig hopped into King Roy's lap. King Roy looked at the frog and smiled. (10) "*Be* careful what you wish for," he said. "You just might get it."

Three pairs of verbs are commonly confused: *lie* and *lay, rise* and *raise,* and *sit* and *set.* Because of the related meanings of each pair, it is important that you distinguish these meanings in order to use the verbs correctly. It is sometimes helpful to consult a dictionary if you are in doubt about which of these verbs to use.

Lie and Lay

Here are the principal parts of the verbs *lie* and *lay.*

Present	Present Participle	Past	Past Participle
lie	(is) lying	lay	(have) lain
lay	(is) laying	laid	(have) laid

Lie is an intransitive verb that means "to rest in a flat position" or "to be in a certain place." *Lie* never has a direct object.

> Our cat always *lies* in the middle of the couch.
> Several books *were lying* on the floor of the closet.

Lay is a transitive verb that means "to place." *Lay* always has a direct object unless the verb is in the passive voice.

Active Voice	The mayor *will lay* the cornerstone for the new gymnasium. (*Cornerstone* is the direct object.)
Passive Voice	After a long delay, the cornerstone *was* finally *laid.*

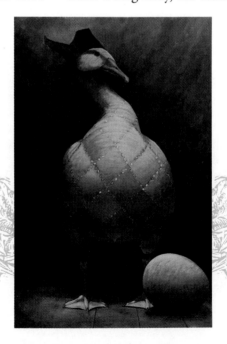

Rise and Raise

Listed below are the principal parts of the verbs *rise* and *raise*.

Present	Present Participle	Past	Past Participle
rise	(is) rising	rose	(have) risen
raise	(is) raising	raised	(have) raised

Rise is an intransitive verb that means "to go upward." *Rise* does not take a direct object.

The water *is rising*. It *has* already *risen* over three inches.

Raise is a transitive verb that means "to lift" or "to make something go up." *Raise* always takes a direct object unless the verb is in the passive voice.

Active Voice   The custodian *raises* the flag every morning. (*Flag* is the direct object.)

Passive Voice   Every morning the flag *is raised*.

Sit and Set

Here are the principal parts of the verbs *sit* and *set*.

Present	Present Participle	Past	Past Participle
sit	(is) sitting	sat	(have) sat
set	(is) setting	set	(have) set

Sit is an intransitive verb that means "to occupy a seat." It does not take a direct object.

Sit next to me on the bus. He *has been sitting* there all day.

Set is a transitive verb that means "to place." *Set* always has a direct object unless the verb is in the passive voice.

Active Voice   The artist *set* a fresh canvas on the easel. (*Canvas* is the direct object.)

Passive Voice   A fresh canvas *was set* on the easel.

Practice Your Skills

A. CONCEPT CHECK

Commonly Confused Verbs Choose the verb in parentheses that correctly completes each sentence.

1. Its reputation as the most beautiful book in the world (sits, sets) the Book of Kells apart.
2. This 1300-year-old book (lies, lays) open for daily viewing.
3. It (sits, sets) on a podium in Trinity College, Dublin, Ireland.

Writing Theme
Ancient Books

4. Daily, a clerk (raises, rises) the book from a glass enclosure.
5. Sealing is necessary because, if the temperature (raises, rises), the aged pages will deteriorate.
6. As in the preparation of many ancient books, scribes (set, sat) for hours hand-copying the pages.
7. Carefully, they (laid, lay) down the four Gospels.
8. Records of local history were (set, sat) down as well.
9. They also (set, sat) tools to work to decorate each page.
10. In many cases they delicately (laid, lain) down gold leaf.
11. In addition, colored inks give the impression the designs are (raised, risen) off the surface of the paper.
12. The Book of Kells has not always (laid, lain) in Dublin.
13. After A.D. 790, the frequency of Viking raids (raised, rose) sharply.
14. Questions (raised, risen) about the book's safety caused it to be moved from Iona to the monastery of Kells.
15. It (laid, lay) there throughout the Dark Ages.

B. PROOFREADING SKILL

Using Verbs Correctly   Proofread the following paragraphs for errors in verb usage as well as other errors in spelling, punctuation, and capitalization. On your paper rewrite the paragraphs correctly.

In ancient Assyria books were wrote on tablets that were put in clay containers. For the Contents to be read, the containers were broke open with a chisel. Little is knowed about how the greeks improved on this early method of bookbinding. It is commonly believed, however, that Athenians used a glue-like substance to hold together leaves of parchment or papyrus.

Regular bookbinding begun with the invention of printing. Unweildy containers gived way to covers made of leather. Kings and queens outdone one another in devising luxurous bindings. It become fashonible to emboss a cover with the owner's coat of arms. Sketches of birds and flowers were drawed and then tooled painstakingly onto the leather.

CHECK POINT
PAGES 674–680

A. Rewrite the following sentences, changing the passive voice to the active voice.

1. Formerly, safaris were held in Kenya by big-game hunters.
2. Elephants, rhinoceroses, wildebeests, giraffes, zebras, antelopes, lions, leopards, and cheetahs were sought by these hunters.

3. Several books and stories about these safaris were written by Ernest Hemingway and other authors.
4. Many hunters were drawn to Africa by these stories.
5. The once large populations of wild African animals have been dramatically reduced by overhunting.
6. Fortunately, many animals are now being saved by conservation efforts.
7. For example, a large wilderness preserve, the Serengeti National Park, was established in Tanzania in 1951 by the British.
8. Six thousand square miles were set aside by the colonial government for this park.
9. Many tourists are attracted to the Serengeti National Park each year.
10. Today, pictures, not pelts, are taken by these visitors.

Poodles of the Serengeti

B. Identify the mood of each italicized verb in the following sentences: *Indicative, Imperative,* or *Subjunctive.*

1. If I *were given* the chance, I would go on safari to the Serengeti.
2. This is what Andrew Calhoun always *said* to himself.
3. Finally, his chance *came.*
4. The editor of a small travel magazine called him and said, *"Go* to the Serengeti, and we *will pay* your expenses.
5. *Do* a story for us on rhinoceroses."
6. The editor asked that pictures *be taken* of the rhinos in their natural habitat.
7. He also *insisted* that Calhoun *get* some close-up portrait and profile shots of the rhinos.
8. "If I *were* you, I would bring back something that *will make* our competitors green with envy," the editor advised.
9. He also suggested that Calhoun *investigate* the illegal poaching of rhinoceroses in East Africa.
10. "But *be* sure to keep yourself out of trouble," he *cautioned.*

C. Choose the verb in parentheses that correctly completes each sentence.

1. Andrew Calhoun (set, sat) on the back of a land rover, heading across the Serengeti plain.
2. The savannah (lay, laid) stretched out to the horizon, its grass as yellow as the pelt of a lion.

Using Verbs   **681**

3. The snowcapped ridges of Mt. Kilimanjaro, which Calhoun had read about in a story by Ernest Hemingway, (rose, raised) in the distance.
4. The land rover passed a pride of lions that were (lying, laying) under a tree, out of the noonday sun.
5. The sun had (risen, raised) high into the sky and was beating down mercilessly.

6. Finally, Calhoun spotted a young rhino where it (lay, laid) dozing in the grass near a watering hole.
7. He (lay, laid) aside the fan that he had been using to cool himself and asked the driver to stop.
8. The rhino (rose, raised) up and backed off to a safe distance, where it stood with lowered head, watching the land rover.
9. Calhoun loaded some high-speed film and (set, sat) the shutter speed very, very high.
10. Then he (rose, raised) the camera to his eye, held his breath, and waited.
11. Suddenly, the rhino charged, and the force of its impact as it hit the land rover (rose, raised) the side of the two-ton truck up off the ground!
12. Before Calhoun knew it, he was (laying, lying) in the grass, staring up at a disgruntled rhino set to charge again.
13. Calhoun's driver had (raised, risen) his gun to shoot the rhino if it suddenly became necessary.
14. However, Calhoun motioned for the driver to (lay, lie) down his gun; then he scrambled into the truck and yelled for the driver to get going.
15. Back home, Calhoun (set, sat) a beautiful close-up shot of the charging rhino on his editor's desk.

A. Using Verbs Correctly Choose the verb in parentheses that correctly completes each sentence.

1. In the past, devastating famines have (came, come) about for many reasons.
2. People have (lost, losed) their crops as a result of war, drought, floods, and insect pests.
3. In addition, wind and rain may have (wore, worn) away fertile topsoil in which farmers (grew, growed) crops.
4. Overpopulation also contributed to famine; it (drived, drove) up prices, making scarce foods unobtainable for many.
5. Such events have often (brung, brought) grief to poor nations, on whom the burden of hunger has (laid, lain) most heavily.
6. In recent years, scientists and relief workers have (fighted, fought) a noble battle against world hunger.
7. In addition, some governments and international groups have (run, ran) massive famine relief efforts that (raised, rose) millions of dollars.
8. If they had not (gave, given) away millions of tons of food, tens of thousands of people would have (gone, went) hungry.
9. Consequently, deaths from famine have (fell, fallen).
10. However, we have not (beat, beaten) world hunger yet.

B. Recognizing Verb Tenses Write the italicized verbs on your paper. Then tell what tense each verb is.

(1) For many decades the United States *has grown* more wheat than any other nation. (2) Other major producers of grain *include* Argentina, Australia, and Canada. (3) Until recently, the Soviets *had produced* most of their own grain. (4) However, for several years now, they *have had* to import large quantities of grain from abroad. (5) Poor harvests and inefficient use of technology *contributed* to the shortfall for the Soviets.

(6) For the foreseeable future, developing nations *will depend* on exports from the major grain-producing countries. (7) However, purchases by large developed countries like the Soviet Union *drive* up prices worldwide. (8) Naturally, the poorer, developing countries *hope* for low rather than high prices.

(9) For years some relief organizations *have been calling* for the creation of a world food bank to address this problem. (10) Perhaps by the end of this century such a bank *will have solved* the problem of providing food at low prices to poor and famine-stricken countries.

Writing Theme
World Hunger

C. Using Verb Forms and Voices Rewrite the following paragraph, changing the italicized verbs to the form or voice shown in parentheses.

(1) Fighting and greed within some countries *impede* (present progressive) hunger relief efforts. (2) For example, in 1984–85 Ethiopia *was struck* (active voice) by a terrible famine. (3) The famine was brief, but it *took* (past emphatic) many lives. (4) At the time, the Ethiopian government *waged* (past progressive) a war against rebels in the north. (5) Relief agencies *sent* (past perfect progressive) food to famine victims in the north. (6) However, the government *stopped* (past progressive) the relief convoys just outside the war zone. (7) Some food *got* (past emphatic) through, but not enough. (8) Much of it *was* often *stolen* and *sold* (active voice, past perfect progressive) by Ethiopian government officials. (9) People around the world *were outraged* (active voice) by the officials' actions. (10) Regrettably, war and vice often *contribute* (present emphatic) to the problem of hunger.

D. Recognizing the Mood of Verbs Identify the mood of the italicized verbs in the following sentences.

1. A reporter recently *asked* an expert on world hunger about future solutions to the problem.
2. The expert suggested that more krill *be harvested.*
3. "What, exactly, *is* krill?" asked the reporter.
4. "It's a tiny shrimplike creature," replied the expert. "If I *were* in the fishing industry, I would be harvesting it.
5. I'd tell everyone, '*Listen,* there are billions of krill in the oceans.'
6. There *are* enough of them to feed several million hungry people annually."
7. "If more krill *were harvested,* would people find them tasty?" the reporter asked.
8. "Oh, yes," the expert replied. "The Russians and Japanese *have been consuming* them for years.
9. *Tell* that to your readers," she added.
10. The expert concluded the interview by asking that readers *be informed* about the nutritional value of krill.

Subject and Verb Agreement

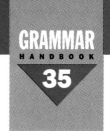

AGREEMENT IN NUMBER

The **number** of a noun, pronoun, or verb indicates whether the word is singular or plural. A word is **singular** in number if it refers to one person or thing. A word is **plural** if it refers to more than one person or thing. In English only nouns, pronouns, and verbs can change number.

The subject and verb of a sentence must agree in number.

If the subject of a sentence is singular, its verb must also be singular. If a subject is plural, then its verb must also be plural. This grammatical harmony between the subject and verb is called **subject-verb agreement.**

> The <u>kitten</u> (singular) <u>likes</u> (singular) catnip.
> The <u>kittens</u> (plural) <u>like</u> (plural) catnip.
> <u>Kate</u> (singular) <u>has</u> (singular) <u>been practicing</u> every day.
> The <u>girls</u> (plural) <u>have</u> (plural) <u>been practicing</u> every day.

The Number of Subjects and Verbs

The subject of a sentence is almost always a noun or pronoun. Determining the number of a noun or pronoun used as a subject is rarely a problem. By now you are familiar with the singular and plural forms of nouns and pronouns.

Except for *be,* the singular and plural forms of verbs should also cause little difficulty. Verbs show a difference between singular and plural only in the third person present tense. The third person singular present form ends in *s.*

Verb Forms

Singular		Plural	
I	sing	we	sing
you	sing	you	sing
he, she (Maria), it	sings	they (the twins)	sing

Grammar Note Nouns ending in *s* are usually plural, whereas verbs ending in *s* are usually singular.

Writing Theme
Riddles

Singular and Plural Forms of *Be* The verb *be* presents special problems in agreement because this verb does not follow any of the usual verb patterns. In the chart below, note that *be* has special forms for the singular and plural in both the present and past tenses and in all three persons.

Forms of Be

	Present Tense		Past Tense	
	Singular	*Plural*	*Singular*	*Plural*
First Person	I am	we are	I was	we were
Second Person	you are	you are	you were	you were
Third Person	he, she, it is	they are	he, she, it was	they were

Practice Your Skills

CONCEPT CHECK

Agreement in Number Write the form of the verb that agrees in number with the subject of each of the following sentences. Then tell whether the verb form is *Singular* or *Plural*.

1. In some cultures, riddles (is, are) more than child's play.
2. In fact, they (represent, represents) an art form.
3. In Greek mythology, a monster known as the Sphinx (destroy, destroys) passers-by who fail to answer her riddle.
4. Her riddle (is, are): "What in the morning goes on four feet, at noon on two, and in the evening on three?"
5. The Greek hero Oedipus (was, were) able to give the right answer: "Man, who in childhood creeps, in manhood walks upright, and in old age uses a cane."
6. In addition, the Anglo-Saxons (was, were) fond of riddles as a pastime.
7. A collection of poems written down around A.D. 975, the Exeter Book, (contain, contains) a set of ninety-five riddles.
8. Unfortunately, the book (offer, offers) no solutions to its readers for the riddles.
9. However, clever readers (have, has) already guessed most of the answers.
10. The riddles (describe, describes) items such as a sword, a shield, a swan, the moon, and ice.

A verb agrees only with its subject.

Occasionally, a word or group of words comes between the subject and the verb. Even though another word may be closer to the verb than the subject is, the verb must still agree in number with its subject. When the words come between the subject and the verb, identify the subject and make sure the verb agrees with it.

The <u>speakers</u> on that car stereo <u>are</u> not <u>working</u> properly. (*Speakers,* not *stereo,* is the subject.)
The <u>plant</u> with purple blossoms <u>is</u> an aster. (*Plant,* not *blossoms,* is the subject.)

The words *with, together with, along with, as well as,* and *in addition to* are prepositions. A phrase beginning with these prepositions does not affect the number of the subject.

That country <u>singer</u>, along with his band, <u>has been</u> on tour for three months. (*Has* agrees with the singular subject *singer.*)
The <u>Prime Minister</u>, together with her top aides, <u>is visiting</u> the United Nations. (*Is* agrees with the singular subject *Prime Minister.*)

Practice Your Skills

A. CONCEPT CHECK

Words Between Subject and Verb   Write the subject of each sentence. Then write the form of the verb that agrees in number with the subject.

1. Words that are derived from a person's name (is, are) called *eponyms*.
2. Many names for articles of clothing (are, is) eponyms.
3. Jules Leotard, as well as the Earl of Cardigan, (is, are) famous because of an article of clothing.
4. The cardigan, a sweater with a front opening lined with buttons, (get, gets) its name from the Earl of Cardigan, a nineteenth-century British general.
5. The one-piece garment worn by performers today (was, were) invented by Jules Leotard, a nineteenth-century acrobat.
6. In addition, our name for slices of bread with a filling (is, are) an eponym.
7. This word for one of the world's most common foods (come, comes) from the eighteenth-century English nobleman, John Montagu—also known as the fourth Earl of Sandwich.
8. The graham cracker, as well as the sandwich, (has, have) its origin in a person's name.
9. This cracker, made from whole wheat flour and other wholesome ingredients, (was, were) the brainchild of a vegetarian minister, Sylvester Graham.
10. Graham, along with his disciples, (was, were) an early believer in natural foods, now widely recommended by nutritionists and other health experts.

B. REVISION SKILL

Making Subjects and Verbs Agree   Rewrite the following sentences, correcting all errors in subject-verb agreement. If a sentence is correct, write *Correct*.

1. The origins of a word is sometimes associated with the name of a specific place.
2. The name for the material used in jeans come from a cloth manufactured in Nimes, a town in southern France.
3. This cloth, first called *serge de Nimes* ("serge from Nimes"), were eventually named denim.
4. A colorfully patterned woolen cloth, along with the designs themselves, is called paisley—from the city of Paisley in the Renfrew District of Scotland.

5. Cities in Germany was the original homes of the frankfurter (Frankfurt) and the hamburger (Hamburg).
6. Less well-known places, along with these famous cities, have been the birthplaces of other English words.
7. For example, a cheese with great popularity in many countries are cheddar, which was named after the English village where it was first made.
8. In addition, specialized vocabulary for a wide variety of actions are also taken from place names.
9. The verb *canter,* which means "gallop gently," is short for Canterbury, a city in England.
10. This word, associated with horses, describe the pace of medieval pilgrims riding to Canterbury.

COMPOUND SUBJECTS

Use a plural verb with most compound subjects joined by *and*.

> Both <u>aluminum</u> and <u>copper</u> <u>are</u> excellent conductors of heat.
> How <u>do</u> your <u>aunt</u> and <u>uncle</u> <u>like</u> living in Albuquerque?

Use a singular verb with a compound subject joined by *and* that is habitually used to refer to a single thing.

> <u>Macaroni and cheese</u> <u>is</u> a favorite dish in our house.
> <u>The horse and buggy</u> <u>is</u> associated with a slower-paced era.

Use a singular verb with a compound subject that is preceded by *each, every,* or *many a.*

> Each <u>car</u> and <u>truck</u> in the lot <u>is</u> on sale this week.
> Every <u>student</u> and <u>teacher</u> <u>has been tested</u> for meningitis.

When the words in a compound subject are joined by *or* or *nor*, the verb agrees with the subject nearer the verb.

> Either my <u>mother</u> or my <u>father</u> <u>drops</u> me off at school in the morning. (The singular verb *drops* agrees with *father,* the subject nearer the verb.)
> A twentieth-century <u>novel</u> or two contemporary <u>plays</u> <u>meet</u> this semester's reading requirements. (The plural verb *meet* agrees with *plays,* the subject nearer the verb.)
> Neither the arresting <u>officers</u> nor the <u>commissioner</u> <u>wants</u> to make a statement to the press. (The singular verb *wants* agrees with *commissioner,* the subject nearer the verb.)

Practice Your Skills

A. CONCEPT CHECK

Agreement with Compound Subjects   Write the form of the verb that agrees in number with the subject of each of the following sentences.

1. During the 1970's Frank Shorter and Bill Rodgers (was, were) America's premier marathon runners.
2. An Olympic gold medal in 1972 and a silver medal in 1976 (was, were) Shorter's top achievements.
3. The Boston Marathon and the New York Marathon (was, were) the sites of Rodger's finest victories.
4. Hard work and dedication (goes, go) into the making of a runner.
5. Two short, fast workouts or one long, slow run (makes, make) up the daily training routine of most competitive marathoners.
6. Neither inclement weather nor minor injuries (prevents, prevent) world-class runners from accomplishing their mileage quota—as much as twenty miles per day.
7. Every major marathon and small-town race (poses, pose) the same challenge—to run as hard as possible for as long as possible.
8. High-school track and field (is, are) where most marathoners get their start.
9. Many a young runner and future Olympian (has, have) been inspired by Shorter and Rodgers.
10. Today Shorter and Rodgers (continues, continue) to race; neither fame nor fortune (has, have) diminished the enthusiasm of these athletes.

B. PROOFREADING SKILL

Agreement with Compound Subjects   Proofread the following paragraph. Rewrite it correcting all errors. Pay particular attention to verb agreement with compound subjects.

> Largely as the result of television, track and field are an area that has grate public appeal. Many an athlete have attempted the challenge offered by the two-day olympic contest, the decathlon. Because running, jumping, and throwing is involved, this event is a supreem test of all-around athletic ability. Since there are nerveracking hours between events, both physical fatigue and mental exhaustion is the price a competetor pays. Interestingly, contestants do not compete against one another, time and distance provides the challenge. In the end, however, neither the fans nor the record are what counts the most. Its the pride of winning for ones country.

C. APPLICATION IN WRITING

Comparison Think of two outstanding athletes, teams, performers, movies, or authors that you can compare. Write a paragraph about the likenesses and differences between the two. In your comparison, use some sentences with compound subjects. Begin at least one sentence with *either* or *neither* and one with *both*.

CHECK POINT
PAGES 685-691

A. Write the correct form of the verb in the following sentences.

1. Years ago, the principles of sanitation (was, were) unknown.
2. Early hospitals (was, were) dirty, crowded, and dark.
3. Neither the medical instruments nor the patient (was, were) clean.
4. Until mid-Victorian times, patients in any hospital (was, were) at risk of dying from infection after surgery.
5. The reason for these infections (was, were) not known until Louis Pasteur discovered that germs caused illness.
6. Joseph Lister (were, was) the first surgeon to understand that antiseptic chemicals could kill germs.
7. Neither antiseptic surgery nor sterilizing techniques (was, were) practiced before the time of Joseph Lister.
8. Both Pasteur and Lister (is, are) considered responsible for introducing modern concepts of sanitation to medicine.
9. Antiseptics now (play, plays) a big part in saving lives.
10. Today, a doctor, along with his or her surgical team, (establish, establishes) a germ-free operation site by using sterile products.

B. Rewrite the following sentences, correcting all errors in subject-verb agreement. If a sentence is correct, write *Correct*.

1. A major health concern today is keeping water pure.
2. Neither waste nor any other contaminants is desirable in water.
3. Germs in water presents a special threat to health.
4. Epidemics of dysentery or cholera is caused by untreated water.
5. Water containing tiny biological organisms are undesirable.
6. Neither filtration nor chlorination alone kills germs.
7. Often, germs in the environment are too small for filters.
8. Carefully measured amounts of chlorine and other chemicals helps disinfect the water supply.
9. One pound of chlorine disinfect 200,000 gallons of water, more water than one person could drink in a thousand years.
10. Chlorination, along with other methods of disinfecting drinking water, are a lifesaver.

Writing Theme
Sanitation

Louis Pasteur in his laboratory

Some indefinite pronouns are always singular; some are always plural. Others may be either singular or plural.

Singular Indefinite Pronouns

another	either	neither	other
anybody	everybody	nobody	somebody
anyone	everyone	no one	someone
anything	everything	nothing	something
each	much	one	

Either of the presidential candidates seems qualified.
Each of them speaks effectively.
Neither of the dressing rooms is available right now.
Everybody plans to attend the rodeo.

Plural Indefinite Pronouns

both	few	many	several

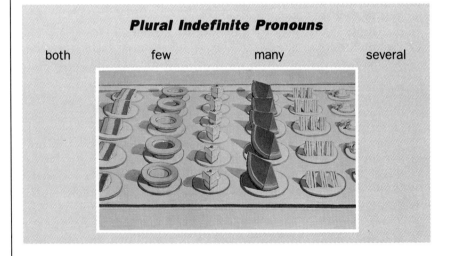

Use a plural verb with a plural indefinite pronoun.

Several in the class were excellent writers.
Both of the dancers were injured.

Singular or Plural Indefinite Pronouns

all	enough	most	plenty
any	more	none	some

These indefinite pronouns are singular when they refer to one thing. They are plural when they refer to several things.

Singular   <u>Most</u> of the ice cream <u>has melted</u>. (*Most* refers to one quantity of ice cream.)
<u>Some</u> of the forest <u>was destroyed</u> by the fire. (*Some* refers to one portion of the forest.)

Plural   <u>Most</u> of the ice cream cones <u>are gone</u>. (*Most* refers to several ice cream cones.)
<u>Some</u> of the trees <u>were</u> hundreds of years old. (*Some* refers to several trees.)

Practice Your Skills

A. CONCEPT CHECK

Agreement with Indefinite Pronouns   Write the subject of each of the following sentences. Then write the form of the verb that agrees in number with the subject.

Writing Theme
National Anthems

1. Many of the world's national anthems (have, has) origins that are not widely known.
2. Several of these tunes (is, are) probably familiar to you.
3. One of these familiar melodies (is, are) "God Save the Queen."
4. Everybody in the United States (recognize, recognizes) it as "My Country 'Tis of Thee," a song based on the British national anthem.
5. Another of our national songs, "The Star-Spangled Banner," (is, are) also of British origin.
6. However, not everyone (know, knows) that the tune of our anthem was taken from a British song, "To Anacreon in Heaven."
7. Some (ask, asks) why its composer chose such a difficult melody.
8. Most (has, have) trouble reaching the song's octave-and-a-half range.
9. The reason for its choice may have been the fact that nearly all of America's citizens in 1814 (was, were) familiar with this tune.
10. Everyone (assume, assumes) that "The Star-Spangled Banner" has always been our anthem, but it didn't become official until 117 years after its composition.

B. REVISION SKILL

Agreement with Indefinite Pronouns   Rewrite the following sentences, correcting all errors in subject-verb agreement. If a sentence is correct, write *Correct*.

1. Much of the historical background about our national anthem are quite dramatic.
2. During wartime in 1814, some of the British forces was attacking Baltimore's Fort McHenry.
3. One of the American prisoners on board a British battleship were Francis Scott Key.
4. Each of the prisoners was a witness to the attack.
5. Everyone on the ship were anxiously watching the U.S. flag fluttering proudly at the fort.
6. Most of the observers was wondering if the flag would go down in defeat.
7. Finally, in the "dawn's early light," several of the prisoners was able to catch a glimpse of Old Glory, tattered but still flying above Fort McHenry.
8. Most of the words of "The Star-Spangled Banner" was written by Key that morning in the form of a poem.
9. Soon, the few on board the ship was able to read Key's poem, entitled "Defence of Fort McHenry."
10. Shortly thereafter, many of the country's newspapers were eager to print it.

C. APPLICATION IN WRITING

A Report on Survey Results   Write a paragraph that conveys the opinions and attitudes of citizens of the United States toward their national anthem. To help you develop your paragraph, use the following results of a poll conducted by *Time*/CNN. As you state the general opinions of most people, use such expressions as "Few say," "Many wish," and "Most want."

Questions	Responses
Is the national anthem of the United States easy to sing?	53 percent said *yes*
Do you know all the words to our national anthem?	64 percent said *yes*
Should "The Star-Spangled Banner" be replaced by another patriotic song, "America, the Beautiful"?	67 percent said *no*

There are several other situations where problems in subject-verb agreement may arise.

Inverted Sentences

Problems in agreement often occur in inverted sentences beginning with *here* and *there;* in questions beginning with *why, where,* and *what;* and in inverted sentences beginning with a phrase.

Even when the subject comes after the verb, it still determines whether the verb should be singular or plural. Study the following examples.

Incorrect	Here is the designs for the homecoming float.
Correct	Here are the designs for the homecoming float.
Incorrect	There is two *t*'s in "regretted."
Correct	There are two *t*'s in "regretted."
Incorrect	Who is those tall people in the parking lot?
Correct	Who are those tall people in the parking lot?
Incorrect	From out of the forest comes two dragons.
Correct	From out of the forest come two dragons.

Usage Note The contractions *here's, there's, what's,* and *where's* contain the singular verb *is.* Use them only with singular subjects.

Incorrect	There's the car keys.
Correct	There are the car keys.
Incorrect	What's the math assignments for next week?
Correct	What are the math assignments for next week?

Sentences with Predicate Nominatives

Use a verb that agrees in number with the subject, not with the predicate nominative.

> Mother's main interest is computers. (*Interest* is the subject and takes a singular verb.)
> Computers are Mother's main interest. (*Computers* is the subject and takes a plural verb.)
> Running in the Olympics was her dream and her goal. (*Running in the Olympics* is the subject and takes a singular verb.)

Sentences with *Don't* and *Doesn't*

Use ***doesn't*** with singular subjects and with the personal pronouns *he, she,* and *it.* Use ***don't*** with plural subjects and with the personal pronouns *I, we, you,* and *they.*

Singular	Doesn't the <u>bus</u> <u>stop</u> at this corner?
	It <u>doesn't</u> <u>run</u> regularly on weekends.
Plural	<u>Don't</u> the <u>buses</u> <u>run</u> on Saturday?
	<u>They</u> <u>don't</u> <u>stop</u> here on weekends.

Grammar Note Remember that *not* and its abbreviation *n't* are adverbs—not part of the verb.

Practice Your Skills

A. CONCEPT CHECK

Agreement Problems Write the form of the verb that agrees in number with the subject of each of the following sentences.

1. How (is, are) shoe sizes determined?
2. There (is, are) several explanations for today's method of foot measurement.
3. What facts (does, do) history provide on this subject?
4. First, there (was, were) less need for shoe sizes before mass production.
5. Traditionally, custom-made shoes (doesn't, don't) require standard measurements.
6. Therefore, measurements of people's feet (wasn't, weren't) a problem until the late nineteenth century.
7. Furthermore, in England and America, inches (has, have) always been the standard unit of measurement.
8. A human foot (was, were) twelve inches—at least, that's what people assumed.
9. What (was, were) the reasons for thinking that?
10. Supposedly, Charlemagne's feet (was, were) the model!
11. From that famous foot (come, comes) the system of sizing for modern shoes.
12. There (is, are) one-third of an inch between two whole-number shoe sizes.
13. Then, what (is, are) the difference between half-number shoe sizes?
14. There (is, are) a new size produced by each one-sixth-inch difference.
15. (Doesn't, Don't) those half sizes make a big difference in comfort, though?

B. PROOFREADING SKILL

Correcting Subject-Verb Agreement Errors Rewrite the following paragraph correcting all errors in subject-verb agreement. Also correct any errors in capitalization, punctuation, and spelling.

There is several facts about standards of human measurment you may not know. Long ago, all measurements was based on the human body. For example, what are the importance of the distance between you're elbow and the tip of your middle finger? From that distance come the standard for the cubit. An early form of measurement. Related to this measurement are the yard, or the length of an extended arm from shoulder to fingertips. Also, from the length of a human foot come the measurement for one foot. Don't this way of measuring seem strange. how many people has a foot twelve inches long? There's always inconsistencies. Peoples arms, hands, and feet all vary in size.

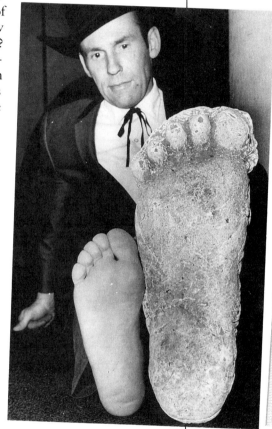

Plaster cast of the footprint of Big Foot, made by photographer Roger Patterson

Collective Nouns as Subjects

A **collective noun** names a group or collection of people or things: *family, choir, crew, herd, faculty.* Depending on its meaning in a sentence, a collective noun may take a singular or plural verb. If a collective noun refers to a group acting together as one unit, use a singular verb. If a collective noun refers to members or parts of a group acting individually, use a plural verb.

Singular	The <u>team</u> <u>is</u> the best in the history of our school. (acting as a unit)
Plural	The <u>team</u> <u>were</u> hurriedly dressing for the game. (acting individually)
Singular	The <u>council</u> <u>has scheduled</u> a meeting for Thursday. (acting as a unit)
Plural	The <u>council</u> <u>have disagreed</u> on the date. (acting individually)

Singular Nouns with Plural Forms

Some nouns are plural in form but are regarded as singular in meaning. That is, they end in *s* as most plural nouns do, but they do not stand for more than one thing: *news, mumps, mathematics.* Therefore, they take a singular verb.

> The stock market <u>news</u> <u>was</u> encouraging.
> <u>Mumps</u> <u>is</u> more serious for adults than for children.

Other nouns end in *s* and take a plural verb even though they refer to one thing: *scissors, pliers, trousers, congratulations.*

> Where <u>are</u> the <u>pliers</u>?
> <u>Congratulations</u> <u>are</u> in order.

Some nouns that end in *s* may be either singular or plural, depending on their meaning in the sentence: *ethics, economics, civics, politics, athletics.* When plural, these words are often preceded by a possessive form or a modifier.

Singular	<u>Ethics</u> <u>consists</u> of a set of values.
Plural	Their <u>ethics</u> <u>are</u> sometimes questionable.

The name of a country or an organization is singular even though it may be plural in form.

> The <u>Philippines</u> <u>consists</u> of thousands of islands and islets.
> The <u>United Nations</u> <u>has televised</u> most of today's sessions.

Titles and Groups of Words as Subjects
Use a singular verb with a title.

The title of a book, play, short story, article, film, TV program, musical composition, or work of art is singular even though it may be plural in form.

> *<u>The Orphans</u>* <u>is</u> the story of twins who attract misfortune.
> *<u>David and Goliath</u>* <u>was</u> painted for the King of France in 1295.

The Honeymooners <u>has become</u> a classic in television situation
    comedies.
"Thistles" <u>contains</u> powerful imagery.

Use a singular verb with any group of words that refers to a single thing or thought.

<u>What we need</u> <u>is</u> votes.
<u>"Because I said so"</u> <u>is</u> a popular phrase.
<u>Canoeing down the white-water rapids</u> <u>was</u> definitely the high-
    light of my family's summer.

Words of Amount and Time as Subjects

Words that refer to amounts are usually singular.

Use a singular verb with nouns or phrases that refer to a period of
time, a weight, a measurement, a fraction, or an amount of money.

Five <u>hours</u> <u>seems</u> a long time to wait.
One hundred <u>pounds</u> of bird seed <u>is</u> in that container.
Ten <u>yards</u> of material <u>is</u> enough for the backdrop.
<u>Two-thirds</u> of the money <u>has</u> already <u>been raised</u>.
A hundred <u>dollars</u> <u>is</u> too much for that jacket.

Use a plural verb when the subject refers to a period of time or
an amount that is thought of as a number of separate units.

Two <u>hours</u> <u>remain</u> before lift-off.
Three <u>quarters</u> <u>were jingling</u> in my pocket.

Practice Your Skills

A. CONCEPT CHECK

Agreement Problems Write the form of the verb that agrees in
number with the subject of each of the following sentences.

Writing Theme
Curious Creatures

1. Year in and year out, the news (include, includes) stories about yet
   another sighting of Bigfoot.
2. Hundreds of stories (has, have) been told about this large, apelike
   creature, but are any of them true?
3. *Monsters of the Mountains,* Jon Jameson's book, (answers, answer) some of these questions about the legends of Bigfoot.
4. Tracking down Bigfoot (has, have) been a hobby of wonderseekers
   for many years.
5. Now, a scientific research team occasionally (travel, travels) to the
   Pacific Northwest to look for the monster.

6. Twenty thickly forested mountains near the coast (is, are) thought to be its home.
7. In such rugged, unforgiving terrain, finding this hairy creature (is, are) not easy.
8. Nevertheless, from time to time a television crew (go, goes) along to film a program about the Bigfoot controversy.
9. Sightings of a similar beast, the Yeti, or Abominable Snowman, have been reported; however, the United States (is, are) the only country where there have been sightings of Bigfoot.
10. What scientists seek (is, are) proof that a Bigfoot, or some other similar creature, exists.
11. Surprisingly, a number of photographs of this shy, mysterious beast (has, have) been taken.
12. However, the scientific community (has, have) dismissed most of this "evidence."
13. "The pictures are too blurry and lack detail" (is, are) the universal response of scientists who have viewed them.
14. Nevertheless, estimating the size of the hypothetical Bigfoot (is, are) possible.
15. Three meters (is, are) a good estimate of the creature's height; its weight may be 800 pounds.

B. PROOFREADING SKILL

Correcting Agreement Problems   The following paragraphs contain several errors in subject-verb agreement, as well as errors in capitalization, punctuation, and spelling. Rewrite the paragraphs, correcting each error.

One of the most famous "monsters" in the world are Nessie, a dragonlike creature that reportedly lives in the murky waters of scotland's Loch Ness. More than three thousand sighting's of Nessie has been recorded. Most of these sightings takes place just before dawn. In the early morning light, a huge snakelike head, as well as a body like that of a camel, supposedly appear.

What's the chances of ever finding and identifying this creature? The probabillity of solving this centuries-old mystery have improved with the use of technology. Recent studies with underwater photographic equipment detects moving shadows that are not identifiable. From this evidence comes new theories about the "monster." There's several theories about nessie. For example, one scientific group believe that the creature is a giant Eel. Several others doesn't agree. However, somewhere on the bottom of loch ness lie the answer.

C. APPLICATION IN WRITING

A Letter to a Professional Organization   Imagine you visited Loch Ness and saw Nessie. Write a letter to the Loch Ness Investigation Bureau. Include specific details. Make certain all your subjects and verbs agree.

RELATIVE PRONOUNS
AS SUBJECTS

A relative pronoun is sometimes the subject of an adjective clause (see pages 607–609). To determine whether to use a singular or a plural verb in the clause, you must first determine the number of the relative pronoun. A relative pronoun stands in place of its antecedent. If the antecedent is plural, so is the relative pronoun. If the antecedent is singular, the relative pronoun is singular.

A relative pronoun agrees with its antecedent in number.

Singular   She is the candidate <u>who</u> <u>has received</u> the most votes.
　　　　　(*Who* refers to the singular antecedent *candidate*.)

Plural   Here is a list of candidates <u>who</u> <u>have</u> already <u>conceded</u>.
　　　　　(*Who* refers to the plural antecedent *candidates*.)

Singular   Ms. Greene is the only one of the coaches <u>who</u> <u>has run</u> in road races. (Only *one* has run races. *Who* refers to the singular antecedent *one*.)

Plural   Len is one of those people <u>who</u> <u>are</u> always <u>coming</u> late.
            (*People* are always coming late. *Who* refers to the plural antecedent *people*.)

The problem of agreement arises in the last two sentences because there are two words that might be the antecedent of the relative pronoun. Remember that the verb in the relative clause will agree with the true antecedent of the relative pronoun.

Practice Your Skills

CONCEPT CHECK

Agreement with Relative Pronouns   Write the form of the verb that agrees in number with the subject of each of the following sentences.

Writing Theme
Unusual Mammals

1. There are some mammals that (has, have) unusual physical features.
2. The narwhal, called a sea unicorn, is an animal that (looks, look) like a mythical creature.
3. It is one species of whales that (lives, live) in the Arctic.
4. However, it is the only one of the aquatic mammals that (has, have) a twisted horn on its head.
5. Some scientists who (studies, study) this creature believe the tusk has a purpose.
6. Apparently, it is a tool that (allows, allow) the narwhal to break ice.
7. There are others who (feels, feel) that the tusk is useless.
8. Between males and females, the male is the only one of the species that (has, have) this ivory horn.
9. Of the narwhal's two teeth, the tusk is the one that (has, have) developed into a projection nine feet long.
10. Today, the Eskimos of Greenland are the only group who (hunt, hunts) the narwhal.
11. They eat the skin, which (is, are) called *muktuk.*
12. In medieval times, it was the tusks that (was, were) believed to be unicorn horns.
13. According to medieval legends, a cup carved from a tusk was the only one of many magical objects that (was, were) capable of preventing poisoning.
14. There existed people in medieval society who (was, were) willing to do anything to obtain a tusk.
15. In any age, the narwhal is a mammal that (intrigues, intrigue) everyone interested in unique sea creatures.

CHECK POINT
PAGES 692–702

A. Write the correct form of the verb in the following sentences.

1. (Doesn't, Don't) everyone love pasta?
2. The proof of this claim is that there (is, are) over one hundred different types and shapes.
3. Some of the most common shapes (includes, include) ribbons, cords, and tubes.
4. From the shapes (comes, come) some interesting names for pasta.
5. "Little worms" (is, are) the meaning of the word *vermicelli,* a kind of very thin noodle.
6. Another name that (reflects, reflect) the shape of pasta is *spaghetti,* meaning "little string."
7. These shapes (doesn't, don't) just contribute colorful names; they also account for pasta's ability to retain heat or hold sauce.
8. Pasta is one of many foods that (is, are) made from semolina, a by-product of the flour-making process.
9. The good news (is, are) that, served without rich sauces, pasta is low in calories and high in certain vitamins.
10. Nobody (agrees, agree) on the best color, shape, or sauce; but nearly everyone (conclude, concludes) that pasta is delicious.

B. Write the correct form of the verb in each sentence.

1. The story of pizza (begins, begin) many hundreds of years ago in Naples, Italy.
2. *Moretum,* a work by the ancient Roman poet Virgil, (gives, give) a description of pizza.
3. This popular food (has, have) many appealing qualities, which (includes, include) convenience, affordability, nutritional value, and good taste.
4. There (is, are) now many regional varieties of pizza.
5. Some of these varieties (is, are) recognized by their distinctive toppings: in Nice, France—black olives; in Naples—mozzarella cheese made from water buffalo milk.
6. Neither of these pizzas, however, (is, are) quite like the Roman pizza, which (has, have) onions, but no tomatoes.
7. The first pizzeria in the United States (was, were) started in New York in 1905.
8. A booming business today (is, are) the pizza delivery services.
9. Over four billion dollars' worth of pizza (is, are) sold each year.
10. Each day people in the United States (eats, eat) seventy-five acres of pizza!

Subject and
Verb Agreement **703**

GRAMMAR
HANDBOOK
35

Writing Theme
Notable
Accomplishments

A. Making Subjects and Verbs Agree Choose the correct verb from the two in parentheses. Then write the word with which the verb agrees.

1. Most of the world's highest peaks (is, are) located in the small landlocked country of Nepal.
2. The news sometimes (carry, carries) stories of people who have climbed Mount Everest, the highest peak in the Himalayas.
3. Twenty-nine thousand feet (is, are) the distance to the top of Mount Everest.
4. (What's, What are) the reasons for climbing this dangerous mountain?
5. Conquering the high peaks (is, are) an extraordinary achievement.
6. Actually, many accomplished mountain climbers (doesn't, don't) use the word *conquer.*
7. None of the over one hundred successful climbers (has, have) changed or "conquered" Mount Everest in any way.
8. Tenzing Norgay and Sir Edmund Hillary are two of these climbers who (has, have) reached the top of Everest.
9. Jim Whittaker, as well as climbers from China and the Soviet Union, (has, have) undertaken a "Peace Climb" of Everest.
10. Neither Whittaker nor the others (has, have) taken the long and dangerous climb lightly.
11. (There's, There are) countless difficulties involved in climbing such a treacherous mountain.
12. At the bottom, each of the climbers (crosses, cross) through a tropical jungle.
13. However, 185 miles through the jungle (is, are) only the first part of the journey!
14. Then, several weeks of the journey (is, are) spent crossing the icefalls.
15. Turning back at these treacherous icefalls (is, are) not at all uncommon.
16. At least two months of physical exertion and courage (is, are) required to reach the top.
17. A lack of oxygen and a resulting decrease in mental abilities (is, are) experienced near the summit.
18. For example, there are stories of climbers who (has, have) taken off their gloves near the top.
19. Either the lack of oxygen or the feelings of exhaustion (causes, cause) the climbers to do something so foolish.
20. For those climbers who (is, are) able to avoid such pitfalls, standing literally on top of the world (is, are) a reward well worth the enormous effort and danger.

In 1974, sculptor Doug Michels combined ten Cadillacs to create a sculpture titled *Cadillac Ranch*, located in the middle of a grainfield in Amarillo, Texas.

B. Solving Problems in Subject-Verb Agreement Choose the correct form of the verb for each sentence.

1. Salvaging autos (is, are) one way to contribute to recycling.
2. According to recent national figures, there (are, is) at least twenty-nine million cars ten years old or older in this country.
3. Twenty-nine million (represent, represents) a considerable increase from just a few years ago.
4. Each of today's junkyards (has, have) its own personality.
5. Some of the junkyards (sell, sells) only parts for specific models; others (deal, deals) only in hubcaps.
6. Computers, which never would have been seen in a junkyard of old, (keep, keeps) track of the rapidly changing inventory in some newer junkyards.
7. Attractive showrooms, steam-cleaned parts, and the free use of power tools (is, are) offered by some junkyards.
8. At some fancier junkyards, neither couples on dates nor a well-dressed businessperson (is, are) a strange sight.
9. "The Riches of Wrecks," a recent magazine article, (tell, tells) about one "junkyard" that is contained within a six-story building.
10. Of course, many a junkyard still (has, have) the typical fierce-eyed mongrel keeping watch at the gate, guarding a mountain of rusty cars and old rubber tires.

C. Correcting Errors in Subject-Verb Agreement Several of the following sentences contain errors in subject-verb agreement. If a sentence has an error, rewrite the sentence correctly. If a sentence does not have an error, write *Correct*.

1. Charlie Brown is only one of the characters that Charles Schulz have created for his much-loved comic strip.

2. "Peanuts" have been around for over a generation now, and there is hardly anyone who don't feel compassion for the struggles of Charlie Brown.
3. Each of Schulz's readers, from children to adults, seem to identify with Charlie's tendency to fail.
4. One of the problems Charlie has are getting his kites to fly.
5. There's always trees in the way, and the kite invariably gets caught in one of them—on purpose, Charlie believes.
6. Then there is Charlie's inability to kick a football or win even a single baseball game.
7. Either the kite or sports give Charlie trouble regularly.
8. However, Charlie has a popularity that have grown even larger through television.
9. He don't have to worry about being unloved.
10. Charlie Brown has millions of friends all over the world.

D. Proofreading This passage contains a number of errors in subject-verb agreement as well as errors in capitalization, punctuation, and spelling. Rewrite the paragraphs, correcting each error.

> One man and his small son runs there fingers over the black wall, touching a name. Another kneel and bow his head. A family are placing flowers and a tiny flag at the base of the wall. The people is visitors at the Vietnam Veterans Memorial in Washington d.c.
>
> Maya Ying Lin, chosen from 1,421 entries in the contest to create a Vietnam War memorial, were only a twenty-two-year-old architecture student at yale at the time. Maya Lin describes her design: "A rift in the earth, a long, polished black stone wall emerging from and receding into the earth." The memorial are actually two walls, two leg's of a V, each 250 feet long. Over 57,000 names—the killed and missing in the war—is carved in the black granite. The list of soldiers are arranged in the order of their deaths from 1959 to 1975. When the memorial was dedicated in 1982 their was a public reading of all the engraved names, which took three days.
>
> Politics were an ever-present factor in the controversial Vietnam War. Inevitably, the wall has been controversial also. Some doesn't like the memorial and would prefer a more traditional statue. Most has found it's simple design profoundly moving. The true meaning of the memorial is clearly expressed by its creator, Maya Lin: "It does not glorify the war or make an antiwar statement. It is a place for private reckoning."

Sketchbook

Before the advent of the mini-cam, any on-the-spot news coverage was rare. People often did not learn about important or exciting events until long after the events had taken place. Imagine yourself as a news reporter with a mini-cam at a famous event in history. Narrate, using vivid active verbs, your report of what happened.

Meeting of the Rails, Promontory Point, Utah, 1869. The Union Pacific and Central Pacific railroads link the nation from coast to coast.

Additional Sketches

A Hollywood producer, filming a documentary of a typical day in your life, has asked you to write a schedule of your daily activities so that the director can prepare for filming. Write a schedule focusing on four "scenes" in your day that most typify you. Describe what you will do and who will be with you in each scene. Make sure that your subjects and verbs agree.

The verbs *lay* and *lie* are often confused. Demonstrate your mastery of the terms by creating a fable—first in the present tense and then in the past tense—about a bricklayer given to telling untruths.

Directions In each of the following sentences, one, two, or none of the underlined sections may be incorrect. Look for errors of grammar, usage, punctuation, spelling, and capitalization. On your paper, write the number of the sentence, the letter of each incorrect underlined section, and the correction. If the sentence contains no errors, write E.

Example   Among the oldest writing in the world are a monument
                        A   **B**
with an inscripshun dating from 4,000 B.C. No error
          C   **D**   **E**

Answer   B—is C—inscription

---

1. During the 1500's and 1600's, children with whooping cough were gave a live frog to
                                                                                              A
   hold in their mouths; this had little positive affect. No error
          B   **C**   **D**   **E**

2. During Africa's colonial period, Beryl Markham frequently flew over Kenya; in fact, she
                                                                        A   **B**
   had flew over the area before much of the land beyond the capitol city of Nairobi had
   C   **D**
   even been mapped. No error
                        E

3. In this century the invention of the microchip had revolutionized the storage and
                        A   **B**   **C**
   retrieval of data. No error
          D   **E**

4. Mark is the only one of our team's wrestlers who have won three state championships,
                                            A   **B**   **C**
   and by the time his wrestling career is over, we expect that he will win his fourth.
   A   **D**
   No error
   E

5. In India most children grow up hearing stories from two long epic poems,
      A   **B**   **C**
   the *Ramayana* and the *Mahabarata*. No error
          D   **E**

6. Because she was African American, Marian Anderson, who had sang with the New York
                                                                        A   **B**
   Philharmonic, was once barred from singing in Constitution Hall in Washington, D.C.
   C   **D**
   No error
   E

7. Several <u>priceless</u> works of <u>art, including</u> one by Rembrandt and one by Vermeer, <u>were</u>
   A B C
   <u>stole</u> from a museum in <u>Boston, Massachusetts</u>. <u>No error</u>
   D E

8. Golda Meir was born in the <u>Soviet Union</u>; taught high school in <u>Milwaukee, Wisconsin;</u>
   A B C
   <u>and</u> then went on to become the <u>Prime Minister</u> of Israel. <u>No error</u>
   D E

9. Although a few people paint <u>a rosey picture</u> for the future of the <u>environment, most</u>
   A B
   emphasize that the planet <u>was becoming</u> <u>perilously</u> overcrowded and polluted.
   C D
   <u>No error</u>
   E

10. <u>There</u> <u>are</u> more than <u>250</u> zoos and wildlife parks in the <u>United States of</u> these, the
    A B C D
    San Diego Zoo is among the most well known. <u>No error</u>
    E

11. <u>Collecting baseball cards</u> became very popular when <u>Topps Chewing Gum Company</u> first
    A B
    included cards with <u>its</u> bubble gum <u>in 1951</u>. <u>No error</u>
    C D E

12. The last emperor of <u>China</u> became a puppet of the Japanese during World War <u>II, but</u> he
    A B
    <u>does not completely give in</u> to the <u>Communist Chinese</u> during the Maoist era. <u>No error</u>
    C D E

13. <u>Justice</u> Sandra Day O'Connor <u>has set</u> on the United States <u>supreme court</u> since <u>1981</u>.
    A B C D
    <u>No error</u>
    E

14. A female seahorse <u>puts</u> <u>her</u> eggs into a pouch on the <u>males'</u> body, and the baby seahorses
    A B C
    <u>hatches</u> there. <u>No error</u>
    D E

15. <u>According to</u> <u>The New York Times, people</u> in the United States <u>have took</u> less and less
    A B C
    time off work <u>during the past few years</u>. <u>No error</u>
    D E

16. The carnival <u>comes</u> <u>to this part of the country</u> every <u>Fall</u>, <u>pitching</u> tents on the edge
    A B C D
    of town. <u>No error</u>
    E

17. The <u>botanist James</u> Stewart said <u>"that he was interested in slime molds"</u> because
    A   B
    botanists and biologists <u>is</u> unsure whether the slime mold <u>is</u> actually a plant or an
    C   D
    animal. <u>No error</u>
    E

18. <u>Both New Jersey</u> and Pennsylvania <u>shares</u> the <u>Deleware River</u> as a <u>boundary</u>. <u>No error</u>
    A   B   C   D   E

19. Venus is close to the <u>earth, but</u> it probably <u>don't</u> have any life because of <u>its</u> high surface
    A   B   C
    <u>temperatures</u>. <u>No error</u>
    D   E

20. The Union of Soviet Socialist Republics <u>are</u> experiencing severe economic difficulties
    A
    during the early 1990's; <u>therefore, a</u> team of <u>Western</u> economists <u>have</u> offered its
    B   C   D
    advisory services to the Soviet government. <u>No error</u>
    E

21. Leg irons or a straightjacket <u>were</u> no obstacle to the great Harry <u>Houdini, who</u> was the
    A   B   C
    <u>greatest</u> escape artist of all time. <u>No error</u>
    D   E

22. Several of the Hindu temples <u>that</u> were carved <u>into</u> rock <u>survives</u> today, although some
    A   B   C
    of their surface decorations <u>has</u> been erased by weathering. <u>No error</u>
    D   E

23. The word *teenage* first became part of the language during the <u>1940's</u>, reflecting the
    A   B
    new thinking <u>that</u> children between the ages of <u>thirteen and nineteen constituted</u> a
    C   D
    special group. <u>No error</u>
    E

24. Seven feet and five inches <u>are</u> the <u>height</u> of the tallest man who ever <u>lived,</u> Robert
    A   B   C
    Wadlow, of <u>Alton, Illinois</u>. <u>No error</u>
    D   E

25. *The Pickwick Papers* <u>are</u> an <u>exceptionally</u> long novel; 863 <u>seem</u> like an <u>extraordinary</u>
    A   B   C   D
    number of pages for one book! <u>No error</u>
    E

Using Pronouns

PRONOUN CASES

Pronouns are words that may be used in place of nouns. Pronouns change form depending on their use in sentences. These changes in pronoun form are called changes in the **case** of the pronouns. There are three cases in English: the **nominative case,** the **objective case,** and the **possessive case.** The personal pronouns are classified below according to case, number (singular and plural), and person (first, second, and third).

Singular

	Nominative	Objective	Possessive
First Person	I	me	my, mine
Second Person	you	you	your, yours
Third Person	he	him	his
	she	her	her, hers
	it	it	its

Plural

	Nominative	Objective	Possessive
First Person	we	us	our, ours
Second Person	you	you	your, yours
Third Person	they	them	their, theirs

The pronouns *who* and *whoever* are classified below according to case.

Nominative	Objective	Possessive
who	whom	whose
whoever	whomever	whosever

Indefinite pronouns change form only in the possessive case. The nominative and objective cases are identical.

Nominative	Objective	Possessive
someone	someone	someone's
everybody	everybody	everybody's
no one	no one	no one's
anything	anything	anything's

The pronouns *this, that, these, those, which,* and *what* do not change their forms to indicate case.

The material in this handbook will explain when to use the various case forms of pronouns.

Practice Your Skills

A. CONCEPT CHECK

Pronoun Case and Person   List italicized pronouns in the passages. Identify a personal pronoun as *First, Second,* or *Third Person; Singular* or *Plural;* and *Nominative, Objective,* or *Possessive* case. Write only the case for *who* and indefinite pronouns.

(1) Some boys taught *me* to play football. . . . (2) *You* went out for a pass, fooling *everyone*. (3) Best, you got to throw yourself mightily at *someone's* running legs. (4) Either you brought *him* down or you hit the ground flat out on *your* chin. . . . (5) Nothing girls did could compare with *it*.

(1) If in that snowy backyard the driver of the black Buick had cut off *our* heads, Mikey's and *mine*, I would have died happy, for nothing has required so much of *me* since as being chased all over Pittsburgh . . . by this sainted, skinny, furious redheaded man *who* wished to have a word with *us*. (2) *I* don't know how *he* found *his* way back to his car.

(1) *This* was for many years the center of the maze. . . . the family's watching through glass the Irish girl skate outside on the street. . . . (2) I watched passive and uncomprehending . . . watched as if the world were a screen on *which* played interesting scenes for *my* pleasure. . . . (3) And the apparently invulnerable girl was . . . part of the Sheehy family, *whose* dark ways were a danger and a crime.

(1) *We* girls chafed, whined, and complained under our parents' strictures. (2) The boys waged open war on *their* parents. (3) The boys' pitched battles with *their* parents were legendary; the punishments *they* endured melted *our* hearts.

Annie Dillard, *An American Childhood*

B. DRAFTING SKILL

Using Pronouns and Point of View   Choose a public event in which you have participated, such as a swim meet, a pep rally, a dramatic production, or a concert. Write a paragraph telling what happened at the event from your point of view. Use first-person pronouns such as *I* and *me*. Then rewrite the paragraph from the third-person point of view, using pronouns such as *he, she, it,* and *they.* Compare the two versions. Which is more formal? Which seems more objective and factual? Which seems more personal? In small discussion groups, share your observations about differences between the two points of view with other students.

Like nouns, pronouns can function as both subjects and predicate nominatives.

Pronouns as Subjects

The nominative form of the pronoun is used as the subject of a verb.

When a pronoun is part of a compound subject, it is often difficult to decide on the appropriate form. To decide which form to use in the compound subject, try each part of the subject separately with the verb.

> Hal and (I, me) kayaked down the Brule. (Hal kayaked; I kayaked, *not* me kayaked.)

The plural forms *we* and *they* sound awkward in many compounds. They can be avoided by rewording the sentence.

Awkward   We and they planned to swim at dawn.
Better   We all planned to swim at dawn.

Pronouns as Predicate Nominatives

A pronoun that follows a linking verb, such as *be* or *become,* is a **predicate pronoun.**

A predicate pronoun takes the nominative case.

It is often difficult to decide on the correct pronoun form to use after the verb *be.* Use the nominative case after verb phrases in which the main verb is a form of *be,* such as *could have been, will be,* and *should be.*

> It *was* **I** whom they called.
> It *must have been* **they** in the sports car.
> We are confident that the winner in the upcoming student council election *will be* **he.**

When using the nominative form sounds awkward, reword the sentence.

Awkward   The winner was she.
Better   She was the winner.

Awkward   The witnesses might have been they.
Better   They might have been the witnesses.

Writing
—TIP—

In informal situations, you may use the objective case after *be,* as in *It is me.* For formal writing, use the nominative case.

Queen Elizabeth I, The Armada Portrait, by Marcus Gheeraerts, 1592

Writing Theme
Queen Elizabeth I

Practice Your Skills

CONCEPT CHECK

Nominative Case Pronouns   Write the correct form of the pronoun for each sentence. Choose from those given in parentheses.

1. "(I, Me) have the heart and stomach of a king," said Elizabeth I of England, whose reign lasted for forty-five years.
2. Historians and (we, us), in the modern world, marvel at the skill of this remarkable historical figure, the daughter of Henry VIII.
3. (She, Her) and her court ruled from 1558 to 1603.
4. Some historians believe that (she, her) and her father were England's greatest monarchs.
5. More specifically, certain scholars think that England's best diplomat was (her, she).
6. (She, her) and her personal courage were celebrated by the poet Edmund Spenser in *The Faerie Queene.*
7. In six books, (he, him) and his epic poetry glorify Elizabeth I and England.
8. Names such as Britomart, Belphoebe, Mercilla, and Gloriana may sound exotic; however, (they, them) are the names Spenser used to represent Elizabeth.
9. (He, Him) and other writers have shown the queen as beloved, yet others have regarded her as a despot.
10. Sir Walter Raleigh was one of her favorite courtiers; it was (he, him) who was said to have placed his cloak across a puddle for her to walk on.

Like nouns, pronouns can also function as objects of verbs, objects of prepositions, or as part of infinitive phrases.

Pronouns as Objects of Verbs

The objective pronoun form is used for a direct or an indirect object.

When a pronoun is part of a compound object, it is often difficult to decide which pronoun form to use. To make your choice, try each part of the object separately with the verb.

Direct Object	The principal called George and (I, me). (called George; called me, *not* I)
Indirect Object	The counselor gave her and (I, me) good advice. (gave her; gave me, *not* gave I)

Pronouns as Objects of Prepositions

The objective pronoun form is used as the object of a preposition.

When a pronoun is a part of the compound object of a preposition, it is often difficult to decide on the appropriate pronoun form. To determine which form is correct, try each pronoun separately in the sentence.

> Will your sister be going with you and (I, me)? (with you; with me, *not* with I)

Use the objective pronoun forms after the preposition *between*.

> between him and me, *not* between he and I

Pronouns with Infinitives

The infinitive is a verb that is preceded by *to*. See pages 592 and 593 for more information about infinitives.

The objective form of the pronoun is used as the subject, object, or predicate pronoun of an infinitive.

> The referee asked *them to observe* the rules. (*Them* is the subject of *to observe*.)
> The team expected the district's MVP *to be her*. (*Her* is the object of *to be*.)

Practice Your Skills

A. CONCEPT CHECK

Objective Case Pronouns Write the correct pronoun from those given in parentheses.

1. For (we, us) and other writers, plagiarism is not funny, but the humorist S. J. Perelman made it seem so.
2. One of his stories centers around a meeting between a young man and the teacher who confronts (he, him) with his plagiarized assignment.
3. The teacher, Miss Cronjager, invites (he, him) to explain his essay about his past.
4. In fairness to her students, she always gives (they, them) a chance to explain.
5. The young man tries to convince (she, her) that an adventure—identical to the one in Kipling's novel *Captains Courageous*—was his own.
6. He explains that he and a friend had spied on suspicious characters and discovered (they, them) to be mutineers.
7. Then he and his parents had moved to the South; fate had bestowed a large inheritance on (he and they, him and them).
8. Soon after, he insisted adamantly, the call of the West had summoned (he, him).
9. There, nothing but raw courage stood between marauding outlaws and (he, him). . . .
10. Next, he tells his teacher, "My family packed (I, me) and my belongings off to Lawrenceville, where I made the varsity team."
11. "Naturally," he later explains, "Miss Cronjager had every right to flunk (I, me)."
12. Perelman, who also wrote material for the zany Marx Brothers, has given (we, us) many moments of pleasure in both books and movies.

B. PROOFREADING SKILL

Correcting Pronoun Errors Rewrite the following paragraph, correcting any errors in pronoun use. Also correct any errors in spelling, punctuation, and capitalization.

> Falling in love over the Telephone perhaps does not seem possible to you and I. Nevertheless, in his story "The Loves of Alonzo Fitz Clarence and Rosannah Ethelton," Mark Twain persuades we to suspend our disbelief. Alonzo, living in Maine, and Rosannah, in San francisco, meet on the telephone when she answers a call from he to his aunt. Rosannahs other suiter,

Sidney Algernon Burley, soon becomes insanely jealous. With his talent for doing impressions, Burley deceives both she and Alonzo, causing a lovers' quarrel. Alonzo suffers grately. the quarrel almost ends everything between he and she—until he figures out what Burley has done. Of course, true love later triumphs for Alonzo and Rosannah, when two ministers ask they to become husband and wife—over the telephone!

C. APPLICATION IN WRITING

A Plot Synopsis   Choose a humorous story or essay, perhaps one by S. J. Perelman, Garrison Keillor, or Erma Bombeck, and write a plot synopsis or summary of it. Briefly outline the main story line or theme, giving just enough information to whet your readers' appetites. Use pronouns in the nominative and objective cases in your brief retelling.

C H E C K   P O I N T
PAGES 711–717

Write the correct form of the pronoun from those given in parentheses. Then write whether the pronoun is in the *Nominative* or *Objective* case.

Writing Theme
Film Biographies

1. Directors and producers of motion pictures have given (us, we) many great biographical films.
2. It was (them, they) who helped glamorize famous lives on the silver screen.
3. Catherine the Great, George M. Cohan, Alexander the Great, and Marie Curie have something in common; (they, them) have each been portrayed in movies.
4. Two films were made about Catherine, Empress of Russia; each depicted (she, her) and her era differently.
5. When a British director made *Catherine the Great,* (him, he) and the actors produced a serious historical work.
6. However, the Hollywood version of Catherine's life focused on the romances between (she, her) and her suitors.
7. Hollywood producers created *The Scarlet Empress* to entertain (we, us).
8. Viewers of other Hollywood movies knew James Cagney for his gangster roles, but then he surprised (they, them).
9. It was (he, him) who portrayed the showman George M. Cohan so convincingly.
10. In fact, his peers awarded (he, him) an Oscar for the role.

James Cagney as George M. Cohan in the movie *Yankee Doodle Dandy*

11. It is fortunate that (we, us) can still view *Yankee Doodle Dandy*.
12. It is more difficult for (we, us) to see *Alexander the Great*, written and directed by Robert Rossen.
13. Alexander III was a great general; (he, him) and his army overthrew the Persian Empire in 334 B.C.
14. One film critic wrote, "Rossen has aimed for greatness, and (he, him) lost honorably."
15. Other critics also gave (he, him) and his film poor reviews.
16. In the cast were Fredric March and Claire Bloom; filmgoers had expected (they, them) to perform brilliantly.
17. A bigger success was a film about Marie Curie and her husband Pierre; it was (they, them) who discovered radium.
18. In portraying Marie Curie, Greer Garson was able to bring (she, her) and her scientific work to life beautifully.
19. This film about the Curies captures the moment when the Nobel Prize committee awarded (they, them) the prize in physics in 1903.
20. *Madame Curie* is a biographical film that has the power both to move and to entertain (us, we) simultaneously.

PRONOUNS IN THE POSSESSIVE CASE

Personal pronouns that show ownership use the possessive case. Possessive pronouns can replace or modify nouns.

The possessive pronouns *mine, ours, yours, his, hers, its,* and *theirs* can be used in place of nouns, as in the following sentences: That is *mine*. *Yours* is blue.

My, our, your, his, her, its, and *their* are used to modify nouns: That is *my* sweater. *Your* sweater is blue.

You will notice that *his* and *its* are used in either situation.

718 Grammar Handbook

Possessive Pronouns Modifying Gerunds

The possessive form of the pronoun is used when the pronoun immediately precedes a gerund.

> *Her running* has improved since the last track meet. (*Running* is a gerund functioning as the subject. The possessive form *her* modifies *running*.)

Present participles, like gerunds, are verbals that end in *-ing*. However, the possessive case is not used before a participle. The nominative or objective case of a pronoun is used before a participle.

> We saw *him running* toward the finish line. (*Running* is a participle modifying *him*.)

To distinguish between a gerund and a present participle, remember this: if the *-ing* word is used as a noun, it is a gerund; if it is used as a modifier, it is a participle. It may also be helpful to ask yourself *Who?* or *What?* of the verb in the sentence.

> We dislike *their playing* the stereo at midnight. (What did we dislike? We disliked the playing. Therefore, *playing* is a gerund, the object of the verb *dislike*. The possessive pronoun *their* should be used.)
> We heard *them playing* the stereo at midnight. (What did we hear? We heard them. Therefore, *playing* is a participle modifying *them*.)

Practice Your Skills

CONCEPT CHECK

Possessive Case Pronouns Choose the correct form of the pronoun from those given in parentheses.

1. In 1948 members of the United Nations gave (them, their) approval of the World Health Organization, or WHO.
2. Thirty years later, WHO and the United Children's Fund held a conference; (their, theirs) was a lofty goal.
3. In (his, him) opening of the conference, the director general of WHO asked participants eight questions about health care.
4. (They, Their) conclusions became the Declaration of Alma-Ata.
5. In (its, it's) ten statements, the declaration states the goal of achieving health for all people by the year 2000.
6. Of key importance to (us, our) reaching this goal is a clear definition of health.
7. Szeming Sze, a Chinese doctor, described (him, his) writing of the definition.

Writing
—**TIP**—

Never use an apostrophe with possessive pronouns. Spellings such as *It's* and *he's* indicate a contraction.

Writing Theme
The World Health Organization

8. He envisioned (their, them) broadening the definition so that it included mental health and disease prevention.
9. The broader definition was used at the 1978 conference, which writer Maggie Black described in (hers, her) book as "a triumph."
10. We marvel at medical progress made during earlier times and wonder if WHO will achieve its goal during (our, ours).

PROBLEMS IN PRONOUN USAGE

Certain situations involving pronouns often cause confusion.

Who and *Whom* in Questions and Clauses

The pronouns *who* and *whom* are used to ask questions or to introduce clauses.

To use *who* and *whom* in questions, it is necessary to understand how the pronoun is functioning in the question.

Who is the nominative form. It is used as the subject of the verb or as a predicate pronoun. *Whom* is the objective form. It is used as the direct object or as the object of a preposition.

> *Who* wrote this novel? (*Who* is the subject.)
> *Whom* will you choose? (*Whom* is the object of *choose*.)

The pronouns *who, whoever, whom, whomever,* and *whose* may be used to introduce noun or adjective clauses. These pronouns also have a function within the clause.

Who and whoever are nominative case pronouns and can act as the subject or predicate pronoun in a clause.

Whom and whomever are in the objective case and can act as the direct object or the object of a preposition in a clause.

The following steps and examples can help to eliminate confusion about the use of *who* and *whom* in subordinate clauses:

1. Isolate the subordinate clause.
2. Determine how the pronoun in question is used in that clause.
3. If the pronoun acts as a subject or predicate pronoun, use *who* or *whoever*. If it acts as an object, use *whom* or *whomever*.

> Galileo Galilei is the scientist (*who, whom*) invented the thermometer.
> 1. The adjective clause is (*who, whom*) *invented the thermometer*.

2. The pronoun is acting as the subject within the clause.
3. *Who* is in the nominative case and is the correct choice.

Pearl Buck is an author *(who, whom)* I admire.
1. The adjective clause is *(who, whom) I admire.*
2. The pronoun is acting as the direct object within the clause.
3. *Whom* is in the objective case and is the correct choice.

A medal was given to *(whoever, whomever)* finished the race.
1. *(Whoever, Whomever) finished the race* is a noun clause acting as the object of the preposition *to.*
2. The pronoun is acting as the subject within the clause.
3. The nominative pronoun *whoever* is the correct choice.

Whose functions as the possessive pronoun within a clause.

This is the artist *whose painting I bought.* (*Whose* is a possessive pronoun modifying *painting* in the clause.)

Practice Your Skills

CONCEPT CHECK

Who* and *Whom   Write the correct form of the pronoun from those given in parentheses.

1. The inventor (who, whom) got movies off to a roaring start was Thomas Edison.
2. Edison, (who, whom) we now consider a genius, introduced the kinetoscope in 1894.

Writing Theme
The Birth of Film

Thomas Edison's dramas of the 1890s included this film of a very long a-a-c-h-h-o-o-o!

The kinetoscope

3. With this instrument, (whoever, whomever) had a nickel could watch a film by peering through a viewer and turning a crank.
4. Two years later, the Lumière brothers, (who, whom) worked in Paris, invented a projector.
5. Consequently, theater owners, (whom, whose) main objective was making a profit, could collect ticket money from (whoever, whomever) they could crowd into their theaters.
6. It was Warner Brothers (who, whom) presented the first sound film in 1923.
7. Consequently, many actors (whom, who) starred in silent films faced a dilemma.
8. Actors (whom, whose) voices didn't match the audience's expectations were out of jobs.
9. For example, silent-screen heartthrob Rudolph Valentino, (who, whom) had received the adulation of millions of fans, quickly lost his popularity when women heard his high, thin voice.
10. Lillian Gish was one actress (whom, who) audiences loved in both silent films and "talkies."
11. Other silent-film stars (who, whom) successfully adjusted to sound were Greta Garbo, Stan Laurel, and Oliver Hardy.
12. As "talkies" developed in the 1930's, two directors (who, whom) the Hollywood studios regularly employed were Alfred Hitchcock and John Ford.
13. (Whoever, Whomever) writes the history of American motion pictures cannot afford to ignore the career of Orson Welles.
14. Welles, (who, whom) was especially interested in the potential of sound and dialogue in motion pictures, is most famous for his landmark film of 1941, *Citizen Kane*.
15. Welles was the director (whom, whose) brilliant experiments with sound had the greatest impact on the development of movies after World War II.

Pronouns with Appositives

The pronouns *we* and *us* are often followed by an appositive, a noun that identifies the pronoun. Phrases such as *we students* or *us players* can cause confusion when you are trying to choose the correct pronoun. To decide whether to use the nominative case *we* or the objective case *us* in this type of construction, drop the appositive, or noun, and read the sentence without it.

> (We, Us) girls can bring the lunch. (We can bring the lunch, *not* Us can bring the lunch.)
> The problem was easy for (we, us) girls. (for us, *not* for we)

Greta Garbo, legendary movie star

Pronouns as Appositives

Pronouns themselves can be used as appositives.

The form of a pronoun used as an appositive is determined by the use of the noun to which it is in apposition.

> The delegates, *Tony* and *I,* want your support. (*Tony* and *I* are in apposition to *delegates,* the subject of *want.* The nominative form *I* is required.)
>
> For the two producers, *Juana* and *him,* the show was a hit. (*Juana* and *him* are in apposition to *producers,* the object of the preposition *for.* The objective form of the pronoun, *him,* is required.)
>
> We gave the neighbors, *Toby* and *her,* a housewarming gift. (*Toby* and *her* are in apposition to *neighbors,* the indirect object of *gave.* The objective form *her* is required.)

To determine which form of the pronoun to use in apposition, try the appositive by itself with the verb or preposition.

> Her friends, Jackie and (he, him), were always calling. (Jackie and he were, *not* Jackie and him were.)
>
> The flowers are from two of your friends, Sally and (I, me). (The flowers are from me, *not* from I.)

Pronouns in Comparisons

Comparisons can be made by using a clause that begins with *than* or *as.* Notice the use of pronouns in the comparisons below.

> Fred is better at chess *than he is.*
> You have as many A's *as she has.*

The final clause in a comparison is sometimes **elliptical,** meaning that some words have been omitted. The use of an elliptical clause can make pronoun choice more difficult.

> Fred is better at chess than he.
> You have as many A's as she.

To decide which pronoun form to use, fill in the unstated words.

> Ricardo plays the trumpet better than (I, me). (Ricardo plays the trumpet better than *I play.*)
>
> Betty was expecting Paul rather than (she, her). (Betty was expecting Paul rather than *Betty was expecting her.*)
>
> We can sing as well as (they, them). (We can sing as well as *they can sing.*)

Practice Your Skills

A. CONCEPT CHECK

Pronouns Write the correct form of the pronoun from those given in parentheses.

1. THOR: (We, Us) Norse gods were venerated as fierce, brave warriors.
2. MORTAL: Some of you immortal beings, however, were beneficial to (us, we) mortals.
3. THOR: Sometimes we were. Most gods, especially Odin and (I, me), were renowned for our strength.
4. MORTAL: Your brother Balder, though, was gentle and innocent. No god was kinder than (he, him).
5. THOR: Mother demanded that everyone in existence, even all the animals and (us, we) gods, swear an oath never to kill Balder.
6. MORTAL: No mother could have been more protective of her son than (she, her).
7. THOR: Yes; but Loki, the source of all evil, was more cunning than (her, she).
8. MORTAL: I remember that story. Through a trick, that pair of cruel deceivers, (he, him) and his brother, killed gentle Balder with a sprig of mistletoe.
9. THOR: Few gods in all Valhalla have been mourned as deeply as (him, he).
10. MORTAL: Although your lives seem very violent compared to the lives of (us, we) mortals, perhaps you reflect the hidden aspects of our own natures.

B. DRAFTING SKILL

Using Pronouns Supply the correct pronouns needed in the following paragraphs.

(1) In our literature class, _____ students of mythology enjoy Native American myths that contain humor. Foremost of all the comical characters is Coyote. (2) These mythical characters, such as _____ and other animals, have human traits and capabilities. (3) The tales of Coyote's very human pranks and cunning tricks are especially appealing to _____ readers. In one myth, Coyote tricks the frog people out of exclusive rights to their water, so that all people can use it. (4) He was far more cunning than _____ .

Coyote, however, does not always win over his opponents. Occasionally, his cleverness fails him. (5) For example, Coyote thought that no one deserved admiration more than _____ .

Coyote Meets the Lone Ranger in a Painted Desert (1978), by Harry Fonseca. Acrylics and glitter on canvas, 30 x 40 in. Private collection

One day, he was so busy seeking admirers that he failed to look where he was walking and fell.

(6) Such tales may hold a message for _____ readers. In any case, Coyote's encounters with his antagonists are always surprising. (7) One never knows whether his opponents will be as clever as _____ —or as foolish. (8) Perhaps that is why so many people, both Native Americans of old and _____ readers of today, have enjoyed the myths about Coyote.

C. APPLICATION IN WRITING

A Dialogue Write a dialogue between two mythical characters. They may argue over who is stronger or wiser, or they may compare feats. Choose actual mythical characters or create your own. Use pronouns both *as* and *with* appositives and in comparisons.

Reflexive Pronouns

A pronoun such as *myself, herself,* or *ourselves* is used reflexively when it refers to a preceding noun or pronoun.

A reflexive pronoun cannot be used by itself; it must have an antecedent in the same sentence.

Incorrect	Myself carried it up the stairs.
Correct	I carried it up the stairs myself. (*I* is the antecedent of *myself.*)
Incorrect	The coach spoke to Tom and myself. (There is no antecedent for *myself.*)
Correct	The coach spoke to Tom and me.

The words *hisself* and *theirselves* are nonstandard.

Incorrect	The boys washed the clothes theirselves.
Correct	The boys washed the clothes themselves.

Practice Your Skills

CONCEPT CHECK

Writing Theme
Historic Moments

Reflexive Pronouns Write the correct pronoun from those given in parentheses.

1. Priscus, the Eastern Roman envoy, counted (himself, hisself) lucky to be dining, not battling, with Attila the Hun.
2. His account states that at 3:00 P.M., "We presented (us, ourselves) in the doorway."
3. Priscus continues his description of the banquet, where Attila's guests clearly held (him, himself) and his power in awe.
4. The most distinguished guests seated (themselves, theirselves) to the right of Attila's couch.
5. A servant said, "Please allow the other servants and (me, myself) to seat you to the left."
6. "We noticed," Priscus continued, "that no other Romans had been invited besides (us, ourselves)."
7. The servants offered the others and (ourselves, us) golden goblets of wine.
8. Attila, however, served (hisself, himself) in a plain wooden goblet.
9. In addition, while we guests fed (us, ourselves) varied delicacies, Attila ate only meat.
10. The long hours of feasting exhausted (me, myself), but the merry-making lasted late into the night."

CHECK POINT
PAGES 718–726

A. Write the correct pronoun from those given in parentheses.

Writing Theme
Accounts of
Pioneer Life

1. No one, in those days, was sadder than (I, me) to reach the wide river.
2. Making and setting up a waterproof ferry is always a long, hard job for (we, us) families.
3. First, we must haul our possessions out of the wagons; anyone (who, whom) knows where to find things afterward will be lucky!
4. Then it is up to (us, ourselves) to help dismantle the wagons to make the ferry.
5. The boys, (whom, whose) job it is to find a long, strong rope, are always eager to help.

6. However, Hiram hurt (hisself, himself) and cannot help the others attach the rope to the waterproof wagon bed.
7. Next, (we, us) women must load our belongings onto the ferry.
8. (We, Our) loading takes many hours.
9. (Who, Whom) should we choose to cross with the children?
10. Hiram is a good choice; (him, his) joking will help the children forget their fears about the crossing.

B. Rewrite the sentences, correcting pronoun errors.

(1) The Miller brothers, Charles and me, left our land claim in order to mine gold. (2) During August 1849, Charles, whom encouraged myself to try mining for gold, obtained over five thousand dollars in gold dust for hisself. (3) Us leaving the claim caused some hardship for Mother and Father. (4) However, no one was happier than them for we boys when we succeeded. (5) Father always said to ourselves, "Some risks must be taken by whomever is going to succeed in this world."

A miner panning for gold along the Colorado River, c. 1898

PRONOUN-ANTECEDENT AGREEMENT

An antecedent is the noun or pronoun for which another pronoun stands and to which it refers.

A pronoun must agree with its antecedent in number, gender, and person.

Agreement in Number   If the antecedent of a pronoun is singular, a singular pronoun is required. If the antecedent is plural, a plural pronoun is required.

The singular indefinite pronouns listed below often cause difficulty. When a singular indefinite pronoun is the antecedent of another pronoun, the second pronoun must be singular. Remember that a prepositional phrase following an indefinite pronoun does not affect the number of any other word in the sentence.

another	anything	everybody	neither	one
anybody	each	everyone	nobody	somebody
anyone	either	everything	no one	someone

Each (singular) of the boys brought *his* (singular) guitar.
No one (singular) has made up *his or her* (singular) mind.

Notice in the example above that the phrase *his or her* is considered singular.

The following indefinite pronouns are plural and are referred to by the plural possessive pronouns *our, your,* and *their.*

both   few   many   several

Both of the countries have improved *their* economies.
Few of us wanted *our* pictures taken.
Many of you do not have *your* eligibility slips.
Of the volunteers, *several* have expressed *their* willingness to distribute food baskets.

The indefinite pronouns *all, some, any,* and *none* may take either a singular or plural pronoun, depending upon the meaning intended.

All the furniture was in *its* original condition.
All the students were taking *their* last examination.

Some of the cider has lost *its* tang.
Some of the children in the refugee camp have heard from *their* parents.

In all of the preceding examples, the indefinite pronouns are used as subjects. Note that the verb as well as any other pronouns referring to the subject agrees in number with that subject.

Incorrect   None of the singers *was* making *their* debuts.
Correct   None of the singers *were* making *their* debuts.
Correct   None of the singers *was* making *his or her* debut.

Two or more singular antecedents joined by *or* or *nor* are referred to by a singular pronoun.

Either Jermaine or Hank will let us use *his* car to drive to the exhibition game.
Neither the cat nor the dog had eaten *its* meal.

Use the noun nearer the verb to determine the pronoun for subjects joined by *or* or *nor*.

Neither the cat nor the dogs had eaten *their* meal.
Neither the dogs nor the cat had eaten *its* meal.

Collective nouns may be referred to by either a singular or plural pronoun. Determine the number from the meaning in the sentence.

The track team *has its* new coach. (The team is thought of as a unified, singular whole.)
The track team *have* worked out in *their* spare time. (Various members act individually.)

Writing
═TIP═

Using a plural pronoun as subject eliminates the need for the *his or her* structure. *All of the drivers were wearing their seat belts.*

Agreement in Gender Masculine gender is indicated by *he, his, him*. Feminine gender is indicated by *she, her, hers*. Neuter gender is indicated by *it* and *its*. A pronoun must be of the same gender as the word to which it refers.

When a singular pronoun must refer to both feminine and masculine antecedents, the phrase *his or her* is acceptable. It is, in fact, preferred by some people who wish to avoid what they consider to be sexist language.

Correct   Each student should have *his* ticket ready.
Correct   Each student should have *his or her* ticket ready.

Agreement in Person A personal pronoun must be in the same person as its antecedent. The words *one, everyone*, and *everybody* are in the third person. They are referred to by *he, his, him, she, her, hers*.

Incorrect   *One* should always wear *your* seat belt.
Correct   *One* should always wear *his or her* seat belt.

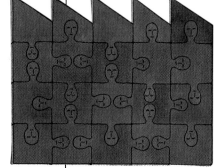

Practice Your Skills

A. CONCEPT CHECK

Pronoun-Antecedent Agreement Find and correct the errors in agreement in these sentences. Write *Correct* if there is no error.

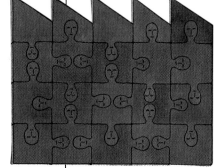
Writing Theme
Remarkable Talents

1. A hundred years ago, neither the works of Gwendolyn Brooks nor her life probably would have received their just acclaim.
2. However, today both her poetry and her novels have taken its place in American literature.
3. Many of you have probably read Brooks's poems in your literature anthologies.
4. All of Brooks's major work has been praised for their powerful originality.
5. For her book *Annie Allen*, Brooks became the first African-American writer to win the Pulitzer Prize.
6. Over the years, neither this work nor Brooks's novel *Maud Martha* has lost their appeal.
7. When Brooks was young, neither her parents nor her mentor, poet James Weldon Johnson, withheld their praise for her talent.
8. Later in Brooks's career, the Library of Congress made her their official consultant for poetry.
9. Meanwhile, few in the world of poetry failed to pursue his or her own exploration of Brooks's vivid writing.
10. Each reader who carefully approaches Brooks's poems can find their own personal meanings in her words.

B. PROOFREADING SKILL

Pronoun-Antecedent Agreement   Revise the paragraph, correcting errors in pronoun-antecedent agreement. Also correct errors in spelling, capitalization, and punctuation.

> if an opportunity arrived, few of us would miss their chance to make a contribution to an art we loved. Neither Marian Anderson nor Sarah Vaughan neglected their opportunity in the field of music. Each of these female singers was recognized early for their talent. Both Anderson and Vaughan began her careers by singing in a Church Choir. Anderson was said to be the greatest contralto of his or her generation. All of the opera lovers of New York were surprized when he or she saw anderson perform at the Metropolitan Opera in 1955. Whereas Anderson succeeded in opera, Vaughan succeeded in jazz, despite her similar beginnings Most of the critic's call Vaughan its "Divine One." She could change the quality of one's voice. Vaughan's voice, extensive in her range, helped create the jazz style known as bebop.

PRONOUN REFERENCE

A writer must always be sure that there is a clear connection between a pronoun and its antecedent. If the pronoun reference is indefinite or ambiguous, the resulting sentence may be confusing, misleading, or even unintentionally humorous.

Indefinite Reference

To avoid any confusion for the reader, every personal pronoun should refer clearly to a definite antecedent.

Indefinite	*It* reports in the newspaper that a strike is likely.
Better	*The newspaper* reports that a strike is likely.
Indefinite	Carmen is running for office because *it* is exciting.
Better	Carmen is running for office because *politics* is exciting.
Indefinite	Read what *they* say about headsets.
Better	Read what *this article* says about headsets.

The pronoun *you* is sometimes used when it is not meant to refer to the person spoken to. The effect is usually confusing.

Indefinite	In that course *you* have fewer exams.
Better	In that course *there are* fewer exams.

Ambiguous Reference

The word *ambiguous* means "having two or more possible meanings." The reference of a pronoun is ambiguous if the pronoun may refer to more than one word. This situation arises whenever a noun or pronoun falls between the pronoun and its true antecedent.

Ambiguous	Take the books off the shelves and dust them. (Which does this directive mean: dust the books or dust the shelves?)
Better	Dust the books after you take them off the shelves.
Ambiguous	The hounds chased the foxes until they were exhausted. (Which animals were exhausted: the hounds or the foxes?)
Better	Until the hounds were exhausted, they chased the foxes.
Ambiguous	Before I could hit the mosquito on your arm, it flew off. (Was it the mosquito or the arm that flew off?)
Better	Before I could kill the mosquito, it flew off your arm.

Practice Your Skills

A. CONCEPT CHECK

Pronoun Reference   Rewrite the sentences to remove all indefinite or ambiguous pronoun references. (There may be more than one way to revise a particular sentence correctly.)

1. They say in a UNESCO report that there are over 700 million television sets in the world.
2. You have over 195 million sets in the U.S. alone.

Writing Theme
Television

3. Companies are developing new methods for producing high-definition television (HDTV) sets because they will permit the clearest television pictures possible.
4. Like the space race, the contest to develop HDTV technology is competitive, and it is heating up.
5. The Japanese and the Europeans have been far ahead of the Americans in this technology, and they have had to make rapid advances to catch up.
6. With HDTV broadcasts offered by the networks, would all viewers without HDTV capability have to buy new sets to receive them?
7. In the early days of television, black-and-white sets competed with color sets, but people did not have to buy them to receive broadcasts.
8. Instead, you could receive color-broadcast programs on a black-and-white set.
9. In those days, when only somewhat primitive sets were available to purchasers, one was likely to have a small circular screen.
10. The sets sported "rabbit ears" antennae, and you were directed to move them around to improve picture quality.
11. A test pattern filled the screen for hours each day until it was replaced by limited evening programming.
12. Rather recently they say a new kind of competition has begun to heat up between the television networks and various telephone companies.
13. Both television networks and telephone companies rushed to develop fiber-optic cables, and they became the center of a dispute.
14. Television interests tried waging a campaign for government support, and it worked.
15. Finally, in 1988 they passed a law that barred the telephone companies from becoming engaged in television broadcasting.

B. PROOFREADING SKILL

Using Pronouns Clearly   Revise the following paragraph, correcting all pronoun references that are indefinite or ambiguous. Also correct any errors in spelling and mechanics.

(1) You take Television for granted in the United States. (2) People in other countries are often amazed to learn of the great number of television networks and cable companies competing for viewers in the u.s. (3) The television networks are owned by the governments in many countries and they control the broadcasts. (4) Recently, however they have made changes. (5) In France, for example, in 1986 only three networks broadcast all the programs on television, and they were all owned by

the government. (6) By 1988 you had six channels—four owned by private companies and two owned by the government. (7) It said in an article that there was also the possibility of a third network channel being added to the two in existence in Austria in Greece (8) In many countries, restriction's against private commersial channels are being dropped, and the governments are welcoming them.

CHECK POINT
PAGES 727–733

PAGES 727–733

Rewrite the sentences, correcting any errors in pronoun usage.

1. Few of us are aware of the story behind one of their everyday household items, the toothbrush.
2. You would be surprised to know how many stages the toothbrush went through in its development.
3. In one article it claims that the earliest known toothbrushes, originally called *chew sticks,* were twigs with one frayed end.
4. Some of these twigs have been unearthed in its original condition.
5. It reports that these primitive toothbrushes can be dated back to 3000 B.C.
6. About A.D. 1498 the Chinese had the idea of gathering bristles from the necks of hogs and attaching them to bamboo handles.
7. However, just about every European who used these first bristle brushes on their teeth complained that they were too firm.
8. European society had their own preference for horsehair brushes, which were softer.
9. As late as the nineteenth century, many Europeans were ignoring toothbrushes altogether; most people preferred to pick his or her teeth clean with metal toothpicks.
10. All of these methods for keeping the teeth clean had its obvious defects.
11. In one book about dentistry it argues that the first successful toothbrush was not actually invented until the 1930's.
12. A breakthrough occurred when Du Pont chemists made its discovery of an artificial "wonder fiber"—nylon.
13. Even with repeated use, none of the nylon used in the new toothbrush bristles lost their stiffness.
14. At first, however, many dentists were reluctant to demonstrate the brushes to their patients or to recommend them; they were too stiff!
15. However, by the early 1950's, Du Pont finally solved the problem when they developed soft nylon for toothbrushes.

GRAMMAR
HANDBOOK
36

Writing Theme
Legendary Figures

A. Using Pronouns Correctly Write the correct form of the pronoun given in parentheses.

1. Everyone has (their, his or her) favorite Greek heroes.
2. Such great heroes were (they, them) that both Heracles and Jason have become some readers' favorites.
3. The myth of Perseus also fascinates (we, us) mythology lovers.
4. Perseus was a mythical hero (who, whom) was the son of the immortal god Zeus and the mortal woman Danae.
5. Acrisius, Danae's father, had received this warning from an oracle: "One day your grandson will kill (yourself, you)."
6. Therefore, no one was more apprehensive at Perseus's birth than (he, him), the grandfather.
7. The grandfather's solution was severe, namely, (him, his) placing of Danae and Perseus in a chest and throwing it into the sea.
8. Fortunately, both mother and son were helped by (his or her, their) rescuer, a kind fisherman from the island of Seriphos.
9. King Polydectes of Seriphos wanted Danae for (him, himself).
10. He tricked the innocent young Perseus, saying, "I want you to promise (myself, me) that you will kill the Gorgon Medusa."
11. (Whoever, Whomever) looked at Medusa's face was immediately turned to stone.
12. The gods Athena and Hermes gave Perseus (his or her, their) aid on this dangerous mission.
13. Perseus responded by telling them, "A great bond will forever exist between you and (I, me) for the aid you have bestowed."
14. While the monster was asleep, Perseus guided (him, himself) by watching the reflections in Athena's shield.
15. (Him, His) beheading of Medusa made Perseus a famous figure of Greek mythology.

B. Correcting Pronoun Errors Rewrite each sentence, correcting all pronoun errors, such as mistakes in pronoun case. If a sentence contains no errors, write *Correct*.

Dear Esteemed Patron,

(1) The interpreter Marina has told ourselves of an astounding legend. (2) It fascinated Hernan Cortes and me. (3) She related the story of Quetzalcoatl, whom is a god of the Aztecs and whose name means "feathered serpent." (4) It seems that this god had promised to return one day from the east to rule themselves. (5) Marina suspects that Montezuma, the emperor, believes in him returning. (6) In addition, many Aztec astrologers who have studied the legend of this god think that Cortes is him. (7) Because Cortes and us have landed in 1519,

the legend may prove useful to us. (8) This is the year in which he had promised to return. (9) Patron, between you and I, this legend may help we Spaniards conquer the Aztecs peacefully. (10) A few of the soldiers may have his misgivings about the power of a legend. (11) To myself, however, the legend is crucial. (12) Montezuma himself is a god to his people, whom are forbidden even to look upon his face. (13) Through flattery, Cortes may be able to convince him that he is Quetzalcoatl. (14) Still, both Cortes and his captains are willing to fight the Aztecs, if necessary, in his quest for power. (15) I hope we do not fight, since no one would be happier than me to claim this land without further bloodshed.

Diego

C. Eliminating Pronoun Errors Rewrite the following paragraphs. Correct all errors in pronoun usage as well as any errors in spelling, capitalization, or punctuation.

Sir Kay look around and said, "Who took my sword?" A knight cannot be seen at a jousting tournament without their sword!"

Wart piped up, "I know where you sord is; I forgot to bring it from the camp."

As Wart dashed threw the town square, he noticed a stone with a sword protruding from it. Wart glanced around to see who it could belong to, but no one was there. As he approached, Wart could see that the sword was inscribed, "Whomever pulls this sword from this stone shall be king of England.

"Oh, well," Wart said to hisself, "I'll just borrow it for the tournament and hope that whoever owns it will understand."

As soon as Wart pulled the sword from the stone, bells rang and a mystical lite appeared. Excited people came running from all directions, asking, "Who pulled the sword from the stone?"

"Look! He holds the sword. It has to be he."

Another cautioned, "Not so fast! Make him do it again so we can be sure it was him."

So Wart, being an agreeable lad, replaced the sword and removed it again the Crowd cheered.

They say that a week later Wart was crowned Arthur, King of England.

On the Lightside

TOM SWIFTIES

Tom Swifties are word puns based on a comic relationship between an adverb and the main idea of a sentence.

Tom Swift, hero of a series of popular novels, was a youthful genius who invented such wonders as electric airplanes. The books are out of vogue now, but the punning word game named in Tom's honor is still going strong. These Tom Swifties will give you the idea [and, perhaps, lead you into creating your own].

"Pass the cards," said Tom ideally.

"I have the mumps," said Tom infectiously.

"You gave me two less than a dozen," said Tom tensely.

"I don't like wilted lettuce," said Tom limply.

"Our ball club needs a man who can hit sixty homers a season," said Tom ruthlessly.

"He's a young M.D.," said Tom internally.

"Gold leaf," said Tom guiltily.

"I'm out of cartridges for my starting gun," said Tom blankly.

"It's the maid's night off," said Tom helplessly.

"The thermostat is set too high," said Tom heatedly.

"The chimney is clogged," said Tom fluently.

"Golly, that old man is bent over," said Tom stupidly.

"Don't you love sleeping outdoors?" said Tom intently.

"I've been stung," said Tom waspishly.

"Let's invite Greg and Gary," said Tom gregariously.

"This boat leaks," said Tom balefully.

"Welcome to my tomb," said Tom cryptically.

"I just returned from Japan," said Tom disorientedly.

"I'll never stick my fist into the lion's cage again," said Tom off-handedly.

"I can't find the oranges," said Tom fruitlessly.

"I lost my trousers," said Tom expansively.

"Are you fond of venison?" said Tom fawningly.

"Here are my Tom Swifty entries," said Tom submissively.

"You've ruined my health." said Tom halfheartedly.

"Is there a quiz today?" asked Tom testily.

"It's just too early to get up," complained Tom mournfully.

"What's the angle?" asked Tom obtusely.

"Is that you?" asked Tom sheepishly.

"It's raining," reported Tom precipitously.

William R. Espy and others

Using Modifiers

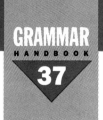

GRAMMAR
H A N D B O O K
37

UNDERSTANDING MODIFIERS

An **adjective** tells *which one, what kind,* or *how many* about a noun or pronoun. An **adverb** tells *how, when, where,* or *to what extent* about a verb, adjective, or other adverb. To decide whether a modifier is an adjective or adverb, determine the part of speech of the word it modifies.

> Garfield the cat is a character in a *popular* cartoon. (The word *popular* modifies the noun *cartoon. Popular* is an adjective.)

> This feisty feline is quite *independent*. (The word *independent* modifies the noun *feline. Independent* is a predicate adjective.)

> Garfield *always* fights for some of his owner's lasagna. (The word *always* modifies the verb *fights. Always* is an adverb.)

> His owner, Jon, is *seldom* victorious. (The word *seldom* modifies the adjective *victorious. Seldom* is an adverb.)

Adjective and Adverb Forms

Adjectives cannot be recognized by any one form or ending. Adverbs, however, are often recognizable because most adverbs are formed by adding *-ly* to adjectives.

Adjective	Adverb
poor	poorly
careful	carefully
sudden	suddenly
excited	excitedly
happy	happily
inquisitive	inquisitively

A few adjectives and adverbs are spelled in the same way. In most of these cases, the adverb form does not end in *-ly*.

Adjective	Adverb
a *straight* course	walks *straight*
a *hard* problem	works *hard*
a *high* note	soars *high*
a *long* journey	lasts *long*
a *late* flight	arrives *late*

Some adverbs have two forms, both of which are considered correct. One form is spelled with *-ly*. The other is not.

Come *quick!*	Please, move *quickly!*
Drive *slow.*	We must be careful and work *slowly.*
Stay *close!*	Follow *closely* or you will get lost.

A few adjectives also end in *-ly:* for example, *friendly, lonely, lovely, lively,* and *ugly.*

Modifiers That Follow Verbs

A word that modifies an action verb, an adjective, or another adverb is always an adverb.

Beyond the castle moat, a beast howled *dreadfully.*
   (*Dreadfully* modifies the action verb *howled*.)

The howl of this beast was *really* dreadful. (*Really* modifies the adjective *dreadful*.)

So dreadfully did the beast howl that the king sent a knight out to slay it. (*So* modifies the adverb *dreadfully.*)

Always use an adverb to modify an action verb. Be careful not to use an adjective to modify an action verb.

Incorrect	The officer stepped *cautious* into the room.
Correct	The officer stepped *cautiously* into the room.
Incorrect	Two hot-air balloons rose *sudden* on the horizon.
Correct	Two hot-air balloons rose *suddenly* on the horizon.
Incorrect	The karate opponents bowed *polite* to each other.
Correct	The karate opponents bowed *politely* to each other.

A linking verb, on the other hand, is usually followed by an adjective rather than an adverb. As you have learned, a predicate adjective follows a linking verb and modifies the subject of the sentence.

The plastic fruit in the bowl appeared *real*. (*Real* is a predicate adjective. It follows the linking verb *appeared,* and it modifies the subject *fruit*.)

A speaker or a writer rarely has a problem when a modifier follows a form of the verb *be,* the most common linking verb. Some linking verbs, however, may also be used as action verbs. When these verbs are used as action verbs, they can be modified by adverbs.

Verbs that can be used as both linking and action verbs include *look, sound, appear, grow, smell, taste,* and *remain.* Look at the examples below.

Linking Verbs	Action Verbs
The lake *looks* choppy.	Laura *looked* quickly at the map.
That note *sounds* flat.	The alarm *sounded* unexpectedly.
Don *appeared* nervous.	A groundhog *appeared* suddenly.
The sky *grew* dark.	The baby *grew* quickly.
You must *remain* calm.	One team member *remained* here.

Practice Your Skills

A. CONCEPT CHECK

Adjectives and Adverbs Write the correct modifier of the two given in parentheses. Label it as an *Adjective* or an *Adverb*. Then write the word it modifies.

> ***Example*** Einstein wrote (extensive, extensively) about the properties of light. extensively, Adverb, wrote

1. The creation of a superlight, first proposed by Albert Einstein in 1917, seemed (impossible, impossibly).
2. Beginning in the 1940's, scientists worked (steady, steadily) to create this powerful light, which they called a *laser*.

3. In 1960 the first laser device that used a ruby rod was built (successful, successfully) by Theodore Maiman.
4. The coherent light produced by the laser was more intense than any produced (previous, previously).
5. Scientists have developed many kinds of lasers whose uses were, only a few decades ago, (unimaginable, unimaginably).
6. Some lasers produce beams so strong that the rays can cut (direct, directly) through steel.
7. Other lasers produce beams (precise, precisely) enough to be used in surgery.
8. Lasers are (remarkable, remarkably) in the ways they have improved surgical techniques.
9. Most laser surgery can be done (rapid, rapidly), without causing any bleeding.
10. Follow the development of lasers (careful, carefully); they are bound to become even more important.

B. REVISION SKILL

Eliminating Unnecessary Modifiers To make your writing clear and concise, be careful to avoid using two modifiers that have the same meaning. Revise the following paragraph by deleting the unnecessary adjectives and adverbs. If a sentence does not require revision, write *Correct*.

> *Example* Lasers have enabled scientists and artists to create exceptionally unique images called holograms.
> Lasers have enabled scientists and artists to create unique images called holograms.

(1) Holography is a recent and new scientific development. (2) In 1948 Dennis Gabor invented holography in his remarkable quest to improve the electron microscope. (3) His extremely brilliant theory, however, was not put into practice until the 1960's. (4) Before the laser was invented, it was hopelessly impossible to create the three-dimensional images called holograms. (5) This unusually different form of photography is achieved by splitting a laser beam. (6) One exactly precise laser beam is directed onto an object and then reflected onto a glass photographic plate. (7) The other beam is accurately reflected onto the plate by a mirror. (8) When the plate is developed, the whole and complete image of the object is engraved on it. (9) To see the hologram, one must direct a minutely tiny laser beam through the plate. (10) The projected image is a weirdly eerie representation of the original object.

C. APPLICATION IN WRITING

Science Fiction Holograms that move are not yet a reality, even though scientists are experimenting with the possibility. Write a scene from a science fiction story about a scientist who uses moving holograms for either good or evil purposes. Use adjectives to describe the characters, the holograms, and the setting of the story. Use adverbs to tell how, when, where, and to what extent the actions and events occur.

COMPARISONS OF ADJECTIVES AND ADVERBS

Every adjective and adverb has a basic form, called the **positive degree.** This is the form of the word you will find in the dictionary. The positive degree is commonly used to describe individual things, groups, or actions.

Positive   Many microcomputers are *light*. Most of them can be transported *easily*.

The **comparative degree** of an adjective or an adverb is used to compare two things, groups, or actions. Notice that in the following sentences two types of computers are compared.

Comparative   A portable computer is *lighter* than a desktop computer. Most portables can be carried *more easily* than most desktop computers.

When deciding whether the comparative is correct, be alert to phrases such as *the other one* that signal the comparison of two things.

The **superlative degree** is used to compare more than two things, groups, or actions. In the following sentences all types of computers are compared.

Superlative   A lap top computer is the *lightest* computer. Of all computers now available, it can be transported the *most easily*.

To make comparisons correctly, remember that the comparative degree is used to compare only two things or groups and that the superlative degree is used to compare three or more things or groups. Specific numbers are not always given in a comparison. At times you must determine how many things are being compared. Would you use the comparative or the superlative form in the following sentence?

> This is the (better, best) restaurant in the city.

You can infer that the comparison is between one restaurant and all other restaurants in the city. Therefore, the superlative form, *best,* should be used. Now try this example.

> Which is (better, best)—the French restaurant or the Italian one?

Since only two restaurants are being compared, the comparative form, *better,* should be used.

Regular Comparisons

Like verbs, modifiers may be regular or irregular. Most adjectives and adverbs are regular and form the comparative and superlative in one of two ways.

Most one-syllable modifiers form the comparative and superlative by adding *-er* and *-est.* There are a few exceptions. Some two-syllable modifiers also form the comparative and superlative in this way.

Positive	Comparative	Superlative
warm	warmer	warmest
close	closer	closest
soon	sooner	soonest
sad	sadder	saddest
true	truer	truest
funny	funnier	funniest

Spelling Note Most dictionaries list the comparative and superlative forms of modifiers in which there is a spelling change, such as the change from *y* to *i* in *funnier, funniest.*

Most modifiers with two syllables and all modifiers with three or more syllables use *more* and *most* to form the comparative and superlative.

Positive	Comparative	Superlative
helpful	more helpful	most helpful
precisely	more precisely	most precisely
optimistic	more optimistic	most optimistic
reliably	more reliably	most reliably

Before   After

For negative comparisons, *less* and *least* are used before the positive form of the modifier.

Positive	Comparative	Superlative
careful	less careful	least careful
comfortable	less comfortable	least comfortable
eagerly	less eagerly	least eagerly
cautiously	less cautiously	least cautiously
impressive	less impressive	least impressive
essential	less essential	least essential

Irregular Comparisons

A few adjectives and adverbs are irregular. Their comparative and superlative forms are not based on the positive form. Because irregular modifiers are used frequently, you should memorize their forms. Study the following list of irregular modifiers.

Positive	Comparative	Superlative
bad	worse	worst
good	better	best
late	later	latest *or* last
little	less	least
many	more	most
much	more	most
well	better	best
ill	worse	worst
far	farther *or* further	farther *or* furthest

Usage Note *Farther* refers to distance, and *further* refers to an addition in time or amount: The distance to town is *farther* than I thought. I won't discuss it *further.*

Practice Your Skills

A. CONCEPT CHECK

Comparative and Superlative Forms Write the correct form of the two modifiers given in parentheses. Identify the correct modifier as *Comparative* or *Superlative*.

1. The (more primitive, most primitive) forms of writing date from about six thousand years ago.
2. Crude rock drawings were the (earliest, most early) written communications.
3. One of the (more interesting, most interesting) rock drawings in the Americas is in New Mexico.

4. The drawing shows a mountain goat standing on all fours and a (less careful, least careful) horse and rider upside down.
5. The picture is one of the (better, best) examples of an ideograph, a picture used to represent an idea.
6. Human beings eventually learned to write ideas (conciser, more concisely) than they could in ideographs.
7. Archaeological discoveries have been the (helpfullest, most helpful) in determining when this first occurred.
8. Because of those discoveries, historians now think that the Sumerians were the (brilliantest, most brilliant) innovators in the development of writing.
9. Invented around 3500 B.C., the Sumerian system is (older, oldest) than even Egyptian hieroglyphics.
10. Later, the Babylonians and Assyrians (further, farther) improved on the Sumerian system of writing.

B. REVISION SKILL

Using Modifiers Correctly Using the correct comparative and superlative forms of adjectives and adverbs can make your writing more understandable. Rewrite the following paragraphs, using correct comparative and superlative forms. If the modifiers in a sentence do not need revision, write *Correct*.

Gold tablet with cuneiform writing from Khorsbad

(1) About the same time that Egyptian hieroglyphics were fascinating European scholars, archaeologists in the Near East were examining one of the more mysterious scripts ever discovered. (2) Cuneiform, a wedge-shaped writing, had been in use earlier than Egyptian hieroglyphics, but information about it had been missing for a thousand years. (3) Of all the samples discovered, the more ancient tablets were found in Mesopotamia.

(4) The better way to describe cuneiform is to say that it looks like bird tracks left in mud. (5) Cuneiform characters were formed by pressing a triangular stylus into a soft clay tablet; then the clay was baked to make it more hard and more strong. (6) Because it has the fewest variations, cuneiform is considered a more elementary form of writing than hieroglyphics. (7) During the years it was used, cuneiform changed least than hieroglyphics. (8) Even though it is one of the more primitive of all written languages, it does have a form of punctuation. (9) One mark that was clearly smaller than the others was used to separate words. (10) Some forms of cuneiform were difficulter to read than others; it took scientists many years to decipher them.

C. APPLICATION IN WRITING

A Comparison Choose two methods or devices for communicating and write a short essay comparing and contrasting them. Use comparative forms of adjectives and adverbs. Possible topics are listed below.

>   newspapers/television news
>   typewriters/word processors
>   radio/television
>   talking on the phone/talking in person

Swiss Alps

C H E C K P O I N T
PAGES 737–745

A. Write the correct modifier of the two modifiers given in parentheses. Then indicate whether the modifier is an *Adjective* or an *Adverb*.

Writing Theme
The Alps

1. The Alps rise (most dramatically, more dramatically) above the land than any other mountain range in Europe.
2. This mountain range, about 750 miles long, has (near, nearly) vertical slopes.
3. By looking (careful, carefully) at a map of Europe, one can see that the Alps extend into seven different countries.
4. Mont Blanc—at 15,771 feet—is a mountain massif, or (principal, principally) mountain mass.

5. The Mer de Glace ("Sea of Ice"), the second (longer, longest) glacier in the Alps, covers about forty square miles of Mont Blanc.
6. From a distance the snowcapped summit appears (calm, calmly).
7. Appearances are deceiving however, since avalanches occur (frequent, frequently).
8. That very danger is perhaps the (greater, greatest) attraction of the peak for some intrepid mountaineers.
9. The (most early, earliest) climbers of Mont Blanc were Jacques Balmat and Michel Paccard in 1786.
10. Today this mountain is the site of the world's (most high, highest) aerial tramway.

B. Rewrite the following sentences, correcting any errors in the use of modifiers. If a sentence contains no error, write *Correct*.

Writing Theme
Greeting Cards

(1) One of the less-known facts in the history of etiquette is that greeting cards have ancient origins. (2) Both the Egyptians and the Romans customary sent greetings on the first day of the new year. (3) Of the two cultures, the Egyptians sent written holiday messages earliest.

(4) Preprinted greeting cards were not widely available until the nineteenth century. (5) Cards were also not sent regular on many holidays. (6) In the mid-1800's the more popular way to send greetings was with handmade cards.

(7) As the pace of life became more fast, however, people began to buy printed cards. (8) Louis Prang was the originator of the greeting-card business with his lavishly complicated printing press. (9) The industry became powerfully enough to create holidays such as Mother's Day and Father's Day.

U SING COMPARISONS
C O R R E C T L Y

These guidelines will help you use comparisons correctly.

Avoid Double Comparisons

The comparative form of a modifier is made either by adding *-er* or by using *more*. It is incorrect to use both.

The superlative form of a modifier is made either by adding *-est* or by using *most*. It is incorrect to use both.

Incorrect   My boat will go much more faster than yours.
Correct   My boat will go much faster than yours.

Incorrect	You should find it more easier to do.
Correct	You should find it easier to do.
Incorrect	It was the most fanciest house I'd ever seen.
Correct	It was the fanciest house I'd ever seen.

Avoid Illogical Comparisons

Illogical or confusing comparisons result if two unrelated items are compared or if something is compared with itself.

The word *other* or the word *else* is required in comparisons of an individual member with the rest of the group.

Illogical	Bill has won more trophies than any student athlete. (Bill is also a student athlete.)
Clear	Bill has won more trophies than any *other* student athlete.
Illogical	Etta is as tall as anyone on the basketball team. (Etta is also on the team.)
Clear	Etta is as tall as anyone *else* on the basketball team.

The word *as* or the word *than* is required after the first modifier in a compound comparison.

Illogical	Tim is as tall if not taller than Estrella.
Awkward	Tim is as tall *as,* if not taller than, Estrella.
Clear	Tim is as tall *as* Estrella, if not taller.
Illogical	Sue's grades are better or at least as good as Helen's.
Clear	Sue's grades are better *than,* or at least as good as, Helen's.
Illogical	The Dodgers' chances of winning the pennant are as good if not better than the Giants'.
Clear	The Dodgers' chances of winning the pennant are as good *as* the Giants', if not better.

Both parts of a comparison must be stated completely if there is any chance of its being misunderstood.

Confusing	I miss her more than Sandra.
Clear	I miss her more than Sandra *does*.
Clear	I miss her more than I *miss* Sandra.
Confusing	Harvard beats Yale more often than Brown.
Clear	Harvard beats Yale more often than Brown *does*.
Clear	Harvard beats Yale more often than it *beats* Brown.
Confusing	Rio is nearer the equator than London.
Clear	Rio is nearer the equator than London *is*.

Win $1,000,000 playing Cash Flow Instant Lottery and you could purchase a dazzling array of durable goods.

Practice Your Skills

A. CONCEPT CHECK

Double and Illogical Comparisons   Find the errors in comparison in the following sentences. Rewrite the sentences correctly.

1. Advertising is the most cheapest and fastest way to inform people about products and services.
2. More is spent in America on advertising than in any country.
3. Each year the sum is more larger than $100 billion.
4. Even in the most earliest colonial days, advertising was important.
5. Handbills were more widely used than any form of advertising.
6. Paul Revere, for example, claimed the false teeth he made were better or at least as good as those made by anyone else.
7. Even then, competition among advertisers became as fierce if not more fierce than competition today.
8. Benjamin Franklin, who owned the *Pennsylvania Gazette,* was the most best known for encouraging advertising.
9. In the early days of magazine publishing, competition in advertising was more greater than you might think.
10. Magazine circulations were as large if not larger than newspaper circulations.
11. By the late 1800's Albert Lasker had devised a more better approach to advertising.
12. He thought that an agency could create a more effective ad than an individual company.

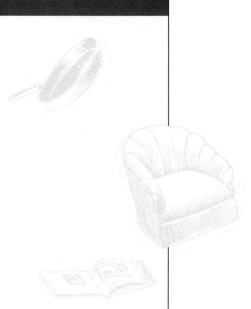

13. By 1910 Lasker's agency was by far the most biggest.
14. By hiring artists and copywriters, he put together a larger staff than any agency in the country.
15. As a result, Lasker's advertising campaigns were more revolutionary and more effective than those of any agency.

B. PROOFREADING SKILL

Correcting Double and Illogical Comparisons The following paragraph contains errors in comparison, in spelling, capitalization, and punctuation. Rewrite the paragraph, correcting all errors.

> Have you noticed that billboard art is becoming even more bolder than in the past? Some billboard figures are as large, if not larger than, the legendary giant paul Bunyan. Others are raised from the background, they seem to pitch their product direct to each passerby. The most strikingest billboard I have seen shows a row of huge sneekers. It's colors are more vibranter than those in any billboard I have seen. Those sneakers would be to large even for Paul Bunyan!

SPECIAL PROBLEMS
WITH MODIFIERS

Certain adjectives and adverbs have forms that can be confusing. In the following section you will learn the correct use of adjectives and adverbs that are often used incorrectly.

This and *These; That* and *Those*

This and *that* modify singular words. *These* and *those* modify plural words. *Kind, sort,* and *type* require a singular modifier.

Incorrect	*These* kind are the best.
Correct	*This* kind is the best.
Incorrect	*These* sort of gloves wear well.
Correct	*This* sort of glove wears well.

Them and *Those*

Those may be either a pronoun or an adjective. *Them* is always a pronoun and never an adjective.

Incorrect	Where did you get *them* statistics?
Correct	Where did you get *those* statistics? (adjective)
Correct	Where did you get *them*? (pronoun)

Bad and *Badly*

Bad is an adjective. It can modify a noun or pronoun. When it is used after linking verbs, it modifies the subject. *Badly* is an adverb. It modifies action verbs.

I felt *bad*. (The adjective *bad* follows a linking verb and modifies the subject *I*.)

The team played *badly*. (The adverb *badly* modifies the action verb *played*.)

Good and *Well*

Good is an adjective. It modifies nouns or pronouns.

Zinnias are a *good* choice for a sunny garden.

Good can also be used as a predicate adjective with linking verbs. It then modifies the subject.

Dad always feels *good* after a brisk walk.

Well can be either an adjective or an adverb. As an adjective, *well* means "in good health," and it can follow a linking verb. As an adverb, *well* modifies an action verb. It tells how the action is performed.

The Vice-President looks *well*. (adjective)
Miguel is sprinting *well* now. (adverb)

The Double Negative

Two negative words used together where only one is necessary is called a *double negative*. A double negative is incorrect.

Incorrect He did*n't* have *no* energy left.
Correct He did*n't* have *any* energy left.
Correct He had no energy left.

Incorrect She did*n't* know *nothing* about the Civil War.
Correct She did*n't* know *anything* about the Civil War.
Correct She knew nothing about the Civil War.

It is incorrect to use *hardly* or *barely* with a negative word.

Incorrect There was*n't hardly* a ticket left for the show.
Correct There was *hardly* a ticket left for the show.

Incorrect Terry could*n't barely* hit the ball.
Correct Terry could *barely* hit the ball.

Practice Your Skills

A. CONCEPT CHECK

Using Modifiers Correctly Write the correct modifier of the two choices given in parentheses.

1. Until recently in India, there were hardly (any, no) tigers left in existence.
2. Hunting and the spread of civilization had destroyed three subspecies (quick, quickly), and the future of two more looked (bad, badly).
3. By (careful, carefully) studying the pugmarks, or tracks, of (those, them) cats that were left, conservationists learned where to establish a protected reserve.
4. Swampy areas south of Nepal were chosen because (these, this) kind of big cat is drawn to water.
5. Also, (them, these) areas aren't much good for (anything, nothing) else.
6. Tourists who haven't (ever, never) seen a tiger can visit the buffer zone around the park.
7. However, it is not (good, well) to go on foot.
8. For some reason, tigers won't do (nothing, anything) harmful to people riding on elephants or in vehicles.
9. The big cat is doing (good, well) under protection.
10. (This, These) type of park may save tigers from extinction.

B. REVISION SKILL

Correcting Errors in Modifier Usage   The misuse of modifiers can confuse readers and make the meaning unclear. Rewrite the following sentences, correcting any error in the use of modifiers. If a sentence contains no error, write *Correct*.

(1) Pandas in the wild didn't always have no problems. (2) These sort of bearlike animal used to live peacefully in the bamboo forests of China. (3) In fact, pandas were not hardly known to Europeans until the early 1900's. (4) The pandas were solitary creatures, surviving good on bamboo stems, leaves, and roots. (5) However, people began to treat the animals bad. (6) Crews cut down the bamboo necessary to these docile creatures. (7) Those people did not have no concern about preserving the pandas' habitats. (8) Others hunted them animals for their fur. (9) As a result, the future of the pandas seemed badly. (10) Now, however, it is good to know that the Chinese people are striving to save them.

CHECK POINT
PAGES 746–752

PAGES 746–752

A. Rewrite the following sentences, correcting all errors in the use of modifiers.

1. Pablo Picasso was one of the most greatest painters of the twentieth century.
2. In the opinion of many experts, Picasso was more original than any modern painter.
3. Even though Picasso was born in Spain, Paris was always nearer his heart than Barcelona.
4. In France he met Georges Braque, who was one year more older than Picasso.
5. Together, them two friends created a new form of art.
6. The style of these sort of painting became known as cubism.
7. In his cubist works Picasso's subjects took on a much more abstract appearance than in his more earlier works.
8. At times, the subject could not barely be distinguished among the overlapping lines and shapes.
9. Picasso, who learned from Braque how to use collage, mastered the technique as good as his friend had.
10. The two men also painted self-portraits, but Picasso painted his in a more greater number of styles than Braque did.
11. Later, when the European political situation grew badly, the friends were separated.

12. The Spanish Civil War in the 1930's was as powerful, if not more powerful, than any other influence on Picasso.
13. In 1937 the small town of Guernica was bombed bad.
14. Picasso didn't hardly know how to respond to this horrible tragedy.
15. The enormous work called *Guernica* is perhaps more emotionally charged than any of Picasso's paintings.

B. Rewrite the following paragraph, correcting all errors in the use of modifiers. Some sentences may contain more than one error or no error.

(1) My brother and I needed money bad, so we persuaded our neighbor to let us paint her garage. (2) We told her that we worked good together and did not finish as slow as professional painters. (3) She agreed, and we headed quickly to the hardware store. (4) A salesperson told us that we should use long-handled roller brushes so that we wouldn't have to climb no risky ladders. (5) However, my brother told him, "We don't like those kind of brush," so the clerk pointed at a bin of short-handled ones. (6) We bought them short-handled brushes and rented an eight-foot construction scaffold. (7) Our painting job was going good when our neighbor came around to offer us refreshments. (8) I turned toward her hastily and fell off the ladder! (9) All them cans of paint and all them brushes landed on top of me. (10) It didn't hurt too bad, but I did get a sore arm and a coat of paint.

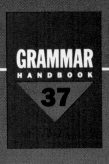

GRAMMAR
HANDBOOK
37

Writing Theme
Inventors and
Inventions

A. Choosing the Correct Modifier Write the correct form of the two choices given in parentheses.

1. Most people haven't (ever, never) learned about the history of some common household items.
2. The umbrella, for example, has a (stranger, more strange) history than many might suppose.
3. (Original, Originally), umbrellas were used in Mesopotamia nearly 3,500 years ago.
4. This fact may seem (peculiar, peculiarly) to those familiar with the region.
5. There is hardly ever (no, any) rain in that area of the world.
6. Umbrellas, however, served (essential, essentially) as sunshades.
7. The (clearest, most clearest) evidence for this fact is that *umbrella* comes from a Latin word that means "shade."
8. In Mesopotamia umbrellas were one of the (more, most) powerful status symbols for the nobility.
9. In Egypt umbrellas had a greater religious symbolism than in (any, any other) country.
10. For the ancient Egyptians umbrellas resembled most (concrete, concretely) the canopy of the sky, which was believed to be formed by the heavenly goddess Nut.
11. The materials used for (them, those) umbrellas included palm fronds and feathers.
12. The Greeks and Romans thought that men should not (ever, never) carry umbrellas.
13. This attitude persisted in Europe (longer, more longer) than anyone might imagine.
14. In about 1750, however, an Englishman named Jonas Hanway set out to make the umbrella (most respectable, more respectable) for gentlemen.
15. If other people thought (bad, badly) of him, Hanway did not care, because he was very wealthy.
16. He decided he would not (ever, never) leave his house without an umbrella, rain or shine.
17. For many years Hanway's friends mocked him as (scornful, scornfully) as strangers did.
18. (Gradual, Gradually), however, Jonas Hanway's new fashion was accepted.
19. People realized that buying an umbrella was (cheaper, more cheaper) than taking coaches when it rained.
20. The (best, better) compliment of all to Jonas Hanway was that, before his death in 1786, Londoners had started to refer (admiring, admiringly) to umbrellas as "Hanways."

B. Using Modifiers Correctly The following sentences contain errors in the use of modifiers. Rewrite each sentence correctly.

1. The ancient origin of sunglasses may seem as peculiarly as the origin of the umbrella.
2. Current tinted glasses are used to reduce the glare of the sun, but initially they served another purpose.
3. At one time smoke tinting was the most easiest method of darkening eyeglasses.
4. This method was developed in China as early, if not earlier than, 1430.
5. Judges wore eyeglasses with these type of lens whenever they tried a difficult case.
6. The judges wanted to conceal their reactions to the evidence as careful as they could.
7. They didn't want no eye movements or expressions to betray their opinions.
8. Fortunately, today's judges no longer wear darkened lenses; modern sunglasses are used quite different.
9. In the 1930's in America, sunglasses were developed to protect military pilots from high-altitude glare that could impair vision bad.
10. Designer sunglasses are now regarded as one of the more glamorous accessories for both men and women.

C. Correcting Errors with Modifiers The following paragraph contains errors in the use of modifiers. Rewrite the paragraph, correcting all errors.

> (1) One can't hardly discuss the subject of inventors without mentioning Thomas Edison. (2) The electric light, the storage battery, the phonograph, and the motion-picture projector—all them inventions are credited to Edison. (3) Edison's impact on industrial America was profoundly, not only because he invented these kind of device, but also because he revolutionized the business of invention. (4) After Edison, the inventor wasn't no longer an isolated individual; instead, the inventor became a member of a scientific team. (5) These new kind of team worked just as good, if not better than, inventors on their own.

D. Proofreading The following paragraphs contain errors in the use of modifiers as well as other mistakes. Rewrite the paragraphs, correcting all errors.

Alfred Nobel left his mark on the world in too dramatically different areas. It seems ironically that the person who invented dynamite would also bequeath a prize for world peace, but Nobel did just that.

Nobel was born in sweden in 1833. His family was in the business of making explosive's, and sometimes there were problems in controlling them dangerous substances. Often, those kind of substances, such as nitroglycerin, would explode inside the Nobel factories. To make the nitroglycerin more stabler, Alfred Nobel mixed it with another material. He called his invention "dinamite."

In 1896, after dynamite and other inventions had made Nobel as rich, if not richer than, the most wealthiest persons in the world, Nobel wrote his will. He didn't leave none of his fortune to his family. Instead, his money was to go direct to men and women who would make outstanding contributions in the areas of literature physics, chemistry, medicine, economics and world piece. So it was that a pioneer in the feild of explosives became the founder of a peace prize.

NAVAHO

Though many Native-American languages have been supplanted by English, the Navaho language

Rainbow Jar, lithograph by R.C. Gorman. Courtesy of Houston Fine Arts Press

continues to play an important role in the lives of the Navaho people. More than 100,000 people speak Navaho, principally on the sprawling Navaho Reservation covering fourteen million acres of Arizona, New Mexico, and Utah.

The Navaho language differs from English in many ways. It is a "tone" language, one in which the pitch used to pronounce a word helps determine its meaning.

In addition, nouns are classified as either animate or inanimate, and words associated with active things have feminine gender while static things have masculine gender. Some verb forms change depending on their direct object. For example, the verb form used to say *holding a ball* is different from the verb form used for *holding a stick.*

Instead of borrowing words from English, the Navaho adapt existing Navaho words and phrases to suit new needs. A car, for example, is a *chidi,* named after the noise a car makes when it starts. A car's headlights are "the eyes of the chidi," its wheels "the legs of the chidi," and its tires "the moccasins of the chidi."

Although many Native-American languages are disappearing due to the dominance of English, the Navaho people are steadfastly holding on to their linguistic heritage.

Sketchbook

You have learned of plans for construction of a twenty-story building just four feet from your house or apartment. Write a letter to the editor of the local newspaper voicing your opinion about the matter. Offer convincing reasons to support your position, and facts and details that explain it. In your letter use all three cases of pronouns.

Additional Sketches

In two paragraphs compare and contrast yourself and one other person. Describe the similarities between you in the first paragraph and differences in the second. Use pronouns with clear referents and modifiers that support your points.

What would Thomas Jefferson think of skyscrapers or Emily Dickinson of space satellites? Write a paragraph or two about today's world from the point of view of some historical or literary American. Use comparative adjectives and adverbs to contrast the past with the present.

Directions In each of the following sentences, one, two, or none of the underlined sections may be incorrect. Look for errors of grammar, usage, punctuation, spelling, and capitalization. On your paper, write the number of the sentence, the letter of each incorrect underlined section, and the correction. If the sentence contains no errors, write E.

> **Example** <u>Of all the</u> ancient <u>cliff dwellings</u> in <u>New Mexico</u>, those at
>   **A**   **B**   **C**
>   Tsankawi are the <u>more</u> interesting. <u>No error</u>
>   **D**   **E**
>
> **Answer** D—most

1. <u>Jules and him</u> <u>read</u> a skit of <u>their's</u> <u>to the drama club.</u> <u>No error</u>
    A   **B**   **C**   **D**   **E**

2. <u>Although a tornado</u> is a smaller windstorm <u>than a hurricane is,</u> <u>a tornado's</u> destructive
      A   **B**   **C**
force <u>is greatest.</u> <u>No error</u>
       D   **E**

3. Because Chris <u>was undefeated</u> in <u>sixteen</u> <u>matches,</u> we expected the next great tennis star
             A   **B**   **C**
<u>to be she.</u> <u>No error</u>
   D   **E**

4. <u>Professor Harvey disagrees</u> with Dr. Jones <u>and I</u> that <u>opinion polls</u> <u>are</u> statistically
         A   **B**   **C**   **D**
significant. <u>No error</u>
          E

5. The <u>most</u> popular night of the week <u>for watching television</u> is <u>Sunday; the</u> least popular
     A   **B**   **C**
night is <u>Friday.</u> <u>No error</u>
       D   **E**

6. <u>Who</u> built <u>many of the great public libraries</u> in <u>America?</u> Andrew Carnegie is <u>whom.</u>
   A   **B**   **C**   **D**
<u>No error</u>
 E

7. Certain inalienable rights are <u>garanteed</u> by the <u>Constitution</u> to all Americans, <u>we</u> citizens
                           A   **B**   **C**
<u>of the United States.</u> <u>No error</u>
     D   **E**

8. The <u>medals</u> went to the <u>fastest</u> <u>swimmers, Lauren</u> and <u>me.</u> <u>No error</u>
     A   **B**   **C**   **D** **E**

9. <u>Those</u> types of cactus bloom at night, and the aroma of <u>their</u> blossoms attracts night
   A   B
   <u>fliers</u> such as bats, <u>which eat</u> the nectar and pollen. <u>No error</u>
   C   D   E

10. <u>Who's</u> going <u>to remove</u> the dishes from the <u>cuboards</u> and wash <u>them</u>? <u>No error</u>
    A   B   C   D   E

11. <u>When</u> Einstein addressed young scientists and <u>students, he</u> encouraged <u>them</u> to pursue a
    A   B   C
    life <u>dedicated to science</u>. <u>No error</u>
         D   E

12. The <u>Twentyeth Amendment</u> to the Constitution states that if the President-elect <u>dies, the</u>
        A   B
    Vice-President-elect shall become President. <u>Himself</u> and no one else shall have all
                                                 C
    powers <u>under the law</u>. <u>No error</u>
           D   E

13. Chinese porcelains <u>have always been considered</u> the finest in the <u>world; that</u> is <u>why</u> the
                       A   B   C
    popular name for fine dishes <u>made in a certain way</u> is china. <u>No error</u>
                                 D   E

14. Henry V and his men fought so <u>brave</u> at Agincourt that there <u>wasn't hardly</u> a person
                                  A   B
    during <u>Shakespeare's time</u> <u>who hadn't heard the story many times</u>. <u>No error</u>
           C   D   E

15. <u>Feed</u> the <u>dogs; neither</u> has had <u>their</u> dinner <u>yet</u>. <u>No error</u>
    A   B   C   D   E

16. <u>Few of us</u> wanted <u>his</u> work subjected to <u>these</u> sort of <u>criticism</u>. <u>No error</u>
    A   B   C   D   E

17. <u>Neither</u> the <u>President</u> nor the <u>Secretary of State</u> would give <u>their</u> views to the press.
    A   B   C   D
    <u>No error</u>
    E

18. <u>Neither Los Angeles nor</u> any of the other <u>cities</u> to the <u>South</u> of Los Angeles have a
    A   B   C
    water supply sufficient for <u>its</u> needs. <u>No error</u>
                                D   E

19. The instructional video on <u>playing the guitar</u> worked out pretty <u>good; it</u> was <u>helpfuller</u>
                               A   B   C
    than any book <u>I could have read</u>. <u>No error</u>
                  D   E

20. <u>This sort of coral</u> causes severe burns and <u>are</u> therefore called <u>"fire coral"</u>; however,
        A   **B**   **C**

    a sting from a bristleworm is <u>more bad</u> than a fire coral burn. <u>No error</u>
                                         D   **E**

21. The <u>capital</u> of North Dakota is <u>Bismarck, and</u> <u>its</u> state song is <u>"North Dakota Hymn."</u>
         A   **B**   **C**   **D**

    <u>No error</u>
    E

22. Amelia Earhart <u>was</u> <u>as brave</u> <u>an aviator</u> <u>as any</u> in history. <u>No error</u>
                       A   **B**   **C**   **D**   **E**

23. <u>At the present time</u> <u>in the United States</u>, <u>women work</u> <u>as many hours if not more than</u>
          A   **B**   **C**   **D**

    men. <u>No error</u>
          E

24. <u>Although the</u> Battle of Gettysburg is often regarded as the turning point in the <u>Civil</u>
         A   **B**

    <u>War, it</u> should be remembered that the war continued for two <u>long, difficult</u> years
      A   **C**

    after that battle. <u>No error</u>
         D   **E**

25. <u>Among the wonders of the ancient world are</u> the pyramids <u>in Egypt</u> the Temple of
                     A   **B**

    Artemis at Epheseus, <u>and</u> the Colossus at Rhodes. Of these wonders, the pyramids are
                           C

    <u>the more</u> well known. <u>No error</u>
       D   **E**

26. A <u>prize</u> <u>will be</u> awarded to <u>whomever</u> writes the <u>best</u> essay. <u>No error</u>
        A   **B**   **C**   **D**   **E**

27. The flood is the <u>least</u> of our <u>worries for</u> the officials have just found <u>toxick</u> waste in <u>our</u>
                    A   **B**   **C**   **D**

    groundwater. <u>No error</u>
              E

28. The diplomats from the <u>United Nations</u> talked <u>with the Iraqi diplomats</u> until <u>they ran</u>
                      A   **B**   **C**

    <u>out</u> of <u>suggestions</u>. <u>No error</u>
     D   **E**

29. <u>Which</u> island <u>has developed</u> <u>its</u> economy <u>more far</u>, Aruba or Martinique? <u>No error</u>
       A   **B**   **C**   **D**   **E**

30. Even though chicken <u>may look well</u> and doesn't smell <u>badly, it</u> contains salmonella
                       A   **B**

    <u>bacteria and</u> should be cleaned <u>thoroughly</u>. <u>No error</u>
       C   **D**   **E**

Capitalization

PEOPLE, PERSONAL TITLES, NATIONALITIES, AND RELIGIONS

A **proper noun** is the name of a specific person, place, thing, or idea. A **common noun** names a general class of people, places, things, or ideas. Proper nouns are capitalized. Common nouns are not. A **proper adjective** is an adjective formed from a proper noun, and is, therefore, also capitalized.

Common Noun	Proper Noun	Proper Adjective
continent	Europe	European
queen	Queen Elizabeth	Elizabethan

Proper nouns and adjectives occur in many compound words. Capitalize only the parts of these words that are capitalized when they stand alone. Do not capitalize prefixes such as *pro-, un-,* and *pre-* attached to proper nouns and adjectives.

pro-Marxist   un-American   pre-Civil War

The following rules will help you identify proper nouns and adjectives and capitalize them correctly.

Names of People and Personal Titles

Capitalize people's names and initials that stand for names.

Elizabeth Dole   **J.P.** Morgan   Lyndon **B.** Johnson

Capitalize titles and abbreviations for titles used before people's names or in direct address.

Reverend Jesse Jackson   **Ms.** Hudson   **Lt.** Harrison
How often should I take this medication, **D**octor?

The abbreviations *Jr.* and *Sr.* are also capitalized after names. In the middle of a sentence, these abbreviations are followed by a comma.

Mr. Ralph Benson, **Sr.,** addressed the class.

In general, do not capitalize a title when it follows a person's name or is used without a proper name.

The doctor wrote a prescription for Amy.

Capitalize a title used without a person's name if it refers to a head of state or a person in another important position.

the **P**resident and **V**ice-**P**resident of the United States
the **P**ope   the **P**rime **M**inister   the **C**hief **J**ustice

The prefix *ex-* and the suffix *-elect* are not capitalized when attached to titles.

ex-**P**resident Carter   the **P**rime **M**inister-elect

Titles of members of the royal or noble classes are not capitalized unless they are used with a person's name or in place of a person's name.

HRH Charles, **P**rince of **W**ales
George Gordon, **L**ord Byron
King Henry II

Family Relationships

Capitalize the titles indicating family relationships when the titles are used as names or as parts of names.

It's hard to believe that **A**unt **M**aria and **M**om are twins.

If the title is preceded by an article or a possessive word, it is not capitalized.

My uncle admitted that being a father can be difficult.

Wedding,
by Malcah Zeldis, 1973

Writing
—— TIP ——

The prefix *ex-* combined with a title is seldom used in formal writing. The word *former* is preferred.

Races, Languages, Nationalities, and Religions

Capitalize the names of races, languages, nationalities, and religions, and any adjectives formed from these names.

Hinduism	**C**aucasian	**C**hinese cooking
French	**H**ebrew	**A**rabian horses

The Supreme Being and Sacred Writings

Capitalize all words referring to God, the Holy Family, and religious scriptures.

the **L**ord	**A**llah	the **T**orah
Christ	the **G**ospel	the **K**oran
the **V**irgin **M**ary	the **O**ld **T**estament	the **T**almud

Capitalize personal pronouns referring to God.

They thanked the Lord for **H**is love and guidance.

Do not capitalize *god* and *goddess* when they refer to multiple deities, such as the gods and goddesses of various mythologies.

Isis was one of several Egyptian nature goddesses.
The Greek god Hades was ruler of the underworld.

The Pronoun I

Always capitalize the pronoun *I*.

I'll probably make the team if **I** improve my free throws.

Practice Your Skills

A. CONCEPT CHECK

Using Capitalization Write the following sentences, using capital letters where necessary.

1. Buddhism is a religion that began in india in the pre-christian era of history.
2. Around twenty-five hundred years ago, the founder of buddhism was born a prince in what is now the nation of nepal.
3. The nepalese prince was originally named siddhartha gautama of the Sakyas.
4. When he was about twenty-nine years old, prince Gautama became ex-prince Gautama, giving up luxury to become a poor monk.
5. His followers gave Gautama the sacred name buddha.
6. All buddhists believe that freedom from desire and worldly things leads to happiness and peace.

7. My uncle chang told me some things i had not known about Buddhism.
8. In some countries, buddhists worship various deities, such as the goddess of mercy.
9. The title dalai lama is given to the supreme leader of buddhists in the country of tibet.
10. Followers of Buddha can read his sermons in the *tipitaka,* a collection of buddhist sacred writings.

B. REVISION SKILL

Errors In Capitalization   Find the words that need capital letters in the following paragraphs. Write them correctly on your paper after the number of the sentence in which they appear.

(1) For centuries the indian people have been divided by struggles between the hindus and the moslems, two groups with vastly different religious beliefs. (2) The moslems, like christians and jews, believe in one god. (3) Founded by a prophet named mohammed, the moslem religion is based on the teachings of the koran, a sacred book similar to the bible. (4) Mosques are churchlike buildings where moslems worship Allah, their name for the supreme being.

(5) In contrast, hindus believe that the creator and his creations are one and the same, and can be worshiped in any form, including animals, water, planets, or stars. (6) Consequently, hindu temples are filled with statues of gods and goddesses—symbols of the faith's three-and-a-half million divinities. (7) The most important of these divine beings are brahma, shiva, and vishnu. (8) A hindu worships alone, searching for the perfect balance in life as taught in the vedas, four sacred books of scripture. (9) On August 15, 1947, hindus and moslems joined together to form a unified indian nation, independent of british rule. (10) The two men most responsible for ending the country's internal struggle were the famous peace-loving hindu, mahatma gandhi, and viceroy of india louis mountbatten, the great-grandson of queen victoria.

Indian bronze sculpture of Shiva Nataraja, early Chola dynasty, c. A.D. 1000. The Metropolitan Museum of Art, Harris Brisbane Dick Fund, 1964

Certain nouns and adjectives that refer to geographical areas or topographical features are capitalized.

Geographical Names

In a geographical name, capitalize the first letter of each word except articles and prepositions.

Continents	**A**ustralia, **S**outh **A**merica, **E**urope, **A**sia, **A**frica, **A**ntarctica
Bodies of Water	**L**ake **O**ntario, the **J**ordan **R**iver, **S**trait of **B**elle **I**sle, **C**ape **C**od **B**ay, the **A**driatic **S**ea, **St**. **G**eorge's **C**hannel
Landforms	the **P**yrenees, the **S**inai **P**eninsula, the **G**rand **C**anyon, the **S**yrian **D**esert, **M**ount **C**onstance, the **P**lains of **A**braham, **R**aton **P**ass, the **R**ocky **M**ountains, **I**sthmus of **P**anama
World Regions	the **O**rient, the **M**iddle **E**ast, the **F**ar **E**ast
Special Terms	the **N**orthern **H**emisphere, the **E**quator, the **T**ropic of **C**ancer, the **N**orth **P**ole
Political Units	the **D**istrict of **C**olumbia, the **W**est **I**ndies, **S**an **F**rancisco, the **R**epublic of **T**exas
Public Areas	**G**ettysburg **N**ational **P**ark, **F**ort **N**iagara, the **B**lue **G**rotto, **M**ount **R**ushmore
Roads and Highways	**M**ain **S**treet, **R**oute 447, **W**est **S**ide **H**ighway, **V**an **B**uren **A**venue, the **O**hio **T**urnpike

Capitalize the word modified by a proper adjective only if the noun and adjective together form a geographical name.

English **C**hannel	**E**nglish accent
the **I**ndian **O**cean	**I**ndian artifacts

Directions and Sections

Capitalize names of sections of the country or the world, and any adjectives that come from those sections.

The Barnetts moved from the **E**ast **C**oast to the **S**outhwest.
Jane is from a **M**idwestern town, but she has an **E**astern accent.

Writing TIP

Do not capitalize words like *city*, *state*, or *county* except as the name of a political unit: "We petitioned the State of Ohio."

Do not capitalize compass directions or adjectives that merely indicate direction or a general location.

Drive south on Pine Street to the first stoplight.
I spent my vacation on the western coast of Yugoslavia.

Bodies of the Universe

Capitalize the names of planets in the solar system and other objects in the universe, except words like *sun* and *moon*.

Neptune	**H**alley's **C**omet	an eclipse of the sun
Jupiter	the **B**ig **D**ipper	a phase of the moon

Capitalize the word *earth* only when it is used in conjunction with the names of other planets. The word *earth* is not capitalized when the article *the* precedes it.

In addition to Earth, Mercury, Venus, Mars, and Pluto are known as the terrestrial planets. They resemble the earth in size, density, and chemical composition.

Structures and Vehicles

Capitalize the names of specific monuments, bridges, and buildings.

the **L**incoln **M**emorial	**A**rch of **T**riumph
the **P**rudential **B**uilding	**T**ower **B**ridge
the **F**lat **I**ron **B**uilding	the **S**tatue of **L**iberty

Capitalize the names of specific ships, trains, airplanes, automobiles, and spacecraft.

Queen Elizabeth II	the *Denver Zephyr*
the *Spirit of St. Louis*	**R**eliant

Practice Your Skills

A. CONCEPT CHECK

Using Capitalization Write the following sentences, using capital letters where necessary. If no capitals are needed, write *Correct*. This exercise covers many of the rules you have studied so far.

1. In ancient times, according to greek and roman writers, there were seven wonders of the world.
2. People from all over the near east and the mediterranean traveled in large numbers to view these wonders.

Writing
——**TIP**——

Underline the names of specific ships, airplanes, trains, and spacecraft, but not automobiles.

Writing Theme
Wonders of the World

3. Considered the first wonder of the world were egypt's pyramids.
4. These ancient tombs are five miles from giza, a town on the bank of the nile river.
5. The Lighthouse of Alexandria, the second wonder, stood on the island of pharos in the harbor of alexandria, on Egypt's northern coast.
6. The third wonder, the Colossus of rhodes, was a huge bronze statue built on the island of Rhodes in the aegean sea.
7. This statue honored Helios, the god of the sun, and stood nearly as tall as the statue of liberty stands.
8. The fourth wonder, a statue of zeus, was also in Greece; fragments from the site are now in the louvre, a museum on rivoli street in paris.
9. The fifth and sixth wonders were located in Asia Minor.
10. The temple of Artemis, the fifth wonder, stood in the Greek city of ephesus.
11. On the southwest coast of Turkey, an enormous tomb was built for Mausolus, an official of the persian empire.
12. This tomb, the Mausoleum of Halicarnassus, was so famous for its size and beauty that the word *mausoleum* now applies to any large tomb.
13. The seventh wonder of the ancient world was the Hanging Gardens of babylon, a city just north of the modern city of hilla.
14. Water from the euphrates river irrigated beautiful flowers and trees in these gardens laid out on high brick terraces.
15. Although the astronauts in flight couldn't see the seven wonders, they did see one of the earth's exceptional spectacles, the great wall of china.

The Great Wall of China

B. REVISION SKILL

Capitalization Errors Rewrite the following paragraph, supplying the necessary capitals.

(1) Few natural wonders in north america can compete with the majesty of niagara falls. (2) The falls are located about halfway along the northward course of the niagara river. (3) Carrying the overflow of four of the five great lakes, the river plunges over a precipice between lake erie and lake ontario into the gorge on either side of goat island. (4) To the east of the small island is the nearly straight line of the american falls. (5) To the south and west, on the river's canadian side, is the graceful curve of horseshoe falls. (6) the horseshoe falls, named for their shape, are also called canadian falls as a result of their location. (7) From rainbow bridge, which is just below the falls, one can observe arcs of color forming on the clouds of spray. (8) The most unusual view, however, is from a boat, the *maid of the mist*. (9) The boat is named in honor of the legendary indian girl whose canoe tumbled over niagara. (10) Her ghostly image is said to appear occasionally in the foaming mist.

ORGANIZATIONS, EVENTS, AND OTHER SUBJECTS

Several other commonly used words and phrases are capitalized. These are grouped into six major categories.

Organizations and Institutions

Capitalize the names of organizations and institutions.

Capitalize all words except prepositions and conjunctions in the names of organizations and institutions. Also capitalize abbreviations of these names.

Democratic **P**arty	**C**entral **I**ntelligence **A**gency **(CIA)**
Sullivan **H**igh **S**chool	**S**ecurities and **E**xchange **C**ommission
Lee **G**lass **C**ompany, **I**nc.	**H**ouse of **R**epresentatives
First **M**ethodist **C**hurch	**T**rans **W**orld **A**irlines **(TWA)**

Do not capitalize words such as *school, company, church, college,* and *hospital* when they are not used as parts of names.

Amnesty International poster

Events, Documents, and Periods of Time

Capitalize the names of historical events, documents, and periods of time.

World **W**ar II	the **H**omestead **A**ct
Bill of **R**ights	the **D**ark **A**ges
the **R**enaissance	the **B**attle of **B**unker **H**ill

Months, Days, and Holidays

Capitalize the names of months, days, and holidays but not the names of seasons.

June   **T**uesday   **M**emorial **D**ay   **w**inter

Time Abbreviations

Capitalize the abbreviations B.C., A.D., A.M., and P.M.

Augustus ruled from 27 B.C. to A.D. 14.
The meeting begins at 9:30 A.M. and ends at 3:00 P.M.

Writing
—TIP—

The abbreviation B.C. always comes after the date; A.D. comes before it.

Awards, Special Events, and Brand Names

Capitalize the names of awards and special events.

Nobel **P**rize   **S**uper **B**owl   **E**mmy **A**ward

Capitalize the brand names of products but not a common noun that follows a brand name.

Springtime air freshener   **G**olden **G**rain cereal

School Subjects and Class Names

Do not capitalize the general names of school subjects. Do capitalize the titles of specific courses and of courses that are followed by a number. School subjects that are languages are always capitalized.

biology	**G**erman
Home **E**conomics 200	**I**ntroduction to **P**sychology

Capitalize class names only when they refer to a specific group or event or when they are used in direct address.

The juniors are selling tickets for the **J**unior **P**rom.
Every spring the **F**reshman **C**lass holds a carnival.
Good luck, **S**eniors, as you graduate and begin new lives.

Practice Your Skills

A. CONCEPT CHECK

Capitalization Errors Write the following sentences, using capital letters where necessary and correcting improperly capitalized words. Refer to all the capitalization rules covered so far in this handbook.

Writing Theme
Immigration

1. In 1776 most americans were of dutch, french, swedish, scotch-irish, and english descent.
2. Citizens of the young Nation generally spoke english, worshiped as protestants, and shared a northern European heritage.
3. In the 1840's roman catholic irish immigrants crossed the atlantic to flee from Famine and harsh british laws.
4. Eastern europeans also hoped to find a new homeland in america.
5. The armenians sought refuge from turkish oppression, while Italians and greeks hoped to overcome poverty.
6. Many polish people wished to escape Foreign rule in their divided country, and jews fled from russian persecution.
7. The Chinese arrived during the 1860's and 1870's to work on construction of the central pacific railroad.
8. While the united states economy was strong, the volume of immigration was very high.
9. Toward the end of the Century, however, the chinese and other newcomers who accepted lower wages were blamed for declining economic conditions.
10. The workingman's party in california urged the Government to pass laws discriminating against specific immigrant groups.
11. The sidewalk ordinance was one such law; it prohibited people who carried merchandise on poles from using sidewalks.
12. The United States congress restricted immigration from certain countries by creating laws such as the chinese exclusion act of 1882.
13. The national origins act of 1924 set specific quotas or restrictions on the number of immigrants allowed from specific countries.
14. Many social reformers, however, tried to help Immigrants.
15. Jane Addams founded hull house, where newcomers could learn english and prepare for american Citizenship.
16. Industrialists such as carnegie steel company's Andrew Carnegie and standard oil company's John d. Rockefeller helped immigrants by funding Public Education Institutions.
17. In spite of the hardships, most immigrants improved their lives and made important Contributions to our diverse american culture.
18. The immigration act of 1965 changed the quotas that discriminated against people from asia.

B. PROOFREADING SKILL

Capitalization Proofread the following paragraph, correcting any errors in punctuation, spelling, and capitalization.

Mr. Schimezi who teaches in the social studies department at eastman high school teaches a course called contemporary social problems. One subject that we discused last Winter was immigration. Mr. Schimezi explained that immigration to the united states is regulated by the imigration and naturalization service (the ins). The responsibility of the ins is to administer laws related to immigration, such as the immigration reform and control act of 1986. Since my parents are both immigrants from guatemala, I decided to write a report on the subject of immigration. In my report, I traced the history of immigration from the period before the revolutionary war to the present day. In the past, few years about half of the immigrants to the united states have come from asian countries, where as 25 percent have come from spanish-speaking countrys. Imigrants have made enormous contributions to american culture. During the spring term, after easter break and just before the senior prom, I got some great news. My report had won the eastman high school excellence in academics award!

The Many Faces of Liberty, detail of quilt by Julia K. Swan

CHECK POINT
PAGES 762–772

A. Rewrite the sentences, adding capital letters where necessary.

1. Many Americans and foreign visitors consider San francisco one of the most beautiful cities in the western hemisphere.
2. San Francisco bay lies east of a peninsula; to the west is the Pacific ocean.

3. Last july aunt Teresa showed us some famous landmarks in the city, including the Golden Gate bridge and chinatown.
4. The Golden gate, a magnificent suspension bridge, links Golden Gate park to the southern tip of Marin county.
5. San Francisco's chinatown, which lies east of Nob hill, is home to the largest chinese community outside asia.
6. Fisherman's wharf, at the northern end of a street called the embarcadero, is known for its many seafood restaurants.
7. Not far from the wharf is ghirardelli square, a shopping complex that was once a chocolate factory.
8. San francisco is famous for steep streets; among the steepest are those on the slopes of Russian hill and telegraph hill.
9. The hills look down on the wharf and on Montgomery street, nicknamed the Wall street of the west and the site of the city's most striking building, the transamerica pyramid.
10. Just south of the financial district is the Presidio, which was originally a spanish army post and is now the headquarters of the U.S. sixth army.
11. My cousin Joe, a member of the freshman class at the university of California at berkeley, told us that in 1906 San Francisco suffered one of the worst disasters in american history.
12. Proud San franciscans quickly rebuilt the city; in 1915 they held the Panama-Pacific international exhibition to honor the opening of the panama canal.

B. APPLICATION IN LITERATURE

Identifying Capitalization Errors In the following paragraph, some capital letters have been changed to lower-case letters, and some lower-case letters have been capitalized. Return the paragraph to its original, correct form by rewriting it and correcting all capitalization errors.

> (1) San Francisco put on a show for me. (2) i saw her . . . from the great road that bypasses sausalito and enters the golden gate bridge. (3) The afternoon Sun painted her white and gold—rising on her hills like a Noble City in a happy dream. (4) A city on hills has it over flatland places. (5) New york makes its own Hills with craning buildings, but this gold and white acropolis [citadel] rising wave on wave against the blue of the pacific sky was a stunning thing, a painted thing like a picture of a medieval italian city which can never have existed.

John Steinbeck, *Travels with Charley*

The first words of a sentence, a quotation, and a line of poetry are capitalized.

Sentences and Poetry

Capitalize the first word of every sentence.

The coach gave his players a pep talk.

Capitalize the first word of every line of poetry.

Whenever Richard Cory went down town,
We people on the pavement looked at him:
He was a gentleman from sole to crown,
Clean favored, and imperially slim.
        Edward Arlington Robinson, "Richard Cory"

Usage Note   Sometimes, especially in modern poetry, the lines of a poem do not begin with capital letters.

Quotations

Capitalize the first word of a direct quotation.

Patrick Henry exclaimed, "**G**ive me liberty or give me death!"

In a **divided quotation,** do not capitalize the first word of the second part unless it starts a new sentence.

"It's true," said Renée, "that appearances can be deceiving."
"It's true," said Renée. "**A**ppearances can be deceiving."

Letter Parts

Capitalize the first word in the greeting of a letter. Also capitalize the title, person's name, and words such as *Sir* and *Madam.*

Dear **M**s. Lopez,   **D**ear **S**ir or **M**adam:

Capitalize only the first word in the complimentary close.

Sincerely yours,   **V**ery truly yours,

Outlines and Titles

Capitalize the first word of each item in an outline and letters that introduce major subsections.

I. **E**ntertainers
    A. Musicians
        1. **V**ocal
        2. **I**nstrumental

Capitalize the first, last, and all other important words in titles. Do not capitalize conjunctions, articles, or prepositions with fewer than five letters.

Book	*To Kill a Mockingbird*
Newspaper	*Miami Herald*
Magazine	*Interview*
Play	*Much Ado About Nothing*
Television Series	*The Oprah Winfrey Show*
Work of Art	*The Last Supper*
Long Musical Work	*The Marriage of Figaro*
Short Story	"**The P**it and the **P**endulum"
Song	"**W**e **A**re the **W**orld"
Chapter	**C**hapter 11, "**The R**ise of **I**slam"

The word *the* at the beginning of a title and the word *magazine* are capitalized only when they are part of the formal name.

The New York Times	the *Springfield Courier*
Audubon Magazine	*Time magazine*

Punctuation Note Titles are either underlined or put in quotation marks. See page 829 for punctuation rules.

Practice Your Skills

A. CONCEPT CHECK

Capitalization Errors In the following literary passage, some capital letters have been changed to lower-case letters, and some lower-case letters have been capitalized. Return the passage to its original, correct form by rewriting it and correcting all errors in capitalization.

> (1) I've read that Navajo, a language related to that of the indians of alaska and northwest canada, has no curse words unless you consider "coyote" cursing. (2) by comparison with other native tongues, it's remarkably free of english and spanish. (3) a navajo Mechanic, for example, has more than two hundred purely navajo terms to describe automobile parts. (4) It might be navajo that will greet the first Extraterrestrial ears to hear from planet earth. (5) On board each *voyager*

Spacecraft traveling toward the edge of the solar system and beyond is a gold-plated, long-playing record. (6) Following an aria from mozart's *magic flute* and chuck berry's "johnny b. goode," is a navajo night Chant, music the conquistadors heard.

William Least Heat Moon, *Blue Highways*

Summer Storm,
by R.C. Gorman
(Navajo Gallery)

B. PROOFREADING SKILL

Capitalization Errors   Proofread and correct all errors in the following letter from an editor at a publishing house to the compiler of a collection of Native American poetry.

dear Ms. Silverfoot:
    thank you very much for your letter of august 20, which i received on monday. I have red through the Selections of Native American poetry that you enclosed. one of my editors echoed my opinion when he said, "they are magnificent literary peaces." i think they are thoroughly apropriate for inclusion in Chapter 2 of *Buffalo grandmother: An Anthology of native american verse.* here are some coments for your consideration.
    I especially like your Choice of the chippewa love song that starts with the line, "a loon i thought it was." can you find another magic formula from the iroquois, one similar to "you

have no right to trouble Me"? i would like to print too examples of short poems of this Kind. by the way, are you familiar with N. Scott momaday's essay titled "The native Voice"? Momaday's piece appears in the *columbia literary history of the united states*. momaday draws attention there to the remarkable story of an Arrowmaker that is told among the members of the kiowa nation. Do You think its possible that we could find a poetic version of this story? In addition please see Momaday's survey for interesting ideas on the work of modern native American poets, for example, simon ortiz and joy harjo.

Sincerely Yours,

Peter Stansbury

C. APPLICATION IN WRITING

Poetry Do some brief research on an interesting aspect of Native American culture and write a short poem about it. Consider that Native American poetry often reflects the importance of and close relation with nature that native cultures value. In some poems, for example, the poet takes on the voice of some creature of nature. You may want to imagine that you are a plant or an animal and, in your poem, speak as that being. Before writing, think about how your chosen object would perceive things.

CHECK POINT
PAGES 774–777

A. Rewrite the following sentences, correcting all capitalization errors.

1. One of the most amusing and suspenseful travel movies ever made is *Around the world In eighty days*.

2. This film, which won the academy award for best picture in 1956, was based on a novel by the french writer Jules verne.

3. Verne's Novel told the adventures of an englishman, Phileas Fogg, who bet the other members of his Club in london that he could circle the globe in Eighty days.

4. In the late Nineteenth Century, most people would have said to fogg, "such a feat is impossible."

5. some of the most exciting scenes in the movie show fogg, who is played by david niven, traveling across America from san francisco to New York.

Writing
——**TIP**——
Native American poetry often does not rhyme. Your poem need not rhyme, but you should use capital letters where necessary.

Writing Theme
Film Entertainment

Walt Disney,
creator of *Fantasia*

B. Rewrite the following
passage, using capital letters where necessary.

(1) born into a midwestern household on december 5,
1901, walter elias disney became one of the best-known creative geniuses of the twentieth century. (2) disney developed
interest in drawing while living on his family's Missouri Farm.
(3) Later he received a smattering of formal art education at
the kansas city art institute. (4) a job at kansas city film ad
company gave disney the experience he needed to open his own
animation company. (5) his animated versions of fairy tales such
as "puss in boots" began a long and successful film career.

(6) four days before christmas in 1937, *snow white and
the seven dwarfs* premiered in hollywood. (7) it was the first
feature-length animated film. (8) during the next three
decades, mr. disney entertained america with hundreds of cartoons and films—from *song of the south* and *alice in wonderland* to *the sword in the stone* and *mary poppins*.

(9) in addition to creating film entertainment, disney
dreamed of an amusement park for people of all ages. (10) this
dream became a reality when disneyland opened on july 17,
1955, in anaheim, california.

GRAMMAR
H A N D B O O K
38

A. Using Capital Letters Correctly   Write the following sentences, capitalizing words as necessary.

1. the date of the first olympic games in greece is uncertain.
2. i was told in a course i took, history of ancient greece, that the olympics began in 776 b.c.
3. the games were held in midsummer every four years; incidentally, the summer season in the part of the northern hemisphere where greece is located occurs at the same time summer occurs in north america.
4. on a modern calendar, the date of the olympics would fall in late july or early august.
5. the period between games was called an olympiad.
6. Although earlier greek calendars were based on nature's timekeepers, the sun and the moon, after about 300 b.c., olympiads became basic units of measuring time.
7. Clearly, the greeks considered the olympics to be more important than other athletic contests at delphi or corinth.
8. in the fifth century b.c., the lyric poet pindar wrote victory odes honoring successful athletes.
9. according to pindar's *odes,* the founder of the games at olympia was the hero heracles.
10. this hero's name is better known in its roman form, hercules.
11. pindar reports that heracles held the first games to celebrate his victory over king augeas.
12. one of the twelve labors of heracles was cleaning the enormous stables where this king kept his horses.
13. the site the hero chose for the games was olympia, a small village in the northwestern peloponnesus peninsula.
14. according to the writer pausanias, however, olympia was chosen because zeus, king of the gods in greek myth, struggled with his father cronus for supreme power there.
15. in any case, a stadium and a temple to zeus were built at olympia on the banks of two rivers, the alpheus and cladeus.
16. at first, the only event in the olympic games was a two-hundred-yard footrace.
17. according to pausanias, "a crown of wild olive was given to the victor at olympia."
18. in the sixth and fifth centuries b.c., such events as boxing and chariot racing were introduced.
19. in athens, olympic victors were honored by the senate in the prytaneum, a building used by distinguished persons.
20. oddly, the marathon was not a part of the early olympic games held in the ancient mediterranean land of greece.

Writing Theme
The Olympics

Capitalization   **779**

B. Capitalizing Correctly Correctly write any words in the following paragraphs that are capitalized incorrectly. Place corrected words after the number of the sentence in which they appear.

(1) "a marathon," Says *webster's new world dictionary,* "Is any long-distance or endurance contest." (2) most runners know the story behind the word *marathon*—the legend of a fierce Battle on the plains near the greek town of marathon in 490 b.c. (3) the athenians caught the invading persian army by surprise, charged the enemy, and saved the greek empire. (4) a greek soldier, pheidippides, was ordered to run from the Battlefield to athens, a distance of twenty-two miles, with news of victory. (5) although pheidippides had no training in running, he managed to reach athens, exclaiming, "rejoice, we conquer!" (6) poor pheidippides promptly collapsed and died, but his name is remembered because his run is considered the first "marathon."

The marathon became an official event in the modern olympic games in 1896. (7) the present standardized marathon distance of 42,195 meters was actually determined by an english princess in london. (8) a marathon was set up to begin at windsor castle and end at white city stadium. (9) her royal highness wished to view the start of the race from her castle window and then see the finish from her stadium seat—a twenty-six-mile span. this distance has remained the same for every olympic marathon since that Summer day in 1908.

(10) the first marathon in the united states was run in new york city, but the best-known american marathon is held each year in boston. (11) thousands of runners have tested their endurance in this famous eastern race, but you might ask, "why would people subject themselves to such a grueling challenge?" (12) to answer this question, consider the case of carl eilenberg, who was ready to quit the 1975 boston marathon when he was halfway up heartbreak hill. (13) a former star runner from syracuse university, tom coulter, ran alongside, and gave carl some memorable words of encouragement. (14) "once you cross the finish line at boston," tom said, "there's nothing you can't do." (15) these words gave carl the strength to continue running and ultimately to finish the race.

On the Lightside

OUT IN LEFT FIELD

"It's Greek to me." "Beat it!" "Not so hot." "Right on." Surprisingly, all of these slang expressions originated with Shakespeare. Slang comes from many less literary sources as well, including sports, jazz and rock music, crime, technology, and foreign languages. Since 1960, more than 22,000 examples have been collected in the periodically updated *Dictionary of American Slang*. This dictionary defines its turf as words and expressions that are used and understood by the majority of the American public but that are not accepted as good, formal usage.

Probably no other area has contributed as much slang to the English language as baseball. Even people who have never rooted for their home team know and use such expressions as "You're

way off base" and "I liked him right off the bat."

Some slang expressions have originated with specific groups, who use the slang to exclude outsiders from their conversations. Several common slang terms have come from the criminal community. Examples include *kidnap,* a combination of "kid" (a small goat) and "napper" (thief); *cop,* from *constable on patrol";* and *hijack,* from the highway robber's demand to a stagecoach driver: "Hands up high, Jack!"

Most slang quickly becomes outdated, although some can remain in the language for centuries without being accepted into standard English. When slang words do become part of the language, it's often hard to remember that their origins may be "out in left field."

End Marks and Commas

END MARKS

End marks are the punctuation marks that indicate the end of a unit of thought. The three kinds of end marks are the period, the question mark, and the exclamation point. The proper use of each end mark is described on the following pages.

The Period

Use a period at the end of all declarative sentences and most imperative sentences.

> More people speak Mandarin Chinese than any other language in the world.
> Please lock the door when you leave.

When an imperative sentence expresses strong emotion or excitement, an exclamation point, rather than a period, is used to end the sentence.

> Watch out!   Let's hurry!

Use a period at the end of an indirect question.

An **indirect question** indicates that someone has asked a question, but it does not give the reader the exact words of the question. (See page 783 for punctuation of direct questions.)

> Jeremy asked whether Amelia Earhart's airplane had ever been located.

Use a period at the end of an abbreviation or an initial.

Sen. Eileen Gramm	Inc.	6:00 A.M. on Oct. 1
Gov. Martha L. Collins	Tues.	3 ft. 2 in.
Mr. John Williams, Jr.	Jan.	2 hr. 35 min.

For abbreviations of metric measurements, acronyms, and abbreviations that are pronounced letter by letter, periods are optional. Use your dictionary to determine whether periods are required in a specific case.

cm	ml	kg	NATO	HUD	IRS	CIA
km	g	L	NASA	UFO	PBS	FBI

Postal abbreviations of state names do not require a period: NY, CA, IL.

Use a period after each number or letter in an outline or a list.

Outline	List
I. Television programs	1. paintbrush
A. Daytime	2. canvas
1. Soap operas	3. watercolors
2. Game shows	
B. Evening	

Use a period between dollars and cents and to indicate a decimal.

$8.57   365.36

The Question Mark

Use a question mark at the end of an interrogative sentence or after a question that is not a complete sentence.

How many days does it take for Mars to orbit the sun?
Your cassettes? I think you left them in the den.
The date? It's the twenty-fifth.

Occasionally, writers may use a question mark to indicate that a declarative sentence is intended to be expressed as a question. In these cases the question mark is a signal to read the sentence with rising inflection.

Declarative	Interrogative
You've finished your work.	You've finished your work?
These are yours.	These are yours?

The Exclamation Point

Use an exclamation point at the end of an exclamatory sentence or after a strong interjection.

An **interjection** consists of one or more words that show feeling or imitate a sound.

What a great game!   That's unbelievable!
Oh, no!   Crash!   Fantastic!   Yes!   Zoom!

When an interjection is followed by a sentence, the sentence may end with a period, a question mark, or an exclamation point.

Wait! I almost forgot my keys.
Wonderful! Will you play that song again?
Look! There's a truck heading toward us!

Practice Your Skills

A. CONCEPT CHECK

End Marks Rewrite the following items, adding periods and other end marks as necessary. If you are unsure about punctuating abbreviations, consult a dictionary.

1. You are in NASA headquarters during a long, slow evening
2. It is Tues, Oct 24, 1995, at 2:30 AM
3. USAF operator Thomas P Allen, Jr, asks you if you can identify the strange objects on his screen
4. Look at those fantastic patterns What do you think they are
5. Quickly, you begin sketching out the alternatives:
   I Unidentified Flying Objects
     A Military or Civilian Aircraft
     B Natural Phenomena
       1 Swamp Gas
       2 Birds
     C Flying Saucers
6. Then, before you can make a decision, the objects disappear, 375 seconds (exactly three and three-quarter seconds, on the timer) after they first appeared on the screen
7. How could anything appear and then disappear that fast
8. Wow Did you see that bizarre action
9. You and Mr Allen stare at the screen as he asks you if what you saw was swamp gas
10. Questions go through your mind Was it swamp gas Was it a flock of birds It must have been one of those; however, in the back of your mind, you wonder

B. PROOFREADING SKILL

Correcting Punctuation Errors Rewrite the following draft of a story, correcting errors in punctuation, capitalization, and spelling.

> At 10:42 AM Robt R Fox, Jr, began to panic He had been running from the aliens for over 2 hrs and still had 3 km to go to reach the Courthouse He wondered weather he had the energy to cover the remaining 2 mi of dark, deserted streets Would he make it Buildings seemed to float past him as he continued down ash St—F W Woolworth's and Bidwell's, Inc Throat parched and head pounding, he spotted the Police Dept lights about 25 yds away Straining, urging his exausted limbs forward, he felt a strange force envelope him For some reason, his voice wouldn't function, but cries swam in his head Someone help me

C. APPLICATION IN WRITING

A Script   Choose your own topic or use one of those listed below and write a script for an exciting scene in a TV episode or a film. In your script, use a variety of sentence types—declarative, exclamatory, imperative, and interrogative.

Story Ideas:

A difficult or dangerous challenge met and overcome
An incident that causes someone to see through prejudice
An incident that causes two estranged people to feel a common
 bond
An invention that turns against its creator

COMMAS: SERIES, INTRODUCTORY
ELEMENTS, AND INTERRUPTERS

Commas can help you express your ideas by slowing down the rhythm of a sentence, showing a shift in thought, or adding clarity. The following rules explain the proper uses of the comma.

Commas in a Series

Use a comma after every item in a series except the last one.

A series consists of three or more items of the same kind.

Words	Benjamin Franklin was a politician, a writer, a scientist, and an inventor.
Phrases	Groups of children played behind the house, on the porch, and in the yard.
Clauses	The paleontologist explained where the dinosaurs lived, what they ate, and how they protected themselves.

Do not use a comma if all parts of the series are joined by the words *and, or,* or *nor.*

All summer we swam and fished and sailed.

Use commas after *first, second,* and so on, when they introduce a series. (Note also the use of semicolons [;] below. For more information on semicolons refer to pages 804–806.)

Our bus stopped at three streets: first, Clark Street; second, Johnson Avenue; and third, Main Street.

Use commas between coordinate adjectives that modify the same noun.

Raging, howling winds whipped the coastline.

To determine whether adjectives are **coordinate**—that is, of equal rank—try placing an *and* between them. If the *and* sounds natural, and if you can reverse the order of the adjectives without changing the meaning, then a comma is needed.

His loud (*and*) whining voice made the audience shudder. (The *and* sounds natural, and the meaning is not changed by reversing the order of the adjectives. Therefore, a comma is needed.)
His loud, whining voice made the audience shudder.

Maria is an experienced (*and*) subway rider. (The *and* sounds awkward, and the adjectives cannot be reversed. No comma is necessary.)
Maria is an experienced subway rider.

In general, it is safe to omit the comma after numbers and adjectives of size, shape, and age.

a big round moon   five tiny wafers

Practice Your Skills

A. CONCEPT CHECK

Commas   Some commas have been omitted from the following literary quotations. Write the word before each missing comma and place the commas correctly.

1. He straightened his shoulders flipped the reins against the horse's shoulder and rode away.   **John Steinbeck**
2. The brother came with his plump healthy wife and two great roaring hungry boys.   **Katherine Anne Porter**
3. Mrs. Proudhammer knew very well what people thought of Mr. Proudhammer. She knew, too, exactly how much she owed in each store she entered how much she was going to be able to pay and what she had to buy.   **James Baldwin**
4. It was true we were at war, observing heatless meatless and wheatless days and conserving sugar.   **Sterling North**
5. Someday Sam, although he knew it so little then, was going to make books, great books, out of all that he was seeing then: the water dappled with silver the bending willows and the great sliding river.   **Mark Twain**

6. [Frederick] Douglass was then twenty-four years old six feet tall with hair like a lion and very handsome. **Langston Hughes**
7. The shaggy little creatures kicked bucked sprang into the air ran through our legs and even hurtled straight up the walls.

James Herriot
8. Hours of wintertime had found me in the treehouse, looking over the schoolyard spying on multitudes of children through a two-power telescope Jem had given me learning their games following Jem's red jacket through wriggling circles of blind man's bluff secretly sharing their misfortunes and minor victories. **Harper Lee**
9. Tarzan ran his brown fingers through his thick black hair cocked his head upon one side and stared. **Edgar Rice Burroughs**
10. She was a lofty dignified conventional lady; and she smelled like an old dictionary among whose pages many flowers have been dried and pressed. **Elizabeth Enright**

B. PROOFREADING SKILL

Using Commas Correctly   Rewrite the following paragraph, correcting all errors in usage, spelling, capitalization, and punctuation. Pay special attention to the use of commas.

Jade Snow Wong has distinguished herself as an author an acomplished artist and an astute busineswoman. She grew up in the bustling colorful section of San francisco known as chinatown. As a girl, she had to learn American custums while her parents followed the more conservative traditional Chinese way of life. In *No Chinese Stranger* she relates the hardship's she faced. In becoming a master potter. The struggles were numerous: first the Chinese veiw that making pottery was unladylike; second the difficulties of mastering the art itself; and third the financial worrys. Discipline produced beautiful . . . pottery aclaimed books and economic independance.

C. APPLICATION IN WRITING

Promotional Copy When an author's book is published, the publisher produces promotional copy for displays, ads, and the book jacket. This information includes any accomplishments or unique characteristics of the writer and lists any previous works. Choose a favorite author or create your own and write brief promotional copy for a recent book. Use commas correctly in your work.

Commas with Introductory Elements

Use a comma after introductory words, mild interjections, or adverbs at the beginning of a sentence.

> Well, I think I can manage the job by myself.
> Yes, I would like some watermelon.
> However, the storm raged for two more days.
> Nonetheless, I expect you and Miguel to be ready for next Saturday's car wash.

Use a comma after a series of prepositional phrases at the beginning of a sentence.

> Before gaining independence in 1960, Nigeria was a colony of Great Britain.
> On the advice of her counselor, Carmen applied for the scholarship.

A single prepositional phrase that begins a sentence may be set off by a comma if it is followed by a natural pause when read.

> After circling the field twice, the plane landed.

A comma is not necessary when there would be almost no pause in speaking, or if the phrase is very short.

> By tomorrow I'll be rested.

Use a comma after verbal phrases at the beginning of a sentence.

> Hoping for victory, the exhausted players pressed on.
> To enhance your appearance, wear colors that complement your complexion.

Use a comma after adverbial clauses at the beginning of a sentence.

> When the concert ended, the audience applauded wildly.

(For more information on verbals and adverbial clauses, see Handbook 32, pages 592–593 and pages 612–613.)

Use a comma after words or phrases that have been transposed, that is, moved to the beginning of a sentence from their normal position.

> Call Serena for directions if necessary. (normal order)
> If necessary, call Serena for directions. (transposed order)

> The birthday card is obviously going to be late. (normal order)
> Obviously, the birthday card is going to be late. (transposed order)

Commas with Interrupters

Use commas to set off nonessential appositives.

Nonessential appositives are words or phrases that add extra information to an already clear and complete sentence.

> The World Series, baseball's toughest competition, is held annually in the fall.
> *Growing Up*, a touching and humorous autobiography, was written by Russell Baker.

Essential appositives, however, are needed to make the sentence clear and complete. Do not use commas with essential appositives.

> The movie *The Color Purple* is based on a novel by Alice Walker.
> The Spanish monk Torquemada was responsible for the infamous Spanish Inquisition.

For further information about appositives, see Handbook 32, pages 589–590.

Use commas to set off words of direct address.

> Erika, please pass the pasta.
> I understand, Ms. Ames, that your hobby is woodworking.
> You've just won the drawing, Mario!

Use commas to set off parenthetical expressions.

Parenthetical expressions are words and phrases used to explain or qualify a statement. Since they interrupt the flow of thought in a sentence, they are set off by commas.

> Our car, I believe, is over there.
> You know, of course, that Yukio is from Japan.
> The Sugar Loaf Mountains, in fact, are located on a peninsula; they rise to a height of 1,325 feet.

The following expressions are often used parenthetically:

of course   consequently   for example
in fact   I believe   on the other hand
by the way   after all   nevertheless
however   moreover   therefore

Conjunctive adverbs such as *nevertheless, therefore,* and *consequently* may be used parenthetically. Since they interrupt the flow of a sentence, they are set off by commas.

> The explorer, nevertheless, completed his hike across the tundra.
> The artist, therefore, has little need for a home computer.
> The rally, consequently, was attended by very few.

Occasionally, words like *however, therefore,* and *consequently* are used to modify a word in a sentence. As modifiers they are essential parts of the sentence and need no commas.

> Pat cannot arrive on time however hard she tries.
> The cast had performed the play the previous semester. They therefore needed little rehearsal.
> Evening rehearsals were consequently eliminated.

For more information on conjunctive adverbs, see Handbook 30, page 556.

Practice Your Skills

A. CONCEPT CHECK

Commas   Rewrite the following sentences, placing commas where necessary.

1. To help visitors become acquainted with the new ostrich exhibit the zoo has printed a special pamphlet.
2. At scheduled times throughout the day guides provide supplementary information.
3. For example ostriches the world's largest living birds are nearly eight feet tall.
4. Before the New Zealand moas died out they were the only birds taller than ostriches.
5. The extinct elephant birds I believe were the only birds heavier than ostriches.
6. By the time an ostrich is mature it can weigh as much as 350 pounds.
7. "Well with such weight how do they fly?" visitors often ask.
8. The answer ladies and gentlemen is that in fact they do not fly.

9. If necessary an ostrich can move very fast on land.
10. Over open ground in Africa ostriches have been clocked at nearly forty miles an hour.
11. Moreover when an ostrich is only a month old it can run as fast as an adult bird.
12. Natural predators mainly lions are no match for such speed.
13. When cornered furthermore an ostrich can deliver a nasty kick.
14. To escape detection both chicks and adults lie with their necks outstretched on the ground.
15. This behavior no doubt gave rise to the legend that ostriches bury their heads in the sand.

B. PROOFREADING SKILL

Using Commas Correctly   Proofread the following paragraph for errors in usage, punctuation, spelling, and mechanics. Pay particular attention to comma errors.

Truly the swift is one of the fastest bird's in the sky. Too visulaize a swift in flight. Imagine a bulet with hinged wings. On the bodies of most birds an outstretched wing has one viseble joint. On a Swift the joint is so close to the body. It is barely noticable. A swift consequently gives the appearence of a narrow curved sword. Louis j Halle the noted naturalist writes that swifts spend most of their lives in the air. Clearly disadvantaged a grounded swift cannot fold it's wings into it's body. Halle notes in fact that a grounded Swift is as helples as a fish out of water.

Use commas to set off the explanatory words of a direct quotation.

Explanatory words are statements that identify the speaker but are not part of the quotation. Use a comma after explanatory words when they precede the quotation.

> The traffic officer said, "Drive east until you reach the first stoplight."

When the explanatory words follow the quotation, a comma belongs at the end of the quotation inside the quotation marks.

> "Drive east until you reach the first stoplight, " the traffic officer said.

In a divided quotation, use a comma within the quotation marks after the first part of the quotation and after the explanatory words.

> "Drive east, " the traffic officer said, "until you reach the first stoplight."

Indirect quotations require no commas.

> The traffic officer said to drive east until you reach the first stoplight.

Commas in Compound Sentences

Use a comma before the conjunction that joins the two main clauses of a compound sentence.

> Guillermo enjoys poetry, but Justine prefers novels.

A comma is not necessary when the main clauses are very short and are joined by the conjunctions *and, but, so, or,* or *nor.*

> Clouds gathered and a storm developed.

A comma does separate clauses joined by *yet* or *for.*

> You said you'd help, yet I finished the project myself.

There is no comma between the parts of a compound predicate.

> Eighty percent of Japan is covered with mountains and cannot be used for agriculture.

Practice Your Skills

A. CONCEPT CHECK

Comma Usage Commas have been left out of the following sentences. Write the word that comes before the missing comma, and place the comma correctly. Some sentences may need more than one comma. If no commas are needed in a sentence, write *Correct*.

1. A noted herpetologist spoke recently at the natural history museum, and he shared his knowledge with the audience.
2. "Four of the world's snake families have venomous members" Dr. Daniel explained.
3. "Our North American rattlesnakes and moccasins" he said "belong to the viper family."
4. Dr. Daniel added "They are pit vipers and those are far more common in America than any other venomous snakes."
5. One member of the audience inquired "Are cobras found only in India or is this snake family found all over the world?"
6. "The family to which cobras belong occurs in every continent except Europe" Dr. Daniel replied.
7. "Other poisonous members of this family" he added "include the African black mamba and the colorful American coral snake."
8. "Most cobras will not attack humans yet these snakes can be extremely dangerous if they feel threatened."
9. Dr. Daniel continued, "The king cobra is probably the most feared snake on earth."
10. He chuckled "The king cobra's large size and hooded threat display may seem frightening but it is actually less aggressive than many other, smaller snakes."

B. REVISION SKILL

Errors in Comma Usage Rewrite the following literary excerpt, adding the fifteen missing commas. You will use several of the comma rules you have learned so far in this lesson. Notice how the use of commas adds clarity and organization to writing.

(1) The doctor said "I was not in when you came this morning. (2) But now at the first chance I have come to see the baby."

(3) Kino stood in the door filling it and hatred raged and flamed in back of his eyes. . . .

(4) "The baby is nearly well now" he said curtly.

(5) The doctor smiled but his eyes in their little lymph-lined hammocks did not smile.

(6) He said "Sometimes my friend the scorpion sting has a curious effect. (7) There will be apparent improvement, and then without warning—pouf!". . . (8) "Sometimes" the doctor went on in a liquid tone "sometimes there will be a withered leg or a blind eye or a crumpled back. (9) Oh I know the sting of the scorpion my friend and I can cure it."

John Steinbeck, *The Pearl*

C. APPLICATION IN WRITING

A Dialogue By personifying the main characters, a mongoose and a cobra, Rudyard Kipling's story "Rikki-Tikki-Tavi" gives readers the unique opportunity to share the thoughts of both these foes. Continue the following conversation between the mongoose, Rikki, and the snake, Nag.

"Who is Nag?" said he. "*I* am Nag. The great God Brahm put his mark upon all our people, when the first cobra spread his hood to keep the sun off Brahm as he slept. Look, and be afraid!". . .

"Well," said Rikki-tikki, and his tail began to fluff up again, "marks or no marks, do you think it is right for you to eat fledglings out of a nest?"

"Let us talk," Nag said. "You eat cobra eggs. Why should I not eat birds?"

Commas with Nonessential Clauses and Phrases

Use commas to set off nonessential clauses.

A **nonessential clause** merely adds extra information to an already complete sentence. An **essential clause** is necessary to complete the meaning of the sentence; if it is dropped, the meaning is unclear. No commas are used with essential clauses.

Nonessential Clause	The Mississippi River, *which empties into the Gulf of Mexico,* is the setting of the musical *Showboat.* (Clause can be dropped.)
Essential Clause	The river *that empties into the Gulf of Mexico* is the Mississippi. (Clause cannot be dropped.)

Notice that *which* is used to introduce nonessential clauses, and *that* is used to introduce essential clauses.

Use commas to set off nonessential participial phrases.

A nonessential participial phrase can be dropped without making the meaning of the sentence unclear or incomplete.

An essential participial phrase is necessary to the meaning of the sentence. No commas are used with essential participial phrases.

Nonessential Participial Phrase	The woman**,** *driving a Ford sedan,* headed down Fir Street at 25 mph. (Dropping the phrase does not change the meaning of the sentence.)
Essential Participial Phrase	The woman *driving a Ford sedan* is my mother. (The phrase identifies a specific woman, so it cannot be dropped without changing the meaning of the sentence.)

Practice Your Skills

A. CONCEPT CHECK

Commas   Rewrite the following sentences, adding the necessary commas. If no commas are needed, write *Correct.*

1. Musical comedies which developed in America in the late nineteenth century remain a popular form of entertainment today.
2. The musicals that have proved most popular are lighthearted and humorous.
3. Many of the best-known songs that people count among their favorites are tunes originating in musicals.
4. The most successful team creating musical comedy during the 1940's and 1950's was Rodgers and Hammerstein.
5. Richard Rodgers's music which was widely admired for its tuneful melodies was ingeniously integrated with Oscar Hammerstein's lyrics.
6. Their early hits which included *Oklahoma!, Carousel,* and *South Pacific* brought Rodgers and Hammerstein unparalleled fame.
7. *South Pacific* was based on two stories that James Michener reported in his *Tales of the South Pacific* a Pulitzer Prize-winning book.
8. Rodgers composing what many critics thought was his best score wrote such songs as "Some Enchanted Evening" and "Younger than Springtime" for this musical.
9. The dancing that the choreographers included added considerably to the show's appeal.
10. Brooks Atkinson writing in *The New York Times* praised *South Pacific* in a rave review.

B. PROOFREADING SKILL

Correcting Comma Errors   Rewrite the passage on the next page, correcting any errors in punctuation, capitalization, and spelling. Pay particular attention to the use of commas.

Writing Theme
American Musical Comedy

Carousel, American musical comedy by Rodgers and Hammerstein

End Marks and Commas   **795**

Authors looking for ideas often find inspiration in the works of other's. The musical *West side story* which tells the story of youthfull lovers thwarted by fate is a modern version of *Romeo and Juliet*. In both plays the atmosphere of violence and hate which sets the stage for certian tragidy is quickly established. Verona's Montague and capulet families who have been feuding with each other have thier counterpart in the rival gangs of New Yorks West Side. Serving as the setting for a major scene in the play Juliets balcony becomes Maria's fire escape in the musical. The theme of starcrossed young love that both plays share is as effective on the musical stage today as it was in Shakespeares time.

East Side, West Side,
All Around the Town,
by Robert Donley

COMMAS: OTHER USES

There are several other situations that call for the use of one or more commas.

Commas in Dates, Place Names, and Letters

In dates, use a comma between the day of the month and the year. When only the month and year are given, no comma is necessary.

October 1, 1948   November 16, 1980   May 1975

When a date is part of a sentence, it is necessary to use a comma after the year, too.

On July 5, 1835, there were snowstorms in New England.

Use a comma between the name of a city or town and the name of its state or country.

Dallas, Texas   Paris, France
Cape May, New Jersey   Sydney, Australia

When an address or place name is part of a sentence, it is necessary to use a comma after each item. Do not put a comma between the name of a state and the ZIP code, however.

Please forward my mail to 3144 Camelback Road, Phoenix, Arizona 85016, where I will reside for two months.

Use a comma after the salutation of a friendly letter. (Use a colon after the salutation of a business letter.) Use a comma after the closing of a friendly letter or a business letter.

Dear Angie,   Yours truly,
Hello Grandpa,   Sincerely,

Commas to Avoid Confusion

Use a comma to separate words or phrases that might be mistakenly joined when read.

In some situations, commas are needed to separate words that may be mistakenly read together. The first situation occurs when the conjunctions *but* and *for* are mistaken for prepositions.

Confusing   I liked all the speeches but one was superb.
Clear   I liked all the speeches, but one was superb.

A second source of confusion is a word that may be an adverb, a preposition, or a conjunction at the beginning of a sentence.

Confusing   Below the earth looked like a quilt.
Clear   Below, the earth looked like a quilt.

A third source of confusion is a noun following a verbal phrase.

Confusing   While sleeping Di dreamed she was attacked by polka
            dots.
Clear   While sleeping, Di dreamed she was attacked by polka
            dots.

Use a comma to indicate the words left out of parallel word groups.

Detroit manufactures cars; Hollywood, dreams.
The day became warm, and our spirits, merry.

Commas with Titles and Numbers

Use commas to set off one or more titles that follow a name. Also use a comma before a business abbreviation and also after it if it is part of a sentence.

I met with John Kane, Jr., regarding the fund-raiser.
My brother worked for Lane and Fox, Inc., for two years.

In numbers of more than three digits, use a comma after every third digit from the right, with the exception of ZIP codes, phone numbers, years, and house numbers.

An estimated crowd of 60,000 people thronged the stadium.

Practice Your Skills

A. CONCEPT CHECK

Comma Usage   The following sentences contain errors in the use of commas. Rewrite each sentence, correcting the errors.

1. Edward Steichen was born on March 27 1879 in the small European country of Luxembourg.
2. When he was three years old, his family emigrated to Hancock Michigan where he went to school.
3. While studying Steichen showed talent for all the arts but the new art of photography intrigued him and soon became his favorite.
4. He helped to organize the Milwaukee Arts Students League Inc. and served as its first president.
5. Steichen began two years of study in Paris France in 1900.
6. He returned to America in the summer of 1902, and at 291 Fifth Avenue New York he set up a studio as a photographer.
7. During this time, Steichen earned a reputation for his portrait photographs for many famous New Yorkers came to sit for him.
8. Besides his photographs of many European notables had already made him famous.
9. During this phase of his career, Steichen became steadily more respected and his photographs more celebrated.
10. He admired all the impressionist painters but Matisse and Cézanne were his favorites.
11. While photographing Steichen helped to introduce these painters to Americans through exhibitions at his New York gallery.
12. In the 1920's, Steichen's photography for such firms as Eastman Kodak Inc. and the J. Walter Thompson agency made notable contributions to advertising.
13. Steichen also served with distinction in World War II for the Navy put him in command of all combat photography.

14. Steichen's most famous exhibition of photographs, "The Family of Man," opened at the Museum of Modern Art in New York City in January, 1955.
15. Within eight years this exhibit had been seen by more than 9000000 people in sixty-nine countries.

B. PROOFREADING SKILL

Correcting Comma Errors Rewrite the following letter, adding commas where they are necessary.

April 24 19—

Dear Holly

    Did you know I'm a celebrity? Before you answer look on page 23 of the April issue of *Photographer* magazine. Can you believe that a girl from Byfield Oregon could win a photo contest that had 2400 entries? Until I heard from the sponsor, Picture This Ltd. I didn't think I had a chance.

    I will be spending the summer studying photography under Gregory Martin Jr. as part of the contest prize. Write to me at L'Hôtel Marquis 73 rue Duret Paris France as often as you can.

Sincerely
Connie

CHECK POINT
PAGES 782–799

A. Rewrite the following sentences, adding periods, question marks, exclamation points, and commas where they are needed. If the punctuation is correct, write *Correct*.

1. One of the most famous theaters ever built was the Globe just outside London England
2. Hoping to attract large audiences the brothers Cuthbert and Richard Burbage built this theater in 1599.
3. William Shakespeare an experienced theater professional by then joined the Burbages in this enterprise.
4. Shakespeare as you doubtless know was a playwright a director an actor and a business manager.
5. How many spectators could the Globe accommodate
6. Like most public theaters of the time the Globe could hold at least 2500 people.
7. Public theaters which were built around roofless courtyards normally contained three levels of galleries.
8. Open to the sky and without artificial lights such theaters held performances only during daylight hours.

9. Because the authorities of the City of London frowned on drama theaters such as the Globe were built in the suburbs.
10. The authorities exercised strict supervision over theaters because they were afraid of raucous unruly crowds of spectators.
11. A large platform that projected into the pit served as the stage of the Globe Theatre.
12. In the pit stood spectators who had paid the cheapest price for admission, probably less than the equivalent of $1.00.
13. "Bravo Bravo" these enthusiastic fans would shout to cheer the actors on.
14. Obviously those who wanted to sit more comfortably in the galleries paid for more expensive tickets.
15. Nearly surrounded by spectators the performers thus had close contact with most of the audience.
16. There were two doorways at the back of the stage; behind these dressing rooms provided a place for quick costume changes.
17. The gallery that hung over the back of the main stage served as an upper stage; it could be used for example for balcony scenes.
18. To accommodate scenes with ghosts and spirits the main stage was equipped with a large trapdoor.
19. "If you want to experience the Globe without traveling to London" writes the noted Shakespeare expert A L Rowse "be sure and see the Folger Shakespeare Library in Washington D C"
20. The summer performances given in the replica of the Globe are certainly worthwhile.

B. Proofread the following paragraph for punctuation errors. For each sentence, list any words that should precede a punctuation mark, and follow each word with the correct punctuation.

(1) *Commedia dell'arte* which is a form of comic theater was performed all across Europe between the years 1400 and 1600 (2) Unlike most actors of today performers of the *commedia* did not memorize written dialogue (3) Instead they improvised which means that they made up their lines as they went along (4) The actor who was clearly the most important in the *commedia* was the clown (5) He had to be an excellent athlete since much of the humor in *commedia* performances came from his gymnastics (6) The clown who was very clever usually played tricks on the other characters (7) *Commedia dell'arte* was very popular; in fact an entire town would often turn out to watch a performance (8) Audiences for the most part could be counted on to fill the hat that was passed around after every show

17th century
actors perform
commedia dell'arte

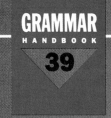

GRAMMAR
H A N D B O O K
39

Writing Theme
Brazil

A. Using Punctuation Correctly Rewrite the following sentences, adding punctuation where necessary.

1. What South American country is almost as large as the US

2. Brazil which occupies nearly half the continent of South America is a wonderfully varied land.

3. Brazil's largest city São Paulo has a population of about 7000000

4. Although São Paulo is larger Rio de Janeiro is probably Brazil's most famous city

5. The vast interior of Brazil is celebrated for its forests rivers and mountains

6. Lining the Atlantic coastline broad white beaches glisten in the sunshine.

7. Throughout Brazil is a country with rich natural resources.

8. This country for example produces about 30 percent of all the world's coffee and more bananas than any other nation.

9. Despite Brazil's huge land area the population is distributed unevenly.

10. The area along the Atlantic coast is heavily populated but the interior has a sparse population.

11. To attract people to the interior the government moved the capital from Rio to the inland city of Brasília in 1960.

12. Brasília which is a showcase for modern Brazilian architecture is now the seat of the national government.

13. How far is Brasília from the coastline

14. Well the distance is about 90056 (nine hundred and fifty-six hundredths) km.

15. Before it became independent in 1822 Brazil was a Portuguese colony.

16. After some years as an empire Brazil became a republic on November 15 1889.

17. Having come from many backgrounds Brazil's population includes people of European descent African Americans and Indians.

18. Indians the original Brazilians now account for less than 1 percent of the population however.

19. For recreation on their holidays many Brazilians enjoy fishing swimming skin diving and attending soccer games.

20. In fact the world's largest soccer stadium is located in Rio and can hold 200000 spectators.

End Marks
and Commas

B. Finding Punctuation Errors Number your paper from 1 to 15. After each number, list any words that should be followed by a punctuation mark; then place the mark correctly.

1. The chief river of South America the Amazon is about 4000 miles long.
2. For much of its course the Amazon flows through Brazil.
3. Entering the Amazon from the Atlantic ocean vessels can sail about 2300 miles to Iquitos Peru.
4. Because the terrain and climate are unfavorable the Amazon region of Brazil is thinly populated.
5. This region however is of great interest to tourists scientists and environmentalists.
6. A government official from Brazil Sen Pedro Xavier was recently interviewed on TV about some of the problems facing the Amazon region.
7. "The Amazon region" he explained "is the site of the largest remaining tropical rain forest in the world."
8. "This rain forest covers about 2700000 square miles" he continued.
9. The interviewer asked "Is the rain forest important We've heard that there is a threat to this area from pressure to develop the region for both tourism and industry."
10. "Once destroyed rain forests can never be replaced" the senator cautioned; "besides about half the world's species of plants and animals live in tropical rain forests."
11. "Senator Xavier what kinds of animals live in the Amazon basin area" inquired the interviewer.
12. "Amazon animals include alligators jaguars anaconda snakes monkeys and parrots" Sen Xavier replied.
13. "For those viewers interested in the scientific potential of the area let me tell you that scientists have found more than 3000 species of plants in one square mile of Amazon rain forest and many of these are being studied for their medicinal value."
14. "Wonderful" exclaimed the interviewer. "I've heard about other important drugs such as curare that are extracted from plants."
15. For anyone interested in obtaining more information about the Amazon Sen Xavier recommended writing to the Brazilian Consulate 630 Fifth Avenue New York New York 10022.

On the Lightside

THE COWBOY

What could be more American than the cowboys of the Wild West? Whether they are lassoing stampeding mustangs on the range or riding bucking

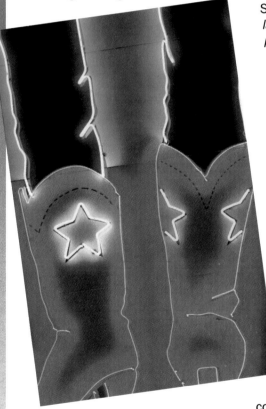

broncos in the rodeo, these buckaroos seem to be American originals. Yet most of the words associated with their world are not original—they were borrowed from other sources.

Buckaroo is a corruption of the Spanish word *vaquero*, the name of the Spanish cattlemen and horse-traders the cowboys encountered on the trails of the West. Spanish is also the source of *lasso, stampede* (from *estampida*), *mustang, lariat* (from *la reata*), *bronco* (Spanish for "rough" or "unruly"), and *rodeo*.

Even *cowboy* was not born on the range. In England during the 1700's, it was a term for boys who tended cattle. Its first use in America came during the Revolutionary War as a derogatory term for Tory soldiers who used cowbells to lure American soldiers and farmers into ambushes. During the Civil War, it was used to describe roustabouts who rustled cattle along the Texas-Mexico border. *Cowboy* also described teenaged boys who served as drovers on long trail drives because older men had been pressed into service as soldiers.

Finally, after the Civil War, the cowboys of the great western cattle drives earned their place in history and folklore. Over time, the other meanings have been forgotten, and what is remembered is *cowboy*'s rich and often romanticized connection to the American West.

Semicolons, Colons, and Other Punctuation

THE SEMICOLON

Like commas, semicolons separate different elements within a sentence. The semicolon, however, signals a more emphatic break than a comma does.

Semicolons Used with Commas

When there are several commas within parts of a compound sentence, use a semicolon to separate the parts. Use a semicolon between main clauses joined by a conjunction if the clause before the conjunction contains commas.

> Jim had done research, taken notes, and made an outline; but he didn't feel ready to begin writing.
> We put out sandwiches, cider, raw vegetables, and potato salad; and still we wondered if there would be enough to eat.

When there are commas within parts of a series, use a semicolon to separate the parts.

> Members of our class come from as far away as Leeds, England; New Dehli, India; and San Juan, Puerto Rico.
> Maris was in charge of the scenery; Roy, the costumes; and Felipe, the directing of the play.
> Eric called the dancers together; reviewed the opening number, solos, and finale; and told them to be ready by seven sharp.

Semicolons Between Main Clauses

Use a semicolon to join the parts of a compound sentence if no coordinating conjunction is used.

A stronger relationship between the clauses is shown by a semicolon rather than by a conjunction such as *and* or *but*.

> Bonita is good at set shots, but I am not.
> Bonita is good at set shots; I am not.

> The cyclone struck with savage fury, and it demolished most of the little coastal town.
> The cyclone struck with savage fury; it demolished most of the little coastal town.

Remember that a semicolon may be used only if clauses are closely related. Do not use a semicolon to join unrelated clauses.

Incorrect   José is a fine athlete; the school fields many teams.
Correct   José is a fine athlete; he has earned letters in golf, swimming, and baseball.

Semicolons and Conjunctive Adverbs

Use a semicolon before a conjunctive adverb or a parenthetical expression that joins the clauses of a compound sentence.

Our treasury was nearly empty; accordingly, we began considering various fund-raising projects.
Many of their talents complemented each other; for example, he played the piano and she sang.

Note that the conjunctive adverb or transitional phrase is followed by a comma in the examples above.

Practice Your Skills

A. CONCEPT CHECK

Semicolons Semicolons have been omitted from the following literary passages. Rewrite the passages, inserting semicolons where they are needed.

1. Learning is not child's play we cannot learn without pain.
   Aristotle
2. Wear your learning like your watch, in a private pocket do not pull it out and strike it, merely to show that you have one.
   Lord Chesterfield
3. She had a painful sense of having missed something, or lost something she felt that somehow the years had cheated her.
   Willa Cather
4. Reading furnishes our mind only with materials of knowledge it is thinking that makes what we read ours.   **John Locke**
5. Nine times out of ten, in the arts as in life, there is actually no truth to be discovered there is only error to be exposed.
   H. L. Mencken
6. When you reread a classic, you do not see more in the book than you did before you see more in you than there was before.
   Clifton Fadiman
7. Books swept me away, one after the other, this way and that I made endless vows according to their lights, for I believed them.
   Annie Dillard

Writing
——TIP——
Many words can be used either as conjunctive adverbs or as interrupters. If the words are used as interrupters, use commas to set them off from the rest of the sentence.

Writing Theme
Books, Learning, and Words

8. Few women even now have been graded at the universities the trials of the professions, army and navy, trade, politics, and diplomacy have hardly tested them. **Virginia Woolf**
9. Mama had not been consulted therefore, she made no comment. **Jade Snow Wong**
10. He who has books is happy he who does not need any is happier. **Chinese Proverb**

B. PROOFREADING SKILL

Using Semicolons Rewrite the following paragraph adding any needed semicolons or other needed punctuation. Correct any errors in usage, mechanics, or spelling.

> Libraries as we know them today have gone through a number of significant changes since the middle ages, so have the books they contain. Medieval books were individually lettered by hand no too copies were identical. These books, which sometimes took years to copy, usually contained valued works. As a result they were highly prized objects. Many of the manuscripts had drawings that accompanied the text. The drawings known as illuminations were often colored with the use of precious substances, for example; gold was used. As well as paints made from powdered presious stones. Because they took so long to produce, medieval books were usualy kept within the library walls. In fact, books were sometimes actually chained to the library desks: to prevent them from being moved.

Illuminated manuscript,
Book of Hours,
c. A.D. 1400

THE COLON

The colon is used to direct the reader's attention forward to what comes next in the sentence. Often a colon introduces an explanation or example.

Use a colon to introduce a list of items.

A colon often follows a word or phrase such as *these, the following,* or *as follows.* A colon is not used when a series of complements or modifiers immediately follows a verb.

> Jim is a member of the following groups: the Drama Club, the Debate Team, the Woodworking Club, and the International Alliance. (list)
> We visited these countries on our trip: Switzerland, France, Spain, Italy, and Austria. (list)

The candidate's attributes are honesty, intelligence, and courage. (series of complements)

The chart shows the primary colors, which are red, yellow, and blue. (series of modifiers)

Do not use a colon after a verb, in the middle of a prepositional phrase, or after *because* or *as* to introduce information.

Incorrect	Mike is interested in: chemistry, photography, and ice hockey.
Correct	These are Mike's interests: chemistry, photography, and ice hockey.
Incorrect	You should bring: paper plates, cups, and napkins.
Correct	You should bring the following items: paper plates, cups, and napkins.
Incorrect	The Constitution designates the President as: commander in chief of the armed forces.
Correct	The Constitution designates the President as commander in chief of the armed forces.

Use a colon to introduce a quotation that lacks explanatory words such as *he said* or *she asked.*

Christine wheeled around angrily: "You're going to regret this decision one day!"

Use a colon to introduce a very long or very formal quotation.

In his Inaugural Address in 1961, President John Kennedy said: "Ask not what your country can do for you—ask what you can do for your country."

Use a colon between two independent clauses when the second explains the first.

Then I knew we were in trouble: none of our boys could match the dive we had just seen.

From then on we understood Ms. Gilroy: she was demanding, but she was fair.

Other Uses of the Colon

Use a colon (1) after the formal salutation of a business letter, (2) between hour and minute figures of clock time, (3) in biblical references to indicate chapter and verse, (4) between the title and subtitle of a book, (5) between numbers referring to volume and pages of books and magazines, and (6) after labels that signal important ideas.

Writing
—TIP—

After a colon, capitalize the first word of a formal statement. Begin an informal statement with a lowercase letter.

Dear Sir or Madam: *The Raven: The Life of Sam Houston*
8:20 P.M.   *National Geographic* 171:348–385
Psalm 23:7   Warning: This substance is harmful if
John 3:16   swallowed.

Practice Your Skills

A. CONCEPT CHECK

Colons Correct the following sentences by adding or deleting colons as necessary.

1. At 700 P.M. on April 6, 1935, thousands of fans watched Bunny Levitt do the near impossible he dunked 499 consecutive free throws.
2. Later, Bunny hooked up with a team known as: the Harlem Globetrotters.
3. The first five members were these Walter ("Toots") Wright, Byron ("Fats") Long, Willis ("Kid") Oliver, Andy Washington, and Al ("Runt") Pullins.
4. Known for their characteristic clowning, they introduced tricks such as the following drop-kicking the ball toward the goal, shooting backward, and dribbling on their knees.
5. However, entertainment was not their only goal they wanted to be viewed as serious athletes.
6. In 1935 they got their break their manager set up a game with the original Celtic team.
7. This game became a serious confrontation because: the Celtics left with a tie score rather than risk defeat.
8. Author Arthur Ashe is familiar with some of the Globetrotters' difficulties "In 1946 major league basketball did not allow any Negro-league teams to enter their domain."
9. Touring over millions of miles, the Globetrotters have performed in: Alaska, Western Europe, North Africa, Central and South America.
10. The "Globies" have been officially recognized as: "ambassadors of good will" by the United States Department of State.

B. PROOFREADING SKILL

Using Correct Punctuation Rewrite the following paragraphs, correcting errors in punctuation, capitalization, and spelling.

Few profesional basketball players created the excitment that Tyrone Bogues did in his first month of play with the National basketball Association (NBA) in 1987. Basketball fans are fascinated by Bogues he is a mere 5-foot-3-inches tall.

Tyrone Bogues

What Bogues lacks in height, however he makes up for with these charteristics speed, skill, and determanation. The shortest legitimite player in nba history. Bogues is not a publisity stunt. In fact, he was a first-round draft choice of the Washington Bullets.

In a preseason matchup against the Los Angeles lakers, Bogues entered the game after the first quarter. the Bullets were trailing 31–22. Racking up twelve points and four assists, he helped shoot the bullets ahead by eight at the half. The Lakers' Magic Johnson sums up Bogues's special talent "You have to be aware of him at all times he's like a Fly that gets in your face when your trying to sleep. Every time you think you've slapped him away, he comes buzzing right back

C. APPLICATION IN WRITING

Research and Documentation   Imagine that you work for a magazine publisher as a fact checker. Marion Huff, one of the magazine's editors, has asked you to check several facts from an article about the Boston Celtics basketball team. Ms. Huff's questions, along with the answers that you found in the library, are listed below.

Question: What is the full title of Joe Fitzgerald's book on the Boston Celtics basketball team? (*That Championship Feeling*. Its subtitle is *The Story of the Boston Celtics*.)

Question: What is the source of this quotation: "But many that are first shall be last; and the last, first"? (the thirty-first verse of the tenth chapter of Mark in the Bible)

Question: Where did David A. Raskin's essay "Unsung Heroes (Underrated Basketball Players)" appear? (on page 35 of volume 81 of *Sport* magazine)

Write a formal letter to Ms. Huff answering her questions. Follow proper business letter form as described on pages 848–849. In your answers, use colons correctly to write out the citations.

THE DASH

Dashes are used to indicate an abrupt change of thought or a pause in a sentence. Dashes show a looser connection to the main idea than commas do. The words, clauses, or phrases set off by dashes merely add extra information to an already complete thought.

Use a dash to show an abrupt break in thought.

> The winner of today's baseball game—assuming we aren't rained out—will play in the regional semifinals.
> The appetizers—supposedly the restaurant's specialty—left us disappointed.

Use a dash to set off a long explanatory statement that interrupts the main thought of the sentence.

> They frantically searched everywhere—under the seats, in the aisle, in the lobby—before Dan finally found the car keys in his pocket.
> The meeting between the two men—they had clashed over the years—was unexpectedly calm and friendly.

Note that in the first example, punctuation occurs within the interrupting statement. Here the dash serves as a guide to the reader, signaling the addition of extra, nonessential information.

Use a dash to set off a summarizing statement from the rest of the sentence.

> Insufficient heating, leaky roofs, cluttered stairways, and unsanitary corridors—for all these violations of the housing code, the landlord was brought into court.
> Photographs of rock-and-roll stars, concert posters, souvenir T-shirts—these covered the walls of her room.

Be careful not to overuse dashes. When used correctly, dashes can add variety and emphasis to your writing. However, too many dashes may make your writing seem choppy and less precise.

When writing dialogue, use a dash to show an abrupt break in thought.

In dialogue, the break in thought is often caused by uncertainty or hesitancy, as in the first example below. Note in the second example how the dash adds a casual, conversational tone to dialogue. People often change their thoughts in midsentence while speaking.

> "Photosynthesis is an action—I mean, it's what happens—well, it's sunlight doing something to chlorophyll."
> "The movie opens with a spectacular shot of the desert—oh, you've already seen it."

Practice Your Skills

CONCEPT CHECK

Dashes Study the passages from literature given below. Dashes have been omitted from these passages. Rewrite the passages, inserting dashes where they originally occurred.

1. Impy left by the back way. Before the scrape of her hard, bare feet had died away on the back porch, a wild shriek I was sure it was hers filled the hollow house. **O. Henry**
2. A man with murder in his heart will murder, or be murdered it comes to the same thing and so I knew I had to leave. **James Baldwin**
3. The third day it was Wednesday of the first week Charles bounced a see-saw onto the head of a little girl and made her bleed, and the teacher made him stay inside all during recess. **Shirley Jackson**
4. The following spring the heavier of the two almost half the tree broke off in a spring gale. **Richard Mabey**
5. I would sit down to this breakfast at a round table in the dining room with my young parents or my beloved Miss Rachel. My father called Tata, the Polish for papa was my most favorite person in the world. **Esther Hautzig**
6. The deep rumble of the produce wagons, coming to the big London markets from the farms generally about three A.M. held no disturbing quality. **Algernon Blackwood**
7. My knowledge made me happy it was like fire in my heart. **Stephen Vincent Benét**
8. I remember I *think* I remember, for I could not have been more than five one frigid day Pa huddled on a stool before the coal stove, took me on his knee, and studied me gravely. **Eugenia Collier**

Writers often use dashes to provide explanation to their readers. The explanatory material added with dashes clarifies the statements being made and keeps the reader from becoming confused.

Semicolons and Other Punctuation **811**

9. I had seen the trick done at entertainments endless times before it's part of the common stock of conjurers but I had not expected it here. **H. G. Wells**

10. Between times he regaled me with spicy stories of the hundreds of thousands they seemed no less numerous to me then of county fairs he had attended in his youth. **Dorothy Canfield**

THE HYPHEN

Use a hyphen in compound numbers from twenty-one to ninety-nine.

thirty-six steps   twenty-eight countries

Use a hyphen in all spelled-out fractions.

a four-fifths majority   one-sixth of the pie

Use a hyphen in certain compound words.

sister-in-law   T-shirt   right-of-way

Use a hyphen between words that make up a compound adjective used before a noun.

We found a well-informed source.

When a compound adjective follows a linking verb, it is usually not hyphenated.

The report seemed well organized.

Some proper nouns and proper adjectives with prefixes and suffixes require a hyphen.

Mexican-style   pre-Roosevelt   pro-Yankees

Use a hyphen if part of a word must be carried over from one line to the next.

Gabriela Dimitrova, a Bulgarian weight lifter, defected to the US after the Women's World Weight Lifting Champion - ship in Daytona Beach, Florida.

The following rules should be observed when hyphenating words:

1. Words are separated by hyphens only between syllables.
2. Only words having two or more syllables can be hyphenated.
3. Each line should have at least two letters of the hyphenated word.

Practice Your Skills

CONCEPT CHECK

Using Hyphens The following newspaper editorial, as it appeared on a word-processing screen, contains several errors in hyphenation. Write correctly all incorrectly hyphenated words.

1 When Brian Styers, a sixteen year old student at Thoma-
2 sville High School in North Carolina, goes to lunch, he isn't
3 concentrating on the menu. His attention is on the trays
4 and other school issued nonbiodegradable plastics. Styers,
5 whose proenvironmental beliefs run deep, won a victor-
6 y for re-cycling recently. Brian's concern was that the pla-
7 tes, cups, and other plastics were contributing to an ever gro-
8 wing problem for landfill areas. He and several other like
9 minded students began staging marches through the school ca-
10 feteria, carrying reusable dishes they brought from home. Br
11 ian and his friends, who had been labeled "tree huggers," figure-
12 d the cost of recycling schemes and contacted the local media
13 for support. In addition, they took a well rehearsed appeal to
14 the School Board. Their efforts paid off. Now the used lunch
15 ware from three Thomasville high schools will be colle-
16 cted and sent to Brooklyn to become rulers, reusa-
17 ble trays, and insulation board. The importance of such rec-
18 ycling efforts becomes clear if one remembers that New-York-
19 City alone produces twenty seven thousand tons of waste ev-
20 ery day.

PARENTHESES

Parentheses enclose material that is only loosely connected to the sentence. Such material interrupts the continuity of the sentence and is nonessential.

Use parentheses to set off supplementary or explanatory material that is loosely related to the sentence.

> I can still clearly recall my high-school graduation twenty years ago (sometimes it seems like only yesterday).

Note the use of parentheses in the following examples:

> Though Loch Ness had been a tourist haven for the rich in Victorian times (the Queen herself journeyed up the loch in a paddle steamer in 1873), it was the road that really opened the area to large numbers of visitors.
> Their father was the twelfth child of a wealthy Englishman (one of whose houses, Claverton Manor, is now the American Museum).
> Inside was a first-aid kit (including boxes of antivenin), a can of beans (invariably rusty), malaria pills, and pliers.

When the supplementary material is more closely related to the sentence, use commas or dashes. Compare the use of punctuation in the following examples:

Commas	The best point of Kate's speech, which she saved for the end, was that every group needs leadership.
Dash	The beef was braised—that is, it was browned and then simmered in a covered container.
Parentheses	Leonardo da Vinci (he was a brilliant scientist and one of the world's greatest artists) wrote: "Those sciences are vain and full of errors which are not born of experiment, the mother of all certainty."

Use parentheses to enclose figures or letters in a list that is part of a sentence.

> A tree is different from a shrub in that it has (1) greater height and (2) a single trunk.
> Is your favorite course (a) English, (b) math, or (c) art?

Use parentheses to identify informally a source of information you use in your writing or to give credit to an author whose ideas or words you are using.

"When the stock market went over the edge of Niagara in October and November, 1929, and the decline in business became alarming, the country turned to the President for action" (Allen 282).

Punctuation with Parentheses

Use punctuation marks inside the parentheses when they belong to the parenthetical material. However, when punctuation marks belong to the main part of the sentence, place them outside the parentheses.

Leo's speech was on disarmament; Barb's, on acting as a career (her favorite subject); Jim's, on slum clearance.
I never guessed (would you have?) that the maid did it.
Sheldon spoke of his victory over Central's debaters (*his* victory!) as if he had been a one-man team.
The tallest man on the team is Seamus (pronounced shay'mɔs!).

CHECK POINT
PAGES 804–815

Rewrite the following sentences, adding semicolons, colons, dashes, and hyphens where necessary.

1. In a sun swept Italian city sometime a little after 100 P.M. on the twenty fourth of August, A.D. 79, the sky suddenly darkened.
2. Showers of hot, wet ash rained down on grass covered slopes the thriving city of Pompeii perished in a single day.
3. Mount Vesuvius it had slumbered for centuries erupted savagely.
4. People misunderstood the explosion they thought the gods were fighting.
5. Pliny, a Roman philosopher, was an eyewitness to the volcanic cloud "Better than any other tree, the pine can give an idea of the shape and appearance of the cloud."
6. Pompeii lay covered in ash for about sixteen and one half centuries still, it was unearthed exactly as it had been on the day of the eruption.
7. Archaeologists found items such as bread in bakery ovens, expensive, vintage wine in jars, and the remains of a beggar seated by the city gates.
8. Pompeii provides a three-dimensional photo a chronicle of every detail of life.
9. Digs have uncovered the following pots, pans, household tools, election slogans, and the scrawlings of unruly boys on walls.

10. Proof exists that a banker he promised the gods a proper sacrifice survived.
11. After the disaster, his portrait, complete with the wart on his cheek, a scene depicting the earthquake, and the bull he sacrificed, and his money chest all these flanked the family altar.
12. The only residents today are crickets nevertheless, thousands of tourists visit annually.
13. You enter through an age old gate.
14. Inside is a museum it was built recently that holds small artifacts.
15. Glass cups, charred peas and beans, baskets of fruit, a box of chestnuts all the little things of Pompeii are preserved for curious eyes.
16. The account books of Caecilius Jucundus are on display he's the banker with the wart on his face.
17. They show an interesting aspect about him he was somewhat greedy.
18. He lent a great deal of money however, he charged very high interest rates.
19. The disaster took a number of lives still, it bestowed a kind of immortality.
20. Pompeii's citizens live on for us Jucundus, the banker, Vesonius, a wool merchant Claudius Elogus, a newlywed and Diomedes, a nobleman.

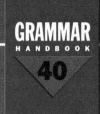

GRAMMAR
H A N D B O O K
40

A. Using Punctuation Correctly Rewrite the following sentences, adding semicolons, colons, dashes, and hyphens as needed.

1. Teenagers in other countries associate the United States with fast foods, such as sodas, hamburgers, and hot dogs, with casual clothing, such as blue jeans and T shirts, and with entertainment, such as movies, TV, and music videos.
2. Hamburgers, music videos, blue jeans these are all parts of what is known as American popular culture.
3. Without question, this popular culture has found world wide appeal recently, an American style fast food restaurant even opened in downtown Moscow.
4. The fast food industry considering that it is a significant contributor to nonbiodegradable waste may not be the best ambassador of American culture.
5. In addition, the nutritional value of some fast food is questionable furthermore, it promotes high fat, high cholesterol, and high salt dietary offerings.
6. Clothing styles blue jeans and T shirts, for example are a less questionable American export.
7. These articles of clothing are comfortable, sturdy, and inexpensive and they are now worn by people all over the world.
8. As one teenager from Italy wrote to her parents' friends, who were visiting the United States "Dear Mr. and Mrs. Moretti I have only one request. Bring me back a pair of jeans!"
9. The irony since both the words *denim* and *jeans* have European origins is that these products seem so American.
10. Nevertheless, these garments with Genoa, Italy, the source of *jeans* and Nimes, France, the origin of *denim* are almost synonymous with America.

Writing Theme
American Popular
Culture

B. Punctuating Sentences Correctly Rewrite the following sentences, adding semicolons, colons, hyphens, and parentheses as they are needed.

1. According to one estimate, in the decade of the 1980's Americans spent nearly twenty three billion dollars on products of the recording industry.
2. Perhaps as much as two thirds of this money was spent by teenage consumers.
3. During this decade the United States produced many well known and popular musical artists.
4. Some pop stars such as Charlie Pride became famous for their musical innovations he's known for his compelling blend of country and rock.

5. The eighties was also a decade of new musical technologies, such as compact discs, digital sound, and music video, and it produced many new musical styles, such as new wave, reggae, and rap.
6. The influence of American popular music can be seen all over the globe for example, American style rap artists and break dancers are common sights on the sidewalks of Tokyo.
7. Perhaps American music exported overseas should carry a label reading, "Warning This product may cause your children to become just like Americans!"
8. American television and movies certainly no surprise are also very popular overseas.
9. Some popular American television exports are: a game shows, b situation comedies, and c made for television movies.
10. Perhaps the most spectacular development in the area of movies during the 1980's was the explosion of videotape sales and rentals by 1990 sixty five out of every one hundred homes in America had VCR's.

C. Proofreading   Rewrite the following passage, correcting errors in capitalization and spelling as well as errors in the use of semicolons, colons, dashes, and hyphens. Add any other punctuation that you find is missing.

> We eat more hamburgers charbroiled and pan-fried than any other nation in the world. Our all American hamburgers, however, began their sizzle on another continent. During the Middle Ages, Tartar Nomads in russia often ate raw meat. To tendarize the meat, they used the folowing recipe place a slab of meat under a saddel; ride on it all day, scrape and shred the meat, and mix it with salt, pepper, and onion juice. The modern version of this delicacy, no longer tenderized under a saddle, is called "steak tartare" German Soldiers from the town of Hamburg picked up the idea at Baltic seaports they brought it home with them. Sometime later, Hamburg cooks had another inspiration, they started broiling the meet. It took, however an american cook experts disagree on who this genius was to introduce hamburger patties to buns. Leave it to an American to come up with a new kind of sandwiche! This introduction was a tremendous success. The rest, as they say, is history.

On the Lightside

FROM HAND TO MOUTH

Language is not always fair. When it comes to matters of right and left, for example, the lefties have been subjected to discrimination. A "right-hand man" is an important person, but a "left-handed compliment" is not really a compliment at all.

Right-handed people have traditionally outnumbered left-handers, so words having to do with the right side have had the upper hand. The supremacy of the right can be traced to the origins of several words. *Dexterous,* meaning "skillful," comes from the Latin *dexter,* meaning "right" or "right hand."

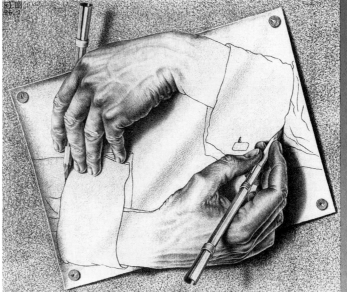

Drawing Hands, by M.C. Escher.

Therefore, someone who is ambidextrous has two right hands, since the Latin *ambi* means "both." *Adroit,* another word meaning "skillful," comes from the French *à droit,* meaning "to the right."

On the other hand, literally, is *sinister.* The word for something evil, corrupt, or dangerous comes from the Latin for "left." *Gauche,* meaning "awkward" or "clumsy," comes from the French for "left." *Gawky,* another word meaning "clumsy," comes from a dialect phrase meaning "left-handed." Even the word *left* itself doesn't get any respect. It comes from the Anglo-Saxon *lef,* which means "weak," since the left hand is weaker than the right hand for the majority of people.

Left-handed people are right to complain that language has not always treated them right.

Apostrophes and Quotation Marks

APOSTROPHES

Apostrophes have several important functions. They are used to indicate possession, to show omitted letters, and to form the plurals of certain items such as numbers.

Using Apostrophes to Indicate Possession

Use apostrophes to form the possessives of singular and plural nouns.

To use apostrophes correctly, you must know whether nouns are singular or plural. To form the possessive of a singular noun, add an apostrophe and an *s* even if the noun ends in *s.*

teacher's   city's   lass's   Chris's

Punctuation Note   Exceptions to this rule about the possessive of singular nouns are *Jesus, Moses,* and names from mythology that end in *s: Jesus', Moses', Zeus', Odysseus'.*

To form the possessive of a plural noun that ends in *s* or *es,* add only an apostrophe. The possessive of a plural noun that does not end in *s* is formed by adding an apostrophe and an *s.*

teachers'   cities'   men's   children's

To form the possessive of a compound noun, add an apostrophe only to the last part of the noun.

A **compound noun** is a noun composed of more than one word. Some compound nouns are written with hyphens between the parts.

notary public + 's = notary public's office
sisters-in-law + 's = sisters-in-law's coats

The possessive forms of nouns such as the *Queen of England* are formed by adding an apostrophe and *s* to the last word only: *the Queen of England's throne.* Your writing will usually be less awkward if you reword and use an *of*-phrase instead.

the throne of the Queen of England

In cases of joint ownership, only the name of the last person mentioned is given the possessive form. Add an apostrophe or an apostrophe and *s*, depending on the spelling of the name.

> Tom and Wes's school
> the actors and dancers' costumes
> Moss and Hart's songs
> Watson and Crick's research

This rule also governs the formation of the possessives of the names of firms and organizations.

> Cross and Hamilton Company's sales force
> Johnson & Johnson's corporate headquarters

If the names of two or more persons are used to show separate ownership, each name is given the possessive form.

> Madison's and Monroe's administrations
> Juana's and Katie's grades
> Gilda Radner's and Lily Tomlin's comic routines

Again, to avoid an awkward sentence, a phrase using the word *of* may be substituted for the possessive form.

> the administrations of Madison and Monroe
> the grades of Juana and Katie
> the comic routines of Gilda Radner and Lily Tomlin

To form the possessive of an indefinite pronoun, add an apostrophe and *s*.

> everyone's   somebody's
> one's   either's

Add an apostrophe and *s* to the last word to form the possessives of compound pronouns like those shown below.

> someone else's turn   no one else's answer

Do not use an apostrophe with a personal pronoun to show possession.

> The raincoat on the couch is hers. Yours is in the closet.
> Is that magazine ours? Its cover is missing.

When nouns expressing time and amount are used as adjectives, they are given the possessive form.

> a month's time   four days' wait   two centuries' tradition

Writing

—TIP—

Underline the plurals of letters, numbers, signs, and words used as words. In print, these items are italicized.

Writing Theme
Earth Day

Using Apostrophes to Show Omissions

Use apostrophes in contractions.

In contractions words are joined and letters are left out. An apostrophe replaces the missing letter or letters.

you'll	= you will or you shall	don't	= do not
what's	= what is or what has	Hank's	= Hank is
she'd	= she would or she had	could've	= could have

Dialogue may use contractions that reflect regional dialects. Apostrophes are used to indicate the missing letters.

"How d'you do, Ma'am!" he shouted. "'Tis a fine mornin'."

Use an apostrophe to show the omission of numerals.

the class of '89   the blizzard of '78

Using Apostrophes for Certain Plurals

Use apostrophes to form the plurals of letters, numerals, signs, and words referred to as words.

How many *r*'s are there in *embarrass?*
Her speech has too many *therefore*'s in it.
To type *$*'s instead of *4*'s, depress the shift key.

Note: The last two rules concerning the use of apostrophes are sometimes considered optional.

Practice Your Skills

A. CONCEPT CHECK

Using Apostrophes Correctly   In the following sentences find the words that have errors in apostrophe usage. Write each word correctly on your paper.

1. Earth Day is a holiday on which the worlds people consider what they can do to protect the environment.
2. The first Earth Day, which took place in the early 70s, was celebrated only in North America.
3. Within twenty years time, however, Earth Day had become a worldwide phenomenon.
4. Many people once held the attitude that the environment wasnt their problem—that it was someone elses business.
5. More people now realize that the condition of our environment is everyones concern.

6. Around the world many special events were devised on one recent Earth Day to celebrate what has been called "the earths birthday party."

7. In one unusual Earth Day event, a team with American, Soviet, and Chinese members climbed Mt. Everest; the climbers purpose was to pick up garbage left at the summit by other teams.

Dennis Hayes, founder of Earth Day

8. In Toulouse, France, the Friends of the Earths sculpture "Monument to the Unknown Refuse," made entirely of garbage, was unveiled.

9. The local governments of Tokyo and Hong Kong used their cities parks for special Earth Day carnivals and concerts.

10. Protesters in Rome lay down in the streets, demanding traffic controls—no *if*s, *and*s, or *but*s about it.

11. In Halifax, Nova Scotia, a crowd gathered to hear a tribute to nature by Noel Kirkwood, the Mirmac Indian nations medicine man.

12. In Beijing, China, the evening news leading report on Earth Day featured a speech on environmental protection.

13. St. Louis and Vancouver's citizens celebrated Earth Day by holding tree plantings.

14. In Chicago, hundreds of children gathered at the Academy of Sciences to attend the institutions' sing-alongs and puppet shows celebrating Earth Day.

15. In Rhode Island, the Childrens' Theatre Ensemble presented a play about Mother Earth.

16. Very youthful environmentalists portrayed a number of Mother Earths problems.

17. Rock-and-roll performers also got into the act; thousands tuned into Paula Abdul's, Alice Cooper's, and Billy Idol's televised concert.

18. Pop singer Paul McCartneys opening statement at his' Earth Day concert in Brazil was, "Save our planet," which he said in Portuguese.

19. In India, Claude Alvares and Ramesh Billorey wrote an Earth Day treatise on an environmentally disastrous dam project; Alvares' and Billorey's book was subtitled *Indias Greatest Planned Environmental Disaster.*

20. Of the participants in Earth Day it might be said, in Jesus's words, that they hoped to give "life unto the world."

B. PROOFREADING SKILL

Correcting Errors with Apostrophes Rewrite the following paragraph, correcting all errors in spelling, capitalization, and punctuation. Pay special attention to the use of apostrophes.

Many scientists feel that in the 90s the well-being of our Planet will depend on the survival of our worlds rain forests. By the end of the 1970s, fourty seven thousand square mile's of rain forest were being destroyed each year, by the 80s the figure had risen to eighty thousand per year. The irony is that we dont even understand the potential of what we are destroying. Tropical rain forests cover only seven percent of the earths surface; but they contain between fifty and eighty persent of it's plant and animal species. Although only a fraction of these forest's thirty million speceis have been identified many have already proved useful. At present twenty-five per cent of the USAs pharmaceutical products are derived from wild plants. Clearly it will be everyones loss if these forests perish.

C. APPLICATION IN WRITING

An Editorial Write an editorial for your school newspaper on an environmental issue of interest to you. Remember that an editorial may either express the views of the writer or try to persuade the reader to see a certain point of view or to take a particular action. Use possessives of some nouns and pronouns in your editorial.

QUOTATION MARKS

Quotation marks are used to set off direct quotations, titles, and words used in special ways.

Direct and Indirect Quotations

Use quotation marks to begin and end a direct quotation.

Ricardo said, "The violinists are ready to perform."

Do not use quotation marks to set off an indirect quotation.

Ricardo said that the violinists are ready to perform.

Punctuation of Direct Quotations

The speaker's words are set off from the rest of the sentence with quotation marks, and the first word of the quotation is capitalized.

"Let's meet at my house next time," Raoul said.
Raoul said, "Let's meet at my house next time."

When the end of the quotation is also the end of the sentence, the period falls inside the quotation marks. Also note the placement of commas in the examples above.

If the quotation is a question or exclamation, the question mark or exclamation point falls inside the quotation marks.

"May I make the poster?" Lola asked.
"I deny everything!" the suspect cried.

Note that no commas are necessary in the examples above.

If the entire sentence is a question or an exclamation, the question mark or exclamation point falls outside the quotation marks.

Did I hear you say, "You're welcome to take an apple"?
It's absurd for anyone to call these thieves "responsible citizens"!

If there is a colon or a semicolon at the close of a quotation, it falls outside the quotation marks.

The committee said that the following states contained "pockets of poverty": Kentucky, West Virginia, and Pennsylvania.
Read the ballad "Sir Patrick Spens"; then write an essay comparing it with Coleridge's poem "Dejection: An Ode."

Both parts of a divided quotation are enclosed in quotation marks. The first word of the second part is not capitalized unless it begins a new sentence.

"Part of my plan," the governor said, "is to reduce property taxes this year."

"You must remember this," the guidance counselor said. "Ten hours of casual work will probably be less effective than five hours of real concentration."

In dialogue, a new paragraph and a new set of quotation marks are used to show a change in speakers.

"My working habits have no pattern," the author said. "Some writers set themselves very strict schedules. I prefer to remain more flexible."

"But you've written five books in five years," the interviewer argued. "You must work very hard every day."

"On the contrary, some days I spend the entire morning putting in a comma," the author replied. "Then I spend the afternoon taking it out."

Single quotation marks are used to enclose a quotation within a quotation.

Jeanne said, "Then she actually said to me, 'I hope I didn't keep you waiting.'"

"The announcer just said, 'More snow throughout the state tonight,'" Len reported.

"Who wrote the song 'Most Likely You Go Your Way and I'll Go Mine'?" asked Jan.

A quotation may sometimes be several paragraphs in length. In long quotations, begin each paragraph with quotation marks. Place quotation marks at the end of the last paragraph only.

Usage Note A quotation of five or more lines can be set off from the rest of the text by indenting ten spaces and double spacing. In this case, no quotation marks are needed.

When a quoted fragment is inserted in a sentence, the first word of the fragment is not capitalized unless it begins a sentence or is a proper noun. No comma is needed to set the phrase apart from the rest of the sentence.

Marc Antony claims that he has "come to bury Caesar, not to praise him." However, his speech has the opposite effect and he knows it.

Practice Your Skills

A. CONCEPT CHECK

Using Quotation Marks Correctly Rewrite the following sentences, correcting any errors in the use of quotation marks, punctuation marks, capitalization, and paragraphing. If a sentence has no errors, write *Correct*.

Writing Theme
Global Communication

1. At a local computer fair, one of the exhibitors asked, "Would you like to try using the computer to contact someone overseas"?
2. "That would be terrific!," I answered, "how do we start?"
3. He began by explaining what he called the "three necessary ingredients for international computer communication": a computer, a modem, and a telephone line.
4. "A modem," he went on, "Is a device that is used for sending computer messages through telephone lines."
5. "Did you say that messages go 'Through telephone lines?" I asked.
6. "That's right." he answered. "The telephone line plugs into the modem and the modem plugs into the computer." "OK," I replied. Let's try it!"
7. He added that "we would need to start the computer and run a telecommunications program."
8. He then explained First, you have to start the telecommunications program and type in the telephone number of the computer that you want to call.
9. "You sit down at the computer, and I'll tell you what to do," he said.
10. Soon we had made contact with another computer owner, Takeo, who lives in Osaka, Japan, and the exhibitor took over the keyboard typing, "So, how are things on the other side of the world"?
11. Takeo's reply then appeared on our screen: "Well, things are dark here. Do you realize that it's the middle of the night in Japan?" "Sorry, we typed back. "That's—how do you say it?—OK, though, because I'm still awake. I've been trying out some new software programs. They are all very complicated. Do you know a good program for computer graphics"?
12. "Sure, I do," the exhibitor typed, "why do you ask?"
13. "I could use one for sales reports." Takeo replied.
14. "Would you leave their name's in my electronic mailbox? I've got to go now, said Takeo. I need to get some sleep."
15. I then thanked the exhibitor for demonstrating his "remarkable machine;" however, he said that it was really nothing and that in the near future, many people will communicate internationally by computer "All the time."

B. REVISION SKILL

Using Quotation Marks in Dialogue The following passage has been changed to include several errors in the use of punctuation (including quotation marks), capitalization, and paragraphing. Rewrite the passage, returning it to its original state by correcting the errors.

(1) He was very thin and dressed in rags. (2) What I remember are his eyes. (3) He had huge, dark eyes. (4) He did not speak. (5) He just stood there, looking up at me. (6) Who are you I asked in Chinese? (7) I am no one. (8) He said. (9) But what is your name I asked? (10) I have no name he said. (11) Where are your parents? (12) I have no parents. (13) But where did you come from I asked, staring at him? (14) I came from nowhere he said. (15) And you are going nowhere? (16) Nowhere he said. (17) Then why come to me? (18) He shook his head, not able to answer. (19) Come in I said finally, you must be hungry. **Pearl S. Buck**

Pearl Buck

C. APPLICATION IN WRITING

A Dialogue Imagine that you are in the middle of a telephone conversation with a friend when suddenly you are interrupted by loud static and a high-pitched tone. A voice says in English, "Go ahead, Detroit. This is Moscow." Write down the conversation you have with a Russian high-school student that you contact because of a technical glitch. Follow the rules for correct punctuation, capitalization, and paragraphing.

Setting Off Titles

Use quotation marks to set off chapter titles and other parts of books and the titles of short stories, essays, short poems, articles, television episodes, and short musical compositions.

Chapter Title	"Chapter 9: The Progressive Spirit"
Short Story	"The Black Cat"
Essay	"The Joys of Science"
Poem	"Mending Wall"
Magazine Article	"Good Food for Healthy Bodies"
Television Episode	"Lucy and Desi in London"
Song	"This Land Is Your Land"

The title of a book, magazine, newspaper, TV series, play, painting, epic poem, or long musical composition is italicized in print. In writing, indicate italics by underlining.

The article appeared in *Newsweek* magazine.
Beowulf is the earliest known epic poem in English.
In her painting *The Bath,* Mary Cassatt evokes feelings of tenderness toward children.
He has the lead in Ossie Davis's play *Purlie Victorious.*
You would recognize Pachelbel's *Canon in D* if you heard it.

Words Used in Special Ways

Use quotation marks to set off words used in special ways and to set off slang.

Writers can show that they are using a word as someone else has used it by enclosing it in quotation marks. Slang words and phrases are also enclosed in quotation marks.

The government official claimed he was "protecting" his country's interests when he lied during his testimony.
The slang of the '80's included such words as "nerd," "awesome," "rad," and "tubular."

A word referred to as a word is italicized in print. In writing, the word is underlined. When a word and its definition appear in a sentence, the word is italicized (or underlined) and the definition is put in quotation marks. Also italicize (or underline) letters or figures referred to as such.

Until then I'd never heard the word *boondoggle.*
Dot your *i*'s and cross your *t*'s.
In music the word *pianissimo* means "very soft."

Punctuation Note When a comma or period immediately follows the quoted word or phrase, the punctuation mark is placed inside the quotation marks. If the quoted word or phrase comes at the end of a question or exclamation, the punctuation mark is placed outside the quotation marks: Is this what you mean by "cool"?

Foreign words and phrases that have not become common in our language are printed in italics: *coup de grace, tempus fugit.*

Many foreign words have become so widely used that they are now part of the English language: spaghetti, gourmet. These words are printed in regular type.

The only way to be sure whether a word or phrase of foreign origin should be printed in italics is to consult the dictionary.

Practice Your Skills

A. CONCEPT CHECK

Quotation Marks Write the following sentences, adding quotation marks and underlining where necessary.

1. What does the word serendipity mean?
2. It is defined as an aptitude for making fortunate discoveries accidentally.
3. As Willard Espy points out in his book O Thou Improper, Thou Uncommon Noun, this word has an unusual history.
4. It seems that Horace Walpole, an English writer and earl, coined the word based on the title of the fairy tale The Three Princes of Serendip.
5. A user of today's slang might say the princes continually lucked out, while Italians would probably use the phrase buona fortuna.
6. Some not-so-lucky accidents produced the word spoonerism.
7. The word, meaning an accidental reversal of sounds, also comes from a name.
8. William A. Spooner, the dean of New College, Oxford, would occasionally transpose sounds and say things like blushing crow when he meant to say crushing blow.
9. This so amused Spooner's students that they began to call such errors spoonerisms, which we now also call bloopers.
10. More examples can be found in D. C. Black's book Spoonerisms, Sycophants, and Sops.

B. APPLICATION IN WRITING

Works Cited Following is a list of sources for a report on unusual word histories. Rewrite the list using the correct form for listing works cited.

Add quotation marks and underlining as needed. You may wish to refer to Workshop 9, "Research Report" on page 287 to review the form for listing works cited.

Books

O Thou Improper, Thou Uncommon Noun by Willard R. Espy
    Clarkson N. Potter, Inc. New York 1978
The Story of American English by J.N. Hook New York
    Harcourt Brace and Jovanovich 1972

Essays and Articles

The Language Mint: Coiners of New Words in March 1990
    Writing by Richard Ledner pages 21–22
English, an entry from the 1988 World Book Encyclopedia
    pages 312–313

C H E C K P O I N T
PAGES 820–831

A. Rewrite the following paragraph correctly. You will find errors in spelling, capitalization, and punctuation. Pay special attention to the use of apostrophes.

Writing Theme
Hockey

One of ice hockeys greatest players is Bobby Orr, the National Hockey Leagues all-time top-scoring Defenseman. Orrs incredible record include's six one-hundred-point season's and more individual honor's and award's than any other player in the NHLs history. Despite Orr's fame, a reporter once remarked, after dinning with orr in one of Bostons downtown restaurants, "Hes so easygoing. I would forget that I was with one of sports greatest superstars."

Orrs thirteen-year career included six operations on his left knee. Finally, even a Surgeons skill couldnt coax the heros knee to respond. Forced to retire early, Bobby Orr became the Hockey Hall of Fames youngest member in September of 79. Their in the Hall of Fame, the famous number 4s sweater remains as a tribute to its' outstanding owner.

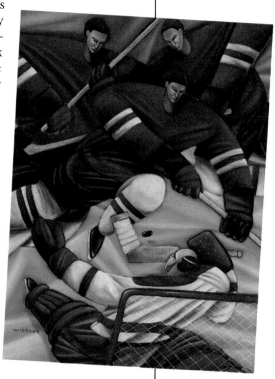

Apostrophes and
Quotation Marks

831

B. Application in Literature Apostrophes and quotation marks have been omitted from the following passages. Rewrite each passage correctly.

(1) A dark silhouette stepped into her path and demanded, Who are you? Where are you going?

(2) Eleni held up her flare and saw more dark figures, ranged all the way up the hill. (3) Eleni Gatzoyiannis, wife of Christos, from the neighborhood of the Perivole, she said, pointing across the ravine. (4) Im trying to find my children.

(5) The figure came closer, and she could see the crown insignia on his two-pointed hat. (6) You cant go any farther, he said. (7) The guerrilla lines are all across the upper half of the village. (8) From here to there is a firing range. (9) But my children are over there! Eleni exclaimed. (10) Well have the whole village by morning, said the soldier. (11) Wait till then.

Nicholas Gage, *Eleni*

(12) Why, Bert Howland, she said, how long have you been sitting here?

(13) All my life, he said. (14) Just waiting here for you. . . .

(15) Flatterer, she said. . . .

(16) Wearing your hair a different way or something, arent you? he asked.

(17) Do you usually notice things like that? she asked.

(18) No, he said. (19) I guess its just the way youre holding your head up. (20) Like you thought I ought to notice something.

Frederick Lang,
"The Beau Catcher"

Using Apostrophes, Quotation Marks, and Italics Rewrite the following transcript of a television interview, correcting any errors in the use of apostrophes, quotation marks, punctuation, italics, and paragraphing.

Writing Theme
Extraterrestrial Life

1. Lets move on to discuss the twelfth episode of the TV series Cosmos, Professor Clark, said Professor Santamarina.

2. I dont remember precisely which episode that is, Joe. Would you refresh my memory asked Professor Clark. And please call me Elizabeth.

3. Fine, Elizabeth. The episode was called Encyclopedia Galactica and dealt with extraterrestrial life he said.

4. Oh, yes, I remember now Professor Clark responded. It was all about speculations that humans are not alone in the universe.

5. "Do you think that theres life on other planets, Joe," continued Professor Clark? "Maybe, answered Professor Santamarina. However, its pretty certain that there isnt life on any of the other planets in our solar system".

6. "How do we know that, asked Professor Clark. "Its simple", he answered, "If you think about it. Mercury and Venus are too hot, and all the other planets atmospheres are too cold.

7. "True, agreed Professor Clark. "but NASAs scientists may be able to use the Hubble telescope to see planets outside this solar system more clearly".

8. "Yes, and dont forget about SETI. As you are aware, SETI means search for extraterrestrial intelligence".

9. "Isnt sending radio waves into space part of a worldwide SETI program"? asked Professor Clark.

10. "Yes, and even Odysseus mythical journey cant compare to the journey radio waves beamed from earth take."

11. "Then theres Harvard Universitys program that listens for radio signals from space". added Professor Clark.

12. Its possible, Elizabeth" continued Professor Santamarina, "That if we do locate planets outside this solar system, perhaps by the late 90s well be able to contact them. This is an instance where my students use of the phrase far out is quite appropriate"!

13. "Then we'll have answers to everybody's questions". Professor Clark said.

14. "Before we bid our viewers adieu, can you tell them where they can learn more about this," she asked?

15. "Michael Hart and Ben Zuckermans book Extraterrestrials: Where Are They? is a good source he responded.

On the Lightside

SHORN WORDS

Many new words are created by the addition of prefixes and suffixes to existing words, but one group of words is created through subtraction. Although television was invented in the 1920's, it wasn't until the 1950's that the

verb *televise* came into the language. Editors made changes in manuscripts long before *edit* existed as a word. These new words are examples of **back-formations.**

Back-formations occur when letters are trimmed from existing words. Often, they are words created by mistake. In the seventeenth century, for example, the word *pease* was mistaken for a plural word because of the "s" sound at the end. The word *pea* came into being as the singular

version, even though *pease* was actually singular. (By the same logic, a new word *chee* might be invented as a singular form of *cheese*.) In other cases, such as the creation of *beg* from *beggar* and *scavenge* from *scavenger,* the letters deleted were mistaken for suffixes, although they really are not.

Mistaken or not, many back-formations have become accepted parts of English. *Bus* came from *omnibus, revolt* came from *revolution, donate* came from *donation, baby-sit* came from *baby-sitter, diagnose* came from *diagnosis,* and *exclaim* came from *exclamation.* In fact, it often seems more logical to assume that the back-formation came first, not the other way around.

Sketchbook

Your local paper has assigned you to interview your favorite celebrity (athlete, artist, entertainer, politician, writer, or other), who has won an award. Begin by citing the name of the celebrity, the name of the award, and the reason for the award. Follow the rules for correct capitalization.

Additional Sketches

Dashes and parentheses are often used in informal writing to help the writer express ideas conversationally. Think of an exciting incident you have experienced or seen. Then write a letter to a friend in which you describe that event. Use correct punctuation, including dashes and parentheses.

Write a phone dialogue between you and a stranger who dialed the wrong number but struck up a conversation anyway. Make sure you use quotation marks and apostrophes correctly.

Directions In each of the following sentences, one, two, or none of the underlined sections many be incorrect. Look for errors of grammar, usage, punctuation, spelling, and capitalization. On your paper, write the number of the sentence, the letter of each incorrect underlined section, and the correction. If the sentence contains no errors, write E.

Example Mark Twains' novel "Huckleberry Finn" has been both
                    A   B   C
praised and censored by school officials. No error
           D   E

Answer A—Twain's B—Huckleberry Finn

---

1. According to a recent survey, 30 percent of Americans have visited Yellowstone Park.
      A   B   C   D
   No error
   E

2. In 1975, when Daniel "Chappie" James, jr., became the first African-American four-star
                                A
   general in the history of the United States military, he excepted the honor with dignity
                      B   C   D
   and pride. No error
            E

3. Recently, mrs. Field published a memoir about how she built a business empire out of
       A   B   C
   making cookies; she entitled the book *One Smart Cookie*. No error
                                 D   E

4. Recently issued spanish language tapes help students learn correct pronunciation,
                    A   B   C
   however, a foreign-language tutor can be even more effective. No error
                               D   E

5. Some of the most interesting national parks in the country include Olympic National
                           A
   Park, which is in the pacific Northwest; Great Smoky Mountain National Park, which is
                    B   C
   in the Appalachian mountain chain, and Haleakala National Park, which is in Hawaii.
                           D
   No error
   E

6. The spacecraft *pioneer I*, which was launched on October 11, 1958 was among the first
              A   B   C   D
   notable planetary probes. No error
                   E

7. At the cathedral of Santiago de Compostela, which is at the end of the pilgrimage route in Spain, pilgrims pray to God and ask him for forgiveness. No error
   A   B   C   D   E

8. Over four trillion gallons of rain fall on the continental United States on an average day.
   A   B   C   D
   No error
   E

9. The United States Supreme Court stands at First and East Capitol Streets in Washington,
        A   B   C   D
   D.C. No error
        E

10. "Easy writing," said Ernest Hemingway, "Makes hard reading." No error
    A   B   C   D   E

11. "These are extraordinary" exclaimed the people who viewed Georgia O'Keeffes works at
         A   B   C
    the Whitney Museum. No error
       D   E

12. To plant carrots, first prepare the soil; second, sow the seeds at a depth of not more
         A   B
    than one fourth inch; third, cover and water the seeds. No error
       C   D   E

13. The State of Alaska lies only 51 mi east of the Siberian mainland across the Bering
       A   B   C   D
    Strait. No error
       E

14. In 1897, most toys could be purchased for less than two dollars; for example, a solid,
         A   B   C
    steel toy wagon started at $115. No error
         D   E

15. Among the few famous people who never graduated from high school are Charlie
    Chaplin, the British actor; Thomas Edison, the American inventor; and Claude Monet,
         A   B   C   D
    the French painter. No error
         E

16. Causing great disruption to sea life two trillion gallons of liquid wastes are dumped in
         A   B   C
    the waters off the United States coast every year. No error
         D   E

17. If <u>your</u> interested in <u>setting up a small business,</u> you can write to the <u>Small Business</u>
         A   **B**   **C**
<u>Administration, 1441</u> L Street, N.W., Washington, <u>D.C. 20416</u> for information and
                                                              D
advice. <u>No error</u>
       E

18. According to Bruce <u>Catton's</u> account of the days just before the outbreak of the Civil
                  A
<u>War, it</u> appears that the main reason for secession <u>was: the</u> failure of the <u>Democratic</u>
  B   **C**   **D**
Convention in Charleston in 1860. <u>No error</u>
                                 E

19. <u>Joseph Montgolfier's and Etienne Montgolfier's</u> first famous <u>hot-air balloon</u> <u>rose up</u> into
                            A   **B**   **C**
the sky and floated away on <u>June 5 1783</u>. <u>No error</u>
                           D   **E**

20. The philosopher <u>Aristotle</u> <u>said</u> <u>"of</u> all an<u>imals, man</u> has the largest brain in proportion
                  A   **B**   **C**
to his <u>size"</u>. <u>No error</u>
       D   **E**

21. <u>Foul Shot</u>, a poem about <u>playing basketball,</u> <u>captures</u> the tension and joy <u>of a winning</u>
   A   **B**   **C**   **D**
<u>moment</u>. <u>No error</u>
          E

22. <u>The ancient Egyptians</u> would wait for the flood waters of the <u>Nile</u> to <u>receed</u> and then
             A   **B**   **C**
<u>would plant their crops</u>. <u>No error</u>
          D   **E**

23. <u>Buckingham Palace</u>, in <u>London, England the</u> home of the <u>Queen of England</u>, has
          A   **B**   **C**
<u>six hundred two rooms</u>. <u>No error</u>
          D   **E**

24. Ernest <u>Hemingways'</u> <u>short stories and novels</u> contain many simple sentences joined by
           A   **B**
<u>and's; he</u> uses these simple sentences to convey strong <u>feellings</u>. <u>No error</u>
  C   **D**   **E**

25. <u>Is it true</u> that Katharine Hepburn <u>said, "Prizes</u> mean <u>nothing. My</u> prize is my <u>work?"</u>
    A   **B**   **C**   **D**
<u>No error</u>
  E

Directions In each of the following sentences, one, two, or none of the underlined sections may be incorrect. Look for errors of grammar, usage, punctuation, spelling, and capitalization. On your paper, write the number of the sentence, the letter of each incorrect underlined section, and the correction. If the sentence contains no errors, write E.

Example The first settlers at <u>Jamestown, Virginia,</u> in 1607 <u>were</u> a
                             A   **B**

group of soldiers and <u>adventerers</u> <u>whom did not know</u> how to grow
                    C   **D**

food. <u>No error</u>
     E

Answer C—adventurers D—who did not know

---

1. Honey is <u>one food</u> that never <u>spoils; in</u> <u>fact, honey</u> found in the tombs of Egyptian
          A   **B**   **C**
   pharaohs <u>is</u> still edible. <u>No error</u>
        D   **E**

2. <u>Extending 1,500 miles</u> <u>through Alaska to British Columbia,</u> <u>engineers keep the Alaska</u>
        A   **B**   **C**   **D**
   <u>Highway open all year.</u> <u>No error</u>
           E

3. The hula hoop is <u>generaly</u> known as the <u>greatest toy fad</u> in <u>history, it was</u> first made
            A   **B**   **C**
   during the <u>1950's.</u> <u>No error</u>
        D   **E**

4. In one fairy <u>tale,</u> <u>a princess,</u> <u>laying</u> still on a golden bed, <u>is woke</u> by a kiss from a prince.
           A   **B**   **C**   **D**
   <u>No error</u>
    E

5. The <u>Chinese</u> leaders ordered troops <u>to surround</u> the <u>square, and</u> the next day the troops
       A   **B**   **C**
   <u>are firing</u> at the people. <u>No error</u>
     D   **E**

6. During the first few years that they were produced, Model-T <u>Fords</u> sold at a brisk pace;
                                         A
   in fact, <u>they</u> accounted for approximately <u>one-half</u> <u>of all the cars sold in 1920.</u> <u>No error</u>
         B   **C**   **D**   **E**

7. <u>In terms of</u> the size of the <u>audience, two</u> of the most popular <u>television-viewing events</u> of
    A   **B**   **C**
   the year are the <u>Super Bowl</u> and the Academy Awards. <u>No error</u>
           D   **E**

8. In several states in the United States. it is illegal to pick wildflowers, start a fire on a
   A   B
   beach or in a park, or light a firecracker. Because some states do not allow these
                                              C
   activities. it is best to know exactly what the laws are in your state before you go hiking
                                D
   or camping. No error
                E

9. To take a good picture. There are a few things you want to avoid. standing too far away,
   A   B   C
   jerking the camera at the last minute, and taking pictures into the sun. Also make sure
                                                                             D
   the background for your photo is uncluttered. No error
                                                 E

10. Each of the reporters at the scene of the fire want to be the first one on the air
                   A   B   C
    with the story. No error
    D   E

11. Scientists used to think that neither marine plants nor animal life exist in the deepest
                           A   B   C
    parts of the ocean. No error
    D   E

12. On the list of endangered species in the United States is the manatee, the American
                                                          A   B
    alligator, the blue pike, the gila troup, the Hawaiian monk seal and the California
                                                  C   D
    condor. No error
            E

13. No one who has an interest in their mental and physical health should take
                                  A   B
    illegal drugs or legal drugs that have not been prescribed by a doctor.
                                    C   D
    No error
    E

14. West Indian food, which was the inspiration for many african-American recipes, often
                      A   B
    tastes strangely to people who are not accustomed to its unusually spicy flavors.
           C   D
    No error
    E

15. Mathematician Edward Kasner named the number 1 followed by 100 zeros a googol; the
    A   B   C
    imaginative people who thought up this name were his nine-year-old nephew and him.
                                                                             D
    No error
    E

16. <u>Who</u> did the children <u>encounter</u> in the <u>Middle East</u> during the famous <u>Children's</u>
     A   **B**   **C**   **D**
    <u>Crusade</u> of 1212? <u>No error</u>
                   E

17. <u>Mercury</u> is hotter <u>than any planet,</u> and <u>Pluto</u> is <u>colder</u> <u>No error</u>
      A   **B**   **C**   **D**   **E**

18. <u>First created</u> by the General Electric Company as a substitute for <u>rubber, Silly</u> Putty was
      A   **B**
    found <u>to be of little industrial use, so</u> it was marketed <u>as a toy.</u> <u>No error</u>
                  C   **D**   **E**

19. At <u>4 17</u> PM on <u>July 20, 1969,</u> Armstrong radioed Houston with the historic message,
      A B   **C**
    "The <u>Eagle</u> has landed." <u>No error</u>
          D   **E**

20. <u>There</u> were <u>not scarcely</u> any tombs in the Valley of the Kings <u>that had not been</u>
      A   **B**   **C**
    <u>plundered or robbed</u> during the many centuries before <u>there</u> excavation. <u>No error</u>
                                               D   **E**

21. Erma Bombeck, Ann <u>Landers, Elizabeth</u> Dole, Ethel <u>Kennedy, and</u> the astronaut
                            A   **B**
    <u>dr. Kathy Sullivan</u> share a common past: they were all <u>Girl Scouts</u> when they were
          C   **D**
    young. <u>No error</u>
            E

22. The pronghorn <u>antelope, which can run at speeds of up to sixty miles per hour, is</u> one
                                              A
    of the <u>fastest</u> land <u>animals</u> but the cheetah <u>is even faster.</u> <u>No error</u>
              B   **C**   **D**   **E**

23. During the nineteenth century, men <u>preceeded</u> women up grand staircases, <u>for fear that</u>
                                   A   **B**
    otherwise the men <u>might see</u> the hems of the <u>womens'</u> dresses. <u>No error</u>
                   C   **D**   **E**

24. The first time <u>that George Gershwin tried</u> <u>to play the piano</u>—<u>when he was ten years</u>
                  A   **B**   **C**
    old—<u>he</u> played an entire song. <u>No error</u>
        D   **E**

25. "Man won't <u>fly,</u>" <u>said</u> Wilbur Wright to his brother Orville in <u>1901,</u> "<u>For</u> a thousand
              A   **B**   **C**
    years." <u>No error</u>
     D   **E**

Appendix

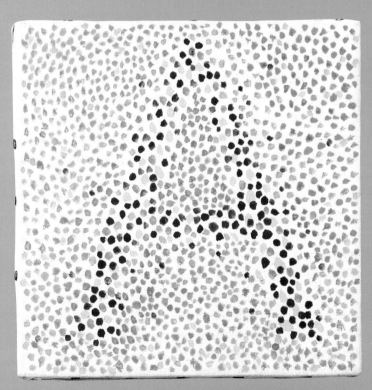

A, Eugene Mihaesco, 1979

IDEAS FOR WRITING

Ideas for writing are everywhere. You need only to recognize and develop them. To help you get your mental wheels rolling, read the following sections and use your thinking skills to generate writing topics. The first section lists ideas by types of writing; the second lists ideas by subject areas.

Narrative
a mistake
an uninvited guest
terror from the sky
a long journey
eyewitness to the news
a great personal success
a biking experience
thrilling entertainment
a narrow escape
making a movie
the final game
meeting an unusual person

Descriptive
wild deer
your favorite place
a photograph you took
tropical fish
a piece of sculpture
what you most like to eat
a car
your own place
an unusual house
the school cafeteria
a big city block
the beach after a storm
a place you dislike
a school in the future
a special person

Literary
a modern tall tale
story of a rescue
a comic monologue
a story for children

a poem about sounds
a script for a puppet show
a self-portrait in verse
a story about an adventure on
   a train
a mystery story
a script for a scene on a TV
   show
a story about a pet
a science fiction adventure

Informative Exposition
Compare you today with you
   five years ago.
Contrast two musicians.
Compare two sports teams.
Compare two movies by the
   same director.
Contrast two places you visit
   frequently.
What causes insomnia?
What causes conflicts
   between parents and
   teenagers?
What are the effects of a
   higher minimum wage?
What causes air pollution?
What are the effects of
   cutting down the rain
   forest?
how to solve your curfew
   problem
what to do about handguns
alternative energy sources
What are some strategies for
   time management?

solving your most important
   problem
finding a summer job

Persuasive
Should school principals
   review articles for student
   newspapers?
fighting the war on drugs
Should force be used in an
   international crisis?
Should state lotteries be
   allowed?
Should school officials be
   allowed to search student
   lockers?
Should the U.S. government
   ration gasoline?
Should parents choose their
   children's schools?

Reports
Olympic Games
life of Mark Twain
the California gold rush
caring for a parrot
origins of rock and roll
Ayers Rock
the destruction of ancient
   Pompeii
the tomb of King Tut
songs of whales
exploring Alaska
the tunnel under the English
   Channel
Teach for America

Ideas for Writing in Subject Areas

Art
origami
handmade paper
Georgia O'Keeffe
urban wall murals
the Taj Mahal
performance art
a favorite painting
role of the artist in society
fine art photographs
furniture design
neon sculpture
history of fashion design
Native American art
decorating a family room

Consumer Education
government warning labels on
    products
copyright laws and
    photocopying
real information in ads
hidden costs of owning a car
quality in sports equipment
buying clothes on a budget
how to complain about
    defective merchandise
the health insurance crisis
starting a small business
how the stock exchange
    works

Health
a first aid or emergency
    procedure
causes and effects of high
    blood pressure
a favorite form of exercise
stress management
genetic testing
stop smoking strategies
prevention of sunburn

home remedies for head colds
a healthy, enjoyable diet
how vitamins work
the controversy over water
    fluorination
allergies

Mathematics
the mathematical discoveries
    of Leonhard Euler
Mayan mathematics
geometry and architecture
the golden ratio
computer spreadsheets
walks guided by the sun
mathematics in the works of
    Albrecht Durer
geometry and music
the origins of algebra
how children learn
    mathematics
how the census works
astronomy and mathematics
how TV ratings are figured

Music
a record review
Compare live and recorded
    music.
experimental music
the "new music"
the life of a twentieth-
    century composer
folk music in the U.S.
ethno-pop or world music
musical sounds vs. noise
the value of rap
history of the Grammy
    Awards
music videos
the life of Mozart
Compare two music schools.

harmony
a favorite group or performer

Science
Why explore space?
new discoveries about the
    universe
Einstein rings
geothermal energy
an important medical
    discovery
self-contained ecosystems
fish farming (aquaculture)
the care and keeping of
    unusual pets
the habitat needs of the bald
    eagle
new ways to reduce air
    pollution
rain forest destruction and
    global warming
biodegradable plastics

Social Science
your neighborhood today and
    100 years ago
Abigail Adams
life in colonial Williamsburg
Stonehenge
global economy
a letter to your city council
    about an issue of impor-
    tance to you
censorship in school and pub-
    lic libraries
Grant and Lee at Appomattox
Alexander the Great
archaeological finds in China
the lost treasures of Mexico
world population trends
researching your family
    history

An outline, whether it follows a specified form or simply groups ideas together logically, can help you organize your ideas for writing. An outline is also useful for taking notes.

Types of Outlines

A **formal outline** shows the main points of a topic, the order in which they are to be presented, and the relationships among them. Formal outlines are useful when writing formal compositions or speeches and when outlining chapters for study.

There are two types of formal outlines: sentence outlines and topic outlines. In a **sentence outline,** each main topic and subtopic is written in a complete sentence. Below is a portion of a sentence outline.

Painting a Landscape in Oils

Introduction — Anyone can paint a simple landscape by following a few step-by-step procedures.

  I. Choose materials and a subject.
    A. Purchase a few basic art supplies.
      1. Buy paints in black, white, and the primary colors.
      2. Buy paper, an eraser, and pencils or charcoal.
      3. Buy canvas, a palette, and brushes.
    B. Beginners should choose a simple subject.
      1. Do not include buildings, people, or animals.
      2. Paint large areas of water, sky, or forest seen from a distance.
  II. Make preliminary sketches of your subject.
    A. Draw canvas-sized sketches of your subject on paper.
    B. Transfer the best sketch to your canvas using light pencil or charcoal.
  III. Paint your landscape.
    A. Decide on the colors you wish to use.
      1. Mix the colors on your palette.
      2. Experiment until you find colors you like.
    B. Begin painting.
      1. Start with light colors, then use darks.
      2. Work over entire canvas rather than in small areas.
      3. Create highlights with light colors.

A **topic outline** uses words or phrases instead of complete sentences. Below is a portion of a topic outline.

First Steps to First Aid

Introduction—to explain the initial actions a person should take when giving first aid.

I. Goals of first aid
  A. To prevent further injury
  B. To ease pain
  C. To soothe fears
II. How to begin giving first aid
  A. Staying calm
  B. Avoiding movement of victim
  C. Preventing shock
    1. Symptoms of shock
    2. Treatment of shock
  D. Reassuring victim

Before making an outline, decide whether a sentence or topic outline better suits your needs. Once you begin, do not mix forms within a given outline.

Correct Outline Form

1. Center the title at the top of the page. Below it, write your thesis statement, or a shortened version of it.
2. Use the arrangement of numerals and letters that you see in the two models for main points and subpoints.
3. When a heading is a subpoint of the previous heading, indent its letter or numeral, placing it directly underneath the first letter in the first word of the previous heading.
4. Either use two or more subheadings or details under a heading or don't use any at all. In other words, for every *A* there should be a *B*, and for every 1, a 2.
5. In a topic outline, keep items of the same rank in parallel form. For instance, if A is a noun, then B and C should also be nouns. However, the form of subtopics does not need to parallel the form of main topics.
6. Begin each item with a capital letter. Do not use end punctuation in a topic outline.

When you use the correct form for your business letter, you make a positive impression on your reader. Following are explanations of the parts of a business letter and examples of two correct business letter forms.

Block Form and Modified Block Form

Use plain, white, 8 ½" × 11" paper for all business letters, whether you handwrite or type them. In **block form,** all parts begin at the left margin. Use this form only when you type the letter not when you handwrite a letter. In **modified block form,** the heading, closing, and signature are aligned near the right margin; the other parts begin at the left margin.

Block Form

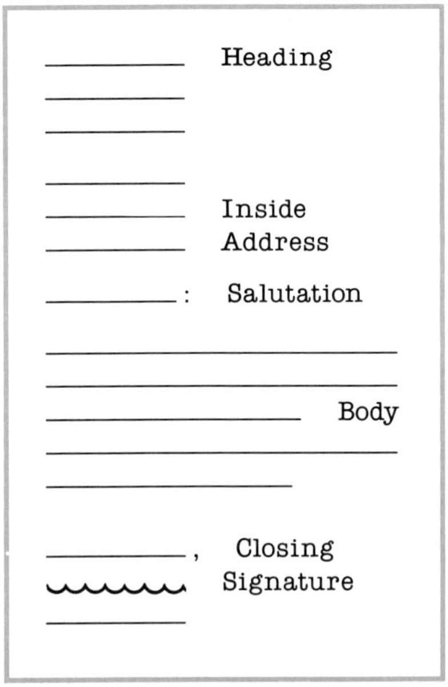

Modified Block Form

Block Form	Modified Block Form
_____ Heading	Heading _____
_____ Inside Address	_____ Inside Address
_____ : Salutation	_____ : Salutation
_____ Body	_____ Body
_____ , Closing Signature	Closing _____ , Signature

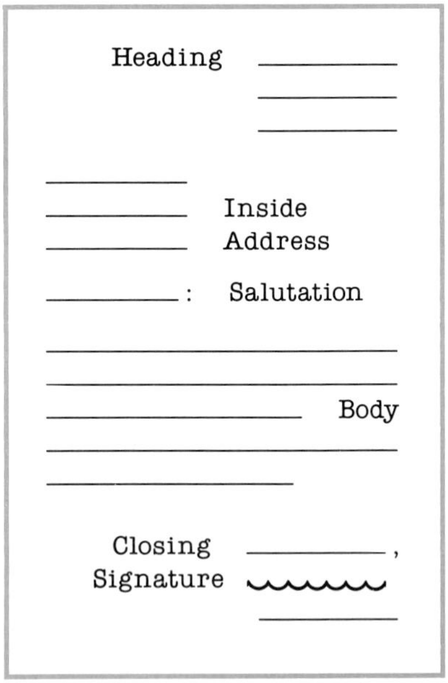

Heading The heading is written at the top of the page. The first line contains your street address; the second line contains your town or city, state, and ZIP code. Separate the city and state with a comma and write out the name of the state. The third line gives the date of the letter. Place the heading at the left or the right margin, depending on whether you use the block form or the modified block form.

Inside Address The inside address tells to whom the letter is being sent. Place the inside address at the left margin at least four lines below the heading. On the first line you should place the name of the receiver. If there is room, place the person's title on the same line, separated from the name by a comma. Otherwise, place the title on the next line. If you do not know the name of the person who will receive your letter, use the person's title or the name of the department. On the succeeding lines, place the company name and address, including the city, state, and ZIP code.

The inside address is important because occasionally a letter is opened by someone other than the addressee, and the envelope is discarded. If this happens, the name and address of the receiver can still be found. Following are two typical inside addresses.

Sylvia Hersh	Customer Service Department
Hersh Publishing Company	ABC Electronics Company
19 First Avenue	4511 River Road
Woodville, Ohio 44006	Greenville, California 90272

Salutation Position the salutation two lines below the inside address. Begin with the word *Dear,* follow it by the name of the person to whom you are writing, and end with a colon. Use only the person's last name, preceded by a title such as *Mr., Mrs., Ms., Dr.,* or *Professor.* If you do not know the person's name, use a general salutation such as *Ladies and Gentlemen.* Another alternative is to write to a department or to a position within a company. The following forms are acceptable.

Dear Mr. Monroe:	Dear Sir or Madam:
Dear Ms. Mizel:	Dear Customer Service Department:
Dear Mrs. Reilly:	Dear Editor:

Body The body, the main part of the letter in which you write your message, begins two spaces below the salutation. The body may contain a single paragraph or several paragraphs. Leave a space between each paragraph.

Closing The closing is placed two lines below the body, in line with the heading. Closings commonly used for business letters include *Sincerely, Sincerely yours,* and *Very truly yours.* Note that only the first word is capitalized and that the closing ends with a comma.

Signature Type or print your name four spaces below the closing, and sign your name in the space between.

USING A WORD PROCESSOR

Word processing, like other uses of computers, is becoming part of our daily lives. A word processor can help you become a better, more effective writer. Here are some techniques to help you use a word processor efficiently.

Goal	Technique	Comment
Keep a notebook of general writing ideas.	Create a file called "notebook." Record ideas, responses to reading, quotes, jokes, incidents, interesting news reports—anything that may later serve as a writing topic.	An electronic notebook provides you with a way to find and retrieve ideas quickly and expand on them freely.
Brainstorm ideas to find a writing topic.	Dim the screen light and freewrite for ten minutes. Print what you have written. Circle ideas you could develop further.	Turning the screen light down is one technique for writing freely without worrying about errors.
Add, replace, or reorder text.	Use the insert, delete, replace, move, cut, and paste commands.	A word processor encourages revision and experimentation because changes are simple and easy to make.
Keep notes to yourself.	Type notes to yourself as you write. Use all capital letters or some device, such as an asterisk, to quickly identify the notes during revision.	Replace the notes with new text as you revise.

Goal	Technique	Comment
Experiment with ways of expressing ideas.	Write a number of alternatives separated by slashes (/). At a later stage, use the search command to find the slashes— places where you will make choices.	As you write, include several alternatives but don't evaluate them. Later, delete or move the words or versions you don't wish to use.
Check your spelling.	Activate the "spelling" command if your program has one. In addition, always proofread carefully.	The program will highlight misspellings, many typing errors, and most proper nouns. Proofread for errors the program cannot catch, such as missing words, punctuation errors, and incorrect words.
Make your paper attractive and readable.	Set margins and line spacing. Insert headings and subheadings. Print a sample page and change the settings if necessary. Insert appropriate page breaks.	Your pages are most readable when page breaks come at natural divisions. Frequent headings and subheadings help break up the text into readable sections.
Make your organization clear.	Use type styles such as underlining, italics, and boldface type to highlight the various headings and subheadings in your paper.	Various type sizes and styles are offered by many word processing programs.

The following response techniques can help you give and receive useful responses as you share your writing with others. These techniques can also help you as the writer to be in charge of the feedback process and to find out what kinds of responses are most useful to you.

How to Use	When to Use
Sharing	
Read your words out loud to a peer. Your purpose is simply to share and to hear how your words sound. Your listeners may ask you to slow down or to read your piece again, but they offer no feedback of any kind.	Do this when you are just exploring and you don't want criticism. Reading to a peer is also useful when your writing is finished and you want to celebrate by sharing it with another person.
Saying Back or Restating	
Ask readers, "What do you hear me saying?" As readers say back what they hear, they are inviting you to figure out better what you really want to say.	Use this type of feedback when you are still exploring and when you want to find ways to change and develop your ideas.
Pointing	
Ask readers to tell you what they like best in your writing. Tell them to be specific and to avoid simply saying, "I liked it."	Use this technique when you want to know what is getting through to your readers or when you want some encouragement and support.

How to Use	When to Use
Summarizing	
Ask readers to tell you what they hear as the main meaning or message in your writing. Make clear that you don't want evaluation of the writing at this time.	Use this technique when you want to know what is getting through to readers.
Responding to Specific Features	
Ask for feedback on specific features of the writing such as the organization, or the persuasive power, or the spelling and punctuation. Ask readers to respond to specific questions, such as, "Are the ideas supported with enough examples?" "Did I persuade you?" "Is the organization clear enough so you could follow the ideas easily?"	Use when you want a quick overview of the strengths and weaknesses of your piece.
Replying	
Discuss the ideas in your writing with your readers. Ask readers to give you their ideas on the topic. Be sure to talk with your peer readers about *what* you have said, not *how* you have said it.	Use this strategy when you want to make your writing richer by using new ideas.
Playing Movies of the Reader's Mind	
Invite readers to tell you what happens inside their heads as they read your writing. Interrupt the reading and ask readers to tell you what they are thinking at the moment of interruption.	This technique is useful at any stage of the writing. Because it can lead to blunt criticism, use this peer response method only when you have a relationship of trust and support with your reader.

Adapted from *Sharing and Responding* by Peter Elbow and Pat Belanoff.

The following section explains many common misuses of individual words. Use this section to make sure you are using words correctly in your writing.

accept, except *Accept* means "to agree to or willingly receive something." *Except* usually means "not including."

> Dawn was *accepted* into the summer science program.
> Every Great Lake *except* Lake Ontario has a shoreline
>   in Michigan.

adapt, adopt *Adapt* means "to make apt or suitable; to adjust." *Adopt* means "to opt or choose as one's own; to accept."

> The writer *adapted* the play for the screen.
> After years of living in Japan, she had *adopted* its culture.

advice, advise *Advice* is a noun that means "counsel given to someone." *Advise* is a verb that means "to give counsel."

> Jim should take some of his own *advice*.
> The mechanic *advised* me to get new brakes for my car.

affect, effect *Affect* means "to move or influence" or "to wear or to pretend to have." *Effect* as a verb means "to bring about." As a noun, effect means "the result of an action."

> The news from South Africa *affected* him deeply.
> The band's singer *affects* a British accent.
> The students tried to *effect* a change in school policy.
> What *effect* did the acidic soil produce in the plants?

all ready, already *All ready* means "completely prepared" or "all are ready." *Already* means "by the given time" or "even now."

> Chang Li is *all ready* for the exhibition of her collages.
> The bands are *all ready* for the parade to begin.
> The lake has *already* frozen over.

all right *All right* is the correct spelling. *Alright* is nonstandard English and should not be used.

> We thought Tammy might have sprained her ankle, but she is
>   *all right*.

a lot is informal and should not be used in formal writing. *Alot* is always incorrect.

among, between   are prepositions. *Between* refers to two people or things. The object of *between* is never singular. *Among* refers to a group of three or more.

>Texas lies *between* Louisiana and New Mexico.
>What are the differences *among* the candidates?

altogether   is an adverb that means "entirely" or "on the whole."

>The news story is *altogether* false.

anywhere, nowhere, somewhere,   and **anyway** are correct. *Anywheres, nowheres, somewheres,* and *anyways* are incorrect.

>I don't see geometry mentioned *anywhere.*
>*Somewhere* in this book is a map of ancient Sumer.
>*Anyway,* this street map is out of date.

borrow, lend   *Borrow* means "to receive something on loan." *Lend* means "to give out temporarily" and is often used with an indirect object.

>She *borrowed* my bicycle.
>Could you *lend* me your umbrella?

bring, take   *Bring* refers to movement toward or with. *Take* refers to movement away from.

>Mom usually *brings* a newspaper home with her.
>Would you please *take* these apples to Donna and Richard?

can, may   *Can* means "to be able or to have the power to do something." *May* means "to have permission to do something." *May* can also mean "possibly will."

>We *may* not use pesticides on our community garden plot.
>Pesticides *may* not be necessary, anyway.
>Vegetables *can* grow nicely without pesticides.

differ from, differ with   *Differ from* means "to be dissimilar." *Differ with* means "to disagree with."

>The racing bicycle *differs* greatly *from* the mountain bicycle.
>I *differ with* her as to the meaning of Hamlet's speech.

different from   is used to compare dissimilar items. *Different than* is nonstandard.

>The hot sauce is much *different from* the yogurt sauce.

farther, further *Farther* means "more distant." *Further* means "additional."

> Robin's putt went *farther* than Jenny's.
> I think you need *further* information.

fewer, less *Fewer* refers to numbers of things that can be counted. *Less* refers to amount or quantity.

> I took *fewer* pictures because I had *less* money for developing.

imply, infer *Imply* means "to suggest something in an indirect way." *Infer* means "to come to a conclusion based on something that has been read or heard."

> Josh *implied* that he would be taking the bus.
> From what the others said, I *inferred* that they would be getting rides.

it's, they're, who's, and **you're** all are contractions, not possessives. The possessive forms are *its, their, whose,* and *your.*

> *You're* eagerly awaited.
> Babylon attained *its* greatest glory around 600 B.C.

kind of, sort of Neither of these two expressions should be followed by the word *a.*

> What *kind of* horse is Scout?
> What *sorts of* animals live in swamps?

The use of these two expressions as adverbs, as in "It's kind of warm today," is informal.

learn, teach *Learn* means to gain knowledge or acquire a skill. *Teach* means "to instruct."

> Jerome is *learning* Portuguese.
> He *teaches* astronomy to seniors at the planetarium.

leave, let *Leave* means "to go away from." *Leave* can be transitive or intransitive, but it is never used in a verb phrase. *Let* is usually used with another verb. It means "to allow to."

> Don't *leave* the refrigerator open.
> She *leaves* for Scotland tomorrow.
> Cyclops wouldn't *let* Odysseus' men *leave* the cave.

like as a conjunction before a clause is incorrect. Use *as* or *as if.*

> Ramon talked *as if* he had a cold.

majority means more than half of a group of things or people that can be counted. It is incorrect to use *majority* in referring to time or distance, as in "The *majority* of our time there was wasted."

> *Most* of our time there was wasted.
> The *majority* of the students study a foreign language.

most, almost *Most* can be a noun, an adjective, or an adverb, but it should never be used in place of *almost,* an adverb that means "nearly."

> *Most* of the students enjoy writing in their journals. (*most* as a noun)
> *Most* mammals give live birth. (*most* as an adjective)
> You missed the *most* exciting part. (*most* as an adverb)
> *Almost* every mammal gives live birth.

of is incorrectly used in a phrase such as *could of.* Examples of correct wordings are *could have, should have,* and *must have. Of* should not follow the verb *had* or the preoposition *off,* as in "Take your coat *off of* the hanger."

> I *must have* missed the phone call.
> If you *had played,* we *would have* won.
> The ball bounced *off* the goal post.

raise, rise *Raise* is a transitive verb that means "to lift" or "to make something go up." It takes a direct object. *Rise* is an intransitive verb that means "to go upward." It does not take a direct object.

> I wanted to *raise* the handlebars on my bike.
> The ocean tides *rise* on a regular schedule.

real, really *Real* is an adjective meaning "actual; true." *Really* is an adverb meaning "in reality; in fact."

> *Real* skill comes from concentration and practice.
> She doesn't *really* know all the facts.

seldom should not be followed by *ever,* as in "We *seldom ever* run more than a mile." *Seldom, rarely, very seldom,* and *hardly ever* all are correct.

> I *seldom* hear traditional jazz.

way refers to distance; *ways* is nonstandard and should not be used in writing.

> The subway was a long *way* from the stadium.

Several strategies can help you improve your spelling. If you write frequently and keep lists of words you are not sure how to spell, your spelling will almost certainly improve. Good spellers also often use mnemonic devices, or memory aids, to help them spell better. For example, you might remember that there is a rat in separate. Proofreading your writing and using a dictionary to look up new and different words is another effective strategy.

The following rules can help you eliminate spelling errors.

The Addition of Prefixes

When a prefix is added to a word, the spelling of the word remains the same. When a prefix creates a double letter, keep both letters.

pre- + arrange = prearrange   co- + operate = cooperate
re- + discover = rediscover   mis- + spell = misspell
anti- + trust = antitrust   il- + logical = illogical

The Suffixes *-ly* and *-ness*

When the suffix *-ly* is added to a word ending in *l*, keep both *l's*. When *-ness* is added to a word ending in *n*, keep both *n's*.

general + -ly = generally   keen + -ness = keenness
truthful + -ly = truthfully   sudden + -ness = suddenness
wool + -ly = woolly   lean + -ness = leanness

Suffixes with Silent *e*

When a suffix beginning with a vowel or *y* is added to a word ending in a silent *e*, the *e* is usually dropped.

make + -ing = making   fascinate + -ion = fascination
knife + -ing = knifing   rose + -y = rosy

When a suffix beginning with a consonant is added to a word ending with a silent *e*, the *e* is usually retained.

home + -less = homeless   divine + -ly = divinely
subtle + -ness = subtleness   lone + -ly = lonely
require + -ment = requirement   fate + -ful = fateful

Exceptions include *truly, argument, ninth, wholly,* and *awful.*

When a suffix beginning with *a* or *o* is added to a word with a final silent *e*, the final *e* is usually retained if it is preceded by a soft *c* or a soft *g*.

bridge + -able = bridgeable
courage + -ous = courageous
peace + -able = peaceable
advantage + -ous = advantageous
outrage + -ous = outrageous
manage + -able = manageable

When a suffix beginning with a vowel is added to words ending in *ee* or *oe*, the final silent *e* is retained.

agree + -ing = agreeing   toe + -ing = toeing
hoe + -ing = hoeing   decree + -ing = decreeing
free + -ing = freeing   see + -ing = seeing

Suffixes with Final *y*

When a suffix is added to a word ending in *y*, and the *y* is preceded by a consonant, the *y* is changed to *i* except with the suffix *-ing*.

silly + -ness = silliness   marry + -age = marriage
happy + -est = happiest   dally + -ing = dallying
carry + -ed = carried   empty + -ing = emptying
merry + -ly = merrily   marry + -ing = marrying

Exceptions include *dryness, shyness,* and *slyness.*

When a suffix is added to a word ending in *y* preceded by a vowel, the *y* usually does not change.

pray + -ing = praying   destroy + -er = destroyer
enjoy + -ing = enjoying   coy + -ness = coyness
gray + -ly = grayly   decay + -ing = decaying

Exceptions include *daily* and *gaily.*

Doubling the Final Consonant

In one-syllable words that end with a single consonant preceded by a single vowel, double the final consonant before adding a suffix beginning with a vowel.

grab + -ing = grabbing   drug + ist = druggist
dig + -er = digger   slim + -est = slimmest

Do not double the final consonant in one-syllable words ending in one consonant preceded by *two* vowels.

treat + -ing = treating feeling + -ing = feeling
loot + -ed = looted clean + -ing = cleaning

In two-syllable words, double the consonant only if both of the following conditions exist:

1. The word ends with a single consonant preceded by a single vowel.
2. The word is accented on the second syllable.

re•gret′ + -ed = regretted
per•mit′ + -ing = permitting
de•ter′ + -ence = deterrence

If the newly formed word is accented on a different syllable, the final consonant is not doubled.

re•fer′ + -ence = ref′•er•ence
prof•′it + -eer = prof•i•teer′

Some words are correct with a single or double consonant: *canceled* or *cancelled, equiped* or *equipped, traveled* or *travelled*. Check your dictionary for the preferred spelling.

Words with *ie* and *ei*

When the sound is long *e* (ē), the word is spelled *ie*, except after *c*.

retrieve pier receive
piece brief conceit

When the sound is long *a* (ā), the word is spelled *ei*.

sleigh neighbor
beige freight

Exceptions include *either, friend, leisure, neither, seize, sieve, species, weird, forfeit, financier,* and *Fahrenheit*.

Words with the *"Seed"* Sound

There are three suffixes in English pronounced "seed." They are spelled -*cede,* -*ceed,* and -*sede.*

-*cede*   accede, antecede, cede, concede, intercede, precede, recede, secede
-*ceed*   exceed, proceed, succeed
-*sede*   supersede

A sentence diagram is a drawing that helps you understand how the parts of a sentence are related. In addition, diagraming sharpens your critical thinking skills by requiring you to analyze sentences, classify their parts, and determine relationships among those parts.

The base for a sentence diagram is made up of a horizontal main line crossed by a short vertical line.

Subjects and Verbs

Place the simple subject on the horizontal main line to the left of the vertical line. Place the simple predicate, or verb, to the right. Capitalize only those words that are capitalized in the sentence. Do not use punctuation except for abbreviations.

We sing.   Thomas has auditioned.

| We | sing | | Thomas | has auditioned |

Interrogative Sentences

In an interrogative sentence, the subject often comes after the verb or after part of the verb phrase. In diagraming, remember to place the subject before the verb to the left of the vertical line.

Has he finished?   Can anyone contribute?

| he | Has finished | | anyone | Can contribute |

Imperative Sentences

In an imperative sentence, the subject is usually not stated. Since commands are given to the person spoken to, the subject is understood to be *you*. To diagram an imperative sentence, place the understood subject *you* to the left of the vertical line. Then enclose *you* in parentheses. Place the verb to the right of the vertical line.

Wait!   Dive!

| (you) | Wait | | (you) | Dive |

Modifiers

Diagram adjectives and adverbs on slanted lines below the words they modify. If an adverb modifies an adjective or another adverb, write the adverb on an L-shaped line connected to the adjective or adverb that it modifies. Keep in mind that words like *not* and *never* are adverbs.

Our awkward waiter spoke too softly.

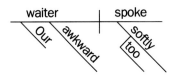

When two or more modifiers are connected by a conjunction, place the modifiers on slanted lines below the words they modify. Connect the slanted lines with a broken line and write the conjunction on it.

A red and yellow parrot chattered loudly.

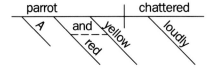

Direct and Indirect Objects

In a diagram, place the direct object on the main line after the verb. Separate the direct object from the verb with a vertical line that does not extend below the main line. Place indirect objects below the verb on lines parallel to the main lines and connected to the main line by slanted lines, as you see here.

My barber gave me a compliment.

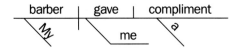

Subject Complements

Place a predicate nominative or a predicate adjective on the main line after the verb. Separate the subject complement from the verb with a slanted line that extends in the direction of the subject.

Mary undoubtedly will be our next president.
(Predicate nominative)

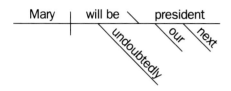

George had always seemed more or less reliable.
(Predicate adjective)

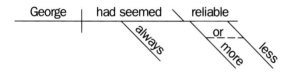

Sentences with Compound Parts

To diagram compound parts, place the parts on parallel horizontal lines as shown below. Then connect the parallel lines with a broken line. On the broken line, write the conjunction that connects the compound parts. Attach the compound parts to the main line with solid diagonal lines. The sentence below has a compound subject and a compound verb.

Snakes and lizards have lungs and eat only live food.

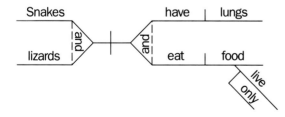

Compound Direct Objects and Indirect Objects To diagram compound direct objects or indirect objects, place the objects on parallel horizontal lines connected with a broken line. Write the conjunction on the line. Attach the compound parts to the main line as shown below.

The magician showed my brother and me her favorite tricks and her most fantastic stunts.

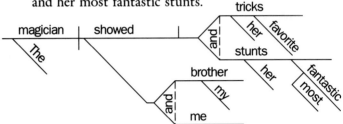

Prepositional Phrases

Draw a slanted line below the word the phrase modifies. From the slanted line, draw a line parallel to the main line. Place the preposition on the slanted line and the object of the preposition on the parallel line. Words that modify the object of the preposition are placed on slanted lines below the object.

Eric painted a portrait of Lester Young.

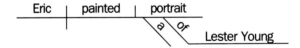

If a preposition has a compound object, place the objects on parallel lines as shown below.

Some stagecoach drivers were known for their determination and their bravery.

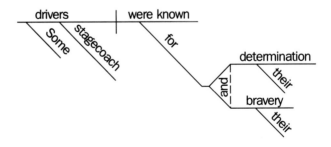

Gerunds and Gerund Phrases

To diagram a gerund, place it on a line drawn as a step (⌐). Put the step on a forked line (人) that stands on the main line. The placement of the forked line varies and is determined by whether the gerund or gerund phrase is used as a subject, a direct object, a predicate nominative, or the object of a preposition. If the gerund phrase includes a direct object or modifiers, place those on lines as shown below.

Exercising daily improves fitness. *(gerund phrase used as subject)*

We enjoyed taking the aptitude test. *(gerund phrase used as direct object)*

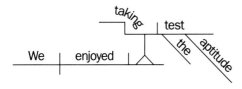

To diagram a gerund or gerund phrase that is the object of a preposition, place the preposition on a slanted line that extends from the modified word. Then place the step and the forked line below the main line as shown below.

After swimming, they relaxed.

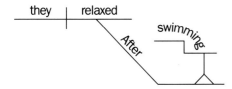

Participles and Participial Phrases

To diagram a participle, place the participle on an angled line below the word it modifies. If the participial phrase includes a direct object, separate the object and the participle with a vertical line. Place modifiers on slanted lines below the words they modify.

Purring softly, the kitten lay down.

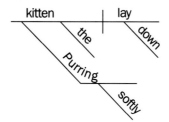

Infinitives and Infinitive Phrases

To diagram an infinitive, place the infinitive on an angled line. Write the word *to* on the slanted part and write the verb on the horizontal part of the angled line. Put the angled line on a forked line that stands on the main line. The placement shows how the infinitive or infinitive phrase is used in the sentence. In the following sentence the infinitive is a direct object.

We want to have a beach party soon.

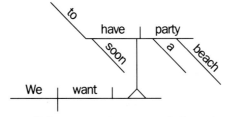

Appositives and Appositive Phrases

To diagram an appositive, place the appositive in parentheses after the word it identifies or explains. Place modifiers on slanted lines below the appositive.

The ostrich, a native bird of Africa, can run swiftly.

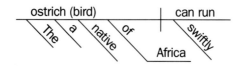

Adjective Clauses

To diagram an adjective clause, place the clause on its own horizontal line below the main line and diagram it as if it were a sentence. Use a broken line to connect the relative pronoun in the adjective clause to the word that the clause modifies.

The route that they took led through Washington.

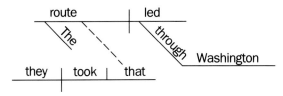

Adverb Clauses

To diagram an adverb clause, place the clause on its own horizontal line below the main line, and diagram the clause as if it were a sentence. Use a broken line to connect the adverb clause to the word it modifies. Write the conjunction on the broken line.

When the car stopped, we lurched forward.

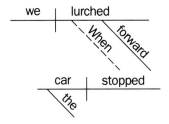

Noun Clauses

To diagram a noun clause, place the clause on a separate line that is attached to the main line with a forked line. The placement of the forked line in the diagram shows how the noun clause is used in the sentence. Diagram the word introducing the noun clause according to its function in the clause.

Juri could not believe what he saw. *(noun clause used as direct object)*

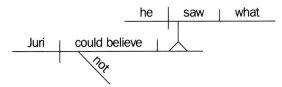

Compound Sentences

To diagram a compound sentence, place the independent clauses on parallel horizontal lines. Use a broken line with a step to connect the verb in one clause to the verb in the other clause. Write the conjunction on the step. If the clauses are joined by a semicolon, leave the step blank.

The game was close, but we finally won.

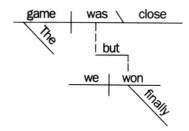

Complex Sentences

To diagram a complex sentence, decide whether the subordinate clause is an adjective clause, an adverb clause, or a noun clause. Then follow the rule for diagraming that kind of clause.

Compound-Complex Sentences

To diagram a compound-complex sentence, diagram the independent clauses first then attach the subordinate clause or clauses to the words they modify. Leave enough room to attach a subordinate clause where it belongs.

Franklin Pierce, our fourteenth President, accidentally collided with an old lady while he was riding on horseback, and a policeman arrested him.

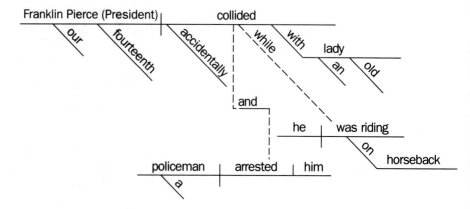

ALLITERATION repetition of beginning sounds of words, usually in poetry but also in prose; for example, the "b" sound in "the silver bell beating, beating."

ANALOGY a comparison usually used to explain an idea or support an argument. For example, an analogy might help explain the movement of blood cells through the body's branching system of blood vessels by comparing it with the daily flow of cars on the system of freeways, roads, and small streets that surrounds a city.

ANALYSIS a way of thinking that involves taking apart, examining, and explaining a subject or idea.

ANECDOTE a brief story, usually told to illustrate a point.

ARGUMENT speaking or writing that takes a position or states an opinion and provides the evidence or reasons to support it—often in a context of opposing points of view.

AUDIENCE the readers or listeners to whom any discourse is directed.

AUTOBIOGRAPHY a biography (life story) told by the person whose life it is.

BIBLIOGRAPHY a list of sources used or recommended (articles, books, encyclopedia) in a research paper or report. Also known as Works Cited.

BRAINSTORMING a way of gathering many ideas by quickly listing them as they occur, without judging their usefulness.

CAUSE AND EFFECT a strategy for analyzing a subject by examining the reasons for specific actions or events or the consequences or results of certain causes.

CHRONOLOGICAL organized according to time sequence.

CLARITY the quality of being clear or as easy to understand as possible.

CLASSIFICATION a type of writing that involves systematically grouping items by some system or principle; frequently involves defining or comparing and contrasting items or groups of items.

CLICHÉ a phrase, figure of speech, or idea used so often that it is predictable, showing little imagination or thought, as in "happy as a lark."

CLUSTERING a brainstorming technique that shows how ideas are connected to one another; gives a quick map of thoughts about a topic.

COHERENCE connectedness, a sense that parts hold together; an essay is coherent when its parts fit together logically and are linked by connecting words and phrases.

COLLABORATION working with other people; giving others support and advice; helping others solve problems.

COLLOQUIAL conversational, linguistically informal; the way people ordinarily speak in conversation.

COMPARISON AND CONTRAST a strategy for thinking or writing that involves explaining, defining, or evaluating subjects by showing how they resemble and differ from each other or from some standard for evaluation.

CONNOTATION the attitudes and feelings associated with a word or idea as opposed to its dictionary definition. The word "determined" differs from "stubborn" in its connotations.

CONTEXT the setting or situation in which something happens, particularly in which words or sentences are uttered or written.

CONTROVERSY a disagreement, often one that has attracted public interest.

COUNTERARGUMENT a refutation, an argument made to oppose (counter) another argument.

CRITICISM discourse (usually an essay) that analyzes something (usually a literary or artistic work) in order to evaluate how it does or does not succeed in communicating its meaning or achieving its purposes.

CUBING a method for discovering ideas about a topic by using six strategies (in any order) to investigate it: describe it, compare it, associate it, analyze it, apply it, argue for or against it.

DEDUCTIVE REASONING deriving a specific conclusion by reasoning from a general premise.

DENOTATION   the literal meaning of a word, without its *connotations*.

DESCRIPTION   an account, usually giving a dominant impression and emphasizing sensory detail, of what it is like to experience some object, scene, or person.

DIALECT   a form of language (usually regional) differing from the standard language in pronunciation, word choice, and syntax. Southern American English or New England English or Australian English are dialects of English.

DIALOGUE   the spoken conversation of fictional characters or actual persons as it is presented in a novel, story, poem, play, or essay.

DOCUMENTATION   naming the documents or other sources used to provide the information reported in an essay or other discourse; usually cited in footnotes or in parentheses.

ELABORATION   the development of an argument, description, narration, or explanation with details, evidence, and other support.

EXPOSITION   writing whose purpose is to explain an idea or teach a process rather than to tell a story, describe something, or argue for a point of view.

EXPRESSIVE   a kind of discourse full of meaning or feeling; often personal writing used by writers to explore ideas.

FICTION   made-up or imaginary happenings, as opposed to statements of fact or nonfiction. Short stories and novels are fiction, even though they may be based on real events. Essays, scientific articles, biographies, news stories are nonfiction.

FIGURATIVE LANGUAGE   language that uses such figures of speech as similes, metaphors, and personification to show one thing as if it were something else.

FORMAL LANGUAGE   careful and somewhat rigid language often used in formal situations such as business communications or school reports.

FREEWRITING   a way of discovering what you know or think or feel by writing rapidly, without stopping, without editing, and without looking back (until you finish) at what you've written.

GENERALIZATION   a statement expressing a principle or drawing a conclusion based on examples or instances.

GLEANING a method of picking up ideas by observing events and by scanning through newspapers, magazines, and books and talking to others in order to find material to write about or to use in writing.

GRAPHIC ORGANIZER a method for visually organizing a complex body of information; includes charts, graphs, outlines, clusters, and tree diagrams.

IMAGERY figurative language and descriptions as the means of vividly rendering experience in language.

INDUCTIVE REASONING a method of thinking or organizing a discourse so that a series of instances or pieces of evidence lead to a conclusion or generalization.

INFERENCE a conclusion derived by reasoning from facts.

INTERPRETATION to explain the meaning of any text, set of facts, object, gesture, or event. To *interpret* something is to try to make sense of it.

INVISIBLE WRITING typing with a dimmed computer screen or writing with an empty ball point pen on a paper that covers a piece of carbon paper and a bottom clean sheet.

JARGON the special language and terminology used by people in the same profession or who share specialized interests; for example, television and radio producers, physicians, and police.

JOURNAL a record of thoughts and impressions mainly for personal use.

KNOWLEDGE INVENTORY a list of statements or phrases representing what a writer knows about a topic, including questions to direct further research.

LEARNING LOG a journal or notebook used in connection with the study of a particular subject where a student records questions, problems, and state of understanding about the subject as it is studied and learned.

LOOPING a process for discovering ideas by freewriting on a topic, stopping to find promising ideas, then producing another freewrite on that subject, repeating the loop several times.

MAPPING See Clustering.

MEMOIR an account of true events told by a narrator who witnessed or participated in the events; usually focussing on the personalities and actions of persons other than the writer.

METAPHOR a figure of speech describing something by speaking of it as if it were something else, without using such terms as "like" or "as" to signal the relationship. To say "the singer was a croaking frog" is to speak *metaphorically.*

MONOLOGUE a speech by one person without interruption by other voices. A *dramatic monologue* reveals the personality and experience of a person through a long speech.

MOOD feeling about a scene or subject created for a reader by a writer's selection of words and details; the mood of a piece of writing may be suspenseful, mysterious, peaceful, fearful, and so on.

NARRATION discourse that tells a story—either made up or true. Some common types of narrative are biographies, short stories, and novels.

NONSEXIST LANGUAGE language free from gender bias, representing the equality of men and women and showing them in both traditional and nontraditional roles.

ONOMATOPOEIA the use of words (usually in poetry) to suggest sounds; the *gurgling* of a stream, the *whispering* of a breeze, the *grinding* of a truck's engine.

PARAPHRASING rewording the meaning expressed in something spoken or written, using other words but retaining all the original ideas.

PARENTHETICAL DOCUMENTATION the placement of citations or other documentation within the text and in parentheses.

PEER RESPONSE response to one's writing provided by other writers who are peers or classmates rather than teachers or other editors.

PERSONIFICATION a figure of speech in which objects, events, abstract ideas, or animals are given human characteristics. "The computer responded smugly" and "the mountain stood imposingly" are examples of personification.

PERSUASION discourse focused on influencing a listener or reader to support a point of view or take an action. Examples of persuasive discourse would include political speeches, advertisements, position papers, editorials, and courtroom speeches by lawyers.

PLAGIARISM presenting the ideas or words of another as if they were one's own. Writers who use the ideas of others will avoid plagiarism by acknowledging their sources.

POINT OF VIEW the viewpoint or perspective through which the reader views the events in a story; defines what a narrator can know and tell about.

PORTFOLIO a place (usually a large folder) where writing is stored for future reference and review or to present for evaluation.

PRÉCIS a short summary of an essay, story, or speech, capturing only the essential elements.

PROOFREADING usually the last stage of the revising or editing process, when a writer checks work to discover typographical and other errors.

PROPAGANDA discourse aimed entirely at persuading an audience, often suggests distortions of truth; usually refers to manipulative political discourse.

PROSE the usual language of speech and writing, lacking the special properties that define poetry; any language use that isn't poetry.

SENSORY DETAIL descriptive detail based on sensory experience— experiences associated with touch, smells, tastes, sights, and sounds.

SIMILE a figure of speech comparing two things that are essentially unlike, signaling the comparison with such words as "like" or "as."

SPATIAL ORDER a pattern of organization based on space used in descriptive writing; for example, a scene may be described from foreground to background, from left to right, from top to bottom.

STYLE refers to those features in a discourse or work of art that identify it as the work of a particular individual, type, period, or artistic philosophy.

SUMMARY presents the theme or central idea in brief form.

SYMBOL a word, object, or action that suggests something other than itself, as a heart can stand for affection or compassion, or in a story a river may suggest the passage of time.

SYNTHESIS refers in writing or thinking to the putting together of ideas or information to reach a conclusion or achieve some insight or find a solution to a problem.

THEME the underlying idea or central concern of a work of art or literature.

THESIS the main point of an essay or other discourse.

TONE the writer's attitude toward a subject—detached, ironic, serious, angry, and so on.

TOPIC SENTENCE a statement expressing the main point of a paragraph; the idea (stated or unstated) around which a paragraph is organized.

TRANSITION a smooth movement from one point to the next, usually marked in discourse with transitional words or phrases like "next," "furthermore," or "on the other hand."

TREE DIAGRAM a visualized plan for an essay, also known as a "branching tree diagram" for the way it shows main and subordinate points as the trunk and main and minor branches of a tree.

TRITE PHRASE a phrase used so commonly that it lacks precise meaning and suggests a lack of imagination, thought, or originality.

UNITY oneness; the concept that in a written work all the parts must form a single whole, held together by a central theme or idea.

VENN DIAGRAM a way of representing the relationship between two items that are distinct but have common or overlapping elements. The diagram consists of two circles drawn with an overlapping section to represent the common elements.

VOICE the personality and distinct way of talking of a writer that allows a reader to "hear" a human personality in a piece of writing.

classification of, in the library, 487–88
italics for titles of, 829
source cards for, 278–79
in Works Cited list, 287
borrow, lend, 855
Brainstorming, 180, 211, 326, 869
to limit a topic, 340
on word processor, 850
Brand names, capitalization of, 770
Bridges, capitalizing names of, 767
bring, take, 855
Browsing, 150–51, 328
Buildings, capitalizing names of, 767
Business letters, 848–49
but, 438, 550

C

Call number, 488
can, may, 855
Capitalization, 762–80
awards, special events, 770
bodies of the universe, 767
brand names, 770
directions, 766–67
in divided quotations, 774
events, documents, periods of
time, 770
family relationships, 763
first words, 774–75
geographical names, 766
I, 764
in letters, 774
months, days, holidays, 770
nationalities and religions, 764
organizations, institutions, 769
in outlines, 774–75
people's names and titles, 762–63
proper nouns and proper adjectives, 524,
542, 762
in quotations, 774
school subjects and class names, 770
structures, vehicles, 767
supreme beings, sacred writings, 764
in titles, 762–63, 774–75
Card catalog, 486, 488–90
computerized, 328, 489
Case
nominative, 711, 713, 720
objective, 711, 715, 720

possessive, 528
Category charts, 333
Cause and effect, 869
fallacies, 153–54
in myths, 165
order, 346
in problem and solution, 183
transitions that show, 380–81
Cause and effect writing, 148–61, 214
drafting, 154–57
evaluation standards, 158
prewriting, 150–54
publishing, 159
reviewing and revising, 157–59
Cause-to-effect pattern, 154
Central idea, restating, 386
Chain of events, creating, 105
Chapter title, in quotation marks, 829
Characters
in autobiographical incident, 32
in monologue, 110, 111
in myth, 165–66
revealing, 112, 452
in tall tale, 50–51
Character sketch, 78–82
drafting, 81
planning, 80–81
publishing, 82
reviewing and revising, 82
Chronological order, 33, 106, 284, 343–44,
362, 869
Clarity, 869
achieving, 47, 141, 402–7
Classification, 124, 346–47
of books, 487–88
paragraphs that classify, 360
See also Exposition: classification
Classificatory writing. *See* Informative/
classificatory writing;
Persuasive/classificatory writing
Class memory album, 37
Clauses, 604–16
adverb, 612–13
in complex sentence, 621–22
in compound-complex sentence, 623
in compound sentence, 619–20
diagraming, 867
elliptical, 613, 723
essential, 608–9
as fragments, 637

independent clauses in, 619
  writing, 159
Compound subjects, 570, 689
  diagraming, 863
  verb agreement with, 689
Compound verbs, 570
  diagraming, 863
Compound words, hyphens in, 812
Computer services as information
    source, 496
Computer Tips, 34, 63, 125, 209, 241, 277,
    288, 321, 328, 351, 365, 435, 462
Conclusions, writing, 232, 386–90
  common types of, 386–88
  for narratives, 388–89
  for persuasive essays, 390
Concrete language, 424–25
Concrete nouns, 524
Conjugation, 660
Conjunctions, 553–56
  coordinating, 553–54
  correlative, 554
  subordinating, 445–46, 555, 612
Conjunctive adverbs, 555–56
  semicolons with, 556, 805
Connotations, 424, 513, 870
Consonance, 427
Consonant, doubling the final, 859–60
Consumer education, writing ideas for, 845
Context, choosing for writing, 61
Context clues, inferring word meaning from,
    456–58
Contractions, apostrophes in, 719, 856
Contrast
  in descriptive writing, 64
  transitions that show, 379
  See also Comparison and contrast, using
Controlling purpose, statement of,
    275, 280–81, 318–19
Controversial issue, 206–21
  drafting, 213–16
  evaluation standards, 216
  prewriting, 208–12
  publishing, 218
  reviewing and revising, 216–18
Controversy, 870
Coordinate adjectives, commas with, 786
Coordinating conjunctions, 553–54
Copy-editing. *See* Proofreading
Correlative conjunctions, 554

Counter argument, 870
Creative thinking, 471–72
  making inferences, 471–72
Crediting sources, 218, 283, 483–84
Critical thinking, 468–70
  evaluating ideas, 468–69
  logical fallacies, identifying, 469–70
Criticism, 870
Cross-curricular writing. *See* Essays in other
    subjects
Cross-reference cards, 488–89
Cubing, 870
Current events, 221

D

Dangling participles, 597
Dashes, 810–11
  in dialogue, 811
  with interrupters, 810
Data, collecting, 230
Dates
  apostrophes for omitted numbers in, 822
  commas in, 796
Decimal points, 783
Declarative sentences, 565
  punctuation of, 782
Deductive reasoning, 870
Definite articles, 542
Definition, writing, 134–37, 319
  in paragraphs, 360–61
  planning and drafting, 136–37
  prewriting, 136
  in problem and solution, 183
  reviewing and publishing, 137
Degree
  of comparisons, 741–43
  transitions that show, 378–79
Demonstrative pronouns, 531
Denotation, 424, 871
Dependent clauses. *See* Subordinate clauses
Description, 58–71, 319, 871
  in art interpretation, 257
  in autobiographical incident, 33
  in field notes, 545
  in interpretive essay, 247
  paragraphs that describe, 361
  See also Observation and description
Descriptive writing
  dialogue in, 64

for writing dialogue, 455
for writing summaries, 482

H

Headings, in letters, 848
Health, ideas for writing about, 845
Historical present tense, 660
Hyphens, 812–13
    and compound nouns, 525
Hypothesis, 168–72
    drafting, 171–72
    formulating, 170–71
    publishing and presenting, 172
    reviewing, 172

I

I, capitalization of, 764
Idea exchange, 327
Ideas
    connecting clearly, 410–11
    during drafting stage, 18
    finding, 322–29
    for writing, 844–45
    See also Main idea; Topic
Idioms, 429, 547
ie and ei, spelling and, 860
Illogical comparisons, 747
Imagery, 872
Imaginative writing. *See* Narrative and
    imaginative writing
Imaging, 323
Inperative mood, 676
Imperative sentences, 565
    diagraming, 861
    punctuation of, 782
    subject in, 575
Implied main idea, 372–73
Implied topic sentence, 359
imply, infer, 856
Importance, organizing by order of, 226, 334
Impromptu method, 497
Indefinite articles, 542
Indefinite pronouns, 531, 692–93
    agreement problems with, 728
Indefinite reference, 730
Independent clauses, 604
    in complex sentences, 621
    in compound-complex sentences, 623
    in compound sentences, 619

semicolons between, 804–5
    in simple sentences, 619
Indexes, 277
Indicative mood, 676
Indirect objects, 578
    diagraming, 862, 864
    noun clauses as, 615
    pronouns as, 715
Indirect questions, periods with, 782
Indirect quotations, 37
Inductive reasoning, 872
Inductive-reasoning frames, 337
infer, imply, 856
Inferring word meaning from context, 456–58
Infinitive phrases, 592–93, 635
    diagraming, 866
Infinitives, 592–93
    diagraming, 866
    split, 593
Informal English, 428
Information, transitions that signal, 381
Information sources. *See* Library and other
    information sources
Informative/classificatory writing
    composition and contrast, 118–32
Informative/descriptive writing
    character sketch, 78–82
    director's notes, 260–64
    interpretive essay, 238–53
    observing situations and events, 58–71
Informative exposition
    cause-effect, exploring, 148–61
    comparison and contrast, 118–32
    cross curricular writing, 304–10
    definition, 58–71
    group discussion, 196–200
    hypothesis, 168–72
    ideas for, 844
    problem-solution, 178–89
    research report, 270–94
    saturation report, 295–96
Informative/narrative writing
    family history, 42–47
    interview, 72–76
    monologue, 108–12
Initials, periods with, 782
Inquiring, 17
Inside address, in letters, 849
Institutions, capitalization of, 769
Intensifiers, 545

O

Objective case pronouns, 711, 715, 720
Objective complements, 579
Objective description, 62
Object of the preposition, 551
  pronouns as, 715
Observation charts, 330
Observation and description
  character sketch, 78–82
  definition, 134–37
  interview, 72–76
  situations and settings, 58–71
Observations, using, 212
Observing, 91, 150, 323
Observing situations and settings, 58–71
  drafting, 63–65
  evaluation standards, 67
  prewriting, 60–63
  publishing, 68
  reviewing and revising, 66–68
of, 857
Onomatopoeia, 94, 427, 873
On the Lightside, 41, 77, 133, 195, 259,
    370, 433, 485, 517, 562, 630, 645,
    736, 757, 781, 803, 819, 834
Opinion poll, 209
Opinions, elaborating with, 367
Opposing viewpoint, examining, 211, 225
Oral presentation, 68, 112, 129, 143, 226,
    227, 416, 497–99
  nonverbal elements, 498
  oral interpretation, 499–500
  oral reports, 497–98
  persuasive speech, 222–27
  verbal elements, 498
Organization, 342–47
  cause-to-effect pattern, 154, 214, 346
  chronological order, 343, 347, 362
  classification, 346–47
  combining methods of, 347–49
  comparison and contrast order, 345-46
  by degree, 345
  of descriptions, 65
  effect-to-cause pattern, 154
  feature-by-feature pattern, 124-25
  main ideas and supporting details, 342–43
  of note cards, 281
  outline, 281–82
  problem and solution, 194, 214, 249
  of research reports, 281–82, 284
  spatial order, 344, 348

subject-by-subject pattern, 124–25
  See also Graphic devices; Outlines
Organizations, capitalizing names of, 769
Outlines, 231, 397, 846–47
  capitalization in, 774–75
  correct form for, 847
  formal, 846
  periods in, 783
  for research reports, 281–82
  sentence, 846
  topic, 282, 847
Overloaded sentence, 410

P

Padded sentences, 412–13
Palindromes, 433
Paragraphs, 357–63, 406–7
  that analyze, 361
  clarity in, 406–7
  coherence in, 357
  that define and classify, 360
  developmental, 360
  elaboration in, 357
  that explain a process, 362
  in fiction, 407
  with logical progression of ideas, 373
  that narrate and describe, 361
  in nonfiction, 406
  structural, 360
  topic sentences, with and without, 358–59
  unity in, 357, 371–74
Parallelism
  and use of commas, 797
Paraphrasing, 248, 279–80, 477,
    482, 873
Parentheses, 814–15
Parenthetical documentation, 283, 873
Parenthetical expressions, punctuation of,
    789
Parenthetical notes, 283
Participial phrases, 595–96, 635
  commas with, 596
  diagraming, 866
  essential/nonessential, 596
Participles, 595–97
  dangling, 597
  diagraming, 866
  misplaced, 597
Parts of speech, 524–61

Passive voice, 436–37, 674–75
Past experience, problem solving, 473
Past participial phrases, using, 173–75
  commas with, 173
Past participles, 597, 649–51, 653–57
Past perfect progressive form, 665
Past perfect tense, 662
Past progressive form, 665
Past tense, 661, 662
Peer readers, questions for, 34, 66, 96, 126,
  157, 184, 216, 248, 285
Peer response, 19, 215, 397–401, 852–53, 873
Perfect tenses, 661, 662–63
Periodicals
  as reference sources, 486, 495
  See also Magazines; Newspapers
Periods, 782–83
Person, pronoun-antecedent agreement in,
  527, 727, 729
Personal goals, determining, 319
Personal pronouns, 186, 527–28
Personal and expressive writing
  autobiographical incident, 26–40
  family history, 42–47
  tall tale, 48–52
Personal issues, 209
Personal techniques for finding ideas,
  322–24
Personification, 426, 873
Persuasion, 874
  controversial issue, 206–21
  editorial, 228–32
  persuasive speech, 222–27
  See also Persuasive/descriptive writing
Persuasive/classificatory writing
  controversial issue, 206–21
  editorial, 228–32
Persuasive/descriptive writing
  advice essay, 190–94
  interpreting art, 254–58
  persuasive speech, 222–27
Persuasive essay (controversial issue),
  206–21
  conclusions for, 390
  evaluation standards, 216–17
Persuasive language, 215
Persuasive speech, 222–27
  planning, 224–25
  reviewing and publishing, 227
  writing, 225–26

Persuasive writing, ideas for, 844
Phrases
  adjective, 586–87
  adverb, 587
  appositive, 201–3, 441, 589–90, 635
  diagraming, 864–66
  eliminating wordy, 412–13
  essential participial, 596
  as fragments, 634–36
  gerund, 600–601, 635
  infinitive, 592–93, 635
  nonessential, 794–95, 635
  participial, 595–96
  past participial, 173–75
  prepositional, 586–87, 635, 788
  present participial, 113–15, 143–45
Place names, commas in, 797
Plagiarism, 874
  avoiding, 283, 483–84
Plays
  capitalization of titles, 775
  dialogue in, 453–54
  underlining or italics for, 829
Plot, planning in short story, 104
Plural pronouns, 527
Plurals, apostrophes to form, 822
P.M., 770
Poems
  titles of, capitalizing, 774
  titles of, in quotation marks, 829
Poetic license, using, 98
Poetry, 88–101
  drafting, 93–95
  evaluation standards, 97
  onomatopoeia in, 94, 427, 873
  prewriting, 90–92
  publishing, 99
  reviewing and revising, 96–98
  shape and form of, 94
  sound devices in, 427
Pointing, 398, 852
Point of view, 447–51, 874
  in character sketch, 81
  in fiction, 447–48
  first, second, and third person, 81, 447–50
  in nonfiction, 449–50
  selecting for short story, 106
  varying, 450–51

Techniques
for peer response, 852–53
Television series
capitalization of titles, 775
quotation marks in episode title, 829
Temporal relationships, transitions that
show, 377
Tense, verb, 37, 68, 660–63
Testimonial, false, 515
Tests
classroom, 501–2
essay, 306–9
standardized, 502–10
that, combining sentences with, 443
that, those, 749
the, 542
capitalization of, 763, 775
them, those, 749
Theme, 875
there, 574
Thesaurus
information in, 492
using to achieve clarity, 402
these, this, 749
Thesis statement, 247, 275, 280–81, 308,
355–56, 875
they're, 856
Third-person point of view, 448, 449
Third-person pronouns, 527
this, these, 749
those, them, 749
Time
capitalization of words of, 770
transitions that show, 376–77
Time line, 46, 165, 333
Time words, 546, 699, 821
Timing, and oral presentations, 227
Titles, personal, 762–63, 798
Titles
capitalization of, 774–75
in italics, 829
quotation marks and, 829
and subject-verb agreement, 698–99
Tone, 227, 422, 875
of interview, 75
Topic
choosing, 16, 30, 61, 122, 141, 151, 273,
317–18
exploring, 122–23
focusing, 338–41

limiting, 340–41
Topic outline, 281–82, 847
Topic sentence, 281, 355–56, 371–72
paragraphs with and without, 358–59
Traditional word order, 83
Trains, capitalization of names of, 767
Transfer, 515
Transition, 875
Transitional devices, 376–82
Transitive verbs, 538, 577
Tree diagrams, 332
Trial-and-error method of problem solving, 473
Trigger words, 324

U

Underlining
names of vehicles, 767
plurals of letters, numbers, signs, and
words, 822
of titles, 829
Unity, 357, 371–75, 875
in longer pieces of writing, 384–85
in paragraphs, 357, 371–74
transitional devices, 376–82
See also Coherence
Unsupported statements, correcting, 408–9

V

Varieties of language, 428–32
dialects, 431
vocabulary variations, 429–31
in writing, 431–32
Vehicles, capitalization of, 767
Venn diagram, 122, 334–35, 875
Verbal phrases, 592–603
commas after, 788
Verbals, 592–603
gerunds, 600–601
infinitives, 592–93
participles, 595–97
Verb phrases, 536
Verbs, 534–38, 649–79
action, 534–35, 649, 739
auxiliary, 534, 536
commonly confused, 678–79
compound, 570
conjugation, 660
diagraming, 861
emphatic forms, 666

ACKNOWLEDGMENTS

Sources of Quoted Materials

26: Random House, Inc.: For an excerpt from *Ake: The Years of Childhood* by Wole Soyinka. Copyright © 1982 by Wole Soyinka. By permission of Random House, Inc. **48:** The University of Chicago Press: Excerpt from *Tall Tale America* by Walter Blair. Copyright 1944, © 1987 by Walter Blair. Reprinted by permission of the author and The University of Chicago Press. **58:** University of New Mexico Press: For an excerpt from *The Way to Rainy Mountain* by N. Scott Momaday. First published in *The Reporter,* January 26, 1967. Copyright © 1969, The University of New Mexico Press. **72:** Random House, Inc.: For an excerpt from *Actors Talk About Acting* by Lewis Funke & John E. Booth, eds. Copyright © 1961 by Lewis Funke & John E. Boothe. By permission of Random House, Inc. **78:** Tribune Media Services: For an excerpt from "The Hidden Songs of a Secret Soul" by Bob Greene, in *The Chicago Sun-Times,* March 3, 1975. **88:** University Press of New England: "Pitcher" by Robert Francis. Copyright © 1959 by Robert Francis. Reprinted from *The Orb Weaver* by permission of University Press of New England. This poem first appeared in *New Poems by American Poets, I.* **102:** Rosemary A. Thurber: "The Unicorn in the Garden" (text and illustration) by James Thurber. Copyright © 1940 James Thurber, Copyright © 1968 Helen Thurber, from *Fables For Our Time,* published by Harper & Row. **108:** International Creative Management: For an excerpt from *The Dark at the Top of The Stairs* by William Inge. By permission of International Creative Management, Inc. **116:** Macmillan Publishing Company. Six sniglets from *Sniglets* by Rich Hall. Copyright © 1984 by Not the Network Company, Inc. Reprinted with permission of Macmillan Publishing Company. **118:** Henry Holt and Company, Inc.: "To an Athlete Dying Young," from "A Shropshire Lad" - Authorised Edition - from *The Collected Poems of A. E. Housman.* Copyright © 1939, 1940, 1965 by Holt, Rinehart and Winston. Copyright © 1967, 1968 by Robert E. Symons. Reprinted by permission of Henry Holt and Company, Inc. **119:** Random House, Inc.: "Ex-Basketball Player," from The Carpentered Hen and Other Tame Creatures by John Updike. Copyright © 1957, 1982 by John Updike. By permission of Alfred A. Knopf, Inc. **162:** Curtis Brown, Ltd.: "Arap Sang and the Cranes" by Humphrey Harman, from *Tales Told Near a Crocodile.* Copyright © 1967 by Humphrey Harman. By permission of Curtis Brown, Ltd. **178:** The New Yorker: For excerpts from "Letter from Mexico City" by Alma Guillermoprieto, from *The New Yorker,* September 17, 1990. Copyright © 1990 Alma Guillermoprieto. Reprinted by permission. **190:** Harper & Row, Publishers, Inc.: For an excerpt from *Girltalk: All the Stuff Your Sister Never Told You* by Carol Weston. Copyright © 1985 by Carol Weston. Reprinted by permission of HarperCollins Publishers. **196:** Time, The Time Inc. Magazine Company: For excerpts from "Struggling for Sanity" by Anastasia Toufexis, from *Time,* October 8, 1990. Copyright © 1990 The Time Inc. Magazine Company. Reprinted by permission. **222:** Princeton University Press: For an excerpt from *Cries for Democracy: Writings and Speeches from the 1989 Chinese Democracy Movement,* edited by Han Minzhu. Copyright © 1990 Princeton University Press. With permission of Princeton University Press. **228:** Omni Publications International Ltd.: For excerpts from "Away With Big-Time Athletics" by Roger M. Williams, from Saturday Review, March 6, 1976. **238:** Harcourt Brace Jovanovich, Inc.: "A Fire-Truck," from *Advice to a Prophet and Other Poems* by Richard Wilbur. Copyright © 1958 and renewed 1986 by Richard Wilbur. First published in *The New Yorker.* Reprinted by permission of Harcourt Brace Jovanovich, Inc. **270:** Discover Publications, Inc.: For an excerpt from "California's Revenge" by Ann Finkbeiner, from *Discover,* September 1990. Copyright © 1990 Discover Publications, Inc. **316:** Warner/Chappell Music, Inc.: "What I Am" by Edie Brickell, Kenneth Withrow, John Houser, John Bush, Alan Aly. Copyright © 1988 WB Music Corp., Geffen Music, Edie Brickell Songs, Withrow Publishing, Enlightened Kitty & Strange Mind Productions. All rights on behalf of Geffen Music, Edie Brickell Music, Withrow Publishing, Enlightened Kitty & Strange Mind Productions administered by WB Music Corp. All rights reserved. Used by permission. **491:** Executor, The Literary Estate of May Swenson: For excerpts from "The Centaur" by May Swenson. Copyright © 1956 and renewed 1984 by May Swenson. Used with permission of the Literary Estate of May Swenson. **562:** Dave Barry: For an excerpt from "What Is and Ain't Grammatical" by Dave Barry. Copyright © 1980 Dave Barry. The authors and editors have made every effort to trace the ownership of all copyrighted material found in this book and to make full acknowledgment for their use.

Illustration and Photography Credits

Commissioned Illustrations: Robin A. Brun: **26/27;** Mark DaGrossa: **644** (map); Mark DaGrossa/Gary Sanders: **533, 595;** John Emery: **xii; 178/179;** Christopher Herrfurth: **116, 268, 302;** James Higgins: **29, 102/103, 228/229, 736;** Gary Sanders: **142** (background); Leslie Staub Shattuck: **24, 35, 52, 77, 95, 142, 156, 157, 158, 217, 287, 380, 479, 483, 495, 515, 589, 620, 656, 664, 678, 701, 733, 748, 778, 781, 832, 835;** Christopher Vallo: **48/49, 56, 138/139, 644.** **Assignment Photography:** France Photography: **42/43, 58/59, 78/79, 88/89, 108/109, 117,**

118/119, 169, 190/191, 206/207; Patterson Graphics: **7, 15, 215, 302, 485, 487, 492, 539;** **Photos and Illustrations: vi:** Kenneth Scallon, Image Bank; **vii:** Jim Whitmer Photography; **viii:** Jeff Kauck Photography; **ix:** Andris Hendrickson Photography; **xi:** Meryl Meisler; **xiii:** AP/World Wide Photos; **xiv:** Phoenix Zoo by Dick George; **xv:** © Mark Allen, Stockworks; **7:** Patterson Graphics; **12:** Superstock; **15:** Jim Whitmer Photography; **16:** Bonnie Learey, Superstock; **19:** Miriam Schaer; **31:** Jim Whitmer Photography; **32:** Tom Jones and Harvey Schmidt; **35:** Terry Widener; **39:** Photograph courtesy of American Hurrah Antiques; **40:** Andrew J. Zito, Image Bank; **41:** Drawing by Donald Reilly; © 1982 The New Yorker Magazine, Inc.; **45:** Neil Shigley; **46:** © Schecter Lee/Esto; **47:** Collection of The Museum of American Folk Art, New York City. Gift of Mr. & Mrs. Philip M. Isaacson; **51:** Leonard Everett Fisher; **52:** Preziosi Postcards; **58:** Spencer Museum of Art-University of Kansas, Letha Churchill Walker Fund; **61:** Jeff Kauck Photography; **62:** Barbara Nessim; **64:** Brad Veley; **66:** Universal Press Syndicate; **71:** Superstock; **73:** *c, bl*Shooting Star; **73:** *tr* The Bettman Archive; **75:** Capital Cities/ABC TV; **76:** Dennis DeBasco, The Graphics Studio; **77:** William Cone; **79:** Judy Pederson; **82:** John Martin, Image Bank; **82:** Margo Feiden Galleries © Al Hirschfeld; **86:** Indianapolis Museum of Art; **91:** David Drapkin; **95:** J.W. Stewart; **98:** Museum of Modern Art, New York; **99:** J.W. Stewart; **101:** Andris Hendrickson Photography; **102/103:** © 1940 James Thurber © Helen Thurber from *Fables for Our Time.* Published by Harper & Row; **105:** Miriam Larsson Kolesar; **107:** *all* UPI/Bettman, Shooting Star; **111:** Spike Nannarello, Shooting Star; **112:** Washington Post Writers Group; **117:** Johnson Space Center **121:** *t* Doane Gregory Photography, Ltd.; *b* Superstock; **124:** The Saatchi Collection, London; **127:** Ken Maryanski; **132:** *tr* UPI/Bettman; *b* Bourse De New York Ph: Guatti, SIPA Press; **133:** Chronicle Features **134/135:** Johnson Space Center; **137:** Ron Brello, Jr.; **141:** Milton Glaser; **142:** Tom Curry; **146:** UPI/Bettman; **148/149:** Guido Alberto Rossi, Image Bank; **153:** Universal Press Syndicate; **155:** Meryl Meisler; **156:** Greg Epperson; **161:** California Institute of Technology, FPG; **162/163:** Randy Mott, KLRU-TV; **165:** Memorial Art Gallery of the University of Rochester: Marion Stratton Gould Fund; **167:** David McCall Johnston; **171:** Vedros & Associates Photography; **172:** Maciek Albrecht; **176:** Washington Post Writers Group; **178/179:** Victor Aleman, FPG; **181:** John Gampert; **183:** Trevor's Campaign; **185:** Suzanne L. Murphy, FPG; **187:** Bob Schatz; **189:** FPG; **193:** Fenollosa - Weld Collection, Museum of Fine Arts - Boston; **195:** Chronicle Features; **196/197:** Tim Bieber; **199:** Daniel Zakroczemski; **204:** UPI/Bettman; **214:** Library of Congress; **217:** AP/Wide World Photos; **221:** UPI/Bettman; **222/223:** Peter Turnley, Black Star; **225:** *t* AP/Wide World Photos; *r* Craig Frazier; **227:** Douglas Bowles, Image Bank; **231:** Stewart Charles Cohen Photography; **232:** Universal Press Syndicate; **236:** Helen Birch Bartlett Memorial Collection, 1926.224, © The Art Institute of Chicago; **237:** *tr* UPI/Bettman; *c* Superstock; *br* UPI/Bettman; **238/239:** Superstock; **241:** *all* Phoenix Zoo by Dick George; **245:** Westlight; **246:** Betsy Everitt; **254/255:** UPI/Bettman; **254:** Museum of Modern Art, New York; **258:** Superstock; **259:** David Richardson; **260/261:** AP/ Wide World Photos; **261:** UPI/Bettman Newsphotos; **263:** Shooting Star; **264:** Dan Brennan; **268:** Ron Garrison, San Diego Zoological Society; **269:** Sheldon Memorial Art Gallery, University of Nebraska - Lincoln; **270/271:** UPI/Bettman; **273:** © Mark Allen, Stockworks; **276:** TSW-Click, Fertility Institute of New Orleans; **278:** Jim Whitmer Photography; **287:** Norman Raincock; **293:** Ken Davies, Masterfile; **294:** Bridgeman, Art Resource; **296:** Sheldon Memorial Art Gallery, University of Nebraska - Lincoln; **304/305:** North Wind Archive; **307:** United Media Reprinted by Permission of UFS, Inc. for Frank & Ernest: Reprinted by permission of NEA, Inc.; **314:** Stanford MacDonald-Wright; **316:** Lester Cohen, Shooting Star; **317:** Jerry Lofaro, Image Bank; **323:** FPG; **324:** Josselin, Image Bank; **326:** Universal Press Syndicate; **331:** *all* Superstock; **334:** *l* Gary Torrisi; *r* Yoram Kahana, Shooting Star; **336:** © David Hockney; **339:** *t* Museum of the American Indian; *b* University Museum,University of Pennsylvania; **341:** Comstock; **344:** Orion, FPG; **345:** © Globus Brothers, The Stock Market; **348:** Superstock; **349:** © D. Bartruff, FPG; **353:** Ben Perini; **356:** © J. Kugler, FPG; **358:** James Tennison, Image Bank; **360:** Curtis Parker; **365:** National Museum of American Art, Art Resource; **370:** Louis LeBlanc, Collection of Texas Southern University; **372:** Guy Billout; **373:** Linda Holland Rathkopf; **374:** Larry Grant, FPG; **377:** Universal Press Syndicate; **378:** Steve Johnson; **379:** Cathy Pavia; **380:** Jay P. Morgan; **389:** The Bettman Archive; **392:** Comstock; **398:** Anthony Russo; **400:** Peter de Seve; **404:** Kenneth Garrett, FPG; **407:** Dave Black, Sportschrome; **410:** Denver Art Museum; **415:** Guy Billout; **419:** The Bettman Archive; **422:** UPI/Bettman; **425:** Tom Lichtenheld; **426:** Nick Koudis, The Stock Market; **429:** Peter Till, Image Bank; **430:** James Porto; **433:** © Schecter Lee/Esto **435:** TSW-Click, Photo by courtesy of Copeland, Douglas, Dyer; **436:** Jim Whitmer Photography; **441:** Daniel Morrison **446:** © 1990 M.C. Escher Heirs/Cordon Art Baarn Holland; **447:** Superstock; **449:** Shooting Star; **451:** © 1987 by David Sipress; **453:** Shooting Star; **455:** FPG; **456:** Westphal Illustration; **460:** Universal Press Syndicate; **461:** Columbus Museum of Art; **463:** Mr. & Mrs. Robert B. McLain Collection; **466:** Jerry N. Uelsmann; **469:** Universal Press Syndicate; **473:** Universal Press Syndicate; **474:** Jim Whitmer Photography; **475:** Brian Bailey, Image Bank; **481:** The Bettman Archive; **483:** The Bettman Archive; **486:** Chronicle Features; **489:** Peter Gridley, FPG; **492:** Courtesy of Gretchen and John Berggruen, San Francisco, CA; **493:** Jill Krementz Inc.; **495:** Katherine Mahoney; **498:** S. Sylvester, FPG; **500:** Martha Swope Photography; **504:** Bob McNeely, SIPA Press; **511:** Paul Schulenberg; **515:** Ralph Morse, Time Life Picture Agency © Time Inc.; **517:** Chronicle Features; **518:** Vivienne Flesher **523:** Universal Press Syndicate; **525:** © The Telegraph

Colour Library, FPG; **529:** Smith College Museum of Art; **530:** Art Resource; **537:** Stan Osolinski, FPG; **544:** Michael Wiliamson; **548:** FPG; **549:** Superstock; **553:** Anita Kunz; **557:** © A. Loginovs, FPG; **559:** Richard Laird, FPG; **564:** Charles Moore, Black Star; **566:** The Bettman Archive; **569:** FPG; **571:** Stephen Johnson, TSW-Click; **573:** Bob Peters; **576:** Comstock; **579:** Illustration from Jules Verne, *From the Earth to the Moon . . . and a Trip around It* (New York: Scribner, Armstrong & Co., 1874); **581:** Museum of Modern Art, New York; **583:** Superstock; **588:** Paul Markow & Associates, FPG; **589:** Universal Press Syndicate; **591:** Museum of Natural History, Smithsonian Institution Photo #47,000; **594:** Otto, FPG; **599:** AP/Wide World Photos; **601:** Dallas Museum of Art, Textile Purchase Fund; **602:** Mark Williams © Index/Stock Int'l Inc.; **606:** Superstock; **609:** Superstock; **611:** © Three Lions, Superstock; **618:** Viesti Associates; **620:** Art Resource; **625:** Monterey Bay Aquarium; **626:** *all* University of Arizona; **630:** Superstock; **634:** Art Resource; **638:** Shooting Star; **641:** Victoria & Albert, Art Resource; **645:** Jim Jacobs; **656:** Stephen Wilkes; **658:** International Tsunami Information Center; **664:** Goddard Space Center, Greenbelt, Maryland; **669:** The Bettman Archive; **671:** Shooting Star; **672:** Metropolitan Museum of Art; **673:** Photo Researchers; **678:** Charley Brown; **681:** Universal Press Syndicate; **682:** Alan Mazzetti; **687:** Carlos Castellanos Illustration, Inc.; **691:** The Bettman Archive; **692:** Stanford University Museum of Art; **697:** AP/Wide World Photos; **701:** Jeffrey Seaver; **705:** D. Luann Brandt; **707:** Library of Congress; **712:** © Martha DiMeo; Viesti Associates; **714:** Bridgeman, Art Resource, Private Collection; **718:** *t* Shooting Star; *bl* Chronicle Features; **721:** *br* George Eastman House; *bl* Library of Congress; **722:** Superstock; **725:** Henry Fonseca; **727:** Seaver Center for Western History Research, Natural History Museum of Los Angeles County; **729:** Yves Lefevre, Image Bank; **731:** Andrew Vracin; **739:** © O'Rear, Westlight; **742:** Alex Tiani; **744:** Giraudon, Art Resource; **745:** Dennis Hall, FPG; **748:** John Craig; **751:** Paul Kratter; **753:** Art Resource; **757:** Houston Fine Arts Press; **758:** Dmitri Kessel, Life Picture Service; **763:** Malcah Zeldis; **765:** Metropolitan Museum of Art, Harris Brisbane Dick Fund, 1964; **768:** FPG; **769:** Frederic Eibner; **772:** Julia K. Swan; **773:** O'Brien & Mayor, FPG; **776:** © R.C. Gorman, Navajo Gallery; **778:** *tl* The Bettman Archive; *tr* John Mattos; **781:** Tribune Media Services; **783:** Elwood H. Smith; **784:** Frank R. Paul; **787:** FPG; **791:** Braldt Bralds; **793:** Guy Billout; **795:** Cinema Collectors; **796:** Collection, Mobil Oil Corporation; **800:** Art Resource; **803:** © Raymond Gendreau, Allstock; **806:** Newberry Library; **809:** David L. Johnson, Sportschrome; **813:** *all* FPG; **816:** *bl* Field Museum of Natural History - Neg # A109999 c Chicago; *c* Metropolitan Museum of Art; **819:** © 1990 M.C. Escher Heirs/Cordon Art Baarn Holland; **823:** John Olson; **824:** FPG; **827:** Yves Lefevre; Image Bank; **828:** *l* UPI/Bettman; *c* Harald Sund, © Time-Life Books B.V., from the *Great Cities* series; **831:** Terry Widener; **832:** Gene Greif; **834:** Connie Geocaris, TSW-Click; **835:** Jeff Greenberg; **843:** Eugene Mihaesco

Cover Photography : Ryan Roessler